Miscellaneous Texas Newspaper Abstracts - Deaths

Volume 2

Michael Kelsey
Nancy Graff Kelsey
Ginny Guinn Parsons

Other Heritage books by Michael Kelsey, Nancy Graff Floyd, and Ginny Guinn Parsons

Marriage and Death Notices from the "South Western Baptist" Newspaper
"The Southern Argus": Obituaries, Death Notices and Implied Deaths, June 1869 - June 1874
Miscellaneous Alabama Newspaper Abstracts - Volume 1
Miscellaneous Alabama Newspaper Abstracts - Volume 2
Miscellaneous Texas Newspaper Abstracts - Deaths, Volume 1

Published 1997 by

HERITAGE BOOKS, INC.
1540E Pointer Ridge Place
Bowie, Maryland 20716
1-800-398-7709

ISBN 0-7884-0781-3

A Complete Catalog Listing Hundreds of Titles
On History, Genealogy, and Americana
Available Free Upon Request

INTRODUCTION

This volume contains abstracts from forty-four newspapers originally published in Texas during the years 1839 through 1881. Included is a German newspaper, *Neu Braunfelser Zeitung,* published in New Braunfels, that has been translated into English.

The authors have abstracted any mention of a death or implied death from death notices and obituaries; articles concerning accidents, murders, epidemics, and Indian depredations; letters written to and published in the local press; and interment, mortuary and sexton reports. Sexton reports recorded the name of the deceased, age, place of birth, and cause of death. Many obituaries chronicle the life of the deceased, place of birth, residences, and date of arrival in Texas. Obituaries for at least ten Revolutionary War soldiers are included in this volume. Formal obituaries were abstracted by deleting material only of non-genealogical importance such as a hymn or praise. In addition to the numerous references to locations across Texas, the newspapers featured in this volume include hundreds of references to the states of Virginia, North Carolina, South Carolina, Georgia, Alabama, Mississippi, Tennessee, Louisiana, Kentucky, Maryland, Missouri, Illinois, Ohio, Massachusetts, Pennsylvania, and New York; and to a lesser degree references to the states of Florida, Michigan, Connecticut, Maine, Indiana, Rhode Island, New Jersey, and the District of Columbia. There are hundreds of references to Germany, England, Canada, Ireland, France, Mexico, and Scotland; and a few references to Prussia, Italy, Switzerland, Poland, Denmark, Austria, Norway, Wales, Sweden, Bohemia, and Moravia.

Every attempt was made by the authors to adhere to accuracy. The newspapers were often difficult to read and contained numerous misspellings. Therefore, the authors recommend consulting the original source. The authors made every attempt to underline surnames that appear more than once on a page, and when multiple appearances of a surname may be easily overlooked. Researchers are encouraged to consult the index for all possible surname spellings.

The abstracts in this volume were made from the archival holdings of: The University of Texas Center for American History, Austin, Texas; The Texas Collection, Baylor University, Waco, Texas; and the newspaper collection of the Temple Public Library, Temple, Texas.

Michael Kelsey
Nancy Graff Kelsey
Ginny Guinn Parsons

ACKNOWLEDGEMENT

We owe considerable appreciation to Shauna Michelle Mowery, Ginny's daughter, for her assistance in preparing this volume. Shauna spent many hours editing, preparing the indexes, and placing the finishing touches on the work. Thank you, Shauna.

We owe considerable appreciation to Eva Lia Graubard of Temple and Houston, Texas, for her assistance in preparing this volume. Eva spent many hours translating information from the *Neu Braunfelser Zeitung* newspaper from German to English. Thank you, Eva.

ABOUT THE AUTHORS

Michael Kelsey, a native Texan, is a resident of Temple, Texas, where he works in the reference department at the Temple Public Library. Since the mid-1980's, he has abstracted genealogical and historical items from 19th century newspapers originally published in Texas, Louisiana, and Alabama. These abstracts are published in books and on microfiche. With this, the sixth book of newspaper abstracts, Mike continues to combine his personal and professional interests in genealogy and history.

Nancy Graff Kelsey, a native Texan, is a resident of Temple, Texas, where she is a Registered Nurse at the Veterans Administration Hospital. With her daughter, Ginny, and granddaughter, Shauna, Nancy has researched her family's history for about 15 years. Nancy is a graduate of El Paso Community College, El Paso, Texas, and St. Edwards University, Austin, Texas.

Ginny Guinn Parsons, a native Texan, lives in Springfield, Virginia. She is employed by the Department of Defense as a Computer Specialist. Ginny is currently Recording Secretary for Henry Clay Chapter, National Society Daughters of the American Revolution, in Annandale, Virginia.

TABLE OF CONTENTS

HOUSTON MORNING STAR
Published daily, Sundays excepted,
at Houston, Republic of Texas.

Issue October 12, 1839
Died: Robert Barr, late Post Master General, at his residence on Friday the 11th inst., at half past nine A.M. It was our fortune to have become acquainted with the deceased soon after his arrival to this country.

Issue October 15, 1839
Died at the city of Austin, 4th inst., Sam. Houston, infant son of Dr. Wm. G. and Louisa L. Lewis.

Died: James Clark, Governor of Kentucky, at his residence, on the morning of the 27th ult. after a painful and lingering illness. He was elected Governor in August 1836. Governor Clark was about 55 or 56 years of age.

Programme of the funeral procession of the late Hon. Robert Barr.

Issue October 16, 1839
Tribute of Respect Temple Lodge #4, Houston, for Robert Barr.

Issue October 18, 1839
A person by the name of Francois L. du Fallois, committed suicide at the Matagorda House the 30th ult. Is not this the first suicide which has been committed in the Republic?

Obituary for Robert Barr... [note: lengthy tribute follows].

Issue October 21, 1839
General Robert Y. Hayne died the 25th of September at Ashvill, North Carolina, of bilious fever.

Died at the residence of ____ [sic] Martin, on Spring Creek, Mr. Thomas C. Dabbs, a respectable citizen of this city. Nashville (Tennessee) papers please copy.

Died yesterday morning (Sunday), Mr. Otto Finke, aged about thirty years. Deceased was a native of Germany but late of Butler county, Pennsylvania. (Pittsburg papers will please notice.)

Matthew Carey died in Philadelphia a few weeks since, in the eightieth year of his age. The immediate cause was an accident, having been thrown from his carriage.

Issue October 22, 1839

Died in this city on the 2nd of October of the prevailing epidemic, S.J. Cook, late of Cooperstown, New York. It will be gratifying to learn that many attended him to his last home, and that over his cold and narrow grave, the solemn and impressive rites of the Episcopal service were performed. He was indeed by strangers honored and by strangers mourn'd.

Issue October 23, 1839

Died in this city this morning at 1:00, Mrs. Aurelia Miller, consort of Christopher Miller, formerly of Hartford, Connecticut.

Issue November 5, 1839

Died in this city, yesterday morning, after a short illness, James Rutherford, aged about forty-five, a native of Scotla[n]d and for two years past a citizen of this city.

Issue November 12, 1839

Died in this city this morning, Mr. E. [Ezekial] Humphreys, publisher of the *Morning Star.* A native of Connecticut. His friends and acquaintances are invited to attend his funeral tomorrow morning at 8 o'clock at the residence of Cruger and Moore. [note: previous issues mention his illness].

Issue November 15, 1839

Tribute of respect from Houston Young Men's Society held November 8th for Henry W. Godfrey. Papers of Petersburg, VA, and Pontotoe, Miss. please copy.

Issue November 16, 1839

Died: John Alexander Newlands, at his residence in the city of Houston, the morning of the 14th of November 1839. By birth a Scotchman, at an early age emigrated to Mexico, from thence he came to this Republic, under the especial care of the lamented Dr. Grant, whose confidence he possessed in an eminent degree. [note: widow mentioned].

Issue November 18, 1839

Died in this city yesterday the 17th of October, Mr. Stephen Brewer of the firm of S.&T.F. Brewer. His friends and also the friends of his brother, T. Frances Brewer, are invited to attend his funeral this afternoon at 3 o'clock from his former residence.

The publication of the *Galvestonian*, it appears, is not discontinued, as was imagined by the melancholy decease of its former editor, John Gladwin; it is now under the direction of David Davis.

Issue November 20, 1839

Died in this city yesterday Mr. B. Christopher. The friends and acquaintances of the deceased and also of Mr. R. Wilkins are respectfully invited to attend his funeral this afternoon at 2 o'clock from the residence of Mr. Wilkins.

Issue November 23, 1839

The friends and acquaintances of Capt. William M. Logan, deceased, are requested to attend his funeral this morning at 11 o'clock to proceed from the City Hotel, November 23.

Issue November 25, 1839

Died in this city yesterday morning (November 22nd) in the 30th year of his age, Capt. Wm. M. Logan, of the county of Liberty. Captain Logan was a lieutenant at the seize of Bexar and he also commanded a volunteer company at the battle of San Jacinto. Was sheriff at the time of his death.

Issue November 29, 1839

Died yesterday afternoon at the residence of Alden A.M. Jackson in this city, Col. – S. Lewis, formerly of New York and late a resident of Montgomery. Came to aid of Texas, participated in most of the war. The friends of the deceased and the community generally are invited to attend the funeral this day at 3 o'clock P.M. from the residence of A.A.M. Jackson.

Issue December 3, 1839

Death of the late City Treasure, C.B. Fanger.

Issue December 3, 1839

Died in this city yesterday, 2nd of December, Mrs. Hannah Vedder, wife of Philip V. Vedder, late of Schenectady, N. York. Funeral this day (Tuesday) at 4 o'clock P.M.

Benefit for Mrs. Farrell, widow of Robert, enabling Mrs. Farrell, and her orphan son, to return to U.S.

Issue December 5, 1839

Report of the free benefit for Mrs. Farrell.

Issue January 3, 1840

The Editor [John W. Eldredge] of the *Star* would inform its readers that having attempted several times during his present indisposition, to discharge the duties of this station, he has come to the conclusion that such attempts are calculated to retard materially, and perhaps prevent entirely his restoration to health. He has, therefore, retired temporarily from the direction of the *Star*.

Issue January 11, 1840

Capt. Reuben Ross on the 24th ult. lost his life in a scuffle in the streets of Gonzales. The cause that led to the affray or any particulars have not been ascertained.

Issue January 15, 1840

Died at his residence on White Oak Bayou, Sun. evening, 12, Henry Trott, late county surveyor of Harrisburg county.

Issue January 18, 1840

Capt. Gilbert Y. Francis, formerly of Virginia, died recently in New Orleans of the yellow fever. He was indeed an eventful and romantic life. The *Natchez Free Trader* states that he has passed through many surprising adventures, and has left a memoir of them for publication. He was in early life attached to the navy, then to the stage -- had travelled over four quarters of the globe [note: list of adventures included] finally revisited his native State and married, and was extensively engaged in Texan operations when death arrested him, still in the prime of life.

Issue January 21, 1840

$250 reward for the apprehension of William R. Bell, John D. Jameson, Dr. James Adams, Henry Augustus C. Pilkington and John Ball who broke jail from this city about 12 o'clock, Saturday night last, 18 January 1840, stealing from some of our citizens 6 or 7 horses.

William R. Bell: formerly from Louisville or Lexington, KY, was committed to jail on the charge of murdering Erasmus D. Rhoton in this city Monday the 24th of December last, 21-24 years old, 5'10"-11" high, dark complexion, dark fair hair [sic]; if discovered, will probably be dressed in a black coat, as he lately purchased one, no doubt intended to prevent being recognized.

John D. Jameson: native of Virginia, formerly a Lieutenant in the Texian army, by trade a tailor, charged with murdering one Wilson in this county January 1839, about 34 years old, 6'1" high, dark complexion, brown eyes, rather speckled, face powder burned, generally wears a brown frock coat rather new, is very much given to drinking and when drunk very quarrelsome.

Dr. James Adams: charged with murder, about 50 years old, 5'9"-10", hair gray, of a feminine voice, fair complexion, full face.

Henry A.C. Pilkington, native of England, charged with grand larceny; about 35-40 years old, 6'1" high, dark complexion.
John Ball: cattle stealing, about 30 years old, 6' high.

John W. Moore, sheriff, Harrisburg county.

Issue January 30, 1840

We are informed by Col. Karnes, who has just arrived in this city, that Col. Benjamin Johnson lost his life recently in the neighborhood of the Rio Grande. The Col. with a party of eight men, when moving on in performance of duty, was suddenly surprised by a party of Cherokees. One individual alone escaped who stated Col. J. with the others were massacred.

On Saturday evening, about sundown, a couple of the soldiers from the fort, by the names of Jones & Cooper, walked to the city; inquiries were made which led to the arrest of Cooper after Jones was absent from roll call Sunday morning. Search was instituted, when the body of Jones was found a short distance from the fort with his head shockingly mangled. He was not sensible when they found him, and died in the course of the day. Cooper has confessed the murder. *Galvestonian.*

Issue February 12, 1840

From a letter from an officer at Ft. Towson. -- We this day buried with honors of war, Gen. George Colbert, the head chief of the Choctaw nation, a man of superior intelligence, the greatest of warriors, and the white man's friend. He was a revolutionary veteran; he served under General Washington in our struggle for independence... He was physically and mentally a great man; although ninety-five years of age, he walked as upright as a man of twenty-five.

Issue February 20, 1840

Departed this life on the 3rd of the present month at her late residence on the Trinity River, Mrs. Elizabeth Whiting, consort of Maj. Samuel Whiting. Mrs. W. was beloved alike for her amiable and endearing qualities of both mind and heart and her death is severely felt and lamented by a large circle of friends and relatives, who must cherish the remembrance of one so endeared to them by the social ties of love and friendship.

Issue February 26, 1840

Announcement of the death of John W. Eldredge, editor. After a lingering sickness of several months arising from an affection of the lungs he expired between twelve and one o'clock this morning. His funeral will take place this afternoon from his late residence near the court house square.

Issue February 27, 1840

Last evening the funeral of Mr. J.W. Eldredge took place. The remains were accompanied to the grave by a large concourse of citizens and the Milam Guards, of which corps he was an esteemed member.

Issue March 4, 1840

Died yesterday in this city, Dr. L.R. Cabell, formerly of Virginia, of pulmonary affection, under which he had lingered for several years past. His funeral will be attended today at 11 o'clock from the residence of Dr. Campbell on Fannin St.

Issue March 20, 1840

John A. Monges. United States consul at the port of Matagorda, died in that town on the 26th ult.

Issue March 23, 1840

We regret to learn, by letter of a recent date from Austin, that William H. Grimes died in that place on the 11th instant.

Issue March 30, 1840

San Antonio -- Killed by Indians:
  Lt. W.M. Dunnington 1st inf.; Pvt. Kaminski of A co.; Pvt. Whitney of E co.; Judge Thompson of Houston; Judge Hood of Bexar; Mr. Casey of Matagorda Co.; and a Mexican, name unknown.
  Wounded: Capt. George T. Howard, 1st Inf.; Capt Mathew Caldwell, 1st inf.; Lt. Edward A. Thompson; Pvt Kelly, Co. L.; Judge Robinson; Mr. Higginbotham; Mr. Morgan and Mr. Carson.

Issue March 31, 1840

The friends and acquaintances of the late J.G. Welschmeyer are requested to attend his funeral this evening at 4 o'clock from the house of Eli Williams.

Issue January 8, 1842

A fatal recontre took place in Brazoria county on the 12th ult. between Col. Willis Alston, Florida, and Dr. John M. Stewart of Brazoria county, which resulted in the immediate death of the latter... We are informed that Alston has since been found dead, having been shot in several places by hands unknown. Stewart left a wife and child.

Issue January 18, 1842

Information wanted: Any person capable of giving information of the place at which Hiram A. Powers, formerly a private in the Texian service, died, will confer a favor upon the friends of the deceased by communicating the same to Mr. G.W. Evans at the store of William M. Rice on Main street. Said

Powers died in this place or its neighborhood of the yellow fever in the summer of 1839.

Issue January 29, 1842

Died in this city on the morning of the 27th inst., Mrs. L.H.S. Ewing, late consort of Dr. A. Ewing and daughter of Rev. H. Reid. This amiable lady was the only child of this unfortunate family. Her afflicted parents only a month and two days since, consigned their only son to the tomb; and they are now alone in a world which we sincerely hope may never prove cold and cheerless to them.

Issue February 1, 1842

We learn that a large party of Indians, a few days since, made a descent upon Rancho de Islitas and Madam Calvillo's rancho, the former about 18 miles below San Antonio and the latter about 35. They killed several persons and carried off some prisoners. Among the latter was a lad of the name of Laughlin, the son of Mr. Laughlin of this city... *Daily Texian.*

Issue February 15, 1842

Died in Victoria, 15th last August, Harriett Ann, daughter of Franklin R. Taylor; aged only 28 days.

Issue February 17, 1842

On next Sabbath morning, a funeral sermon will be preached by the Rev. Mr. Sommers at 11 o'clock in the Presbyterian Church, occasioned by the decease of John R. Reid. Masonic and Odd Fellows are requested to attend.

The Mexican marauders have become exceedingly troublesome on the western frontier, and have broken up the trade with the settlers of the Rio Grande. They have also killed one or two citizens at Aransas Bay; among the victims is a Mr. Pierce, who resided near Capano.

Issue February 22, 1842

Mutiny and murder on board the *San Antonio*, while lying in port at New Orleans on the evening of the 11th inst., in which Lt. Fuller was killed...

Issue March 1, 1842

A week or two since, a party of Comanches passed down the San Antonio below Bexar. They were pursued by a party of eight Mexicans and overtaken a few miles from the mouth of the Medina... One Mexican, old Capt. Sanchez, about sixty years old, was killed by a gigantic Indian. The son of the Capt. Sanchez shot the Indian through the head just as his father fell.

A gentleman from Austin brings the intelligence that Mr. Fox was lately killed within two hundred yards of the corporate limits of that city by three Indians while ploughing in his field. This man had no arms and of course fell an easy victim.

Shipwreck. *San Luis Advocate*. The British brig *Buoyant*, Captain Wollasten wrecked off Velasco... The captain, the first and second mates were drowned...

Issue March 10, 1842
Died: Mr. D.H. Fitch, formerly editor of this paper. The young gentleman emigrated to the Republic in the autumn of 1839. Last summer he was attacked with a pulmonary complaint that gradually exhausted his powers.

The friends and acquaintances of D.H. Fitch, deceased, are respectfully invited to attend his funeral this morning at 10 o'clock, from his late residence on Court House Square.

Issue March 24, 1842
Capt. Cairnes and five men were surprised on the Nueces about ten days ago by a party of Mexicans. The Capt. and two men were killed...

Issue March 31, 1842
Died in this city on the 30th inst., Henry Markham, formerly of Auburn, New York and late of Clinton, Michigan. He contracted a severe fever while on his journey to Texas and lived but a few weeks after his arrival. His friends and acquaintances are requested to attend his funeral, which will take place at 10 o'clock this morning from the *Telegraph* building.

Issue May 10, 1842
A young man named Flonrnoy/Flournoy Hunt was killed near Harrisburg on Saturday last by a pistol shot by a young man named Black. It will be recollected that no less than three persons have been killed in broils at race tracks within three years: Mr. Syms at Nacogdoches, Mr. J. Vance at Houston, and Mr. Hunt at Harrisburg.

Issue May 12, 1842
Mr. C. VanNess was killed by the accidental discharge of a gun. He was riding with his friend, Mr. Robinson, a few miles below Bexar, and the horse of the latter suddenly started and threw his yauger on the pommel of his saddle with such violence that it went off, and the ball passed into the side of Mr. VanNess. He lingered until the next morning and expired.

Issue May 14, 1842
A.S. Macdonald was killed at Corpus Christi, a few weeks since, owing to the accidental discharge of a gun. He was Chief Justice of Victoria county and highly respected in the West.

Issue June 2, 1842
Mr. Lynch, Lynched. A man named Lynch, who had for some months past been the terror of the whole neighborhood of San Felipe, was hung without judge a few days ago. He had killed one or two citizens, and threatened the lives of several others and had eluded the strictest search of the civil officers of the county...

Issue June 4, 1842
Lieut. Governor Boggs was shot by some villain, about three weeks since, at Independence, while sitting in his room in the evening. The ball passed through his lower jaw into the brain, and is considered mortal. A reward of $500 has been offered by the citizens of Independence for the murderer.

Issue June 7, 1842
Death of Judge Scott: The shafts of death have lately fallen rapidly and thick around and several of our most eminent citizens are numbered among his victims. Last not least of the number is the Hon. John Scott, late Recorder of Houston. He was a native of North Carolina.

Issue June 9, 1842
Another hero at San Jacinto gone. The Hon. Isaac N. Moreland, late Chief Justice of Harris county and the commander of the Artillery Co. in the battle of San Jacinto, died in this city yesterday morning.

Issue June 21, 1842
Dr. Ira Abeny, late of Washington county, Texas, was drowned in the Arkansas River near Lewisburg on the 19th ult. by the upsetting of a canoe.

Issue June 25, 1842
The Hon. W.H. Laudrum was shot at while returning from the race track about one mile west of San Augustine, was shot by some person concealed in a thicket near the road and severely wounded.

Issue June 30, 1842
Col. W.H. Patton was killed on the 12th inst. at his residence upon the San Antonio river about thirty-five miles below the city of San Antonio. On the morning of his death, about sunrise, he went to the river as he was accustomed to do, to wash, when he was fired upon by a party of Mexicans

and instantly killed. A man by the name of Eaton, who had gone to Col. Patton's the day previous on some business for Mr. H. Arnold, went with Col. Patton and was killed at the same time...

Issue July 9, 1842

Gen. H. Atkinson died at the Jefferson barracks near St. Louis on the 14th ult.

Issue July 16, 1842

A report has reached us that Castro, the Lipan Chief, died lately of a fever near Austin.

Issue July 19, 1842

A party of twelve Indians on the 19th inst. went to the house of Judge Janes, about two miles from Austin, and as they pretended they were Tonkawas, the Judge ventured out with his little boy to talk with them; a man named Haskins also accompanied him. While out at his gate talking, they shot him and Haskins and seized his eldest son and were about to scalp them when a man in the house appeared at the door with a rifle. Mrs. Janes also pointed a gun at them and they fled, taking with them, however, the little boy.

Issue July 28, 1842

We have learned with bitter regret that a quarrel lately occurred at Lamar between Capt. Hickey of the *Natchez* and Capt. Stevenson of the St. Louis Volunteers. It arose from a dispute about a boat used in the transportation of the troops from Live Oak Point to Lamar. Capt. Hickey was dangerously and it is feared mortally wounded.

Issue August 4, 1842

A small party of Indians visited the settlement on Peach Creek a few miles west of Austin a few days since, and killed Mr. Addison Gillespie and another man whose name we have not learned.

From the *Sabine Advocate:* We are informed that the free booter, Jim Strickland was shot through the head, a few days ago, by a company of gentlemen from the Trinity river who were in pursuit of several negroes decoyed off by Jim, his brother Henry, and another individual, belonging to the Strickland company, one of whom they also killed. It was the same Jim Strickland and his brother Henry, who in attempting to assassinate Col. Straw at his own house, in Shelby county, shot a boy by the name of Buckner; also several weeks previous to this, he lay in ambuscade and shot a worthy citizen of Shelby county by the name of Middleton.

Issue August 11, 1842

We learn from a gentleman who arrived a few days since from Austin, that Capt. Dolson and Mr. Black of San Antonio were lately killed by Indians near Austin. They were out in company with ten others to hunt bears and were surprised and killed by the savages.

It is our painful duty to announce the death of Col. John H. Moore, so long and so favorably known in the history of our frontier warfare. Immediately after his return from the pursuit of a party of Indians that lately made a descent upon the settlements on Cummin's creek, he was attacked by an inflammatory fever, caused by fatigue and exposure he had undergone and so violent was the disease, that it terminated fatally in about two days. Thus has he fallen a noble martyr to the country he delighted to serve. His last campaign is over. His merits and achievements are registered in ever during characters; and long after the perfidious tribes who so frequently called forth his avenging arm, shall have melted away, his memory will be cherished by his grateful countrymen.

Issue August 23, 1842

Robertson county: Mr. Dread Dawson, well known as one of the oldest and wealthiest settlers of that county, died lately at his residence.

Issue September 10, 1842

We learn from the *Colorado Gazette*, that Baron Ernest Philabeaucourt, who arrived at Matagorda in last March with his family and twenty other emigrants from France, committed suicide lately while on board the sloop *Cutler* on her trip from Galveston to Matagorda.

Issue September 15, 1842

Capt. Prier and Mr. Donovan were killed by Indians near Austin on the 3d inst.

Issue September 29, 1842

Nathaniel Watrous, Representative elect for the county of Travis, died at Austin on the 19th inst. of congestive fever.

Col. Caldwell states that Col. Seguin has killed three sick men at Sulphur Springs; one was Dr. Smithers the other two Americans were McDonald and Rhea.

11

Issue October 11, 1842

A.C. Allen, who arrived on Friday evening from Bexar, has informed us that the brother of Gen. Vasques was mortally wounded on the Salado. He died a day or two after the battle and was buried on the Medina. Cordova was also killed.

Issue October 22, 1842

Died in this city on the 6th inst. of congestive fever, George R. Mercer, a native of Edinburgh, Scotland.

The schooner *Charlotte* arrived at Galveston on the 19th from New Orleans, and brought papers from that city of the 15th inst. They contain the intelligence of the loss of the steam ship *Merchant*. She left New Orleans on the 2nd inst. for Galveston with seventy passengers and on entering the Gulf encountered a heavy gale which caused her to leak so badly that on the morning of the 4th inst. she was run ashore on Raccoon Island when she immediately went to pieces. Three of the crew and a negro were drowned. A Mr. Barker, who was supposed to be deranged, shot himself immediately after the accident...

Issue October 25, 1842

New Orleans Bulletin -- Died yesterday morning at 7 o'clock on board the Texian sloop of war *Austin*, of congestive fever, after an illness of fifteen days, Capt. Robert Oliver.

Issue November 10, 1842

A man named White, who resided about two miles north of Austin, was killed a few days since by Indians. He was found dead near the foot of the mountain, and a short distance from him the tracks of moccasins were found, and a large trail of blood indicating that an Indian had been killed by him and dragged away.

Issue November 19, 1842

We learn from a gentleman from San Augustine that Mr. Napoleon B. Garner was killed in that city about a fortnight ago by Gen. J. Pinkney Henderson...

Issue December 1, 1842

Died on Thursday evening the 17th inst. at his residence in Austin county, Joseph C. Gentry, in the fiftieth year of his age; formerly of Dayton, Ohio.

Issue December 29, 1842

The body of a man was found on the 26th inst., in Bray's bayou about five miles from this city. A jury of inquest was held on Wednesday last and the body was recognized by Mr. DeChene as that of a frenchman who put up at his hotel a few days ago. It was found that the unfortunate man had been shot through the head.

Issue January 3, 1843

Died on the 19th of December at her residence on Galveston Bay, Mrs. Sarah Britton, late widow of Whitney Britton, deceased.

Issue January 5, 1843

It will be recollected that a large party of Indians passed down the San Antonio to the bay of Aransas about the same time that the Mexican army, under Vasquez, captured Bexar last spring. These Indians killed Mr. and Mrs. Gilleland, near Copano, and carried off their two children, but on their return from the coast were intercepted by the company under the command of Col. Owen and the children recaptured.

$100 reward to any person who will arrest and lodge in any place of security a man named Pouvais, charged as the murderer of a young frenchman whose name is unknown and who was killed near this city Monday the 26th of December, 1842. Said Pouvais is about five feet, ten inches high, is a frenchman and speaks very little english, dark complexion, black hair, black eyes, eye brows heavy, and a mole on the right side of his nose just between the eye brows. Said Pouvais came out from New Orleans by the *Neptune* under the pretence he wished to purchase a large quantity of hides. He returned on the *Neptune* on the 30th December from Galveston to New Orleans. The young frenchman who was murdered was recently an overseer on a plantation near Plaquemine in Louisiana...

Issue January 14, 1843

A party of about twenty Indians lately came to Austin, killed a man named Bell, and captured a Mr. Coleman, but the latter made his escape. They were pursued and three of them were killed by a party of citizens from Austin.

The coast fever is still raging among the Mexican troops, and several citizens of the United States have fallen victim to it. Capt. B.L. Hutton of the steamboat *Champion*, died on board that vessel at Tobasco, after the boat arrived at that port from Campeachy. One of the engineers died also and the owner, supercargo, and all the crew were so ill when last herd from that the vessel could not return to New Orleans.

Issue January 19, 1843

Died: Col. Matthew Caldwell, the hero of the Salado, at his residence in Gonzales on the 28th of December 1842, in the forty-third year of his age... Col. Caldwell was a native of North Carolina and emigrated to Gonzales county in 1830... buried with military honors, 30 December. [note: condensed].

Issue February 7, 1843

The bodies of Captain Webber, J.H. Auld, Mr. McConnell and Captain Clark, formerly of the steamer *Correo*, were found near Boliver Point, a few days since, who were lost on the schooner *Gen. Pike*, which capsized off Galveston about three weeks ago.

Issue February 21, 1843

$100 reward: Whereas, Mrs. Cannada, an amiable and highly respectable lady of this city was basely murdered in her own house on the evening of the 18th of February... The city council offers a reward of $100 to any person or persons who will deliver to the sheriff of this county the murderer...

Freshet in Red River... The steamer *Hunter*, from the vicinity of Jonesboro, arrived at the Raft, bringing intelligence that the entire country from Dooley's Ferry (Ark) to Jonesboro was completely overflowed, and that the river was still rising... We regret to state likewise that many lives were lost. At Jonesboro, a place almost entirely deserted, the family of Col. Johnson was supposed to be drowned. When the colonel and his family were last seen, they were on top of his house, surrounded by the waters, and beyond the reach of aid, and were undoubtedly finally engulfed... Col. Milam, of Kentucky, was drowned a short distance from Jonesboro, and many others were probably swept away, of whom we have no account.

Issue February 23, 1843

The City Sexton reported two deaths since last communication, to wit: B.S. Burke, son of A.J. and E. L. Burke, aged 11 months, and Mrs. Elizabeth Kennedy, who came up to a violent death by some person unknown.

Issue February 28, 1843

Zebediah Payne, who was arrested and taken to Tennessee by Mr. Crossman of Galveston a few months since, charged with the murder of William Coltart [in the county of Franklin on 10th June 1840] has been convicted, sentenced and executed. At the same time, Willis G. Carroll was sentenced and executed. [note: condensed].

Issue March 23, 1843

Maj. J.B. Ransom was recently killed by a shot from his own gun (near Waco Village). Our information states that he was out on a buffalo hunt, and while descending a steep hill placed his gun before him for support; but it unfortunately slipped and went off; the ball passing directly through his head, killing him instantly.

Suffering from cold. The *Galveston Times* mentions that a man was frozen to death near the dwelling of Mr. Parish, on Galveston Bay, on the morning of the 15th. The name of the deceased was Campbell, formerly a Captain in Lafite's service.

Issue March 30, 1843

Departed this life on the morning of the 28th inst., at half past five o'clock, James Izod Niles, infant son of J.W. and Alesannah Niles, aged two years, two months, fourteen days.

The *Planter's Gazette* mentions that the skeleton of a man and a horse were found a few weeks since in the bottom of the San Bernard, near the steam saw mill. The man had evidently been hung, as a lariat was hanging just over the bones, and a bullet hole was discovered in the skull of the horse... A shaving box was found with the initials J.S. and it is said that the box has been identified as the one formerly belonging to Mr. J. Sloan, who was in that neighborhood about three years ago and suddenly disappeared.

Issue April 6, 1843

We have learned with feeling of the most bitter regret that Col. James R. Cook, of Washington, was killed on the 31st ult by his friend Mr. Adkins...

Issue April 20, 1843

The City Sexton reported but one death for the last two weeks, to wit: Johnson Jackson, a pauper.

Issue April 22, 1843

Texian Navy --The ship *Austin* and brig *Wharton* were at New Orleans on the 15th, and upon the eve of sailing for Campeachy. The *Tropic* of that day says they would have sailed on the night of the 14th inst, but for the necessity that existed of disposing of the mutineers before the Court Martial on the *Austin*.

This Court Martial was instituted for the trial of the men who mutinied on board the *San Antonio* about one year ago, which resulted in the death of Lieut. Fuller. Four of the men were tried on the 14th, viz: Antonio Landois, James Hudgens, Wm. Barrington, and Issac Allen. Three other prisoners remain, who were probably tried on the 15th. The leader and instigator of the mutiny, named Oswald, escaped from the parish jail in New Orleans several months ago, and another mutineer named Pumpelly, died in prison in New Orleans last winter. The latter, it is said, killed Lieut. Fuller.

Issue April 27, 1843

Mr. J.S. Phelps in a letter addressed to the editor of the *Northern Standard* and written at Bird's Fort, states that a Mr. Sloat, a white man, and Jack Joy and Capt. McCullough, two Delawares, arrived at the fort on the 27th of March from the Waco and Keachie Villages. They stated that while at those villages a war party came in with three scalps, one of which had some grey hairs, another was of a dark color and the third they did not go near enough to distinguish. It is supposed these scalps were taken from the bodies of Dr. Calder and Messrs. Clements and Whistler who were killed near Peter's colony some weeks since...

Gen. Henderson was indicted before the District Court of San Augustine for the murder of N.B. Garner, and his trial took place on the sixth of April and was concluded on the 8th, when the jury after retiring about five minutes returned with a verdict of not guilty. R.B. Wallis, District Attorney pro tem, and E.W. Cullen appeared in behalf of the Republic, and Messrs. Rusk, Reily, Wheeler, and Scurry for the defendant.

Issue April 29, 1843

News from the United States and Mexico: The news in relation to the Texian prisoners, in the main, is gloomy enough, especially as regards those retaken who belong to Col. Fisher's command. The order to decimate the number retaken (165) we are fearful has been carried into effect near Matamorous. The report is that seventeen were shot.

We have heard it stated that of this number, young Crittendon came near being one. Fortunately, however, the cutter *Woodbury*, brought an order for his release in season to save his life. The *Vincennes* touched at Tampico on the 13th inst., with the expectation of finding him there, but he had left three days before for the city of Mexico. Not a doubt can be entertained of his safety. We have been unable to learn the names of those shot.

Col. Fisher, Gen. Green, Capt. Reese, and Messrs. Shephard, VanNess, and Hancock, had arrived at Perote, with such of the men as accompanied them, some eighteen in all. Fisher and Green are chained together, with heavier irons than the rest, and are compelled to work with the other prisoners carrying sand, &c. A young brother of Capt. Reese has been released to Gen. Thompson.

Col. Fisher with four of his officers were about a mile in advance when the attack upon the guard at Salado commenced. Dr. Brenham and Messrs. Lyons, Rice, and Higginson were killed dead on the spot---poor Fitzgerald was mortally wounded, but survived some two or three days...

Dr. Booker, one of the San Antonio prisoners and a meritorious men, was accidently killed at Perote about the 1st inst. by a drunken Mexican soldier. The latter pointed his gun with the intention of shooting one of his own officers; but unfortunately the ball lodged in the breast of Dr. B., who survived a few days.

Mutineer in the Navy. The court martial lately held on board the ship *Austin* in New Orleans, sentenced four of the mutineers to death... Antonio Landois --guilty of all charges and specification and sentenced to suffer death, unanimously. James Hudgins --guilty of all charges and specification and sentenced to suffer death, unanimously. Isaac Allen --guilty of the 1st and 3d charges, sentenced to suffer death, unanimously. William Simpson --guilty and sentenced to suffer death...

Issue May 9, 1843

A party of seven or eight Mexicans attempted to steal some horses near Seguin about a fortnight since, but were discovered by the citizens who immediately pursued them, killed two, wounded two or three others, and it supposed that one was drowned in the Guadalupe. The two who were killed were recognized. Their names are Rubrio and Garza of Bexar.

Richard Jackson, one of the prisoners captured at Bexar last autumn, died at Perote on the first of April last.

Issue May 11, 1843

City Council. The report of the City Sexton stating that but one death had occurred within the city for the last three weeks, viz: Henry Simmons, who died of consumption.

Issue June 1, 1843

Died on Wednesday, May 31st, of chronic bronchitis, William H. Trott, aged 23 years. His friends and acquaintances are invited to attend his funeral this evening at four o'clock from the residence of Philip Thompson.

Issue June 3, 1843

An Imposter -- a German by the name of Rhinehart appeared in Fannin county a few weeks ago and represented that he was the agent of a company of wealthy Germans, who were about landing at Jonesborough, in Red River county... The people of that section were delighted to learn that a large company of wealthy Germans were soon to settle among them, and many placed implicit credit in his statements. But soon after he had started the teams for Jonesborough, he set out in the direction of the Brazos and nothing has been heard from him since. We are inclined to believe this man to be insane, and it is not improbable that this was the individual whose body was recently found near the Falls of the Brazos, and who it was supposed starved to death.

Issue June 13, 1843

Died of bronchitis on the 6th inst. at Allenwood, Galveston Bay, Rowland Allen, aged 62 years. He met his fate with great resignation, rejoicing that the hour was at hand when his spirit would take its flight to a world of bliss.

Issue June 17, 1843

MURDER -- Col. John O'Brien was lately shot with a rifle ball while standing in the door of his house at Anahuac by some person concealed in the bushes near the place. He expired a few moments after receiving the wound. Mr. Ferguson, who was standing with him, was also shot and dangerously wounded with a charge of buck shot at the same time. It is feared that Mr. Ferguson can survive his wounds only a few days.

The late American Charge d'Affaires, Hon. Joseph Eves, died at Galveston on the 16th inst. of consumption. He had not a single enemy in the Republic. His funeral was attended by the largest concourse of citizens ever seen at Galveston.

Issue June 27, 1843

Dr. Hagan, late editor of the *Vicksburg Sentinel*, was killed at Vicksburg on the 7th inst. by Mr. D.W. Adams. It appears that Dr. Hagan had published an article reflecting the character of Judge Adams, the father of D.W. Adams, and the latter armed himself and met Dr. Hagan while on his way from his boarding house to his office just after dinner. Adams struck the doctor with a cane, a scuffle ensued, and both parties fell. Adams drew a pistol and shot the former in the back of the head, killing him instantly. Dr. Hagan was unarmed. Adams has been arrested.

Issue June 30, 1843

The *Galveston News* mentions that Ferdinand Diderich, a native of Poland, was shot on the 20th of June by a German named Huffmaster whilst in the act of committing a robbery on the premises of Mr. E. Kaufman, merchant, on the Strand, and died almost instantly. Huffmaster being employed as a watchman by E. Kaufman.

Issue July 6, 1843
A Frenchman named Jean Joseph Jeaneau was drowned on the 17th ult. while attempting to ford the Colorado opposite to Austin.

Issue July 10, 1843
The City Sexton reports but two deaths had occurred within the last three weeks, to-wit: a child of F. Herring's, and a black boy from Colorado county who came to the city sick.

Issue July 13, 1843
Homicide or Murder -- an elderly gentleman named Bartlet Fry, who resided on the Attoyae, was killed in San Augustine county on the 29th ult. by John Garner. We have not learned the particulars of this melancholy occurrence.

Death by lightning -- *Richmond Star*... The bolt that accompanied it struck a house in Butchertown killing a young man named Thomas Jones, instantly. He was standing at an open window, as was his custom after meals, when he was struck-the bolt passing from his head along his person to the shoe, ripping it off and setting his clothes on fire. [note: mentions a sister and a brother named James].

Issue July 18, 1843
Died in Cincinnati, Ohio, the 25th June at half past 9 o'clock of chronic diarrhea, Mary Folger, consort of John S. Stansbury and daughter of Moses and Judith Coffin, in her 25th year.

Commodore Edwin W. Moore of the Texian Navy... is a native of this place. He is the son of Thomas Moore, deceased, and a nephew of the late Alexander Moore. He is now a little upwards of 30 years of age...

Issue August 3, 1843
Horrid Tragedy -- It is with feelings of the most painful emotion that we are compelled to record one of the most bloody and shocking affrays that has ever disgraced any portion of Texas. Mr. Sneed, who arrived on the 29th ult. from Bastrop, has informed us that Capt. Mark B. Lewis, a Mr. Nolan and a Mr. Peyton were all killed in an affray at Austin a few days since! [note: condensed].

The City Sexton reported one death since his last communication to the Board, to wit: Joseph D. Rogers of Montgomery county, who came to the city sick; disease, bilious remittent fever.

Issue August 12, 1843

A German named William Weigand was accidentally drowned while bathing in the Bayou in this city on Thursday evening.

Issue August 24, 1843

Four men were killed by Indians; their names are John H. Davis, Elisha C. Simons, Frances Sharpe, and a man named Caldwell, of Paris, Lamar county.

Died: Miss Rebecca Ann Lamar, daughter of our ex-president. She was in her sixteenth year and died on the 29th of July at Macon, Georgia.

Issue August 31, 1843

City Council. The treasurer was ordered to pay G.M. Taylor for sundries for Mrs. McMahan; C.H. Jaeger for medical attendance; Brown & Conger for sundries; S.D. Staats for burying Mrs. McMahan; S.D. Staats for burying a pauper named Robinson.

Issue September 5, 1843

Mr. Hueston late editor of the *Baton Rouge Gazette* was lately killed in a disgraceful duel by Mr. LaBranch, formerly Charge d'Affaires to Texas.

Issue September 7, 1843

Trouble among the Cherokees -- all is consternation among the Cherokees, owning to the murder of John Ross. The particulars of his death are not known. It is supposed that he was killed by the friends of Ridge, who was killed about two years ago by the adherents of the Ross party. Fears are entertained that the death of Ross will lead to a civil war among the Cherokees.

The City Sexton reports three deaths have occurred within the last three weeks, to wit: an infant child of Joseph Reynolds; Mrs. McMahan, disease monomania; one Robinson, a pauper, disease not known.

Issue September 9, 1843

Died in this city on the 6th inst. of pulmonary consumption, Mrs. Leathe G. Mott, formerly of Smithland, Kentucky.

Issue September 19, 1843

Col. L.P. Cook, who was engaged in the late melancholy affray at Austin, has been arrested for the murder of Capt. Lewis. Col. Cook is in close confinement and will not be admitted to bail.

Died in this city on the 15th inst., John B. Cochran, son of Mr. O.J. Cochran, aged 18 years.

Issue September 21, 1843

Died in this city on the 15th inst. of congestive fever, Francis P. Herring, formerly of Georgia.

City Council-the treasurer to pay S.D. Staats for burying a pauper named Herring.

The City Sexton reports but three deaths have occurred within the last two weeks, to wit: Mrs. L.G. Mott, John B. Cochran, and F.P. Herring.

Issue September 26, 1843

The trial of Col. L.P. Cook indicted for the murder of Capt. Lewis has been transferred to Bastrop county.

Issue September 28, 1843

City Council. Treasurer to pay S.D. Staats to burying a pauper named Brittle.

The City Sexton reports but two deaths within the last week, to wit: Mrs. Busby, and an infant child of Samuel Pascal.

Issue October 3, 1843

We learn from the *Civilian* that a man named Tyson, a gardener, was murdered and thrown into a well, and the house occupied by himself and a German named Henry Weyers, burned to the ground on the morning of the 26th ult. A German named Charles Henninger stands committed to make his trail at the District Court for the act. [note: occurred in Galveston].

The *Sarah Barnes* is a total wreck having been lost at sea on the 25th ult.... Messrs. Henry S. Dagget, of N.O., Jas. Potter, and the woman [Adaline] were drowned... One of the men who drifted on to the Island says two men were taken off the raft he was on by sharks, and thinks Blair of Galveston was one of them, though others think he (Blair) was on the same raft with the captain... Fears are entertained that Capt. Frankland [note: see Franklin] and his associates are all lost...

The trial of Col. L.P. Cook was not concluded during the session of the Court at Bastrop. He was arraigned on the charge of being accessary to the murder of Mr. Peyton. He is also indicted for the murder of Capt. Lewis.

Issue October 5, 1843

City council. The treasurer to pay Hon. A.P. Thompson for the fees on the estate of Mrs. Julia McMahan.

Issue October 24, 1843

We regret to announce that Charles R. Alexander, formerly one of the editors of the *Diamond*, and Robert H. Brenham, formerly one of the editors of the *Tropic*, lately died of yellow fever in New Orleans. The latter was a brother of the chivalrous Dr. Brenham who fell in the struggle to liberate our prisoners at Saltillo.

Issue November 2, 1843

George Barret, indicted for the murder of Peyton and Lewis, effected his escape from prison in Austin on the evening of the 19th ult.

Issue November 4, 1843

Indictment for murder have been found by the Grand Jury of Galveston county against Charles Heniker, J.W. Pilant, and a German named Hoffmaster. [note: condensed].

Issue November 28, 1843

Charles Heninger was on the 11th inst. sentenced by Judge Morris to be hung on the 8th of December next for the murder of Mr. Tyson. Hoffmester was also sentenced to be hung on the first Monday in August next: but as there are many palliating circumstances in his favor, it is not improbable that he will be pardoned by the President.

Issue December 7, 1843

Death of Pete Whetstone: This noted freebooter, that for many years has been an object of terror and hatred on the frontier of Texas, was recently killed in his own house, 20 miles from eastern Shreveport, on Sunday 9th November. He has left three sons to have grown up amid scenes of crime and bloodshed. It is said not less than twenty persons have been murdered by Whetstone during the last fifteen years.

Issue December 14, 1843

Charles Heninger was hung at Galveston on the 8th inst. He confessed his guilt on the day previous to his death, but expressed no remorse for the horrid crime.

Issue December 26, 1843

Died on the 21st inst. at his residence of consumption, Joseph M. Robinson, merchant of this city, native of Pennsylvania; aged thirty-five years.

Issue December 28, 1843

City council. The Treasurer to pay Dr. A. Ewing to professional service to ad[?]ed to H.T. Wooddy during his last illness, S.D. Staats to burying d[itto?]

Issue December 30, 1843

Died in this city on the 27th inst., George G. Gazlay, a native of New York, aged 36 years. His friends and acquaintances are especially invited to attend his funeral from his late residence this evening at 3 o'clock.

Bexar -- We learn from a gentleman who recently arrived from Bexar that business of that city continues very dull. A few traders have arrived from the Rio Grande within the last six or eight weeks, but they brought only a few hundred dollars to purchase goods. They confirmed a report circulated a few weeks since about Agaton, the bandit who has long been a terror to the border settlers, was killed about three months since while in pursuit of a party of settlers. The latter, having received intelligence that he was following their trail to attack them, suddenly turned back and lay in ambush in a thicket. Agaton and a few followers soon after appeared and while passing, intent on capturing his supposed victims, was shot down and killed instantly.

Issue January 4, 1844

City Council. Alderman Raadel, in reply to a question from Alderman Chanch, respecting the money advanced by the City Council to defray the expenses of the late Mrs. McMahan's illness and burial, stated that so soon as the Secretary of the Council furnished him with the proper evidences of indebtness and that he has the authority of the Probate Judge, the same shall be paid into the City Treasury immediately.

Issue January 9, 1843

Indians... It will be recollected that Judge Janes was murdered at his own door by a party of strange Indians who enticed him out, pretending that they were Tonkewns.

Issue January 11, 1844

Hoffmeister, who was sentenced to be hung at the last term of the District Court at Galveston, has been pardoned by the President.

Issue January 13, 1844

Died Thursday, January 11th, Josiah G. Moore, son of A.G. Moore (of a scald) in the fourth year of his age.

Issue January 20, 1844

Prisoners at Perote who have died. John Trapnall, Joseph Simons, James S. White, Norman Woods, Zachias Wilson, S.B. Bennett, Z. Island [?][sic], A.F. Burras, Wm. H. Vanhorn, J.P. Wyatt, Wm. Miller, D.A. Hollowell, and John Clement Grosjean, of Missouri.

Senate met. A bill for the relief of M.E. Goodwyn, Louise Ann Harris, Eliza V. Harris and other heirs of Robert W. Harris, deceased.

Issue January 23, 1844

House of Representatives. A joint resolution for the relief of the heirs of John Hebbins/Hubins, read 3d time and passed.

A message from the Senate informing the House of the passage of a bill for the relief of Maria W. Goodwin &c. and heirs of Robert W. Harris, deceased.

Issue January 30, 1844

Loss of the Schooner *Galveston* -- Fears are entertained that the schooner *Galveston* has been wrecked and that all on board have perished. This vessel sailed from Galveston for New Orleans on the 15th January, and on the night following, a Norther came up suddenly and it is believed she capsized before those on board could make any preparations to escape. The *News* gives the following as the list of those who were on board: Capt. Wm. Ricketts; mate and three hands, names unknown. Passengers, Midshipman Bryant, formerly of Texas Navy; Mr. Degeurs, wife and child; Mr. Klein, and a German female, name unknown.

Senate. A joint resolution for the relief of Sarah N. Hubert -- read 1st time.

Issue February 1, 1844

The *Caddo Gazette* says: A few days since Judge Hansford was most cruelly murdered in Harrison county, Texas, by an old gentleman, named Mosely, and his son-in-law, whose name is Bullard.

Issue February 8, 1844

Indians!... a party of hostile savages or white men worse than savages, attacked the house of Mr. Wm. B. Wilson on Little River about twenty-five miles above Nashville, killed and scalped a negro and stole twenty-five horses.

Hon. George W. Wright of Red River has not attended Congress during any part of the late session, having been prevented from the discharge of his official duties by a dangerous illness.

Issue February 17, 1844

Perote, Jan. 13,1844. Leonidas Saunders of Montgomery county, Texas, died last night of the prevailing epidemic. Mr. S. was Chief Justice of that county when he left it, and I will venture to say that no one can be found in his district more worthy to fill his office -- in short, he was a well-informed, amiable gentleman. There are many others yet sick in the hospital, many of them dangerously.

Issue February 22, 1844

Small Pox... This loathsome disease has made its appearance in Austin county and there is reason to fear that it will spread rapidly, owing to the fact that many children in the vicinity have not been vaccinated. It first appeared in the family of Mr. Thomas Bell, whose wife and child were dangerously sick with the disease at the last account. They caught it from a Mr. Newton, who recently arrived from Alabama.

Issue February 24, 1844

The *Galveston News* mentions that on the morning of the 22d ult. "the shattered fragments of two chests were picked up on the beach at Bolivar, one of which contained the following articles: --a speaking trumpet, having engraved upon it, "1842, from G.H. Stewart to Hugh Larkin," a "protection" for Hugh Larkin, who is described to be a native of Baltimore, aged 26, light complexion, brown hair and blue eyes, with a scar over his right eye; a miniature of a person corresponding with the above description; several books, ordinary clothing, a pair of shoes and sundry other small trinkets."

"It is supposed that the articles may have belonged to someone on board the *Galveston*."

Issue February 27, 1844

Gov. Reynolds of Missouri committed suicide on the 9th inst.

Hon. Albert Hoa, Senator of Louisiana, died lately at New Orleans. His funeral took place on the 16th inst. and the papers mention that the funeral procession was one of the largest witnessed in the city.

The Death of a Brave and Good Man -- ...Doctor Ridgely, whose recent death has been noticed in most of the papers of the Union, was one of those noble, brave and pure souled men...

Issue February 29, 1844

The *Harrison Times* says that the examination of Mosely and others before J.W. Maulding, Justice of the Peace, on a charge of killing John Hansford, was concluded on the 26th Jan.

Issue March 12, 1844

There have been several outrages among the negroes upon two or three of the plantations on the Brazos within the last month. The overseer on the plantation of Mr. Burdit, near Richmond, was killed by one of the slaves, who attacked him while at work. Two negroes on the plantation of Mr. Terrey attacked the latter with knives and axes by Mr. Terry, with admirable courage defended himself with a large heavy whip until he drew a pistol and shot one so as to disable him. With a well directed blow of his whip he broke the arm of the other and compelled him to submit.

Issue March 14, 1844

On Friday the 1st inst. between 3 and 4 o'clock in the morning, the Steamers *Buckeye* and *DeSoto* came in contact with each other near the mouth of Red River... sixty or seventy persons were drowned including whites and blacks. Among the lost were a daughter of Mr. Hynes (of Alexandria) aged 10 years, his sister-in-law, and Miss Smith (a young lady raised by Mr. H.) Mr. Hynes also lost 15 negroes. Mr. John Blunt lost his wife, child and seven negroes. Mr. A. McKenzie lost his wife, 7 children and 4 negroes, and Col. King lost 2 child [sic]. Mr. Beard attempted to swim ashore with his nephew on his back, both were drowned.

Issue March 16, 1844

Mier Prisoners -- Within the last two or three months twenty of the prisoners have died, and at last accounts sixty-two were employed carrying sand and other articles to repair the walls of the Castle. Among the late victims to disease was French S. Grey, formerly a noted lawyer of Bexar... He was captured while attending his professional duties in the court at Bexar, in the fall of 1842, and had been in captivity nearly two years. His remains were decently buried in the *ditch* of the Castle of Perote.

Issue March 21, 1844

Gen. Felix Huston/Hoston, late of Texas, is reported to have been killed in a duel at New Orleans.

Issue March 28, 1844

Most Horrid Indian Murder -- Mr. Monsey, Mr. Jamison, Mrs. Monsey, were killed by Indians on the morning of the 20th of February, in Fannin county. Two sons of Mr. Monsey are missing, one about sixteen years old, the other about twelve. [note: condensed].

Issue April 9, 1844

The negro who lately murdered the overseer on the plantation of Mr. Burdet was shot dead on the evening of the same day that the murder was committed.

A young man named Coffee was drowned a few days since in the Brazos near Richmond. He was crossing the river in a pirogue, with another man, and the latter fell overboard, upsetting the pirogue. Mr. Coffee was unable to swim and was drowned. His companion held on to the pirogue and was saved.

Issue April 11, 1844

The trail of John Garner for the murder of Bartlett Fry was concluded at San Augustine on Thursday the 28th ult. Two or three days were occupied in empannelling a Jury, nearly every man in the county having expressed an opinion relative to the guilt of the prisoner; and on Thursday evening reported they could not agree. The Court decreed a mistrial and admitted the prisoner to bail in the sum of five thousand dollars for his appearance at the next term of the District Court.

Issue April 13, 1844

Died at the residence of Leonard W. Groce on the 8th of April, 1844, Mrs. Jane C. Reid, the wife of the Rev. H. Reid, aged 53 years, 4 months and 25 days.

The funeral sermon of Mrs. Reid will be preached tomorrow morning by the Rev. Mr. Gillet at eleven o'clock in the Presbyterian Church in this city.

Issue April 20, 1844

We learn from J.P. Lowry that three of the Mier prisoners died at Matamoros last year. Their names were M. McAulay, Lynn Bobb, and James Barben. Mr. McAulay was formerly a citizen of this county and was highly esteemed by all who knew him.

Issue April 25, 1844

Murderer of Chavis -- The trial of John McDaniel, who was arrested last spring near Independence, charged with the murder of Chavis the Santa Fe trader, was lately concluded at St. Louis. He was found guilty of murder in the first degree, and was remanded to jail and a guard of sixty men, with loaded rifles ordered, for forty days.

Issue May 2, 1844

A white man has lately been arrested at the Falls of the Brazos, charged as the murderer of the three Indians that were killed on the plantation of Mr. Stroud, about a fortnight since. It is reported that he murdered them while sleeping in their beds, and on being discovered by an Indian, he raised the cry of "Indians" and when the neighbors came he reported that the murders were committed by wild Indians. The persons murdered were two women and one child. They were Muscogus or Creeks, and had resided on the plantation of Mr. Stroud for one or two years.

Issue May 11, 1844

At a meeting of the members of the Bar of the Fourth Judicial District and officers of the Court of Bexar County, held at the Court House in San Antonio on the 9th day of March 1844, to pay a suitable Tribute of Respect to the memory of their late friend and associate John R. Cunningham, Attorney at Law of Bexar, who died on 20th September 1842 whilst on his march as a prisoner from this place to Mexico.

Issue May 16, 1844

We learn from the *LaGrange Intelligencer* that the hostile Indians have recently been committing depredations on the San Gabriel... One of the men found murdered was a Mr. Mercer.

Issue May 18, 1844

Indian Murders: Little did we think a few weeks since, when recording the barbarous massacre of Mr. Monsey and his family in Fannin county, that we should so soon be compelled to record another massacre even more atrocious and appalling. We learn from Mr. Beaty and Mr. Stevens, that Dr. Kinney, Mr. Castleberry, and Mr. Courteney, have all been murdered near their residence on the Brushy by a party of Wacoes. [note: condensed].

Issue May 23, 1844

Our former statement of murders committed by the Indians is confirmed; with the exception that Mr. Courtney is not among the slain.

Issue June 8, 1844

The body of Mr. B. Canfield, whose residence is about 9 miles from Houston at Piny Point, was found in Buffalo Bayou, a short distance below his dwelling, on the 6th inst. He went out to catch some fish the day before, and not returning, a search was instituted. The body was found by three gentlemen who went from Houston for that purpose. He had been shot in the face and neck with fourteen buck shot by some person unknown, and the Jury returned a verdict accordingly. Appearances show that he was shot in a sitting posture near the edge of the water on a steep bank. The foot steps as well as the range of the ball holes, prove that the assassin discharged the fatal shot from an eminence on the opposite bank, 40 feet higher than his victim was sitting.

Issue June 11, 1844

Galveston News. From Corpus Christi: The Indians returned again on the 30th and surrounded the whole Caballada belonging to the citizens of the Ranche... of the whites, George Gleason and two Mexicans were killed.

Issue June 15, 1844

Judge Earl of South Carolina died suddenly of a stroke of paralysis on the 24th ult. at Greenville.

Death of a Veteran – Mr. John Jacobus VanVorst died at Schenectady, N.Y., on the 23d ult. at the advanced age of 103 years, 4 months, and 4 days. It is stated that he never used ardent spirits. During the Revolutionary War he commuted that part of his rations for money.

Administrator's Notice. Estate of John Belden, dec., of Harris county. J. DeCordova, Admin.

Issue June 18, 1844

The venerable Dr. James Thacher died at Plymouth, Mass., on the 23d ult. During the Revolutionary War he entered the army as surgeon, and continued to serve in that capacity to the end of the war. He was present at many of the principal battles of the Revolution, and terminated his services at Yorktown. He was an eye-witness of the execution of Andre, and has fully described the scene in his Military Journal. Dr. Thacher was the author of several approved medical works, but was probably better known to the public as the author of the "Military Journal" and the "History of Plymouth."

Issue June 20, 1844

The Galveston papers give an account of suicide committed by J.R. Dufour, by shooting himself with a pistol. Mr. D. is said to have been a highly respectable merchant of that city. Some domestic troubles occasioned the fatal act that terminated his existence.

Issue July 9, 1844

The execution of John and David McDaniel and Joseph Brown has been suspended by the President to the 12th of July.

Issue July 18, 1844

The City Sexton reports the number of deaths since the first of January 1844 to this date, the 13th July 1844, being 6 months and 13 days:
Josiah G. Moore, 4 years, of a scald.
J.B. Cassidy, 45 years, dropsy.
Miss Francis Freil, 6 years, 8 months, inflammation of brain.
Warren, negro boy, 19 years, sore throat.
John N. Wilson, 29 years, of fever.
Isaac, negro man, 40 years, dropsy.
Louisa Adelaide Thompson, 10 months, 13 days, inflammation of brain.
Rebecca Louisa Tomkins, 13 months, 5 days, of fever.
Augustine Kemper, 40 years, disease unknown.

Andrew Lewson/Letson/Lettson, 45 years, of consumption.
An infant of J. Utz, 18 hours, disease unknown.
Robert Levenhagen, 28 years, of conjestive fever.
Thomas Ellis, 40 years, disease unknown.

Issue July 25, 1844
The City Sexton reports for the past week one death, to wit: Milley, a negress, belonging to J.J. Crawford, aged 24 years, of disease of the head.

Issue August 3, 1844
Died on the 30th ult. at half past 1 o'clock a.m., Maj. Philemon Waters, in the 48th year of his age. Maj. Waters had impaired his health from excessive exposure in traveling. In this situation he returned to the plantation of his brother, Col J.W. Waters, about 15 miles below Richmond on the Brazos, where after a short illness he expired with congestive fever. He has left a widow and six children, who reside in Mobile, Alabama. It is but a few weeks since he took leave of them to visit this country, where he designed to settle.

He was a native of Newberry Dist., South Carolina. His father and grandfather served in the war of the Revolution. The former held a Captaincy, and the latter commission of Major under Gen. Washington.

Two brothers of the latter were killed by the tories in the partizan war of South Carolina and another brother held the rank of Col. and served in the Northern army. Although Maj. Waters was not a resident citizen of this country, yet he has long been among the most active and efficient friends of Texas. Whenever a call has been made upon the patriotic citizens of Mobile to send us assistance in time of our distress, he has always been our able and successful advocate. He was a member of the Methodist Episcopal Church of Alabama.

Issue August 6, 1844
Judge Patrick C. Jack is no more. He died in this city on the 4th inst. at the hour of 6 o'clock p.m. Judge Jack came to Texas in the year 1832. In him, his country has lost a powerful advocate, and our judiciary one of its most talented, popular and impartial judges. [note: condensed].

Issue August 8, 1844
We regret to state that Dr. Stephen H. Everett, who came passenger by the last trip of the New York from Galveston, died yesterday at the St. Charles Hotel. Dr. E. was a native of New York...

Issue August 10, 1844
The City Sexton presented his bi-weekly report, to wit:
July 29th, a Mulatto child named Betsey, belonging to J.C. Sheffield, died in child birth.

July 31st, Captain John Manson, a native of Scotland, aged about 34 years, of Billious Fever.

July 31st, Miss Cathrine Kenard, native of Germany, aged about 18 years, of Bilious Remittent Fever.

August 1st, Joseph Schmidt, a native of France, aged 28 years.

August 1st, Sephe Schmidt, a native of France, aged 26 years.

The last two named persons died of Fever and from want of medical attention, which they refused.

August 1st, Windle Buck, a native of Germany, aged about 54 years, of Bilious Fever.

August 1st, an infant child of T.W. Bennett.

Issue August 15, 1844

The City Sexton reported the following deaths for the past week, viz:

August 4, Hon. P.C. Jack, aged 35 years, of Typhus Fever.

August 5, David Campbell, aged 6 years, of fever, son of R.C. Campbell, Esq.

August 6, James Rather, aged 49 years, of fever.

August 9, Samuel Kelly, aged 33 years, Billious Fever.

August 9, A black boy named Arnold, aged 6 years, belonging to J.B. Johnson, drowned Buffalo Buffalo [sic].

August 10, Mrs. S.G. Howell, 40 years, conjestive fever.

Issue August 20, 1844

Commander J.T.K. Lothrop of the Navy of Texas died at Washington on the 14th inst. of billious fever. He was a native of Massachusetts and a descendant in the maternal line from Kirkland, one of the early pilgrim fathers...

The Hon. Tilghman A. Howard [of Illinois], minister to this Republic from the U.S., died at Washington on the 16th inst.

The City Sexton reports the following deaths, viz:

August 11, Geo. H. Dutton, of fever, aged 22 years.

August 11, Mrs. Chenault, of fever, aged 30 years.

August 11, Antonion, a Mexican, of fever, aged 28 years.

August 11, John Blessmann, of fever, about 12 years.

August 12, J.V. Uglow, of fever, about 35 years.

August 12, J.B. Young, son of J.A. Young, 2 years 7 months.

August 13, --- Turner, came from the country sick, of fever, aged 28 or 30 years.

August 15, Col. J.P. Lowrey, 35 years.

August 16, John Bishop, came from the country sick, of fever, aged 28 years.

August 17, Julia Tyler, of fever, aged 13 years.

Issue August 24, 1844

The Hon. William H. Jack departed this life on the morning of the 20th inst. at the plantation of Gov. Runnels on the Brazos. He had contracted the epidemic that has prevailed in Galveston and died with the black vomit... The two brothers have departed together - together they lived - together they struggled hand in hand in the great cause of liberty, and together they have retired from the theater of action. *Par nobile fratrum*. Like the two Whartons, neither could survive the other.

James P. Lowrey died at the Old Capitol on the evening of the 16th inst. [note: lengthy praise given]. Col. Lowrey was a native of Tennessee, and had, in early life, removed to Mississippi, where he had acquired high honors at the Bar. His emigration to Texas was as late as 1838.

Hon. Richard Morris, Judge of this District, died on Monday last at 10 p.m. of the disease which has recently prevailed here, its last and most lamented victim... No man in the community could have died whose loss would have been more generally and seriously felt, or whose place it would be more difficult to supply. As a judge he was not only the pride and ornament of his District, but of the Supreme Court, where his opinions were of the first authority. *Civilian.*

Issue August 27, 1844

Died on the 25th inst., Frances Elizabeth, eldest daughter of Daniel G. and Hester E. Wheeler of this city, aged 4 years and 5 months.

An election will be held at the City Hotel on Saturday the 31st day of August inst., to fill the vacancy of Alderman of Ward No. 1, occasioned by the death of Robert Levenhagen, dec., Houston.

Issue August 29, 1844

Administrators notice. Estate of Charles Scarborough late of this county, deceased. A.W. Ridgeway, adm.

City Sexton report:
August 19, Carolina Simmler, aged 1 year, 7 months, of Hooping cough.
August 20, Infant child of Nelson Davis, aged 26 days.
August 21, Catherine Henrietta Ewing, aged 5 years, of Fever.
August 21, Turner, aged 50 years, of consumption.

September 10, 1844

The report of the City Sexton states that three deaths occurred during the past week, viz:
September 1st, Mrs. Martha Ann Bryan, aged 28 years, of fever.

September 1st, Mrs. Margary B. Simmons, aged 23 years, of fever.
September 2d, Mary H. Bohannon, aged 60 years, of fever.

Issue September 12, 1844
Tribute of Respect for Commander J.T.K. Lothrop. We sympathize in the sorrows of that widowed and absent mother in the irreparable loss she has sustained by the early fall of her son.

Issue September 14, 1844
$500 reward for the apprehension and safe keeping of James L. Dawson, late Creek Agent, who from all appearances premeditatedly murdered Seaborn Hill, who has long been a trader in the Creek Nation. Two hundred dollars will be given for the apprehension of his accomplice and brother-in-law John R. Baylor.

Issue September 17, 1844
The City Sexton reports but two deaths occurred during the last week, to wit:
September 8th, James Wilson, aged 34 years, of fever.
September 12th, Mrs. Susan M. Kuykendall, aged 28 years, of fever.

Issue September 19, 1844
Died in this city on the morning of the 16th inst. in the 35th year of his age, Warren S. Depew, a native of Herkimer county, New York, and for the last several years a citizen of this place.

Issue September 24, 1844
A correspondent of the *Planter*, speaking of the recent visitation of sickness and death among our citizens, uses the following just language in relation to Wm. H. Jack: Mr. Jack was one of the highest order of intellect. At the Bar, in the Senate, before the Hastings, he was a match for any man... He was the Calhoun of Texas...

Issue September 28, 1844
We see the funeral of Mrs. E.C. Franklin, consort of Judge B.E. Franklin of Galveston. The burial took place on the 25th inst.

Address on the occasion of the funeral of J.T.K. Lothrop... He was a native of Massachusetts, but reared and educated in the State of New York, whither his parents had emigrated while he was quite young. He was a lineal descendant of Kirkland, one of the Pilgrim Fathers, who disgusted with the licentiousness, the despotism, and religious persecutions of the english throne, left the land of their birth... When our Revolution broke out, he readily abandoned home, friends, and all, and came to our rescue...

Issue October 5, 1844

All persons having claims against the estate of Henry Reinermann, dec., will present and prove them... Louise Reinermann, executrix.

Issue October 10, 1844

The City Sexton reports the deaths that have taken place in this city since 14th September to date:
September 15, Warren S. Depew, 35 years, of fever.
September 20, R. Hampshire, aged 50 years, of fever.
September 24, Mrs. Teresa Uglow, aged 31 years, of consumption.
September 26, Elizabeth B. Brown, aged 45 years, of fever.
October 2, Theodore Schimpf, aged 2 years, of diarhoe.
October 5, Joseph Blessman, aged 19 years, of fever.

Administrators Notice. Estate of Ellen Milligan, dec. Justin Castanie.

Issue October 12, 1844

Died on the 6th ultimo in this country, Ex-Governor Moore of Alabama, and also formerly a Senator from that state in the United States Congress. He died in his 61st year, soon after his emigration to this country. *Harrison Times.*

Issue October 15, 1844

Administrators notice. Harris county. Estate of J.J. Crawford. C.D. Crenshaw.

Administrators Notice. Harris county. Estate of Richard Hampshar, dec. Richard Mockett.

Administrators Notice. Brazoria county. Estate of Patrick C. Jack. R.J. Towns.

Administrators Notice. Estate of Joseph H. Boone. Fort Bend county. J.H. Boone.

Issue October 17, 1844

We have been informed that Mr. Carin Brennin was waylaid and shot in Washington county, near Jacksonville, on Monday 30th ult. The victim who has thus cruelly been murdered, received the shot just below the right shoulder blade-the ball coming out on the left side of the breast. A man by the name of Daniel Meadows, who has been arrested on suspicion and committed to jail at Brenham, is the assassin. The evidence before the committing court was very strong, although entirely circumstantial—*LaGrange Intelligencer*, October 10th.

Miscellaneous Texas Newspaper Abstracts - Deaths --- Vol 2

Issue October 19, 1844
Resolutions of regret for the death of the death of Hon. Richard Morris and the Hon. William H. Jack, one of the oldest members of the profession in the Republic.

Another Revolutionary Hero Gone -- Col. Gen. Gill of Chester District, South Carolina, died on the 8th of August and was buried with military honors. Col. Gill served under Gen. Green and was in several engagements during the revolution, particularly that of the Eutaw Springs.

Issue October 22, 1844
Probate Sale. Harris county. Estate of John Marks, deceased. Thomas Baily, administrator.

Issue October 31, 1844
Probate Sale. Fort Bend county, at the residence of Mrs. Bundick on Oyster Creek, the property of S.C. Bundick, dec.

Issue November 2, 1844
Premeditated Murder on the 8th by John Arnold on Wm. Stephenson, a citizen of west Liberty. Arnold is about 30 years old, 5' 8 or 10 inches. It is believed Arnold is not his name, but Gormond.

Affecting letter -- The following is a letter written by Mrs. Stone on the death of her husband, the late Colonel Stone -- Saratoga Springs, Aug. 30, 1844, Gerardus Clark, Dear Sir, ... To the last he spoke with the kindest interest of his associates in the Board of Education, and wished very much to dictate a farewell letter to them, giving them his views on one or two topics which he thought important.

I entreated him to spare himself. He two or three times spoke to my brother Dr. Wayland (of Brown University), who was with us, to the same effect, and he for the same reason declined being his amanuensis... He suffered greatly during his illness, physically and mentally... it was my privilege to attend upon him till the last... [note: condensed] With great respect, S.P. Stone.

Issue November 9, 1844
We find the following in the *American Eagle*, Memphis, Tennessee. The last sentence shows that the allusion to the afflicting mortality was intended for political effect. It is thus southern journals go hand in hand with Northern Abolitionists in traducing our country. We can say to the *Eagle* that we want no army here, and least of all an army of his Northern confederates: "Fatal Honors -- within four years, four ministers from the United States to Texas

35

have died, viz: Mr. Flood and Gen. Murphy of Ohio, Judge Eve of Kentucky, and General Howard of Indiana. Mr. Greene, our Consul at Galveston, died a short time ago. Still the Polkites want to send our brave army to bleach that country with their bones."

Issue November 14, 1844

We learn that two children of Mrs. Simpson, a widow lady living in Austin, were captured and carried off. A party of men left in pursuit of the savages, but from the nature of the country, and the impossibility of following the trail for any distance in the mountains, we have no idea that they will be overtaken. The oldest child was a girl of 14 years and the other a boy of about 12. *LaGrange Intelligencer.*

Issue November 21, 1844

On Friday next will take place the execution of the negro, Castro, belonging to Judge Campbell. This negro has been convicted, during the present term of court, of the murder of Mr. Canfield last summer.

The *Harrison Times* mentions the death of the Hon. Isaac VanZandt, the information being derived from "a source entitled to credence."

Issue December 14, 1844

Col. Thos. W. Nibbs died at his plantation on Oyster Creek, near Richmond, on the 11th int. He had for some time been suffering from feeble health, and a debilitated constitution; the immediate cause of his death, however, was a violent cold brought on by exposure, and occasioning an excessive swelling of the glands of the throat. Col. Nibbs was among the early settlers of this country, and shared largely in the troubles and privations of our revolutionary struggle. He was a native of South Carolina but had, for some years, been a citizen of Alabama, until he finally made Texas the home of his adoption... He has left an aged mother, a widow and children...

Issue December 28, 1844

Death of Murrell -- The death of this "land pirate" is announced as having lately taken place in Pikesville, Tenn. -- A pretty strong proof that he is not living in Texas. "He died of consumption, and denied to the last moment of his life that he was guilty of the principal charges against him."

A letter from the West states -- "We are not in fear of the Mexicans -- parties of them are often coming into the Ranch to trade. But the Caranchua Indians are a great annoyance to us; one of them was killed by Mr. Gleen on the upper island last summer, and four have lately been killed on the San Antonio river. They have again commenced hostilities on the whites by killing a white man (Mr. Kemper) near Victoria and burning his house."

Issue January 14, 1845

Died yesterday afternoon, Charles, infant son of Thos. F. and Martha Gravis; aged 1 year, 2 months, 13 days. The friends and acquaintances of the family are respectfully invited to attend the funeral today at 12 o'clock from the residence of John N.O. Smith on Prairie Street.

Issue January 18, 1845

A disease similar to influenza has been prevailing around Washington county for several weeks. One of the latest victims was Hon. J.W. <u>Smith</u> from Bexar. He died on the 13th inst.

Issue January 23, 1845

Murder at Virginia Point: We have hitherto, for prudential motives, neglected to mention that a most shocking murder was committed at Virginia Point on the night of the 10th inst. The persons murdered were Mr. Simeon Bateman, one of the oldest and most wealthy settlers of Gonzales county, and Mr. Mathew Jett, a gallant soldier who had distinguished himself in many bloody engagements at the West. They were murdered while asleep in their camp by a man named Shultz, who went on the *New York* to New Orleans a day or two after the murder was committed...

We learn from the register that the children of Mrs. Simpson were captured by hostile Indians a few months since, are now in the possession of the Toweash and Wacoe Indians in the Wichetaw mountains...

Issue January 30, 1845

We learn from the *Washington Register* that one of the children of Mrs. Simpson, a boy of about twelve years old, who was lately captured by Indians near Austin, has been restored... His sister was murdered by these fiendish savages on the night they were taken from Austin.

Issue February 1, 1845

Senate. On the motion of Senator Caldwell, resolved, that the Secretary of State pay the expenses of the funeral of the late John W. <u>Smith</u> out of the contingent fund of the Senate.

Issue February 8, 1845

We regret to mention that a small party of Indians have been committing depredations on Chambers' Creek in Robertson county. It is believed that they have murdered Maj. Baxter, who has been missing from the settlement at the head of that creek for some days. A party of the settlers went out lately to search for him and found an arm severed from the body and numbers of cattle slaughtered... The Indians are supposed to be Wacoes.

Issue February 27, 1845

The steamboat *Pathfinder* was burnt on the 15th of February near Grand Gulf and several persons were drowned or perished in the flames... The names of the persons lost were: S.S. Caldwell, Huggins and Buttler of Grenada, (Miss.), Mr. Carleton of Tallahatchee, Mr. Pinchback of Ill., together with the stewart and one of the crew, names unknown.

Issue March 8, 1845

The *Northern Standard* states that the skeleton of a man was lately found on the Sister Grove Fork of the Trinity, about ten miles from Throckmorton's settlement, in a northeasterly direction. Some military buttons were found among the bones, and near them a tin cup marked P. Jefferson, and below it, the word Russel. It is supposed that the deceased was formerly a soldier in Col. Cooke's Regiment, and perished during the expedition to survey the military road. The relics of a large encampment were near the skeleton.

Murderer arrested -- We have hitherto neglected to mention the murderer Shultz, who fled from Galveston a few weeks since, has been arrested in Alabama, and was imprisoned to await a requisition from the President of Texas to the Governor of that state. It is believed that he will be given up immediately to the officers of Texas who may be sent to take him in charge.

Issue March 25, 1845

The *Shreveport Gazette* of February 26th states that A.M. Scott, superintendent of the mill of a Mr. Cutliff in Caddo Parish, while attempting to chastise a negro was knocked down by the latter with a frower and immediately killed... and lately a Mr. Wilson, in Harrison county, was murdered by his slaves.

Issue April 5, 1845

City Council. To pay A.W. Ridgeway, for burying a pauper named Fanning.

Issue April 19, 1845

Died at their temporary residence in this city on Thursday the 17th inst. after 5 days illness of putrid sore throat, aged 21 years, 7 months, Cathrine Teresa, the beloved wife of Capt. Tobias A. Grant of Colorado county. But seven days past this then happy pair landed on our shores (with five other members of their family emigrants from England)...

Indian Skirmish in the Cross Timbers: We learn from the *Northern Standard* that the treacherous Indians have recommenced hostilities upon the frontier settlement in the Cross Timbers. It appears that a party of savages, supposed to be Creeks or Cherokees from the United States, made an attack upon one of the settlements, and in the skirmish which ensued, an old gentlemen named Underwood, his little son, and a boy named Price were killed...

Issue June 12, 1845

More Indian Murders: We have learned with bitter regret that the sons of Mr. Hornsby and Mr. Atkinson were murdered by Indians near Austin on Saturday last. The Indians came upon them while they were fishing in the river and killed them with spears. The body of Mr. Atkinson was found on Monday morning pierced with seven wounds.

Issue June 17, 1845

Disgraceful Broil. We have learned with regret that a most shameful row occurred at LaGrange, in Fayette county, on the day of the election for delegates to the convention. Several persons, who had previously been regarded as decent men, were rolling in the dirt, scratching and tearing each other's clothes and faces, but this was the least of the disgraceful part of the affair. A duel occurred, which resulted in the death of Mr. Gardenier, late Sheriff of the county.

Issue June 17, 1845

Estill's defeat. One of the most remarkable pioneer fights in the history of the West was that waged by Captain James Estill and seventeen of his associates on 22d March 1782 with a party of Wyandotte Indians, twenty-five in number. Sixty-three years almost have elapsed since; yet one of the actors in that sanguinary struggle, Rev. Joseph Proctor of Estill county, Kentucky, survived to the 2d December last, dying in the full enjoyment of his faculties in the 90th year of his age. His wife, the partner of his early privations and toils, and nearly as old as himself, deceased six months previously. [note: account of battle given]. He joined the Methodist Episcopal Church in a fort in Madison county, Kentucky, under the preaching of Rev. James Hawkins. He was ordained by Bishop Anthony in Clarke county, Kentucky 1809. He was buried with military honors.

Estate of Malcolm McCauley. Harris county. Land in Refugio, Harris, Montgomery counties offered for sale. H.G. Pannell, adm.

Administrator Notice. Fort Bend county. Estate of W.N. Rick, dec. John Patton, adm.

Issue June 24, 1845

The suspicions that the Comanches committed the depredations a few weeks since near Austin are still further confirmed. We learn that a party of the friends of Mr. Hornsby pursued the murderers of his son and traced them to an encampment of the Comanches. They searched the camp and found a fishing line which was recognized by Mr. Hornsby as the identical line that his son had taken with him to the river on the morning that he was murdered.

Issue June 28, 1845

The Indian who murdered young Mr. Hornsby has been discovered and it now appears that the murder was committed to satiate his revenge for an injury inflicted upon him by Capt. Coleman in the skirmish on the Pedernales last summer... He boasted that he had killed Miss Simpson, at Austin, last summer. [note: condensed].

Issue July 1, 1845

Died on Tuesday evening the 12th inst. of congestive fever, Miss Sarah Ann Smith, daughter of Mrs. Woodruff.

Died on Sunday night, 22nd, of congestive fever, Mrs. Sarah Woodruff, mother of the above.

The N.O. *Jeffersonian* says: -- "General Jackson died on Sunday, 8th, at 6 o'clock p.m. When our informant left Nashville the drums were beating in token of the event and preparations were being made for the celebration. Business was entirely suspended. Two hours before, he requested that there might be no military pomp or pageantry displayed at his funeral. One hour before the event he ceased to speak, but his great faculties were as unconcluded as ever -- he expired with his immortal mind as clear and strong, as when his iron frame was unimpaired. General Houston arrived at the Hermitage four hours after the decease and was to superintend Gen. Jackson's obsequies. For many hours previously large crowds congregated about Hermitage. We are further informed that he expired in the arms of Jas. W. Breedlove, Esq., of this city."

The citizens of Galveston have set apart the 4th day of July for public demonstrations of respect to the memory of the illustrated dead.

Accident -- We learn from the *Montgomery Patriot* that Col. Joshua Hadley, for many years a citizen of that county, recently met his death by a fall from his horse. —Col. H. was much esteemed, and his sudden death is sincerely lamented by his fellow citizens.

The City Council, as will be seen in their proceedings, have taken the necessary steps to pay proper funeral honors on the occasion of the death of the venerated Sage and Patriot, Andrew Jackson. Our citizens will readily concur in any measures the Board may think proper to adopt in commemoration of the event. We have been informed that the 4th of July has been fixed upon as the day of celebrating the obsequies. There seems to us a harsh incongruity in mingling with the glad and triumphant feelings, naturally awakened by the recurrence of that day, the mournful pageantry of a funeral.

Issue July 3, 1845

City council. The following bills were read and ordered to be paid: James B. Hogan, bill on acc't Wm. Steger, a pauper, now deceased; H.S. Bachelder, do.; A.W. Ridgeway, burying do; Dr. A. Ewing for attendance on Wm. Steger.

The City Sexton presented his semi-annual report of deaths that had taken place in the city, commencing January 1st, 1845, viz:

March 1, a negro man belonging to Dr. Ewing, accidently drowned.
March 18, a child of J.W. White, of whooping cough, aged 7 months.
March 20, an infant of A.J. Burke, of whooping cough.
March 21, M. Fannin, of consumption, aged 45 years, a native of Ireland.
March 22, S.W. Welsch, of pleusery, aged 45 years, a native of Ireland.
March 26, James Mathews, sore throat, aged 38 years, a native of Georgia.
April 7, a Mexican named Morales, disease unknown, aged 50 years.
April 17, Mrs. C.T. Grant, sore throat, aged 21 years, a native of England.
April 19, H.W. Sperry, of apoplexy, aged 24 years, a native of Connecticut.
May 9, a negro woman belonging to J.A. Southmayd, drowned in Bayou.
May 21, a negro infant at Maj. Moore's.
June 12, Sarah Ann Smith, congestive fever, aged 13 years.
June 22, Mrs. John Woodruff, of fever, aged about 50 years.
June 22, Wm. Stegger, of consumption, aged about 40 years, from Alabama.

Administrators Notice. Harris county. Estate of Andrew Larsson. A.P. Thompson.

Administrators Notice. Austin county. Estate of George W. Reynolds. Cornelius Ennis, co-admin. with T.C. Reynolds.

Dr. Wm. C. Ridgeway, respectfully informs the citizens of Austin [not clear] and the adjoining counties, that he has permanently located himself at the former residence of Wm. Pettus, dec., on the waters of Mill Creek and near the town of Industry, where he will be found at all times unless away on professional business.

P.S. Owing to the derangement of money matters and the extreme low price of cotton, his professional services will be very moderate. References as to capability, &c. given with the greatest pleasure.

Issue July 8, 1845

It is with sorrow, after having lately thrown off the habiliments of mourning for a departed patriot of our motherland, we again assume the somber weeds on the occasion of the death of one who stood high in the esteem and affection of the people of Texas. The Hon. K.L. Anderson, vice-President of the Republic, died at Fanthorpe's, Montgomery county, on Thursday last of fever. Col. Anderson was uniformly distinguished as a warm advocate of the popular measure of Annexation: and it is sad to record the death of such men at the very time that the great object for which they so ardently strove is so near its consummation.

Celebration of the fourth. -- In the forenoon of the 4th, the arrangements adopted by the Committee appointed for that purpose for paying funeral honors to General Andrew Jackson, were carried out with complete and happy effect. The proceedings throughout were conducted in the most solemn and appropriate manner, and an unusually large concourse of citizens and strangers united on the occasion.

At noon, great numbers partook of a magnificent barbecue provided by our hospitable fellow-citizens, Mr. Sam'l Barron and Col. R. Wilson, at their residence; where also the regular target firing of the Milam Guards took place.

The celebration in the afternoon, by the pupils of the different Sunday Schools, excited much interest. Appropriate addresses were delivered at the Methodist church, after which they returned to the Presbyterian church, where a most sumptuous banquet was provided for the children and all comers.

The orations considering the short time given for preparation, were worthy of all praise; and the day passed off without the occurrence of an accident of any sort to mar the solemnity or harmony of the different celebrations.

Joint Resolution tendering to Gen. Andrew Jackson the tribute of a nation's gratitude... Resolved by the Senate and House of Representatives of the Republic of Texas in Congress assembled, that in the name and in behalf of the people of the Republic of Texas, we hereby tender to General Andrew Jackson the unfeigned tribute of a nation's gratitude.

Issue July 10, 1845

Col. Samuel B. Marshall of Nashville, Tennessee, died at Galveston on the 28th ult. He was on his way to Washington City with despatches from Maj. Donelson to the U.S. Government. Col. Marshall was formerly Marshal of the Western District of Tennessee and was for many years a personal and political friend of General Jackson.

Died in this place on the 1st inst., Col. Samuel Chiles, formerly of Washington City and recently of St. Louis, Missouri, where his family now reside.

[note: left side of article illegible] --op *Tom Jack* arrived at Galveston from Cor----- the Indians killed a young man ---- Kinney, within a mile of the ranche.

Issue July 15, 1845

The party of Comanches that lately encamped near Austin has retired towards the sources of the Colorado. They were followed by Mr. Sloat, the Indian agent, to the mouth of Pecan Bayou. Their trail indicated that they had fled in great haste. It is evident that they have become greatly alarmed since they have learned that the citizens of Austin have discovered that some of their party committed the murder of Mr. Hornsby and Mr. Atkinson. Fears are entertained that they intend to resume hostilities; and some of the Delawares report that they have formed a league with the Wacoes against the whites. The people of the frontier have become so fully convinced that they are hostile, that they are determined to attack any party that is found near the settlements.

Issue July 17, 1845

Board of Health. Houston. The City Sexton presented a list of deaths for the past two weeks, viz:

Col. Sam'l Childs, of St. Louis, MO, aged 50 years, of inflammation
A negro man named John, belonging to Col. Andrews, of dropsy.
A negro woman, belonging to J.W. Cloud, of whooping cough.

Extracts of letters giving some interesting incidents of the last illness of Gen. Jackson.

On the day before his death, he franked a letter to the Hon. Thomas F. Marshall of Kentucky, which had been written under his direction by his adopted son, in reply to anxious inquiries concerning the state of his health. His last letter, in his own hand, was that which he wrote to the President on the 5th or 6th inst. He seemed to be conscious that his time had come on Saturday evening for he intimated as much to his physician by saying: "My life is drawing rapidly to a close and I shall expire in the hope that the liberties of my country may endure forever and that my enemies (if I have any) may find peace."

At the breakfast hour of the morning on which he died he swooned away and the household became much alarmed -- white and black rallying to his room in tears; but he revived in a few moments, and he opened his eyes, met the glance of his adopted daughter at his bed side, saying: "Do not weep; it is true my suffering are great, but they are not so great as were those of Christ upon the cross; I shall soon be relieved." He then called upon the members of his family respectively, and addressed each of them in the kindness language of love and exhortation. He missed his two little adopted grandchildren, and inquired of them. He was informed that they were at Sunday School. He requested that they should be sent for. In a few minutes they came in, and received his prayer and blessing. He then called in all his servants and exhorted them to embrace the religion of christ, giving them most wholesome advice. The scene was painfully affecting; for he now seemed perfectly conscious that he could last but a few hours longer.

Two or three minutes before his last breath, he asked his adopted son to adjust the pillow beneath his head. Up to the last moment, he maintained the most unshaken reliance in a blissful immortality -- a certain reunion with his beloved wife and all his christian friends in heaven. Clearly, clearly, he was ready to die. [note: condensed].

Issue July 19, 1845

Kenneth L. Anderson, Vice President of the Republic, departed this life on the evening of the 3rd inst. at Fanthorp's in the county of Montgomery and was there buried yesterday with Masonic honors. [leaves widow and children] Washington, July 5, 1854.

Santa Fe -- Gov. Armijo has been superseded, and Chavis, brother to one of that name who was killed by McDaniel and his confederates two years ago, appointed in his place.

Issue July 24, 1845
[note: date of issue is not clear].

Col. Josiah H. Vose of the 4th reg. U.S. Inf. died suddenly on the 15th inst. at New Orleans of an affection of the breast. He had just returned to his quarters from a parade when he dropped lifeless. Col. V. was sixty-one years of age; had been thirty-three years in the service.

Issue July 25, 1845
[note: date of issue is not clear].

The City Sexton reported the death of a negro infant, four days old, belonging to Daniel Shipman.

Issue August 5, 1845

The City Sexton reports the death of a negro woman belonging to Geo. Allen, died in child bed.

Issue August 12, 1845

The City Sexton reports but one death -- an infant child of Mr. J. Whiteside, of the measles.

Miscellaneous Texas Newspaper Abstracts - Deaths --- Vol 2

Issue August 21, 1845
Estate of John N. Wilson, dec., Harris county. Notice is hereby given to William Wilson, Edward Wilson, Charles Wilson, and Joseph W. Wilson, who are residents of the city of Baltimore, state of Maryland, Mary Wilson, the mother of decedent, has applied for a division of property between the heirs.

Issue August 26, 1845
We have learned that a most brutal murder was committed a short time since in the neighborhood of Groce's Retreat, Montgomery county. Mr. Nathan Taylor was shot down in his own house... Mr. T. was formerly a merchant in Galveston, where he had done business for several years. He has left a most amiable wife and a large circle of friends to mourn his untimely death.

Issue October 18, 1845
DIED -- On the 2d inst. at the residence of Mr. [?] Wilson, on the Navasoto, of congestive fever, Captain Benjamin Sloat, Indian Agent.

Issue November 13, 1845
Died at the house of John A. Ragsdale in Fort Bend county on the 31st of October, 1845, Calvin F. Keith, an amiable and pious young man who was acting as Colportiour under the auspices of the American Tract Society. Mr. Keith had much endeared himself to the christian community by his very exemplary christian deportment and persevering efforts in the promotion of the noble enterprize in which he was engaged. Though far from the country of his nativity, he was surrounded by christian friends, and cheered by the hopes of the gospel in his dying moments. His end was peace. He was interred in the family burying ground of Mrs. Mary E. Bell, near West Columbia. Mr. K. was a native of North Bridge Water, Massachusetts.

Issue November 27, 1845
Capt. Charles L. Dorcher died in New Orleans on the 14th of November.

Issue November 29, 1845
A horrid affray took place in the bar-room of the St. Louis Hotel in New Orleans in which Joseph B. Carson was shot dead by a man named T.M. Wadsworth. -- Wadsworth was immediately arrested and committed by Recorder Genois on a charge of murder.

Parents should repeatedly caution their children never to point a gun loaded or unloaded at any person... A few days since a boy living in Gates county, North Carolina, who was amusing himself with a gun, which he supposed to be empty, placed a cap on the nipple, and, turning to a young lady named Mary Overman, said playfully--"Cousin Mary, I'm going to shoot you," firing the gun at the same moment. The contents lodged in the poor girl's face, tearing away the entire side of it. Two hours afterwards she expired after having suffered the most excruciating agony. *Picayune*.

Issue December 8, 1845

Dr. Houghton of Detroit was drowned in Lake Superior on the night of the 13th inst. [note: condensed].

Died in this city on the 26th day of November, John W. Niles, aged 41 years. Baltimore papers please copy.

Issue December 13, 1845

The difficulties among the Cherokees are increasing. Great numbers of the treaty party have fled across the line to the adjoining settlements to escape destruction. -- Three cherokees named Tom Watie, Joseph Swimmer Stroin [sic] have been killed by the Ross party. A large band of the Ross party are constantly under arms patrolling the country to exterminate the adherents of the unfortunate Starrs.

Issue December 16, 1845

We have received a letter from Mr. Ingram of Victoria in which he mentions that fears are entertained there that Capt. Ketchum of the U.S. Army has been murdered between Victoria and Corpus Christi. He started alone from Victoria on the 25th ult. intending to proceed directly to the camp of the U.S. Army at Corpus Christi. He was mounted on an excellent horse and could easily have reached the camp in four days. But accounts have been received from Corpus Christi to the 7th inst. and nothing has been heard of him. It is believed he has been assassinated on the road or has been murdered by Indians. He had been engaged for some weeks past purchasing cattle for the Army, and as an impression prevailed that he had a large sum of money by him, it is quite probable that he has been waylaid and killed by robbers. It is possible, but scarcely probable, that he has missed his way and gone by some of the prairie paths towards the coast or towards Bexar. The people of Victoria, however, are confident that he has been assassinated between that place and the San Antonio river.

Issue December 20, 1845

We have received a letter from Lt. E. Hayne, dated Corpus Christi, 17th December, in which he mentions that during the late inclement weather there has been some sickness and a few deaths in the American camp. Col. Allen of the 2nd dragoon's was buried on the 7th inst.

Died in Corpus Christi, 1 December 1845, of inflammation of the bowels, James Edgar, for a long time a citizen of Houston. Mr. Edgar was one of the late Santa Fe prisoners and had been engaged in many of the short Indian conflicts prior to that time. He was interred with the honors of war by the Mier and Santa Fe prisoners, aided by the talented band of music attached to the 3rd Reg. U.S. Service, which had been most generously sent by Col. Huchcock for the occasion.... Newark and New Jersey papers please copy.

Issue December 30, 1845

Captive Boy -- The *Austin Register* mentions that a captive white boy has been found among the Kickapoos by the Delaware Chief Jim Shaw. He was purchased from the Comanches by the Kickapoos, and it is supposed to be the son of Col. Colmac, whose widow was murdered near Austin about six years ago. Some of the friends of Col. Colman intend to purchase him of the Kickapoos.

Issue January 1, 1846

A young man named Shean was lost overboard from the Steamboat *Spartan* on her return from Galveston on the night of the 29th ult. He was the only son of his widowed mother who was on board. Her extreme grief at this shocking catastrophe can be better imagined than described.

TELEGRAPH & TEXAS REGISTER
Published at Houston, Texas.

Issue July 5, 1847

Died on Sunday the 27th ult., Mary A., only child of Benj. F. and Gertrude E. Tankersly, of this city; aged 15 months and 4 days.

Issue July 19, 1847

A man by the name of Downs was killed by another named Triplett, in Gonzales, some two or three weeks since. *Victoria Advocate* gives an account... Downs was not a citizen of this county.

The steamer *Ann Chase* burst one of her boilers near Sabine Pass... killing Firman V. Carmichael, a Private in Co. A 4th Reg. of Indiana Vol. and James Dolan, a boat hand, belonging to Pittsburg.

Issue August 9, 1847

The *Caddo Gazette* of the 25th of June announces the death of Samuel R. Hinton, who was drowned in the Red River while attempting to escape from the party that was endeavoring to transport him to Alabama.

Issue August 23, 1847

Health of Galveston. The editor of the *News* asserts that a case of yellow fever has occurred at Galveston is incorrect... death of Capt. Thompson as a case of this disease, brought direct from Tampico... no resemblance to Yellow Fever.

Issue August 30, 1847

$1000 reward: To anyone who will apprehend within this state and deliver to the officers of justice at Chulahoma, Mississippi, William M. Sledge, who at this place on the 10th inst. killed Joseph Echols. Said Sledge is a young man about 27-30 years of age, 5'6-7" high, dark complexion, spare built, bald head, but wears a wig, speaks in a quick sharp voice, is very genteel in his dress. Said Sledge has a very recently marked scar on his forehead, extending down toward the right or left ear, which he received the 10th inst. Chulahoma, Mississippi.

$375 reward: Whereas Montgomery Williams, late of Wharton county, did on the 28th of July murder James A. Colvin.

Said Montgomery Williams is about 22 years of age, about 6'2" high, of slender form, light hair, and hazel eyes, and rather swarthy complexion... It is probable that he may attempt to get to the state of Mississippi where he has relatives... Wharton.

Liberty county, September term 1847. Estate of John T. Pinckney, dec., James Butler, adm. Petition for an order of sale of land.

Liberty county, September term 1847. Estate of Joseph Coit, dec., A.W. Dismuke, adm'r: Petition for order of sale of lands.

Issue August 30, 1847

Board of Health Houston. City Sexton reports one death Mrs. Weiser, a German.

The *Natchitoches Chronicle* of the 14th mentions a report that Mr. Russell, editor of the *Red Lander*, has been killed by Mr. Kendall, editor of the *Shield*, of San Augustine. "He was shot while standing in his office door the latter part of last week."

Issue September 6, 1847

Board of Health Houston. City Sexton. Interments for the week ending this day:
August 22, Aubrey, a German, of fever.
August 23, Mrs. Stratton.

August 26, a german infant.
August 26, a colored infant belonging to Mrs. Jane Dunn.

Issue September 13, 1847

Died in San Augustine, Eastern Texas, on the 10th of August, the Rev. James Russell, editor & proprietor of the *Red Lander*. Mr. Russell emigrated from Scotland to the United States...

Died at Victoria on the 6th of August last, Wm. B. Sutton, son of Mrs. J.K.T. Walton of Washington county, aged about 20 years.

Issue September 23, 1847

It is with unfeigned regret that we are called upon to announce the death of our much esteemed brother, editor James W. Dallam, late conductor of the *Matagorda Herald.* He died of yellow fever at New Orleans, whether he had gone to procure the necessary materials for commencing a new paper at Indian Point. *Victoria Advocate.*

Issue September 30, 1847

The *Matagorda Flag* mentions a report that Capt. G.K. Lewis had been murdered at a place called the Wells while on his way from Corpus Christi to Guerrero.

Issue October 21, 1847

We have learned with regret that Gen. Darnell's son, a lad of 18 years of age, recently died at the General's residence in Shelby county.

Issue October 28, 1847

Preamble & Resolutions of Holland Lodge #1 Free Masons on the death of Hon. Isaac VanZandt.

Interments, Houston:
September 3, Madam Gubner, German.
9, Mrs. H. Bond.
18, Miss Miller, who came from Seneschall's, out of town.
18, John Curtail, died of broken-leg, out of town.
22, Fushe, German.
23, John Daly, Irishman.
23, Marie Louise, German.
24, Reed Fushe, 2d, German.

October 2, Madam Bheringer, German.
    7, Infant child of Gentry.
    11, I. VanZandt.
    13, H. Thayer.
    14, L. Wakeley.
    18, Keohn, German.
    23, Dykemann, German.
    23, Madam Broker.

Issue November 18, 1847

Physicians of Houston express their regret on the death of Doctor S.O. Young, who departed this life on the 10th inst. at half-past eleven o'clock. Deeply sympathize with wife.

Issue December 2, 1847

Shocking casualty. Little girl about 13, step-daughter of Mr. Shely, was dreadfully burned a few days since in this city.

Issue December 16, 1847

The remains of the lamented Capt. Walker, who fell in the desperate battle of Huamantla, were brought to this city on the 12th inst...

Issue December 20, 1847

Liberty county, probate court January term 1847. This is to notify all persons interested in the said estate of Alexander S. Roberts, dec., that Matilda Garner, administratrix of the estate of Jordon West, dec., having filed her petition for an order of sale of a sufficient amount of the property belonging to said estate to pay or satisfy her claim as administratrix aforesaid...

Liberty county: Probate court, January term 1948. Bryan Danzay, the administrator of the said Mary C. Swinney, dec., having filed his petition for an order of sale of the headright land certificate of said deceased.

Issue January 20, 1848

Senator Fairfield, of Maine, died at Washington on the 25th ult...

Liberty county: Probate court to January term 1848. To the unknown heirs and all others interested in the estate of James Grant, dec.
    William J. Mills, adm. of the estate of the said James Grant, dec., having filed at the November term 1846 for an order of sale of lands belonging to said estate.

Issue February 10, 1848

The remains of M. [Magnus] T. Rogers, late representative of this county, were brought to this city on Tuesday the 1st inst.

Issue March 2, 1848

Horrible death. Dr. Isaac Hamberlin, a most worthy man and an old citizen of this county came to his death in a most horrible and shocking manner... A large bear in the thick cane... *Yazoo City Whig*.

Issue March 9, 1848

We learn from a gentleman who arrived recently from Austin that the notorious Eppes, charged as the murderer of Mr. Muir of Virginia, was lately arrested at the Falls of the Brazos.

Issue March 23, 1848

Liberty county. Probate court to March term 1848. Jonas Butler, administrator of the estate of John T. Pinckney, dec., having filed his account current with said estate at the July term...

Liberty county. Probate court to March term 1848. John E. Chassaigne, adm. for the estate of A.A. Cardel, dec.

Liberty county. Probate court to March term 1848. Petition for partition. Estate of Andrew Weaver, dec. Aaron L. Barrm, admin.

Liberty county. Probate court to March term 1848. Barkley Townsend, admin. of the estate of William M. Logan, dec., has filed his account in our said court on final settlement with his said interstate...

Liberty county. Probate court to March term 1848. Riley R. Rhodes, admin. of the estate of Ephraim Thompson, dec.

Liberty county. Probate court to March term 1848. Mary E.A. Read, admin of the estate of Alfred Carrall, dec.

Issue March 30, 1848

The *Galveston News* of the 24th [?] inst. comes to us in mourning for that of Maj. Bache, a late Senator at the Galveston district, who expired at Austin on the 17th inst. at 4 o'clock pm.

Issue April 13, 1848

Order of the Procession Masonic Fraternity, Hon. Richard Bache...

Issue April 27, 1848

Died in this city Sunday the 23rd inst., Edward Henry, youngest son of Elizabeth M. and Francis Moore, Jr.

Issue June 1, 1848

Liberty county, admin. notice. On the 30th November 1847, the undersigned was duly appointed admin. of the estate of Edward Dorr, late of said county, dec. James Butler, admin.

Issue June 15, 1848

A man named Thomas Moriarty, a native of Ireland, was recently drowned in the bayou, a short distance below the landing in this city.

Issue June 22, 1848

Liberty county. Probate court May term 1848. To the sheriff of Polk county. You are hereby commanded to take into your custody the body of Benjamin P. Hardin, and so to provide that you have him before the Hon. Probate Court in and for the county of Liberty at the next term therefore, to be holden at the court house in the town of Liberty on the last Monday in July next, then and there to make a showing of his acts and doing as admin. of the estate of James Clements, dec.

Issue June 29, 1848

Died on the night of the 19th inst., a young child of John Shea of this city.

Masonic Resolutions, Graham Lodge, death of F.W. Hubert...

Issue July 6, 1848

Died on 15th June, William Adolphus, son of Thomas G. & Eliza Green, aged 8 years.

Issue August 10, 1848

We learn from the *Victoria Advocate* that a difficulty occurred in DeWitt county, lately, between Messrs. Poinsett and Brissett, partners in trade. Poinsett shot Brissett in the thigh with a revolving pistol, and the latter seized a gun, shot Poinsett through the head, killing him instantly.

Issue August 24, 1848

A little child, aged about 6 years, son of Mr. Jourdan of this city, was accidentally poisoned a few days since. A quantity of poisoned molasses had been set out near the house of a neighbor to destroy ants. In two days the poor little innocent was a corpse.

Issue September 14, 1848

Health of the city. Several persons have died at the Columbus Hotel. Mr. Cabanis, his wife, and 4 others have died. None assumed to be yellow fever. [note: condensed].

Issue September 28, 1848

Houston City Sexton:
September 18, Mena Frescher, 20, German.

18, A. McFarland, 69, Irishman.

18, W.B. Reeves, Jr., 13, U.S.

19, Madam Raunscheutz, German.

19, Robert Trimble, U.S.

Interments, Houston Cemetery:
September 8, Madam Cabannis, a German.

10, Caspar Cabannis, a German.

10, -- Bowman.

11, Enoch King.

13, --[?] Dechanne, 2 months.

13, --[?] Hoffman, 3 years.

15, Thomas ---, Wales.

16, F. Thiel, a German.

16, Joshua Shea, Jr., 11 years.

Issue October 5, 1848

We have learned that the Hon. W.S. Rayner, late Representative of Fort Bend county, died at his residence in Richmond, 23d September, of congestive fever. Native of South Carolina, emigrated to Texas about six years ago.

We learned with pain that the Rev. J.M.K. Hunter, on his return from this city to his residence at Columbia, was taken sick at Mr. Terry's on the Brazos and died a few days since. An estimable young man who accompanied him, C.D. Runnels, also sickened and died at same place.

City Sexton report. Interments in the Houston Cemetery from Friday 22nd to Thursday 28th, inclusive:
Sept. 22, Dougan, U.S.

22, Erdmann/Erdmanu, German.

22, Myer, German.

22, Hildeger, German.

23, James, U.S.

23, Edw. Brown, U.S.

24, Ratcliffe, U.S.

25, John Wannie, German.

25, Mde. Becllmann, German.

Sept. 25, H.L. Bassett, U.S.
25, Wm. Gangawa, U.S.
26, John O. Bracken, U.S.
27, Mich'l Larkin, Ireland.
27, Ed. Stafford, 9 years, U.S.
27, Infant of Jos. Stafford.
27, Block, German.
28, I/L. W. Kemper, U.S.
29, Stewart Pipkin, U.S.

Issue October 12, 1848

Died in Brazoria county on the 27th ult. in the 18th year of his age, Davis Runnels, son of the late H.W. Runnels of Mississippi... Lately returned home to his mother, residing in the city of Houston.

City Sexton's report of the interments from Friday 29th Sept. to Thursday 5th October, inclusive:
September 29, Jas. T. Hogan, 19 years, U.S.
30, --- Wilson, U.S.
30, J. Morris, U.S.
30, Herman Strabbleman, Germany.
30, Mde. Cramar/Cramor, Germany.
30, Mde. Hildeger, Germany.
October 1, Jos. Thompson, U.S.
1, Wm. Armmia [?], Germany.
1, --- Isheutreger, Germany.
1, D. Lockhard, Germany.
1, a negro, belonging to Dr. Bryan.
2, James Miller, 6 [?] years, U.S.
2, M.C. Robinson, U.S.
2, Unknown, Germany.
2, Unknown, Germany.
3, Samuel Hart, Ireland.
3, --- Hoffman, U.S.
3, P.A. Ackerman, U.S.
4, John Clark, 6 years, U.S.
4, Infant of Ramerschautz, Germany.
5, Nancy, Indian girl.

Issue October 19, 1848

We learn that on last Monday week, two young men by the name of Davis (brothers) were inhumanly murdered at their own house, upon the head waters of the Clayto, about the upper corner of DeWitt and Goliad counties... [note: mentions older brother]. *Victoria Advocate*.

The Sexton reports the following deaths from the 6th to the 12th October, inclusive:

October 6, Wm. Cleveland, U.S.
> 6, James Fisher, U.S.
> 6, Burke, Germany.
> 7, James Hopson, England.
> 7, B. Scott, U.S.
> 8, John Cheek, U.S.
> 8, Davis, U.S.
> 9, John Huffman, U.S.
> 9, Mrs. Robinson, U.S.
> 9, Bone, U.S.
> 9, Wilhelm, Germany.
> 9, Dan'l Hamblin, U.S.
> 10, Nolan, 7 years, Texas.
> 10, Ernst Clar, Germany.
> 10, name unknown, Germany.
> 11, J.L. Wilson, U.S.
> 11, Miller, U.S.

Issue November 2, 1848

The sexton reports the following deaths from Friday the 20th to 26th October, inclusive:

October 20, John Pither, Germany.
> 21, T. Hadgel, Germany.
> 21, Madame Shiley, Germany.
> 23, woman, unknown, Germany.
> 24, man, unknown, Germany.
> 26, Madame Urban, Germany.

Issue November 9, 1848

We learn from the *Huntsville Banner* that Col. J. Bennet, lately died at his residence in Navarro county... At battle of Jacinto.

Report of Interments from the 27th October to Thursday Nov. 2d, inclusive:

October 29, Mrs. Cooke, U.S.
> 29, Ernst Blobel, Germany.
> 29, Mary Markun, Germany.
> 31, Mrs. Nobles, U.S.

November 1, woman, unknown, Germany.
> 1, Infant of Dr. Estel, Texas.
> 2, Col. Wm. S. Wallace, U.S.

John Bergin, City Sexton.

Issue November 30, 1848

Died in Austin county on Wednesday the 15th inst., infant son of Col. Thomas B. White, aged one year.

Wm. Jones of this city was shot with a pistol through the breast on Wednesday morning in the bar room of the City Hotel by David Allen. He expired in a few moments after receiving the wound.

Dr. H.B. Kelsey of Marshall is dead. Editor, Minister, Mason...

Issue January 18, 1849

Died near this city suddenly on the morning of the 10th inst. of apoplexy, James Evett Chapman, formerly of the British Navy and recently clerk in the Quarter Master's Dept. at Vera Cruz.

Issue February 15, 1849

Died in this city on the 31st of January 1849, Robert Caldwell, aged 43 years. Baltimore and New York papers please copy.

Issue May 10, 1849

Departed this life on the 7th inst., Julia, daughter of Joshua and Betty O. Hendy; aged 1 year and 22 days.

Issue July 5, 1849

A very valuable negro man owned by J.J. Cain of this city died of lockjaw on Sunday last.

Issue July 12, 1849

We are pained to announce that Rufus Chandler was killed on Sunday morning the 10th ult... in the streets of Rusk by Gen. Joseph L. Hogg.

Issue October 19, 1849

Died on the morning of the 4th inst. in New Orleans of bronchitis, Andrew Briscoe, formerly chief justice of this county.

Liberty county. October term 1849. The undersigned admin. of the estate of John T. Pinkney, dec., hereby gives notice to all persons that he will file his account current with the said estate, upon final settlement at the October term of said court, and ask for a discharge from the further admin. of the said estate of John T. Pinkney, dec. James Butler, adm.

Issue January 3, 1850

From the *Western Texian*: [note: condensed from a letter]. Killed by the Indians: Solomon, Garner and John Woodley.

Issue February 14, 1850

Died at Torrey's trading house, Texas, on the 4th day of January last, Emanuel R. Seibrat[?] aged 34 years, a native of Harrisburg, Penn.

The body of a person was found on the Washington road a few days since a few miles above Mr. Hamblin's. The stage driver, who found it, brought it on to the nearest house. Some letters were found in the pockets of the unfortunate man indicate that his name was MacDonald and he was on his way to New Orleans to return to his family. He emigrated to Texas a few months since from Missouri and brought a large flock of Merino sheep.

Died in this city, 8 February 1850, of consumption, James B. Williams, of the house of Groesbeck, Williams & Cooke. James B. Williams was born in South Deerfield, Massachusetts, 8 July 1824. At the age of 10 years, as nearly as can be ascertained, he became a resident of Albany, New York. There his residence continued until, in consequence of impaired health, he was advised by his physicians and others to try the effects of a milder climate. Accordingly, on the 20th of June 1847, then bid adieu to kindred and friends and arrived in this city on the 7th of the following March...

Issue March 7, 1850

[note: condensed from a letter]. Murdered by Indians, David Torrey.

The *Victoria Advocate* contains a very affecting account of the death of Mr. Robinson, who emigrated from that place to California but a year ago.

Died of small pox on the 20th of February last in New Orleans, William A. Chance of Burleson county, Texas.

Issue April 18, 1850

Died in Stockton, California, on the 5th of February 1850, William G. Evans, late a citizen of this place.

We have received the melancholy intelligence of the sudden death of Mr. Gerard Hayden of Rutersville, Fayette Co. On Thursday the 4th inst. while engaged in planting a piece of rented land a short distance from his own, feeling ill, he left his hands and returned to his camp; and on the return of the servants to the camp on Friday night, they found it burned up, and the body of Mr. Hayden nearly consumed. His remains were conveyed to Rutersville and buried on the 7th inst... [note: condensed].

Issue April 25, 1850

Died in this city on the 10th inst. of hydrocephalus, Edward Wingate Collins, aged 13 months; the son of Dr. John Collins and Margaret Jane Collins of Crockett, Houston county, Texas.

Issue May 2, 1850

Gen. John T. Moore, once Marshall of the State of Kentucky and well known in some of the heavy land transactions connected with the early history of Texas, died at the Tremont House, in this city, on Wednesday, at an advanced age.

Issue May 9, 1850

Grimes Co., April 16, 1850. Tribute of Respect to the memory of Ophelia S. Hunt. Died 6 April 1850 at her father's residence in Grimes county. Wife of Dr. J.G. Hunt, and eldest daughter of W.B. Loftin, aged 23 years.

Issue July 25, 1850

Died on the 17th ult. at the residence of her husband in Washington county, Mrs. Elizabeth Miller, in the 26th year of her age.

Issue August 21, 1850

Mr. D. Williams was killed a few days since, at his late residence on Oyster Creek in Ft. Bend county, by a young man who had for some months been living with him.

Issue October 23, 1850

William Nibbs, son of the late Col. Nibbs of Ft. Bend county, was killed on the 13th inst. by a young man named Beckum.

Issue November 13, 1850

We regret to announce the death of Horace Baldwin, formerly Mayor of Houston. He died at Galveston on the 8th inst. after a short illness of only 22 hours.

Issue December 20, 1850

Mr. James Qinn was killed in this city on Wednesday morning by the caving in of a bank of sand in which he was digging.

Issue January 3, 1851

Died at Cedar Bayou on the 6th inst., Mrs. Sarah E. Hamilton, wife of J.R. Hamilton and mother of Rev. W.S. Hamilton of the Texas conference, in the 57th year of her age. Was a native of New Jersey and emigrated to the south in 1826...

Issue January 17, 1851

Died on the 5th inst. at the residence of S.F. Noble, one mile from this city, after an illness of 9 days, Dr. William G. Lewis, a native of Philadelphia. Dr. Lewis emigrated to Texas in 1836 and at that time was assistant surgeon in the Texas Army.

Issue March 21, 1851

Died. Major Gen. George M. Brooke, commanding the 8th Military Dept. of the United States. He died at his residence in this city on the morning of the 9th inst. at half past 2 o'clock of internal mortification... *San Antonio Ledger.*

Issue April 25, 1851

Died on the 2nd inst. at the house of her father in Brenham, Texas, Eliza M. Wilkins, oldest daughter of Elizabeth D. and John B. Wilkins, aged 16 years. Deceased was born in Lowndes county, Alabama, from which place she emigrated with her parents to Texas in 1844.

Issue May 9, 1851

The murder of Mr. Neil Bowen, who was shot through a window in Brenham, a short time since, has created quite an excitement in Washington county, and fears are entertained that the old feuds between the regulators and the Murrell gang will be revived.

Died in this city on the morning of the 3rd inst. Fanny Caroline, youngest daughter of Elizabeth M. and Frances Moore, Jr., aged 15 months.

Issue May 16, 1851

Lone Star. Three men were drowned in Elm Creek in Milam county. One by the name of Dally, 75 years of age, a citizen of that county. One a traveler from Virginia, who had in his saddle bags a letter of introduction to a gentlemen from Austin. The other, nothing has been found to give information of who he is.

Died in this city on the 5th inst., Capt. J.N.O. Smith, aged 36 years, after lingering illness of 20 months. His disease was consumption. Capt. Smith was a soldier in the army of San Jacinto.

Issue May 30, 1851

Cameron, Texas, 17 May 1851. Died in this place on the 10th inst. of pulmonary consumption, Mrs. Ann Bowles, consort of J.P. Bowles and daughter of John Hobson, near Nashville, Tennessee.

Issue June 6, 1851

We see it stated in the New Orleans papers that Mr. Morrisett of Alabama, who lately died at Hodge's Bend on the Brazos, fell a victim to the effects of cholera. This, we are informed, is a mistake. He was very much fatigued and hungry when he reached the Brazos and ate very heartily of fish that had been caught in the neighboring ponds, and which were considered to be wholesome. His disease was, in all probability, caused by the fish he ate, and at any other season would have been regarded as a case of cholera morbus.

An estimable young man named G.B. Higginbotham, lost his life on the 6th ult. at Camden, Alabama, by the accidental discharge of a gun, which slipped off a piazza as he was loading it.

Issue June 20, 1851

Mr. Albert Barton was drowned near Ft. Graham about the 1st inst. while attempting to cross the Brazos in the ferry boat. The boat sunk and he was swept down by the current and lost. Two other men were on board but they swam ashore. He has left a wife and two children to deplore his loss.

Issue June 27, 1851

Col. G.W. Hockley died at the residence of Col. Kinney at Corpus Christi on the 9th inst.

Issue July 4, 1851

We are pained to announce the death of Mrs. M.R. Gray, who died in this city on the morning of the 1st.inst. at the residence of her son Peter W. Gray.

We regret to state that Mr. Michael Connelly, of this city, accidentally fell through the hatchway of the steamer *Reliance* a few days since and was killed.

Issue August 22, 1851

Died at the residence of his father in Polk county on the 3rd of August, Charles William, eldest son of Henry F. and Lucinda E. Gillett; aged 8 years and 5 months.

Issue September 5, 1851

Died on Friday the 29th ult. at Lynchburg, Mr. David P. Penn, an old and much loved citizen of Harris Co., Texas.

Issue September 12, 1851

Capt. James Dunn, formerly of Alabama but for the last 17 years a citizen of Robertson Co., Texas, died at his residence on the 27th of August.

Issue October 3, 1851

Died at Huntsville, Texas, the 23rd of September, Rev. Hamilton Scott, pastor of the O.S. Presbyterian church of that place. Mr. Scott came from Ohio to Texas in December 1849 and soon settled in Huntsville where he afterwards married the daughter of Rev. Daniel Baker, D.D.

Issue November 7, 1851

Died in this city on the 27th of October, Frances Susan, daughter of James F. and Henrietta M. Cruger, aged 3 days.

Issue November 18, 1851

We learn from the *Matagorda Tribune* that on Sunday the 2nd inst., a difficulty occurred between James F. Martin, Sheriff of Colorado co., and Francis Waldeman, which resulted in the death of the latter.

Issue December 19, 1851

An interesting little girl child of Mr. L. Reynolds of Bastrop, about 3 years old, lately fell with its head into a post hole, partly filled with water and was suffocated before it was discovered.

A man named Ragsdale shot down a teamster named Smith while sitting at his camp fire near Bastrop about a week since. The two brothers of Mr. Smith immediately pursued Ragsdale and captured him. The citizens in the neighborhood assembled the next morning, examined the prisoner, and condemned him to be hung. A rope was fastened to a branch of a tree and Ragsdale was hung up, until life was extinct. Mr. Smith had died in the mean time.

A man was arrested on the Washington road a few days since on the suspicion that he is one of the murderers of Mr. Wayland, who was killed in Grimes co., a few weeks since.

Issue December 26, 1851

Died at his residence on Oyster Creek of chronic diarrhea, Hiram L. Ayrick, aged 30 years. The deceased emigrated from Mississippi to Texas about a year since.

Issue January 2, 1852

Died in Montgomery, Montgomery county, Texas, on the 24th of December 1851, David S. Boyd, a native of New York.

Issue March 5, 1852

Mr. James F. Jordon, who lately emigrated to Texas from Murray county, Tennessee, committed suicide on the 21st inst. at his residence near LaGrange.

Issue April 23, 1852

A young man named Gordon M. Griffin was immediately killed on the Montgomery road on Monday last. He was riding on the fore part of his wagon, when the fore-wheels suddenly fell into a deep hole in the road and he was thrown directly under one of the wheels, which passed entirely over his body. He lingered until Tuesday morning and died.

Issue May 14, 1852

A man named James Brown, a German, was hung at Hall's Bluff, on the Trinity, a few days since, by a party of citizens.

Issue July 16, 1852

Capt. William S. Hansborough was killed in this city on the morning of Tuesday last at the Old Capitol by H. Runnels, son of Gov. Runnels, formerly of Mississippi.

Issue November 26, 1852

Yellow fever at Indianola: About 3 three weeks since, Mr. Little of Chappell Hill visited Indianola and on his way home was taken sick. He, however, proceeded on his journey and died at Chappell Hill a day or two after his arrival.

Our community was thrown into great consternation on Thursday last by the perpetration of one of the most horrid murders that shock humanity and makes the blood run cold within our veins; perpetrated by a man calling himself David Butler, upon the person of Thomas McGuire, both strangers in this community.

Issue December 3, 1852

The *Galveston News* mentions that one of the passengers on board the steamer *Texas*, while she was lying at anchor off Matagorda bar, came to his death by the accidental discharge of a rifle that had been loaded for the purpose of shooting porpoises. The name of the gentleman was Shotwell, a native of New York but recently from Tennessee.

Issue December 10, 1852

Died at the residence of Mr. James Bailey in this city on the 6th inst., Miss C.A. Bailey, aged 15 years, daughter of David Bailey of Pekin, Illinois.

THE OLD CAPITOL
Published at Columbia, Texas.

Issue December 17, 1887

The death of Hon. A. Underwood, which sad event occurred Friday the 18th ult. at his residence in this place. Deceased had been a citizen of Brazoria county for over fifty years... leaves widow and four children, all grown.

Issue January 7, 1888

Dr. Spencer of Barclay, Bell co., a most respectable citizen, died suddenly of heart disease just after eating a hearty supper.

Huntsville. January 4th. Reliable news reaches here from Madison co., thirty miles west of here, that a mob of 200 or 300 men went to the town of Madisonville yesterday and shot down one Will Bobo on the public square in presence of the sheriff. The mob went from there to the house of one Red Page and took him out and hanged him. Also, shot Alf. Whiting, it is supposed, fatally. Killed one other party, name unknown...

CLEBURNE BULLETIN
Published weekly at Cleburne, Johnson County, Texas.
A.J. Byrd, editor and manager.

Issue August 13, 1880

Texas Notes: Col. J.R. Pickard of Stephensville is dead.

Martin L. Mynett, a notorious desperado, who was wanted in Johnson co. for cattle stealing, was shot and killed while resisting arrest in Montague county.

We are pained to announce the death of Allie Bell, infant daughter of W.R. and S.E. Nix, at Glenrose last Saturday night.

Issue August 20, 1880

Louis Daross of Cuero, DeWitt county, was bitten the other day by a large spider and the gentleman is likely to die from it.

Mr. Howell, who lived five miles east of Cleburne, is dead; cause dropsy.

Mr. W.H. Earle and family have the sympathy of this office in the loss of their little infant babe.

Capt. Fred Voight of Nacogdoches, ex-Senator and ex-Superintendent of the Capitol Grounds, was drowned Aug. 5th in the Angelina river while attempting to cross on horseback.

Issue August 27, 1880

Tribute of Respect. Barnsville school, Johnson county, Texas, August 22nd, on the death of William Burran, who breathed his last, Saturday night, 21st inst.

Died of congestion of the bowels near Marystown at the residence of Mr. Isaac Jackson in this county, W.H. Key, late of Tenn. Mr. Key was 22 years old.

Died in this city, a little eight months old child of Mr. Longacor, of general debility.

On Thursday the 18th inst., the friends of John E. Odom were called to pay the last tribute of respect to the remains of his estimable wife, Elizabeth Odom, who died on the 19th at her pleasant home in Johnson county, Texas, aged 43 years, 2 months, 4 days.

Items from Caddo. The first born and only child of Samuel and Lizzie Foster, formerly of Caddo, but now of Fort Worth, was buried here last Thursday the 12th.

Issue September 3, 1880

Deaths reported by Gray and Blair, undertakers.
   W.P. Summery's child, 10 months old, six miles south of town, on the 31st.
   Miss M.L. Peters, ten miles below town, died of pneumonia on the 1st.
   A child of Mr. Hiram Chism, 9 months old with congestion of the bowels, six miles N.W. of Cleburne on the 29th of last month.

Issue September 10, 1880

A child of Mr. O.E. Walker was buried in Grand View on Friday last.
   The late Rev. O. Fisher, had been a minister of the Gospel in Texas for forty years. He died at Austin a few days ago.

Deaths. (Reported by Gray and Blair, undertakers.)
   [?]. C. Donnell's child, died 5 milest Northeast of Cleburne, September 3rd.
   [?]. K. Garner's child about one year old, eight miles Southeast, September the 3rd.

[?]. Bullock's child months old [sic], (teething) eight miles South of the city, on September the 7th.

Daughter of S. T. Lightfoot, six years old, died of diphtheria six miles from the city, September 8th.

Issue September 17, 1880

Deaths. (Reported by Gray and Blair, undertakers.)

A. Holland, 62 years old, malarial fever, at Covington, Sept 11.

Child of J. H. Thompson, 10 days old, 8 miles south of the city.

Miss A. Blair, 18 years old, congestion, 4 miles east of the city.

J. Nixon's daughter, 5 years old, congestion, 5 miles northeast of the city, on 12th instant.

A son of J. F. Roots, 16 months old, congestion of the bowels, 1 1-2 miles east of the city, on the 12th inst.

James Ewing's son, 20 months old, congestion of the bowels, 9 miles west of the city, on the 15th.

A son of L. Q. Roby, 14 months old, cholera infantum, in the southern part of the city, on the 15th instant.

Parties have at last been arrested for the murder of Mattie Woods and Alf Hodge at Morgan, Bosque co.

It now appears that two sons of Judge Fossett, Joe Wright and Ed. Nicolls, did the deed, and robbed the murdered parties of four hundred dollars.

From Grand View -- Mrs. Odom, wife of T. C. Odom and daughter of our fellow townsman Col. J. T. Wade, died on last Sunday morning.

Issue September 24, 1880

Deaths reported by Gray & Blair.

Esq. Cope's mother, 72 years old, near Caddo on the 20th.

A granddaughter of C.P. Starratt, living one and a half miles of the city, 9 months old, on the 22nd.

Infant of T.P. Richardson, 8 days old, six miles east of the city, on the 22nd.

In the city on the 18th, Miss Belle Yancy, of congestion, in the 18th year of her age.

The "pale horse and his rider" have lately visited our community and with sad hearts and tearful eyes their coming is bemoaned. Mrs. Richards, who for twenty weeks has been suffering with consumption and confined to her bed, died on Wednesday the 18th inst. and was buried the next day at the Caddo cemetery. ...preceded to the spirit land by her husband who died of the same disease more than a year ago... [note: condensed; mentions young daughters].

Miss Sallie Hayden died on last Saturday and was followed to her grave on Sunday by a number of weeping friends.

Cross Timbers News: Mrs. Nancy Cope, wife of the late I/L.A. Cope, died this morning. She leaves many children and grandchildren to lament her loss.

Mr. W.A. Thompson of Waxahachie, was thrown from his horse a day or so ago, and was instantly killed.

One Hawley, a full-blooded Creek Indian, was executed at Eufala, I. T., a few days ago. The Indians do not use the gallows. The condemned man stood erect, with a small piece of white card board pinned on his left breast over the heart. Ten paces in front of him stood the executioner, with a six-shooter. Two shots did the work...

Sicklist: There is sickness in Dr. Beverly's family. Mrs. Ham, his daughter, has been quite ill.

Col. S. H. Bowen, formerly a citizen of Cleburne, died on the 14th at Gainsville, Texas. Ulceration of the stomach was the fatal disease that caused his demise.

Issue October 8, 1880
Waco Examiner: Ellen Colton, alias Georgia Noble, a courtesan, aged 22, died by her own hand in a house of prostitution on North Second St., yesterday morning at 4 o'clock. Morphine was the agent employed...

Issue October 15, 1880
Died in this city on Sunday, October 10th, at the residence of W.D. Beverly, his daughter, Mrs. H.T. Ham...

Gin Accidents. -- Mr. W. H. Harris, near Grand View, was the unfortunate victim of the gin last Saturday. He was attempting to clean the ribs of his gin, whilst the same was in motion, when his arm was caught and drawn in upon the saws and fearfully larcerated. Since, his arm, or what was left of it, has been amputated. Drs. Wagley and Greenwell performed the surgical operation. The surgeons think Mr. Harris' injuries extremely dangerous.

Another similar accident occurred last week at Mr. Mose Barnes' gin. A negro boy, about seventeen years old, was caught by the shaft in some way, and the life beat out of him.

Issue October 29, 1880

Died on Saturday, October 23, 1880, of congestion, Nathaniel Wallace Haggard, son of Calvin and S.A. Haggard, aged 11 years, 9 months, 20 days.

Gin Accidents. -- Frank (Doc) Duncan, whom everybody knows, and by the way a very unfortunate man, already bereft of a leg, was made again a victim on Saturday last, by becoming mixed up with the saws of Frank Files' gin, and it was thought by Dr. Chambers that the amputation of an arm would follow the accident.

And we learn also since writing the above that a Mr. McCollum, was so terribly mangled at a gin near Milford that he has since died.

Issue November 5, 1880

Williamson Harris, of Waco, and a son of Mr. B. F. Harris, formerly postmaster of Cleburne, died on the 26th ult.

The case of Abe Rothschild, for the murder of "Diamond Bessie," will get a hearing at the present term of the Harrison county court. The case has been set for the 24th inst...

Gus Burney, of Whitney, whom we noticed last week as being shot and mortally wounded at a bagnio in that place, died on the 27th. He was the youngest son of the late Hon. Geo. E. Burney of Waco.

Col. Chas. Lewis, one of the oldest, wealthiest and most prominent citizens of Robertson county, died at his home in Hearne the other day. Col. Lewis was in Cleburne but a short time since, looking after landed interests in this county, and looked the very picture of health. In his death the citizens of Robertson sustain a great loss.

Issue November 12, 1880

N.H. Bone or Boone [sic] of Mansfield was frozen to death on the prairie between Fort Worth and Cleburne on the 6th.

Marystown, November 10, 1880: Mr. Robert Ham and wife lost by death their infant daughter on the 4th inst., aged 2 weeks.

Issue November 19, 1880

Mr. John R. Murphy, who has for sometime resided near Marystown in this county, was killed on last Monday by a runaway team... leaves a wife and six children.

Mr. L.D. Bartley, an old citizen... was suddenly attacked with disease of the heart and in a few moments was no more.

Capt. Charles Bickley, long connected with the Texas Press, died in New Orleans a few days ago...

Issue December 3, 1880

Jack and Tom Jones, who killed George Morse at Calvert, were tried at Cameron last week, and acquitted. Jack Jones was sheriff of the county at the time of the killing.

Issue January 7, 1881

On last Monday night, "Aunt Bettie," a negro woman, was frozen to death, on the margin of the creek just west of the square...

Col. J. J. Cathings. In our issue of Dec. 24th, we noted the fact that the above named gentleman was injured in a cotton gin, and gave utterance of the hope for his recovery; but now we are called upon to chronicle the death of Col. Gathings [sic], which occurred Dec. 24, 1880, at his residence in Hill county. ...kind and indulgent husband and father, and his bereaved family has our heartfelt sympathy.

Issue January 27, 1881

Died. In Waxahachie, Jan'y 20th, Mrs. Nancy C. Walker.
In Galveston, Mrs. Tho. M. Jack, on the 17th.
In Washington county, 13th, Mrs. W. H. Robertson.
In Denton, Mrs. Callie Batch, quite suddenly.
In Grayson, Mrs. Ann Potts, aged 73 years.
In Smith county, Col. Joe P. Smith, an old resident.
At Calvert, last week, Mr. L. K. Preston, an old resident.
On Jan. 20, Mrs. Ann Eliza Hooker, wife of R. M. Hooker, who lives five miles south of Cleburne. She was thirty-six years of age, was an estimable lady... Many followed her remains to the Cleburne cemetary where they were interred on the 21st inst. Rev. Oscar Hightower, officiating at the funeral service.

Issue February 4, 1881

Died. Yesterday about noon the infant daughter of Mr. and Mrs. John Brobst, aged 3 months. The funeral will take place from the family residence, one north Wilhite St. at 10 o'clock to-day.

Issue February 11, 1881

Deaths. Reported by Gray and Blair, undertakers.
    John D. Allard, infant son of Mr. and Mrs. Allard, residing four miles west of Cleburne. Died January 31.
    This is the only death that Messrs. Gray and Blair have to report occurring within fifteen days past, and speaks well for this community...

Issue February 25, 1881

State vs. Alf Kenner. Assault to murder. Continued by consent.

Reported by Gray and Blair, undertakers.

Mrs. F. M. Weathered, residing near Fort Graham, Hill co., died Feb'y 21st, 1881.

Infant child of B. F. Williams, of Johnson co., died Feb'y 21st, 1881.

On the 11th, in Seymor, Baylor Co., Mr. B. F. and M. A. Wilbanks lost their little Dora Osborne Wilbanks, aged 2 years and one month, congestion the cause.

It is with regret that we chronicle the death of William Canter of this vicinity. Mr. C. was the victim of a merchant who mistook him for a burglar. So far as we know no blame attaches to any one in this sad affair.

Deaths. Reported by Gray and Blair, undertakers.

J. H. Nelson, of Cleburne, Texas; died Feb. 27, aged 61 years.

William Canter, of Lane's Prairie, died Feb. 28, aged 30 years.

Mr. Mittie Gatewood, wife Wm. Gatewood, of Nolands river; [note: age illegible].

Tribute of Respect. ...our worthy brother, Jessee H. Nelson, who died at 9 o'clock p.m. on the 27th of February, 1881, who though not a member of our Lodge had endeared himself to us by his uniform walk in life.

Brother Nelson was about 62 years old, was a member of Tompkinsville Lodge No. 321, of F.&A.M. in Kentucky. It was his request that Cleburne Lodge No. 315 bury him, which was done with the usual Masonic Honors... G. H. Maxey, J. A. Willingham, Andrew Young, committee.

Issue March 6, 1881

Deaths. Reported by Gray and Blair, undertakers.

Mrs. Thomas, residing five miles east of Cleburne, died on the 12th March.

Mrs. Wm. Tartar, died at the family residence 6 miles south of Cleburne, on the 16th March.

Mr. Graphy, residing near Caddo, died on Wednesday, 16th day of March.

Infant of Mr. and Mrs. L. Black, 7 miles north-west of Cleburne, died on the 12th March.

THE FAR WEST
Published at LaGrange, Fayette county.
Texas. Vol. 1, #1 dated February 13, 1847. Published by M. Austin Martin.

Issue May 22, 1847
On Tuesday last, Alfred English, aged 28 years, a Private in Capt. B. McCullough's company, in attempting to leap his horse over a pair of bars at Mr. Hill's, about two miles from this place, was thrown and immediately killed. We learn he was a native of Cincinnati, O., and had lived for sometime in New Orleans. He has relatives in both of these cities. He was buried the following day in our village burying ground.

THE LAGRANGE PAPER
Published at LaGrange, Fayette county, Texas
by W.B. M'Clellan.

Issue February 24, 1855
Volume I, #1
John Hyde, a notorious and desperate character, was arrested in this county a few days ago by Sheriff Cowser, upon affidavit of Richard A. Barkley, charging him with the murder of Levi W. Young in Bastrop county, Texas, on the 14th day of September 1853...

Issue March 10, 1855
Died in the town of Columbus on the 12th February, Joel D. Kolbe, in the 24th year, leaving aged parents and numerous friends... The deceased was an only child of the Rev. A.J.D. Kolbe and wife Elizabeth Kolbe, citizens of this county...

Issue March 31, 1855
Departed this life on the 22nd inst., Miss Elizabeth B. Nichols. The daughter of Wm. B. Nichols, aged 16 years, 1 month and 8 days.

Execution of Bob: On yesterday J.A. Fitz, the acting sheriff of our county, executed by hanging near the grave-yard, the negro man Bob, who was found guilty and sentenced at the recent term of our court for the brutal murder of his master, the late D.D. McSween, of this county.

Issue May 5, 1855
Richard D. Chisholm died at Clinton on the 8th inst., aged about sixty years... He resided for the last twenty five years or more at or near his late residence in DeWitt county.

Issue May 26, 1855

Died in this place on the 8th inst. of scarlet fever, Elizabeth C. Norton, only daughter of James J. Norton, deceased, and Martha K. Norton, widow and relict of the said James, in the 8th year of her age.

Issue June 16, 1855

Egypt, Texas, 14 May 1855, drowned: On the 10th of May, a man was drowned in the West Bernard while attempting to cross upon his horse, the water being very high. He was taken out the next day and buried when papers were found about him, showing his name to be John N. McClutchin... He was a member of the Sons of Temperance at Middlebrook, Virginia.

THE TEXAS RANGER AND BRAZOS GUARD

Published at Washington, Texas, Tuesdays, by J. Lancaster; volume I, #1 is dated January 16, 1849.

Issue March 9, 1849

By a gentleman from Liberty county we learn that Mr. Jackson, the owner of Sour Lake in Jefferson county, is supposed to have been murdered... He went to Louisville with a drove of horses and crossed the Sabine about two weeks ago on his return home with eighteen hundred dollars in his possession since which time he has not been heard of.

THE LONE STAR

Issue April 5, 1851

Fatal affray in Sabine county: On Monday last, as a Mr. Lovin was returning from Milam to his residence in Sabine county in company with his son, William, and nephew, he fell in with a youth named Hoffman at or near Patroon bridge. Lovin soon commenced abusing Hoffman by calling him among other names, a thief. Young Hoffman remarked to the old man that his being drunk alone saved him from a whipping, and turned to speak to William Lovin when the old man drew a pistol on him and fired, the ball penetrating his body. Hoffman staggered back, with his rifle in his hand, when he received two other shots, one in the neck, supposed to have been fired by the young Lovins. He then raised his rifle and fired at old Lovin (who was running) shooting him through the body and killing him instantly... *San Augustine Herald.*

Mr. J. Dozell, an old and respectable planter of Copiah county, Mississippi, was cruelly murdered on the 11th ult., it is thought by one of his own slaves.

Issue July 12, 1851

Mr. Salucas Askew, an overseer of Dr. R.R. Peebles, in attempting to whip a servant girl, was assaulted by a negro man and stabbed twice to the heart...

Issue October 23, 1852

Died on the 17th inst. between Houston and Washington, Mrs. Mary Trabue, wife of Mr. Daniel Trabue of Washington, late of St. Louis. St. Louis papers please copy.

Issue November 13, 1852

Died 31 October, Mrs. Eliza W. Miller, consort of Dr. J.B. Miller of Ft. Bend county.

[Died] At San Augustine, October 24th, Miss Matilda C.B. Stovall.

Issue November 20, 1852

Our community was thrown into great consternation on Thursday last, by the perpetration of one of those horrid murders that shock humanity and make the blood run cold within our veins; perpetrated by a man calling himself David Butler, upon the person of Thomas McGuire, both strangers in this community. *La Vaca Commercial.*

Our community was plunged into mourning on Tuesday last by the melancholy intelligence that day Dr. Edward Ragland had been killed by John A.J. Hamilton, both of Mission Valley, in this county... *Texan Advocate.*

Issue November 27, 1852

Dallas county: The *Leon Pioneer* states that a man named Kelly shot a man named Preston in the town of Dallas on the 11th inst. The two had disputed over a game of cards, when Kelly went and got a shot gun and deliberately fired at Preston, wounding him in the left breast, after which he mounted his horse and rode off. A man named Tilly was killed by G.B. Hardwick, within a few days of the above occurrence.

GOLIAD EXPRESS
Published at Goliad, Texas.

Issue July 11, 1857

Frank Bowden, of Eastern Texas, is dead.

Issue September 5, 1857

Another suicide: A letter has been received in this city from Richmond, says the *News* of yesterday, announcing the death by suicide of James D. Pentecost of Fort Bend county... *Galveston Herald,* August 19th.

GOLIAD MESSENGER
Published at Goliad, Texas.

Issue November 12, 1864
Died in this city after a protracted sickness on the 8th inst., Mrs. Mary Bridge, daughter of the late W.B. McCampbell. She was born in Blount county, East Tennessee, 26 December 1808. She was converted to God, and died in the faith and hope of the gospel of Christ. Her only anxiety was with reference to her three children.

GOLIAD GUARD
Published at Goliad, Texas.

Issue June 13, 1874
Died in Goliad on the 5th of June 1874, Mr. J.D. Ryan, aged 73 years. Deceased was an old and respected citizen of Goliad. He had been in feeble health for several years and lingered until last Friday week ago, when he was "gathered to his fathers."

THE FRONTIER NEWS
Published at Weatherford, Texas
by C.E. VanHorn & Co.

Issue August 19, 1858
Died at his father's residence in Parker county, Texas, near 8 o'clock P.M. on the 31st of July 1858 of apoplectic fits, Daniel Pratt, aged 1 year, 9 months and 9 days. Only son of Mr. J.S. and Jane A. Wampler.

INDEPENDENT MONITOR
Published at Sulphur Springs, Texas, Hopkins county.

Issue December 1, 1860
Fell dead in the pulpit: On Sunday the 14th inst., Rev. Mr. McNeil/McNeel, a Presbyterian minister, fell dead while preaching in the Brick church near Mr. Statenboro's in the southern portion of Dallas county, Alabama. It is supposed it is a disease of the heart.

Four men in jail in Neb City were, on the 16th, taken out in nothing seen or heard of them until about noon, when the lifeless body of Philip McGuire was found suspended by the neck from a limb of a tree from that place. Pinned upon his neck was a cord on which was written "hanged for his many rascalities."

Killed -- Mr. Stansel, a horse trader belonging to this city, was killed at Leon Springs, this county, Monday last, by Squire Plehwe[?] of that town. As we underlined this matter, a trial was going on before Phehwe[?] ___ which Stansel resisted the constable, firing several pistol shots at him, whereupon Plenwe[?] went into ____ took down his gun and shot him. *San Antonio Herald.*

Issue December 6, 1866
Hopkins county. Estate of Wm. B. White, dec. A. J. Cannedy, George Starr, adm.

SOUTHERN CONFEDERACY
Published at Seguin, Texas.

Issue February 8, 1861
We are pained to learn of the death of Gen. John D. Pitts, who left Austin for home in fine health a few days ago, spending the night with his friend, Thomas F. McKinney. At breakfast, we learn, he was well when he took his seat but was soon stricken with paralysis and died in twenty-four hours. Hays county has lost a useful citizen.

Issue February 15, 1861
We deeply regret to learn of the death of Rev. James C. Wilson of Gonzales, who departed this life on the 7th inst.

Issue February 22, 1861
The *Advocate* (Palestine) says that the examining court, after 2 days investigation, committed the negro boy Martin for the murder of Wm. D. Westcott of New Orleans.

Issue March 15, 1861
On Wednesday, March 6th, Mr. Robert Woodfolk was killed in Texana, Jackson county, in a difficulty with Mr. H. Flournoy and R.S., his son, and the elder Flourney, wounded.

Issue April 12, 1861

We deeply regret to chronicle the death of Oscar Dalton, editor of the *Crockett Printer*, who died at his residence in Crockett on Monday night, 25th ult. The *Printer* was a universal favorite throughout Texas and its editor occupied a warm place in the hearts of his contemporaries. Good bye, poor Dalton, and may God protect the widow and orphans.

Issue April 19, 1861

Died in this county on the 5th of April, Mrs. Elizabeth, consort of W.D. Foy, in the 24th year of her age.

Died at the residence of Gen. J.R. Jefferson on the morning of the 18th inst., Mr. Ben. Morrison of Louisiana, aged 21 years.

Issue April 26, 1861

The same paper (*Galveston News*) learns of a homicide committed at Port Sullivan about three miles above Milican's in Brazos county. It appears that a grocery was kept there by a man named Adams, who had a quarrel with a Mr. Evetts, and each had threatened to shoot the other the day previous. Evetts came to Adams' store on Monday and shot him dead as he was opening his door.

Died this morning at 2 1/2 o'clock at the residence of Gen. Jefferson of congestion of the lungs, Mr. George Elgin of New Orleans, aged 22 years.

Issue May 3, 1861

We were pained to learn of the death of our fellow county-man, C.L. Cox, who was drowned on the Escondida creek on Thursday the 25th of April... Leaves a wife and one daughter, 7 or 8 years old. Mr. Cox's mother had just reached his house, from Tennessee, on the day of the news of his death reached Seguin.

Issue May 6, 1861

Tribute of Respect for C.L. Cox.

Issue May 11, 1861

The Late Oscar Dalton. [note: starts with poem].

    The mournful intelligence of the death of Oscar Dalton, which we received at Galveston, caused deep feeling of sorrow among a host of friends there, where he was so long and so favorably known. Although being for months in intimate connection with him, and knowing the feeble state of his health, we were shocked at the announcement, and confess our inability to do that justice to his memory which a less disinterested party might evince. To return to the scene of our mutual labors -- to gaze upon his vacant chair -- to look upon his little household goods, whom the ruthless hand of violence have deprived of their only earthly protector -- some of them too young to know their irreparable loss, to recall to memory the once happy father, the devoted husband and trusty friend -- to think that he "now sleeps the sleep that knows no waking," might have but little effect upon a stranger who knew not his worth, but to us these recollections conjure up the most poignant sorrows... He was a essentially a domestic man, and the fire-side was his world. With his little ones clustering around him like tender vines around the sturdy tree, the toils and vexations of every day life were forgotten in the heaven of domestic enjoyment -- and the purity of his heart was evinced by his child like simplicity, as he shared their evening sports, till wearied with play, one by one, -- their little eye-lids closed, and they sell into the land of dreams, to listen to angel whispers....

Mr. Dalton was born in New Orleans, and not in Baton Rouge as was erroneously stated in a previous notice of his demise--- *Printer*

Issue June 14, 1861

A young man, William Mills, was drowned in the Guadalupe river a few miles below Seguin some days ago.

Issue June 21, 1861

F.C. Hauser, formerly of Salem, North Carolina, died at the residence of Dr. J.R. Johnson in this place on Friday. He had been ill for three weeks with typhoid fever.

Issue August 23, 1861

Departed this life August 5, 1861, in the 26th year of her age, Mrs. E.L/l. Benton, consort of Capt. Nat Benton and daughter of John and Laura Harris. She immigrated from Tennessee with her parents... She left parents, husband, brothers, sisters, three children.

THE McKINNEY MESSENGER
Thomas & Darnall, publishers & proprietors.

Issue November 16, 1866

The *Paris Press* gives an account of a shocking murder which was perpetrated in Lamar county on the night of the 7th inst. The unfortunate victim was a Mr. John B. Duncan, who lived about three miles west of Paris. An old woman (part Indian) by the name of Matilda Winters and her son, Nelson Winters, who for some years had been inmates of Mr. Duncan's family, are charged with the murder...

CASTROVILLE ERA
Published at Castroville, Texas
by Morrison & Wallace.

Issue December 18, 1877
Austin Statesman 12th: Deputy Sheriff William Smythson, of Bastrop county, was killed by his saddle horse in Elgin last Sunday.

THE GREENVILLE INDEPENDENT
Published at Greenville, Hunt county, Texas
by Tom R. Burnett and Chas. W. Geers.

Issue May 2, 1868
Mr. Joseph Caldwell, one of our patrons, and a very nice, genteel, intelligent man, so far as our acquaintance extends, while returning from Greenville to his home, some ten miles in the county, on Monday last, met and shot and killed a Mr. Graham, one of his neighbors.

DENTON MONITOR
Published at Denton, Texas,
Burnett & Geers, proprietors; Tom R. Burnett, editor.

Issue June 13, 1868
The *Waco Examiner* reports the killing of a Mr. Powers by a Mr. Morrison at Stephenville.

The *Henderson Times* reports the killing of James Brewster, a dwarf, only 36" high, by one Joe Cocke, a ruffian.

We learn more of the particulars of the killing scrape in the southeast portion of this county since last issue. A misunderstanding had sprung between Edwards and McCoun when the latter threatened to kill the former if he did not make some satisfaction in matter, and visited his house as is supposed for that purpose. Edwards, seeing his enemy before him armed, ran toward the house for his gun, but was caught at the door by McCoun, pulled out into the yard and shot. A daughter of Edwards who was milking at the time, seeing the danger her father was in, ran to the spot with an ax and struck several blows at McCoun, wounding him severely about the head... Edwards died. An old gentleman named Noah Aiken, who went to the house next day after some things with his wagon, while taking his load(ed) gun from the wagon was shot in the arm, the amputation of which caused his death.

HOUSTON TRI-WEEKLY UNION
Published at Houston, Texas.

Issue January 20, 1869
The *Waco Register* of the 13th has an account of the killing of a notorious character known as Wild Bill Miller. The sheriff of Coryell county, aided by a posse, attempted to arrest him, but he, resisting, was shot, from the effects of which he died.

THE FLEA
Published at Jacksboro, Texas.

Issue April 15, 1869
Mr. Henson, who killed a soldier at this place in November 1867, has been released from the post guard house...

THE FRONTIER ECHO
Published at Jacksboro, Texas.

Issue July 14, 1875
Sulphur Springs Gazette, 3rd: James Whiting came to an untimely death upon the prairie about one mile west of town last Sabbath evening. He was found by John VanVickle a few moments before he breathed his last. A bottle of whiskey near by indicated the cause.

Gatesville, Sunday 3rd: ...mentions the examining trial of Bill Wilson, indicted for the murder of James Armstrong.

Sudden death: of James Hefner on last Saturday morning... Worked on the farm of J.W. Rubel. [note: condensed].

Issue August 11, 1875
Marshall Herald, 3rd: Yesterday Walter Hunt was accidently shot by Arthur Young in front of the residence of Ed. Clark, in the edge of town on the Gilmer road. The two boys, aged about fourteen years each, were out hunting. The shot took effect in the bowels.

FAYETTE COUNTY RECORD
Published at LaGrange, Texas.

Issue December 16, 1873
We are informed that the body of Mr. Robinson, whose death by drowning was announced in the *Record*, has been discovered.

PALESTINE ADVOCATE
Published at Palestine, Texas.

Issue March 17, 1881
Volume 28, #12

A Mr. Wade died of pneumonia the 12th inst. on the farm of Mrs. T.S. Parker, two miles south of Palestine. Mr. Wade had been but a few weeks in the county but was an old resident of the state and a relative of Col. Wade, a San Jacinto veteran, who died in southern Texas a few months ago.

BUSY BEE
"Official paper of Blanco County."
Marion and Craft, prop. and publishers.

Issue August 21, 1875
$500 is the reward offered for the apprehension of Jack Post, who shot John Spelse near Honey Grove on the 28th of July.

W.J. Jeffrys', who killed a man named McFail in Comanche county a little over a year ago, was killed in Llano county by Wild Bill [Miller?]. The governor had offered a reward of $250 for Jeffry's scalp.

Information is wanted of one Jno E. Naff, or J. Emmet Naff, as Samuel W. Foyey, of the Cherokee nation is now under sentence of death for murdering him and denies that he killed him. Any information in regard to said Naff, addressed to the Independent office at Ft. Smith, Ark. will be thankfully received.

79

HEMPSTEAD WEEKLY COUNTRYMAN
Published Hempstead, Austin County, Texas.
J.G. <u>Rankin</u>, prop.

Issue September 3, 1869

Jim Stapp, Gain Peas, Jim Bell, Charles Moore, Ruthland Jones, Tobe Pool, Jim Zansford, have been disposed of by the regulators of Victoria County, as horse and cattle thieves.

On the 18th inst., Warren Lawless of Bell county was arrested by the military at Waco on suspicion of having killed freedman Tom Wilson near Waco, in July 1868. Mr. Lawless showed conclusively that he was not the lawless man he was accused of being and was accordingly released.

Ellis Hill, a young man of Moulton, Ala., recently killed Thomas McKelvey, cutting his throat with a pen knife.

A little son of Mr. Bracewell of Newman, Georgia, the other day, playfully attached the halter of a mule around his neck. The mule took fright at something, ran away, and the boy literally torn to pieces.

The brothers McGehu and their cousin, in route for Mexico with a considerable amount of money, are reported killed west of San Antonio.

Round Top, Fayette county, was the scene of an unfortunate difficulty on the night of the 23rd ult. between two young men, Patton <u>Rankin</u> and Walter Holt. Rankin killed, Holt mortally wounded.

The deceased was an own cousin of the editor hereof and the occurrence is a source of deep regret to us.

Mrs. Oscar Gray, the wife of one of the prisoners in the stockade at Jefferson, died Saturday week after a lingering illness. He was allowed to visit her during her last hours and to witness the final sad offices of burial.

Tribute of Respect at stated meeting of Bellville Lodge No. 223, held at the Lodge Room in Bellville, August 21, 1869 for Dr. E.T. Bonney, who died on the night of 6 August 1869, a good physician and an exemplary Mason. Little orphan son, mother, sister, and brother.

We stand corrected...[?] There is some difference between killing and being killed. We congratulate Mr. Zion Barton that our informant was mistaken and take pleasure in saying to our readers that Mr. Barton was the individual who killed the horse thief.

Dave and Ralph (negroes), father and son, had a shooting match at Fairfield on the 14th. The son shot the father in the mouth.

The *McKinney Messenger* says Mr. James Loving, an old and highly esteemed citizen of Dallas county, was recently murdered by a desperado named Hays.

Issue September 24, 1869
Sheriff Sneed of Hill County was killed recently.

More arrests. Marshall Browning, assistant of the military, arrested two men, John Talbott and James Stevenson, in this county last week, who are charged with complicity to the murder of some negroes and U.S. Soldiers. Stevenson was badly wounded and surrendered. They were taken to Brenham and placed under guard on the Federal camps.

CUERO STAR
Published at Cuero, Texas.

Issue December 31, 1873
Killed. We learned from passengers up on a train yesterday that Mr. Wiley Pridgen of Thomastown station was perfectly riddled with buck-shot about 11 o'clock yesterday. No one can find out who did the shooting. Mr. P. was an old Texan and has lived in this county for many years.

BEAUMONT BANNER
Published at Beaumont, Texas
A.N. Vaughan, prop.

Issue December 11, 1860
Fell Dead in the Pulpit. On Sunday the 14th inst., the Rev. Mr. McNeel/McNeil, a presbyterian minister, fell dead while preaching in the Brick church, near Statenboro's in the southern portion of Dallas county, Ala. It is supposed it was from a disease of the heart.

Issue January 8, 1861
Estate of Stephen W. Turner, dec., in Orange county. R.A. Neyland will present for probate a certain nuncupative will made by deceased in his last illness.

Jefferson county. James E. Armstrong, adm. of Robert F. Green and Henry R. Green.

Obit. Died at his residence in Beaumont, Thursday morning, 3rd last., Hon. E.A.M. Gray, 49 years, 1 month, 24 days. Native of Petersburg, Va. Graduate of Princeton. Bar at age 20. Moved to Ala. one year, then MS, Ark for 3 years. To this place, 1853. Wife, five children. [note: condensed].

Adm. notice. Susan Frazier, dec., Orange co.

BROWNSVILLE JOURNAL
Published at Brownsville, Texas.

Issue July 13, 1864
Pedro Garcia, a Private in First Texas Cavalry, was shot Wednesday, June 22, in garrison at Brownsville, in pursuance to the sentence of a court martial. He was executed for desertion when on picket duty and for firing on the guard that arrested him.

THE LEON PIONEER
Published at Centreville, Texas.
Wood, Horn & co. Publishers.

Issue August 16, 1854
About $1600 reward is offered to the apprehension of Munroe Black, the murderer of Barnes at Ft. Graham in Hill co.

More killing. A party of gentlemen were in our town on Monday from Wheelock in search of a man named Miller, who they said had killed a negro in the skirts of that village a few days previously. Miller it seems was seeking a chance to kill the owner of the slave, Mr. T. Johnson, and failing to meet with an opportunity to do so, in an excuse of rage and passion killed the poor negro, who chanced to fall his way. Citizens of Texas how long are these things to be tolerated.

HARRISON FLAG
Published at Marshall, Texas
by W.G. Barrett proprietor.

Issue January 11, 1868

Mrs. Mariam Luxton, mother of Lt. General Forrest, died the 12th inst. at Navasota, Texas, aged sixty-four.

Clarksville Standard: On the last day of 1867, at merrymaking in Whitett's drinking saloon, Hardy Barry, an old citizen was shot in the arm by Capt. Thomas Lennox and died on Thursday night.

Died in Harrison county, 24 December 1867, Lizzie Swanson Webb, infant of John W. and Elizabeth Webb, aged twenty-four days.

Issue February 15, 1868

Grayson county: James Perryman, of this county, left Sherman Tuesday evening last, with a two-horse wagon to go to his home about five miles from town; sometime after dark the horse came home without the driver; a search was made the next morning and the man was found dead within 1/2 mile of home.

Capt. Steven W. Webb died January 31, 1868; born June 6, 1832.

Died in Waco, Texas, the 4th of December, Mr. G.B. Woods, formerly of Harrison county.

Issue March 7, 1868

Homicide at Dangerfield: Sgt. C.H. Pearson, of the 6th U.S. Cavalry, was killed at that place Sunday evening the 1st inst. by a man named English.

Issue March 14, 1868

The *Paris Vindicator* of the 25th ult. says that John Dennis, a well known citizen of Lamar county, was bush whacked and killed on the Friday previous on Red River.

Issue March 20, 1868

We published yesterday (Wednesday) an article from the *Rusk Observer* in reference to a murder in Panola county about the 1st of February. We learn this morning through the Freedmen's Bureau, at this place, that the name of the murdered man was McCloud and that he was killed by W.A. Coyle and another man.

Miscellaneous Texas Newspaper Abstracts - Deaths --- Vol 2

Issue April 3, 1868
Died in Ft. Worth, Friday the 20th of March, 1868, Mrs. Minerva J. VanZandt, wife of Maj. K.M. VanZandt.

WEEKLY HARRISON FLAG
Published at Marshall, Texas.

Issue April 10, 1868
The evening of the 2nd inst., Mr. W.R.D. Ward and Mr. Ely were attacked and murdered on the road ten miles below Henderson on the Nacogdoches road by Willis Poe and Harris Robinson.

Judge Thadeus B. Reese died very suddenly in Jefferson on Thursday night the 2nd inst. of an apoplectic fit.

Issue May 8, 1868
A man has been found dead some two weeks since near Bolivar, Mississippi, whose body was in such a state of putrefaction that no personal identity could be discovered as to who he was, except for a certification of registration bearing the name J.R. Barnes of Upshur county, Texas.

Issue May 28, 1868
About 1:00 Sunday night, a freedman in the employ of Judge Mason of this place, named James Ellis, was shot and killed by unknown persons.

Issue June 18, 1868
Col. Grimes of Sherman committed suicide by shooting himself in the region of the heart, a short time since.

Issue July 9, 1868
Mr. Harry McDonald, a blacksmith by trade, committed suicide by swallowing laudanum in Jefferson the evening of the 30th of June.

Issue July 16, 1868
Died in Jefferson, Saturday the 11th inst., after a short illness, in the 20th year of her life, Miss Rosa D. Britt, only daughter of Mrs. Mary S. Todd.

Issue July 30, 1868
Died Wednesday, July the 29th, 1868, Miss Octavia Virginia Hall, eldest daughter of Col. M.J. Hall of Marshall, Texas.

Issue August 6, 1868
A Mr. Wall killed Reading W. Black of Uvalde.

Issue August 20, 1868

Died: W.B. Ochiltree, at his residence in the city of Jefferson, in the month of December last.

Tribute of respect on the death of John M. Henderson.

Issue August 27, 1868

Died: Andrew Carver, old and esteemed citizen of Harrison county.

Dudley W. Jones, Col. of the 9th Tx. Reg., and one of the editors of the *Ku Klux Vedetta*, died in Houston the 14th of August; aged 26.

Galveston News: Mrs. M.C. Dial, wife of Dr. W.H. Dial, formerly of Marshall, died in that city the 16th of August.

Issue September 10, 1868

Died in Marshall the morning of the 7th of September, Mrs. Louisa R.C. Barrett, relict of the late Capt. John W. Barrett, aged 56. Leaves three children (one the editors of the *Harrison Flag*), and two daughters.

Issue September 17, 1868

Obituary of R.C. Banett; came to Texas 1837 and to this county in 1838.

Issue October 1, 1868

Gen. T.C. Hindman has been assassinated at his residence in Helena, Arkansas, by one Robbins of Springfield, Missouri.

Mr. M.D. Ball, proprietor of the *Texas Gladiator*, published at Anderson, Grimes county, was shot and killed Saturday last by Mr. B. Goodrich.

From the *Henderson Times*: Horrible affair, four men killed: Sunday the 13th, Mat Shaddon was killed by his brother-in-law John Elliot. Early Wednesday morning four brothers of Shaddon went to the house of Hayden Phillips together with some five other parties in search of Elijah Phillips and Elliot where the party shot and killed Hayden Phillips and a son-in-law of Hayden Phillips was also killed.

Issue October 8, 1868

New Orleans: On Saturday morning the 26th of September a negro named Edward Desforges, alias Forest, was killed in a personal altercation in the French Market by a white man named Arthur Guerin.

Two young men, Mr. Brownlee and Ogden, were shot by negroes about ten miles above Shreveport, Louisiana, on Wednesday morning the 13th ult. Mr. Ogden died in a short while, and there was no hope of Mr. Brownlee's recovery.

Issue October 29, 1868
On last Saturday morning, Capt. W.H. Mullins, of Tyler, committed suicide by shooting himself in the left breast near the heart with a pistol.

The youngest son of Mr. J. Lancaster, editor of the *Navasota Ranger*, was recently taken out of his bed and murdered.

Mr. John Rain, old and universally esteemed citizen of this county, died at his residence last Sunday the 25th of October.

Issue November 5, 1868
Dr. William Trabue, who killed Mr. J. Cherry, in Panola several weeks ago, made his escape the night of the 24th of October and being discovered the 26th, six miles from Shelbyville, Texas, was shot and killed.

Died at the residence of her husband, fourteen miles west of Marshall, the 4th of November, Mrs. S.J. Jones, wife of John S. Jones.

Issue November 26, 1868
Mr. Dan Sanford, city marshall of Jefferson, was killed in that place Friday by Mr. W.E. Rose. The deceased was quietly eating his dinner at a restaurant, when his slayer, being in a state of intoxication, drew his six shooter and fired upon him.

Issue December 13, 1868
Died: Mrs. Sarah Jane Jones, born October 10, 1825, and professed the religion of Jesus Christ in Dresden, Tennessee; married December 23, 1841, Col. John S. Jones and emigrated to Texas and settled in Harrison county, 1848.

Died at the residence of her husband, Dr. L.S. Rayfield at Jefferson, Texas, the morning of the 25th of November, Mary Virginia, daughter of the late Hon. W.S. Todd and Eliza A. Hudgins; aged 26 years.

Issue December 17, 1868
Mr. Lafayette Cook, living 7 or 8 miles west of Henderson, Rusk county, committed suicide by shooting himself with an infield rifle a few days ago. Leaves a wife and four children.

Issue December 24, 1868
Col. Eli Baxter, formerly of Marshall, died in Bellville, Austin county, the 13th inst.

Issue January 7, 1869
Jefferson, Texas; a posse of soldiers killed Capt. William Perry.

Issue January 14, 1869
Cullen M. Baker and a man named Kirby were shot and killed the 6th of January.

George W. Reynold, associate editor of the *Brenham Banner*, shot and killed a soldier named Davis.

Issue January 28, 1869
Henderson county: On Monday night last week, John Nelson and his son Reily were killed near Belview by two negroes, Henry Bell and John Loyd.

Last Sunday night a young man named Charley Man was killed about a mile from Dangerfield by a man named Blakey.

Drowned: The wife of Private Kenny, of company "C" 29th U.S.I., and her infant.

On the morning of October 30th, 1868, Cullen Baker, with ten or twelve men, killed Mr. James Salmon.

Issue February 4, 1869
Near Rock Ford, on the Bois d'arc, Wednesday of the past week, a party of men, in camp, made a wager over a pistol in a shooting match, which resulted in Verner killing Grider and Tumalt.

Issue February 11, 1869
Last Saturday, five miles west of Marshall, on the Henderson road, a number of negroes were conveying the corpse of a child, to be interned, when a young man named Tobe Crain, being intoxicated, joined the procession. When he reached the grave he fired his pistol among the crowd killing a negro boy and wounding a man in the face. Crain rode back to a grocery store, where a negro shot him. Crain then rode to a field where he was later found lying on the ground and some negroes shot him three or four more times killing him.

Issue February 18, 1869

Galveston: Mrs. Sallie Roach, widow of the late Bracy Roach, residing near Crump's Ferry on the Brazos river in Austin county, was killed the night of the 3rd inst.

The *Mittie Stephens*, Capt. Kellogg, burned on the lake (Ferry Lake) near Swanson's Landing, about 1/2 past 12 Thursday night. One hundred and four passengers, sixty-one of whom were lost. Lost were, crew: George Remer, 1st clerk; Charles Welr, 1st engineer; Thomas Mulligan, 2nd engineer; M.M. Gill, striker; Peter Fisher, James Gardener and John Battese, colored firemen. Passengers: Mrs. Jackson and three children; Mrs. T.L. Lyon and son Frank; Mr. & Mrs. Lewis and three children; one unknown lady from Grand Ecore; W.A. Broadwell, New Orleans; J.C. Christian, Mr. Boykin, Mr. Ash and Mr. New., deck passengers: James Johnson, Nancy Bradford, Henry Ashley, Sidney Ashley, Robert Phillips, Martha A. Phillips, Alex Phillips. Deck crew: William Murphy, Joseph Ganes, Andrew Gallighan, Thomas Ryan, Pat Reily, Nat Buchanan, Jim Hill, Henry Hicks, Peter Engine, and six not known. Cabin crew: A. Baptiste, Napoleon Washington, Charles Bedford, John Smith, and Dennis Williams; Robert Franklin, 2nd porter; G.W. Hughes, 1st cook; Charles Crane, baker; Ann Collins, chambermaid.

Tribute of respect for William Snediker, aged 15; from the Swamp Eagle Wigwam #1, I.O. of R.M.

Issue March 4, 1869

Henry Jacobs, well known police officer of New Orleans, was killed in Mobile, Wednesday.

A son of Hardin Hart was killed at Greenville, a few days since, by the sheriff of Hunt county.

Issue March 18, 1869

Died in Marshall, Tuesday, March 16, 1869, Mrs. Mattie R. Parish, wife of Mr. Lee H. Parish of this place.

Died in Marshall, Wednesday evening, March 17th, Mrs. Anna Brown, widow of Capt. Phil Brown. Her burial will take place this evening at 4:00 at the Marshall cemetery.

Issue April 8, 1869

Hung the 26th of March, John Thompson and William O. Blackmore at Sherman for murdering a stranger, January last.

Issue April 22, 1869

Died in Upshur county the morning of the 5th of April, Mrs. N.E. Hagler, wife of Ralph Hagler.

Died in Elysian Fields, Harrison county, Tuesday morning, April 13th, Edward Smith, aged 79; native of South Carolina.

From the *Waco Register*: Clark Jones and a man named Nelson were hung in Marlin, Falls county, the 13th. The former charged with the murder of the Howards. The latter for the killing of a man named Wallace. There were said to be about 5,000 persons to witness the execution.

Issue September 23, 1869

Man Killed: On Friday evening the 3rd, James T. Browning, Marshall of Hempstead, arrested a man named Samuel S. Huff of Co. B 4th Cavalry, supposed to be a deserter from the federal troops stationed in Texas. Huff made an attempt to escape by running and was shot in the bowels. Huff died the next day.

JEFFERSON HOME ADVOCATE
Published at Jefferon, Texas.
F.J. Patill, editor.

Issue February 27,1869

In a shooting affair in Houston, 13th inst. between Mr. Kinney of the *Houston Times* and Mr. Tracy of the *Union*, a son, 14, of Rev. Alex. Hinkle was accidently shot in the groin, and is thought to be mortally wounded. Bro. Hinkle is a member of the East Texas Conference, was stationed a number of years ago in Marshall.

Issue March 5, 1869

Died Sunday morning, Alford Baldis, only son of Rev. Alexander and Mrs. L.H. Hinkle from the effects of a pistol shot. He was about twelve.

Issue March 13, 1869

Died Sunday morning, Alfred Balford, only son of Rev. Alexander and Mrs. L.H. Hinkle, from the effects of a pistol shot wound. Age about 12 years. From the *Houston Times*.

Issue April 8, 1869

At Gussettville, Live Oak county: We learn from the *San Antonio Herald*, Tom Dolan killed his uncle, Patrick Fox, by stabbing him in the belly.

Issue April 16, 1869
The *Waxachachie Argus* announces the killing of the desperado Bickerstaff and one of his confederates named Thompson, by the citizens of Alvarado, Johnson county, on the 5th inst.

Issue April 23, 1869
Five negroes were taken from the jail and hung in Henderson last Tuesday morning at 11:00 by a mob; they had murdered Col. Green.

Issue May 7, 1869
From the *Sherman Courier:* John Thompson and William O. Blackmore were hung the 26th of March.

Issue May 14, 1869
The Supreme Court has confirmed the decision of the District Court in the cases against Robinson and Poe charged with murder of Ward and Ely. The *Jimplecute* learns from Gen Buell that they are to be hanged on the 11th proximo in Marshall.

Issue May 21, 1869
Col. Lewis, an old Texan, and prominent lawyer, died at his residence in this city on last Saturday morning.

Issue June 25, 1869
Death of Benj. T. Cullin. Died about two weeks ago, aged twelve years and two months, pa - Rev. D.P. Cullin. John Adams, Millberry.

Warren, youngest son of S.W. and Nannie J. Stone, departed this life June 15, 1869.

The "Tribute" by Nettie Campbell in memory of Emma Bradshaw, who was burned to death by the upsetting of a kerosene lamp, will appear next week.

Issue July 2, 1869
Tribute of respect for Emma Bradshaw, who was unfortunately burned to death by the upsetting of a kerosene lamp. Read at the close of Prof. Ragsdale's School. Pittsburg, Upshur county.

Most of our young readers remember the great excitement caused several months ago by the murder of Col. Ward of Marshall while passing through Rusk county with a large sum of money... Poe and Robinson were hung. [note: condensed].

Issue July 16, 1869

Death in a church. The Darlington S.C. *Democrate* relates the sudden death in a church at Timmonsville. Mrs. Powers, wife of Thomas Powers, and grand-daughter of the late Rev. Wm. Brockington, fell from her seat with an infant in her arms. The infant lives but the mother is in the grave...

Issue August 13, 1869

Military commission No. 2 is in session in this city for the trail of Mr. Rose, charged with the murder of Mr. Sanford.

Issue October 15, 1869

Daily South Western: The 6th inst., Mr. Cas. A. Gray, who shot and killed Wm. G. Pickens some time since at Summer Grove in this parish, was arrested at Prairieville, Texas.

Shreveport Daily South Western: The 1st inst., Robt. McCracken killed a German named "Dick" at Keachi.

Issue October 29, 1869

Died at her residence in Upshur county, the 6th of October, 1869, Mrs. Mary S.C. Hicks, wife of James T. Hicks, aged 22 years.

Issue December 4, 1869

Little Tommy Barber, son of Col. Barber, formerly sheriff of Washington county, was killed by his pony at Brenham, November 16th.

Issue December 11, 1869

Milam, Sabine county: A few days since, Mr. Thornhill's child, 10 or 12 months of age, caught fire and died.

Issue December 18, 1869

On the 12th ult., Elijah Kinsey of Nacogdoches county, while in his cotton field picking cotton, dropped dead.

Issue January 1, 1870

Died the 24th of November, at the residence of W.K. Mayberry, in Jefferson, Julien S. Foscue, aged 29 years.

Issue January 8, 1870

Died at night of the 20th of November, 1869, Albert, only child of R.B. and Anna Barnes; aged 13 months, 18 days.

Issue January 15, 1870

Died the 29th of November, 1869, at Mount Pleasant, Richard, son of W.R. and M.B. McLean; aged 3 years, 4 months and 9 days.

RED LANDER
Published at San Augustine, Texas.

Issue July 8, 1841

An unfortunate accident occurred in the camp of the Santa Fe pioneers Saturday evening last, Mr. Andrew Jackson Davis, volunteer, lost his life.

A man by the name of Meadows was shot in the town of Milam, Monday last, by Allison A. Lewis of the same county.

Col. W.S. Jordan, hero of Saltillo, died at New Orleans the 22nd inst.

Issue July 22, 1841

Jackson's trial, 12th of July, of Charles W. Jackson for the murder of Joseph G. Goodbread of Shelby county. [note: no details provided].

Died in this county Sunday evening last, Mr. John Cartwright, age 54.

Issue July 20, 1841

Died July 10, 1841, six miles north of the town of Nacogdoches of congestive fever, Henry, son of Solomon and Martha Wolfe; aged 11 years.

Died in this county the 22nd inst., Mrs. Anne Holman; aged 58 years.

Issue August 12, 1841

We learn from a gentleman from Kingsborough that a Mr. McIver, the same that was arraigned and tried for the murder of Joseph Shanks last term at Crockett, was himself murdered at Kingsborough by a man named Burrus. Burrus was killed by a man named Burton.

Issue August 19, 1841

Died in this county the 9th inst., Thomas J. Rusk, infant of Thomas H. and Sarah Garner; aged 2 months, 9 days.

Issue October 14, 1841

Shelby county: When overtaken by the Regulators, a man by the name of Bledsoe, killed and a man by the name of Strickland attempted to make his escape and was shot and badly wounded; three others by the name of McFadden were taken and brought back to Shelbyville and two of them were hung Saturday last.

Died: Gen. Nathaniel Smith, September 17th last, at his residence near this place. Age 50 and died of typhus fever; his last illness continued only three days. [note: condensed; marriage notice above obit, gives marriage of Col. James Carr, attorney, of Houston county and Mary Myers Hunter, eldest daughter of the late General Nathaniel Smith, of Burnet county].

Issue April 14, 1842

Sabine county. A man named David Huffman was killed.

Issue October 20, 1842

Died at the residence of her father the evening of the 10th inst., Miss Frances, eldest daughter of John G. Love.

Died in Sabine co., Saturday last, Charles Morse.

Issue October 27, 1842

Died at New Orleans, Fielding Culp, late midshipman of the Texas Navy.

Issue November 10, 1842

William L. Province, notoriously known as a horse and negro thief on both sides of the Sabine, was killed about a month ago by Gross Welch.

Issue February 9, 1843

Died at the residence of J.J. Hennise the 23rd of January last, John E. Pennington, age 49, a citizen of Arkansas.

Issue April 15, 1843

Killed Monday night, a man named Jefferson Haggerty, by the sheriff's deputy, while trying to escape from custody.

A few weeks ago Samuel Damon and Capt. Heard, when examining the San Bernard, Colorado county, found the remains of a skeleton of a man and horse within a few miles of the steam mill. The man had been hung, as the lariat was still hanging over the bones and a bullet hole was in the skull of the horse. A shaving box with the initials J.S. was found. It is conjectured to be the remains of J. Sloan, who was in that neighborhood some two or three years ago.

Issue August 5, 1843
Died in this city, Wednesday the 2nd inst., Christopher Winder.

Died in this county, Thursday last, at the residence of Hezekial Cartwright, John Cartwright, age 23 years.

Issue September 2, 1843
Died at the residence of his father 2 miles west of San Augustine, John C. Garrett, only son of William Garrett, age 9 years.

Issue September 9, 1843
Died in this city, Monday last, James Tabor, age 37.

Died in this county at the residence of John Nicholson, widow Mary McIver, age 77.

Died in Nacogdoches county, Saturday the 24th inst., Mrs. Sarah M. Eubanks, age 19.

Died in this city, Thursday last, Isaac Campbell, age 30 years.

Issue September 23, 1843
Died yesterday, J.C. de St. Romes; one of the gallant band who in 1814-15 turned out to defend Louisiana.

Died in this county, Monday the 11th inst, John W. Holman, age 30.

Died Sunday last, Mrs. Esther Edwards, age 51.

Died in the neighborhood of Douglass, Nacogdoches County, Rev. M. Moore, age 48.

Issue November 4, 1843
Died or lost on the *Sarah Barnes*: Capt. Charles Franklin of Galveston; James Potter, Houston; H.S. Daggett, New Orleans; James Boyd, Matagordo;— Martin, Matagordo; Dr. Cosgrave, Brazos; William Mehin, fireman; James McDonough; William Mure, deckhand; Alexander Isbel, cook; John Dean, 2nd engineer.

Issue November 25, 1843
Escaped prisoners: Charles Toby, who was confined to the jail at Brazoria for the murder of Stephen Hard, has escaped.

Issue December 23, 1843

Died yesterday morning at 5 o'clock at the residence of his brother 3 miles east of this city, Sanford Holman; age about 28.

Issue January 13, 1844

Died in Sabine county, Friday, Mrs. Martha Renfro, wife of David Renfro; age 32.

Issue January 27, 1844

Died at this residence the 24th inst, Rev. Sumner Bacon; age about 60. He was the first to preach the gospel of Jesus Christ at variance with the Catholic church of Mexico.

Died in this county the 20th inst., Chesley C. Johnson, age 22 years.

Issue February 24, 1844

Died Thursday the 4th of January in Houston county, Mary Ann, consort of Col. S.L.B. Jasper.

Issue March 2, 1844

Shelbyville, February 7, 1844: Died Monday morning the 5th inst., Mrs. Sarah S. Northcut; aged [?]8, consort of N.W. Northcut.

Issue March 9, 1844

A man named Varner, his son, and a Mexican named Gonzales were killed at the residence of Varner about 60 miles north west of Henderson in Nacogdoches county the 22nd of February.

Issue April 13, 1844

Died, Capt. French S. Grey, February last.

Died in this city the 6th inst., Mrs. Hannah A.G. Slaughter, consort of William H. Slaughter, age 36 years, 6 months.

Issue May 18, 1844

Shelbyville, May 9, 1844; confession of William Wells, Shelby co., May 8, 1844: That in the month of March of the present year, I was employed by John Haley, Sr., formerly of this county near the town of Alabama on the Trinity river, to kill one Wat Mooman, known as a Captain of a regulating company of this county, for $1,000. I proceeded then to the town of Douglass in Nacogdoches. I met John M. Bradley of Shelby who pledged the reward that Haley offered. I left Douglass with John M. Bradley, John Haley, Sr., Nat Smyth, Josephus Moore, Thomas Garner, Ben Hines, and Bill York to the residence of John M. Bradley in Shelby county. The next day at Shelbyville

I met Amos and Joseph Hall. They told me a certain Henry Runnells shot and killed their brother and hired one Stanfield to kill another brother of theirs. That if I would kill Runnells, they would pay me $500, which I agreed. I met one James Secres, alias James Smyth. We over took Runnells on the way to Shreveport and Smyth shot him with a shot gun. [note: condensed].

Issue June 8, 1844
Died in this city the 5th inst., John Calvin, youngest son of William H. and the late Hannah A.G. Slaughter, age 4 years, 3 months and 14 days.

Issue June 22, 1844
Died: Mrs. Penelope Thomas; born December 22, 1813; died June 17, 1844.

Died in this city the 20th inst., William, son of Mrs. Riannah and the late William B. Patterson [?], age 3 years, 3 months.

Issue August 24, 1844
Died the 4th inst. at his residence in Nacogdoches, Mr. Robert Le[?]maird, age 60.

Issue September 14, 1844
A murderer killed: A man named Stone, who killed a Mr. Pruett in Rusk county sometime since, made his escape the day of the barbecue at Nacogdoches. He was over taken near Ft. Jesup and killed.

Issue October 19, 1844
Died Sunday evening the 13th, Mr. Louis M. Flatau, merchant of this city, formerly of Berlin, Prussia; age about 26. He had been a resident in this city for the last four years. Died from the accidental discharge of a gun. Left wife and friends.

Issue October 26, 1844
The 12th inst., a party of Indians near Seguin killed John Berimendi.

Ex-Governor Moore of Alabama died recently in Marshall county, age 61.

Mr. Battle, Sr. of Shreveport, Louisiana, and his negro fell in a well and drowned.

Issue November 16, 1844
Died in this city the 4th inst., Laura A. Ford, age 16 months, 2 days.

Issue December 7, 1844

Died in this city Tuesday the 3rd inst., Thomas R., infant son of S. and Jane Brooks, age 3 months.

Issue December 14, 1844

A lawless gang of men in Fredrictown, Madison county, recently broke open the jail and hung a man named Abraham Smith.

Issue January 4, 1845

Died in this county the 30th ult., Mary Ann Houston Daniel, daughter of William and Martha Daniel; aged 3 years, 1 month, 9 days.

Issue May 15, 1845

Died in this city the 12th inst., Henry D., son of Dexter and Cornelia Watson; age 15 months.

Issue September 11, 1845

Died in Lexington, Kentucky, the 28th of July last, Alexander M. Davis, late chief justice of this county.

Died in this city at the residence of Mrs. Layton, Monday night the 28th inst., Judge A.M. Davis of San Augustine, Texas. Lexington, Kentucky papers please copy.

Issue March 13, 1847

Died at the residence of her father, Maj. Lemuel Bullock, Thursday morning the 4th inst., Mrs. Elizabeth O. Whittlesey; age 27. Consort of E.A. Whittlesey of Sabine Town, Texas.

Died Tuesday the 9th inst. at the residence of her mother (Mrs. Cartwright), Mrs. C.G. Holman.

Issue December 9, 1854

Tribute of respect on the death of Horatio McHanks.

NATIONAL VINDICATOR

Issue December 16, 1843

Died at the residence of Dr. E. Smith on the Guadalupe river, Gonzalas county, the 27th November ult., Charles Earley Smith, age 8 months, 13 days.

Issue July 6, 1844

Died at his residence in this place after a long and painful illness on the 3rd inst., Maj. Asa Brigham, age 56.

TEXAS NATIONAL REGISTER
Published at Washington, Texas.

Issue December 7, 1844
Died in Shelby county the 4th ult., Hon. John Dial.

Died near Oakville, Lawrence county, Alabama, the 18th of October last, Mrs. Catharine Miller, in the forty-sixth year of her age.

Died in this place 1st inst., Judge John Lockhart, formerly of Marengo county, Alabama, in the 63d year of his age.

Issue December 14, 1844
Departed this life in Bennett's Prairie, Montgomery county, Texas, the 24th of August 1844, Mrs. Emily E., consort of Ezekiel Henry, age 20. Native of Bibb county, Alabama, and a member of the Baptist church. Left a disconsolate husband and one child.

Issue December 21, 1844
Died in this neighborhood the 19th inst., Alfred Woolf, late of Marengo county, Alabama. Age about 27.

Died Sunday the 15th inst., Mrs. Elizabeth Dieterich, consort of F. Dieterich of this place.

Issue January 4, 1845
Died at his residence in the neighborhood of this place the 1st inst., Capt. John W. Hall, age 59 and a native of South Carolina, whence he removed to Louisiana with his father. Came to Texas 1812. He was in the Battle of Salado and also in the Battle of New Orleans. He settled his family in 1822 on the spot where he died and where he encamped in 1812. He founded the town of Washington. He was interned with Masonic honors and both houses of Congress adjourned as a mark of respect.

Died at Gonzalas the 11th ult., Ezekiel Williams, for a number of years clerk of the county court, native of Delaware. Emigrated to Texas 1835.

Died in Harrison county the 28th ult., Mrs. Eliza Jane Brown Saunders, consort of Mr. Thomas C. Saunders, age 17. Native of Tuscaloosa, Alabama.

Issue January 11, 1845
Died the morning of the 5th inst., John Hall, age 40, chief clerk of the Department of State.

Died in Sabine county, the 14th ult., Harriett Missouri, age 18 months, daughter of Frances and Col. William Means.

Issue January 18, 1845
We learn that Mr. Simon Bateman, one of the oldest settlers on the Guadalupe, near Gonzalas, and Mr. Matthew Jett, a settler on the Medina and for the last year attached to Capt. Hay's Co. were barbarously murdered on the night of the 10th inst. near Virginia Point.

Died in the town of Washington, Sunday the 12th inst., John W. Smith, Senator from Bexar county.

Issue January 25, 1845
Died at this place the evening of the 22nd inst., Hon. Gustavus A. Parker, member of the House of Rep. from Ft. Bend county; native of Georgia and came to Texas spring of 1836 at the head of a company of men, for the purpose of sustaining our country in its struggle for independence and free government.

Died in this place the 21st inst., Frances C. Cabler, age 61.

Died in this neighborhood the 23rd inst., Alexander Lockhart, son of the late Judge John Lockhart; age 15 years.

Issue February 8, 1845
Died the 5th inst., P.C. Jenkins, a worthy citizen of this place; leaving an amiable family to mourn his loss.

Issue February 22, 1845
Died Thursday morning last near the town of Washington, Robert Williamson Hall, youngest son of John W. Hall, deceased; age 15 years.

Issue March 1, 1845
Died in this place the morning of the 26th ult., S. Ewing, eldest son of Nathaniel Norwood, age 11 years. Alabama papers please copy.

Issue March 8, 1845
Died in this place on the morning of the 3rd inst., Susan Charlotte, daughter of Nathaniel Norwood; age 4 years.

Issue March 22, 1845
Died Monday the 17th inst., Henry Thomas, youngest son of Dr. A. Moore; age 9 years, 9 months.

Murderer arrested. The murderer Shultz, who fled Galveston a few weeks since, has been arrested in Alabama.

Issue May 1, 1845

On Friday night last, a rencontre took place between two hostile parties of citizens on the premises of Col. Walton about 7 miles east of this place, which resulted in the death of two men and the third being dangerously wounded. The names of the killed were John L. Laguire and John Nix, the latter has left a wife and several small children. Mr. Strickland, the person wounded, still survives, but his recovery is doubtful.

Issue May 29, 1845

J.L. Nicholson, who was indicted for the murder of Mr. Luguire, has been acquitted. His trial for the murder of Mr. Nix, who was killed at the same time, has been postponed.

Issue June 5, 1845

Camp, who was indicted in this county for the murder of James H. Harrison, was shot on Saturday last while in the custody of the deputy sheriff. He has obtained a change of venue from this county to Rusk, where he was carried for trial... *Harrison Times*. May 8.

We have heard of the melancholy death of Mrs. J.M. Fisk of Brazoria. In proceeding from Brazoria to her father's (Gov. H. Smith) she was thrown from her horse and survived but a few hours. Husband and infant child. *Brazos Planter.*

Issue June 12, 1845

We learn that Daniel Hornsby and ---- Adkinson, while fishing in the Colorado about nine miles below Austin, on Saturday last, were killed by a party of Indians. The body of Hornsby has not been found.

Issue June 19, 1845

Died the 17th inst. at his boarding house in this town, Geo. F. Thornton, age 23. Profession an attorney. Residence amongst us for a few weeks.

Died: Phileman, youngest son and child of Mrs. Harriet A. Jenkins, at her residence in this place, of croup the night of the 14th inst., age 3 years, 6 months.

The Hon. John Campbell, for many years a distinguished member of Congress, from the Pee-dee district, South Carolina, died at his residence the 19th ult.

Issue July 3, 1845

From the *Montgomery Patriot*: On Saturday the 11th inst., the body of a man named Jefferson Richards was found on the road between Mr. Ray's and Groce's Retreat. The general impression is he committed suicide.

Issue July 10, 1845

Died Thursday the 3rd inst. at one quarter before 3:00 P.M. at Fanthorp's, Montgomery county, K. [Kenneth] L. Anderson, vice president of the Republic; native of North Carolina and was about 40 years old. Buried with Masonic honors. [note: almost entire page is regarding his death].

Issue July 17, 1845

James Kinney, eldest son of Rev. Mr. Kinney of Austin county, was lately murdered by Indians near Corpus Christi.

Issue July 24, 1845

We learned the death of Dr. D.A. Perry of this county on the morning of Monday last. He rode from his residence toward his plantation, a distance of half a mile... Several hours after his departure, his horse returned. His family instituted a search. His body was found. Head horribly mutilated... a negro, formerly the property of Dr. Perry is believed to have perpetrated the murder. Dr. Perry left a widow and large family. Buried with Masonic honors.

P.S. We have just learned that the guilt of the negro has been ascertained. Yesterday, he confessed and was hung.

Issue July 31, 1845

Died Monday last, very suddenly, Ann Maria, only daughter of Mary and Henry Bailey; age 13 years, 5 months, and formerly of Providence, Rhode Island.

Issue August 7, 1845

We learn that W.W.T. Smith, American Counsel at Matagorda, was washed from his horse and drowned a few days since in attempting to pass the Bayou between Indian Point and Pass Cavallo.

Col. Josiah H. Voss/Vose, of the 4th Regt. U.S. Inf., died suddenly on the 15th inst. at New Orleans of an affection of the breast. Age 61.

Issue August 28, 1845

We regret to learn that Mr. Nathan Taylor, a worthy citizen of Montgomery county, was killed by an unseen hand Friday evening last, while setting in his own house and engaged in a game of chess with his lady. The assassin approached the house under cover of the darkness and shot his unsuspecting victim instantly dead.

Died in Bailey's Prairie the 26th ult., Frederic S., son of Dr. R.M. and Mrs. Collins, age about 4 years.

Died in Bailey's Prairie, Sunday the 10th inst., William, son of the Hon. S.W. Perkins, age about 4 years.

Issue September 11, 1845
At the time of the murder of Nathan Taylor, three of his neighbors, John Gilbert, P.R. Lilly, and G.W. Loftis, happened to be absent on business. Justices Knott and Jones upon full and careful investigation declared them guiltless.

Issue September 18, 1845
Died in Washington county the 9th inst., Mrs. Mary Sims; native of Halifax county, Virginia. Age 69.

A son of Amos Kendall was lately killed in an affray at Washington City by a man named Elliott.

Issue September 25, 1845
Murdered at Crockett, Houston county, Monday, September 8th, 1845. Charles Henry Nelson was murdered by Robert T. Gage. Gage was born in Georgia and the greater part of his early youth in Green county, Alabama, and in Holmes county, Mississippi. Came to Texas in 1839 to Harrison county, from there removed to Ft. Houston, thence to this place 3 years ago. We learn he went back to Mississippi. Mr. Nelson was a native of Maine, we think near Banger. Gage is a little over 39[?] years old 5'10"-6', red or sandy hair, his beard quite red.

Issue October 2, 1845
Died Saturday the 20th ult. at his residence on the Trinity, Col. William Bledsoe.

Issue November 29, 1845
Died on 31st October in Fort Bend county of a chronic affection of the lungs Calvin F. Keith, a native of Mass., aged about 21/24. Mr. K. came to Texas last April as a book-agent.

Issue December 17, 1845
White boy Among the Indians... Supposed to be son of Col. Colman, whose widow was killed at her residence on the Colorado some time in 1839.

TEXIAN ADVOCATE
Published on Thursdays at Victoria, Texas.

Issue October 12, 1848
The last *Houston Telegraph* announces the death of the Rev. Mr. Hunter. We suppose it must be Mr. Hunter of Brazoria, a minister of eminent abilities in the Presbyterian Church. If so, that church and the country has sustained the loss of a valuable citizen.

The Hon. Wm. S. Rayner, late a Representative from Fort Bend county, died at his residence in Richmond on the 23d ult. of congestive fever. He was a native of South Carolina and was esteemed by those who knew him.

We regret to learn that a party of three men were attacked by a band of Indians on the road between Goliad and San Antonio, near the *Cabaca*, on last Friday, and two of them killed, and the other escaping with three arrows shot into his person! The name of one of the deceased is Biven, the wounded one Joseph Ware; but the name of the other deceased person we have not heard.

A SHOOTING SCRAPE. A difficulty occurred at Bell's Mill in the Cherokee Nation, near the line, on the 12th, between M. Hazen, a white man, and who, for many years, has been a citizen of Crawford county, Ark. and a half-breed Cherokee, named Joseph Pardue, in which the latter was shot. The half-breed commenced the quarrel.

Issue September 26, 1850
The *Lavaca Journal* says Mr. Turner, the young man who was knocked down in the streets of our city a few days ago by H.P. Savery, died today at about 3 o'clock. It is reported that Savery has left for parts unknown.

The Rev. Bishop Bascom of the Methodist conference, died at Louisville, KY, on Saturday the 7th inst.

Issue October 24, 1850
Died in Galveston, about the 12 inst., after a short but severe illness, Mrs. Eliza G. Smith, of this place, consort of Mr. John M. Smith, now of California; aged about 26 years. The deceased was on a visit to Galveston for the benefit of her health...

Sudden death, at the Tremont House, Galveston, Mrs. Eliza G. Smith. She went over on the *Portland* on the 7th instant, was taken sick in Galveston, and died in two or three days.

Miscellaneous Texas Newspaper Abstracts - Deaths --- Vol 2

Issue October 31, 1850

Died in this place on Friday morning last after a protracted illness, Mr. Geo. W. Harrison, aged about 50 years. Mr. H. was born in Virginia where he resided until about the year 1845, when he emigrated to Washington county, Arkansas; and in 1846 he removed to this State... Buried with Masonic honors. Victoria Lodge # 40. Left a large family.

Died in this place on Sunday evening last, after an illness of several months, Mrs. Esther Arnold, aged about 70 years. The deceased emigrated to Texas from Illinois in 1848. She was the mother of our esteemed fellow citizen, Capt. J.O. Wheeler.

Issue November 7, 1850

E. Fitzgerald of Corpus Christi died recently at that place.

Mr. Thomas of Brownsville, who arrived here a few days since, gives us the following account of a supposed Indian outrage. He says that about ten miles the other side of the [?]. There were three trunks and a tool chest near the spot. On one of the trunks was marked with the name of John Horton. Female clothing scattered around... *Nueces Valley.*

Issue November 14, 1850

Mr. James Fay of Iowa, who came passenger on the *Maria Burt* from New Orleans to Galveston, died at the latter place on the 28th October. His effects, said to be of some value, have been placed in the care of the Probate Judge of Galveston county.

Issue November 28, 1850

We learn from the *Western Texan* that Arnold Henckel, formerly sheriff of Comal county, committed suicide by hanging himself in his own stable on the 16th inst. It seems he got up earlier than usual, wrote out a disposition of sundry papers on hand, went out at day break to feed his horse as customary, and was found half an hour thereafter, with life extinct. It is said he assigned in writing, as the cause for committing the fatal deed, that he could not live longer with honor to himself. He leaves a young wife and child.

Escape of a convict - We learn, says the *Galveston Journal*, that Wm. Turner, convicted of the murder of John Tanent in Bexar county, had escaped from the penitentiary at Huntsville...

Murders in Eastern Texas. A most atrocious murder was perpetrated at Nacogdoches a few weeks ago... a young man by the name of Shanks was paying attention to a young lady of Nacogdoches... It appears that Marshall had also an attachment for the same lady, though unknown to his cousin... A few days later he [Marshall] saw her and immediately drew a pistol and shot her in the back. [note: condensed].

Brutal assassination -- On Sunday night, six heathens entered the Palo Alton House, media distant between this city and Point Isabel, and brutaly murdured its occupant, an old man of sixty years of age... We have been unable to ascertain the name of the victim, but learn that he had occupied the house for some months, was a resident of Texas since 1836, and bore a very exemplary character.

Since the above was in type we learn that the murdured man was Colton and that the assassins were all Mexicans. *Rio Grand Sentinel.*

Issue December 12, 1850
The *Galveston News* says - "Captain Horace Baldwin died last Friday morning after a short and distressing illness of only 16 hours. He was attacked the day previous with many of the symptoms of cholera, but there appears to be some difference of opinion as to the proper name of the disease. If it was cholera, it was certainly the only case of the kind that has ever originated in this city; and we believe it is admitted on all hands that Galveston was never more free from any epidemic than at present."

Issue January 23, 1851
Dreadful Tragedy in Memphis, which was enacted in that city on New Year's day. John K. Chester, the city recorder, was shot and instantly killed by a negro, belonging to a Mr. Herron near Coffeeville. A son of some 17 or 18 years was rendered a raving maniac on seeing his dead father. [note: condensed].

Issue March 13, 1851
On Tuesday evening, an express from San Antonio reached this place, bearing the mournful intelligence of the death of General Brooke. This veteran soldier breathed his last at San Antonio, on Sunday morning last, at 3 o'clock. His sickness was short, but severe... He now sleeps beneath the soil of Texas.

Died at his residence in San Antonio, on Sunday morning 4th inst., at half-past 2 o'clock, Gen. George Mercer Brooke, aged about 65 years. General Brooke was a native of Virginia, entered the army as Captain in the year 1808. [note: condensed].

A willful and horrible murder was perpetrated in the neighborhood of Col. Stevens' in De Witt county about the 4th inst. upon the person of an American named Richardson or Richmond by some Rio Grande Mexicans...

Samuel Lott of Seguin, one of Capt McCulloch's Rangers, died suddenly in that place Sunday last. [note: condensed].

The trial of William S. Gorman of Goliad on the charge of killing William Spencer of De Witt county in January 1848, came off in this place on Monday last. Verdict of acquittal.

Issue April 17, 1851

Died at his residence near this place on the 2nd inst., Mr. Nathan Grover, in the 64th year of his age. Mr. Grover was a native of Mass., and emigrated to this state from Ohio in 1840.

Judge Carr, the oldest American resident of St. Louis, MO, died in that city 31st ult.

The *North Carolinian* on the 22d ult. gives the following particulars of the murder of Tilghman Hunt, a resident of Guilford county and negro trader, near Fayetteville, N.C...

Brinkley Bishop, found guilty of the murder of Turner Smith at the last term of Bibb Superior court, Georgia, and sentenced to be hung, has been respited by Gov. Towns until the 12th December next.

Issue May 8, 1851

California. On the 7th March, a young man named Hugh McClure was murdered by the Indians on the Nevada road near Rough and Ready.

Issue May 15, 1851

Moving Incidents. On Thursday morning last, a daughter [Charlotte Elizabeth] of Major Andrews of Mission Valley was married to Wm. Preston Stapp of the same place. About noon of that day, a son of Major Andrews', a young physician, died; a few hours later he received two letters, one informing him of the death of another son, in Kentucky, and the other communicating the intelligence of the decease of another favorite relative in that State.

Issue June 5, 1851

Christopher Strong of Charlotte, Tenn., recently deceased, bequeathed seven thousand dollars to religious institutions, liberated all his slaves, and made provision to carry them to Liberia.

Issue July 24, 1851

The last New Orleans newspapers bring us the sorrowful and heart sickening details of a duel recently fought in that city between Col. T.G. Hunt and J.W. Frost, in which the latter fell, mortally wounded, upon the second fire, and died in fifteen minutes. The victim in this unhappy conflict was one of the editors of the *New Orleans Cresent*. According to the revised statutes the unhappy survivor is liable to the death penalty, and the seconds are regarded as accomplices.

Instant death of Mrs. Matilda Baker and the mortally wounding of her husband, William Baker... Negro, runaway slave, stabbed her, the knife entering just above the left nipple, severing the arteries of the axiller, producing hemorrhage and almost instant death; and after stabbing Mr. Baker four times, he fled. Five little children home during the horrid tragedy. There is not the distant hope of his recovery. The tragic event makes orphans of six children, the eldest of whom is scarcely grown. *Texas State Gazette*. [note: condensed].

On Friday last, the junior editor of this paper received by despatch telegraphic to New Orleans and thence by mail, the melancholy tiding of the death of his mother-in-law, Mrs. Elizabeth R. Jones. She died on the 9th inst. at the age of about 57 years at Newport, Ky...

Issue August 7, 1851

Dr. Hunt, the surviving party of the late duel in New Orleans, has placed himself in the hands of the law and given bond to the amount of ten thousand dollars for his appearance at the next fall term of court.

We are informed by a gentleman lately from Austin that the negro who murdered Mr. Baker and his wife near that city has been arrested. He was caught prowling around Austin... They took him from prison, tried him before a committee of twelve men, convicted him of the awful crime, and then hung him to a limb.

Issue November 1, 1851

[Began publication on Saturdays]

The scarlet fever is prevailing in this place. There have been three deaths from the disease during the week -- all children. One a daughter of A.D. Beatty, the others, two daughters of John J. Linn.

Taylor Murphy was executed at Campbellsville, Ky., on October 8th. He was convicted of the murder of his wife, and afterwards burning her remains upon the hearth of his own house. He wrote out a confession of the murder of his wife and seven of his own infant children. Hanging is a fit ending for such a career of crime.

The Hon. Thomas C. Hackett died after a lingering illness at Marietta, Ga., on the 9th ult.

Crittenden, Ky., death of a wife and murder of her child... Mr. Hall was married to a sister of his wife, but a few months deceased... His second wife delivered a child in two months after marriage... The wife died and was buried... Hall, hearing of the discoveries made, effected his escape.

Issue January 3, 1852
Died on the 21st December of congestion of the brain, Mrs. Ann R. Jones, consort of Capt. Augustus H. Jones, of Gonzalas... husband and five children.

Issue February 14, 1852
Died in this place on Thursday morning last of neumonia, Mary L., daughter of Mr. A.M. and Mrs. Sarah C. Ciaaro, in the 9th[?] year of her age.

Died in Jackson county on the 22nd January last, Mr. William Bracken [?].

Died at the residence of Mrs. E.L. Mills in Jackson county on the 6th inst., Mr. Levi Williams.

Issue March 6, 1852
FOUL MURDER AT LOCKHART: Mr. Granville H. Stiner, sheriff of Caldwell county, was shot down in his own store about two weeks ago by a fellow by the name of Hoskins.

Another Indian Outrage. On yesterday the body of one of our Mexican citizens, Mr. Navarro, was brought into our city for interment. He with others was out on the "Chacon" for the purpose of hunting wild cattle and was killed by the Indians while setting at his camp fire on the 24th inst. near dark. *San Antonio Ledger*.

Issue April 3, 1852
We learn that a young man named William Duggan was drowned on the 15th ult. while attempting to cross the San Antonio river at Carlos' Ranch in this county... Mr. D. was from the state of New York and was a stranger in this county.

The Jonesboro' (Tenn.) *Democrat*. A disease similar to the cold plague broke out in the family of Rev. Wm. Reed of Washington co. of which three of his children died within a few hours after they were attacked. A fourth child was attacked and died. A. Sligar's family also suffered from the same disease.

Died in this place on the 22nd ult. of newmonia, Mr. John Garrett, a German, aged 23 years, formerly a resident of Jackson county.

Issue May 22, 1852
We learn that Matthew St Clair Clarke, an old and highly esteemed citizen of Washington, died in that city on the 6th inst. He had been for several years Clerk of the House of Representatives.

Murders -- We are informed by a letter from Bastrop, dated 2d, that a man named Joel Forbus was shot in the street in that town and killed instantly, on the morning the letter was written by a woman--Mrs. Slocum.

Another -- Letter to the editor by a gentleman from Williamson county. A gentleman by the name of Donald Smith, a Scotchman, I think one of the Mier prisoners, had resided about Bastrop... Accompanied by a young man who gave his name as John Franks, who said he had an uncle in Bastrop... The neighbors became suspicious... The skull broke into pieces with an axe... said Smith was murdered by John Franks...

Issue June 12, 1852
We are pained to learn that Mrs. Sophia Jones of Gonzalas county, mother of the Hon. Wm. E. Jones, died at Port Lavaca on Monday evening last of cholera. This lady had been sick several days at Indianola and was brought up to Lavaca in a carriage, when she became worse, and seemed to realize that death was upon her.

We are pained also to hear that Augustus Jones, aged 2 years, son of Capt. Augustus Jones of Gonzalas county, and grandson of Mrs. Sophia Jones, whose death is given above, died on Tuesday evening at the same place of cholera...

Capt. Jerry Smith, Jr. Drowned -- We regret to learn that this young man, so favorably know in Western Texas, was drowned at Galveston in the fore part of this week, having fallen from the guards of the steamer *Louisiana*, while lying at the wharf at that place. Every effort was made to rescue him but in vain. His body was found on the day following his death.

Important from the Rio Grande. Steamer *Comanche* fired into again... Mr. Brashear was dangerously wounded, the little son was only wounded, a boy of some four years...

Phillip Rogers, a merchant of Rio Grand City, while standing behind his counter, was stabbed to the heart and killed by a Mexican...

G.N. Clark, who recently arrived at Brownsville, from New Orleans, was found dead in old Fort Brown, on the 16th instant, and it was evident he had been murdered. The coroner's jury returned a verdict that the deceased came to his death by shots fired from a gun or pistol by some person or persons unknown.

A serious accident happened to A. McFadin of Brownsville on the 16th inst. As the stage that he was driving was about starting for Point Isabel, the horse took fright, and after running for some distance the coach upset and Mr. McFadin was thrown a distance of fifteen feet, upon a lot of lumber and iron, breaking his collar bone, and bruising him severely.

Issue July 10, 1852

Died on the 3rd inst., John Adolphus, aged 2 years, 4 months and 10 days, child of L.G. and Margarete J. Davis.

On the same day at the residence of L.G. Davis, Dr. William S. Bake, in the 29th year of his age, formerly of Laurens District, South Carolina.

Murder -- We learn that the body of French Louis (well known about this place) was found a day or two since just below Chocolate on the Indianola road, where he had been murdered, his brains appearing to have been knocked out with some heavy weapon. He had a wagon with him loaded for gentlemen here. No clue as to the perpetrator of the murder or the reason therefore is known to exist.

Issue September 4, 1852

Died in this city on Friday, 9th of July, Major Michael Hancock Chevallie, late of Texas. Maj. Chevallie was a native of Richmond, Virginia, from whence he emigrated to Texas in 1836 at the age of 14 years. He was one of the original company of Texas Rangers who under command of Col. Jack Hays were the pride of Texas and the terror of her enemies... *San Joaquin Republician.* [note: condensed].

Issue September 18, 1852

We learn from Mr. Smith, just arrived from El Paso, the mournful intelligence of the death of H.H. Norr, for several years a practicing physician in this place. The doctor died in Chihuahua some time in July last.

James E. Byers of Maysville, Ky. was recently killed at that city by J.B. Casey of Covington.

Issue September 25, 1852

Died in this place on the 13th inst. after a painful illness, Charles Holbrook, aged about 7 years, and son of Mr. and Mrs. A.B. Holbrook.

The disease of which this interesting child died not only baffled the best medical skill but was of so strange a character that our physicians could not even determine what it was-- For sixteen days and nights the brave little fellow endured the most intense suffering-the pain being chiefly contained to the head. The parents are absent in the East, whither they went for the benefit of the mother's health, which for many years had been wretched, but which at last accounts was rapidly improving.

We learn that James Powers, of Refugio county, the Empresario of the old colony of that name, died recently, at his residence. Mr. P. emigrated to Texas as early as 1825 or '26 and has been a member of different legislative bodies in the State and Republic. *Ind. Bulletin.*

Issue October 23, 1852

Died in Port LaVaca on the 15th inst., William Irvin, attorney at law, for the last 3 years a citizen of that place and formerly of Ohio...*Indianola Bulletin.*

We are sorry to hear of the death of Louis Hipp of Seguin. He died yesterday morning at the residence of Mrs. Terry, fifteen miles below this place. He was on his way from Indianola, accompanied by his wife, to his home in Seguin. We learn that his disease was remittent fever.

A duel was fought near Lexington, Kentucky, on the 5th inst. between Benjamin Johnson and T. White, in which the latter was killed at the first fire. The weapons were shot guns and the distance fifty paces.

Issue November 27, 1852

Died at Corpus Christi on the 27th of October last, Co. T.B. Ives, formerly of Yallabusha county, Mississippi, in the 52nd year of his age. He was a member of the Masonic fraternity and Methodist church. At one time he was lapped in the luxury of a wealth which was dissipated in a lavish and prodigal charity, as much as by unfortunate speculation. At another time we see him the leader of his political party in North Mississippi...

The Hon. David Randall of the Fifth Judicial District in Louisiana died in Donaldsonville, in that state, on the 6th instant.

Died in this place of consumption on Tuesday night last, Mr. Am'l [Sam'l?] B. Mixon, aged 43 years. Mr. Mixon was an old and respectable citizen of Victoria and a member of the Lodge of I.O.O.F., in this place, by whom he was buried.

Died in this place at 4 o'clock on Thursday morning last after a short illness, Elizabeth, daughter of Mr. Richard and Mrs. Elizabeth Owens, in the 7th year of her age.

Issue March 19, 1853
Kate Hayes, the distinguished Irish songstress was not murdered in San Francisco as reported a few days since, but on the contrary was married to Col. Jack Hays - the celebrated Texas Ranger - quite a difference between getting married and being murdered. Ky. Papers, what a lie!—Bulletin.

Issue March 26, 1853
On the 14th ult., Mr. George Sharp of Burnsville, Dallas county, Alabama, was murdered by a man named Noles. Noles had been guilty of the infamous crime of incest with two of his daughters, and a warrant had been issued for his apprehension. Sharp had been deputized to serve the warrant and in the performance of his duty, he, on the 14th ult, with a posse of men, proceeded to the house of Noles, about two miles west of Burnsville, for the purpose of arresting him...

Died on the 5th of March at the residence of Mr. Perry on the San Antonio, Morgan O'Brien, in the 45th year of his age.

Issue June 18, 1853
Who wants cattle? On the 11th day of July next, J.O. Wheeler, as administrator on the estate of M.H. Hardy, deceased, will sell twelve hundred head of stock cattle on a credit of twelve months. This is an excellent stock of gentle cattle. He will also sell one hundred head of good beef cattle. Here is a great chance for speculation - on a credit. Who wants it?

Issue September 24, 1853
Died in Victoria, Texas, on the 18th September, after an illness of seven days, Mr. C. Cowan Shive, aged 25 years. [note: mentions parents living in Mississippi and that a brother, name not given, died in Victoria some three weeks before]. Graduated Davidson College, in North Carolina, in 1850. Mr. C. Shive had married in North Carolina on the 9th of August last. In the spring of 1852 he was chosen Principal of the Preparatory department of Aranama College at Goliad... [note: condensed].

[Died] In this place on Friday, September 16th, William, son of Nelson & Roxanna Maynard, aged 13 years and 8 months.

[Died] In this town on the 18th of dysentery, Samuel W. VanNorman, an old and esteemed citizen. The writer first knew him as a prominent citizen of the country, in the summer of 1840... has held several responsible public offices. Wife died little over a year ago, leaves three small children. Member of the Baptist church.

We understand there is considerable sickness in the town of Goliad and its vicinity -- the flux has made its appearance, but most of the sickness originates from colds. Two or three deaths have occurred; one person, Col. Gibson, at the advanced age of between ninety-five and one hundred years.

Issue October 15, 1853

Died in Goliad, Goliad county, Texas, on the 21st of September last, Josephine Helen, daughter of E. Percy and Ann Howe, in the 3rd year of her age.

Departed this life September 11th at his residence in Goliad, Col. John Gibson, aged 90 years. The subject of our notice was borne in 1763, in the State of North Carolina... He enlisted in the Revolutionary War at age 16 under Gen. Anthony Wayne... father fell at King's Mountain. He left a widow of eighty winters, to mourn her loss --- soon to follow. [note: condensed].

TEXAS ITEMS M.M.K. writes us from Goliad, Sept. 24, that the flux is prevailing very fatally in that village. Five deaths have occurred during the last week. Among them Rev. Mr. Whithy, an old settler, and Col. John T. Gibson, an old revolutionary soldier, aged 93 years.

Doctor Haynie, whose letter of the 27th ult. we published, giving information of the appearance of the fatal epidemic yellow fever at Lavaca, and also his partner, Doctor Johnson, are both dead.

On the 26th a daughter of D.H. Rankin, editor of the *Brenham Enquirer*, was suddenly hurried from life under the most heart-rending circumstances... [note: description of the occurrence given]. Apron had taken fire; 8 years, 8 days.

Issue April 8, 1854

Suicide -- a young man named Bell, says the *Texian Mercury*, committed suicide in the lower part of this county, on the Cibolo, on Wednesday the 22nd inst. He placed the muzzle of a rifle against his side and pulled the trigger with his foot. We have not learned the cause that prompted him to commit the deed.

Issue September 23, 1854

E. Percy Howe. The death of this gentleman, coupled as it is with the death of eldest son, is a heavy and sad misfortunate to a large and dependent family... He conducted the *Marshall County Republican, Dollar Democrat, Pine Knot,* and a paper called the *Stingaree* in Mississippi. On his way to Texas, the vessel in which himself and family were passengers was wrecked on Mustang Island, and his printing materials together with his furniture and clothing were all a total loss. In this destitute condition, he obtained a situation in the Ranger Office, but from causes with which we are unacquainted, soon gave it up, and removed to Galveston, where he became connected with the *Times.* Thus in the midst of summer, and unacclimated, he was forced by misfortune to brook the dangers of the epidemic in that city, where he fell, in his efforts to secure an honest living, a victim to yellow fever. *State Gazette.*

Issue January 18, 1862

Died at his residence in this place on the 15th January, 1862, of consumption, Henry C. Coulson, aged 33 years... He leaves a wife and two children. His stay amongst us has been but a few years.

Obituary. Camp Henry McCulloch, near Victoria, Texas. Ed. *Advocate* - - the announcement this morning that our sutler H.C. Coulson had died last evening has produced a gloom of sadness in this camp that proves how dear to the hearts of the members of this regiment is his memory. Born and reared amongst those we now regard as our enemies, he no sooner became one of our number in the South, than he manifested at all times a deep interest in the welfare of his adopted home... The widow and orphans have the sympathies of this regiment... Company "B."

The death of our illustrious fellow citizen, the Hon. John Hemphill, at Richmond on the 4th inst., is a cause for national grief -- a void is made which cannot be filled.

Lieut J.R. Parsons of Coopwood's Spy Company, died of small box [sic] at Fort Fillmore, Texas, on the morning of the 22d ult. He was 43 years of age, and a native of Staunton, Virginia.

Col. Cooper, of the immortal 8th Georgia Regiment, was killed by a fall from his horse near Manassas on the 23d ult.

Latest News. Richmond. The body of Col. Hugh McLeod is in this city, en route to Texas. He died at Dumfries on the 3d inst. Col. McLeod was a native Georgian and commanded the celebrated Santa Fe expedition under President Lamar.

Issue May 24, 1862

On Monday night last, Mr. Elijah Bennett, who kept a ferry above town, was crossing the river in his boat when about half way over it was struck by some drift wood coming down with the freshet. The shock precipitated Mr. Bennett into the river, and he was drowned. His body was recovered on Thursday morning. He leaves a large family.

The editor of this paper has received a letter from Capt. G.J. Hampton, of the Victoria Volunteers, dated New Mexico, April 25th, from which we extract the following:

I drop you a few lines to inform you of our boys and their welfare. The loss of my Company (C) was three killed and three wounded. Alex. Montgomery, A. Hannar, J.F. Henson, killed and B.N. White, L.J. Bartlett and Sam Brown wounded. White wounded in the foot, Brown in the leg.

The Captain, in speaking of young Montgomery's death, says "He was loved by all who knew him; he fought as brave as man ever did, and fell like a soldier, at his post." We condole with the widowed and bereaved mother in her affliction, who has thus had taken from her only son.

Ben. N. White, who was wounded, and is no doubt, a prisoner, is the only son of the editor of this paper. We hope that, as Gen. Canby has proved himself, from all accounts, a brave soldier and a generous enemy, that Ben will soon be with his parents and friends --- Pub.

Issue March 28, 1863

My Boy will Ne'er Return. Dedicated to the memory of J. Henson, Co. [?] 4th Regiment Sibley's Brigade, one of the lamented lost at Glorietta... [note: poem follows; signed by Mittie, Melino].

We are pained to learn that Judge John P. McKenney, of the 14th District, died at Wharton on the 11th March.

Hon. H.L. Pinckney, the founder of the *Charleston Mercury*, died in that city on the 3d inst. He was formerly a member of the U.S. Congress from that district. It was his father who submitted the "Constitution of the United States" to the Congress in 1797. Hon. Wm. Elliott, another prominent South Carolinian, is dead.

Issue October 1, 1864

Died in Victoria on the evening of the 14th September, 1864, at his residence, Mr. Nathaniel Thompson Gaines, in the 44th year of his age, leaving a widow and little boy of some three summers... Deceased was born in Charleston, Virginia; was the son of (3rd child) of Herbert Prince Gaines, and Sarah E. Crutchfield, natives of Virginia... Deceased was married in September 1859 to Mrs. Turner, widow of R.W. Turner and daughter of Mr. A.F. Hall of

Victoria. Uncle Judge P.T. Crutchfield. In battle of Buena Vista. His father was a graduate of William and Mary, profession lawyer. Leaves an elder brother and a sister with families in Little Rock, a younger brother with family in Kemper city, in this county. Last tribute of affectionate brother. [note: condensed].

We have just learned with deep regret of the death of James Sampson, the only child of Mr. Allen Sampson, of this county. A mere youth, he joined the 6th Texas Infantry, he at last succumbs on the blood-drenched fields of Georgia.

Issue October 17, 1864

Unprovoked Killing -- Last Tuesday our community was shocked by the shooting down of a man by an intoxicated groggery keeper without the least provocation. James Freil, who perpetrated the murderous deed, being intoxicated, invited his victim to take a drink, which he declined, whereupon he seized him by the beard, dragging him towards the bar, and after some altercation, drew a pistol and shot him through the head, killing him instantly. The deceased was a solider by the name of Jacob Andrews, who, after having served faithfully in the army for three years, obtained a furlough to visit his home at Castroville and was on his way... *S.A. Herald*, 8th.

Issue October 22, 1864

Died at Sabine Pass on the 13th Sept. after an illness of two weeks, Ginella and Helena, daughters of Rev. J.F. and Mrs. Brunow/Brudow [?], formerly of Victoria. Ginella was about five, and Helena, two years of age.

The *Huntsville Item* says: We see by the *Austin Gazette* that Dr. Lyman Cronkrite, formerly an itinerant dentist, is dead. He is gone to a land where tooth-carpentry is unknown, and where the shrieks of his victims will no more horrify the ear. May the D.D.S. rest be peace [note: unclear].

James Freil, whom we published as killing Jacob Andrews, a soldier, in San Antonio, we see by the *Herald*, has been admitted to bail in the sum of five thousand dollars-- There appears to be mitigating circumstances in the case, according to a correspondent of the *Herald*.

September 24, 1875
EXTRA EDITION - THE INDIANOLA STORM

[Note: Indianola, located on the shores of Matagorda Bay, was settled by German immigrants in 1844. Citizens were forced to endure epidemics of yellow fever and other diseases, Indian attacks, a Civil War blockade, and a series of storms, hurricanes, and cyclones, one of the worst of which occurred on Thursday, September 16, 1875. After this storm, the *Advocate* dispatched a special reporter to the scene and following is an abstract of the *Advocate's* extra edition of September 24, 1875, covering the "day of danger and night of horror", "frightful destruction of property", and "terrible loss of life" experienced in Indianola.

The Victoria party, including the *Advocate* representative, which left for Indianola on Saturday night last, arrived at its destination, nearly forty miles distant, at 9 o'clock Sunday morning, having been in the saddle since 9 o'clock the evening before, with the exception of an hour spent in resting the horses. The last six or seven miles of the ride bore evidences of the terrible strength of the current which had swept over that part of the route. Salt water filled the marshes and low places on the prairie, and as Indianola drew near, the wrecks of schooners, the shattered fragments of lonely prairie ranches and remnants of fences were visible everywhere. The railroad track for four or five miles was scattered away to the west, and much of the embankments were entirely destroyed. Sections of the track, four or five bars long, were swept like bubbles from their positions for hundreds of yards, and one stretch of a mile or more not a vestige of either tie or iron remains in sight, but was probably carried into the lake a mile distant.

West of Indianola, and between the railroad and Powderhorn Lake, where once a number of buildings stood, but one solitary dwelling remains, and it in a shattered condition. Near here stands a locomotive engine and tender, while along side the track a passenger coach lies in an inverted position, while one set of its trucks remains on the track just where the car had stood.

Once into the stricken town evidences of the extent of the awful catastrophe began to present themselves. Houses, torn and shattered, were on every side, often several squares from the original site, fences wrenched from their fastenings, mingled shrubbery and trees, lay piled in masses everywhere. The scene from the bridge was one of desolation, of wreck and ruin.

Topography. In order to give the reader a better idea of the calamity, a few descriptive remarks upon the topography of Indianola and vicinity may be of use. The reef, on the extreme southern limit of which the town is situated, is about four miles long, the lower part running nearly north and south, while further up it tends more to the westward. The beach of the bay above Indianola sweeps around until it forms a coast running nearly due east and west, and is then at almost right angles with that in front of the town. To the south the bay coast tends to the eastward until Alligator Head is reached, beyond which there are numerous inlets and points. In the rear is a series of connected lakes and bayous, not generally full of water, a conjunction of which is made at the lower point of the town with a wide and deep bayou, from its peculiar shape called Powderhorn. This bayou connects and is the channel through which Powderhorn Lake, a half mile above discharges into the bay just immediately at the lower point of the town. About midway of the reef the water of previous years had cut a channel directly across, but ordinarily there was little or no water there, and but seldom were there interruptions of travel from one end of the island to the other. On the northern part of the reef stands what is called Oldtown, or Indianola proper, which at one time was the leading shipping point, and enjoyed the distinction of being the county seat of Calhoun county until transferred to what was then called Powderhorn, now Indianola. To the rear of Oldtown, across a shallow lake or bayou, is the highest land for some miles, a portion of which during the late storm, was not submerged.

The Storm -- Its Nature. Atmospheric disturbances are classed under several distinctive heads, with the cyclone as the climax, or severest character of storm known. The highest speed of a hurricane is fixed at eighty miles an hour, while the cyclone travels at a much greater speed, having two motions, the one rotary and the other in a straight direction. A cyclone is reported to have passed over the Gulf to the south of Indianola three years ago, traveling at the rate of one hundred and twenty-six miles an hour, while it is estimated by the officer in charge at the U. S. observatory at Indianola the one of Thursday moved at a speed less rapid, or from one hundred to one hundred and twenty miles an hour. His observations marked the speed of [note: unclear] northeast and at 10 o'clock Thursday night at eight-eight miles, but at that time the abrupt change to the north west destroyed the instruments and rendered it impossible for him to make any further notes. His opinion classes it as a cyclone, the exact center of the lines of progress of which must have been in the neighborhood of Indianola.

Indianola. The town of Indianola is principally comprised in one long street, running with the reef nearly north and south. Formerly another street existed on the bay front, but successive encroachments of the water rendered it impracticable. West of Main street, one or two short streets ran parallel with the reef, while across a low marsh was situated the railroad depot, machine shops, etc., near Powderhorn bayou. The railroad track runs across and connects with the wharf extending out into the bay. The business portion lies principally on the lower part of Main street near the wharf.

Wednesday's Storm. On Wednesday, the 15th inst., the storm which was known to have been gathering in this latitude, and which had been prognosticated by the heavy banks of clouds that for some days had hung over this section, commenced, a heavy northeast wind being its most prominent distinguishing feature, accompanied by an almost steady rain. It was early noticed the bay was being rapidly filled, but as it was a usual occurrence at the period of the autumnal equinox, no uneasiness was felt. Later in the evening the water had progressed to a higher point than ever known, but the wind, which had increased to a gale, was confidently expected to decrease in violence as the sun went down, and the citizens of Indianola slept undisturbed, in the hope that the morrow would bring a cessation of the storm. During Wednesday night, however, the steady southeasterly wind increased, and daylight Thursday morning found the eastern side of town submerged, and the water breaking over Main street in many places. The wind, while heavy, had not yet become more than a gale, and was blowing with but a tithe of the fierceness of the day and night following.

Thursday's Cyclone. Daylight on Thursday, the 16th inst., dawned upon the stricken town and its now anxious citizens. The gale had become first a hurricane and then a cyclone, and the waters of the bay, lashed to fury, rushed angrily westward over the town, and far out into the prairie beyond. All the forenoon boats were busily employed in transferring people from the lower part of Main street to points further up, where it was thought less danger existed, while in many of the stores and business houses efforts were made to render valuable goods as safe as possible. By noon the water had increased to several feet in depth, and was pouring through the cross streets like a mill [note: word unclear] race. It was now evident that there no longer existed any hope to save property from destruction. Life, and life alone, was worth struggling for, and every possible effort was now turned to the preservation of those in danger. The current rendered it impossible to retain footing for an instant without assistance, and life lines were stretched along Main street, across the torrents running through the cross streets. Boats, loaded with women and children, were drawn by ropes up Main street to the upper part of town, which was thought to be the safest. Many accidents occurred, and fearful danger had up to this time been experienced, but as the night drew on, to be long remembered by a nation so direful were the events destined to mark it as one of horror and suffering, the already fearful situation become trebly worse. At this time the water had risen to fully five feet in depth, and the highest points on the reef were submerged. Many of those who had been removed earlier were again in danger, and the buildings thought the strongest and best able to stand the immense pressure of the rushing flood were made the refuge of many who had been compelled to abandon their houses. During the afternoon most of the buildings along the bay front had succumbed to the fury of the storm, the dwelling house of Mr. George Seeligson being among the first, about 2 o'clock.

The Night of Horror. The horrors of the situation at night can scarcely be imagined, it was far beyond a description. Added to the terrible condition, houses which had been made the refuge of large numbers under the supposition that they offered better chances for safety and security, began to give way. Many of these buildings contained from twelve or fifteen to sixty persons, whose only hope for life was in the strength of their place of refuge.

Under this accumulation of hardships, the intrepid conduct seen on every hand stood out in bold relief as a prominent feature. Neck deep in water, the buildings reeling and tottering, despairing of life and beyond the reach of human aid, amid the howling of the wind and frenzied onset of the waves, with all the storied courage of the Anglo-Saxon race, men, women and even children faced the angered elements in their mad carouse, and calmly awaited an expected doom. Heroism beyond that of charging columns of trained warriors sinks into abjectness and deserves not the name when compared with the steady courage displayed under circumstances so frightful and danger so appalling. Husbands gathered their families or remnants of families to the safest places possible, and then rushed to the assistance of others; youths and even young girls, with steady nerve resolutely risked themselves to aid others from being swept away, and in some instances met the death they had so unselfishly attempted to avert from others.

From the time darkness closed upon the scene and midnight a large portion of the loss of life and destruction of property took place. The water was filled with buildings in all stages of demolition hurrying rapidly westward, into the bayou and out on the prairie beyond. Clinging desperately among the debris, and with it being swept away, were dozens of persons who had been percipitated into the flood by the falling of the houses they occupied. Numerous instances of heroic struggles with the current are told, and the few who live to recount the story of their fearful journey tell of heart-rending scenes of death among the angry, surging waves and rushing wrecks. Near the lower part of the reef one building carried with it thirty-one people, men, women and children, and with it were swept into and across Powderhorn Lake. Eleven only survive, leaving twenty-one to be added to the list of missing. Many like incidents occurred, sickening in details and horrible to relate. A number of persons were saved by being carried against the wreck of the depot buildings, which [note: words are not clear] together where they fell. One young man, while clinging here saw his sister swept by almost within his reach, but could render no assistance, and she sank in his sight.

About 12 o'clock the wind changed from Northeast to Northwest, and continued with increased violence. By this change of direction the shattered remnants of the unfortunate town were exposed anew to danger from another point. The vast volume of water which for eighteen hours had been pouring out of the bay ten feet in depth over the reef, until the salt water from the Gulf extended for miles inland, submerging even the highest points several feet, not only relieved of the enormous pressure of the force which had urged it forward, but subjected to the action of the same power, was first checked and then turned back in its course, and thrown again across the reef into the bay. The immense power of the cyclone and terrible rush of water at this stage can be comparatively judged by the fact that the water which consumed eighteen hours in its passage to the west required only about one-third as long to return with the wind in the northwest. Buildings which had stoutly withstood the deluge from the east were swept into the bay by the returning water; others crumbled where they stood, and the scattered wrecks floated with the outgoing tide. Many persons were carried out into the bay clinging to pieces of the wreck or on hastily constructed rafts. Wm. Coffin, and his wife and two children, were carried in the direction of the pass. The two children were lost, the mother died of exhaustion, and Mr. Coffin, after a night of fearful danger, was drifted on the beach, where he watched by his dead wife until the storm was over. Of the two children the body of the eldest was found by Mr. Tom Allen on Sunday about six miles west of Indianola, and buried. The new concrete building belonging to Mr. Tom Coutret, occupied by Alexander as a dry goods store, was washed down towards the last carrying with it Robt. Blossman, Mr. Monseratte, Ed. Crossland, Wm. Trayler, Wm. Terry, and others. All were saved, although Mr. Terry was swept into the bay, but was caught by a counter current and carried back into town, where he was extricated from his perilous position and thus escaped.

The Dawn of Friday. Friday's dawn came at length, and cold and dreary though it was, stricken hearts were lifted up in thankfulness. Almost immediately after the wind had changed a perceptible decrease was distinguishable in the depth of the flood, and by 6 o'clock on Friday morning the streets were free from water. The first gleams of the coming day shone down on the pitable sight of a wrecked and ruined town. A thriving little city of 2000 inhabitants, with its handsome residences and happy homes, its warehouse stored with the varied products known to commerce, its costly churches and splendid marts of business, streets, pavements and gardens, all a shattered and unsightly ruin, while nearly two hundred of its citizens had gone down amid the raging waves and howling hurricane. The scene was desolate, and the stout hearts which had so unshrinkingly braved the terrors of Thursday night felt their first and only weakness when the succeeding morning exhibited the full extent of the catastrophe...

On Saturday morning burying parties succeeded in crossing Powderhorn Bayou and proceeded to examine the lower bay beach and the shores of Powderhorn Lake. Many bodies were found and buried where they lay. From the best sources at hand it is estimated that nearly one hundred bodies have been recovered and interred, very few of which were identified. It is thought many were carried out into the bay by the returning water, many of them will be drifted by incoming tides on the beach for miles along the coast.

The Missing. The following is the list of persons missing from Indianola. It will perhaps be found incomplete, and will, it is thought, probably be somewhat increased as soon as a thorough canvass of the matter can be made. It is possible, too, that there may be a very few names in the list through error, as it is thought a chance exists that some may have been rescued from the bay, information of which has not yet reached here. Still the list is believed to be correct in the main, although it is more than probable that important alterations will be necessary. It includes one hundred whites, and fifty-eight blacks, summing up a total of one hundred and fifty-eight:

Whites in Indianola: Rev and Mrs. Jope, Misses Josie and Annie Jope, and Davenport Lee, son of Mrs. Jope, and two orphan boys, members of the Jope family; Rev. Mr. Homberg, wife and child; Mrs. Wm. Coffin and two children; Mrs. Pat Madden and three children; Miss Rebecca Hanna; Fred. Goeffert; Joseph Coutret, wife and child; Mrs. James Morrison; Mrs. Mike Brennan and two children; Mr. ---- [sic] Peters, wife and son; Mr. M. Haller and wife; Willie and Tennie Cahill; two children of Mr. Thomas Clements, drowned in his arms; Alex. Schmidt, stewart of the hospital; Missess Barbara and Minnie Simon; Mrs. Kelley and daughter; Mrs. Herd and three children; Mrs. Chas. Ernst and child; three children of Mr. Alex. Cole; Mr. E. W. R. Jones and wife of Saluria, attending court at Indianola; James Strang; [note: page is creased and the following names are unclear and difficult to read] Mrs. Emory Foote; Mrs. Catherine McGrath and two children; a Mrs. Smith and daughter Bridget; Mr. Robert Moore, daughter, and infant child of Corinne Miller; Capt. Thos. Harrison and three children; Dennis McMahon; Mr. ---- [sic] Winkleman, drowned in hospital; Mrs. Perry and Amelia Perry, her daughter; Peter, other name unknown, called Spanish Pete; Capt. Barton; A. Dinter; Mr. --- [sic] Clark; two children of Mrs. Kale; Chas. Walker, wife and four children; unknown Spaniard and wife; Mrs. Alfred Co---, mother of Arthur and William Coffin/Collin; Dr. J. H. Leake, who fractured his leg jumping from a window, and was rendered helpless and drowned, and Dr. J. K. McCreary, the quarantine officer of Indianola [note: it appears as though there is a line that is not legible], were lost at Saluria. Mr. John S. Hicks and Dr. Hall at the white, Mr. Thomas Mayne. and Ed. Fink at the red light, keepers of the two light houses in the bay, were lost, and both lighthouses destroyed.

Decrow's Point: Thos. Decrow and wife; Mr. Geo. Humphrey and three children; Mrs. Cherry; James Collins; Mrs. John Humphreys. The loss of life at Saluria is reported as fearful. The most authentic accounts indicate that of about forty-three persons more than thirty were lost. Our list of those living below Indianola who were saved is as follows: Henry Nichols; Miss Olivia Decrow, who was visiting Saluria in attendance upon a sick friend; Mr. and Mrs. Hill, and two daughters; Phut Decrow, swept away, but rescued; Judge Hawes and Walker Hawes and family; Kemp and daughter; S. K. Brown and family; Horton and family; Wilkerson and family. The above list was prepared on Tuesday morning, at which time the reporter left. Later news may make material alterations.

Colored: The preparation of a list of the colored people lost was necessarily beset with obstacles, the leading one of which was the disposition of those of that class interrogated to include in the list every one they did not know to be saved. The report, however, will it is thought, be found in the main correct, as far as it goes, as it is probable there have been omissions made. It includes the names of 58 persons: Jobe Green and three children; Fannie Jones; Julia Williams and three children; Wallace Lewis, wife and one child; Charity Daniels; Charley and Harriet Jordan; Ed. Williams, wife and three children; Harriet Jones; Grant Gibbs and son; Henry Rutledge, --ve years old; [note: one line not legible]; Mollie Williams; Dave Walter; John Young and wife; Wm. Turner and wife Sarah; Emily Antoine; Charity McDuffy; infant child of Kitty Gray's; Wm. Turner and four members of his family, (three saved); Mrs. Phil Jones and child; Rev. John Nelson, wife and three children; Elizabeth Mitchell; Emily Autville; Alexander and Maria Anderson; Rev. and Mrs. J. Lucomb; Berry Bateman; Sarah Green; Julia Loyd and three children; Lilly Ebley.

The Destruction of Property. It is impossible to give anything more than a very imperfect account of the pecuniary losses involved. Even those buildings which still remain are shook and wrenched until almost valueless, without considerable and expensive repairs. None escaped damage, and perhaps not more than three or four retained their positions on the blocks, such was the fierceness of the current.

The *Bulletin* office and building was destroyed, the broken presses being about all that remains of a complete printing office...

The courthouse escaped without serious damage, and the jail, immediately next, lost a portion of its tin roofing. Of all the churches, six or seven in number, but one, the Presbyterian, is standing, and it severely shaken and leaning to the south. The Catholic Church was crushed together, or "telescoped" and totally destroyed, the sanctuary alone remaining in its position. The Masonic building was washed away, entailing a heavy loss on the fraternity at Indianola.

Where formerly stood the livery stable belonging to Charles Hubble and the hotel of Pat Smith, is a deep bayou connecting the bay with the lakes in the rear, and which necessitates a long detour around near where the depot stood to avoid. Two blocks above, another bayou connects the lakes with the bay, and with the rising tide fills the low places in the rear of the town with water. [note: continues with lengthy list of businesses and churches damaged or destroyed during the storm; in most cases owner's name is included].

Organized Relief. The destruction of both water and provisions rendered immediate assistance imperatively necessary. Early on Monday the first supply of food and water arrived from Victoria, and on Tuesday the Cuero committee arrived. Arrangements were made by the Victoria committee to communicate regularly with the railroad terminus, twelve miles distant, and supplies are being sent forward to the destitute. Morgan's steamers offer to carry all the suffers who desire to leave free of charge. A number have accepted the invitations of friends and are now in Victoria, while a considerable party have been transferred to Cuero and elsewhere.

Escaped Prisoners. During the violence of the storm the jail became filled with water, and the prisoners, Bill Taylor (charged with the murder of Sutton), George Blackburn (charged with rape), and the two Ruschau's (theft of cattle) were removed to a place of safety and placed under guard. On Monday night they effected their escape by knocking down the guard and are now at large.

Oldtown. The destruction of property at Oldtown was great, although fortunately no lives were lost there. Two residents of the place drowned elsewhere. Nearly all the houses were more or less damaged, and all that part of the reef bears marks of the furiousness of the storm. But three or four houses remain on the blocks, and some were saved with difficulty. [note: continues with a list of buildings destroyed during the storm, including owner's name].

The only four houses in Oldtown still on their blocks are those of Mr. Garner, the Foster place, Waidig and August Miller.

The two persons lost from Oldtown are Thomas Mayne, at the lighthouse in the bay, and — Winkelman in the hospital at Indianola.

A Mr. Piejat, had a large herd of sheep on the reef, most of which were drowned. During the storm a schooner loaded with cotton was swept through the town and wrecked, and her cargo scattered along the coast...

Mass Meeting of Our Citizens! Aid Voted to the Distressed People of Indianola. The fears expressed in our last week's issue of the injuries which Thursday's storm would occasion on the bay, seems to have been fully shared in by all of our people alike, and with the greatest anxiety they sought and discussed on Saturday every rumor coming from that direction, which tended to give information of the fate of Lavaca, Indianola or Saluria. Nothing, however, but the vaguest reports were afloat until near night, when Messrs. Thomas Sterne, Jr., and Ed. Thompson rode into town from ill-fated Indianola, and for the first time acquainted our anxious people of the disastrous fortune which had befallen this unhappy place. The excitement on our streets now reached fever-heat, for many had friends living there, and others had relatives, while all our people moved by the feeling of humanity, that spirit which is so deeply implanted in the breast of man, of every country and clime, were shocked at the recital of those calamitous details of the suffering and woe which had visited a sister city. A mass meeting of our citizens was called at 7-1/2 o'clock, within one hour after the sad news reached our town, of which we publish the following minutes. This meeting was the largest ever called together in this city:

Court House. Saturday Eve., Sept. 18, 1875. At a meeting of the citizens of Victoria, called to render immediate assistance to the distressed people of Indianola, during this hour of their sad, unexpected and unparalleled loss of life and property, Mr. A. Levi was called to the chair, and E. D. Linn appointed Secretary. The chair stated the object of the meeting... [note: continues with a list of resolutions of assistance to the citizens of Indianola from the citizens of Victoria]. Volunteers being called on to go to the assistance of Indianola, the following gentlemen were immediately enrolled: Ed. Thompson, Ed. Stapp, H. A. Glenn, Lee Owens, Wm. Sutherland, J. E. J. Moody, Peter Malitz, I. P. Kibbe, Chas. Schugart and W. S. Glass, Jr. ...A. Levi, Chm'n. E. D. Linn, Secretary.

Subsequent Meeting, Court House, Sunday Morning, Sept. 19, 1875. At the call of the chairman, the adjourned meeting of citizens assembled this morning to hear the statements of Col. Geo. P. Finlay, respecting the condition of that distressed people, and to devise ways and means to forward food and clothing to the sufferers. The meeting hearing the report of the sad and heart rending scenes transpiring during the storm which swept away one-third of Indianola, given by Col. Finlay, who was himself a survivor, it was resolved that an Executive Committee of seven persons be appointed by the chair, who shall be empowered to act on behalf of the citizens of Victoria in forwarding provisions and clothing to the people of Indianola. The following gentleman were appointed: J. E. Carpenter, F. E. Sibley, John Mahon, A. Goldman, W. J. McNamara, G. A. Levi and Chas A. Wertheimer. It was moved and carried that the Secretary of this meeting be instructed to open a subscription list for cash, to aid the Executive Committee in carrying out the wishes of this meeting. The following persons came forward and subscribed the amounts opposite their names [note: continues with a lengthy list of names and amounts]. ...A. Levi, Chm'n, E. D. Linn, Secretary.

The praise worthy spirit which actuated our people during this excitement, we can not refrain from here recording. On Sunday, although the day of rest, our city presented a lively scene, for every body seemed determined to out do his neighbor in rendering the aid call for. The Executive Committee could not have done more in so short a time. Without intending to discriminate, we would notice also Messrs. E. Melchoir and L. Ditmar, who went from house to house and obtained large quantities of bread and other provisions, and C.L. Thurmond, who was active in getting off wagons. There was no lagging, and there are many more names deserving of notice, but we will not write them because too numerous. It gives us pleasure enough to know our city has shown the most commendable spirit in this matter. Large supplies of flour, coffee, bacon, meal, etc, were forwarded on the train on Sunday, and a number of wagons were dispatched to the Chocolate station to convey the supplies to Indianola. Much suffering was alleviated by this prompt action of our citizens.

Issue July 20, 1876

From Goliad. Eight days ago a man named Styles, who had only been in this county two or three months, having came, as it would appear from papers found on him, from Lavaca county, was killed by unknown parties on the Coletto. No clue to the guilty parties.

Painful Accident. A sad and painful accident occurred in the eastern portion of our city last Monday, which resulted in the death of Fred. Gaugler, a young son of our worthy German citizen, Martin Gaugler... The wagon proceeded but a short distance before Fred. lost his balance and was thrown under the front wheel, which passing directly over his chest, crushed out his young life. He was near the age of seven.

Issue July 27, 1876
From Colettoville. Killed last week at Fred. Meyer's, near the mouth of Hog creek, in Goliad county, W.O. Stiles, who has been living with Bill Davidson...

Issue August 10, 1876
We are informed that a shooting affray occurred at Refugio on Thursday of last week, which resulted in the killing of John McGrew, and the wounding of a Mexican -name unlearned- by Phil Porter. We have not been furnished with full details, but are told that Porter acted in self defense.

Issue August 17, 1876
We are pained to hear of the death in Mission Valley on yesterday morning of our most estimable lady, Mrs. Ferdinand Fenner, of this county.

Died in this city Monday the 15th inst. after a painful illness of some weeks, August Degener, in the 66th year of his age. The deceased has been living at this place for several years, engaged in the lumber business with Messrs. Westoff & Co. He was a brother to Hon. E. Degener, former Congressman of this district. He was a veteran of the Mexican War.

A correspondent of the *Goliad Guard*, writing from Refugio, gives the following particulars of the killing referred to in the *Advocate* of last week.
Quite a sad affair occurred in our quite little village yesterday. About 3 o'clock p.m. at the saloon of Chas. Berkowitz, known as the "Bull's Head", two persons, John H. McGrew and Phil Porter, while drinking, got into a friendly dispute about who was the best man... A Mexican named Honora/Zamora was taken to the hotel and McGrew was taken to his brother-in-law's, Wm. Doughty, and died about 5 p.m. [note: condensed].

Issue August 31, 1876
Died on July 18, 1876 in Dallas, Texas, of congestive chill, Sarah B. Culbreath, in the 28th year of her age. She was the daughter of Mrs. Margaret Jenkins, formerly of this place. She leaves a husband and three little children, mother and brother.

Miscellaneous Texas Newspaper Abstracts - Deaths --- Vol 2

Issue September 14, 1876

Hon. Ed. Randle, Senator from Washington county district in the Thirteenth and Fourteenth Legislature, died suddenly in Austin last week.

Don Jose Maria Cardenas died at his residence in Atascosa county last week, aged 80 years. He fought for the independence of Texas.

Homicide at Cuero. On Monday, there occurred at our neighboring town of Cuero a difficulty which resulted in the shooting of a man named DeMorse by a young man named Ryan. The difficulty had its origin in a cattle trade, which proving unsatisfactory, provoked hard words and a personal recontre. DeMorse was advancing on Ryan with an upraised quirt, when the latter drew his pistol and fired four shoots, three taking effect at equal distances in a line from the shirt collar to the waistband, producing death almost instantly.

In Victoria, Texas, September 8th, 1876 at 2 o'clock p.m. after a long and painful illness, Susan Linn, second daughter of Mrs. Susan T. and the late James A. Moody, ages 27 years, 3 months and 23 days. Yarmouth, Nova Scotia, papers please copy.

Issue September 21, 1876

We hear a report going the rounds on our streets that two men were found dead one day this week in the vicinity of Yorktown - one supposed to have been Dr. Brassel, a person who has been living for several years in Yorktown. This report is not yet fully confirmed.

Issue September 28, 1876

From Goliad. While at Middletown, we heard from parties who live in Dewitt county that a few nights ago Dr. Brassell and son, of Yorktown, were visited by a body of armed men, taken a few hundred yards from their house and shot. We heard nothing derogatory to the character of these persons thus killed - on the contrary that their character was good, except some local prejudices against them.

Issue October 5, 1876

The death of Gen. Bragg is announced as having taken place suddenly at Galveston, September 27. Apparently in usual good health he was walking across the street when he suddenly he staggered and fell, living but a short time after first attacked. His body was taken to Mobile for burial.

The Brassell killing... In the dead hour of night a band of masked men surround the peaceful home of an old man and dragging him from the midst of his family, without apparent cause or reason - without word or warning shoot him down, dead - within thirty steps of his door. This old man had recently left the state of Georgia...

Killing at Clinton. Intelligence reached us on yesterday of the killing of Martin King, jailor at Clinton, DeWitt county...

Issue October 12, 1876

On last Friday, Henry Kuhne, Sen., died suddenly in this city. Came to his death with paralysis of the heart, superinduced by excessive use of ardent spirits. It appears that this unfortunate man had attempted to take his own life by poisoning on Tuesday previous but was relieved. The deceased then drank excessively of whisky. He was an old citizen and leaves a family.

Issue October 19, 1876

From Jackson county. We are informed that Mr. Woodward, the person upon whom the recent attempted assassination was made, has since died of the injuries inflicted... The deceased was an old and peaceable citizen, and his death is regretted by the entire community in which he lives.

Mr. George Wages, whose painful illness was alluded to a few days ago, died night before last at the residence of Mrs. Northway. He was buried with masonic honors. Mr. Wages suffered from a severe pain in his toe, which was superinduced by trimming a corn. He leaves a wife and nine [?] children [note: unclear]... *San Antonio*...

Issue October 26, 1876

Died at the residence of her parents on the Coletto Creek, in this county, on Sunday the 22d inst. after a short illness, Minnie <u>Warden</u>, in the eleventh year of her age.

Issue November 9, 1876

Died in Victoria county, October 25th, 1876 Minnie, daughter of J.C. and Mary <u>Warden</u>, aged 10 years and 7 months.

Issue December 9, 1876

Died recently after a brief illness of four days, Mrs. Mary Scott, wife of D.B/R. Scott, at their residence in Milam county, one and a half miles south of Rockdale. She leaves a husband and six children to mourn her loss; having resided in the county for seventeen years and in the state for thirty odd years. Mrs. Scott was born in the state of Tennessee, 20th November 1810, and died 20 November 1876. *Rockdale Messenger.*

TEXAN MERCURY
Published at Seguin, Texas.
Edited by H.T. Burke.

Issue September 24, 1853
We are credibly informed that Col. William Wallace, of San Antonio, was shot at his rancho on the Cibolo, by a Mexican, on last Sabbath, which we are told is likely to result in the death of Col. Wallace.

Issue October 1, 1853
Mr. Levi W. Young, a citizen of Bastrop county, was waylaid and shot on the 14th ult. as he was going from his residence to the town of Bastrop... Mr. Young leaves a wife and five children. The Masonic fraternity have offered a reward.

Died at Indianola on the 24th ult. of the yellow fever, Mr. B.F. Southern.

Issue October 15, 1853
Died at Galveston, the 28th ult., H.H. Smith, editor of the *Galveston Journal.*
    Obituary: The death of Horatio H. Smith, the editor of this paper, who expired on the morning of Wednesday, September 28th, at 6 A.M., of the prevailing epidemic. Mr. Smith was born at Sackett's Harbor, New York, and resided several years in Union City, Michigan, prior to his removal to this State... Mr. Smith was 33 years old... he leaves a widow and an infant daughter. *Weekly Journal*, Galveston.

It is reported that Moses Evans, the celebrated "Wild Man of the Woods" died at Washington recently. He was a land-locator and extensively known in Western Texas.

Two young men named Butler and Goacher, on the 7th inst., fell out and fought. Butler struck Goacher with a pistol, holding the barrel in his hand. The force of the blow was such, that the cock of the pistol was buried in Goacher's skull, and at the same time, by the discharge of the pistol, Butler received the contents in his abdomen. The news reached town yesterday evening that Butler had died, and Goacher was not expected to recover. This happened at the place of Mrs. Young, in the lower part of the county. *Bastrop Advertiser.*

From the *Port Lavaca Commercial* of the 4th... Already seventeen of our most useful and worthy citizens have fallen victims to the terrible destroyer, the yellow fever, among them, we are grieved to state, is our beloved fellow citizen, Doctor Moses Johnson...

SICKNESS IN HOUSTON: The sickness in Houston is not abating. There were seven interments on Monday, the same number Tuesday, and five deaths on Tuesday night. Mr. Schrimp, who has been dangerously sick, is now recovering; also the Rev. Mr. Petway, and Mrs. Petway. The Rev. Mr. Cameron, editor of the *Banner*, is sick, but not dangerously. Mr. Remington, known to the public by several patented inventions, is understood to be dangerously sick...

Issue October 29, 1853

We learn that the bodies of two men, a Mr. Dickerson and his son, residing in the southern part of this country, were found in the road on the 23rd ult., pierced with buckshot. They have left families with several children. *San Augustine Herald.*

Issue November 12, 1953

Sam. Wilson, who was shot recently in Lockhart by Mr. Robertson, has since died.

The *Advocate* of the fifth inst. thinks that not more than thirty -if so many- cases of yellow fever have occurred. The names of those who have died are Mr. S. Sutton, Dr. Bonney and child, Mr. French.

Issue November 26, 1853

The *Austin Gazette* announces the death of Dr. T.N. Sutherland, member-elect to the House of Rep. from the counties of Cameron and Hidalgo. Dr. Sutherland died of brain-fever, on his way to Austin to join the legislature.

An affray occurred on the 19th inst. at Mr. Johnson's Ferry, 3 miles above this place, between a man of the name of James B. Johnson, from Burleson county, and Alfred Hampton, of this county. A difficulty originated in reference to crossing the ferry, when Johnson obtained a gun, and threatened to shoot. Hampton and another man approached and seized the gun for the purpose of disarming Johnson when the latter inflicted a wound on Hampton's neck. Hampton is not wounded dangerously, though in a dangerous state.

Dr. Alexander Ewing, formerly Surgeon General of the Army of Texas, died recently in Houston.

Issue December 10, 1853

It becomes our painful duty to announce the death of Dr. Z.M. Anderson, who was killed by the accidental discharge of his fowling-piece, on the evening of Thursday the 8th inst. Leaves an afflicted partner and an only babe.

Departed this life, on Thursday evening last, Doctor Zebulon M. Anderson, of Seguin, aged 25 years. The deceased was a native of the State of Virginia, and located in Seguin about 2 years since... He leaves an estimable and bereaved companion, and one child, a little daughter...

Issue December 17, 1853

The residence of Mr. James McAllister, of Gonzales county, was consumed by fire on Saturday the 3rd inst., so says the *Inquirer*. The same paper states that a man named Smith, from Virginia, was found dead about six miles above the town of Gonzales on the morning of the 9th. He was addicted to intemperance.

A correspondence of the *Nueces Valley* states that yellow fever is raging in Brownsville and Matamoras. Lieutenant Dungan, Co. B Fourth Artillery USA, died of the prevailing epidemic on the 11th ult.

Issue December 24, 1853

From the *Western Texas* -- Lino Flores and Antonio Quino, accused of the murder of C. de la Garza, have been found guilty in the first degree.

Issue January 14, 1854

On Friday the 13th ult., says the *San Antonio Ledger*, a man named Lard, was found dead near the grave yard of the San Pedro. He had been stabbed in the left breast and in the right side. The supposed murderer, one Esteban, has been arrested.

Issue January 28, 1854

A murder was committed in Grayson county on the 10th ult. A man named Davis left the village of Kentucky Town, on horseback, with three others, one named Umphries; the others, Jamieson, in a wagon. They had all been drinking. A difficulty occurred on the way, and the three attacked Davis. They then dragged him to a thicket, off the road, and Umphries fled. The other two were seen, by a man passing that way, returning to their wagon, and hastily driving away. The body was discovered, and the Jamiesons were arrested...

Issue February 11, 1854

Tribute of respect from Prairie Lea Lodge #114 A.F. & A.M. held on 31 January 1854 on the death of Col. Thomas J. Hardeman.

James T. Lytle, Senator from Lavaca, who has for sometime been in ill health, is dead. He had left Austin several weeks ago in consequence of declining health.

Justis Dunn drowned himself in the bayou, below the foot of the Famine street, he was about 56, a cabinet maker, had been in the city 5-6 months. Friends in Madison, Indiana. *Spirit of the Age.*

The *Leon Pioneer* says that the grand jury of Hill county has found a bill of indictment against Dr. Steiner for the murder of Major Arnold.

Issue February 18, 1854

A young man named James Perry was accidentally killed on the railroad at Harrisburg on Wednesday... Mr. Perry was from Boston and intended to return in a few weeks. *Telegraph.*

Issue February 25, 1854

We learn that Byrd Smith, who was recently stabbed in the eye in an affray in Gonzalas, has since died.

On Wednesday night of the 18th January, says the *Telegraph*, a lunatic named Pate killed his son, John W. Pate, while sleeping. He used a Collins' axe-box.

Issue March 11, 1854

The property of the estate of Louis Hipp, deceased, that was advertised for sale on the seventh inst., embracing eleven, unimproved back, town lots, sold for the sum of $617.

Issue April 1, 1854

SUICIDE: A young man named Bell committed suicide in the lower part of this county, on the Cibolo, on Wednesday the 22nd inst...

Col. Stem, formerly Indian agent, was killed by Indians 4 miles from Ft. Belknap, while riding in a buggy. *Western Texan.*

Issue April 15, 1854

Died on the 6th of April, Martha, infant daughter of John F. and (the late) Martha Bruce, formerly of Portsmouth, N.H. In January 1853, a dying mother intrusted to Mrs. T.W. Wilson, of Seguin, the daughter whom it had been decreed she should not nourish, then but 24 days old...

We learn from Mr. J.M. Smith, who came over from Austin by Tuesday night's stage, that a Mr. Gwinn had been shot by Capt. Grumbles. The weapon used was a shot-gun loaded with buck-shot, eight of which were lodged in Gwinn's body, breaking his arm and causing what was deemed a mortal wound. *San Antonio Ledger.*

Issue April 22, 1854

The *Ranger* says that E.J. Hendrick of Grimes county was shot in the streets of Washington by G.W. McLees. The weapon used was a double-barreled shot-gun.

The honorable David <u>Gage</u>, Senator from Rusk, died at his residence, 26th ult.

Issue April 29, 1854

Maj. Neighbors, Indian agent, in a letter to the *San Antonio Ledger* says there is little doubt the party of Indians were Wichitas who killed Mr. Forrester and children. The Mormons on the head of the Guadalupe, had a fight with them and killed four.

The Honorable David <u>Gage</u>, Senator from Rusk, died at his residence, 26th ult.

Issue May 6, 1854

We learn that Mr. Posey of the *LaGrange Monument*, who has been some time suffering from consumption, is dead.

We are again called upon to record a scene of bloodshed in our city. On Tuesday morning last, a rencontre occurred in front of the Metropolitan Hotel, between William H. Cleveland, son of Capt. J.T. Cleveland, and George J. Durham, in which the former was almost instantly killed by a pistol shot. On the previous day angry words passed between the parties and as Durham was walking down the street past the hotel on the morning above named, young Cleveland made an attack upon him with a walking cane, with the sad result we have already mentioned... *State Gazette*.

Issue May 20, 1854

The *Galveston Civilian* records the death of one of its oldest and best citizens of that place which occurred on the night of the 13th ult. Mr. J.A. Kauffman retired to his bed about 10 o'clock in the evening and was discovered next morning, at day break, lying in the alley near his house, dead, and his face and head much lacerated. Jury verdict, died causes unknown, supposed to be accident.

The *Marshall Republican* learns that Doctor Hamilton G. Graves, living near the north east corner of Cherokee county, was waylaid and shot in the back and killed.

Issue June 3, 1854

The *Banner* [Houston] says a man named Read was killed at the railroad depot at Stafford's Point on the 14th ult. by a man named Herring.

Issue June 10, 1854

HOMICIDE: James Tomerlin was murdered on last Monday the 29th ult. about three miles west of this place; five buck shot or balls having entered various parts of his body, from the effects of which he survived only a short time. The facts as developed before an examining court, before whom William W. Montgomery was charged, and undergoing examination for the perpetration of this deed, were in substance about as follows: Tomerlin and his son were on their way to town; on arriving near Montgomery's house, William Tomerlin, (the son who was riding with the deceased) swears he was suddenly surprised by the report of a gun; on looking around he saw his father in the act of falling from his horse, and in the thick bunch of bushes, some ten or fifteen paces off, he saw Montgomery standing with a double barrel shot gun presented and smoke proceeding from the muzzle. Montgomery and the deceased had been enmity for some time. *Lockhart Clarion.*

Simeon M. Rogers and M.S. Ragland, son of Judge Ragland, were struck by lightning. Rogers left a wife and two infant children. Ragland leaves a widow and a twin brother.

Issue June 24, 1854

W.S. McFarland certifies that a man called "Kentuck" has confessed to him that he assisted the Indians in the murder of the Forrester family. It is possible Mrs. Forrester may recognize him... *Western Texan.*

Issue March 10, 1855

A man by the name of Joseph Bell was arrested in this town on last Tuesday night on the charge of having killed a man by the name of Crowly, in Clinton, Louisiana, in the fall or winter of 1852... *Gonzalas Inquirer.*

Issue June 16, 1855

At Dripping Springs, some 40 miles westwardly from Austin, Mr. Walker and a negro were attacked by a party of five Indians, apparently. Mr. W. was killed and the mule the negro was riding was shot from under him. He fled and was pursued but managed to escape... *State Times.* [note: condensed].

A German named Nuttenhaver, living on the Quihi, was attacked by one of his cattle. He died in less than an hour. *San Antonio Texan.*

WASHINGTON AMERICAN
Published at Washington, Texas
by G.W. Perkins & Co., G.W. Crawford, editor.
Published every Friday.
First issue dated Vol I #1, November 1, 1855.

Issue November 8, 1855
A lad about 17 years of age by the name of Hill, a mail rider on the Chappell Hill route, accidently shot and dangerously wounded himself in this place last night. He is not in the habit of carrying arms, but was fearing an attack from some Germans in Austin county.

In the District Court of Robertson county, T.A. Johnson, John Johnson, and Earle Brown, were acquitted of the charge of murder of W.D. Miller.

Issue November 16, 1855
Burwell and Burnes, indicted for the murder of Wm. Bird in the District Court of Austin county, were convicted of murder in the first degree.

Issue November 23, 1855
The *Huntsville Presbyterian* of the 3rd inst. says a few days ago, Mr. Jas. Baily, a grocery keeper at Danville, was murdered [by] Mr. J.B. Caperton. Cause-whiskey.

Issue November 30, 1855
We learn from the *Waco Beacon* that the grand jury brought in an indictment for man-slaughter, in the case of Bryant for the murder of Kell, which took place in Bosque county, 29th or 30th of October.

Issue December 7, 1855
The funeral of Mr. Wm. E. Finch will take place today at 10 o'clock A.M. at the residence of Mrs. Stephen Locket. He will be buried with Masonic honors. B.F. Wilson, W.M.; L.M. Minor, Sect'y.

We learn that J. Shelby Young of Brenham committed suicide a few days since by shooting himself with a pistol through the heart.

Issue December 21, 1855
The *Nueces Valley* says that on the 1st a Mexican named Antonio Pelasho entered the house of another named Juan Aguila and bid him good morning when the latter drew a knife and stabbed his wife and then rushed upon

Pelasho, plunging his knife into his body and killing him instantly. He also cut another woman. He is in the hands of the sheriff. Jealousy is supposed to have caused this brutal murder.

Died in this place on the 7th instant at the residence of W.Y. McFarland Esq., Mrs. Mary L. Summers, wife of Mr. Sam. H. Summers of LaGrange, Texas, and eldest daughter of Mr. William Brown, of Shelbyville, Tennessee, in the 25th year of her age. Her health had been extremely delicate for the past three years, her last sickness was of three weeks duration and her sufferings were severe. Member Methodist E. Church. She has left a husband and two lovely and interesting little daughters.

Our readers will recollect that B.J. Forlson of this county was killed some months since and that Hugh Cooper was arrested. The trial is now over and the verdict is guilty. *Prairie Blade*.
We learn that Cooper has been lodged in the Grimes county jail.

Issue January 4, 1856
Died at the residence of Sam Holiday, two miles from this city, on the 21st ult. after a lingering illness, Mrs. Ellen, consort of Titus Holiday.

Died on the 25th at the residence of her father, near Rock Island, of Typhoid Pneumonia, Miss Ruth Gates, daughter of Amos Gates, Esq., in the 18th year of her age...

Issue January 11, 1856
Judge Munger's death: The Judge died last Tuesday evening of scarlet fever... Bereaved widow and orphan children.

Died in this city at the residence of her husband of putrid sore throat, Mrs. Elizabeth, wife of J.L. Stevenson. She was buried by the Samaritan Order, of which she was a consistent member.

Issue January 18, 1856
Gifford was stabbed in Rusk on the 8th inst. by Wm. Reynolds. His life is despaired of. So says the *Palestine American*.

Tribute of Respect-Cartmell Lodge, Mrs. Elizabeth Stevenson.

Issue January 25, 1856
We learn through Mr. Hanks that a difficulty occurred at a race track in Grimes county a few days since in which Mr. Robt. Barker and William Cobb, were killed, and four other persons were dangerously wounded.

Issue February 1, 1856

We learn from the *Tri-Weekly Telegraph* that Mr. Levi Pitts, of this county, died near Houston a few days since.

Issue February 15, 1856

It becomes our painful task this week to chronicle the death of our worthy and esteemed friend and fellow citizen, R.E. Lott, son of R.A. Lott of this city, who departed this life on Saturday night last at about 10 minutes of 1 o'clock. He leaves kind and affectionate parents, sisters, brothers.

Fall term District Court at Waco, Presley Bryant for murder... He was waylaid a few days since in the county of Johnson, by three men, at a time when he least expected danger and was shot dead.

Issue February 22, 1856

Died in this city of scarlet fever on the 9th inst., Mr. Royal E. Lott, in the 27th year of his age. The deceased was born in the State of Florida and emigrated to Texas at an early period...

Issue February 29, 1856

Tribute of Respect from Brenham, Cartmell Lodge I.O.O.F. held Tuesday February 19, 1856 on the death of A.J. McDade. [note: beloved mother mentioned].

Issue March 7, 1856

A Mrs. Smith, of Waco, accidently caught fire to her dress in Waco a short time since and was so badly burned that she died soon after.

Issue March 19, 1856

Affray - by a gentleman from Eagle Pass we learn that a man by the name of H. Sample was killed there a few days ago by another named Augustine; several shots, we learn, passed between the parties. *San Antonio Texan.*

Issue March 26, 1856

We are informed that Blake Thompson, the murderer of Finnin at Austin three years since, is now in jail in Tennessee.

Issue April 2, 1856

Tribute of Respect from Brenham chapter #5 on the death of Nelson H. Munger, Judge of First Judicial District.

We are requested to state Rev. Dr. Morriss of the P.E. Church will preach the funeral sermon of Mrs. Titus Holliday at the Methodist church, in this place, on next Sunday.

Issue April 16, 1856

A dreadful accident occurred at the steam mill of Messrs. Crocheron & Co. On Monday last, a young man named Carter was killed. He was caught in the wheel band. *Bastrop Advertiser.*

A letter to the *Christian Advocate* states Mrs. Napp and her two children were drowned in the Brazos in attempting to cross the ferry near Port Sullivan.

Issue April 23, 1856

The case of the State against Dozier for the murder of Lane has been continued by the defence.

Issue April 30, 1856

On Tuesday evening, John Barnett had the misfortune, whether justifiable or not, to send to his long home William Lowther. Soon after Barnett was lodged in jail to await the judgement of his peers and of the law. Anything more than a bare statement of the leading facts of this melancholy affair, would be, previous to the trial, ill-timed and improper. The prisoner on the evening of the unfortunate tragedy, which has spread gloom over our community, was seen in a state of reeling intoxication. About supper hour he was taken to the room of Drs. Weston and Weaver and laid in bed. Sometime after, young Lowther entered the room to arrange his costume for the evening party. While standing before the mirror, no doubt thinking of the gay scene for which he was preparing the stillness of the hour was broken by imprecations and the startling report of a pistol. The ill-fated Lowther, with heavy noise, fell to the ground never to rise or speak again... *Richmond Sun.*

We are informed that Fernand Cotton was killed by N.K. Killum at the white Sulphur Spring in Grimes county on last Friday.

We learn, says *Houston Telegraph,* that the jail at Halletsville was broken open by two persons and that Dr. Bellows, imprisoned for the murder of Mr. Fly, made his escape. The parties, engaged in thus letting out the caged bird, were caught and now occupy the doctor's late quarters.

Issue May 7, 1856

Died on Friday, May 2, 1856, of scarlet fever, at 5 o'clock P.M., Thomas Adney Perkins, first born of G.W. and Magdaline A. Perkins, born February 21, 1853; aged 3 years, 2 months, 11 days.

We regret to see in the Austin papers the death of Hon. Hardy Holman. He was a good man.

Mrs. Hope, wife of Richard Hope of this vicinity, died on last Sunday. She leaves an affectionate husband.

Issue May 14, 1856

We learn that Mr. John Macnamara died yesterday at the residence of John Spann and will be buried today at half past 10 o'clock A.M.

Mrs. Rusk, wife of Gen. Thos. J. Rusk, United States Senator of Texas, died at Nacogdoches on the 25th of April.

The *Shreveport Democrat* -- death of an old black man Jim -- usually known as Dr. Jim, died Saturday the 19th, one hundred twenty-four [sic], three months, and twenty-five days. Born December 24, 1781 in Fredericksburg, Virginia, and slave of Capt. John Carter, Rev. War officer. He was well acquainted with Gen. Washington.

Issue May 21, 1856

H.V. [Henry] Robertson died at his residence near Independence on Monday evening.

Terrible and destructive storm. Nine persons killed.
    The severest and most terrible storm that has ever visited this country, passed through a portion of this county, on Tuesday evening last. At Cedar Hill, a small village fifteen miles from this place, it seemed to have attained its greatest power, and its destruction was terrible. Nine persons were killed almost instantly in this small village and a great many wounded. Every house in the village was leveled with the ground and some of the houses were blown entirely away. Wm. Horn furnishes us with the particulars.
    List of killed:
        John Hart, his wife and child.
        J. Berry (merchant) his wife and child.
        Mrs. Dickson (residing at Berry's).
        Mrs. Allen.
        A negro girl.
        Among the wounded we have only learned the names of--
        Old man Hart.
        Henderson Hart (skull fractured).
        Mr. Hall, who was at Brotherton's at the time, was slightly injured.
        [note: damage to buildings also given]. *Dallas Herald.*

Issue June 18, 1856

We regret to learn that a man named Melton was shot at Cameron a few days since by a person named Roberts; both of the above parties were of the order usually denominated "sportsmen".

Mr. Ingram was killed by Mr. Stuckey on the 24th ult. in Grimes county.

Issue June 25, 1856

OBITUARY: At a called meeting of Milam Lodge #11 of Free and Accepted Masons, held at their lodge room in the town of Independence on the 20th of May A.D. 1856, brothers H. Clark, G.J. Duncan, and J.B. Robertson were appointed a committee to draft resolutions expressing the sense of the lodge at the loss it had sustained in the death of brother Henry V. Robertson, who departed this life at his residence near this place at a quarter past 2 o'clock P.M. on the 19th inst...

Died at the residence of her husband in DeWitt county, Texas, of typhoid fever on the 29th of May 1856, Mrs. Julia A., wife of J.W. Wynne, and daughter of Capt. R.H. Harper, of Washington, Texas. She leaves a husband and three small children.

The yellow fever was prevailing at St. Domingo at the latest dates. On the 12th ult., Mr. Thomas H. Smith, mate of schooner *Bandel*, of Fredericksburg, died.

Charles T. Layton, aged 18 years, a relative of the captain, died on the same day.

Jno. K. Hyde, the murderer of Charles Butler, will be hung.

Issue July 2, 1856

Died of paralysis in the town of Houston, Tuesday the 24th ult., John F. Crawford. Mr. Crawford was born in Rockbridge county, Virginia, in 1798; he moved to Tennessee in 1812; to Mississippi in 1820; thence to Texas in 1840... Mr. Crawford died, leaving four children... from Houston his remains will be removed to Rock Island, in this county... In battle of Horse Shoe. Five-year member of the Methodist church.

From the *Liberty Gazette* we learn of two murders in the East: on the Sabine river, near Madison, one Sam Ashworth, a free negro, in a skiff with another, made an attack on two others, the county clerk of Orange and one S.A. Deputy, was shot three times and fell in the Sabine, the negro murderer had escaped... Then in the town of Liberty, D.M. Wall attacked M.A. Praytor with a hack knife, mortally wounding him in the side... The *Nacogdoches Chronicle* gives a horrible assassination in that county on the person of Geo. B. Perry, while plowing in the field, one Simon Bruton shot him twice...*San Antonio Herald*. Mr. Wright and 5 or 6 others on their way to El Paso with a drove of cattle were killed by Indians at Devils Creek...

Issue July 16, 1856

A lady named Mrs. Curtis died very suddenly about 12 o'clock today. She had only been in this city about a month and had opened a millinery near Dr. Labadie's on Market St. Very little appears to be known about her. She represented herself as having a husband in California and is supposed to have been some 35-40 years of age. We learn she took two powders and died soon after. *Galveston News.*

Issue August 27, 1856

Died at the residence of her husband, E.M. Alexander, on Friday, August 22nd, Mrs. Eleanor A. Alexander, in the 31st year of her age, leaving a husband, six children and numerous friends.

Distressing intelligence. The annexed account of the loss of steamship *Nautilus*, with all on board, we clip from the *Confederate*. It will be seen also, that the entire village on Last Island, was destroyed by the same gale. Nearly two hundred souls have perished on the Island.

The following is the list of those on board as far as we have been able to ascertain by inquiry. Rev. Jerome Twichell of Houston; Rev. Mr. Vedre of Galveston; Capt. Thompson and son of the *Nautilus*; John and Henry Ker, pursers, do; Mr. F. Johnson, Engineer of the *Nautilus*; Capt. McGoven of Galveston; Thomas H. Maloney of Galveston; Thomas L. McNeill of Mobile; Capt. Mure of New Orleans; Andrew Marsh of New Orleans; Judge J. Scott of Anderson, Texas; Master Dossatt of St. Mary's College, Galveston; J.P. Ellis of Washington, Texas; Adolph Half of Liberty, Texas; S.J. Ingram of LaGrange, Texas; R.P. Dearer of North Carolina; Mr. R. Graves of Wheelock, Texas; Miss H. Gay, of Wheelock, Texas; H. Bullock of Fayette, Texas; Micajah Thomas of Houston, Texas; Mrs. Micajah Thomas of do do; J.M. Adams of Marshal, Ala; W.A. Kiruin of Freestone, Texas; S. Newman of Marshal, Ala.; C.H. Short of New Orleans.

Issue September 3, 1856

The friends of H.C. Fountain and Capt. R.A. Lott will no doubt be grieved to learn of recent death of an infant son of the former. Lived 18 hours.

Issue September 10, 1856

The *Liberty Gazette* of the 1st says: "The mail-rider from Woodville to Liberty informs us that a man named Smith, his wife, and a young lady were killed by some unknown person or persons on the evening of Tuesday last. The occurrence took place on the Angelina river between the town of Marion in Angelina county [sic]...

Issue November 5, 1856

We were pained to learn of the decease of Wm. F. Hunt, son of the venerable Dr. Hunt, of this county, on the 5th of September 1856, at Spring Bank on the Red River in Arkansas. The deceased was born in Greenville county, near Williamsborough, North Carolina, on the 17th of August, 1822, and emigrated to Texas at an early day. He now sleeps on the bank of the Red River.

Died on the 21st, Ida R., adopted daughter of Rufus H. and Sarah Felder, aged 4 months...

At Richmond, Fort Bend county, an affray took place on the evening of the 16th, between John F. Walker and Patrick Cunningham, in which the latter received a severe cut on the arm and also a stab in the back. Cunningham lingered until the morning of the 22nd when he died. The parties were in a state of intoxication at the time of the affray.

The *Civilian* says: *Daily Courier*, Bastrop county. Franklin Lewis, indicted for murder of his negro Henry, was acquitted. Cornelius C. Hemphill was indicted for murder of George A. Gamble.

Issue November 19, 1856

We regret to learn, says the *Brenham Enquirer*, that Mr. John Crenshaw, a worthy citizen of this county, which engaged in erecting a chimney on his premises, a few days since, fell from the scaffold, breaking his back, which accident proved fatal.

Dr. J.L. Burwell committed suicide while laboring under temporary insanity, in Alexandria, Virginia, on the 22nd inst., by cutting his throat with a pen knife. Dr. B. was the son of George H. Burwell of Clarke county, Virginia.

At San Antonio on last Wednesday week, an affray took place between Charles Cameron, a clerk in one of the Government Departments, and a Michael Keef, which resulted in the death of the latter. The difficulty originated at a dance in Alamo City. Cameron is in jail.

Tribute of respect at Baylor Lodge #125 held at their Lodge Room at Gay Hill, November 9, 1856, on the death of Wm. T. Hunt.

Issue November 26, 1856

We learn from the *News* that Maj. Moses Park died in Galveston on Saturday last. Maj. Park was an old citizen of Texas and was greatly respected.

The *Savannah News*, alluding to the death there of Catherine Ritters at age 105 and 8 months, says that a few years before her death, her eyesight was fully restored as were also her teeth of which she had a full set.

State Times on Wednesday last, Narcissa Burnham of Austin was found dead in bed. Suffered neuralgic affection. Over dose chloroform.

Issue December 3, 1856
On Monday, 24th November, an old man by the name of Flesher living on the head of Brushy, about forty miles above Austin, was killed near the county line between Travis and Williamson... Shot by some person unknown.

Died November 23, 1856, Mrs. Francis Rhodes, widow of the Rev. Thomas Rhodes, at her residence, three miles south-east of the town of Washington, Texas; aged 74 years, 9 months. She lived the life of a christian and died without a struggle. Although her affliction was great, suffering from a cancer, she bore it to the last with Christian fortitude. W.A.T.R.

Issue December 10, 1856
Died on Thursday the 4th inst. at the residence of James McMiller of consumption, Mr. H.W. Jones. Mr. Jones was about 32 years of age and partner of the house of Burtis, Jones & co. of New York...

Issue December 17, 1856
On Saturday night last about 9 o'clock, a man by the name of Stafford killed his companion by the name of Beasely at the house of Randolph Walker, five miles from Bastrop, by stabbing him in the left side... [note: condensed].

Tribute of Respect for Hon. Abner S. Lipscomb. [note: tribute of respect also in issue December 30, 1856].

Issue December 30, 1856
William L. Gresham, the subject of this brief sketch, was born in the state of Georgia on the 29th of June 1819, and died of consumption, after an illness of nearly 13 years, on the 18th of December 1856, near Washington, Texas. Associated with Presbyterian church; left aged father.

Issue January 13, 1857
It is our painful duty to announce the death of our late talented and excellent fellow citizen, James R. Jenkins. Mr. Jenkins has been for twenty years a brilliant member of the Washington Bar. Died at his residence, near Independence.

Miss Anna M. Lachause, daughter of Jas. M. Lachause of New York, died on board the *Arago* on the 3rd ult. after a short illness.

Issue January 20, 1857

We regret to learn of the death of our esteemed fellow citizen, Alfred McMillan. Mr. McMillan has been suffering for some time from a lingering illness.

Issue January 27, 1857

James R. Jenkins departed this life at his residence near Independence at 4 o'clock A.M. on Monday, January 5, 1857. Aged 46 years. The deceased was a son of a revolutionary officer, Capt. Jenkins, and was born in Green county, Georgia. He embraced religion early in life, and became an active member of the Baptist church. He was educated at Mercer University, at Penfield, Georgia, during the Presidency of that great and good man B.M. Sanders... Mr. Jenkins studied law in LaGrange, under Gen. Haraldson and in the fall of 1836 he emigrated to Texas, and in the spring of 1837, settled in Washington, and commenced the practice of law in partnership with his friend George W. Horton from the same state...

Died at Orange Springs, [F]lorida, in the 34th year of his age, the Rev. J.B. Stitler, former pastor of the Baptist church, in this place. Mr. Stitler met death on the 25th of December last...

Issue February 3, 1857

It was our melancholy task in the last number of our paper to announce the death of the Rev. J.B. Stiteler, who departed this life, in Florida on the 25th day of December last, in the 32nd year of his age. Symptoms of consumption. Declining health drove him from Texas. At the time of his death Mr. Stiteler was a citizen of Savannah, Georgia, and had left that city temporarily in search of health... For several years preceding his death, he was the pastor of the Baptist church at this place... He was also at the time Professor of Natural Sciences in Baylor University... He left behind him a wife and three infant children...

Issue February 24, 1857

The *Victoria Advocate* of the 7th inst. says: A friend writes to us that B. Brooking was shot by John Wardick at Goliad on Monday the 2nd inst. and was killed instantly. Brooking leaves a wife and several interesting children.

Issue March 24, 1857

At Hallettsville recently, R. Kelly received several stabs, inflicted by Newton Hicks, who fled and was arrested. The wounds, though severe, were thought not to be mortal.

Died at his residence near Washington on the night of the 17th inst., Col. Leonidas B. Aldridge, in the 44th year of his age. Col. Aldridge was a native of Green county, North Carolina. In 1828, he, together with his mother, emigrated to Tipton county, Tennessee, where he continued to reside until 1850, when he removed to this place, where he resided till his death. He leaves a wife and seven children. *Memphis Eagle & Enquirer* please copy.

Dr. Christopher Columbus Jones was killed last Saturday. Mr. Jones was a preacher and had abducted off the wife of Mr. Sherrel... Mr. Bell, a brother of his wife, started to Clarksville to get there before Jones and his sister should leave. He found them at the hotel where she was stopping. Mr. Bell... shot him through the heart.

Issue April 7, 1857
The *Rusk Enquirer* notices the murder of a man named Findley by Mr. Rainwater on the 14th ult.

Suicide: The *Telegraph* notes the suicide of Mr. B. Love of Washington county recently in Houston. He appears to have been delirious from illness.

Issue April 14, 1857
From the *True Issue* we learn of a most brutal assault upon the person of three unprotected females: Mrs. W.H. Mathews and daughters. The incarnate fiend, one Edmond Raymond, making his escape.

Issue April 28, 1857
We regret to learn of the death of James Irvin of Bellville, Austin county. It appears that he fell from the upper deck of a steamer ascending the Mississippi, and is supposed to have been struck by the wheel.

Issue May 12, 1857
The *Galveston Herald* of Wednesday morning, May 6th, has the following: On Monday evening, the son of Mr. Wm. Hudson, an interesting boy of 6 years, was playing about the cistern, and it is thought that in raising the lid he fell in and was drowned...

The same paper says, "We are sorry to hear that an accident occurred to a little daughter of Mr. Daniel Phillips yesterday afternoon, about sun-set. She was playing near Mr. Kauffman's new building, where carpenters were at work, when it is supposed that a block fell from the scaffold, struck her on the head, and prostrated her. It is feared she will die."

145

Issue June 30, 1857

Mr. Wm. Skailes, second clerk of Gen. Rusk, was drowned at Brazos Santiago, on the 22nd. He was bathing in shallow water and is supposed to have taken a fit.

Issue August 4, 1857

Nacogdoches Chronicle of the 30th July, 1857: A great calamity has befallen the state of Texas. One of her most distinguished and noble sons has fallen. Thomas J. Rusk is no more. The cause of death was a gun shot (rifle) wound on the fore part of the head, inflicted from a rifle gun held in his own hands and discharged by himself...

TEXAS RANGER
Also known as **LONE STAR AND TEXAS RANGER**; and
TEXAS RANGER AND LONE STAR
Published at Washington, Texas.

Issue October 6, 1852

TRIBUTE OF RESPECT: Dr. John Ellis departed this life a few weeks since, of congestive fever, at his home in Burleson county, Texas, in the 39th year of his age... We learn from our friend, Judge J.G. Thomas, that the deceased was born in North Alabama, and attached himself to the Presbyterian church when quite a boy, of which church he had ever been a consistent member. We became acquainted with Dr. Ellis in 1842 in the county of Chickasaw, Mississippi, where he became our family physician. He it was, who stood by us at the marriage alter; he it was, who met us again in Texas after a separation of years and attended the birth of a daughter and he it was, who near three years after, saw that darling child close its eyes in death, and conveyed it to the tomb. He then returned to his home in Burleson county, assuring us that he would return to Washington in three weeks, but ere that time elapsed, his spirit had taken flight to another and happier world... Aberdeen, Houston and Columbus, Mississippi papers, also North Alabama, are requested by the friends of Dr. Ellis to give the above an insertion in their respective journals. Leaves a widowed aunt, brother, nephew, nieces.

Issue March 25, 1853

Tribute of respect: At a regular communication of Murchison Chapter Mason #18, Brenham, held in the chapter room in the town of LaGrange, December 11, 1852... [note: gives a report on the death of fellow member General J.S. Mayfield].

Died on Sunday, M. Emma, daughter of Wm. T. Austin of this place, after a short illness.

Issue April 1, 1853

Mr. William Muldrew of Grimes county was assassinated on the evening of the 28th ult. The deceased was undressing to retire for the night when he was shot through a window by someone as yet unknown.

The Masonic Fraternity will on the 29th raise and reintern the remains of their deceased brother Rev. Martin Kuter/Kutor/Ruter/Rutor.

Issue May 26, 1853

Bill Fitzgerld (says the *Texan*) who has made himself quite notorious in San Antonio, in times gone by, committed a cowardly and brutal murder on Wiley Robinson at Eagle Pass and then fled to the river and crossed into Mexico...

On the 26th ultimo, Col. James Torrey, living a few miles west of Lexington, Mississippi, was shot by his son-in-law, Mr. Fletcher Harrington... A dispatch to the *Carrollton Flag* states that Torrey was about to stab his wife, when Harrington interfered. Torrey turned on him with his knife when the latter shot him.

Issue June 2, 1853

MEMPHIS EAGLE & ENQUIRER, 13th ult: We regret to learn that a difficulty occurred on Wednesday evening last at A.T. Well's store on Main St. between John F. Sale and Mr. Thomas A. Fisher, both of this city, in which the former received a pistol wound in his knee. Mr. Sale had previously assaulted Mr. Fisher with a stick...

Issue June 9, 1853

A man by the name of Robinson, formerly of Memphis but now residing in the vicinity of Hernando in this State, shot his own daughter on the 11th inst. He was said to be a drinking, worthless character; had previously separated from his wife, who likewise drank... Wife had property. Robinson sold negro belonging to child. She died the next morning. [note: condensed]. *Holly Springs Miss. Times.*

Mr. Editor: It becomes my painful duty to announce the death of our much esteemed friend Joseph D. McCutchan, who departed this life April 30th, 1853, in the 30th year of his age; leaving a wife, a little boy, and a numerous circle of friends... He embraced religion in Carroll county, Mississippi, in 1839, and attached himself to the Presbyterian church... The subject of this imperfect memoir was born in Wilson county, Tennessee, July 18th, 1823, and emigrated to Texas, in company with his brother, in January 1841. Soon after his arrival into this, then young, Republic he entered her ranks as a soldier and was ever ready to defend her rights. He was one of the unfortunate company, who at the battle of Mier, fell into the hands of that monster of tyranny, Santa Anna... M. Yell.

We notice, a few days ago, in some paper, we forget which, that Blake Thompson, who murdered Finnin in Austin last year, had gotten into a difficulty in Arkansas, recently, and was killed...

Issue June 16, 1853

Trial of John A.J. Hamilton for murder; appearance of the prisoner, legal sparring, fatal effects of intemperance &c:

Thursday, May 26th, 1853: After the usual preliminaries, the District Court, this morning took up the case of the State vs. J.A.J. Hamilton charged with the murder of Dr. Edwards Ragland, both of Victoria county, where the offence is charged to have been committed. The accused appeared in court dressed in a blood-red hunting shirt, with two pistols, and (or what appeared to be) a bowie knife, under the shirt, attached to a belt buckled around his person. He appeared to be about 35 years of age, six feet in height, narrow head, high forehead, a milky blue eye, the lower part of his face, covered with a course thick beard, extending from a line drawn horizontally from the top of the upper lip round to the ears, down to as far as the eye of the observer could perceive... [note: condensed].

Another murderous tragedy in County. A gun-smith, a German named Malitz, had his house broken open and robbed on Saturday night last by two persons supposed to be deserters. Malitz pursued them and is supposed to have been murdered by them... *Victoria Advocate.*

Issue June 23, 1853

The death of Major George Sutherlan of Jackson county is announced in the *Indianola Bulletin*. He came to Texas from Alabama in 1829; was at the storming of San Antonio in 1835; at San Jacinto. Represented Jackson county in 1837 and also in 1843-44.

[The Texas Ranger becomes the]
TEXAS RANGER AND LONE STAR

Issue July 14, 1853

We regret to learn that the difficulty heretofore existing between Jas. P. Johnston, county clerk of Burleson county, and Capt. Snell, postmaster at Caldwell, has terminated by the death of Mr. Johnston. The parties are said to have met on the public square at Caldwell, with double barrell shot guns, and Mr. J. was killed on the first fire by Capt. Snell.

Obituary on the death of Mr. John Allcorn. Another old Texian has fallen; and after the dangers and hardships of nearly 30 years on the frontier, he quietly sleeps in the bosom of our mother earth. Our deceased friend was the son of Elijah and Nancy Allcorn, and was born in Franklin county, Georgia, May 20, 1799. He emigrated to Texas as with his parents in 1822, when the fair land was under the nominal dominions of Priest ridden Mexico, but under the real dominion of the prowling wolf and the roaming Comanche. He died of typhoid fever on the 7th of June, 1853, after a painful illness of 22 days. He was a devoted Baptist and a Royal Arch Mason...

His funeral sermon was preached by the Rev. Rufus C. Burleson, at his residence, after which his corpse was carried to the family burying ground near Jefferson Allcorn's, and buried with Masonic honors. Joined Baptist Church. Wife and child.

Died on the 4 inst. by the accidental discharge of a gun, Albert Yerger Upshaw, son of Col. A.M.M. Upshaw of Washington county, aged 17 years, 8 months, 22 days.

Died at her residence in Austin county, Texas, on 1st July, Nancy Black, daughter of Gregor McGregor of Argyle, Scotland, aged 60. Emigrated to North Carolina in 1841 where she has three brothers living. In Texas past three years.

[The Texas Ranger and Lone Star becomes the]
LONE STAR AND TEXAS RANGER

Issue July 23, 1853

Died on the 12th inst. at the residence of her father in Austin county near Rock Island, Texas, Miss Jane J. Shaw, daughter of Wm. C. and Elizabeth Shaw, deceased, aged 15 years, 10 months and 16 days. She has left a fond stepmother, kind sisters and brothers, who deeply lament her loss... Rock Island, July 15, 1853.

The *Indianola Bulletin* announces the sudden melancholy death of Charles J. Mitchell, late editor of the *Victoria Advocate*, occasioned by injuries received from jumping off a wharf while bathing at Lavaca, 28th ult.

In our last paper we stated that James P. Johnson of Caldwell was killed in a street fight by Capt. Snell. Not the case. Friends interference prevented serious consequences.

Issue August 20, 1853

A gentleman recently from the upper Brazos informs us that at Moseley's Landing in Burleson county, a man by the name of Brazle was killed a few days since by a Mr. Smith. It seems that the deputy Sheriff was endeavoring to arrest a Dr. Lucky, who was secreted at the house of Brazle. Brazle endeavored to shoot the officer, when Mr. Smith, who had been summoned to assist in the arrest, fired upon and killed him.

Issue September 3, 1853

Another "Ranger" Gone. Died at the residence of Hon. R.E.B. Baylor, in Washington county, on the 4 August, Dr. Henry W. Baylor, aged 30 years.

A native of Kentucky and emigrated to Texas in 1840, since which he has been actively engaged in the border warfare upon our Western frontier. As a youth he was with Col. J.H. Moore in his campaign against the Comanches in 1840. He died suddenly of congestion of brain... For the last four years he never retired at night without reading a chapter in the Bible. Leaves a wife and interesting and beautiful little daughter.

Issue September 10, 1853

Died at the residence of Capt. S. Duty in Burleson county on the 10th ult., Dr. Henry S. Munson, aged 40 years. Dr. M. emigrated to Texas in 1836 and was with her time of darkness and troubles.

An affray resulting in the death of a man named Harris happened at Seguin some time last week... It appears Harris and Roberson had gambled and both attempted to draw weapons, but were prevented from using them. Afterwards Roberson shot at Harris from behind the house but missed; Roberson then ran into the tavern and snapped at him with a double-barrel shot gun. Harris attempting all the time to evade him, Roberson then snatched a bowie-knife from a bystander and rushed upon him inflicting five wounds, either one of which would have killed. Harris's pistol was not in a condition to be used, and of this fact it is said Roberson was aware. *Bastrop Advertiser.*

Issue October 1, 1853

Mr. Harry R.W. Hill, whose death we mentioned in our last paper, was Grand Master of the G. Lodge of Masons of Louisiana...

On last Saturday, Mr. Jacob Haller died at Chappel Hill of yellow fever contracted at Houston. On the following Monday, Mr. E.W. Nichols, clerk of Mr. Kavanaugh, died at the same place of the same disease...

Pro. Ruter of Chappell Hill College died of yellow fever at Galveston on the 16th...

Miscellaneous Texas Newspaper Abstracts - Deaths — Vol 2

Issue October 8, 1853

Died of yellow fever, 16 September, at residence of her uncle, Rev. Charles Gillette in Anderson, Grimes county, Miss Ellen M. Gillette of Granby, Hartford county, Conn., aged 17. Her illness was contracted while passing through Houston...

Died in LaGrange, 4 inst., of inflammation of the brain, William Brown, infant son of Samuel H. and Mary L. Summers; age five months.

Issue October 15, 1853

Probable fatal rencountre: We learn from a friend in yesterday from Marshall that a dispute arose opposite the court house in that place between Mr. Coburn, an elderly gentleman, and a Mr. Hide, a young lawyer, touching the merits of candidates for election to the legislature. The latter gentleman, having over indulged in the mantling glass at the height of his excitement, drew a "derringer" and discharged it at Mr. Coburn. Before the friends of the parties could intercede, Mr. C. drew from his side pocket a bowie knife and inflicted several wounds upon Mr. H., from the effects of which he is not expected to recover.

San Augustine Herald: We learn that the bodies of two men, a Mr. Dickerson and his son, residing in the southern part of this county, were found in the road on the 23rd ultimo, pierced with buckshot... It is supposed they were waylaid. They left families with several children.

Tribute of Respect. Masons. P.S. Ruter.

The recent killing of Major Arnold of the second dragoons by assistant surgeon Steiner: We have a history of this horrible affair by a private letter direct from Fort Graham, Texas, where it occurred. It seems that Dr. Steiner and Lt. Bingham, from drinking, fell to quarrelling, so disturbing the garrison as to compel the commander, Major Arnold, to go to them and order them to their respective quarters. Steiner then told A. that if he placed him under arrest he would kill him. This threat being taken as a mere ebullition of passion Arnold took no notice of it, and the quarrellers went to their respective quarters. On the next day, when they had time to cool their passions, Arnold sent the Adjutant of the post with an order to arrest both. They were found at Lieut. Bingham's quarters, apparently about to renew the quarrel. Steiner, on reading the order for his arrest gave himself up, and again remarked that he would kill any man who should arrest him, and desired to see Arnold. The Adjutant advised him not to go over to A's quarters, least he might commit himself by using violent and insubordinate language. But he persisted in going there. In a few moments the Adjutant heard pistol shots there (six), and rushing over, found Arnold laying weltering in blood in the passage between his two rooms...

Died on the 1st/12th inst. at the residence of Samuel [?], near Independence, Earl [?], oldest son of George William & Elizabeth <u>Chapman</u>, late of Quincy, IL. On the 8th inst., Imogene Norwoode, infant daughter of Henry E. and Catherine J. Lockett, of this place.

Died near Independence, Earl <u>Chapman</u>, oldest son of George Wm. and Elizabeth Chapman, late of Quincy, Ill.

Issue October 22, 1853

From Mississippi: *Jackson Mississippian* of the 7th inst: Mr. Levi Wheeler of this city was stabbed mortally on Tuesday evening last by Mr. C.E. Cline, one of the attendants sent here with the physicians from New Orleans by the Howard Association...

Died on the 13th inst. at his late residence near Chapel Hill, Mr. William H.[?] Slaughter, aged 34 years. The deceased was a native of Kentucky... The victim of a slow lingering death (pulmonary consumption). He was fully aware of his apparent end... *Hopkinsville Press* please copy.

Died 14th inst. at his late residence in this county near Warren, Major James H. Cocke, 56 years old. Employed by War Department at Washington for a number of years. Marshall city of Mobile, Collector of the Port of Galveston and lastly Marshall of the State of Texas... He died after a short illness of congestive chills.

Issue November 5, 1853

Died at Goliad, 21st, Josephine Helen, daughter of Percy and Ann Howe, late of Gainsville, MS.

Issue December 15, 1853

W.R. O'Neal was shot by some men named of Buck near Buckville in Carroll county, Mississippi, on the 8th.

Died of consumption on the 18th of November, 1853, Mrs. Sarah Jane, wife of Mr. Orlando Harris... She was the daughter of Anne and Joseph Banner. She was a native of South Carolina, and obtained her education chiefly in the female department of Baylor University... She was gifted in painting and poetry. Independence.

Died at his residence in Grimes county, Texas, on Monday the 14th November of yellow fever, our beloved brother, John H. Dunham, in the 26th year of his age, he was born in Tennessee, 19th September, A.D. 1828, and emigrated to this country at an early day with the family of Dunhams... Mason. He leaves an afflicted wife and two tender little children...

Dr. L/J. B. Miller, formerly Secretary of the Treasury of the Republic of Texas and one of the oldest settlers of Austin colony, died recently near Richmond, on the Brazos of yellow fever.

L.B. Harper died on the 11/14 inst. at the residence of his father, Capt. Richard Harper, near this place. He was formerly from near Memphis, Tenn.

Issue December 29, 1853
The *Cassville (Georgia) Standard,* records a horrible suicide, committed in that place on the 19th ult. The unfortunate man, Jeremiah <u>King</u>, by name, was from Charleston...

Issue January 5, 1854
A man named Spotts was killed accidently (report says) in Anderson, Grimes county, last week, by a man named Barker. The deceased formerly lived at Gate's steam mill in this county. He leaves a wife and two or three children.

Issue February 16, 1854
The *Lynchburg* (Virginia) *Express* states that a young man named Cocke was arrested in Richmond a few days ago, who in 1851 shot a young man named Wm. B. Sanderson at Holly Springs, Mississippi. [note: condensed].

The *Savannah Evening Post* of the 26th gives an account of a horrible suicide committed in Cassville by a Mr. <u>King</u>...

Issue February 23, 1854
Died at the residence of Daniel Meador, two miles south of Washington, Washington county, Texas, on the 14th of February of consumption, Charles B. Salmon of Steubenville, Jefferson county, Ohio, in the 22 year of his age.

Died at the residence of Doc'r J.B. Robertson in Independence, Washington county, Texas, on the morning of the 30th of January, 1854, Mrs. Amelia Ruth Morgan, consort of Dempsey A. Morgan, of Burleson county, in the 22nd year of her age. The subject of this brief notice was born on the 7th day of December 1832, in Davies county, Kentucky, emigrated with her father's family to Texas, in the fall of 1837, and settled in Burleson county, where the family lived, (encountering all the hardships and inconveniences of a new country) until the spring of 1844, when she was deprived of her dearest earthly friend by the death of her mother... Married to D.A. Morgan (late of Edgefield District, South Carolina) in December 1852. Her last illness was long and intense.

Issue March 2, 1854

Departed this life on Thursday the 23rd inst. at 5 o'clock A.M. in this place, at the residence of his brother, Hardin White, after a lingering illness, Anderson White, aged 35 years, 4 months. The subject of this sketch was born in Bledsoe county, Tennessee, on the 11th of November 1819, and in 1840 immigrated to this place from Alabama...

Issue March 9, 1854

A murder was committed in Grayson county on the 10th ult. A man named Davis left the village of Kentucky Town, on horseback, with three others, one named Umphries, the two others Jamieson, in a wagon. They had all been drinking. A difficulty occurred on the way, and the three attacked Davis... *Seguin Mercury.*

From the *Leon Pioneer* of the 1st inst., we understand that Mr. E.T. Robinson, of this place, was shot at Madisonville, Madison county, on Monday evening (27th ult.) and dangerously, if not fatally, wounded. He was shot by a Mr. McIver of that county, who, also, had his arm broken.

Issue March 30, 1854

From the *San Antonio Ledger.* Mrs. Wall, wife of a soldier who went with Messrs. J.R. Sweet & co's El Paso train, was killed by indians at the Spring near the first crossing of the Limpa... Wall and his wife and child had strolled off a short distance from the train when they were suddenly surrounded by Indians... The Indians shot and scalped her...

Died on the 11th instant at Chappell Hill, Texas, Mrs. Mary Ann Tunstall, wife of Dr. W.L. Tunstall, in the 29th year of her age.

Died on the 14th inst., Thomas George, son of Dr. W.L. Tunstall and Mrs. Mary Ann Tunstall, deceased, two days after the death of his mother, aged 2 years and 5 months.

We are pained to announce that a German named Wilhelm Bower was killed at the Railroad house on the Cypress on Sunday by Mr. John Boon...

A man named Augustus Wilbar, residing in West Randolph, killed his wife on the morning of the 22nd ult. by beating out her brains with an axe. He then cut his own throat from ear to ear. Seven children are left parentless by this shocking tragedy.

Issue April 6, 1854

P.S. we stop the press to announce with regret, the killing of E.J. Hendrick, of Grimes county, who was shot down in our [?], this afternoon, by G.W. McLees. McLees assigns as a reason for killing Hendrick that deceased had threatened his life.

Another Revolution Patriot Gone. There died on 22d February 1854 in county of Goochland near Powell's Tavern, an old man 92, James Gray. He had all his faculties of mind in a perfect state. Member of Methodist church. [note: condensed].

Issue April 27, 1854

We understand that Dr. Hamilton G. Graves, living in the north-east corner of Cherokee county, while on his road home on the first of April, was waylaid and killed; having been shot in the back.

We glean the following particulars of this inhuman massacre from the *Western Texan*, published at San Antonio, of the 20th inst. The blood must boil with revenge on perusal of the article. We have just listened to one of the most heart rending recitals that it has ever been our painful duty to hear or read. On yesterday, April 16th, Mr. James Forester and family consisting of his wife and four children were enjoying the Sabbath day in their humble cottage which is situated in this county, and about 18 miles north west from San Antonio, and also accompanying them was a neighbor, who was a single man and whose residence was only a mile distance, when on a sudden a cow made her appearance, and from the actions of the cow they concluded that all was not right. Upon examining her they found that she had been shot with several arrows, and fearing that indians might be near, the single man proposed to return to his house and bring over his most costly effects to the residence of Mr. Forester. He accordingly left for this purpose, but had not been gone but a few minutes when three indians made their appearance at the door, well armed with rifles, knives, etc., and demanded something to eat.

Mr. Forester proceeded to comply with their demand, and had hardly turned, when one of the indians shot him through the heart, he fell dead without hardly a struggle, the blood gushing through the wound and also his mouth and nose. The mother with her child in her arms, two years and a half old, sprang to the door, but before she could escape, she was knocked down with a gun, receiving a blow on the back of her head, and they supposing her dead, commenced their other depredations, she immediately sprang out of the door without her child, and started for the bushes which were near by. As she turned the corner of the house, she was met by one of her children a girl about 12 years old, who had been to play near by, and attracted by the noise, was coming to the house, she screamed to the girl to run, and the child being frightened, instead of fleeing, ran immediately into the house, and the mother secreted herself in the bushes. She had hardly secured herself, when the dreadful cries of her four little children at the house, and actuated by those feelings known only to a fond and devoted mother when her children are in such an awful situation, she thoughtless of danger, rushed to the house and coming to the back part where she could look through, she saw a sight too horrible to relate.

One of the savages had her oldest daughter, a girl of 14 years of age, by the hair of her head, here the poor woman commenced wringing her hands and wailing she could not relate what followed, it was too horrible, and God grant that we may not be pained to hear such another tragedy related, and too, by a mother about her children. Seeing there was no hope of saving her family she fled and arrived in San Antonio this morning...

Issue May 4, 1854

Wm. H. Cleveland, son of Capt. J.T. Cleveland, was shot down in the streets of Austin by George J. Durham, and instantly expired. Mr. Cleveland made an attack on Mr. D. with a walking cane, which led to the killing.

Issue May 11, 1854

Noah Cheek departed this life at his residence of consumption in Washington county, near the town of Washington, on 26/28 April 1854, 35 years, 10 months, 6 days. Born in Laurens District South Carolina, moved to Ala, Lownds county, with his father, Randol Cheek, at about the age of 17. In 1840, came to Texas. 29 April 1847 married Evaline Baldridge. Left wife and two little sons. He was confined to bed about 3 months...

Issue May 25, 1854

The *Gazette* says that last week a man named William Dummitt was killed near Belton by John Bowls... The parties had a misunderstanding in Belton that evening and Bowls had returned home; and as Dummitt was also passing home by the house of B., the latter came out and shot him. Bowls fled and was at large...

On Monday the 15th inst., a man named Isaac Hogan was killed at Moseley's ferry, in Burleson county, by Dr. Marcellus Harris.

Tribute of respect from Milam Lodge #11 in the death of Thomas W. Blakey.

The Frequency of Homicides. A few days ago a man named Odum deliberately shot down an unarmed German named Suhr residing on Buffalo Bayou.

A rencounter between Absolom Reed and John Heran took place at the Harrisburg Railroad depot which resulted in the death of the former.

Virgil A. Steward, who captured the notorious Murrell, died on the 6th inst. at his residence in Wharton county, Texas.

Issue June 1, 1854
Last week at Vine Grove Post Office in this county, Jas. Holt, postmaster, was killed by a man named Forrest who had been employed as a stage driver on the route...

Issue June 8, 1854
Mike Finnin murdered: Nearly everybody about Washington have heard of Mike Finnin, the sportsman. We regret to say that he has been most brutally and fiendishly murdered by a Col. Bunch, who we learn is a desperate and reckless man; but too great a coward to meet Mike face to face. He was assassinated at Aberdeen, Mississippi, on the 12th of May...

The funeral sermon of Mr. Noah Cheek will be preached in the Methodist church in this place on next Sabbath by Rev. Rufus C. Burleson of Baylor University.

Issue June 15, 1854
Death of Capt. Wm. Wood: This gentleman, one of the officers commanding a company at the battle of San Jacinto, died this morning at the Pierce House... His remains will go down to the battle ground. *Houston Telegraph.*

Issue June 22, 1854
From the *Central Texan* of June 17th: We regret to learn that Mr. M.P. Mize was killed at Weaver's Store, in the lower part of this county, by Edward Howel on Wednesday evening last...

Issue June 29, 1854
Died on Monday the 26th inst. of pulmonary consumption, Horace B. Hurlburt, aged 36 years... To the grave by the masonic fraternity. San Augustine & Nacogdoches papers please copy.

We learn from the *Houston Mississippi Argus* of the 24th ult. that Mr. Roy Chandler of Chickasaw was lately thrown from his horse and the injuries were so severe as to cause his death...

A most horrid murder was committed at Ft. Graham, in Hill county, about the 8th inst. Munroe Black, it is said, shot a man, by the name of Barns, through the head. [note: condensed].

Issue July 13, 1854

We learn that Black, the murderer that robbed Thos. Harrison near Ft. Graham, and escaped has been overtaken. He was shot down and died immediately.

Issue July 20, 1854

Died near Chappell Hill, Texas, at 4 o'clock P.M. on the 12th July, Mrs. Caroline Elizabeth Flewellen, consort of Doct. R.T. Flewellen, aged 23 years and 25 days. Texas & Georgia papers please copy.

Tribute of Respect from Chappell Hill on the death of D.B. Carson, who died 30 ult. Masonic condolence.

On the San Marcos river at Duncan's ferry, John Duncan was shot by T.D. Netherly.

In our last weeks issue we stated that Thos. Harrison died at Marlin. We are pleased to learn from a gentleman from Springfield that Mr. Harrison is not dead but alive and kicking.

A.M. Graham, living on the Medina River 15 miles from San Antonio, was killed on the 10th by three Mexicans because he tried to prevent them from cutting timber on his own land.

Thomas Ritchie, respected editor, died in Washington City, 3 July. Established *Richmond Enquirer* in 1804...

Issue July 27, 1854

We learn from Antonio Rivers that James Wiseman was killed at Madisonville on Monday evening last by a man of the name of Nash...

Issue August 3, 1854

On the 22nd inst., Joseph Bates of Montgomery county killed Stock Davis at Houston...

Maj. Houston of Cuero was shot dead at that town by M.G. Jacobs.

Conrad Frillman, a dissipated German, killed a man recently at Port Lavaca, named Wingate or Shawnee Bill.

Mason Tribute of respect for Wm. C. Gould, who died on the 19th inst...

Issue August 10, 1854

We are deeply pained to learn from the *Clarksville Standard* of the 8th inst., that a most horrid and heart rending murder was committed in that place on the 2nd inst. It appears that Mr. Charles H. Peabody, an honest, intelligent and inoffensive citizen of Clarksville had recently been guilty of some slight indiscretions at the house of one Husbands and his son-in-law, Weston...

Affairs stood thus until on Sunday evening the 2nd inst., as Mr. Peabody was passing the house of Husbands and Weston, he was set upon by several armed men, fired upon with a pistol, and knocked down with brick-bats, and then attempting to escape from his numerous assailants, was caught and held down by the hair of the head by Husbands, and whilst in this position, totally unarmed and helpless, Weston advanced upon him with a drawn pistol and putting it within a few inches of his (Peabody's) back fired, the ball ranging downwards towards the heart. The unfortunate man breathed his last within five minutes afterwards, with the single exclamation "Oh, God I am a dead man"...

Tribute of Respect. Washington Lodge #18 Masonic. W.C. Gould died Wednesday morning, 18th inst.

Tribute of Respect. Washington Lodge #18 Masonic. H.B. Hurlbert died 26 Jan 1854.

Issue August 17, 1854

We regret to see by the *Huntsville Item* that Ann, daughter of the late Dr. Goree, and wife of Mr. Barclay, died in that place on the 4th inst.

Died in this place at the residence of Mr. B.B. Baxter on the night of the 10th inst., Mrs. Sarah Perdue, in the 64th year of her age.

Departed this life in the vicinity of this place on the 19th ult., Capt. Wm. C. Gould, of dropsy and disease of the throat, in the 41st year of his age... was a native of Baltimore and for the last 13 years a resident of this State, the latter part of which he was engaged in the mercantile business in this place... He leaves an only daughter, father, mother, sisters and brothers... Remains conveyed to tomb by the Masons in Galveston by his wife.

G. Jacobs, who killed Maj. Robt. B. Houston in DeWitt county on the 15th ult., was arrested 8 miles below this place on Saturday.

Issue August 24, 1854

Died on the 19th of August, 1854, at the residence of his brother, Mr. Newton Mays, near Belton, Bell county, John K. Mays, in the 23rd year of his age, from contagion of the brain. The deceased, who lived for a short period amongst us, was a native of Alabama, from whence he emigrated last winter to Texas to seek a home on our bountiful soil... was a member of the Presbyterian Church.

Departed this life Sunday morning, August 6th, Mattie M., infant daughter of W.P. and M.L. Rogers, aged 8 months and 13 days.

Issue September 8, 1854
Tribute of respect. Baylor Lodge #125 Masons on the death of Patrick Gorman...

Issue September 15, 1854
From the *Gonzales Enquirer*: We earn that a rencontre took place between Mr. Augustus Hemphill and Mr. O.H. Ship of this county on the [?] ult. Mr. Hemphill was dangerously, it is feared fatally injured...

Issue September 21, 1854
From the *Telegraph*: W.H. Harrison was arrested yesterday and examined before magistrates for stabbing, with a bowie-knife, with intent to kill, an Italian named John Arto, who keeps an oyster saloon near the Houston House...

On yesterday, about 9 o'clock, a fatal rencontre took place between Mr. George P. Finlay, editor of the *LaVaca Register* and Mr. Henry Jordan, commission merchant of this place, which resulted in the death of the latter by being shot with a double-barrel shot gun and a revolver in the hands of Finlay...

Issue October 5, 1854
Effects of the storm: At Lynchburg and San Jacinto, at the head of Galveston Bay, the *Houston Star* says the water spread over the flats, from Colonel Washington's to Judge Burnett's place and on the San Jacinto side to the high lands near the Battle Ground. During the storm on Tuesday night, the dwelling house of Mr. Depperman, a clerk of Col. Washington's, was blown over and carried off with the current, and the entire family, consisting of Mr. and Mrs. Depperman and their two children, were drowned. Great damage was done to property in the vicinity. The two-story dwelling of I.W. Brashear, on the Battle Ground, was blown down, and the occupants, Mr. and Mrs. Coleman, were injured. The warehouse of Mr. Hiram Brown, on the wharf at San Jacinto, was blown over; Mr. Brown's house, on Brown's Island, was blown over; one side of the ways of Hand & Millar's ship-yard was carried away...

At San Louis Island, the house of Capt. Burr was blown down and a number of cattle drowned. The house of Mrs. Follet, on the peninsula west of Galveston Bay, was a good deal injured.

The town of Valasco and Quintana, at the mouth of the Brazos, suffered a good deal, particularly Quintana, where we learn the store of Capt. R. Brown was blown down, and its contents greatly injured. A good deal other damage is reported to have taken place.

Matagorda is in ruins: Our correspondent says, but two houses are left standing, those of Col. Williams and Mrs. Sartwell. He gives the following particulars: The steamboat *Kate Ward* was lost and Capt. Wm. J. Ward, his two brothers, and nine of the crew drowned. The new steamboat *Colorado*, nearly finished, is 300 yards from water now. The schooner *Tom Payne* wrecked and Captain (Frank Hulsman) drowned. Four lives were lost in the town, Mrs. Duffy, Mr. Merryman, and a negro woman and child...

Issue October 12, 1854
We regret to learn that Maj. Thomas J. Smith, an old citizen who resides at Austin, was killed at Brenham on Monday by Thos. Cooper, who has escaped. Smith was one of the Mier prisoners.

Issue October 19, 1854
A few weeks since, Ashton Hazelrigg shot Mr. Easley in the head with a pistol in Morgan county, Kentucky. Easley died on the spot... now one of them is "food for worms and the other a candidate for the gallows."

Issue November 9, 1854
We regret to announce the death of Mr. P.P. Brown, a citizen of this place. He left here about three weeks since with a party consisting of his two little sons and two other persons to visit the Guadalupe country.

Issue November 18, 1854
Died in this town at the residence of Mrs. George, Miss Priscilla A. George, of Sumpter county, Alabama, in the 21st year of her age..

Also on the 13th, Mrs. Mary C., wife of Capt. B.M. Hatfield.

Great Excitement in Navarro county, a man hung: The following statement of this tragedy we gather from the *Leon Pioneer*. From Mr. Wm. Lockhart, just from Navarro, we learn that Gillilan was the principal witness against Wells, and not Morgan, as stated in the following article:

We mention on last week that considerable excitement existed in Navarro county, in consequence of the supposed thief of two negro men belonging to Col. Elliot of that county, and that parties in the neighborhood, one at least, had been arrested under suspicion of being guilty, but had escaped.

From Mr. John T. Grisham of this county, who has just arrived from the neighborhood of Elliot's, we learn the following further particulars:

It seems that soon after the negroes were missing, that circumstances transpired which induced Elliott and some of his neighbors to suspicion two men who were in his employ of being concerned in the thief. The circumstances that led to the suspicion of these men seem to have transpired through a cook of Elliott's, the mother of the negro boys, who told that the boys had been persuaded off by these men, with the understanding that they were to be sold and restolen for two or three times, and finally to be carried to Mexico, where they could be free. A third party, who is now at large with the negroes, it seems was to do the running and selling, and afterwards to return and divide proceeds with the other two. The plan to prevent detection was, to black the negroes, they being very bright mulattoes.

On the strength of this, one of the men in the employ of Elliott was arrested by a posse of the citizens, and was induced to make a confession corroborating, in every particulars just related. He stated further, that he and the other man, Wells, had become uneasy about the matter, and had resolved to murder Col. Elliott. The plan was for him to decoy Elliott into the bottom, where they were getting timber, under the pretence of showing them where the lines ran, for fear that they would trespass on land that did not belong to him, and that Wells was to shoot him from ambush. Elliott corroborates that statement, and says he refused to go on account of suspicion of foul play, knowing at the time the men knew the lines of his land better than he did.

After getting this confession, search was immediately made by various parties for Wells but without, it was said, succeeding in arresting him. On Friday the 27th ult., his body was found in Chamber's creek, by some persons who were engaged in building a bridge, and who were hunting oxen at the time, and were attracted to the spot by a gang of buzzards. When found he was floating near the surface of the water, between a forked limb, which had to all appearances been placed over him for the purpose of holding the body to the bottom. Around his neck was the print of a rope. His abdomen had been ripped open and his bowels torn out, thus leaving little doubt but he was hanged, afterwards his body thrown in the creek for concealment. The body, from appearances, had been in the creek but a short time, probably fourteen or twenty hours.

The parties, or some of them, engaged in the search for Wells, are suspicioned of the murder, and their lives are threatened. One or two of them have gone to Corsicana and demanded a trial, alleging their innocence. When our informant left, the greatest excitement prevailed, and it was feared that bloodshed would ensue. By the hand of Dr. Carter we have received a copy of the report of the Coroner's Jury, that held inquest, on the 29th ult., over the body of J.H. Wells, found in Chamber's creek, as related in another place.

The Jury says that the deceased "came to his death on or about the 19th of the month (October), by violent hands, there being a mark around his neck"...

Issue November 23, 1854

Dr. A.J. Miller of Rusk county, a member of Capt. Boggiss Co. of Rangers, was shot at Waco on the 16th inst. by W.E. Long of that town...

Issue January 23, 1855

A fatal affray took place lately in Chickasaw county, Mississippi, between W.W. Woodward and Jas. Simington, which resulted in the death of the former by a bowie knife in the hands of the latter.

The death of Dr. Thomas Elgin of Austin is announced in the *State Times.*

Issue February 17, 1855

Arrest of a murderer: John Hyde, a notorious and desperate character, was arrested in this county a few days ago by Sheriff Cowser, upon the affidavit of Richard A. Barkley, charging him with the murder of Levi W. Young in Bastrop county, Texas, on the 14th day of September 1853...

Issue February 24, 1855

Fatal Affray in Navarro: We are under obligations to Mr. Johnson of Springfield for information of an unfortunate and fatal affray between William Love and Doctor Wm. N. Anderson, of that county, that resulted in the untimely death of the latter. The encounter was caused by an old feud of long standing. The parties met in the public road, and after the exchange of a few exciting words, simultaneously fired at each other. The fire of Anderson proved ineffectual; but that of Love took effect in the right side of Anderson, and inflicted a mortal wound. This occurred on the evening of the 8th and Doctor Anderson survived until the morning of the 9th inst...

Issue March 17, 1855

The *Columbus (Mississippi) Democrat*, records the death at that place, on the 20th ult., of Joseph Seawell Jones, familiarly and widely known as Shocco Jones.

Issue March 31, 1855

A telegraphic dispatch dated Jackson, Mississippi, March 24th, says: Col. A.K. McClung, the celebrated duelist, shot himself through the heart, causing instant death, at the Eagle Hotel in this place today.

Death of Roger Barton: This distinguished lawyer expired at his residence, five miles north of Holly Springs, Mississippi, on Sunday the 4th inst...

Died at the residence of A.H. Wood in Washington county on the 21st inst., Mrs. B.T. Bone, wife of John Bone, late of Galveston, in her 21st year...

Issue April 7, 1855

We learn from Capt. M.K. Snell of Burleson county that the remains of Mr. W.O. Wilson, deceased, will be buried with Masonic honors on the 3rd Sunday in April next, eight miles east of Caldwell...

Issue April 21, 1855

We learn that Robert Wood, one of the members of Capt. Roger's Company of Rangers, was accidentally killed in camp...

Departed this life on the night of the 14th inst. in the 23rd year of her age, Mrs. Martha Harris, daughter of Judge Gregg, deceased, of Burleson county...

A case of deliberate murder: We have been shown a letter dated Wheelock, the 4th inst., and proceed to give its account of a dreadful murder in as few words as possible as follows: Sometime last summer, a difficulty occurred at Wheelock, Robertson county, between T.A. Johnson and Wm. D. Miller, and it was reported that each carried arms and made attempts against the life of the other. Johnson was aided by a man by the name of Lewis Tubbs, and Miller for a time left the State. He returned to Wheelock a few weeks since, and on the 2nd of this month, was murdered in the streets of that place. About half past nine in the morning he was walking along the street not suspecting any danger, when he was shot through the body with two balls, from an adjoining store, by Lewis Tubbs. He did not fall immediately, and J.A. Johnson, his brother John Johnson and Early Brown, who were all well armed on the opposite side of the street, pursued him, and was again shot by Johnson. He lived eight or nine hours, but the shot from Tubbs proved fatal.
  None of the murderers has been arrested on the 5th inst. They left Wheelock and were understood to be together, armed and desperate, and declared they will not be taken.
  Wm. D. Miller was a native of Madison county, Kentucky, about thirty years of age, of highly respectable family, formerly a member of the Kentucky Legislature, a lawyer by profession, and of much more than ordinary ability...

On Monday night the 12th inst., a serious affray occurred in Helena. It appears that several persons had congregated at a "whiskey shop" and a dispute arose between a man by the name of Bell and another named Holt, when Bell was stabbed by Holt, so that he died of the wounds soon after. Holt we are informed made his escape, and has not since been recovered. Bell has left a wife and eight or ten children to mourn his untimely death. Holt also had a family...

Issue April 28, 1855

Capt. G.K. Lewis was killed at Corpus Christi on the 14th inst. by J.C. Yarington...

Issue May 5, 1855

The *Nueces Valley* says Andy Walker, a distinguished Ranger who had served in many a hard fight on the frontier, died at Corpus Christi on the 15th inst...

Issue May 24, 1855

The Georgia papers announce the death of Walter T. Colquitt. It occurred at Macon on the 7th inst...On the morning of May the sixth, an affray took place in one of the drinking and gambling establishments of our city. It seems that there had been a misunderstanding between Joseph Malloy and Terry O'Neal, and as generally the case, each of the parties had their backers. It appears from the statement of witnesses that Malloy and his party armed themselves and following O'Neal to the grocery where the difficulty occurred. O'Neal and those with him went out door after drinking and met the opposite party; when Malloy remarked "that they now had met". Upon this O'Neal said "that he was a better man than Malloy in any way." Malloy told him to strip, when O'Neal stepped back and drew, or made a motion to draw his revolver, but did not present it. At this moment, Malloy drew his pistol and shot at O'Neal, once or twice, one of the loads containing two balls, passed through O'Neal's left arm, between the wrist and elbow and also one in the hand of W.G. Tobin, who was one of the party of O'Neal. Tobin remarked to Malloy "you have [?]" and so saying he drew his revolver and shot Malloy through the body, killing him on the spot...

Issue June 7, 1855

Died on the 15th of May at his residence in Brazos county in this state, Doct. Alva Payne, after a lingering illness, in the 56 year of his age. Notice is further given that Marshall Payne, a son of the above deceased, left his home in Washington county, in this state, sometime in the month of February 1854, for parts unknown...

Issue June 23, 1855

Died in this place on the 21st inst., Mrs. Elizabeth Baxter, consort of Rev. B.B. Baxter, of this town.

Died on the 10th inst., Mr. R.M. Hannay, postmaster and merchant of Rock Island, Austin county. He died of congestion while on a visit to the city of Austin.

Died in the city of Austin on the 14th inst., Major. J. Hampton, late editor and proprietor of the *Texas State Gazette*.

We learn from Mr. Wm. S. Johnson that four Indians accompanied by an unarmed white man, attacked the overseer and a negro belonging to Judge W.E. Jones, about New Braunfels on the Guadalupe, on Saturday week. The overseer, Mr. Laughlin, was killed ...

Issue June 30, 1855

We regret, says the *Virginia Herald* of the 28th ult., to announce the death of Col. John Thom, who died at his residence in Culpepper county on Tuesday last, in the 85th year of his age...

Issue August 5, 1855

Died in this place, on the 26th ultimo, of pulmonary consumption, Mr. John Griffin, of Buckinghamshire, England, in the 50th year of his age. Mr. Griffin emigrated to America in the year 1832, and has resided in Texas for the last 12 years. Like many other victims of consumption, he had spent much of the latter part of his life, travelling and removing from place to place in search of health, till 5 years ago he settled in the town of Washington, determined to devote his few remaining days in providing a comfortable home for his wife and family...

Died at her residence in Washington county, Texas, on the 4th instant, Mrs. Nancy Ann Moses, consort of Norton Moses, aged 25 years and 6 months. Mrs. Moses died firm in the Christian faith which disrobes death of all its terrors. She left a husband and four little children...

Issue August 11, 1855

Departed this life at her residence in Washington county on the 22nd inst. at 11 o'clock P.M., Mrs. Pamella Foster, in the 72nd year of her age. The subject of this notice was born in the State of Virginia, but emigrated in her youth to Abbeville District, South Carolina, where in the year ____ she intermarried with James Foster, of the latter state. From South Carolina she emigrated with her husband and family to Mississippi Territory, thence to Texas in the year 1832...

TRUE ISSUE
Published at LaGrange, Texas.

Issue December 20, 1856

Obituary: Mrs. Eliza A. Satterfield, daughter of Mr. William A. and Mrs. Ann W. Clark, was born in Notaway county, Virginia, February 25th, 1827. Having received a refined education, she married Mr. Jno. N. Satterfield, in September 1849. She emigrated with her husband to Texas in 1850, and died at their residence, in Fayette county, of a pulmonary affection, November 7, 1856, aged 28 years, 9 months, and 18 days. Mrs. S. has left a kind husband, an infant son...

We learn that Mr. Green living on the upper Blanco, while collecting his hogs in the woods, was shot at and killed by a person whose name we are not informed of... Mr. Green was shot through the heart... *Gazette*.

On Saturday night last about 9 o'clock a man by the name of Stafford killed another by the name of Beasely at the house of Randolph Walker, five miles from Bastrop, by stabbing him in the left side. The particulars as they have been stated to us by those who were on the spot before the unfortunate man died are substantially as follows:

It seems that the murderer and the deceased had been carousing in this town during the day. A short time after dark they started home. When about two hundred yards from the house of Mr. Walker, Beasely fell from his horse. His companion rode on to Walker's, and informed those whom he found there of the facts, stating that if he was not cared for, he would freeze to death, the weather being extremely cold. Some of the inmates of the house, went to the assistance of the drunken man, brought him in, and laid him on the floor in front of the fire. Stafford at this time was sitting near by. In a very short time the deceased in stretching out his limbs, accidentally kicked Stafford on the knee. The ruffian murderer, without a single word, immediately jumped upon his helpless comrade, and stabbed him as above stated. He then deliberately walked out of the door to where his horse was hitched, but returned immediately to inquire if his victim was dead, adding "If he is not I will finish him." Old man Walker took down his gun to shoot the murderer, but was unfortunately deterred by others who were in the house. Stafford then fled...

Issue May 8, 1857

We learn from a friend who is just in from Lexington that a serious difficulty took place at Mr. Cradler's 3-1/2 miles from Lexington on last Friday, growing out of a mule theft committed by one Jesse S. Miller from Mrs. Nunn, a widow lady living on the Yegua. Constable Johnson and a gentleman by the name of W.B.M. Barbee, went to arrest Miller and J.H. Carraway, who was an accomplice in the theft, and after arriving at the residence of Mrs. Cradler's, where the fiends were secreted, Mr. Barbee concluded to peep in at the cracks of the logs and see if he discovered them, whereupon Carraway fired at him, the shot taking effect in the forehead, but not considered mortal. Barbee returned to the other side of the house where Johnson was, and being rather slow in getting out of the way, received another shot from the hands of Carraway in the abdomen, after which he (Carraway) attempted to escape, but constable Johnson getting sight of him, fired at him, his shot taking effect in the thigh, Miller escaped. Both men, Barbee and Carraway, have since died from the effects of the wounds... *Bastrop Advertiser*.

Issue June 19, 1857

With feelings of deep regret we record the particulars of an accident, which occurred in this place on last Wednesday evening and which resulted in the immediate death of a little boy, son of John and Sarah Munden, of this city. The deceased, Thomas Jefferson, a boy some 7 or 8 years of age, and a little negro boy 4 or 5 years old were at play in a room where several guns were deposited. The report of a gun attracted the family to the spot of the tragic scene, where they were appalled to see the unfortunate boy in the agonies of death. The little negro upon being interrogated stated as plainly as he could that they had been handling the guns, and that he had taken up the lightest one and pointed it at Thomas and pulled the trigger, but did not know it would hurt him. *Harrison Flag.*

Tribute of Respect. Fayette Union Lodge No. 11 of the I.O. of G.S. & D. of S., Janetta Harrison, wife of Rev. Dr. R.P., while temporarily residing at Rutersville College. She was one of our Charter Members.

Issue December 12, 1857

Tribute of respect from the LaGrange Union Sabbath School upon the death of our beloved Brother and Superintendent E.V. McAshan...

Issue August 21, 1858

Last Sunday, a difficulty occurred between a Mr. Mathew Scoby and Caleb Willburn, who were neighbors, who lived on the San Antonio river in this county, which resulted in the killing of Willburn by Scoby. The deceased leaves a wife and several children in rather destitute circumstances. *Victoria Advocate.*

Lamar Enquirer... Two men by the names of Newton Rozell and Irvin Castleberry got into a difficulty about some cider, which resulted in the death of the latter. He died at nine o'clock on Thursday night.

Issue February 12, 1859

Died at his residence in Fayette county, Texas, on the 1st day of February 1859, Maj. Thomas Shaw, who was born April 6th, 1789. He was brought up in Sumner county, Tennessee, and afterwards resided in Humphreys and subsequently in Hardeman county, in the same state...

Issue July 23, 1859

A funeral discourse, occasioned by the death of Miss Mary Frances Penn, will be preached in the Methodist church on the Sabbath next 10 1/2 A.M. by the Rev. H.S. Thrall. [note: long poem given].

Died at the residence of her mother, Mrs. E.Y. Hopson, on Sunday the 17th inst., Miss Josephina M. King. She was born in Covington, Kentucky, on the 24th day of December 1837, and at the time of her demise was 21 years, 6 months and 23 days old...

Issue January 20, 1860

Death of the Oldest Inhabitant. The *Victoria Advocate* announces the death of Señor Alexandro de la Garza, aged 110 years and 3 days. He lived and died on the Arinosa river, Victoria county.

Issue February 7, 1861

Col. J.R. Burns, who was convicted at the November term of the District Court of Colorado County of the crime of murder in the first degree in the killing of Cola Bruin in this county about one year ago, has been pardoned.

Issue September 5, 1861

Died near Fayetteville, at the residence of Judge Compton's on the 20th August, James Daniel Lyle, infant son of Mary M. & D. Lyle, aged 2 years, 7 months. *Louisville Journal, Shelbyville News*, and Victoria papers will please copy.

The *Colorado Citizen* learns that D.W. Denney, formerly of this place, died at Beaumont, the terminus of the railroad, where the soldiers commenced their march on foot, of palpitations of the heart.

We learn that Mr. Nunn, member of the Bastrop Co. Rangers, while under the influence of whiskey at Alleyton on last Tuesday, seriously, if not fatally, stabbed in the neck Mr. Estes.

Issue July 31, 1862

At a meeting of the Journeymen Printers of the city of Austin held on the evening of the 16th inst. to express their deep regret for the death of Col. John Marshall of the 4th Texas Regiment and late editor of the *Austin State Gazette*... [note: widow and children mentioned].

Issue February 12, 1863

The body of Mr. Weinert, who was one of the persons drowned in the Colorado river, Sunday evening the 1st inst., in attempting to cross in a skiff, was found just below town Friday last. Remains interred in the cemetery on Saturday by the Masonic Fraternity.

Issue November 12, 1864

In Memory of Mrs. Elizabeth Ledbetter... born in the state of North Carolina on the 19th day of December 1838 and in the year 1851, having lost her parents, she came with her brother to Fayette county, Texas, and in the year 1860 she was married to Wm. H. Ledbetter, a member of the bar of LaGrange... her childhood name was Bettie Pope... two children, Willie and Olivia.

Died on the 8th inst., Robert, son of Dr. R.S. Shannon, of this county, aged 2 years.

Died at his residence in Fayette county, after a long and painful illness, on the 20th October last, Mr. Edwin L. Moore... Mr. Moore was born in Halifax county, North Carolina, on the 29th January, 1797 and in 1837 removed to Sumpter county, Alabama; and in 1839 he moved to Fayette county, Texas...

STATE RIGHTS DEMOCRAT
Published at LaGrange, Texas.

Issue March 7, 1861

Died on the 28th ult., Ellen, infant daughter of Mr. and Mrs. L.W. Moore, of this county.

Died on the 1st inst., Miss Sydney Jones, at the residence of her father in this county.

Died on the 2nd inst., Miss Francis E. Nichols, at the residence of her mother in LaGrange.

Issue August 25, 1866

Col. Jno. Rutherford, an old distinguished and universally esteemed citizen of Virginia, died suddenly on the 3rd August in Richmond... He was 74 years of age and of Scotch descent.

The *Herald* says that Thos. F. Corry, lately killed at the Spencer House, Cincinnati, was during the war a resident of Bexar county.

From Tennessee: A drunken fray occurred on the old Cairo road, two miles east of Gallatin, on last Sunday week, in which a man named William H. Pollard, was killed by a gun shot discharged by John H. Chambers...

Itaska, infant daughter of Rev. E.E. and Mrs. Sarah Blackwell, died on the 10th inst. 5ys, 8ms, 20d.

Cloud, the sheriff of Austin county, killed a Mr. Abbott a few days since.

Issue September 7, 1866

San Antonio Herald. A serious disturbance occurred at the Calaveros ranch near that city on the 29th ult. At a dance, McMahan was killed, and Byrd, the carriage driver, was wounded.

Issue September 14, 1866

Judge Buckner Harris died on Peach creek on the 19th ult.

Maj. Frank Weeks of Gonzales county died at La Messilla, New Mexico, lately.

Mississippi News: From the *Lexington Advertiser* of the 24th... on the evening of the 21st inst., Mr. R.H. Baughn and Dr. W.F. Ashley... engaged in a personal difficulty at the variety store of Mr. John Crosa, in which rencontre Dr. Ashley was twice shot at the hands of Mr. Baughn with a pistol, one ball penetrating the right arm, and the other going through the aorta just above the heart, from which he instantly died...

Issue September 28, 1866

Gen. E.S.C. Robertson was tried at the recent term of the district court of Bell county, charged with the killing of Julius C. Lynch in 1862, and acquitted.

Mississippi News: A difficulty occurred a few miles from Grenada, a few days since, in which Mr. Thomas J. Robinson killed his brother-in-law, Mr. Edward P. Williams. The *Carroll Conservative* of the 25th ult., chronicles the death of three most worthy citizens, Mr. W. Hemingway, J.M. Hamilton, and Frances Eubank. All were old citizens and men of large families.

Issue October 2, 1866

Ten Confederate soldiers were reinterred at Georgetown, Kentucky. Among them were Capt. John Black and Wm. Ganehill of Texas.

Issue October 5, 1866

Died in this place on the evening of the 23rd inst., Lee Clark, son of Thomas C. and L. Jennie Gregory, of congestion of the lungs; aged 4 years, 3 months, and 3 days.

Mississippi... The death of Mrs. Frank Smith, a most estimable lady of Canton, is announced. She was passing through New Orleans, on her return from the coast, where she had gone for the benefit of her health, when she was attacked by cholera, and became its victim.

Issue October 19, 1866

Mississippi... An altercation took place on the 25th ult., at Vicksburg, between Morris Walsh and Wm. Rose, in which the former was instantly killed by the latter, having received three shots.

Issue October 26, 1866

The *Goliad Intelligencer* says that Sarah Hasdorff (better known as Sally Scull) was killed by her husband at their residence, some forty miles south west of that place, a short time since.

Maj. A.M. Haskell of Galveston died of cholera in New Orleans on the 9th inst.; in Confederate war; wife and three interesting children.

Died on Thursday the 11th inst. of chronic abscess, after protracted suffering endured with christian patience, Robt. F. Gregory, eldest son of D.G. Gregory, aged 36 years. He leaves a widow and five children and a large circle of relations and friends to mourn his loss.

The venerable old citizen, Mr. J.C. Eccles is no more! He died at his residence in this place on the morning of the 19th inst. Mr. Eccles, we believe, was one of the oldest citizens of LaGrange...

We understand that Mr. Richard Walter, a merchant at High Hill in this county, was assassinated and robbed near that place on the 12th inst...

Issue November 16, 1866

Died in this place on the 10th inst. of cholera morbus, little Pressly P., infant son of Mr. E.S. and Mary A. Hine, aged near 2 years. Mississippi papers will please copy.

Deputy Sheriff Kroeger arrested Jonathan and A. Lindley, father and son, on the Atuacosa, last week. They are charged with the murder of T. Duncan of Bell county.

Issue November 23, 1866

A man named Martin Tate, living in Cumberland county, Virginia, three miles west of Harrisburg, died on the night of the 28th of hydrophobia. He had been bitten by a rabid dog nine weeks ago; died in the most terrible agonies.

The steamer *Henry Von Phul* was entirely destroyed by fire on the Mississippi on the 13th. One gentleman and his son, aged about seven years, who were on their way to their home in Texas, supposed perished, as they were not seen afterwards. J.C. Harrell, Round Top, Fayette county, was also lost.

On the 13th, Capt. Roff, deputy sheriff of Washington county, was severely cut and stabbed while arresting a soldier for an attempt at burglary.

Issue November 30, 1866

The *San Antonio Express* says that a little son of Mr. Myer of that city fell into the river and was drowned a few days ago... It also states that a negro woman, named Amanda Stephens, who had been attending a protracted meeting got her mind tangled on religious subjects, and the balance wheel was moved slightly off the pivot, and she ended her mortal career by jumping into the river and making for herself a watery grave on the 19th.

The *Liberty Gazette* announced the death of Major J.M. Hall, an old citizen of Texas, at Liberty of cholera on Saturday evening last.

The *Waco Register* says that Miss L.O. Yell of that county, a young lady 14 years of age, was killed a few days ago by being thrown from a buggy.

The *Brazos Signal* says that Mr. T.W. Hunter, who was tried at the recent term of court at Columbus for homicide, was after a fair and partial trial, honorably acquitted. He was one of the original Three Hundred of the Austin Colonists.

The *Brenham Inquirer* of the 24th announces the death of the wife of Mr. John Ewing of that place.

Died at 6 o'clock P.M. on the 25th November at his residence in LaGrange, E.S. Hine, after an illness of 15 days... The subject of this notice was born in Limestone county, Alabama, in 1824, where his life was spent till a few months since, when he was induced to emigrate to this state with a view of recuperating his fortunes, which the late war so sadly shattered. In 1858 he became a member of the M.E. church. His death was calm and peaceful.

At Monroe, Louisiana, on the 26th September, 1866, passed from earth to heaven dear little Laurence, son of John and Annie Byrne, aged 3 years and 27 days... He was a child of the covenant, having been dedicated to God in baptism by his pious mother at Round Top, Texas, in March 1864...

Issue December 7, 1866

Mr. Lee C. Steadman, proprietor of the Overton Hotel at Memphis, died suddenly a few days ago of disease of the heart.

We understand that a Mr. Simmons, living over in the edge of Colorado county, shot and killed his brother-in-law, whose name we did not learn...

Issue December 14, 1866

Tribute of Respect Lyons Lodge No. 195. Died on the 25th of last June, at his residence in Fayette county after an illness of 2 years, James Morrow...

Issue January 11, 1867

The *Ranger* says Mr. W.G. Council of Navasota was waylaid and shot by some one on the night of the 26th ult. as he was entering his yard gate. Twelve or more bullets or large shot entered the legs a little above the knees causing terrible wounds. Amputation was resorted to, and Mr. Council died a few hours afterwards. The assassin has not been detected.

A most diabolical murder took place in Hill county on the 20th ult. Six men entered the house of J.W.P. Doyle, killed him and his son Rufus, then robbed the house...Capt. B. Bradberry of Port Lavaca and Capt. J.M. Hall of Austin, both old Texians, are dead.

Frank Erickson of Memphis was killed by Jos. Burton at Somerville on the 27th.

Maj. Jerome Wilson of Gen. Hood's staff died from cholera lately at Memphis.

Excerpt abstracted from a letter dated Columbus, January 4th, 1867... There was some excitement here a few days since, caused by the arrest of an "American citizen of African [de]scent" as one of the murderers of Mr. Newman and family, who lived in the edge of Lavaca county near Oakland. Mr. Newman and wife and child and a negro girl were all killed by means of an axe and knife, while in their beds and the house set on fire and the bodies almost entirely consumed... Mr. Newman was a German, formerly lived in Columbus, was a good mechanic...

Issue February 7, 1867

Maj. Jas. W. Scott, an old Texian and highly esteemed citizen of Houston, died at his home last Saturday.

Issue February 22, 1867

From the *Athens (Alabama) Post*... Tribute of respect upon the death of our worthy brother and former junior warden, Edward S. Hine, who died in LaGrange, Texas, on the 5th of November 1866, which place he had but recently adopted as his home.

Issue March 22, 1867

A wagoner, T.J. Delany, in route from Alleyton to Bastrop was killed by the falling of a tree. The deceased built a fire at the root of a tree and during the night the tree fell across his breast killing him instantly. Mr. D. lived on Clear Creek in Bastrop county.

Dr. N.D. Labadie, an old citizen of Galveston, died in that city on the 13th.

The funeral sermon of Mrs. A.C.G. Haynie will be preached by Rev. Q.M. Menifee at the Methodist church, 29th inst.

Issue March 29, 1867

Died: Mrs. Melissa McKinnie at the residence of her husband, four miles of [sic] LaGrange on the 26th inst.

The *McKinney Enquirer* says Mr. Huffmans, living near Decatur in this county [Collin], was drowned last week.

Issue April 5, 1867

The *Brazos Signal* says that a New Yorker, J.B. Johnson, was found dead in the Island City Hotel last Saturday morning. He had been drinking very hard.

Mrs. Ann Well of near Mantua, Collin county, was burned to death on the 4th.

A Mr. French, who had recently removed to Denton county, was drowned a few days since in crossing the Big Elm.

Issue April 12, 1867

An old man by the name of Simmons was shot and killed by his son a short distance from Rutersville in this county on the evening of the 4th. On the day he was killed he had beaten his wife severely... [note: mentions three sons].

Serious Accident: Mr. Moon, at the plantation of Mr. John Pinchboak, on Monday last, in attempting to shoot a cat, the gun exploded, lacerating his right hand to such an extent that amputation was necessary. Drs. Hamilton and Lewellyn were called in and performed the operation. The mutilated hand can be seen at their office, second door east of the National Hotel. From the *Columbus Times* of the 6th inst.

Issue May 3, 1867

Mrs. Martha Gregory, consort of Capt. A.S. Gregory, died at her residence in this place last Wednesday and her remains were followed to the cemetery last evening. We tender Capt. Gregory our condolence.

175

W.A. VanAlstyne, an old citizen of Houston and a brother to our townsman J.A. VanAlstyne, died at his residence in that city, Thursday the 25th.

Issue May 10, 1867
Mr. John Folts, an old citizen of Columbus, died in that place a few days ago.

Lt. Seth H. Griffin, whose head was split open by a saber in the hands of a negro sergeant in the late mutiny at San Antonio, died. He was buried with military honors.

Issue May 17, 1867
Death has claimed another of our old citizens and R.S. Snell is one of us no more. He died at his residence near this place last sunday after a protracted illness and was buried by the Odd Fellows fraternity, of which he was a member, on Monday. He leaves a wife and children...

Issue May 31, 1867
Tribute of respect for R.S. Snell.

Issue June 7, 1867
FROM THE WACO REGISTER, White man killed by a negro: On last Saturday, a Mr. R.H. Morrison, who lives on the Conner place, ten miles below Waco, was shot by a negro boy by the name of Dick, at the ferry at this place. Mr. M. died on Sunday night from the effects of the wounds. Dick attempted to escape, but is now in the custody of the military authorities... He leaves a young and interesting widow.

The Galveston Civilian says a young man named Smith committed suicide in the house of M'dme Vic Morton. Cause, loved a courtesan named Ida Howard.

Issue June 14, 1867
The Herald says that a fearful tornado passed through the north part of Dallas county on the 26th ult. in the vicinity of Breckenridge killing and wounding a number of persons and destroying a great amount of property. Among the killed was a child of Benjamin Prigmore, and Volney Coldwell, his wife and three of their children. There were also two negroes killed at Coldwell's residence, making in all eight persons lost in this terrible tragedy...

Alabama Items: Huntsville Independent, 17th ult., relates the killing of Egbert Wiggins and Raynor Betts, negroes. Betts was abusing his wife, Wiggins interfered, and Betts immediately shot and mortally wounded him. He fled and was overtaken and arrested, but he resisted and was shot dead.

Miscellaneous Texas Newspaper Abstracts - Deaths — Vol 2

Issue July 5, 1867

Mr. William Keith, a well known citizen of Bosque county, has been killed by the Indians. Mr. Keith was found dead and scalped. No other injury being found upon the body.

Died at Fayetteville on the morning of the third inst., an infant son of J.W. McGehee.

Rev. W.A. Leonard, a minister in the Methodist church, died at Houston on the 25th ult.

Died on the 24th ult., Mrs. Lucy H., consort of Jas. L. Blackwell, in the 71st year of her age. The deceased was a native of Virginia, and a resident of Texas for the past 14 years and for 20 years a consistent member of the Baptist church.

Died enroute from New Orleans to Mobile on his 59th birthday, Charles G. Bowen... Brother Bowen was happily converted and connected with the Methodist Episcopal church in Madison county, Alabama, A.D. 1833...

Issue August 30, 1867

Died at the residence of her grandfather G.W. Penn, Esq., Abietta, aged 3 years and 8 months, only child of Mr. E.S. and Mrs. Fannie J. Alley.

Minna Tipton died 15 August 1867.

The *Herald* says yesterday morning a man was found lying dead on the side of the road leading to Bandera - about nine miles from San Antonio. He was recognized as a man whose sister lived some distance. The man's name was Milsted and it was rumored that a dose of tartar emetic had been administrated to him...

In front of G. Friedberger's store, Dr. J.P. Brash mortally stabbed L. Lindsay, an attorney.

The *Columbus Times* gives a rather meager account of the killing of T.J. Roberts by Phocian Tate...

Sickness in town. Four deaths at LaGrange. Mrs. H. Bradshaw. Mr. - - Richers died of congestion chills, and Mr. -- Sayers, Charley Marckmann, and little Fannie Franklin have died of a very malignant type of billious fever. Mr. Sayers, a New Yorker we believe, had lately come to our town from Lockhart, Texas. Mr. Marckmann was a young merchant of our place. Served with Hood's Brigade, wounded and left for dead at Gettysburg.

177

The *Telegraph* says that Tho's Cotton killed his brother, Jas. Cotton, in a personal difficulty in Montgomery county.

Issue December 6, 1867

Mortuary report, as revised by Drs. Blakemore and McGown. Those marked * died of other diseases than yellow fever; those marked with ! died out of town; and those marked with a # were non-residents of LaGrange.

August: 17th, Prof. F.C. Wilkie *; 23rd, Adolph Richers *; 27th, C. Sayers & Mrs. Bradshaw *; 28th, C.R. Marckmann & little Fannie Franklin; 29th, S. Potter, Jas. Nicholson and C. Conard.

September: 1st, Felix Altman; 2nd, James, little son of J.W. White; 3rd, Bertha Walter and child of Tips; 4th, C. Walter, August Merrem, Martha Trombowsky, child of B. Zanders, Siegfried Zanders and Jas. W. Mathews; 6th, --- Brown #; Zeb M.P. French, Theo Harigel; 7th, Julius Tips, Charles P. Smith, John Phillips, Mrs. F.P. Hood, Clay Price *, child of W.W. Little *, B. Simon and Mrs. Zellers; 8th, Edward Pelzer; 9th, Theo Carter, child of I. Meyenberg, Mrs. B. Simon, N. Turnage!, Mrs. I. Meyenberg, Alex Carter, col., Mrs. G. Pauli, ____Fandanki #, and a negro child; 10th, Henry Moore, G.C. Reagan, Johnson #, Norman Ujffy, Mrs. H. Moore, Martha Bowers; 11th, G. Koening, E.B. Turnage, Mr. S.L. Rack, J. Burton, Mrs. Weinert, ____ Weinert, Jo Gardner, Mrs. L. Norton, Mrs. A. Walter. 12th, child of Chas. Herman, Leslie Savage, Wm. Hermes' child, C. Troumbowski, Mr. Footh, V. Korn, August Frede, T.E. Carter, G. Matschke, Richard Croom. 13th, Mrs. D. Hermes, Mrs. C. Melcher, Miss Anne Moore, C. Schroeder, Mrs. W.B. Price, I. Fadanski #, I.G. Tanner, Frank Cox !. 14th, Tom Patton !, P/R. Bennett, Mrs. Hittle, Mr. Harrison #, son of I. Meyenberg, Mrs. A. Fredo/Frede. 15th, Wm. DeWarren #, Dr. Amos Hough, Mrs. D. Koenig, child of I. Meyenberg, Mrs. M. Schwartz #. 16th, R. Reichel, ____Willerford #, F. Pfeffereorn, John a negro. 17th, K. Simon, David Lafon, child of C. Gobel. 18th, Anna Seeberger, Mrs. Tom Patton !, H. Levine, Wm. Webb, Jr. 19th, J.P. Ackerman, ____ Gobel, Sr., F.P. Hood, Mrs. J. Morton, little girl of John Carragee *, son of L. Hellman. 20th, David Phillips. 21st, Chas. Kiefer. 22nd, Judge Ben Shropshire. 23rd, John Carragee *, Mr. S. Potter, Mrs. L. Hellman. 24th, C. Urbach, Mrs. C. Urbach, negro woman and child. 25th, child of Frank Meyer, L. Harigel. 26th, Miss Loughridge, and negro. 27th, Mrs. J.P. Ackerman, child of C. Urbach, Dr. S.H. Doxey, Mrs. S.H. Doxey, negro woman and child. 28th, Negro man and woman. 29th, a stranger # at Goebel's, J. Reynolds #, Mrs. C. Schroeder, Mrs. H. Harigel, J.H. Ujffy !, Mrs. C. Goebel, and a negro girl. 30th, Miss Mattie Reagan, Mrs. Florian Meyer, Mrs. Short, Hermann Reichel, and a son of C. Schroeder.

October: 1st, negro woman; 2nd, child of C. Schroeder and also an infant of C.R. Dickinson *, and Mrs. G.C. Reagan. 5th, a negro man. 6th, Robert Stroud. 7th, son and daughter of H. Harigel. 8th, Dr. Musgrove Evans, daughter of Dr. A. Hough, an infant of C. Goebel *, and a negro woman. 9th, Florian Meyer, Mrs. Schivarke #. 12th, Fr. Thies !., 13th, Mrs. Dr. Amos Hough, and a negro girl. 14th, Miss Kate Carter. 15th, Negro girl. 17th, A. Seeberger, and a child of C. Goebel. 19th, G.E. Meinert *, Emma Scholtz, and a negro man. 21st, Simon Kirk #, son of C. Leesemann, Harry McClellan!. 22nd, a negro child. 24th, Mrs. L. Witschke *, daughter of V. Korn *, and a negro woman. 26th, a negro man. 27th, a negro woman 103 years old *. November: 21st, Samuel D. Bradshaw *.

The *Columbus Mississippi Index,* November 6th, reports the death of Rev. Thos. Wolstenholme, in the 73d year of his age. At his death he was said to be the oldest Odd Fellow in America; he had belonged to the order over 50 years.

We announce the death of James W. Mathews, late editor of the *LaGrange New Era,* on the 4th of September, it is supposed of congestion of the brain, after a few hours illness.

Issue January 3, 1868
Town-talk says the two brothers Collins, who were recently in the LaGrange jail charged with robbery, were both killed by a man named Dean during the holidays.

It is rumored that a difficulty occurred on the 31st between Ferdinand Loessin and Noah Tutsthe, some ten miles from LaGrange, in which the latter was killed.

Issue January 10, 1868
The name of Mr. R.C. Gibbs, of Galveston, Texas, appears among the killed, by the late railroad accident at Augusta, New York.

On the 16th September, little Hattie Estes, aged 3 years and 7 months, daughter of the late John C. Carragee, died from the effects of a dose of morphine, which her mother unfortunately mistook and gave to her for quinine.
    After a painful illness of nearly three months duration, Mr. John C. Carragee, late of Coffeeville, Mississippi, died at this place, on the 23rd September. Mr. Carragee was a native of the county Westmeath, Ireland, but came to this United States when only 17 years of years... He settled at

Coffeeville, Mississippi, where he resided for upwards of twenty years. He leaves a widow and two children. He was attacked by the prevailing epidemic, yellow fever.

J.D. Hunt, adm'r of the estate of his father, will sell some fine stock, farming utensils, etc.

Letter from Oso, Fayette county. One of the brightest members of our society was taken from us, Quinn Menifer. We all mourn the death of Parker Hood. We deeply regret the death of Young Tuttle, we think the murder unjustifiable. He fell into bad company and it cost him his life.

Issue January 24, 1868

The *Tyler Reporter* announces the death of Col. B.T. Selman of that city. He died on the 5th. Able lawyer.

A man named Alfred Colton was killed in a house of ill-frame in San Antonio on the 13th. His murderer, William Smith, made his escape.

Issue January 31, 1868

Suicide appears to have become an epidemic in Galveston. On Tuesday, two men "shuffled off the mortal" by taking morphine, and resolving "not to be," flew to "ills they know not of." One of these was Mr. Giffeths, of Dallas county, who took morphine to quite his nerves, which were unstrung by drink, and by some means took more than the proper quantity. The other was James Day, a circus performer. He was out of money and out of employment; he took morphine and killed himself... *Journal* of the 25th.

As the wife of Mr. J.B. Bailey of Van Buren county, Arkansas, was chopping some wood one day last week, she made a mislick with the axe, tripped up and fell backwards on a knotty stick of wood breaking her back, which caused death almost instantaneously.

Issue February 7, 1868

Virginia papers contain notices of the death of Mr. John Henry of Charlotte, last survivor, save one of the children of Patrick Henry...

The *Lavaca Commerical* says that Valentine Cook, who was murdered in Victoria, was from DeWitt county... Only son of Rev. T.F. Cook.

Miscellaneous Texas Newspaper Abstracts - Deaths --- Vol 2

Issue March 13, 1868

Military outrage in Gonzales: We have before us a copy of the *Gonzales Enquirer* giving an account of one of the most humiliating and shocking outrages, we dare say, that was ever perpetrated upon the soil of Texas. It seems that a squad of Federal soldiers stationed there, all of a sudden and without provocation, began visiting grogshops, beer saloons, etc., and insulting and quarrelsome towards citizens... After severely beating the post-master and firing at him through the walls and the windows, riddling the mail and beating in the window panes with their pistols, they went to the hotel, entered and commenced beating in the doors and firing into the rooms. In one of the second story rooms asleep was a physician by the name of Cunningham, living near Belmont. The noise roused him, and he opened his door and asked them what they meant. They pushed open his bedroom door and dragged him out, and after beating him severely, the Sergeant ordered him out to repeat the Lord's prayer and give three cheers for the Union, which the poor fellow did. They then brought him into the street and finally shot him dead...

Issue May 1, 1868

B.B. Lee was shot and killed at Hempstead on Tuesday last.

At Round Top on last Saturday, Mack Jones was killed by a man named Moore. Dispute about some cattle between Moore and a brother Andrew Jones...

Issue May 8, 1868

W.D. Williams of Waco, Texas, is dead.

Died at his residence near Oso, May 2, 1868, Mr. N. Burns. Father Burns would have attained, had he lived a few days longer, his 74th year; forty-year member of Methodist church.

Issue June 12, 1868

We are informed that J.O. Cassidy shot and instantly killed Mr. Ghans, a dry goods merchant at Brenham, on Tuesday morning last. Cassidy has resided in this state since 1857; and during the past 3 years has been in the employ of Messrs. Whittlesey & Co. of this city. Mr. Ghans and Cassidy have occupied the same store. Ghans accused Cassidy of stealing. Cassidy surrendered...

Issue October 29, 1868

From Mississippi: A man named Rickey was shot Sunday night, near Pontotoc.

The *Gazette* announces the death of Mrs. Rodgers, wife of the Rev. B.A. Rodgers, rector of St. David's church in Austin, which occurred on the night of the 21st after a long and painful illness.

Issue November 12, 1869

Died suddenly at Nuncation, Warwickshire, England, on the 3rd ult., Mr. Thomas Owen, late of Arley, England. The deceased was for some time a resident of this county and was well known to the citizens of LaGrange...

We regret to announce the death of little Hugh Hill, only son of the late John C. Hill and Mrs. Elizabeth Hill, his surviving wife. He died on Wednesday evening last from an attack of congestion, aged about three years.

Issue November 19, 1869

Burr Harrington, the son of Maj. S.J. Harrington and the late E.N. Harrington, deceased, was born in Tuscumbia, Alabama, on the 23rd day of October, 1850, and departed this life after a brief but violent attack of hemorrhagic malarial fever on Saturday the 13th day of November, 1869, at 8 o'clock in the evening... resting place in the LaGrange cemetery...

A drunken negro, Allen McKnight, attacked an Irishman named Jack Ryan, at Independence. Ryan, in self defence, shot and killed the negro.

Issue February 4, 1870

The Houston papers announce the death in that city on the 28th inst. of Mrs. House, wife of Mr. T.W. House.

GALVESTON CIVILIAN AND GAZETTE
Published at Galveston, Texas.
Editor, H. Stuart.

Issue October 19, 1838

Quinn, tried at the present session of the Brazoria Circuit Court on an indictment for the murder of a man named Buchanan, has been convicted of manslaughter.

The case of Humphreys, indicted for the murder of Capt. Powel, was continued.

Miscellaneous Texas Newspaper Abstracts - Deaths --- Vol 2

Issue January 11, 1839

Stop the murders. 1,000 dollars reward will be paid by the undersigned for the apprehension of John Step and Solomon Step, who murdered Martin Farley, Sr. on the 8th October near Wolf's Ferry, Hardin county, Tennessee. [note: description of John and Solomon given]. The Steps formerly resided in Cherokee Country in Georgia. Salley Farley, Henderson G. Farley, Jackson Farley, Samuel Lenox.

Issue May 17, 1839

Late in May or early in June 1837, five or six young men occupied the same bed room one night at the boarding house of Mrs. Mann at Houston. In the morning one of the number, Chauncey Goodridge, missed a one thousand dollar bank note... one of the lodgers was suspected... he was called upon to specify the person upon whom his suspicions rested... he designated a Mr. Lawrence, a young man from the city of New York, of great respectability and to whom M.M. Noah had been or perhaps was then guardian, for we believe he had not attained his 21st year... a challenge was passed by Lawrence... the parties met and Lawrence was killed.

C.M. Stanley, who had been one of the lodgers where the thief had occurred, acted as the second of Lawrence and saw him shot.

Stanley remained in Houston... In November he went to Mr. Doswell, who was about to leave for New Orleans, and gave him a thousand dollar bank bill... Doswell's suspicions were excited... He mentioned the circumstance to Maj. Holman, who had seen the note in the hands of Lawrence and from description believed that sent by Stanley to be the same.

Dr. Niles F. Smith, knew the destitute condition of Stanley and strongly believed in his guilt. In the mean time poor Goodridge, stung by remorse at the death of Lawrence, became almost a madman, wandered to San Antonio where he quarrelled with a gambler named Allen. Afterward the gambler shot him in his bed, then plunged a bowie knife through him so as to pin him to the mattress.

Stanley is the son of the ex-Governor of Carolina of that name, and has had a brother in the American Congress for several years. The family of the best standing, but we learn that he has been a renegade for several years.

Issue January 18, 1840

Died in this city on Wednesday, Mrs. Ann E., wife of John J. Carson. New York papers please copy.

Capt. Ross, whose recent connection with the Federalists of Mexico has made him somewhat conspicuous, was shot in a quarrel a few days ago at Gonzales by a man named M'Coullough, brother to the man of the same name killed by Ross in a duel.

All those endebted to the estate of Jas. B. Bodine, dec., are notified to come forward. A. Turner, admin.

Alexander Ewell applied for letters of admin. estate of Benjamin D. Jones, dec.

Letters of admin for estate of W.W. Pace, dec. John E. Jeffers, Adm'r.

Letters of admin for estate of Philip M'Laughlin.

David B. Fowler. Letters of Admin. Estate of Stephen Prescott.

Issue November 4, 1840
Clark L. Owen, admin. estate of Colonel Pinckney Caldwell, dec. Texana.

Issue January 4, 1843
John Wace Browning, native of England. Information requested. Left New Orleans for this Republic towards close of 1840, and was in Houston in January 1841. Supposed to have been in Austin about the month of September 1841. Distressed parents. Communicate to Capt. Elliot at Galveston.

Issue February 1, 1843
A small schooner of 45 tons called the *Gen. Pike* and owned by Capt. Webber and Messrs. Rains and Downing left Buffalo Bayou for Galveston on the 13th ult. and is supposed to have swamped in a gale... The bodies of Capt. Webber, Capt. Clark, formerly of the steamer *Correo*, Henry Coombs and another not recognized, have been found. Jos. H. Auld and a man named M'Connell were also on board, one of whose bodies is still missing.

Issue February 8, 1843
There are in the U.S. just one hundred soldiers of the Revolution on the pension list over one hundred years of age. The oldest man on the list is Michael Hale of Union county, Pennsy., who is in his 115th year.

Issue February 15, 1843
Fatal accident: Three days ago, two little boys, one a son of A.F. James, some ten years old, the other an orphan named Wm. Gordon, aged about 8, playing with power in the back yard of the store of Messrs. Raymond and Marston, upon which the residence of Mr. James also opens, when fire was by some means communicated to the whole mass, which exploded with a shock, mangling the oldest boy in a shocking manner, so that he expired the same evening; much injury to the other.

Miscellaneous Texas Newspaper Abstracts - Deaths -- Vol 2

Issue February 18, 1843
Red River has been higher than ever before known - ten feet higher than the flood of 1840 - and in the neighborhood of Jonesborough one hundred persons are estimated to have been drowned in the bottoms -- among them Col. Thomas and family of Jonesborough, Col. Milam (a brother to the hero of the Alamo), his wife and sister.

Issue February 22, 1843
Zebulon Payne, arrested and taken to Tennessee some months since by Mr. Crossman of this city to stand his trail for the murder of Mr. Coltant, has been convicted, sentenced and executed.

Issue March 18, 1843
The morning of Wednesday last was warm and pleasant; but a few minutes before one a Northwester suddenly came up and continued to blow with great violence until Thursday evening, accompanied during the most of Wednesday by an exceeding cold rain... A man named Campbell, perished of cold before night on Wednesday...

Issue March 25, 1843
J.B. Ransom (formerly a citizen of this place) who accompanied the Commissioners to the Waco Village as secretary, was killed a few days since at the village by the accidental discharge of his own gun. *Houstonian.*

Issue April 8, 1843
We regret to learn that a rencounter, resulting fatally, occurred in Washington on the 31st ult. between Col. James R. Cook and a Mr. Adkins.

Issue April 15, 1843
Rev. Ira Parker died in this city on Thursday evening, leaving a sick wife and destitute family... Persons in this part of the town who may wish to assist them with things necessary to their condition can leave the same with Albert Ball on Tremont street.

Issue April 29, 1843
Dr. Booker, one of the San Antonio prisoners and a brave and meritorious man, was accidentally killed at Perote about the 1st inst. by a drunken Mexican soldier.

Issue May 31, 1843
Lost my San Jacinto Donation claim, No. 1[?]5 [note: page creased], for six hundred and forty acres of land, supposed to have been in the possession of Col. Smith when he was murdered by the Indians. Jno. M. Allen.

Issue June 10, 1843

We deeply regret to state that Hon. J.M. Eve, the late incumbent, is hopelessly ill of consumption and is not expected to survive more than a few days at farthest...

Mrs. Shelton, the widow of the late Col. Shelton of Mississippi, who committed suicide some short time ago, has at last been released of her sufferings by death. The disgrace and suicide of her husband were too much for her true woman's nature, and she died of a broken heart.

Issue July 15, 1843

Died on the 1st July on board the brig. *Wharton*, Lt. J. P. Lansing, Texas Navy, a native of New York. The body having been brought to this city will be interred this evening at 4 o'clock with military honors. The procession will start from Menard's Wharf. The public are invited to attend.

$100 reward. Littleberry B. Franks and Lucius Johnson, who were in my custody charged with the murder of Henry Castledine, did, on the evening of Monday last, escape from the guard during the storm and darkness of the night. This is to give notice to the citizens of the Republic, that anyone apprehending either or both, and delivering them to my custody at the county jail in Milam county, will be entitled to a reward of fifty dollars for each. Littleberry B. Franks is six feet high, light complexion, red whiskers, sandy colored hair and thin visage.

Lucius Johnson is 5 feet 8 or 9 inches high, fair complexion, white eye brows, with a downcast, stoops in the shoulders. Ordera Watson, sheriff of Milam county.

Issue July 22, 1843

Died at Harrisburg on Monday the 9th inst., Alfred John, son of E.D. John of this city.

Issue July 29, 1843

A man by the name of Wigginton, recently from Texas, was found dead in his bed this morning. When discovered, he was in a complete state of decomposition. He had been complaining of indisposition the day previous. A coroner's inquest was called over him, but we have not heard the result of their verdict-- *N.O. Courier.*

Issue September 2, 1843

A man named Thomas Wells, formerly a sailor on one of our navy vessels, was stabbed to death in this city on Saturday evening by J.W. Pilant, formerly a gambler at Houston. The parties, it seems, quarrelled and fought about a bet of two bits at a game of cards.

Pilant was arrested and committed by Justice James for trial at the District Court, but was brought out Monday on a wit of *habeas corpus* and admitted to bail by Judge Morris in the sum of $90,000--(old Treasury Notes)

Stephen Hard, who kept a house of entertainment at the West end of the Island, was, we learn, shot dead on Sunday by a man named Toby.

Mr. Asa Hill, an old gentleman of Rutersville, and one of the prisoners taken by the Mexicans at Mier, arrived here by the brig *Sam Houston* on Wednesday having being released by Santa Anna in consequence of his age and the helpless condition of his family at home. Mr. Hill had two sons (boys) who distinguished themselves at Mier. One of them was, for his bravery in the battle, liberated and adopted by Gen. Ampudia, who, when he was ordered to Yucatan, turned him over to Santa Anna, who designs educating and rearing him as his own child. The other is yet in the hospital of his wounds and Santa Anna promised to have him provided for. The father, whois a poor man with a family of twelve, was perfectly willing to leave them. Mr. Hill furnishes the following list of men (Mier prisoners) who have died in the hospital of Santiago; viz:
> Benj Middleton, of Trinity.
> J.J. Blanton, Rutersville.
> Robert Smith, do.
> J. Shipman, Brazos.
> John Owens, Brazoria.
> Thos Caldwell, San Jacinto.
> Died at Saltillo:
> Burnet Bryan, Fort Bend.
> Robt Beard, do.
> Sam McChellan, Trinity.
> Chas Hill, do.
> ---- Kauffman, Bastrop.
> Allen Holderman, do.
> ---- Martin, Victoria.
> Perry, Randolph, Lewis, Wm Mitchel, and 16 other men (names not recollected) were lost in the mountains.

We have been pained exceeding at the account, contained in the New Orleans papers, of a duel between Hon. Alcee La Branche, late U.S. Charge d'Affaires to Texas, and Mr. Heuston, an editor of Louisiana, in which the latter was shot dead, at the fourth fire, double barrelled guns being used.

Singular Case -- A negro boy, the property of Andrew H. Jordan of Columbia, Miss, died in Louisville, KY, on the 9th inst. The editor of the *Advertiser* says of him: ...he was four years old in April last; and four feet one inch in height; was born in Mississippi, of parents in no respect remarkable for any deviation from the ordinary size and temperament. He completed his first year -- when he began developing in a manner that excited the astonishment of all who saw him. His hair grew surprising rapidly over his entire body and face, giving him whiskers and beard as luxuriant as an adult. His body assumed the muscular development of athletic manhood, his strength enabling him at four years of age, to lift 200 pounds dead weight with ease... His hands and feet were more taper and symmetrical than any of his race we ever saw. He fell victim to pleurisy.

Information requested. The relatives of William Quin, by trade a bricklayer, native of the town of Ballyshannon, county of Donegal Ireland, 35 years of age, dark complexion and stoutly made, are anxious of information concerning him. Said Quin emigrated to Texas in 1833...

Republic of Texas -- Galveston county. Elizabeth Hard/Hand filed for letters of admin. on the estate of her late husband Stephen Hard/Hand, dec.

Issue September 16, 1843
Died on Sunday the 10th September at Galveston, Willis, only son of John A. and Sophia L. Settle, aged 12 mo.

Issue October 7, 1843
Loss of the *Sarah Barnes*. [note: condensed from a lengthy article]... There were 31 souls on board the *Sarah Barnes* -12 reached the yawl and 19 the rafts. To wit: in the yawl -- Alex. G. Abell, (bearer of despatches for the U.S. Government); Benj. P. Hartshorn; F. Pinkard; Henry S. Daggett; James Potter; passengers, a woman in the steerage, name unknown; Michael Mathews, 1st engineer; Charles Cloud, mate; Henry Stewart, Stewart; Thomas Green, cabin boy; James Locklin, deck hand, servant boy, Allen ___ 12. On the rafts were W. Boyd; J.W. Blain/Blair, R. Martin of Ala-- passengers. Charles Frankland, Captain; Thompson Riley, clerk; John Dean, 2d engineer; Peter Gorman, bar-keeper; four firemen, names unknown, 4 deck hands, names unknown, and ship's cook, named Aleck ___, 3 deck passengers, names unknown -- 19 on the rafts -- in all 31. ...three of our number had sunk in a watery grave! James Potter, from Houston; Henry Daggett, from N.O.; and a woman from Houston, name unknown, were the sufferers. ...Five men have reached Galveston by means of the rafts -- to wit: Thompson Riley, clerk; Peter Gorman, barkeeper; Jno. Dean, 2d engineer -- Carlton and Farmer 5 [sic]. In the yawl nine escaped, making 14 in all. The remaining 17 were doubtless drowned. ...The Survivors Of The Yawl.

Henry S. Daggett (aged 28 years) of the firm of Eager, Daggett & Bennett, New Orleans, came to Galveston a short time since on a visit to his mother and sister, who reside in this city... The father of Mr. Daggett was a sea captain, and the son had followed the sea for three years when a youth, besides making frequent voyages in after life...

Republic of Texas. County of Galveston. Eleanor Payne Frankland, praying for letters of administration upon the estate of her late husband, Charles Frankland, late of Galveston county.

Issue October 14, 1843

Col. L.P. Cook -- The trial of Col. L.P. Cook was not concluded during the session of the court at Bastrop. He was arraigned on the charge of being accessary to the murder of Mr. Peyton, and the case was submitted to a jury, but as the jury could not agree before the court adjourned, they were discharged and he will remain in custody until the next term. He is also indicted for the murder of Capt. Lewis and will probably be tried on this charge at the next term. *Star.*

Issue October 28, 1843

We regret to learn that Mr. Torry, one of the agents who went out on a tour among the Indian tribes in order to bring them into the Council, died at the treaty ground of fever.

The late Murders in this county.--The G[rand] Jury at [the] recent session of the District Court---[note: page creased] against Louis P. Cook and George [Ba]rrett, as [pr]incipals and accessories for the willfu[l] [mu]rder of Capt. Mark B. Lewis and Alexander Peyton. Their trials however did not come off, the time of the Court occupied in the discussion of points of law...

The Grand Jury subsequently brought into court a "true bill" against Charles F. King, the sheriff, as a party to the murder.

Louis P. Cook changed the venue in the case of the murder of A [note: page creased] Peyton, to Bastrop county, where the trial came off. It was a mistrial, eleven of the jurors, it is said, being in favor of a verdict of guilty, and only one against it.

Cook is confined in Bastrop jail and Barrett here.--Austin paper.

Issue November 4, 1843

The jury yesterday brought in a verdict of guilty in the case of the Republic against Charles Heninger for the murder of Benjamin Tyson in the county some weeks since.

Indictments for murder have been found by the grand jury of this county against Charles Henniker, J.W. Pilant, and a German named Hoffmaster.

Letter of admin. estate of John O'Brian, dec. J.S. Sydnor, adm.

Issue November 25, 1843
Administrators notice. Estate of John S. Cash. Galen Hodges. Matagorda.

Issue December 9, 1843
Charles Henniker was hung yesterday... [note: page folded].

Notice. Estate of Joseph Taylor, dec. Jefferson county. David Garner, Admin.

Notice. Estate of Danl W. Krim. Jas P. Sherwood, Admin.

Issue January 13, 1844
We regret to learn that Thomas Bryson died a few days since at Mr. Stevenson's, near Washington, while on his way to the latter place with despatches from Galveston.

Issue January 27, 1844
Wreck: The schr. *Galveston*, Capt. Rickets, of this city, sailed for New Orleans on the 15th inst., and it is believed was struck by a squall and capsized the night following, all on board perishing... A portion of the deck and other parts of the vessel, which have been identified, have drifted ashore on Pelican Island and Point Bolivar. There were on board besides the Capt., the mate and three or four hands, whose names we cannot learn; young Bryant, a midshipman, who distinguished himself, and was wounded in the naval action between Texian and Mexican vessels off Campeachy; Mr. Degurs, wife, and child; Mr. Klein and perhaps one or two other persons not known here.

James Scott, a laborer on board the *Irene*, was struck by a bale of cotton, which was rolled into the hold of that vessel on Wednesday, and died of the injury on the following morning.

Died on Thursday last, 18th inst., Miss Mary Ann Dalton, daughter of Mr. Ellis Pledger, of this city, in the 15th year of her age.
[Died] On Saturday the 20th inst., Mr. Ellis Pledger, in his forty-eighth year.

Issue February 3, 1844
Shocking Murder -- The *Caddo Gazette* says that a few days since Judge Hansford was most cruelly murdered in Harrison county, Texas, by an old gentleman named Mosely, and his son-in-law, whose name is Bullard. [note: circumstances are given].

Letters of Administration to the undersigned on the estate of James D. Owen, dec'd, late of Jackson county. Clark L. Owen.

Letters of administration granted to the undersigned for the estate of William Ryan dec'd late of Jackson county. Clark L. Owen.

Issue February 10, 1844
Gen. Murphy, the U.S. Charge d'Affaires, who has been in this city for some months past, left on Thursday on board the Dayton for Houston. We understand his health is bad and he hopes to be benefitted by a change of location. He may extend his visit to Washington.

Issue February 17, 1844
Hon. W.H. Jack, who has recently been dangerous sick, was convalescent at the last accounts.

Issue February 24, 1844
Died on the 21st January at the residence of Mrs. S.A. Wharton in the town of Brazoria, Mrs. Ann S. Dabney, in the 23rd year of her age...

Issue March 2, 1844
Gov. Reynolds, of Missouri, committed suicide on 9th Feb. by shooting himself.

Issue March 30, 1844
Red Lander: Murders on the Frontier. — A man by the name of Varner, his son, and a Mexican named Gonzales, were killed at the residence of Varner, about sixty miles north west of Henderson, in Nacogdoches county, on the 22d February. [note: circumstances are related].

Issue April 20, 1844
Died on Thursday last, Mr. A.L. Crossman, a citizen of Galveston.

Issue May 11, 1844
J.W. Pilant was tried in the District Court of Galveston county on Thursday last, charged with murder of George Wells, and acquitted.

Issue May 15, 1844
Republic of Texas. County of Galveston. Jacob L. Briggs presented the will of Catherine Vorrith, dec.

Issue May 25, 1844
Died on Thursday morning, 24th May, J.A.T. Fry, of this city.

The undersigned was appointed Administrator of the estate of Patrick Usher, dec'd, late of Jackson county. Clark L. Owen.

The Vicksburg papers state that a sister of Mr. Hagan, the editor who was recently killed in a duel at that place, has arrived there...for the support of her and her mother, who were wholly dependant on the brother and son. A similar subscription was taken up for the family of Huston, the La. editor, killed in the duel with LaBranche.

Issue June 1, 1844

Died on yesterday evening, Miss Mary Ann, daughter of Mrs. Jeannette Scott, formerly of Edinborough, Scotland, aged 22 years. The friends and acquaintances of her brother-in-law, Mr. D.R. Robertson, are respectfully invited to attend her funeral from his residence on Tremont St. at 10 o'clock this morning.

Died -- On Thursday morning last (30th ult.), Mrs. Margaret, consort of S. Kirkland/Kirklane of this city.

Issue June 12, 1844

Died in this city on yesterday evening at the Planters Hotel, Mr. Isaac Allen, one of the San Antonio Prisoners, who arrived here on the *Poinsett*. The citizens are invited to attend his funeral this morning at 9 o'clock from the Methodist church.

Died on the 1st inst. at the residence of Mr. Broach, near Gonzales, F.T. Wells, late Purser in the Navy of Texas.

Assassination: The body of Mr. B. Canfield, whose residence is about nine miles from Houston at Piny Point, was found in Buffalo Bayou a short distance below his dwelling the 6th inst. He went out to catch some fish the day before, and not returning, a search was instituted. The body was found by three gentlemen who went from Houston for that purpose. Upon examination it was discovered that he had been shot by some person unknown and the jury returned a verdict accordingly... *Houston Star*.

The undersigned administrator of the estate of Dean Murch will present his accounts for final settlement at the Probate Court Galveston county. David N. Terheun.

Issue June 15, 1844

J. R. Dufour of this city committed suicide on Tuesday night by shooting himself.

Miscellaneous Texas Newspaper Abstracts - Deaths --- Vol 2

Issue June 22, 1844
Recent skirmish with the Indians, who recently visited Corpus Christi and were pursued from that place... This chief, a fine looking fellow, had been wounded some time before by Juan Ramorez, a fine little Mexican clerk of Col. Kinney... Before they could load again, the Indians were on them and G. Gleason was almost instantly killed.

Issue June 29, 1844
Died at Cedar Point on the 17th inst., Gulian Clement Yates, oldest son of A.J. Yates, aged 11 years and 8 months.

Issue July 6, 1844
Died in Galveston on the 4th inst., Kendall Salsbury, late mate of the American barque *William Ivy*.

Hon. Tilghman A. Howard of Illinois has been appointed U.S. Charge d'Affaires to Texas and confirmed by the Senate. He may be expected here by the 20th inst.

Issue July 20, 1844
Died on Thursday evening last, Mr. J.P. Burger [note: page folded], a citizen of Galveston.

Hon. Wm. S. Murphy, late U.S. Charge d'affairs to Texas, died on Friday night.

The *Houston Democrat* of Saturday says -- "Three slaves, John, Castro, and Hester were yesterday examined before Chief Justice Thompson on suspicion of having murdered or been concerned in the murder of B. Canfield on the 7th ult. They were fully committed for trial."

Probate court. G[alveston] county. Estate of P.W. Grayson.

Administrators notice. Estate of Wm. Hall.

Issue July 27, 1844
Died on Saturday morning last in this city, Gen. W.S. Murphy, late Charge d'Affaires of the U. States in Texas.

[Died] On Wednesday night last, Mr. P.G. Street, a worthy and valuable citizen, in the prime of life.

193

Died in this city on Wednesday 24th inst., of bilious fever, after an illness of 28 days, John C. Michie, of Halifax county, Virginia. The *Richmond Enquirer* will please copy.

Died -- We regret to state that Dr. Stephen H. Everett, who came passenger by the last trip of the *New York* from Galveston, died yesterday at the St. Charles Hotel. Dr. E. was a native of the State of New York, and for several years past resided in Texas, where he had filled several important offices. He was a signer of the Declaration of Independence of the young Republic and was for some time President of the Senate. *N.O. Bee.*

Issue August 3, 1844
Died on the 28th ult., A.M. Green, U.S. Consul at this port.

[Died] on the 23rd ult., R.D. Sebring, editor of the *News*.

[Died] on the 28th, Judge E. Andrews, of this city.

N.O. Bulletin... Most atrocious murder, committed in the last month at the Creek agency in Arkansas by Capt. Dawson of the U.S. Army and agent of the Creeks, upon the person of S. Hill of the firm of T.B. Eastland & Co., but residing at the Agency... Dawson becoming deeply enraged went to Hill's house, and, without previous warning, slaughtered him in the presence of his wife -- and fled as was supposed for Texas.

Notice. It having been reported, much to my injury, that there was a great deal of sickness in my house, and that there were six to eight in it dying a day, this is publicily to pronounce the person who reported such a story to be a base liar and the truth is not in him. I have had but three of my boarders sick, and no one has died except Gen. Murphy, who had been in bad health for the ast [sic] year. J. C. Shaw.

Issue August 10, 1844
By the last arrival from Houston we learn that Hon. P.C. Jack died at that place on Sunday last. His loss from the Judicial Bench will be seriously felt and difficult to repair; the country will lament in his premature demise one of its best citizens, and a large circle of devoted friends and relatives have sustained a bereavement which they will long remember with sorrow.

Miscellaneous Texas Newspaper Abstracts - Deaths — Vol 2

Issue August 17, 1844

Died at his residence in this city on the 6th of August of the yellow fever, Maj. Talliaferro S. Howard, in the 45th year of his age. Maj. Howard emigrated to Texas from Mississippi in 1840, and recently settled in Galveston, where he bade fair to become a useful and valuable citizen... He left a wife and seven promising children to lament his loss.

Died in this city on the 10th inst., Pamelia Richardson Allen, youngest daughter of J.M. and Mary Allen, aged 4 years, 7 months and 12 days. New York and St. Louis papers please copy.

Issue August 24, 1844

Just after our Wednesday's paper had been printed the Houston boat arrived with the news of the death of Hon. Tilghman A. Howard, U.S. Charge d' Affaires to this government, which occurred, near Washington, on the 16th inst. from fever. The Secretaries of State and War gave him every attention during his sickness, and were with him when he died. The President, who knew Gen. H. in the U. States, was an old personal and political friend, was unfortunately absent.

Commander J.T.K. Lothrop of the Texas Navy died at Washington on the 14th inst. He was an active and popular officer, and has left many friends to mourn him, both among his old companions in arms and our private citizens.

Issue August 31, 1844

Departed this life on Wednesday the 14th inst. at twenty minutes past 9 o'clock P.M. at this place of billious fever, Commander J.T.K. Lothrop, of the Navy of Texas. Capt. Lothrop was a native of the state of Massachusetts. His parents whilst he was an infant, moved to Utica, in the state of New York, where the subject of this obituary was reared and educated... He was a direct descendant, in the maternal line, from Kirkland, one of the early pilgrim fathers... (he was but 30 years of age).

Died Thursday evening last in this city, Col. Henry Ware, a distinguished hero of San Jacinto.

Hon. Wm. H. Jack died at the plantation of Gov. Runnels, on the Brassos, of fever on the 20th inst.

Hon. Richard Morris, Judge of this District, died on Monday last at 10 p.m. of the disease which has recently prevailed here, its last and most lamented victim... No man in the community could have died whose loss would have been more generally and seriously felt, or whose place it would be more difficult to supply...

Lt. H.F. Porter of the U.S. schooner *Flirt*, late from this port, died in the harbor Charleston of yellow fever just after the arrival of the vessel. He was a son of the late commodore Porter.

Issue September 7, 1844

Died on Wednesday evening last, Mrs. Penelope, consort of G. Borden, Jr., of this vicinity.

Maj. Edward B. Ely, Agent for the contractors of Trinity Colony, died in the colony on the 7th July of bilious fever.

Issue September 14, 1844

Mr. R. Holbein fell overboard from the sloop *Sarah Foyle* in the Bay above Red Fish Bar on Saturday and was drowned before he could be picked up.

Issue September 21, 1844

Commodore Dallas of the U. St. Navy died on board the frigate *Savannah*, in Callao Bay, on the 3d day of June of paralysis. He had been in the navy nearly 39 years, and was a brother to Hon. George M. Dallas.

Issue September 28, 1844

Ex-Governor Moore of Alabama died recently in Marshall county, in the 61st year of his age-- He had but recently removed to this country.

Adminstratrix Sale at the house of the late Stephen Hard, all the personal estate of Stephen Hard, dec. Elizabeth Hard.

Issue October 5, 1844

Administratrix's Notice. Estate of Taliaferro S. Howard, dec. Elizabeth Howard.

Issue October 19, 1844

Notice: Died in the employ of the undersigned, Liberty county, Texas in the spring of 1838, Peter F. Edwards, late of the army of Texas, leaving two sisters in Virginia, who he wished to be benefited by his services here, and have papers and can make the proof that will entitle them to a quantity of land in this country, and have been several years trying in vain to reach them with information. August 7, 1844. I hope some friendly paper in Virginia will give the above circulation. Mat. Hubert.

Issue October 26, 1844

Coroner's Inquest -- On Monday last on the Peninsula, an Inquest was held upon the body of Benjamin Franklin Love, who was found murdered on the beach... He was overtaken by James Duncan, who was on his way to the Pass. A few words were passed between them, and a scuffle ensued... He fell dead upon the beach and Duncan went on his way as if nothing had occurred. Immediately after the coroner's jury had rendered their verdict, an officer hurried to the Pass to take Duncan into custody, but has not yet returned.--*Matagorda Despatch.*

Administrators Notice. Estate of Edmund Andrews, late of the county of Galveston. Jonas Butler, admin.

Issue November 16, 1844
Died at Montgomery of congestive fever on the 20th October, Mr. Joshua Keoys, Printer, a native of Ireland, but recently publisher of the *Star of Assumption* Attakapas, La. Louisiana papers will please copy. [note: see Keays].

Issue November 30, 1844
Administratrix's Notice. Estate of Benjamin Whitson, dec. Probate Court of Jackson county. Martha Whitson, adm'x.

Admin. Notice. Estate of James McKnight, dec., late of county of Galveston. Wm. H. Sandusky, admin.

Issue December 14, 1844
Mr. E. Miller, a steerage passenger on the schr. *Wm. Bryan* from New Orleans, died after the arrival of the vessel here on Friday last.

Admin. Notice. Republic of Texas. County of Jasper. Estate of Dr. Stephen H. Everett, dec., late of said county. Z. Wms. Eddy, adm'r.

Must be sold for cash... Persons wishing to engage in the avocation of Printing cannot find any point presenting greater prospects than at the town of Montgomery... the undersigned having lost her husband (Joshua Keays) on the 20th Oct. last is now forced to sell for cash to enable her to return to Ireland having no relatives either in the United States or Texas. Mary Keays.

Issue December 21, 1844
Republic of Texas. County of Galveston. Mrs. Jhouana Quitte having made application for letters of admin. on the estate of her dec. husband, Charles Quitte.

Issue December 5, 1846
Admin. notice. estate of John Dinsmore, dec. Galveston county. I.S. Savage, adm'r.

Issue April 21, 1847

The undersigned will present their account in the estate of James O'Leary for settlement. Jeremiah Kirby, admin. Mary Kirby, admin'x.

Appointed admin. estate of Mary Lee Harvey, dec. Galveston county. David Harvey, adm'r.

Issue June 26, 1847

A letter dated the 3d of the present month, the editor of the *Huntsville Banner*, describes an affair which sounds more like the reaction of some craggy Dutch romance writer, than serious truth -- yet true the story may be, as it is credited by the writer:

A most unnatural and horrible murder was committed a few days ago in Cherokee county... a man by the name of Jones and his wife had lived unhappily together for several years. Jones had frequently threatened to take their child and give it to his mother, declaring that his wife was unfit and unworthy to have it. During one of their quarrels he endeavored to get possession of their child, which in the scuffle between the father and mother, was killed. The infuriated wretch then turned upon his poor wife, and catching her by the throat with one hand and beating her with the other killed her... Jones was taken to the county seat and was handed over to the brothers of his murdered wife, who without further ceremony, bury him upon a gibbet. Jones' father a respectable and pious old man, found the body and buried it decently...

The Massachusetts volunteer put in prison at Matamoros for killing Capt. Myers, who refused him. whiskey, has made his escape. One of his companions has killed a woman in Matamoros for the same offence.

Some of the papers have stated that Wilkinson, the man at whose house the great poisoning case occurred in Shelby county, was hung by Lynch law. This is a mistake... Of the seventy persons who were poisoned at the wedding in Shelby county, twenty have died... One fact looks very suspicious and goes towards proving the guilt of Wilkinson.

Issue July 10, 1847

Killed by lightning -- Thomas H. Williams and David Watson were killed by lightning near Hickory Wythe, Fayette county, Tenn. on the 16th inst. They were under a hickory tree the shade of which they sought to protect them from a storm, and the lightning striking the tree passed to them.

The remains of General Howard of Indiana (the U.S. Minister to Texas who died at Washington on the Brazos in 1844) which were recently carried back in conformity with a resolution of the legislature of that State, arrived and were buried at Rockville on the second of June.

A man named James Mays, a Virginian by birth but a long resident of Texas, was shot recently at Monterey by the guard while attempting to escape from the guard house.

Died in Houston, June 26th, J.R. Capers, late of Alabama.

Died at the same place on the 27th, Mary Asenath, infant daughter of Mr. & Mrs. B.F. Tankersly.

Died in Galveston, June 25, Thomas L. Martin, infant son of Mrs. O.D. Johnson, aged 10 months and 20 days.

Died of consumption at the residence of Mr. T.H. Duggan, near Seguin, Guadalupe county, William B. Wilson, aged 24 years -- Mr. W. was a native of Barren county, KY.

Return of an Indian Captive -- William Lyons, whose mother, a widow, resides on the upper Navidad, in the county of Fayette. The *Advocate* says--This young man, at the age of 12 years, was captured at his mother's house, and his father murdered in October, 1837. His brother, Dewitt Lyons, had accompanied every campaign into the mountains since his captivity in the hopes of recovering him. We learn that young Lyons, in dress, manners and in a considerable extent in his general appearance, is Indian. He speaks his mother tongue very indifferently, but it is thought will acquire it as well as ever, in a few weeks...

Issue August 14, 1847

The U.S. ship *Raritan*, Capt. French Forrest, from the squadron in the Gulf of Mexico, arrived at Hampton Roads on the 22d ult. Sixty of the ship's company were sick with the fever. Capt. Edson, of the marines, Midshipman Storer, and seventeen hands, died on the passage.

Maj. Chevalic of the Texas Rangers met with a very serious accident a few days since at Saltillo, from which it is feared he will not recover. He was about starting to Parras, and while on horseback was taken with a fit and fell to the ground, receiving severe and serious injuries thereby.

Indian Hostilities on the Santa Fe Route... It is with regret that I have to report five of our best men killed: Privates Arledge, Dickhart, Gaskill, Short, and Vlake, and Sergeant Bishor and privates Lovelace and Vankaster are severely wounded; Privates Bush, <u>Wilson</u>, and Ward, slightly. [note: condensed].

Funeral Rites of American Heroes. George Lincoln, Capt. 8th Reg. Inft'y U.S.A. Fell at Buena Vista, Mexico February 23, 1847, aged 29 years. [note: condensed].

On Tuesday the 20th ult., the remains of Col Wm. R. McKee, Lieut Col. H. Clay, Capt Wm. T. Willis, Capt. W.H. Maxey, Adjt. E.M. Vaughn, Lt. Jos. Powell, W.W. Bayles, Wm. Thwaits, N. Ramey, Thos Weigert, Alex. G. Morgan, C. Jones, H. Carty, T. McH. Dozier, H. Trotter, C.B. Thompson, and W.T. Green, who fell courageously fighting the country's battles, and died in the service, were interred in the state grounds of the Frankfort, Ky. Cemetery. [note: condensed].

Col. Hardin -- the remains of Col. Hardin, who fell at Buena Vista, were interred with imposing honors at Jacksonville, Ill, late the place of his residence, on the 14th ult. The funeral eulogy was delivered by Richard Yeates. The beautiful grey charger which bore him through the campaign was led in the procession.

Issue November 6, 1847

List of interments for the week ending November 4th:

October 28th	Dan'l Jenkins	aged 35	U.S.
October 28th	John Moro	aged 35	Germany
October 28th	Mr. Rose	aged 40	Germany
October 28th	Charles S. Savage	aged 20	U.S.
October 28th	Matthew Rowe	aged 47	Georgia, U.S.
October 28th	George Kink	aged 59	Germany
October 28th	Christiana Hoback	aged 25	Germany
October 28th	John H. Mills	aged 18 days	U.S.
October 28th	Fred. Opperman	aged 12	Germany
October 28th	Maria Kried	aged 40	Germany
October 28th	a man unknown	aged [??]	Germany
October 29th	John Stauffle	aged 53	Germany
October 29th	Thos. J. Melvin	aged 20	New York
October 29th	Fred. Ladambear	aged 6 weeks	
October 9th	Eliza Fink	aged 8	Germany
October 29th	F.X. Jeannotat	aged 62	France
October 29th	a child of William R. <u>Wilson</u>'s aged 2 years		U.S.
October 30th	Mrs. Kronz		Germany
October 30th	Michael Suey	aged 44	Germany
October 30th	Ludwig Petoi	aged 55	France
October 30th	Mary Stopleberg	aged 22	Germany

October 30th	Minna Stample	aged 30	Germany
October 30th	a child of		
	J.J. Thompson's	aged 3 years	U.S.
October 31st	Joseph Eagely	aged 17	Germany
October 31st	Jostena Abert	aged 25	Germany
October 31st	Lewe Oldendroff	aged 4 months	
October 31st	C. Louisa Shattuck	aged 17	U.S.
October 31st	Reid Malincrodft	aged 27	Germany
October 31st	C. Painter		Germany
October 31st	Caroline Short	aged 40	Germany
October 31st	Jacob Johen		Germany
October 31st	J. Gomet		France
November 1st	William Grodbread	aged 24	Germany
November 1st	a child of C. Baudin's		
November 1st	J. Goodlow	aged 21	Cincinnati, Ohio
November 2nd	Gus. Tobel	aged 30	Germany
November 2nd	J. Bechsoppf		Germany
November 2nd	Ann M. Mathee	aged 28	Germany

Hon. Alex. A. Everett, American Minister, died at Canton on the 29th of June.

Issue November 20, 1847

Capt. Brown of the schr. *J.G. McNeel* was drowned by the swamping of a boat on the Brazos bar a few days since.

List of interments for week ending November 18th:

November 11th	A man unknown,		Germany
November 11th	John P. Davie	aged 20 months	U.S.
November 11th	a negro child	aged 2 years	
November 12th	Andrew Marx	aged 64	Germany
November 12th	Mrs. E. Brown	aged 37	U.S.
November 12th	Rob't Miller	aged 50	England
November 12th	J. Herzfield	aged 14	Germany
November 12th	Chas. Cinckle	aged 43	Germany
November 13th	Wm. Yager	aged 42	Germany
November 13th	Hankin Frauget	aged 14	Germany
November 13th	Joseph Crane	aged 35	U.S.
November 13th	Geo. Gifford	aged 17 months	U.S.
November 13th	P. Rolata	aged 21	Germany
November 14th	James Burke	aged 55	U.S.
November 15th	a German child	aged 4	
November 15th	E.W.H. Cors	aged 31	Germany
November 15th	....Christiana	aged 42	Germany
November 15th	Henry Schinl	aged 6	Germany

November 16th	....Stoppleberg	aged 22 days	Germany
November 16th	E. Cattinger	aged 45	Germany
November 17th	C. Maix	....	Germany
November 17th	C. Shaver	aged 27	Germany

John Griffin, City Sexton.

December 11, 1847

List of interments in the city for the week ending 9 December 1847:

December 2nd	Mary Jane Menard	aged 33	U.S.
December 4th	a female named Stamann		Germany
December 5th	Fritz Kliuker	aged 5	Germany
December 6th	negro boy belonging to J.S. Sydnor		
December 7th	Mary Moller	aged 9	Germany

John Griffin, City Sexton.

The remains of Capt. Walker now repose at the Odd Fellows Hall opposite Baudin's, where they will remain until 10 o'clock tonight, to give an opportunity to those who may desire to touch the bier of the brave soldier and pay honor to his remains. The procession will form at 9 o'clock tomorrow and march to the Baptist church -- from thence, after the ceremonies at 12 o'clock, the remains will be removed to the boat.

Issue December 18, 1847

The Comanches made a descent on the Mexican Settlements near Parras in force. Sixty of the Texian cavalry under the command of Maj. Lowe, charged on a hundred and twenty of them, killing about thirty. W.H. Bell was killed in the charge, McMurty and two others wounded.

Capt. Sam'l H. Walker. At 10 o'clock on Saturday the Order of Odd fellows and a large number of the citizens proceeded on procession to the Baptist Church, where an eulogy on the life and character of Capt. Walker was delivered by Robert Howard and divine service performed by Rev. M. Huckins. From thence the body was carried in procession to the steamer *Reliance* in charge L.P. Sundburg and Richard C. Barry, to be delivered by them to the Order at Houston, from which point it will be transported to San Antonio.

Capt. Walker's Remains --- When the remains of the gallant Walker were taken to Puebla, the botch of a carpenter made the coffin too small, whereupon Lieut. Clinton, of Scott's company, 1st P., off with his uniform, rolled up his sleeves, and made him a coffin himself. He is a carpenter, you will recollect, from Mopamensing or Southwark, in Philadelphia -- Lieut. Breese of same company, who is a blacksmith, entered a smithery and made the nails. So much for Pennsylvania volunteers.

List of interments for the week ending December 16.

Dec. 11-Joseph Leimiller	aged 33	Germany
Dec. 12-Carl Voo	aged 23	Germany
Dec. 12-Dr. Russell		U.S.

Died -- At Brazoria on Wednesday the 8th inst., Charles Schleight, aged about 38 years.

GALVESTON DAILY NEWS
Published at Houston, Texas.
Established 1842.

Issue February 21, 1865
Died in this city on Saturday morning the 18th inst., Mr. John H. Johnston, in the 51st year of his age, much respected...

Issue February 26, 1865

The man who was badly injured by the accident of the Galveston train on Wednesday, was the brakeman, Henry Sholiboh, who died a few minutes after.

Issue February 28, 1865
Preamble and Resolutions on the Death of P.G. Reynolds. Adopted by the R.W. Grand Lodge I.O.O.F. State of Texas.

Issue March 4, 1865
We regret to learn of the killing, by a stroke of lightning on the 4th of February, of Henry Karnes Brown, aged 16 years; son of W.A. Brown of Uvalde county... *San Antonio Herald.*

Issue March 5, 1865
Hempstead, March 4th: Our little place was today much aroused by a difficulty between Capt. Logan, Enrolling Officer of Austin county, and Mr. E.S. Buck, which resulted in the death of the latter, who was stabbed several times in the breast. Mr. Buck formerly lived at Chappell Hill.

Issue March 17, 1865
We were gratified on yesterday to meet with Mr. Wm. Penny, formerly a citizen of Galveston, some twelve years ago. While he was quite a youth his family removed to California, where his parents both died... His birth place was Galveston, his father formerly a merchant.

203

Issue March 22, 1865

Died of consumption on the 15th of March, 1865, Maj. Joseph Wallis, aged 64 years [?], after an illness of two years. Chappell Hill, March 17, 1865.

Issue March 26, 1865

Died of [?] tetanus in the city of Houston on the 19th day of March inst., Lt. George Clinton Duncan, of Spaight's Regt. Texas Vol. Inf., in the 34th year of his age. Lt. Duncan was a native of Virginia, but from early youth a citizen of Talladega county, Alabama, whence he removed to Texas in 1859...

Issue March 28, 1865

Died October 20th at 10 o'clock p.m. of wounds received in the battle of October 7th, 1864, on the Darbytown road near Richmond, Virginia, 1st Lt. Robert R. Armstrong, Co. L 1st Regt. Tx Vol., a native of Newcastleton, Roxburghshire, Scotland, aged about 28 years...

Issue March 29, 1865

The *Austin State Gazette* says Mr. James R. Jackson, for a number of years a resident of Austin, was killed on Saturday night last by a knife, in the hands of Alfred Robinson (better known as Beaut Robinson) a citizen of this county.

The coroner's jury returned a verdict to the effect that Mr. J. came to his death from wounds inflicted by a knife or sharp instruments.

Issue March 30, 1865

The death of Capt. Peter Dowd, an old resident of the Rio Grande, is reported. He was much respected.

Issue April 7, 1865

We have reported one among the heaviest national calamities with which our country has been visited during the war in the death of Gen. John A. Wharton. He was shot through the heart at the Fannin House in this city at the hour of 10 o'clock yesterday morning by Col. George Baylor... aged mother [note: testimony before the jury of inquest also given].

Issue April 12, 1865

Died in Galveston, April 7th, Fannie Elizabeth, infant daughter of Robert and Hannah Dickey, aged 15 months and 2 days.

Issue April 13, 1865

Died at his residence near this city, April 10th, 1865, of typhoid fever, Capt. A.T. Morse, of the firm of A.T. and J.B. Morse, Druggists, of Houston. Capt. Morse was born in the city of New Haven, Conn., October 1801, but was raised in South Carolina; thence the family emigrated to Alabama, thence to Mississippi. The last 13 years of his life have been spent in Texas...

Loss of the Schooner *Eliza Catherine* and six lives. Brazoria county April 8, 1865. The names of the missing crew are as follows: R. Boyle, Capt.; August Torbert, mate; A.W.H. Sanford, supercargo; C. Lambert, Julius Osker & Antonio DeSilver, seamen.

Issue April 14, 1865

General Wharton's birth day was 5 July 1829. [note: was given incorrectly in notice of his death].

Gen. T.J. Chambers, old and distinguished citizen of Texas, was assassinated in his bed-room in Chambers county on the night of 15th March in the presence of his wife and children by being shot in the right side of his face and head with twenty-nine shots of different sizes. He died instantly.

General Chambers was born in Orange Co. Virginia in 1802. At the age of 21 he was admitted to the bar of Kentucky. [note: condensed].

Issue April 16, 1865

The friends of Col. John S. Sydnor and family are invited to attend the funeral of Walter McNair, son of Columbia Sydnor and the late Robert H. McNair, from their rooms at the Fannin House this Sunday afternoon at half past 4 o'clock. [died after a distressing sickness from typhoid fever, for about two months.] Houston, April 16, 1865.

(From the *News*) In recording the names of those who honored their country, and were by their country honored, we should take into consideration the fact, that at the same time, that heroes win battles and glory, the mothers who early matured their pride and ambition, should stand first on the record.

Mrs. General Sydney Sherman, late deceased, the wife of a brave and patriotic Texian, and the mother of Lt. S.A. Sherman... deserves to be placed high on the list of those who rank as Southern patriots. The wife of one hero and the mother of another has a patent in the heart of every honest man to be called a heroine.

Misfortune with her dolorous train, has of late years constantly attached itself to her, and the death of her cherished son at the battle of Galveston added the finishing stroke, and she lingered for a period, the fatality broke her heart.

Issue April 18, 1865

Died at his residence in San Jacinto, April 14, 1865, of dropsy, Mr. J.C. Habermehl, aged 54 years... He was buried with Masonic honors.

Five of the six unfortunate crew of the ill-fated schooner *Eliza Catherine* drifted ashore near this place on the 11th and 12th inst. and were as decently buried on the Gulf shore as the circumstances would admit by Capt. Dunn's company. Two of the bodies bore incontestible evidence of having lived some days after the schooner went to pieces, and one of them appeared to have been dead but a few hours when found on the beach. This gives hope that probably the sixth man may have been picked up by the blockader off the mouth of the Brazos.

Issue April 19, 1865

Died in Millican, Texas, on the 15th inst. in her 20th year, Miss Ada, 3rd daughter of John H. & Eliza P. LePert. Whilst riding on horseback on the afternoon of the 14th, her saddle turned and she was thrown against a stump, causing concussion of the brain. She lingered in an unconscious state for eight hours, when death ensued. Parents, sisters, and many friends mourn her untimely fate.

Issue April 29, 1865

Died in this city on the night of the 26th inst., Mr. G.T. McIntosh of Co. F, 24th Tx Cavalry, in the 19th year of his age.

Issue May 4, 1865

Victoria Advocate: Mr. Hogan James, living on the Garcitas, in this county, was shot and killed on Thursday last by a man named O'Daniel.

Issue May 7, 1865

Col. Eddar, the state agent for the state of Arkansas, died in Brownsville after an illness of about a week.

Issue May 10, 1865

We regret to learn, by a letter from Judge D.G. Burnet, that his only son (Maj. Burnet) was killed in the defence of Spanish Fort in Mobile Bay on the 21st of April.

We regret to learn that the wife of Lt. Gov. Stockdale died at her residence near the city of Austin on the 27th ult.

Issue May 16, 1865

Galveston, May 15th, 1865: Last Saturday afternoon the person known as Dr. Macelmurray, was shot and killed in this city, on the street, in front of the old ice house (Morian Hall) by Mr. Sutton, the person who obtained the confession from Macelmurray of the murder of Mr. Neibor's negro woman last Christmas eve. [note: condensed].

Miscellaneous Texas Newspaper Abstracts - Deaths --- Vol 2

Issue June 6, 1865
Died on Friday the 26th ult., in Washington county, after a short but violent illness, David Kaufman, in the 19th year of his age. He was the son of Hon. David S. Kaufman. He leaves a sister and brother.

Issue June 10, 1865
Gov. John Milton, of Florida, committed suicide at his residence in Mariana, Florida, about the 1st of April by shooting himself through the heart.

Issue June 13, 1865
Died on the 8th inst. at the residence of his father, Edward Pearsall, son of G.W. and V.C. Strother, of Galveston, aged 15 1/2 months. It is a singular coincidence that they lost another child at the exact, same age, not five hours difference.

Issue June 27, 1865
We copy from the *San Antonio Herald* of the 17th: We are pained to be called upon to chronicle the untimely death of Capt. Charles Bouldin, who was killed in an unfortunate difficulty between the deceased and a German named Leu. The deceased was a brother of Mr. Bouldin, of the firm of Bouldin, Riggs & Walker of this city, and a brother-in-law of A.W. Terrill of Austin.

Died near Chappell Hill on the 23rd of June, Hood, infant son of I.E. & S.C. Wallis, aged 16 months and 17 days.

A man by the name of Albert Robinson was shot and killed on the 20th inst. by some person who we suppose was a stranger to the deceased. Mr. James Jackson of Austin was killed some little time ago in a difficulty with the deceased, Robinson... A man, by the name of Thos. Slaughter, who was supposed to have been one of the Austin party, was found on the Austin road, about a mile and a half from the city, on the same evening, dead.

San Antonio Herald: On Sunday morning last a German named Herman living near the head of the river, shot and killed his brother. The survivor was arrested. It appears that the brothers had a quarrel, in the course of which Gregory, the one on trial, was attacked and bitten by three dogs belonging to his brother Michael -- that presently Gregory shot and killed two of the dogs, when Michael got his gun and shot at but missed Gregory. The latter then advanced upon Michael, who attacked him with a sabre, and in the conflict which ensued, Michael was shot, surviving but a few minutes.

We understand that a difficulty occurred in Columbus a few days since, between Mr. Harris and N. Womble, in which the latter shot Harris through the shoulder, and was in turn shot by the son of Mr. Harris, and survived only a few hours. We have been unable to learn the particulars, only that Harris is not seriously hurt.

Issue June 29, 1865
Died in Grimes county June 18th, Edwin Brenard, son of John and E. Eveline Stoneham, aged 9 years, 2 months, 28 days.

Issue July 4, 1865
Departed this life on Saturday night the 24th of June, 1865, at his residence in Houston, Kosciusco Morgan, the only son of Col. James Morgan of Galveston Bay, in the 44th year of his age. Mr. Morgan was a native of Murfreesboro, North Carolina, and was educated at New Haven... Besides his surviving father, a wife, and six children mourn their irremediable loss...

Issue July 7, 1865
James Jackson, son of the rebel Governor Clairborne F. Jackson, has been killed by militiamen in Audrian County. He was charged with being a guerilla.

William Mull, a printer, died suddenly in St. Louis on the 2nd from an attack of cholera, the physician pronouncing it to be a clear case of asiatic cholera.

Issue July 11, 1865
Died in this city on the morning of the 21st inst., Frank Wilson, youngest and idolized son of William R. & Amanda E. Wilson.

Issue July 13, 1865
Clarksville Standard of the 24th: Elias Miller, a grocery keeper in our town, was killed this morning by two discharges from a shot gun in the hands of Marcos J. Anderson, a jeweler...

Issue July 15, 1865
From the *San Antonio Herald* of the 8th: On Friday evening an unfortunate difficulty occurred between Col. Z. Vanward and Mr. Stoerbeeck, a German, (both of this city) in which four or five shots were exchanged, resulting in two wounds being inflicted upon the person of Stoerbeeck; one in the wrist and one in the breast, which bids fair to be mortal. Stoerbeeck was a music teacher.

Died at her residence in Harrisburg on Sunday evening the 9th inst., Mrs. Mary A. Gray, wife of Mr. J.W. Gray, formerly of Lynchburg, Virginia and before the war, of Galveston... a lady deservedly esteemed by her numerous friends, who with her bereaved husband and orphan family of seven children, sincerely mourn their loss. Mrs. Gray was a native of Scottsville, Virginia, and at the time of her death, was in the 44th year of her age.

Issue July 18, 1865
Died on the 13th inst. after a long and painful illness, Mattie Bennetta, infant daughter of Edward Cane and Lucretia Dealy, aged 10 months and 14 days.

Issue July 19, 1865
Mrs. Bryan, wife of Dr. Louis A. Bryan, died in Galveston on Sunday, and her remains were brought to Houston by the train on Monday and buried on the evening of the same day. Dr. Bryan is well known to the people of Texas as one of their greatest benefactors. He has had charge of the Texas Hospital in Mississippi and Alabama for the past three years, and had only returned to Galveston on Thursday last, on his way home with his estimable lady, who took sick but two or three days before her death.

Issue July 20, 1865
Died on the 17th of July 1865 at Galveston, Mrs. Jane Frederick, wife of Julius Frederick.

Remarkable death from being poisoned by a fly. Coronor Collin held an inquest yesterday on the body of Chas. Schweiger, German butcher, 40 years of age... *New York World.*

Issue July 21, 1865
San Antonio News of the 4th: Information has reached us that three men, Germans, on their way from Fredricksburg to Castroville, each with a wagon loaded with flour, were attacked and killed by Indians somewhere below Bandera Pass. The name of one of them is Louis Mann.

A short time since, two persons whose names are given as Gebhard and Koening were killed upon the Eagle Pass road near the Sabinal.

Died on the 14th after an illness of nineteen days, Mrs. Sue L. Halton, wife of Dr. N.G. Halton, leaving a husband and four children. *Henderson Times* please copy.

Issue July 27, 1865

We are pained to learn from Mr. Robert Clark that the grave of his child, in the Episcopal church yard of this city, had been dug out and the coffin opened, though the contents were not disturbed.

Issue July 29, 1865

Died at the residence of her father-in-law, Mrs. Lula M. Newell, wife of John E. Newell. This worthy Christian lady was born in Port Gibson, Mississippi, October 15, 1846, was married October 3, 1864, and died July 24, 1865... She leaves an infant ten days old... Richmond.

Issue August 3, 1865

We have information that on Friday last (21st), a man named Henry Meier, was killed by Indians on the road between Fredericksburg and Sisterdale...

Issue August 5, 1865

San Antonio News. A man by the name of Fiers was murdered near Mr. Bass's on the Gilmer Road, about two weeks ago... The murder undoubtly supposed he had money when in reality he had but five dollars in specie.

Issue August 8, 1865

On the morning of the 1st, the body of Charles Smith was found about seven miles below Fredericksburg, having been dead apparently some hours...

On Tuesday the 25th inst. at about noon, the house of Mr. Charles Ginseng, fifteen miles above Fredericksburg at the Squaw Creek settlement, was attacked by a party of Indians numbering about fifteen; Mr. Ginseng was killed, his wife was ravished, scalped and cut with knives in three places upon her body and one of their children was carried away a captive. Mrs. Ginseng survived at the last account and it was thought she would recover.

We regret to learn of a homicide in Walker county, a few days ago, in which a Mr. Dick Williams killed a man named Goodrich, who had threatened his life, for acts committed in the reign of the Confederacy...

Issue August 12, 1865

Dr. A.J. Cornett, a citizen of Dallas, Dallas county, Texas, and formerly a merchant of Crockett, died at the Holman House on the 20th ult., aged 48 years.

Issue August 13, 1865

The funeral of Miss Mary Nash was largely attended last evening by her numerous friends.

Issue August 15, 1865

Some little commotion was observed in our city on Sunday morning, occasioned by a reported death from yellow fever on the previous evening. The deceased was a young man from Burlington, Iowa, named John Robinson... The physicians who attended on and examined the case reported it to have been a well defined case of congestive bilious fever...

Issue August 17, 1865

Austin Intelligencer of the 11th: Miss Augusta Bahn, aged 28, oldest daughter of Mr. A. Bahn, of this city, was drowned at the upper ford of the river last Sunday morning...

Issue August 18, 1865

The *San Antonio News* on the 11th says: We have information that Mr. Grinder was shot a few days ago in the daytime, while sitting in the gallery of his house at the crossing of the Rio Frio on the Eagle Pass road from this place. No particulars were given.

Issue August 22, 1865

The *Clarksville Standard* contains a circumstantial account of the killing of a man named Taylor, a returned confederate soldier, by the paramour of his wife, a physician in good practice and of otherwise respectable character. He decoyed his victim into the woods and then shot him.

Issue August 25, 1865

Died at Waverly, Walker county, Texas, August 20, 1865, of apoplexy of the lungs, Mrs. Sarah Hill, wife of Col. John Hill, aged 51 years [note: age not clear].

Issue August 27, 1865

San Antonio Herald: We have received a letter from Charles Lewis, dated at Fredericksburg, August 10th, from which we learn that the Indians killed nine persons on the head of Spring Creek, recently. One named McDonald, another Taylor, four children and three women.

Issue August 29, 1865

The *Dallas Herald* on the 19th informs us that a fatal rencontre took place in the lower part of that county near Lancaster on the morning in which Mr. H.F.C. Johnson, of Pleasant Run, and a Capt. Coffee, of Collin county, were killed...

Issue September 1, 1865

Died at Liberty, Texas on the 3rd of August, 1865, William G. Shepherd, late of the C.S.A., aged about 21 years...

From a private letter we learn that our respected friend and fellow citizen, Dr. J.C. Jordan, died at South Port, Indiana, on the 21st day of April last, of disease of the heart, under which he had been suffering during the last three years... The doctor was a native of Alabama and served as an Army physician during the war with Mexico. After peace was established between the U.S. and Mexico he emigrated to Texas and made Galveston his adopted home...

Issue September 7, 1865
Mrs. Ursula P. Thompson, daughter of Susan and Dickie Chappell, and wife of Hiram Thompson, was born in Christian county, Kentucky the 21st of October, 1815, and died in Chappell Hill, August 14, 1865. Sister Thompson made a profession of religion in Cadiz, Kentucky, during the ministry of Rev. Abraham Long...

Issue September 8, 1865
Archibald S. Ruthven is dead. He died in Scotland, July 28th. He became a citizen of Galveston in 1839 and has resided in Texas ever since... [note: born Scotland 1813; member of the Masons; grand secretary from 1846-1860].

Died at Washington on the 25th of August 1865, Mrs. Elizabeth Seely, wife of Rev. R.S. Seely, of South Carolina... Member of the Episcopal Church...

Issue September 15, 1865
Died near Houston on the morning of the 11th inst., Imogene L., only child of L.F. and Mary Jane Harris, aged 3 years, 11 months, 2 days.

Issue September 16, 1865
After sunrise, the mornings glory expands - midday comes - it wilts. So has Rebecca, the third daughter of P.J. and Emma Mahan.

Issue September 17, 1865
San Antonio News 9th: On Tuesday last, Mr. Julius Haenel, of this city, took his life by a shot from a pistol... leaves a loving family.

Issue September 20, 1865
Died at Sour Lake, Texas, on the 5th inst., Sophronia Ann Cash, wife of H.J.B. Cash of Brazoria county... Her husband is left to comfort the cares of this life with five helpless children... She was a native of Georgia and in her 29th year of age...

Issue September 23, 1865
Died in the city of Houston, September 13th, 1865, Charles Robert, infant son of C.H. and Eugenia Leman, aged 1 year, 4 months, 13 days.

Issue September 24, 1865

Betsy Wilder, a negro woman, died in Richmond, age 108... [note: mentions a son, age 90].

The Frontier -- From a citizen of this county lately from Wise we learn that the frontier is in an unpleasant state; trouble with bushwhackers, who lately hanged Capt. Hagler of Montague; and with Indians, who have taken horses in and around Decator, and killed others, and who lately killed a white boy near Prairie Point, Wise county. The citizens have asked for a protecting force of Federals, but got none as yet. --*Clarksville Standard.*

Issue September 30, 1865

Died in this city on the evening of the 28th inst., Alexander, infant son of John Brashear.

Died at White Rock, McLellan county, Texas August 29, 1865, Miss Emeline J. Flint, of Alexandria, Louisiana.

Issue October 5, 1865

The storm which we referred to as doing so much damage in Orange, extended to Calcasieu, destroying plantations, houses, and lives... We have the following names of the killed: Lt. Harris, Serg. Willis, Mr. & Mrs. Lowell, Mr. Lewis, Mrs. Thayer, mother and daughter, an infant of Mrs. Ketchum, Emma and Henry Goss, children; a daughter of Capt. Nelson, Galveston; Mrs. Lambert, daughter and son; Mrs. Mitchell and three children, Isham Reeves, a daughter of Mrs. Wilson and two negroes.

...I have seen in the *Telegraph*, as an item of news, the hanging of Capt. G.W. Hegler, by some Union men of the frontier...

Issue October 6, 1865

Charles H. Loftin, aged 20 years, son of W.B. Loftin, was killed by lightning September 4th, 1865, a few miles east of Lake Charles, Louisiana.

Issue October 8, 1865

In Fayetteville, Fayette county, September 30, 1865, Andrew Jackson died, son of E. and Annie J. Rice/Rich, aged 4 years, 3 months and 2 days.

Issue October 13, 1865

Dr. A. Patter, a resident dentist of Galveston for the last ten years and much respected by all, died very suddenly yesterday morning. After taking some active exercise, he went in his house and laid down and died in a few minutes, without any previous illness. The physician pronounced that he died of a disease of the heart.

Issue October 14, 1865

Died at his residence near the city of Austin on the 3rd inst. of asthma, Robert J. Townes. Judge Townes was born in Amelia county, Virginia, on the 20th of February 1810. He emigrated to Texas in 1836, locating in Brazoria county in the practice of the law... He leaves a family of seven children to mourn his loss... [note: condensed].

Issue October 15, 1865

Between 9 and 10 o'clock yesterday afternoon, the city was agitated by a report that Col. J.E. Kirby, of Austin county, near Hempstead, had been killed in our Provost Marshall's office by a pistol fired by Mr. John Steele...

Issue October 20, 1865

Died on Tuesday morning, October 17th 1865, of typhoid pneumonia after a short illness, Mrs. Amelia D. Raby, formerly of Terrebonne Parish, Louisiana.

Issue October 25, 1865

Died in Harrisburg on the 25th of September, 1865, after a short and sudden illness, Alice Spooner, aged 18 years.

Died in the city of Houston of brain fever on the night of the 19th October 1865, George Edward, the only son of Helen M. and the late Lieut. Rottenstein, aged six years and twenty-five days.

Issue October 26, 1865

Died on the night of the 24th of October 1865, at the residence of Mrs. Maria Jameson, in the city of Houston, Alexander Willett, only son of Mrs. Eliza McEbine, aged 10 years, 1 month, 9 days.

Letter from Gonzales, October 10, 1865.:. a shocking murder was committed in the eastern part of this county on the 10th inst. by a man named Page residing somewhere near Texana, Jackson county. It seems that three brothers named Heller, Germans, had gone down to that county and stolen Page's daughter, for a wife of one them and as they were returning, Page overtook them and camped with them... While they were asleep that night, Page stole their pistols from under their heads and killed one of the brothers...

Issue October 27, 1865

Died. At Col. E.M. Sandord's Wharton, Texas, on the 27th ult., William Saunders, aged about 38 years.

Captain Saunders was born in Greene county, Alabama, came to Texas in 1857, was connected with the cotton gin business and wa a member of the firm of Mather, Hughes, and Saunders... He leaves a widow with three small children...

Issue November 8, 1865

Death of Mr. W.W. Morris: At about midnight on the 5th inst., he was found lying near the door of Mr. Clark's store on Main St., his neck broken, and he dead... Mr. Morris was about fifty years of age, was born in the state of New York and came to Texas some six years ago; since which time, he has been the Chief Engineer and Superintendent of the Texas and New Orleans Railroad.

Died at her residence in Washington county, Texas, on the 3 October 1865, Mrs. Mary A. Dawson, wife of Col. John H. Dawson.

Issue November 9, 1865

Peter White, an old and respected citizen of Goliad county, and T. Craig, visited B. Osgood, of that county to see about his abusing his wife, who was Craig's sister. Mr. White reproved Osgood for his conduct, received an abrupt reply and struck at him with a stick. Osgood drew a pistol and shot White, and Craig at once shot Osgood. Both White and Osgood were killed.

Issue November 11, 1865

Died at the residence of Mr. William Janes on the 2nd inst., Mrs. M.J. Clark, in the 22nd year of her age; daughter of Mr. Janes, and consort of M.H. Clark... Fort Bend, 11 November 1865.

Issue November 17, 1865

Died in the city of Houston on Sunday the 12th inst. after a weeks illness, Mrs. Sophia Price, widow of John Price, deceased, in the 61st year of her age. She was a native of Tennessee and came with her father to this state in 1840 and resided in Galveston for over twenty years...

Issue November 26, 1865

Died on November 6th, 1865, in Robertson county, Texas, Mrs. Rebecca Beeson, wife of John A. Beeson and daughter of Col. David Cole of Perry county, Alabama... She was born in South Carolina, 15 July 1818, and died at the age of 47 years, 3 months and 21 days. She left a husband and six children. New Orleans papers please copy.

Issue November 29, 1865

Died on Thursday the 16th November in Huntsville, Mrs. A.M. Baker, daughter of Col. Joseph Bates of Brazoria county.

Issue December 3, 1865

Died Saturday evening, 19 November 1865, of a gunshot wound accidentally received while hunting on the same day, Fulsh[?]ar/Fulansar Moore, aged 10 years, 6/8 months and 11 days; only son of Mrs. Mary A. Wimberly, of Fort Bend county.

Issue December 6, 1865

Died near Livingston, Polk county, on the 15th October 1865, Margaret Elizabeth, consort of Dr/De. Willis, in the 34th year of her age... left husband and helpless children.

Issue December 10, 1865

Died on the 3rd inst. at his residence in Colorado county, Albert A. Williamson, aged 38 years, 3 months.

Died on the 9th at the residence of R.D. Carr, Andrew Livingston, formerly of Natchez, Mississippi.

Issue December 15, 1865

Died yesterday morning (14th inst.) at half past 7 o'clock after a short and painful illness, Mrs. Mary Ellen Bodman. The friends of the family are respectfully invited to attend her funeral, from the residence of H.A. Bodman, opposite the Fannin House, this morning at 10 o'clock.

Issue December 31, 1865

We regret to hear of the death of Col. John McClarty of Henderson.

Issue March 24, 1866
Published in Galveston, Texas.

The funeral of Samuel D. Mills, formerly a respected citizen of Galveston, but residing more recently near Houston, took place here yesterday at noon, from the residence of his uncle, Robt. Mills, under the direction of the Masonic Fraternity. Mr. Mills was killed a few days since at his home, fifteen miles from Houston, by a German named Snyder, sometimes called Grobecker. He shot the deceased twice in the breast...

Francis Tait Bonds, daughter of Rev. M.C. & Ann Conoly, was born in North Carolina, June 12, 1842, married in Washington county, Texas, September 24, 1864, and died at the residence of her husband, Capt. A.B. Bonds in Colorado county, Texas, February 21, 1866. Father, mother, sisters, brothers and friends mourn thee dear Fannie! But the husband and the motherless daughter; who can tell the bitterness of their woe?

Issue March 27, 1866

Died in Galveston on Sunday the 28th inst. of measles, Wharton, infant son of Hon. Jno. W. and Mrs. Annie P. Harris, aged 11 months and 3 days.

The verdict of the coroner's jury in the case of Mrs <u>Kauder</u>, found dead in her room last Sunday morning, has not yet transpired...two negro men in jail. Mrs. Kauder was the wife of Frank Kauder, and old citizen and formerly an Alderman. She was found to have been under the influence of chloroform shortly before her death, by the physicians who made the Post Mortem examination and marks detected upon her neck leads to the supposition that she was strangled to death after being stupefied with chloroform.

Issue March 28, 1866

W.L. Miller, for many years a citizen of New Orleans, was buried Monday, having died at the rooms of R. Jones, on the Strand, who gave him every attention and medical assistance during his short illness...

Issue March 29, 1866

The Coroner's Jury in the case of Mrs. <u>Kauder</u> rendered the following verdict: We, the jury of inquest, find that Mrs. Ann Harris, or Kauder, came to her death from causes unknown to us.

Verdict of the jury of inquest held on the 26th day of March, on the body of Henry Kaddo, a colored man, about twenty years of age. We the jury, from evidence before us, find that said Henry Kaddo, came to his death from a pistol shot, in his own hands.

Issue March 31, 1866

The *Liberty Gazette* says G.W. Jelks was shot and killed at the residence of Mrs. Gibson in that place on the night of the 24th. Wm. W. Gibson was arrested...

Issue April 3, 1866

F.J. Ward, of the 3rd Michigan Inf., was drowned on the 24th ult. while bathing in the river at San Antonio.

Issue April 4, 1866

The *Banner* (Brenham) says Mr. Alex. Green was killed near Union Hill, Washington county a few days ago, by a negro, who gives his name as Jack Givens.

Mr. D.D. Crumpler of Brenham died suddenly on the 26th... He was sitting in his chair, conversing cheerfully, when he fell suddenly to the floor and expired immediately. The *Banner* says he was an old and respected citizen.

Issue April 5, 1866

Died: Mrs. J.F. Montgomery. She departed this life in peace on the 20th of March, 1866, after a brief illness... leaves her husband, three little children and her honored parents... Before she died, she told her loved ones that she would soon go to her sweet little daughter, who died a short time before... and now, with her "Kate" she calmly sits down; their gentle brows decked with the saints immortal crown.

A dispatch from Houston last evening gives the gratifying information that Dan. Groesbecker, who murdered Saml. D. Mills some two weeks ago has been arrested and is now in the Houston jail.

Issue April 8, 1866

F.W.T. Harrison, who departed this life at his residence in this city on the 13th ult., was a native Alabamian, born in Blount county (if we are rightly informed) September 17, 1820. When but a youth he came to Texas just too late to participate in the battle of San Jacinto... in the month of August, in 1846, he was married to Ann E., only daughter of Dr. Quinby of Montgomery... [note: condensed].

Issue April 12, 1866

A young man named McClelland, a nephew of S.G. Powell, was murdered by the freedman on his plantation in Brazoria county, recently. Mr. Powell who is now in this city, received the intelligence by telegram, yesterday.

Issue April 13, 1866

Letter from Houston. The examination of Grobecker for the killing of Mills, terminated in the accused being sent to jail, and bail refused.

Elias J. Rogillio, living with his mother seven miles from Natchez on the Pine ridge road, was taken from his home by a party of negroes and murdered. His mutilated body found in the bushes near the house. Several negroes have been arrested. One of them was found to be in possession of the watch of the murdered man.

Issue April 19, 1866

A freedman was lodged in jail at Victoria, a few days since, says the *Advocate*, for shooting at a citizen, Mr. Snyder.

Issue April 20, 1866

We regret to learn that our old and much esteemed fellow citizen, Dr. Labadie, is seriously sick. He was taken unwell just one week today and his physicians now pronounce it a mild case of small pox, or perhaps varioloid... He is in the back room of his house and all communication carefully guarded against...

Issue April 21, 1866

Died on the 29th March at Fair View, Washington county, Texas, Emma, eldest daughter of D.S. and Mary Ann McNeese, aged 10 months, 20 days.

Died on the 5th day of April, 1866, at Fair View, Washington county, Texas, Mary Ann, consort of D. McNeese, aged 32 years and 9 months.

Yesterday morning about ten o'clock, Lewis Wedemeyer, a lad three and a half years of age, the son of Carston Wedemeyer, an industrious ship carpenter, was found drowned in a well on the unclosed lot on the corner of Market and Twenty-ninth street, by his uncle, Lambert Bodden..

Issue May 1, 1866

Mr. Henry Bennett, one of the old citizens of Galveston, died on Sunday morning about 4 o'clock and was buried at 5 P.M.... Mr. Bennett was born in Auburn, New York, September 26, 1813 and has been a resident of Galveston over twenty years... He had suffered for years from a naturally feeble constitution.

Died in the town of Gonzales on the 22nd of March, Mrs. Julia Turner, consort of Col. Amasa Turner of Lavaca county, in the 66th year of her age. The subject of this notice came to this state with her husband from Mobile, Alabama in 1837, resided in Galveston and vicinity for several years, afterwards at Oakland in Lavaca county. Fifteen years ago she became a member of the Methodist church...

Tribute of respect: Whereas in the dispensation of a Wise Providence, our fellow townsman, Dr. N.H. Boring, has been called suddenly from our midst by a railroad accident... meeting of the citizens of Chappell Hill, April 25, 1866.

Issue May 2, 1866

The valuable property of the late Mrs. Osterman, on Broadway, was sold yesterday...

Issue May 5, 1866

Funeral Notice: We are requested to announce that the funeral of Mr. F.W.T. Harrison, late of this city, deceased, will be preached at the Methodist church, next Sabbath, 11 o'clock A.M.

Issue May 9, 1866

The *Times* says a citizen of Old Town, near Indianola, named Wittenberg, was shot while at supper a few days since. He died on the second day following. The *Times* hears also of a rumor of the assassination of a young man, named Weisiger, in Victoria county. The young man was a son of Dr. Weisiger, a prominent citizen.

Issue May 10, 1866

The Houston papers announce the death at his residence in that city Monday night last, Hon. A.N. Jordan, formerly State Senator from that district.

Issue May 11, 1866

The funeral of Col. John P. Waters takes place today at 4 P.M. from the residence of his uncle, Col. J.D. Waters. The deceased served in the Mexican War... He received a severe wound and has since resided on his uncle's plantation in Fort Bend county, where he died after a severe illness. His remains were brought by the train last night.

Letter from Houston. Tribute of Respect for Hon. A.N. Jordan...

A very unfortunate and fatal accident occurred on Monday evening at Harman's saw-mill, Harrisburg. Zach Harman fell against a circular saw in motion, and had his thigh horribly mutilated, his arteries severed, and expired the same night. He was formerly a member of Company D, 4th Texas Infantry, Hood's Brigade...

Issue May 15, 1866

Hon. J.W. Texada, member of the House of Representatives from Rapides Parish, La, was shot by his brother T.J. Texada, a few days since. The physicians pronounced the wound mortal. The difficulty originated in politics.

The facts in the case of the murder of Louis H.D. Helfenstein night before last are these... After being shot he ran down from the church towards the corner and fell upon some oyster shells... At this place Dr. Randle found him, and from here he was conveyed to his home. He died of his wounds yesterday morning... verdict that Louis N. Helfenstein came to his death on the night of the 13th of May, 1866 from a pistol shot in the hands of Joe Fletcher, a colored soldier... Mr. Helfenstein was a native of Germany, and a clerk in the hardware store of J.P. Davie... We saw him late in the afternoon of that day walking down Tremont Street, pleasantly chatting with his little daughter, as he held her by the hand.

Issue May 16, 1866

Mrs. Amanda M. White, wife of Col. T.B. White of Galveston, who died at the residence of her husband in this city on the evening of the 9th inst., was the daughter of Arthur S. and --- Hogan, and was born in Smith county, Tennessee, May 1, 1815. Her parents having removed to Alabama, she was, in early life, married to Wm. E. Walker, esq., of Tuscumbia, with whom she removed to Macon, Mississippi, where the principal portion of her mature life was spent. Her children were born and here she became a widow by the death of her husband. Subsequently, she removed to Washington county, Texas, where in 1863 she became the wife of Col. White... Mrs. White's children, with the exception of one daughter, had gone before her to the spirit land...

The *Ranchero*. We learn that the body of a man was found in the ship yard of Mr. Powers near Clarksville day before yesterday. The person referred to was Mr. Pillman of the firm of H.S. Pillman & co... He was a Polander by birth. He left a young widow...

Issue May 18, 1866

Letter from Houston. Case of the State versus Michael Flock was called and brought to trial. Michael Flock is charged with the murder of policeman Foley in 1860; the evidence, in short, was, that some time in March 1860, on the occasion of a great fire in Houston, the defendant, having gotten under the influence of liquor, interfered with the deceased while in the discharge of his duty, whereupon the policeman Foley knocked him down with a stick; the defendant, after saying he intended to kill Foley, betook himself to his home, about seven blocks distant, procured a double barreled shot gun, returned to the market house, the scene of the former occurrence, took his position behind a safe and other furniture, and upon the appearance of Foley, fired both barrels of his gun, killing the deceased almost instantly... The defense relied on principally was partial and temporary insanity caused by drunkenness, and appeals to the clemency of the jury. There was no verdict, the jury being unable to agree.

Gov. Allen died in the City of Mexico on the 20th. We published the report some twelve days since, and we now have the confirmation. The kind-hearted exile is at rest... have ere now outweighed in his behalf all the treason which made him a fugitive from his native land and caused him to find a burial place among strangers.

Gov. Allen was native of Virginia -- He removed to Mississippi in his early manhood, and afterwards to Louisiana. He left a luxurious home to join the army on the breaking out of the war; and was wounded in several battles, among others those of Sinloh and Baton Rouge. He was about fifty years of age and a widower. He leaves on relatives in Louisiana, but the whole State will mourn his death.

Issue May 20, 1866

The friends of Gov. Allen, in New Orleans, have held a meeting to arrange for the removal of his remains from Mexico to Louisiana. A communication, written by order of Gen. Canby and stating that he had no objection to the removal, was read at the meeting.

Issue May 23, 1866

Letter from Houston. The case of the State versus John Steele occupied the time of the District Court on Friday and Saturday. The accused was charged with the murder of J.E. Kirby. The line of defense rested upon two grounds, justifiable homicide and partial and temporary insanity from monomania or delusion, but mainly the former ground... The jury after an absence of about half an hour, returned a verdict of not guilty; the verdict received with applause from the spectators.

The case of the State vs. Groebecker, for the murder of Lawrence Mills, is set for today.

The case of the State vs. G.W. Baylor for the murder of John A. Wharton, was continued on defendant's affidavit.

Issue May 24, 1866

We learn by private letters that Dr. Allen of Corpus Christi committed suicide in that place recently, cause not known, supposed to be some family troubles. We also learn that Mr. Shire of the same place was murdered in cold blood the other day by a noted desperado named Garner. The citizens became so exasperated that they seized Garner and hung him at once.

Issue May 25, 1866

An unfortunate affair occurred in the county Monday. Robert Jones had a difficulty with a negro on his plantation and on the negroes drawing a knife, Jones shot him dead. *LaGrange New Era.*

Death of Theodore Clapp.-- The *Times* of New Orleans has an appreciative obituary notice of Dr. Clapp who died on the 18th at Louisville, Ky. He became widely known during his long pastorate at New Orleans. He was born in Easthampton, Massachusetts, in 1792; graduated at Yale College in 1814. [note: condensed].

Issue May 26, 1866

Letter from Houston. The jury in the District Court in the case of the State vs. Groebaker, for the murder of Mills, assesses the punishment at two years in the penitentiary.

222

Issue May 29, 1866

Died, Sunday, May 27th, at the residence of his brother, Clinton Wells, James K. Wells, native of Baltimore, Maryland; aged 22 years, after an illness of four weeks of typhoid fever...[note: also appeared in issue May 30, 1866].

Issue May 30, 1866

Letter from Brazoria county. Brazoria county. Eds. News. It was my privilege on yesterday to be present on the sad and solemn occasion of the reinterment of the remains of the late Major George W. McNeil, in the family cemetery, at the house of his father. Death has dealt heavily with the father since the commencement of our troubles; first a young and gallant son, loved by all that knew him, died in the service far away from his home; then a cherished and loved wife. And last, the gifted and gallant son, whose obsequies I witnessed. He deserves a more extended notice.

You know from our history that the family of McNeil were amongst the earliest letters [sic] in Austin Colony. The father of the deceased J.G. McNeil was an active and energetic participant in all the trials and hardships of that adventurous band that made the first mark of civilization in the wilderness of Texas. You are familiar with what they suffered and how they triumphed. The success of that small band of pioneers, and the consequences growing out of it, find no parallel in history. Honored be their name in all time to come.

The father of the deceased settled where he now resides about 1830. As patriot, citizen, neighbor, friend, and father, he commands the respect and esteem of all who knew him.

The son we now mourn was born on the 27th of September 1837; his early education was in Texas; at the proper age he was sent to Princeton, where he remained three years; education completed at Rutger's College, New Jersey.

When war came upon us, he was amongst the first that rallied to the Confederate standard. He joined the company of the lamented Wharton, and was elected first Lieutenant. Fell into an ambush and was slain on the 7th May 1864 at Gordon's bridge, near Alexandria, having received many wounds. It is a singular fact that his dead body fell into the hands of old college friends in the Federal army. They arranged his corpse neatly, covered the wounds on his face with plaster, fastened his hands on his breast with ribbon, intending to have him interred with decent propriety. They were driven away before this could be effected, leaving his personal effects upon him, taking his purse, containing his money, which was returned to his father by Gen. Lawler. I mention this as a rare act of cruelty shown to our dead bythe enemy. He was buried near Dr. Gordon's garden, who had his grave enclosed and cared for; when his father went for his remains, he received at the hands of the doctor every possible hospitality and assistance on the sad occasion. His great kindness deeply touched the father. He has left to mourn him a young lovely and interesting wife with two small children, one born after his death...

Issue May 31, 1866

A most atrocious murder was perpetrated on Saturday the 5th at Robinson's mill, in Ellis county. Charles Macklin, a discharged Federal soldier, in the employment of Bell & Robinson at the flouring mill, was shot by Stephen Meredith, a boy about nineteen years of age. The murderer, we are informed, has escaped, but the police are in hot pursuit. He is about five feet seven inches high, light hair, blue eyes, and has a ringworm on the right cheek and neck. *Waco Register.*

Issue June 1, 1866

To the memory of the Rev. Dr. H/N.[?] H. Boring. Died April 24th 1866 from wounds received in a Railroad accident at Chappell Hill, Texas... [note: condensed; mentions father, mother, brothers, sisters]

Issue June 3, 1866

An inquest was held yesterday on the --- Wharf upon the body of John Powers, lately waiter at the Island City Hotel. Deceased was drowned while laboring a fit, caused by intoxication. He had been in the water about twelve hours but had been missing since the 31st ult. There were no -- violence upon his person. A verdict in accordance with these facts was rendered by the Corner's jury.

Issue June 5, 1866

The *Ranchero* gives an account of the murder, Sunday week, of Dr. Morse, who was in charge of the military hospital at Brownsville. The Doctor, with his orderly, had started out to visit a camp some three miles from Brownsville, and was waylaid and attacked at Rancho Viejo. A lasso was thrown over him by a party of outlaws, when they dragged him into the chaparral, where he was murdered and rifled of all he had. The negro orderly succeeded in making his escape, though he was pursued. The body of the doctor was found and interred the next day. Three of the outlaws were identified by the negro and arrested.

Issue June 7, 1866

Letter from the Country. Long Point, Washington county. A horrible affair took place at Round Top, about fifteen miles west of this place, on Tuesday night, May 29th. The wife and daughter of a German tailor, named Krimpke, was found with their heads split open with an axe or hatchet. The house is surrounded by other dwellings, and no noise or alarm was heard during the tragedy. No cause can be assigned for the horrible deed, as the family were poor and had no money in the house. The husband was absent at a neighbor's at the time, and returned to find his family murdered... The perpetrators are generally believed to have been vicious negroes...

From Corpus Christi. Assassination of a Merchant. A few days since a man by the name of James Garner, a murderous pest to the public, assassinated a merchant in Corpus Christi, Mr. Scheuer, brother to a man of the same name who was murdered on the Rio Grande.

Mr. Scheuer was standing in his store when Garner rode up to the door and shot him through the heart, with a revolver. This having been Garner's third or fourth murder, the people of the place seized him, and before his victim was cold, he was dangling to a limb.

Mr. Scheuer was an excellent citizen, and had given Garner no provocation to commit the diabolical act. *Matamoros Ranchero.*

Dr. Morse, who had charge of the Military Hospital at Brownsville, was murdered on the evening of the 28th ult in sight of that place. With his negro orderly, the doctor had started out to visit a camp some three miles from Brownsville, on the Rancho Viejo road, and when two and a half miles out, he was assaulted by a squad of outlaws, dragged into the chaparral, and murdered, and his person rifled of everything of value. A great number arrests were made, but all had been released, except three men identified — or suppose to be — by the negro orderly.

Issue June 8, 1866
Died on the 7th June, 1866, at Galveston, infant son, William, of Mr. and Mrs. Wm. Hawley, aged 1 year, 6 months and 26 days. Houston papers and New Orleans papers please copy.

Issue June 9, 1866
Died yesterday morning at 10 o'clock, Roberta E. Lee, infant daughter of Emily C. and J.H. McCormick... funeral this Saturday morning at 9 o'clock.

Died in this city on the 8th inst., Robert Lee, infant son of Mr. and Mrs. J.J. Jenny. The funeral will take place this afternoon at 4 o'clock from the residence of Mrs. Baumgarten near Close's foundry.

Issue June 23, 1866
From the *Nagcodoches Chronicle.* We learn that our neighbors over in Angelina county had another frolic, somewhat serious in its consequences. James Windham and McMullin, (sheriff for said county) were killed; the latter in his official capacity, endeavoring to preserve peace.

John Stovall (slightly wounded) shot Gilly, who was supposed mortally wounded, but is now recovering. Ely Windham, supposed wounded, also recovering. James Ewing slightly wounded...

Died on the 15th June at Wallisville, Willie, aged six years, son of Sarah L. and S.B. Wallis.

Issue June 24, 1866

The *McKinney Messenger* has a letter from Ft. Arbuckle, written by John Field, U.S. Indian agent, in which he says two little white boys, one about ten and the other about six years old, have been delivered to him by the Indians. The eldest of the boys says his name is Jimmy; the younger calls himself Sammy. They say they are the sons of Mr. Robin Hunter, and that two men and one woman (their aunt Caroline) were killed at the time of their capture. They were captured by the Noconie band of Comanches somewhere in the vicinity of Comanche Peak.

A correspondent of the *San Antonio Ledger* says Maj. H.P. Darling, Thomas Cossa, an Englishman, Wm. H.V. Smith, late of Navarro county, two negro boys, and two Mexicans were murdered by the Indians, recently at or near the rancho of Maj. Darling, on the Eagle Pass and Laredo road, about forty miles above Laredo. The place is known as the Salado Rancho...

We were mistaken in our last in giving an account of the cause of the killing on Nelson by Carlson. Nelson had been an Union man but joined the Confederates. He had not assisted in the conscription of Carlson. Carlson has escaped; Gov. Hamilton offers two hundred and fifty dollars for his arrest. The brother of Nelson offers the same amount.

The *Express* learns that Thomas J. Kerr, for some years past a resident of Kerr county, was murdered near Bandera on the 1st inst. He was cut in fourteen places. The pantaloons, which contained fifty or sixty dollars specie in the pockets, were taken from the body.

Issue June 26, 1866

Died at Bolivar Point, on the main land, Isaac McGary, of Huntsville, Texas, on the 22nd inst. of hemorrhage. Mr. McGary was born in Ohio, January 18, 1800, came to Texas at an early time, perhaps 1826, and was an actor in the stirring scenes of early Texas history. United with Episcopal church some twelve or fifteen years ago at Huntsville. Youthful son...

Capt. Howell Leight (formerly sutler at Fort Chadbourne, from Maryland, and brother of Capt. A. Kerr Leight, who died in this city in 1864 of yellow fever) died suddenly at the Island City Hotel Friday evening last, and his funeral took place on Saturday, attended by many friends.

Issue June 29, 1866

August, or Auguste, a Frenchman, and a man named DePruy, also a Frenchman, started in a fisherman's boat to the east end of the island, to drag their seine Wednesday evening. Late in the evening DePruy was discovered by the Pilot Boat waving his hat. The boat was sent after him, and found him *minus* his shirt and standing in the water to his middle. August was not with him nor in the boat, which latter was left at anchor. The man was brought to town by the pilot boat and explained the absence of his comrade to the satisfaction of one of the pilots who understood Spanish. We were unable to obtain this explanation from the pilot, although we asked him for it, any farther than that he said his comrade had been drowned.

The boat was brought down to town by a citizen of the place, who found on board shoes, shirt and pantaloons of the missing Auguste, a revolver with one barrel discharged, a bottle with some whiskey, a knife, some spots and stains upon the deck, which he believes to be blood... Auguste gave a statement so confused and apparently conflicting that suspicious were aroused, and he was arrested. The case will be examined on Saturday the 30th.

A coroner's jury of inquest held on the body of Dr. Ash find that he came to his death by a gun shot wound from the hands of N. Lavine, in defence of self and family, the deceased attempting to enter the house occupied by Lavine about 12 o'clock at night.

It appears that deceased being temporarily insane, left the Palmetto House about 11 o'clock in a hack and went in the neighborhood of Lavine's. He left the hack, and getting back into a quarrel with the hackman, shot him in the shoulder. He immediately ran down the nearest alley into Lavine's back yard and endeavored to get into the house in order to evade pursuit, and in his endeavors to enter the house was shot. Dr. A. was a gentleman of high respectability and excellent character and was of a family of high standing. That he was temporarily insane there is not a doubt.

Issue July 1, 1866

The Jury of Inquest in the case of Alfred Lafenillade, the fisherman, who was missing, and appeared to be drowned or murdered, rendered the following verdict:

We, the Jury of Inquest, held on June 30, 1866, upon the body of Alfred Lafenillade, find that said deceased came to his death by a pistol shot and knife in the hands of Pierre Dupuy, now a prisoner. Deceased was found by some fisherman late Friday night who secured the body to a pole, which they planted in the mud. The Coroner (Dr. Walters) and his jury found upon arriving at the place that the body was tied to a 64 lb. iron weight, his throat cut, and shot through the right--[note: unclear]

The Frenchman Dupuy, accused of killing —, was arraigned by the Justice, Mr. James [?] Seawell... Accused has been staying at Mrs. Mary Hordes. [note: deposition of witnesses given] His wife was in the old country...

Issue July 5, 1866

John Murphy, a hackman and for some time back driver of an express wagon, was killed yesterday, about noon, by a woman named Helen Black, an Englishwoman, lately from New Orleans to Galveston. The man had quarreled with her in the morning at her house, where he had gone, she said to get whiskey, accompanied by two soldiers, and she had slapped his face, when he went away and returned about noon. Either at the first meeting or the last, the deceased is charged with having knocked her down. The last time he came she was cooking and had her cook knife in hand. He is charged with having then called her a —[not clear], and she followed him from her house to Lang's Saloon, knife in hand, for the purpose, she alleges, of having him arrested. Arrived at the Saloon, she called Officer McCann, who was passing down Merchants' street, to arrest the deceased, who was just coming out of the saloon, but as he came out, she preceding him, he caught her by the shoulders, the policeman says, as if to apologize, when she commenced cutting him with the knife. Policeman saw her make two or three cuts before he could seize her and wrest the knife from her hand, and arrested her forthwith. The man died in a few minutes.

The Coroner's Jury, in substance, present that John Murphy came to his death from wounds inflicted with a knife by Helen Black. The Coroner committed her to jail upon her failure to give bond of $5000 to answer at court.

Since writing the above, we learn that the accused has procured bail.

Issue July 7, 1866

Sorry are we to record the fact that on Monday last, the day of the election, late in the afternoon, a difficulty originated between two of our fellow countrymen, H. Tom and W.W. Little, resulting in the death of the latter. *Seguin Western Texian.*

Issue July 17, 1866

Memphis. July 12. A duel was fought this evening at the Mississippi line between Alonzo Greenlaw and A.H. Taylor of this city. The latter was killed at the first fire.

Louisville, July 12. Chas. S. Woodruff, recently a merchant of Grenada, Miss, has been arrested by order of Gen. Thomas for supposed complicity in the assassination of Lieut. Blanding of the Freedmen's Bureau at that place in April last. Later reports say Woodruff goes to Grenada as a witness against the assailants of Blanding.

Issue July 18, 1866

Died in this city at 5 o'clock P.M. on the 16th inst., Ernestine Mason, daughter of Joseph E. Mason, aged 2 years and 1 week. New Orleans papers copy.

Issue July 19, 1866

Paul [?] Helterich [?] for many years a highly respected citizen of Galveston, Surveyor of the county and a civil engineer, died at 11 am yesterday after a very brief illness, said ----bilious fever. He was a native of Hesse Cassel but resided in Galveston for many years...buried yesterday with Masonic honors.

---- another sudden death of Thos A. Stanwood, an old citizen ---- physician of our city died last evening about half past five. He had been ill for several days but was not suppose to be dangerous. The cause of his death was probably excessive bleeding from an attempt to bleed himself, which was followed by a succession of spasms which terminated fatally. He has left a widow and an orphan daughter to mourn their loss. His funeral will probably take place today but we have not learned the hour.

Issue July 20, 1866

The *Gonzales Inquirer* reports the death of an old Texian, J.B. Patrick. He was a native of Missouri and came to Texas with DeWitt's colony in the fall of 1828. Lived almost whole time in Gonzales. He was a member of the Masonic brotherhood.

Issue July 21, 1866

The *Victoria Advocate* says a letter to the Postmaster there announces the murder of Judge David Murphree, an esteemed citizen of DeWitt county, near Osceola, St. Clair county, Missouri, about the 8th of last month.

Judge Murphree left here some months since on a trip to Virginia, taking with him his daughter and a young lady from this place. These he left there, and proceeded on his way to Missouri, where he expected to meet a party who had a considerable stock of horses and mules belonging to him, and met his death as above before he joined them.

The letter gives no particulars, other than that the body was found and identified by letters and papers – that a gold watch and $28 or $30 was found on the deceased, and that the money was expended in its decent interment; but not a word as to the nature of the wounds that caused death, or clue as to the perpetrators of the horrid deed.

Issue July 24, 1866

The coroner, Dr. Walters, held an inquest upon the body of Mr. McCarten, found two miles and a half below the city, near the Railroad track. No one was able to recognize him until his wife came from Virginia Point searching for him. He was a carpenter in the employee of G.H. & H.H.R.

From Mexico. From the *Mexican Railway Era*. The issue of the 20th says that Lafayette <u>Cotton</u>, formerly of Galveston, but many years resident in Mexico, died recently at Vera Cruz of yellow fever.

Miss Lucy J. Adams, aged 17 years, daughter of W.J. and E.P. Adams, formerly of Nashville, died at Carlotta on the 6th ult. of pneumonia.

The paper of the same date [23d] announces the death at Tuxpan, May 26, of Peyton D. Nowlin, of Austin, Texas. He was a brave Confederate soldier, an only son, aged 26 years. The *Era* says "he died as a Christian, caressed by countrymen, honored by strangers, and was interred in a manner worthy of his character."

Issue July 25, 1866

We were informed late yesterday evening that Charles Atkins, a well known citizen, is in a very dangerous condition, caused by the sting of a centipede.

The verdict of the jury if inquest, held upon the body of R. Morris, who died suddenly while bathing in the Gulf on Saturday evening, found that he had came to his death from a fit. Coroner Walters informed us that it was evidence at the inquest, that the deceased was with some six friends bathing in the Gulf, he being the last one to go in, and when first noticed by his comrades was lying face down in two feet of water. When turned over froth was observed on his lips and he was immediately dragged ashore, and every effort made to resuscitate him, but without success. He was a shoemaker by trade, and had been a citizen of Galveston about fourteen years.

Issue July 27, 1866

Letter from Mexico... I am sorry to say that the yellow fever is still very bad in Vera Cruz, and generally fatal to emigrants, not so much to the violent grade of the disease but from want of good physicians... I have known only three americans who have died lately, Mr. Lafayette <u>Cotton</u> from Richmond, Texas; Frederick Keazer, of Georgia; both at Vera Cruz; and John Lineham, of Matamoros, at this place. I am sorry to learn by letter received from Tuspan, several day since, of the death of Peyton Nowlan, the only son of Col. P.W. Nowlan, of Austin, and brother-in-law to C.H. Randolph, our former State Treasurer; and of John W. Dacy, of LaGrange, Texas. Mr. Nowlan had just brought out Judge Randolph's family to him at this place, and was returning, and intending, as he told me a few hours before he left, to bring out this fall a saw mill and planting machine, and establish himself near here permanently. His death will be a heavy loss to his aged parents and sisters... He was, so I was informed by my correspondent, attended during his last illness by Col. L. P. Butler, of Tyler.

Issue July 28, 1866

Died in Harris county on the 24th inst. of congestive chill, William Henry, son of Geo. W. McMahan of said county, aged 10 years, 6 months...

Issue July 31, 1866

Died in this county yesterday at 6.p.m., Amelia, daughter of Mr. & Mrs. M.P. Munyan, late of Chappell Hill.

Issue August 2, 1866

The *Shreveport Gazette* of the 20th gives an account of an attack made on the premises of Mr. Cane, who resides 3 miles from Shreveport on the Texas road, on the Tuesday night previous by a party of 10 or 15 negroes dressed in Federal uniform. He was killed by a well directed shot. The negroes rushed in the house, broke into the trucks, and carried off some specie, and other things they valued.

A case of genuine Asiatic cholera, terminative fatally, is reported by the *Houston Telegraph*. The unfortunate person was a Mr. Dale of Brenham on his way home from New York, stopped at the Fennin House. On Monday he was attacked and died the same day... He may have contracted it at Galveston if he went out to quarantine camp six or seven days ago.

Issue August 4, 1866

Died in this city of croup at 7 1/2 o'clock A.M. on August 3, 1866, Henry Arlington, infant son of Joseph and Mary Helm, aged four years. The funeral will take place from the Rust cottage this morning at 9 1/2 o'clock. New Orleans papers please copy.

Issue August 5, 1866

John Marshall placed the muzzle of the pistol to his right temple, sprang the trigger, and received the charge, the ball passing through the head... The deceased was but recently married and leaves a young and interesting widow to mourn his sad and untimely death. He had evidently been suffering from mental aberration for a day or so. [note: condensed from a letter dated Millican, August 2, 1866].

We deeply regret to learn, as many others will, that C.A. Bulkley, well known in this city and throughout a large part of Texas, died at Mullican on the 2d inst. He had recently lost all his family within the past three or four months... The death of Mr. Bulkley was undoubtly hastened by his heavy afflictions.

Issue August 7, 1866

Died August 1st at the residence of Mr. R.G. Kyle, Fort Bend county, Texas, Mrs. F.A. Ragsdale in her 74th year. For the last fifty-five years of her life, she was a strict member of the Methodist church. Memphis and Shreveport papers please copy.

Issue August 8, 1866

A tragical affair occurred at Gilbert Jackson's Mill in the upper edge of Falls county last Sunday morning. Collins, who is employed by Mr. Jackson as superintendent of his saw mill, shot and killed Miskill. Miskill had threatened the life of Collins.

Issue August 10, 1866

Sexton's report.

Jno Neterson, aged 24 years, buried 2d of July, disease congestive fever.
John Graves, aged 49 years, buried 3d of July, disease of heart.
Henry A. Helen, aged 4 years, buried 4th of July, disease cramp.
George W. Roberts, aged 4 days, buried 5th of July, disease not known.
Ward Green, (negro) aged 2 years, buried 5th of July, disease dysentery.
Henry Anderson, (negro) aged 60 years, buried 5th of July, disease old age.
--- Taylor, aged 30 years, buried 5th of July, disease not known.
Frederick Stoppelburg, aged 50 years, buried 6th of July, disease cholera morbus.
Mary Jane Jay, aged 4 years, buried 7th of July, disease dysentery.
Wm. Young, aged 23 years, buried 7th of July, disease cholera morbus.
Leana Burney, (negro) aged 23 years, buried 7th of July, disease dropsy.
Dan Waters, aged 30 years, buried 7th of July, disease dropsy.
Mary Shelton (negro) aged 81 years, buried 7th of July, disease cholera.
Charley Stoppelburg, aged 13 years, buried 8th of July, disease cholera morbus.
William, (negro) aged 8 years, buried 8th of July, disease cholera morbus.
Jake, (negro) aged 25 years, buried 8th of July, disease flux.
Edward Fisher, aged 9 months, buried 8 of July, disease cholera morbus.
Henry Jenkins, (negro) aged 40 years, buried 8th of July, disease cholera morbus.
Mary Hameun, aged 3 years, buried 8th of July, disease cholera morbus.
Dick Hamilton, (negro) aged 24 years, disease cramp cholic.

The above is the report of the City Sexton, not including the nativity of the deceased persons and some other unimportant particulars which were contained in it. It will be noticed that of the ten deaths from cramps and cholera morbus, 5 were children, and 3 were negroes. It is advised by physicians that as the fatal sickness in nearly every instance is brought about by eating unwholesome food or dissipation, therefore, great caution as to food and temperate habits should be strictly observed and followed.

The Mayor avers his determination to enforce the city ordinance requiring the attendant physician to report to the City Sexton in each fatal case, the name, age, nativity &c of the deceased, as well as the disease of which the person died.

Interments Aug 9th

Mary Ann Edwards, (negro) 25 years, cholera.

Wallace, (negro) 25 years, cholera.

Georgiana Cobern, (infant) 1 hour.

The Sexton reports that Edwards and Wallace had no attendant physician, and he did not know whether to report the disease as cholera or cholera morbus, no one having certified to him what the disease was; but reports it cholera, as they died somewhat suddenly with all cholera symptoms.

Issue August 12, 1866

Headquarters, Dep't of Texas. Galveston, Texas. Aug. 11, 1866. It is with much regret that Major General Commanding announces to this command the sudden death of Major P.W.L. Plympton, Brevet Lieut. Col. U.S. Army, which took place at an early hour this (Saturday) morning.

Col. Plympton graduated at West Point in 1847, and soon after joined his regiment, the 7th Infantry, then commanded by his father, at the city of Mexico. [note: service record given]. His funeral will take place at 6 o'clock this evening.

By command of Major General Wright.

Issue August 14, 1866

Sexton's report. Interments for Aug. 11, 1866.

Peter W.L. Plympton, cholera, Brevet Lt. Col. U.S.A.

Josephine Simon, spasms, negro child.

Mary Dormy, cholera morbus.

Henry Dormy, cholera morbus.

Mrs. M.O. Quarffle, cholera morbus.

Issue August 15, 1866

Sexton's report. Interments August 12th:

Mr. [?] Dormey, cholera morbus.

Interments August 13th:

Elizabeth Frazier, teething.

John Thomas Cabban, croup.

Charles Hughes, cholera.

John Bush, diseased lungs.

Louisa Young, congestive fever.

Daniel Young, cholera.

Issue August 16, 1866

The funeral of James W. Moore takes place this morning at 10 o'clock from his late residence. He died yesterday forenoon after a painful illness of three weeks duration. He had lived in Texas twenty-six years, participating in the struggle for independence from Mexico, having come to the assistance of the patriots with his brother, Com. Moore, and actively engaging with him in the naval operations of 1840'41. After independence, he became a permanent citizen of Galveston, and for many terms filled the office of District Clerk. He was a faithful and efficient officer, a citizen of unblemished integrity and a high-toned gentleman, whose demise a large circle of friends will learn with the deepest regret and sympathy for his bereaved family.

Issue August 18, 1866

Died at Galveston August 17, 1866, at 7 o'clock P.M., Capt. Wm. Dwyer, of steamer *Silver Cloud*. Funeral will take place from the *Silver Cloud* at 10 o'clock today.

Issue August 21, 1866

Sexton's Report. Interments Aug. 18th, 19th, 20th 1866: Capt. Wm. Dwier 18th, chronic dysentery; Jack McDonell, 18th, dysentery, negro; Caroline Coburn, 19th, worm fever, negro child, four years old; Capt George Wilson, 20th, cholera morbus; Nancy Hunt, 20th, dysentery; negro [?]; Doyle, 20th, cholera (from hospital); G. Welkes, 20th, cholera (from hospital); unknown woman, 20th, swamp fever.

Mar[?]a Wilson, the friends and acquaintances of Capt. Hezekiah Wilson are respectfully invited to attend the funeral of his late consort from his residence on Market street.

Yesterday, being set for the obsequies of Senator Gwinn [Guinn], no legislative business was transacted.

Issue August 22, 1866

I regret to announce that Senator Gwin [note: James Washington Guinn] of Angelina county, died yesterday at the residence of Mr. N.C. Raymond. His sickness, I learn, was billious fever brought on by too much exposure. Several other members have been sick from the same cause, but are now getting better. Senator Gwin has represented his county in the Legislature for many years and was one of the oldest and most respected Senators. He has a younger brother [note: Robert Henry Gwin/Guinn] here who is a Senator from another eastern district. The funeral takes place to-day. W.R. [note: the following information is a correction to that provided for James Washington Guinn in the authors' publication "Miscellaneous Texas Newspaper Abstracts - Deaths, Volume 1: James Washington Guinn married

234

Catherine Ann Dobson. His parents were John Guinn and Rachel Shields. He lived in Greene county, TN, Haywood county, NC, and Randolph county, AL, before coming to Texas. He is buried in the State Cemetery at Austin, Texas.].

Died on board of sail vessel between Indianola and Decrow's Point of cholera, Mrs. Carrie C. Ballou, daughter of Charles and Mary Ann Block, of this city.

Issue January 1, 1867

The Tornado - The *Rusk Observer* gives some further particulars of the tornado. The wife of Capt. Saddler, living on Ioni Creek, fifteen miles from Crockett, was instantly killed and her husband badly wounded. His house, fencing and considerable amount of cotton were destroyed. Not far from this place, the house of Mrs. Thomas, a widow, was blown down.

Military funeral. -- The remains of the late H.H. Wilson, Lieutenant of the 6th Reg. U.S. Cav'l, who died in Austin recently, passed through here yesterday, en route for Washington, and were escorted to the boat by a company of the 17th U.S. Infantry. Mr. Wilson was the son of Senator Wilson of Mass. and said to have been a young officer of fine promise.

Issue January 2, 1867

Murder and robbery in Hill county: Hillsboro, Texas, December 24, 1866: On the night of the 20th inst. about twelve miles northeast of Hillsboro, a party numbering nine men stopped at Judge J.W.P. Doyle's about dark on the evening above mentioned and asked permission to stay all night... Judge Doyle told them they could stay... upon entering the room one of them... remarked to his comrades that now is the time to commence and drew his pistol and shot down Judge Doyle's eldest son... several shots were fired at Judge Doyle and other members of the family... Judge Doyle ran off about 200 yards and fell dead... [note: condensed].

The *Huntsville Item* records the shooting and killing of Mr. George Grant of that place on the night of the 22d ult. by Mr. Wm. L. Evans...

The *Ranger* says Mr. W. G. Council of Navasota was waylaid and shot by someone, on the night of the 26th ult., as he was entering his yard gate. Twelve or more bullets or large shot entered the legs a little above the knees, causing terrible wounds. Amputation was resorted to and Mr. Council died a few hours afterwards. The assassin has not been detected.

Issue January 3, 1867

Prof. John R. Crow was killed at Henderson by the falling of the Masonic Institute Building during the late storm...

Cutting affair. -- Billy Farrell, on the night of the first, was severely cut by a knife about the region of the abdomen. A man named Dowdy or Doughty has been arrested and lodged in jail, supposed to be the offender.

Capt. Wm. Purdom. -- We regret that the gentleman whose name heads this paragraph has been confined to his bed for several days with a severe attack of pneumonia and is now improving, although still confined to his room.

The Doyle murder and robbery. We find in the *Waco Register* of the 29th a letter from Mrs. Doyle, widow of the gentleman whose murder by a gang of robbers was noticed in our last issue. The letter is dated Hillsboro, Hill county, Texas, December 23, 1866. We give it entire:

My husband, J.W. P. Doyle of this county, was robbed and murdered on the 20th instant. The amount taken was as follows: eight drafts for four thousand each, about ten dollars in currency and two thousand five hundred in specie... I will give to any parties all the specie and currency, if they will apprehend the assassins and return them to this county, together with the drafts and notes on private parties to be turned over to me.

I furthermore warn all persons not to trade for said drafts as they have been stolen. [descriptions of men given, but no names,]   Mary Ann Doyle.

Issue January 4, 1867
Lavaca, December 27, 1867... It is my painful duty to convey to you the sad intelligence of the death of Capt. David Bradbury which took place this morning from general paralysis of the whole system. He was an old citizen of Texas... Geo. P. Finlay.

Issue January 5, 1867
Edward Lecuyer, a frenchman by birth, took passage on the steamship *Matagorda* from Galveston to New Orleans, December 1, 1866, and died during the passage and was buried at Brashear, Louisiana. By letters found on his person it appears that he had recently lived in Houston, Texas.

Issue January 6, 1867
An inquest held by Coroner Hannay on the body of Wm. Farrell, January 5, 1867... Capt. Doughty, the person who arrested, and supposed to have killed Farrell, has been discharged from custody.

Issue January 10, 1867
Died at his residence in Pittsville, Fort Bend county, on Monday, January 7th, Theophilus Simonton, in the 55th year of his age. His funeral takes place Wednesday the 9th inst...

Houston. B.E. Jamison, a well known citizen, was found dead in his chair this morning. His death was doubtless caused by apoplexy.

Issue January 13, 1867

Coroner's Inquest -- An inquest was held yesterday morning by Coroner Hannay on the body of Mrs. Maria D. Yerger, consort of the late Dr. Yerger, of this city.

Mrs. Yerger has been in ill health for some time past, and her relatives, thinking she was remaining unusually long in bed, went to her room to ascertain the cause, when they found she was dead.

Verdict of the jury: "That the deceased came to her death by cramps in the stomach, caused by general debility."

Issue January 15, 1867

Murder and Arson, Huckberry, Texas, January 10, 1867: One of the most shocking, cruel and heart rending murders was committed on the night of the 26th December last, that has ever occurred in Lavaca county... the assassins crept into the house of John Newman and cut the throats of himself, wife and infant child, and a little negro girl about twelve years old and then set the house on fire... suspicions resting upon two negroes, Marshall Matthews and Levi Blackly... they were arrested, ordered to jail and placed under guard. On the way to Halletsville, the prisoners attempted to escape and both were killed...

Issue January 20, 1867

The *McKinney Enquirer* records a fight at Black Jack Grove, Hopkins county, on Christmas, in which three men were killed. Their names were Frye, Newcome, and Brumley.

Issue January 30, 1867

Died on Sunday evening the 20th inst. in Huntsville, Walker county, after a brief illness, F.M. Baker, aged 28 years. The deceased was a younger brother of the Hon. James A. Baker and Capt. Andrew M. Baker of Huntsville and of Dr. G.M. Baker of Galveston...

Issue February 2, 1867

A man named Thurston was killed last Monday at Hockley by a Mr. McMahan, citizen of Anderson...

By a gentleman just down from Fayette county we have intelligence of a very unfortunate difficulty resulting in the sudden death of Dr. Pope, a very highly esteemed citizen, which occurred on Monday night last in the office of the Bureau Agent at LaGrange. James Pope, brother to Dr. Pope, was engaged in an altercation with a negro in the office and drew a pistol... in the scuffle... the weapon was accidentally discharged, mortally wounding Dr. Pope.

Issue February 3, 1867
The *San Antonio Herald* gives the particulars of the killing of Mr. Kennedy by Mr. William Edgar, on the El Paso road, a short time since...

The funeral of John H. Frosh, the youngest son of our fellow citizen, Mr. Lawrence Frosh, will take place at 4 P.M. today. He was sixteen years old. He was only taken sick about twenty-four hours before his death, with pneumonia...

Issue February 10, 1867
Died on the 26th January, 1867, Mrs. Mary A. Walton, consort of Col. Walton, aged 66 years and 29 days. She came from New York to Mobile in 1827 and emigrated to Galveston, Texas in 1840... She died at Oaklands, Victoria, county...

Issue February 14, 1867
Mr. H.L. Sunier, the well known restaurant keeper, died very suddenly about 11 o'clock, night before last.

Issue February 15, 1867
Died at his residence (commercial restaurant), February 12th, Mr. Henry Louis Sunier. New Orleans papers please copy.

Died on the morning of Saturday, February 2, 1867, at the family homestead, near Long Point, Washington county, Texas, Mrs. Sarah, consort of Dr. Gideon Lincecum, aged 71 years.

Issue February 21, 1867
A youth named Conring, about sixteen years old, committed suicide a few days since at Comal Springs...

Issue February 22, 1867
Died in this city of pneumonia on Saturday the 16th inst., Capt. James Noble, formerly of the U.S. Navy, aged sixty-one years. Charleston, South Carolina, and Indianapolis, Indiana, papers please copy.

Mr. Nathan Dow and son of Erath county were killed by Indians on the 23rd ult. They were engaged in hauling rails.

Issue February 23, 1867
Died at the residence of his father in this city on the morning of the 22nd inst., Zachary T. Cleveland, in the 21st year of his age. His funeral will take place from the residence of Judge J.A.H. Cleveland this morning at 10 o'clock.

Mr. Warren Adams, just returned from Waco, informs us that a man named Gregory was killed near Marlin, Falls county, last week, by a youth nineteen years of age, named Pilkin.

Issue February 26, 1867
Died at his residence on Broadway, Nathan Smith, in the eighty-seventh year of his age.

Died at the Island Hotel, February 24, 1867, of consumption, Edward H. Eaton (late of Louisville, Kentucky) aged thirty-nine years.

Issue February 28, 1867
The *Waco Register* says Mr. H.M. Hood, one of the north west citizens of that place, was shot and killed in his blacksmith shop on the 18th by a man named Gray.

Issue March 1, 1867
Tribute to the memory of C.T. Bannerman, who departed this life on the morning of the 6th of February 1867, of pneumonia, aged 35 years and 6 months.

Issue March 6, 1867
Died in Richmond on the 18th of February, after an illness of seventeen days, David Randon, aged 13 months 18 days, youngest son of Mr. and Mrs. Walter Andrus.

Issue March 12, 1867
Murder: We learn from the *Brownsville Courier* that a negro soldier named Andrew Johnson of Co. G 117th U.S.C.T. was killed by a negro citizen there a few days since.

Issue March 13, 1867
Mr. William Zumlin, a prominent citizen of Jefferson, was killed and a Mr. Summers severely wounded in a difficulty at a restaurant in that place on the 27th ult.

The Man Found Dead – The soldier whose body was found day before yesterday on Broadway near 16th street turns out to be one Hinds, late of Company G. 17th U.S. Infantry. A post mortem examination on the body found no marks of violence, and state that he died from watery fusion on the brain.

Issue March 14, 1867

Still another of the old citizens of Galveston has gone. Dr. N.D. Labadie, whose sickness we noticed some two weeks ago, has finally fallen a victim to that fatal disease, the typhoid fever, after having suffered for near six weeks. He first came to Texas about 1839. In Battle of Jacinto... [note: nice tribute given].

Issue March 17, 1867

Died on the 16th inst. in this city, Mrs. L.A. McAuley, wife of Geo. W. McAuley. The funeral will take place from the residence of her husband on Ave H today at 3 o'clock.

Letter from Houston. The death of the lamented Dr. Labadie, of your city has cast a gloom over the whole state. Few men tried harder than he did to obey the commands of the Golden Rule, and to act the part of a christian citizen towards humanity. We met him in this city a few weeks ago where he came to attend the obsequies of Gen. A.S. Johnson, and was at that time in good spirits.

Issue March 19, 1867

Dr. Hannay was notified on Sunday morning of a man having died suddenly at the Island City Hotel. Collecting together a jury, the jurors returned the following verdict: That the deceased, J.B. Johnston, came to his death from the effect of excessive drinking of intoxicating liquors. We have been informed that Mr. Johnston was from New York and in the employ of Mr. Chalmers of that city and at the time of his death was employed at the Island City Hotel for the purpose of putting up a patent annunciator.

A discharged negro soldier murdered by three white soldiers: Dan Parker, a negro, and formerly a member of Co."I" 36th U.S.C.I., was killed... [note: lengthy description of incident given]. Parker is described as a quiet, inoffensive man, and at the time of his death was employed as a stevedore on Central Wharf. Jas. Hewson was arrested.

Issue March 24, 1867

The *San Antonio Express* says an old man named Gerdes was murdered by the Lipans near Quihi on the 14th. His body had eleven lance wounds.

Issue March 27, 1867

The *Enquirer* says Mrs. Ann Well of near Mantua, Collin county, was burned to death on the 4th. Standing near the fire in the kitchen, her dress caught in a flame and she was burned so severe as to cause her death the next day.

A Mr. French, who had recently removed to Denton county, was drowned a few days since in crossing the Big Elm.

The Governor has information of a raid into Palo Pinto and Jack counties on the 21st of February, by a party of about twenty Indians, at which time they murdered a Mr. Ross and his son, a lad of eleven years of age, and a Mr. Hightour...

Issue March 29, 1867

The *San Antonio Express* says a Mr. Pendleton, living near Tyan's ranch, was killed by Indians a few days since...

Death of an ancient negress -- Aunt Winnie, lately the property of Col. W.J. Holt of Bedford, died on Monday last, aged 118 years. This old servant woman had been in the family of Col. Holt for two generations and remained with him until a few weeks since. She was in full possession of her faculties and could thread a needle readily. She knew everybody that she had ever known. She died peacefully sitting in her chair. *Lynchburg Virginian.*

Issue March 30, 1867

The *Corpus Christi Advertiser* announces the death there on the 18th of Judge Frederick Belden, an old and respected citizen.

The *San Antonio Ledger* says: Francisco Granadez, who died last Wednesday, was born, raised, lived 82 years, and died in his little jacal, east side of the Main Plaza.

The trial of J. Hewson, a United States solider, for the murder of Dan Parker, a negro, has been postponed due to sickness of several witnesses.

Issue April 1, 1867

Died at Galveston, Sunday morning, March 31, in the 46th year of her age, Mary, beloved wife of Dr. John Moore, late of Tyler, Texas.

Issue April 3, 1867

Departed this life on the 23rd ult. after a short illness, Mrs. Mary Robinson, wife of Col. W.T. Robinson, Huntsville, Texas... [note: mentions children].

Issue April 10, 1867

Col. W.D.C. Hall died night before last at his place on the Island, about fifteen miles to the westward of this city. We learn that he was with a fit of apoplexy on Monday night, and died before morning. He first came to this country in 1812 and emigrated with Col. M'Gee in his unfortunate attempt to revolutionize this country... He was probably near eighty years old... [note: condensed].

Issue April 12, 1867

Died at his residence near this city on the evening of the 10th inst., Col. T.W. Winter, formerly of Tuscumbia, Alabama. Memphis, Tennessee and North Alabama papers please copy.

We regret to announce the loss of another valuable citizen in the person of Col. T.W. Winter, who died at his residence on the Island, east of the city, day before yesterday. He came to this state from Mississippi some years ago, and settled as a planter in Washington county. [note: mentions amiable wife and daughter].

Issue April 13, 1867

The *McKinney Enquirer* gives an account of the sudden death of a man by the name of R.C. Jones, who was a stranger there, and had come in hunt of a horse which he said had been stolen from him in Dallas county. He stopped with a Capt. Wardon. After waiting for Jones to come to him, he went in search of him, and came upon him in a thicket, lying dead in the path. A jury was summoned, and rendered a verdict of death by apoplexy. A letter was found on his person directed to Miss Anna Kelly, Waxahatchie, Ellis county, Texas. Capt. Wardon had his body well dressed and nicely buried and will show his grave to any of deceased friends, or answer letters concerning him. Deceased was about twenty-five years old, weighed 130 pounds, dark complected, and was possessed of a good education.

The *Fairfield Pioneer* of the 2d inst. informs us that a difficulty occurred in that place on that day between Dr. W.A. Milner and Mr. P.L.C. Davis, in which the latter was shot through the heart and expired in a short time.

Judge Tate, of LaGrange, Texas, who killed J.J. Bryant in the rotunda of the St. Charles Hotel, New Orleans, some months since, has been tried and acquitted.

Issue April 16, 1867

Died in this city on yesterday after a brief illness, Mrs. Minerva Patrick Daniel, wife of Dr. F.E. Daniel. Mississippi papers please copy. The friends and acquaintances of the family are respectfully invited to attend her funeral from corner of Mechanic and 13th st's, today at 2 o'clock P.M.

Issue April 18, 1867

Phillip Carrer, an industrious, peaceable, German citizen of Dhanis, Medina county, was killed in cold blood by a teamster of a train encamped there on last Monday.

Issue April 19, 1867

A difficulty occurred last Thursday evening upon the streets of Brenham between Dr. Ben Stones and Mr. Henry Lockett, in which the former gentleman was shot and badly, if not fatally wounded. The firing was with a double barreled gun, and five buckshot took effect in the region of the left hip, from which they have not yet been extracted. The hip-bone, we learn, is badly fractured, and the Dr. -- if he survives at all, will probably be a cripple for life. Both Dr. Stones, and Mr. Lockett are merchants of Brenham.

Issue April 25, 1867

The *San Antonio Herald* says Geo. Libby, who had been confined in the Centreville jail for killing Phillip Kenser at Dhonis, has been forcibly taken from the jail by a mob and hung.

Issue April 30, 1867

Sunday, our city was the scene of another cold blooded murder. James Green, a teamster in the employ of the Government, was shot in the mouth by a pistol in the hands of J. Anderson Parker, formerly stewart of the steamboat *Como*. The affair happened at a low brothel in the eastern part of the city... It appeared that Green and Parker quarrelled about a negro woman named Molly Harris...

Issue May 1, 1867

Died at the residence of Col. Wm. F. Henderson, Bolivar Point, April 28, 1867, of general debility, Annie Mary, infant daughter of Hon. Geo. F. and Mrs. Annie M. Alford, of this city.

J.H. Darnall, an old and respected merchant of Clarksville and a member of the Masonic and Odd Fellows societies, died recently, in the 53rd year of his age.

Issue May 4, 1867

San Antonio Herald: Mr. George W. Dawson, originally from New York, was killed by Indians sometime last month near San Augustine Spring, about sixty miles north of El Paso...

Issue May 7, 1867

Died, Monday, May 6, 1867, Miss Jessie M. Hill, aged twenty-two years. Her friends and acquaintances are invited to attend her funeral this afternoon at 4 o'clock from the residence of her brother-in-law, Mr. John Wolston.

Issue May 8, 1867

Yesterday, about 1 o'clock, a gentleman named N.J. Hackney, committed suicide by taking morphine and laudanum at Jones's ticket office on Central Wharf. Just before he died, he directed Mr. Starr S. Jones to get to his brother in New Orleans the following letter. Dear Dave. We have always been favorites with each other... Be kind to my poor darling children - their mother liked you well. They are orphans now, indeed. Remember me fondly, to all my brothers and sisters. Tell Carrie [brother's wife] a last good bye. I have never been the same since I lost my Mary. Remember me kindly to Lizzie. Tell my own darling Annie as a last farewell for me, may she too be ever happy. Tell Kate goodbye. [note: letter condensed; he also left a letter to the Masonic fraternity.]. The deceased died from the effect of laudanum and morphine.

Issue May 22, 1867

The remains of Judge W.D. Mitchell, who died at Tuxpan, Mexico, on the 22nd ult., were buried at Richmond, Texas with Masonic honors on the 13th.

Issue May 23, 1867

Suicide: On Monday a man named Wm. Oelsner applied to Mr. J.W. Frank, president of the Hebrew Benevolent Society, and stated that he was a stranger in the city, had formerly resided in Cleveland, Ohio, and desired that assistance might be given him. Tuesday, he complained of being sick, and Mr. Frank directed Dr. Randle to visit him, which he did... he was informed his patient was dead... he was an Odd Fellow and bore a certificate of travel issued from Concordia Lodge #13, Zanesville, Ohio, dated November 29, 1866. [note: article condensed; mentions wife and son].

A sailor, Harry Sullivan, fell out of a second story window, and being carried to the City Hospital, died.

Issue May 27, 1867

Tribute of Respect for John J. Jamison.

We regret to learn of the death of Don Carlos Chacon, Spanish Consul at this port, which took place yesterday at the Hospital of the Sisters of Charity. His disease is said to have been congestion of the brain.

Issue May 28, 1867

Died in this city on the 24th inst., A. Blair Smith, aged eighteen years, son of John Blair and Mirean H. Smith of Louisiana. New Orleans and Natchitoches papers please copy.

Issue May 29, 1867

Mount Pleasant Express, man killed: On Saturday evening last, a wagoner by the name of G.W. Corley, supposed to be from Fannin county... was shot and killed by James Cloud.

Drowned - a gentleman named Jno. Dean was accidently knocked overboard from a sail boat on Sunday last, a short distance below Lynchburg, and before he could be rescued was drowned. The body was afterwards recovered by means of trappling irons, taken ashore and buried.

Funeral notice. Died at 12 o'clock M. Tuesday, May 28th, J. Pendergast, aged 46. The funeral will take place at 2 P.M. from the residence of the deceased on 24th st. between Postoffice and Church streets. Friends of the family are invited to attend.

Issue May 30, 1867

Died in this city May 28th, Emma, infant daughter of Dr. F.E. Daniel. Jackson, Mississippi papers please copy.

Tribute of Respect, Bricklayers' Benevolent Union, for John Pendergast.

On last Saturday, a Mr. R.H. Morrison, who lives on the Connor place, ten miles below Waco, was shot by a negro boy by the name of Dick, at the ferry at this place. Mr. M. died on Sunday night, from the effects of the wounds. He leaves a young and interesting widow. [note: condensed].

The Grand Jury dismissed Wm. Stanton, accused of killing Swift, up the Trinity river.

Issue May 31, 1867

Died in the city of Galveston on the 25th inst. of old age, Mrs. Phoebe Crain, in the eighty-first year of her age. She died a true Christian. New York papers please copy.

Issue June 1, 1867

Jas. Hewson, company I, 17th U.S. Infantry, was tried yesterday. He was accused of having murdered Dan Parker, a negro, and formerly a soldier... The jury retired, and after remaining out over two hours, returned and rendered the verdict of "not guilty," and the prisoner was released.

Issue June 2, 1867

The schooner *Stevens* was capsized, drowning two of the crew. The names of the unfortunate men are James Gaffin, an Irishman, residing in Jersey City, and John Rigin, who leaves a widowed mother in Somerset county, Maryland. No trace of the bodies had been discovered up to the 29th ult.

Mortuary report: Jacob Webster, 65, a native of Texas, died.

Issue June 4, 1867

Died at Indianola June 1st, Mrs. C. Lang, formerly an old resident of this city.

Georgetown Watchman. We learn from a private letter to a lady of this town, that a disastrous affair occurred at the foot of the Staked Plains, date not given, in which a large drove of beeves, belonging mostly to Ben. Gooch, was driven off by the Indians, and four white men killed. A lady, a Mrs. Whitehead, was taken prisoner; her husband, Mr. Whitehead, was badly wounded and supposed to be killed, but has since come in. One of the men killed was found entirely skinned. [note: this occurred in Mason county].

The body of R.H. Kennark was found on Sunday morning on Centre street, opposite the Washington Hotel... He was a native of Poland. He came to the city from Brazoria county... The captain of the vessel that brought him here states that he was an educated man and was en route for New Orleans.

A Mr. Lyons was killed Friday last at Millican by a man named Blair.

The *Waco Spectator* says the negro, Dick, who shot Mr. Morrison near the Waco ferry, recently, endeavors to make the impression that the gun was discharged accidently; but some remarks made previously by the black man show that it was his intention to murder the white man. The negro is in custody.

Issue June 5, 1867

Prairie Plains, Grimes county, May 29, 1867: On last evening about sundown, Mr. Washington Hoke shot Mr. John Driscol in the back of the head, the ball ranging upward... He lived till about 10 o'clock last night. The difficulty arose on account of the said Driscol having sung a song that was not agreeable to the said Hoke's sister, Sunday night three weeks ago...

Bellville Countryman. Ernest, a child of Ella's, a negro woman living at the Manning house, died on Tuesday night last. Its death was caused by taking an overdose of laudanum...

The *Waco Register* learns from Hill county that Sam M. Matlock and M.H. Alexander, two of the murderers of Judge Doyle and son in Hill county under aggravated circumstances, were found hanging to a limb of a pecan tree within a few hundred yards of the graves of their victims...

Issue June 7, 1867
Died in Millican, May 23rd, Lilly Durant, aged 19 months, only daughter of James B. and Emma Durant.

Issue June 8, 1867
C.S. Lablond drowned in the cistern attached to the house of Mr. McCormick on 16th street. Painter by trade and addicted to the habits of intemperance. [note: condensed].

Issue June 11, 1867
Died on Sunday evening, June 9th, Ida Lee, infant twin daughter of Hamilton and Maggie Blagge, aged 11 months, 4 days. New York papers please copy.

Murder: The *Waco Register* is pained to learn that Maj. Manning was shot by some unknown person near Cotton Gin, Limestone county, on the 1st. He was living at last accounts, but the wound is said to be mortal. [note: later account reported his wounds as not serious and the Maj. survived].

We learn that a Mrs. Rosa Hamilton was most brutally murdered in Johnson county one day last week by her own brother-in-law. This lady was the wife of Rufus Hamilton, who killed Lt. Powell in Johnson county sometime during the war, who was himself killed by the deputy sheriff of Guadalupe county at Seguin last summer or fall...

Issue June 13, 1867
The *Waco Register* learns that Jesse Rose, a young man about eighteen or twenty years old and of high repute as a peaceable good citizen, was shot and killed near Dyer's Mill, in Hill county, a short time since, by a man named Sellers, who is represented as a desperate character and has not been arrested.

The *Dallas Herald* of the 1st inst. says the storm which visited that section on the previous Sunday night was one of the severest since the "Cedar Hill Hurricane" of 1857. No harm was done in and about Dallas, but in the vicinity of Breckenridge and along Duck Creek the storm left its sad marks in a desolate country and in the destruction of many lives. Some of the family of Mr. James Jackson were injured, and Mr. John Cranston, who was staying there, was badly hurt. One of Mr. Benjamin Prigmore's children was killed and others injured. Out of nine persons in the house of Volney Coldwell, eight were killed, viz: Mr. Coldwell, his wife, four children and two negroes. The residence of Mrs. Huffman, O.P. Simms, Jas. Jackson, Benj. Prigmore, V. Coldwell, A.T. Coldwell, A.T. Pickett, Dr. Cloud, Bailey Harris, Mr. Pruitt, Mr. Lovelace, Mr. Marr, were blown down. Vast injury was done to fencing and crops.

In Tarrant, the storm was very destructive. The *Herald* hears of as many as fourteen houses blown down along the village creek valley. A Mr. Randall is known to have been killed, and some fifteen or twenty persons to have been badly hurt.

Issue June 15, 1867

Died in London, May 18th, of hypertrophy of the heart, Rev. Stephen Kay, D.D. of the Episcopal church. Dr. Kay was well known in this city and state, having lived here during the war.

Issue June 16, 1867

Died, Marion Elizabeth, youngest daughter of W.T. and Laura Clark.

Issue June 18, 1867

Died in this city on the 16th of June, John William, infant son of John H. and Ellen Stoner, aged 3 months, 25 days. *St. Louis (Mo.) Republican* please copy.

[Died] in this city on Sunday morning, June 16th, John, youngest son of A.J. and Fannie J. Walker; aged 8 months, 15 days.

Issue June 21, 1867

The *Bastrop Advertiser* reports that Mr. Ham. White, an old and respected citizen, was killed by some unknown person on the evening of the 12th about eight miles west of town.

A family in Hill county recently heard shrieks in the direction taken by Mack Hamilton and a lady, who had just passed, as if on a journey. Next morning the body of the murdered woman was found cast in a pool of water, stripped of clothing, a bullet-hole in the head, throat cut, and three stabs in the breast. Hamilton stopped and asked the family above mentioned for milk, and as it was near nightfall he was invited to stop, but he refused. He is supposed to have committed the murder. The woman was his brother's widow. We quote from a letter from the *Waco Register*.

Issue June 22, 1867

Died at Clinton, Texas, on the evening of the 15th of May, 1867, after a painful illness of four days, Mrs. Ella Virginia Friend, wife of Wm. R. Friend, in the 24th year of her age. Mobile papers please copy.

Distressing Accident -- Yesterday morning, Mrs. Gordon, the mother of Capt. Gordon of the steamer *Ruthven*, had occasion to draw some water from the cistern attached to her house. Whilst in the act of doing so she lost her balance and was precipitated head-foremost into the water below, and before her friends could render assistance was drowned. Mrs. Gordon was an aged lady, and much respected and esteemed in the community.

Issue June 25, 1867

Murder. The *Telegraph* of Sunday has the particulars of the killing of an unknown white man at the Brashear residence, near Houston, on Friday afternoon. A colored man saw the murder, and testified that two white men were quarreling, when one of them jumped over a fence, secured an axe, and immediately dealt the other several blows with it, knocking him down and splitting his head open after he had fallen. From papers found on the murdered man, his name supposed to be Ab. Berry. Efforts are being made to arrest the murderer.

Issue June 29, 1867

Departed this life Tuesday morning, June 26th, at 5 1/2 o'clock, William Turner, oldest son of William and Annie Strickland; in the 21st year of his age.

Issue June 30, 1867

Died. We understand late last evening that Joseph Perry, scalded by the boiler explosion near the depot, died of his injuries.

Issue July 2, 1867

William Keith, a well known citizen of Bosque county, was recently killed and scalped by the Indians.

A little fellow of twelve years, Daniel Cheers, whose parents reside in Galveston, fell over the bow. He was going up country in company of the family of Dr. McClanahan of Polk county.

Issue July 7, 1867

Death of Hon. C.C. Herbert -- We have been informed by a gentleman just from Columbus, Texas, that Hon. C.C. Herbert was killed there on Friday last, in a bar-room, by a man named Speers. Herbert, as is supposed in jest, made some threat against Speers, when the latter went off and got a pistol, and returned immediately, shot Herbert dead on the spot.

We are also informed that the Federal guard of the place soon afterwards shot and killed Speers.

Mr. Herbert was a member of the Confederate Congress and had been elected since the war to the Congress of the United States.

Issue July 9, 1867

Homicide — On Sunday morning last, between eight and nine o'clock, a barkeeper by the name of C.I. Tripp entered the store of W.S. Stephens, and, after a few words passed between the parties, Tripp discharged two barrels of a six-shooter, the contents taking effect in either side of Mr. Stephens' breast. After committing the deed, Mr. Tripp made his escape. Mr. Tripp [sic] lingered about four hours in great pain, when he expired. His remains were followed to the grave on Monday morning, by his relatives, the Masonic, and a large number of sympathizing friends. *Mt. Pleasant (Texas) Press*, 15th.

Issue July 11, 1867

The *Civilian* has seen a letter from Mr. Henry Seeligson at Indianola, of July 4th, stating that Dr. Dibble and Mr. Vance have both died and also the youngest son of Gen. Woodward. Later information says Mr. Aug. L. Dibble, the partner of Mr. Seeligson, is dead, and that there were thirteen deaths on the 5th inst. The prevailing opinion is that this sickness is yellow fever, others think it is a severe type of billious fever.

Joseph Welsh, for a long time an engineer on the Morgan steamers, dropped down yesterday morning upon the deck of the steam tug *E. Reed* in an apoplectic fit and died. He was an accomplished machinist.

Issue July 13, 1867

Died at 3 P.M. yesterday, E. Malone, aged 41 years. The funeral will take place 4 1/2 P.M. today from his residence on Ave G, Winnie St.

The members of the Galveston Lodge No. 3 I.O.O.F. will meet at their Hall to attend the funeral of Edward Malone.

Clarksville Standard: Died, W.T. Skinner, of poisoning... informed that he lived at Pilot Point, Denton county. [note: condensed].

Issue July 18, 1867

Died in New York, July 15, 1867, Edward Nichols, of the firm of Nichols & Bro. of this city.

The *Columbus Times* published where Col. C.C. Herbert was killed on the night of the 5th inst... The Corner's Jury say in reference to the killing of Spear afterwards, that it was done by a posse summoned by the Sheriff to arrest said Spear for the murder of Herbert. They also say that Spear was a dangerous man and came to his death by resisting the lawful authority of the State.

Col. Herbert was buried at Reed's Bend, about twelve miles below Columbus, where his wife was buried only a few weeks since.

Issue July 20, 1867

Died in Keachi, Louisiana, of pneumonia, on the 10th day of January, 1867, Col. Anderson Floyd Crawford, in the 38th year of his age. Col. Crawford was a son of Maj. Joel Crawford and a native of Sparta, Georgia. [note: widow and children mentioned].

The *Journal* of the 13th says all the prisoners confined to Belton jail escaped on the previous Saturday night: Spence, a freedman, charged with the murder of Mr. Gillespie; Albert Gillespie, charged with the complicity in the same murder; John Riley, alias Richardson, committed on a charge of horse stealing; Scott, a deserter, committed by the Federal authorities. He has been recovered.

Rev. Thos. F. Cook of the Western Texas Conference, son of the celebrated Valentine Cook, of Kentucky, died at his home near Texana, about two weeks since. The *Lavaca Commercial* of the 12th contains a handsome obituary notice of the deceased written, we presume, by Rev. H.S. Thrall.

The *Mobile Tribune* of the 16th says Geo. A. Hillard, a well known and respected citizen, committed suicide by shooting himself with a pistol on the night of the 13th. Distress on account of pecuniary affairs is supposed to be the cause.

Issue July 21, 1867

Dr. J.L. Bryan, an old and respected citizen of Houston, died there on the 19th. He removed from Houston some years ago, and resided a while near Baytown, but went back to the city after the war, and resumed the practice of his profession as a dentist. He leaves a wife and several children.

We have mentioned that a man named Skinner died recently near Clarksville, Texas, saying that he had been poisoned. The *Clarksville Standard* says he was a respectable citizen of Pilot Point, Denton county, and was returning from Arkansas, where he had received money for a drove of cattle, which he had sold there last fall. A man named Garvland or Garvin, was accompanying him... Skinner's brother and a friend have been down and given the proper attention to his affairs.

Issue July 23, 1867

Robert R. Rennall, deputy sheriff of Caddo Parish, Louisiana, was waylaid on Saturday last, by a negro named Cash, and shot in the back. Mr. Rennall lingered until Monday night, when he died. The murderer is still at large.

Miscellaneous Texas Newspaper Abstracts - Deaths --- Vol 2

Issue July 24, 1867

The *Tyler Reporter* says Justice Donley has been engaged for six days in trying A.C. Middleton, charged with murder of Mrs. Eliza L. McClanahan of Van Zandt county.

Funeral -- The funeral of Wm. G. Casseady will take place at 10 o'clock a.m. today. Mr. Casseady was for many years a resident of this city and a compositor in this office. He departed this life yesterday evening at 4 o'clock, leaving a bereaved and grief stricken family to mourn a great loss.

Issue July 25, 1867

Died in this city, Susan, the beloved wife of Chas. Dalian, of inflammation of the bowels, after a short illness, fortified by the sacrament of the Catholic Church. The funeral will take place from the residence of her husband on Market St., between 17th & 18th st's, this morning at 10 o'clock. New Orleans papers please copy.

Issue July 27, 1867

Died at 2 1/2 o'clock A.M., July 26th, Mary Seymour, only child of Isabella and H.R. Giffney; aged 2 months and 16 days. New Orleans papers please copy.

List of Burials at Galveston, July 25: Frederick Ripke, teething; Susanna Dalian, inflammation; Emma Dressel, typhus fever; Matilta Laid, teething.

Issue July 30, 1867

Died on Thursday morning, July 25, 1867, Maud Lee, only daughter of Col. R.R. and Ellen E. Lawther of this city; aged 14 months and 5 days.

The *Dallas Herald* says an old and respected citizen, Capt. J.L. Peak, was murdered there in cold blood on the 16th by a man named Wilson, who was at once arrested and committed to jail.

We regret to learn from the *Gazette* that Wilson H., son of Judge C.S. Cleveland, died at his home in Liberty of congestive fever on the 18th, in the 18th year of his age. He was a young man of much promise. We sincerely sympathize with his relatives in their bereavement.

A German named August Kobbe, residing here some few months, was discovered dead in his bed on Sunday morning at his boarding house, near Market St & 24th St... Suicide by poison... Miss Carrie was about to be married to Mr. Kobbe, but for some reason or other she recently left him, and took up with another. [note: condensed; suicide letter was also published].

Sent to the Hospital -- Night before last, Chas. McLean was found in a helpless condition in front of the Washington Hotel. He stated that he was suffering with chills and fever. He was taken to the City Hospital.

Accident -- On Sunday night, a porter in the store of B.R. Davis fell through a hatchway from the third story to the basement. When picked up, his skull was found to be fractured. He was taken to the Hospital, but was not expected to survive.

Mortality Report -- The following are the deaths for July 27th and 28th, as reported by the City Sexton:
Saturday, July 27-Julius Reissner, aged 24; Henry S. Baldwin, aged 16, whooping cough; Levi Wood, aged 7 months, congestive chills; Jas. St. John, aged 32, congestive billious fever; Fredrick Wagnor, aged 26, dysentery.
Sunday, July 28-Frederick Kress, yellow fever; Joseph Levei, congestion brain; Henry <u>Franklin</u>, billious fever; Jaso Sabner, cholera morbus; Francis Lang, yellow fever; A. Kobbe, suicide.

Deaths in the Police Force -- We are informed by the Chief of Police that two of his men are defunct. Their names are John C. Waggoner and Henry <u>Franklin</u>.

Issue July 31, 1867
Mentions the death of W.G. Casseady, a Galveston printer.

The *Countryman*, now published in Hempstead, announces the death of J.C. McDade, assessor and collector of the county of Austin.

Mortality Report -- The following are the deaths for July 29th, as reported by the City Sexton: C.S. Keley, 49, congestion of brain; John Wagner, 22, yellow fever; Paul Lang, 22, yellow fever; Man unknown, congestion of brain; Mrs. Antonio Frank, 65, billious fever; Wm. Marid, 36, dysentery.

Issue August 1, 1867
There was only one death reported day before yesterday, and that was a little child named Mary C. Schroder, three months old, who died of congestion of the brain.

Died yesterday. -- Officer Smith of the police force died yesterday at 3 o'clock of yellow fever. He was an efficient police officer, and we regret his sudden demise.

Issue August 3, 1867

Died on Thursday, August 1st, at 12 1/2 o'clock, Walter S., only child of Walter M. & Maggie E. Robinson; aged 2 months, 18 days.

Funeral -- J.R. Pointer, a compositor in the office of the *Bulletin*, was buried yesterday morning at 9 a.m. by the Members of the Typographical Union. He died of the prevailing disease, the night before, having been attacked on Wednesday last. Mr. Pointer, a native of Bedford county, Virginia, came to our city since the war. He was a most estimable man and gentleman having made many warm friends among his associates during the short time he has been a resident of our city.

Issue August 4, 1867

Capt. A.S. McLain -- This officer was buried yesterday morning, having fallen victim to the prevailing disease. Capt. McLain, as Chief of Police, has been an energetic officer, always faithful to the duties, and alive to the responsibilities of his station.

Mortuary Report -- We have obtained the following names and disease of the persons buried yesterday, Saturday, August 23d, [sic] 1867: S. Loeb, yellow fever; Frank Muller, yellow fever; Albertine Miller, yellow fever; A.S. McLain, yellow fever; Negro infant, age one hour; Gus. Douglass, yellow fever.

Issue August 6, 1867

The negro sailors of the American bark *Wallace* murdered the second mate, Michael Ryan, of Philadelphia, at Havana on the 25th ult.

Interments -- The following is a list of the names of the persons buried Sunday and yesterday, their ages, and the disease of which they died, furnished by the City Sexton:
Sunday, August 4th: Mrs. H. Wintzel, yellow fever; John Hallins, yellow fever; Moses Levi, yellow fever; Morris Schramber, yellow fever; Infant of Mrs. Thomas, still-born.
Monday, July [sic] 5th: John Ernfeld, aged 24, yellow fever; Louisa Thomas, 38, yellow fever; Eliza Harmon, 3, yellow fever; John Miller, 44, yellow fever; Edward St. John, 25, yellow fever; Mrs. Vott, 24, yellow fever; Alfred Wilson, 26, yellow fever; John Morris, 28, yellow fever; Jacob Gorman, 20, yellow fever.
In addition to the above, Dr. Taylor, Medical Director for this District, was buried by the military. He died of yellow fever.

Issue August 7, 1867

Alfred Morrill, aged about twenty, and his younger brother, about fourteen years of age, were murdered by two Mexicans at Ramirena Rancho, some forty miles from Corpus Christi, sometime last month. The murdered boys came to Texas from Philadelphia about a year ago, and in company with a younger brother, were engaged in sheep raising. *Corpus Christi Advertiser.*

Issue August 8, 1867

The *Columbus (Colorado Co.) Times* of the 3rd records the killing of Mr. L.G. DeGraffenried and a young man named Hudson in the edge of the county of Fayette on the previous Wednesday. [note: condensed].

We deeply regret to hear of the death of Capt. S.A. Benton, editor of the *Indianola Times*. He fell a victim to the epidemic there... He began his editorial career in this state at Richmond... The same paper adds that Mrs. Benton's father, Rev. J.H.D. Moore, died in Richmond during the past year... and that only last week her niece and namesake, the daughter of Mrs. Col. Peters, of Richmond, died in Jackson county... [note: condensed].

Issue August 9, 1867

We learn that the celebrated Dr. H. Parker was killed a few days ago by Lt. Plummer at Prairie Lea. The Dr. had been arrested and was attempting to escape when the Lieut. fired upon him, killing him instantly.

Issue August 10, 1867

The *Chronicle* feelingly records the death on 28th inst. of Wm. Voigt, brother of the editor, useful citizen and Mason.

Issue August 11, 1867

Died in this city of yellow fever on Saturday, 10th of August, James C. Brown, aged 28 years. Richmond, Virginia papers please copy.

Died: Sarah, youngest daughter of Wm. E. & Sarah Wheelwright; aged 18 years, of New Orleans, Louisiana, of yellow fever, on Saturday morning at 2 o'clock A.M. New Orleans papers please copy.

Mortuary Report -- The following is a list of the names of the persons buried yesterday, August 10th, 1867, furnished by the City Sexton: H.B. Simpson, aged 28, yellow fever; Helmoth Saber, aged 28, yellow fever; Bully. Durr, 28, yellow fever; A. Connolly, aged 28, yellow fever; Thomas Dewney, 22, yellow fever; Mr. Thomas, –, yellow fever; J.T. Strong, 40, yellow fever; James Horan, 38, yellow fever; William Hawley, 38, yellow fever; Sarah F. Wainwright, 18, yellow fever; W.H. Ramsey, 20, yellow fever; Julia Kelly, 23, yellow fever; Massie (colored), 35, yellow fever;

F. Leonard, 31, yellow fever; J. Hermann, --, yellow fever; D.D. Finley, 30, yellow fever; L. [?] Max, 23, yellow fever; J. [?] Beshard, 37, yellow fever; Maj. W.B. Jolly, 25, yellow fever; Cora E. Honey, 3yr, 10m, yellow fever; Edward Kath, 23, yellow fever; Richard Bates, 21, yellow fever; James Brown, 28, yellow fever; Catherine Wanberg, 25, conges. fever.

Father Holman, an old Methodist preacher, for many years a resident of Louisville, Ky, and widely known, died at his brother's residence in Indiana on the 1st, aged seventy-seven years.

THE TEXAS DEAD: The *Macon Telegraph* is publishing a list of Confederate dead on Chickamauga battle field. The number from Tennessee is 268; from Louisiana 40; from Mississippi 111. The list will be continued. The following are the names as far as yet gathered, of the dead of Texas:
Capt. J.S. Sexon, co. ___, 15th regt.
Capt. J.W. Cannon, co. ___, 10th regt.
Lieut. S.A. Williams, co. ___, ___ regt.
Lieut. A. Hamilton, co. C, 9th regt. cav.
Lieut. S. Fitch, co. ___, 9th regt. cavalry.
Lieut. L.A. Williams, co. ___, 32d regt. cav.
_____ Crawford, co. ___, ___ regt.
E.D. Prey, co. B, 15th regt.
Unknown, co. ___, 15th regt.
J.M. Kelton, co. ___, 15th regt.
W.R. Bruce, co. F, 9th regt. cavalry.
J.M. Harris, co. I, 9th regt. cavalry.
J.M. Boons, co. ___, 9th regt. cavalry.
J.S. Errin, co. E, 14th regt. cavalry.
W.W. Gregg, co. C, 14th regt. cavalry.
W.W. Gaston, co. K, 14th regt. cavalry.
B. Lynch, co. G, 14th regt. cavalry.
J.F. Campbell, co. F, 14th regt. cavalry.
C.C. Wair, co. c, 10th regt cavalry.
J.H. Homes, co. I, 10th regt. cavalry.
R. Hulin, co. ___, 32d regt. cavalry.
J.R.T., [sic] co. ___, 32d regt. cavalry.
Y. Bowlin, co. F, 10th regt. cavalry.
Unknown, co. ___, 10th regt. cavalry.
Three Unknown, co. ___, 1st regt.
R.S. Hall, co. ___, ___ regt.
R.R. Chaste, co. ___, ___ regt.
N.H. Mendenhall, co. H, 1st regt.
1st Serg't. E.O. Wood, co. C, 4th regt.
Serg't. T.T. Moore, co. K, 24th regt. cav.

W.C. Canall, co. I, 4th regt.
W.P. Mynatt, co. G., 18th regt.
Corg'l [sic] C. Cuppler, co. K, 24th regt. cav.
W.H. Crawford, co. G, 18th regt. cavalry.
Addison Gibbs, co. G, 18th regt. cavalry.
T.J. Short, co. D, 24th regt.
D.R.D., [sic] co. ___, ___ regt.
D.W. Holland, co. A, 15th regt.
B.V. Lay, co. G, 10th regt.
W.G. Moss, co. D, 1st regt.
R.G. Robertson, co. G, 6th regt.
W.R. Deane, co. H, 10th regt.
C. Steele, co. A, 15th regt.
G.W. Simmons, co. H, 15th regt.
J.M. Cason, co. I, 18th regt.
N. Allen, co. D, 24th regt.
Unknown, co. G, 18th regt.
W. Lettemer, co. F, 24th regt.
W. Murry, co. F, 18th regt.
E.J.M. Hapson, co. G, 10th regt.
H.E.T., [sic] co. ___, 18th regt.
J. Childress, co. E, 9th regt.
56 Unknown. Total 111.

Issue August 13, 1867

Mortuary Report -- The following is the list of burials Sunday and yesterday, August 11th and 12th, 1867, obtained from the City Sexton:
Conrad Neibour, 69, yellow fever; Thomas Docket, 23, yellow fever; Beman [?] Halkrauth, 25, yellow fever; F.O. Nitsche, 26, yellow fever; Henry Ohrmnair, 35, yellow fever; P.[?] Strickman, 28, (col.), yellow fever; B.F. Clark, 26, yellow fever; Henry Mooney, 35, yellow fever; Thomas Lynch, 28, yellow fever; Geo. Williams, 26, yellow fever; G.W. Thompson, 35, yellow fever; Robt. Martin, 21, yellow fever; O. Blum, 28, yellow fever; Patrick Cronin, 30, yellow fever; Joseph Hertz, 21, yellow fever; May Marcus, 22, yellow fever; John Schonholts, 33, yellow fever; Jane R. Newell, 12, yellow fever; W. Planed, 40, suicide; James McQuinn, 35, syphilis, Mary Richards, infant, 16 mos., teething. 13 foreign born, 8 native born.

August 12: Jacob Sayrt, 40, yellow fever; Mrs. M. Magrouz, 35, yellow fever; Fred Ploem, 36, yellow fever; M. Young, 31, yellow fever; C. Hahu, 22, yellow fever; J. Klapt, 28, yellow fever; Thomas O'Neil, 31, yellow fever; John Rooney, 34, yellow fever; Jacob Careleman, 40, yellow fever; Mathew O. Hick, 21, yellow fever; John Shean, 25, yellow fever; Joseph Bauhoff, 27, yellow fever; Patrick Fitzgerald, 48, yellow fever; James Hide, 30, yellow fever; S. Anotine, 29, yellow fever; Mr. Idelman, 00 [sic], yellow fever;

Charles Garland, 4, yellow fever; Frank E. Terry, 5, yellow fever; John M. Nash, 9, yellow fever; M.A. McPherson, 16, yellow fever. 16 foreign born, 4 natives of Texas, 1 negro.

The Hospitals -- Hereafter the Military as well as the City and Marine Hospital will be under the control of Dr. Greensville Dowell, this gentleman having obtained a contract to run the former as surgeon in charge, the position made vacant by the death of Col. Taylor.

Missing Papers -- Theopolis O'Clair, a house builder, died of yellow fever yesterday morning, and since his death his book of memoranda, in which he kept his accounts, contracts and money is missing. His watch and some letters and papers were found in possession of the friend who sat up with him. Where is his other friend with the memoranda, etc?

Scene in a sick room -- An englishman, a porter at the establishment of J.A. Sauters, whilst he was delirious with fever during the temporary absence of his nurse, arose from his bed and attacking Mrs. Sauters, who was waiting for the return of the nurse, threw her down and would have strangled her to death had not immediate assistance arrived. The sick man died within twenty minutes after he was put back to bed.

Young Charles Cooper, who was in this city from his childhood, but not found [?] here for the past seven years, died on Sunday night. He was attended by Dr. Robinson who says it was a most unmistakable case of yellow fever. We understand he had visited this city a few days before he was taken sick.

From the *Millican News Letter* of the 10th: We have been informed that a shooting affair came off some eight miles from Owensville, in Robinson county, last week, between a gentleman named Able, a planter, and Ethridge, his overseer, in which the latter was shot and killed.

We learn that a Mr. Mosely of Byran was knocked in the head with a billiard cue by one of his associates while the two were disputing about the game, and is likely to die from the effects of the wound. The party who struck him has been arrested.

Issue August 14, 1867
Died in Galveston on the 24th of July, 1867, of brain fever, Hunter, infant daughter of J.E. & S.C. Wallis, aged 15 months, 3 days.

The *Dallas Herald* learns that two hundred Indians drove off between three hundred and five hundred head of horses from Parker and Wise counties about the 20th ult. On that day they attacked the residence of a man named Briscoe, living near the line of the two counties, killed the old man and his wife and carried off their five children into captivity.

Three young men named Johnson, Carlton, and Proffitt were killed by about one hundred Indians at Patrick Ranche, in Young county, on the Clear Fork of the Brazos on the 17th ult. This is the same Ranche from which Mrs. Patrick and family and a negro woman and three children were taken by the great Indian raid of 1863. The Indians making this last raid seemed to have presumed on the difficulty of crossing the soldiers at Fort Belknap to the west side of the Brazos.

We report the burial of George <u>Wilson</u>, engineer of Washington Steam Fire Engine. A large number of firemen attended his funeral.

William Goggan, an estimable gentleman, died, and was buried yesterday.

Horrible Outrage. -- D. Messer, keeper of a bar-room and boarding house about a block east of the 2d ward market, died about 1 a.m. yesterday, and his wife died yesterday evening. Whilst the attendants were gone from the room in which the woman's body was laid out, a man named Meyer, who was drunk, was caught, it is charged, committing an outrage which cannot be related. The report went out upon the street that such an outrage had been committed, and a crowd gathered, and would have hung the drunken man to the nearest lamp-post had he not been arrested and carried to jail. He had been a friend of the deceased and the policeman who saw him thought he was merely exhibiting his sorrow over the death of his friend. An examination will probably be had to day, and the horrible charge substantiated or disproved.

Mortuary Report: The following is a list of the names of the persons buried yesterday, August 13th, 1867, furnished by the City Sexton:
Mary Fagan, aged 26, yellow fever.
Mrs. D. Alexander, 20, yellow fever.
Henry Long, 30, yellow fever.
Mary Maren, 20, yellow fever.
William Graham, 50, yellow fever.
Thomas Kelly, 48, yellow fever.
August Kleinker, 3, yellow fever.
George <u>Wilson</u>, 28, yellow fever.
Samuel Clesser, 35, yellow fever
P. Bording, 25, yellow fever.
Jessy Jones, 12, yellow fever.
Lizzie Flood, 21, yellow fever.

Patsy Mann, 20, yellow fever.
J.M. Essner, 33, yellow fever.
Joseph Dowsey, 50, yellow fever.
Klimapue, 28, yellow fever.
James McGill, 40, yellow fever.
David <u>Messer</u>, 33, yellow fever.
William Goggan, 26, yellow fever.
John Smith, 40, yellow fever.
Mary Holman, 28, yellow fever.
Clara R. Baehr, 31, yellow fever.
Jacob Brock, 20, yellow fever.
James McDonald, 28, yellow fever.
Nat Weems, 28, yellow fever.
Mrs. <u>Messer</u>, 27, yellow fever.
Walter Massey, __, yellow fever.
Adule Wells, 40, yellow fever.
Peter L. Flett, 38, congestive chill.
Michael Hussey, 9, lockjaw.
Draw Housa, 48, flux.

Issue August 15, 1867

Died in this city at 5 o'clock P.M. yesterday of yellow fever, Capt. W.N. Ledyard. His funeral will take place from his residence this morning at 10 o'clock.

The scourge has destroyed the life of no more estimable, beloved and gallant gentleman than W.N. Ledyard, who died yesterday evening. His partner in business, Maj. White, is down with the fever.

Notice. The Officers and Members of the Island Steam Fire Engine Co. No. 2 are hereby requested to meet at their Hall this (Thursday) morning at 6 o'clock to attend the funeral of the late I.V. King.

Dr. Parker. -- We have already recorded the killing of Dr. Parker, an intelligent negro, who was in the habit of warning the freedmen of this State against the Radicals... We hope to be able to lay the full particulars of the killing before our readers in a few days.

MORTUARY REPORT: The following is the list of burials yesterday, August 14th, officially reported by the City Sexton:
Mrs. Louisa Wolff, 25, yellow fever.
Mrs. Levy, 26, yellow fever.
Mrs. Heyman, 23, yellow fever.
Charley Alrod, 23, yellow fever.
H. Britchsnider, ___, yellow fever.

Harman Schriver, 38, yellow fever.
Emile Ney, 28, yellow fever.
Andrew Preacher, 41, yellow fever.
Elizabeth Garland, 36, yellow fever.
Henry Kelso, 23, yellow fever.
Walter Mapson, 17 months, yellow fever.
Antone Oberle, 48, yellow fever.
___ Shumaker, 31, yellow fever.
Mr. Lichtenstein, 26, yellow fever.
Luseinda Creary, 18, yellow fever.
Franz Sucharveck, 20, yellow fever.
Simon Wail, 28, yellow fever.
Wm. Hildebrands, 35, yellow fever.
Mrs. Louise Lavine, 22, yellow fever.
Simon Weil, 26, yellow fever.
M. Johaima, 60, yellow fever.
J. DeBrow, 21, yellow fever.
Mrs. Thompson, 24, yellow fever.
Mrs. F. Burguess, 37, yellow fever.
Henry Esau, 23, yellow fever.
Mr. John, 40, yellow fever.
James Murphy, 23, yellow fever.
Negro man, 50, yellow fever.
Richard Holden, 31, billious fever.

Issue August 16, 1867

Died on the 12th inst., Mr. James H. Hyde [?] of county Clare, Ireland. The deceased was lately of Cook county, Illinois.

Died in Galveston, August 15th at 3 o'clock A.M. of yellow fever, Dr. R.G. Salmon, late of Brazoria, Texas; aged 47 years.

The Fever. -- The *Indianola Bulletin* of the 8th says: We have a letter from Corpus Christi which states that several deaths have occurred from yellow fever; among them Mrs. Polan and Mr. Eastwood, both known in this place.

Col. Davis, U.S. Deputy Marshall, was buried last night at 8 o'clock. He died of the prevailing disease.

Echoes From Houston. Yesterday exhibited an increase in the number of interments as follows:
August 15: I.C. Spence, 50, general debility; Mr. Lewis, yellow fever; Mr. Glascoe, yellow fever; Mr. Schwaah, yellow fever; Daughter of Judge Thomas, age and disease unknown.

August 16: Rhoda Todd, col., 19 [?], child birth.

Mrs. Dr. J.M. Sledge died Friday last in this city and was taken to Brenham for interment. She was a most estimable lady, and leaves a large circle of sorrowing friends.

MORTUARY REPORT: The following is the list of burials yesterday, August 15th, officially reported by the City Sexton:
James Murphy, 26, yellow fever.
James Pratt, 25, yellow fever.
H.S. Cimmarger, 50, yellow fever.
I.V. King, 35, yellow fever.
R.G. Salmon, 30, yellow fever.
W.N. Ledyard, 30, yellow fever.
George Burr, 22, yellow fever.
L.A. Westphall, 29, yellow fever.
Anderson Thomas, 19, yellow fever.
Frederick Haller, 23, yellow fever.
Joe Decoe, 26, yellow fever.
W. Ehrman, 37, yellow fever.
James Finnegan, 23, yellow fever.
Charles Banks, 36, yellow fever.
J. Neibou's son, 10, yellow fever.
H.M. Davie, 27, yellow fever.
Wm. Dummerry, 42, yellow fever.
P. Leiberman, 23, yellow fever.
Mrs. Zaadoc, 37, yellow fever.
Augusta Dilks, 41, yellow fever.
Thos. H. Hawkins, 22, brain fever.

Issue August 17, 1867

Died on Friday, August 16th, at 12 1/2 o'clock, of yellow fever, Charles H. Fondi/Fundi; aged about 28 years, formerly a resident of New Orleans & Mobile, Alabama.

[Died] On Friday, August 16th, of the epidemic, Wm. Eldridge, infant son of Matilda and Thomas Compton; aged 4 years, 8 months and 21 days.

In the unavoidable haste with which the Sexton's reports are written and published, errors not infrequently occur... For instance, in our yesterday morning's report by the Sexton, the name of H.M. Davie is given by mistake for Col. H.M. Davis, Deputy U.S. Marshall, whose death was announced in a separate paragraph.

MORTUARY REPORT: The following is the list of burials yesterday, August 16th, as furnished by the City Sexton:

Mr. Groot, 23, yellow fever.
Thomas Hunt, 26, yellow fever.
J. Weiss, 33, yellow fever.
Louisa Grape, 36, yellow fever.
James B. Brown, 10, yellow fever.
Wm. Baudman, 27, yellow fever.
Wilhelmina Braush, 28, yellow fever.
William Brown, 31, yellow fever.
Madam Burch, 20, yellow fever.
J.L. Wallis, 14, yellow fever.
Mary A. Anderson, 22, yellow fever.
Henry Tate, 32, yellow fever.
Edward Albert, 23, yellow fever.
Samuel Nichols, 28, yellow fever.
Mr. Tife, 40, yellow fever.
Dan Lyons, 35, yellow fever.
Boy Auguste, 6, yellow fever.
Christian Rhodefield, 51, yellow fever.
George Trouwitter, 24, yellow fever.
Mrs. Hublin Negries, 45, yellow fever.
Aleck Edmundson, 24, yellow fever.
Charles N. Fonda, 28, yellow fever.
Willie A. Compton, 4 6m. [sic], yellow fever.
Rudolph Nushon, 31, yellow fever.
A. Garland, 32, yellow fever.
Mrs. M.A. Thompson, 54, yellow fever.
Inf't. of W.M. Burnet, still born.
Mary Hyen, 18, typhoid fever.
Joseph Bush, 15m., convulsions.
Charley Menard, 78, Old age.
Samuel L. Berry, 39, Inflam. Bowels.
Jtephen [sic] J. Nagle, 36, Cong'n Brain.
H. Kure, 37, Dysentery.
Pauline Kure, 8, fever.

We notice that the statement we made the other day on the authority of Dr. Robinson, that young Charles Cooper of Houston died of yellow fever, is contradicted, on the hypothesis that he had the yellow fever before, and that it cannot be taken a second time.

Issue August 18, 1867

Died at 8 o'clock A.M., August 16th, of congestion of the lungs, Samuel L. Berry, aged 39 years. Born in Scott county, Illinois. Winchester and Jacksonville, Ill. papers please copy.

The *Palestine Advocate* records the killing there on the 31st ult. of Mr. Milam, a citizen of Anderson county, by a U.S. soldier... [note: condensed]

Echoes from Houston. Mary Marshall, 45, died of cancer, a colored woman.

Hon. R.L. Waddill, long a resident of Collin county, formerly of Hopkinsville, Kentucky, died at his residence near McKinney on the 5th inst.

MORTUARY REPORT: The following is the list of burials yesterday, August 17th, furnished by the City Sexton:
Andrew Alston, 32, yellow fever.
Clement Fonleron, 20, yellow fever.
Madeline Miller, 15, yellow fever.
John Gibson, 30, yellow fever.
Theodore Lockman, 24, yellow fever.
Mrs. Mary O'Brien, unk., yellow fever.
J. Finegan, 40, yellow fever.
[?]. Maury, 36, yellow fever.
Wm. Wagner, 39, yellow fever.
Wm. Zimmerman, 24, yellow fever.
James Coyne, 28, yellow fever.
Moses, 45, yellow fever.
H.C. Smith, 18, yellow fever.
J. Emeline Pound, 67, yellow fever.
John McChane, 32, yellow fever.
Annie Condor, 22, yellow fever.
Theodore Mix, 36, yellow fever.
Mr. Grant, 26, yellow fever.
Fred Besberd, 20, yellow fever.
F. Wassoms, 31, yellow fever.
Ch[??]les Zadow, 32, yellow fever.
Samuel Ambler, 20, yellow fever.
Antone [unclear] Gillhe, 18, yellow fever.
Kate Long, 22, yellow fever.
R. [?] Lackland, 32, yellow fever.
Charles [unclear] Powers, 22, yellow fever.
[??] Khun, 10, convulsions.

Issue August 20, 1867

A letter in the *Mt. Pleasant (Titus co.) Press* says -- on the 23d of last month, W.G. Kirkman, with three U.S. soldiers, went to the eastern portion of Davis county to arrest a desperado named Baker... Baker fired the first shot, killing Private Albert E. Titus, Co. C, 20th Infantry immediately... W.G. Kirkman, with eleven soldiers, made an attempt to arrest Baker... Baker was a deserter from the Confederate Army... [note: condensed].

Mr. John A. Lidstone, the younger brother of our old fellow citizen, died early Sunday morning after a sickness of about forty hours. His funeral took place at 11 A.M. the same day from the residence of Mr. E.L. Ufford.

In the list of recent yellow fever deaths, we notice the names of Maj. Wilke and Andrew Fleming. The latter was a young man, and came to this state as agent for the publishing house of J.P. Morton & Co., of Louisville, Kentucky...
    Mr. Andrew Fleming of New Orleans died on Sunday evening of the prevailing epidemic... He was a native of Ireland and for many years past a resident of New Orleans, where he was well known as the head of a book house... A young wife and child are left... He was one of the survivors of the famous "8th Louisiana.

"The epidemic. Among those attacked yesterday we hear of Major B. Rush Plumly and Capt. Perry, Chief of Police. Capt. Dan. Striker, late Captain of the Night Watch, was not expected to survive. (Quite a number of the police are down.)

The following is the list of burials Sunday, August 18th, 1867, officially reported by the City Sexton:
Catherine Bonet, 30, yellow fever, France.
Mr. Boston, 22, yellow fever, Mass.
Geo. Tan, 20, yellow fever, German.
H. Wilke, 29, yellow fever, German.
William Wilson, 20, yellow fever, U.S.
J.E. Abbots, 10, yellow fever, New York.
Lawrence Cavanaugh, 30, yellow fever, Texas.
Mark Morris, 30, yellow fever, Genoa.
Thomas Farley, 28, yellow fever, Ireland.
James Wilson, 21, yellow fever, U.S.
William J. Carter, 22, yellow fever, Kentucky.
Thos. J. Smith, 23, yellow fever, Tennessee.
John A. Lidstone, 26, yellow fever, England.
Martha St. Blondine, 24, yellow fever, France.
Adolph Bumbuhl, 29, yellow fever, German.
Christine Keigher, 27, yellow fever, German.

Dora, 19, yellow fever, not known.
J.B. Cheesborough, 39, S. Carolina.
Thomas Kelly, 20, yellow fever, Ireland.
Lloyd J. Harrison, 17, yellow fever, Texas.
Henrietta Volst, 30, yellow fever, German.
A.F. Compton, 28, yellow fever, Texas.
Byram Russel, 25, typhoid fever, Alabama.
Gustava Silversand, 4, typhus fever, German.
Richard Veitgen, 22, inflammation of brain, German.
    Monday, August 19th:
Eliza Sulfolk, [??], yellow fever, German.
Julius Miller, 28, yellow fever, _____
Andrew Flemming, 27, yellow fever, La., U.S.
Patrick Murphy, 28, yellow fever, N.Y.
Mary Francis Abbot, 30, yellow fever, _____
Charles F. Williams, __, yellow fever, France.
Joseph Darby, __, yellow fever, German.
Joseph Tenss, 22, yellow fever, German.
Kate Cana, 9m, 18 days, yellow fever, Ireland.
Patrick Tobbs, 39, yellow fever, U.S.
Charles Jones, 26, yellow fever, Italy.
Austin Such, 20, yellow fever, ___.
James F. Soyre, 51, yellow fever, Baltim'e.
Edward Williams, 50, yellow fever, Ireland.
John Harberg, 19, yellow fever, German.
William Polvgt, 39, yellow fever, German.
Maria Whiting, 60, yellow fever, Virginia.
C.G. Lounds/Lownds, 30, yellow fever, Virginia.
Jimmy Nichols, 2, yellow fever, Texas.
Mr. Wilbergard, 36, yellow fever, German.
Pauline Krannerg, 27, yellow fever, German.
Joseph Marks, 33, yellow fever, Poland.
Emelia Brennan, 1y 14 d, yellow fever, Texas.
Wm. T. Elwick, 37, yellow fever, England.
Emily Curry, 25, yellow fever, U.S.
John Eisenhert, 30, yellow fever, _____
Henry C. Cate, 37, yellow fever, N.Y.
T.T. Bullerty, 37, yellow fever, Ireland.
Mary E. Pound, 4, yellow fever, Texas.
Ernest Pelter, 34, yellow fever, German.
Sally Day, 14, yellow fever, Texas.
Charles Neibour, 9, yellow fever, Texas.
Fred. Ladwicks, 9, typhus fever, German.
Wilhelmina Nieburh, 7m, teething, Texas.

Miscellaneous Texas Newspaper Abstracts - Deaths — Vol 2

Issue August 21, 1867

MORTUARY REPORT: The following is the list of burials Tuesday, August 20th, officially reported by the City Sexton:

Charles Anderson, 32, yellow fever, U.S.

Mrs. Windham, ___, yellow fever, U.S.

S.A. Thompson, 21, yellow fever, Tennessee.

E. Harvey, 37, congestion brain, Phillad.

Albert Page (col'd) 5, yellow fever, Texas.

Capt. Dan Striker, 29, yellow fever, N.J.

Wm. Grave, (col.) 28, yellow fever, Miss.

Catherine Dubner, 47, yellow fever, Germ'y.

Julius Brickman, 18, yellow fever, Germ'y.

Eley Dolley, (col.) 50, yellow fever, Ballm'c.

C.F. Graves, 8 1/2, yellow fever, Galves'n.

George A. Eaton, 45, yellow fever, U.S.

Mary Volst, 6, yellow fever, Texas.

Eliza Hill, (col.) 15, yellow fever, Texas.

E.F. Conklim, 33, yellow fever, N.Y.

Anna Schuelder, 2 1/2, yellow fever, Galves'n.

Henry Lausen, 6, yellow fever, Galvest'n.

R. Anderson, 30/80, yellow fever, N.Y.

Joe Stamps, (col.), 28, yellow fever, U.S.

Pat Egan, 24, yellow fever, Ireland.

Eugene Palauis, 8, yellow fever, France.

Pat Howe, 35, yellow fever, U.S.

Martin Moran, 34, yellow fever, Austria.

A. Hoffman, yellow fever, U.S.

Edith Gonzales 6, inflammation stomach, Texas.

Infant of Jos. Aiken, 1 day,—— Gal'ton.

Of above 23 yellow fever; 3 other diseases; 8 females; 18 males; 6 City Hospital; 8 Howard Association patients; and 5 colored.

Issue August 22, 1867

Rev. James McLeod. This gentleman, well known and highly esteemed throughout the State, died, as already announced, at the residence of his mother-in-law, Mrs. Wynne, of Houston, on the 19th inst. He was an extensive planter on the Brazos, near Pittville, and had been for many years, up to the time of his death, a popular and useful minister of the M.E. Church, South.

His loss, as a citizen, as a minister, as a man and as a relative and friend, will be severely felt.

Mortuary Report--The following is a list of burials yesterday, August 21, as furnished by the City Sexton:
Pat Perry, 47, yellow fever, N.C.
Patrick McGillick, 27, yellow fever, Missouri.
John Masterson, 26, yellow fever, Denmr'k.
T.N. Hyde, 18, yellow fever, Texas.
Charles Waddle, 40, yellow fever, Virginia.
Frank Joseph, 4, yellow fever, Texas.
Mrs. H. Westerlage, 23, yellow fever, German.
Henry McDonnell, 34, yellow fever, Ireland.
Edward Moench, 32, yellow fever, German.
Wm. Robinson, 25, yellow fever, Alabama.
Eliza Ward, 22, yellow fever, England.
John Greer, 37, yellow fever, N.Y.
A. Maury 24, yellow fever, France.
Henry Allen, 24, yellow fever, England.
Joseph Finley, 24, yellow fever, England.
J.W. Hill, 23, yellow fever, Ala.
James L. Shotwell, 48, yellow fever, Ala.
M.E. Green, 21, Syphilis, German
John Fanthorp, 21, yellow fever, German
Frank O. Derwin, yellow fever, German.
Eve Gould, 9, inflammation lungs, New Orleans.
Herman Boutsch, 1 year, 9 ms, congestive fever, Texas.
Of the above--2 females; 20 males; 19 yellow fever; 3 other diseases; 3 negroes; 2 Howard Association patients; 4 from the City Hospital. Total 22.

Echoes from Houston: Sexton reports:
Aug. 21 A.H. Torbert, 35 years, typhoid fever.
Aug. 21 Daughter of Henry Lane, 13 years, inflammation of the bowels.

Issue August 23, 1867
Mortuary Report. -- The following is the list of burials Wednesday, August 22d, officially reported by the City Sexton:
Chas. Ehrenberg, 34, yellow fever,--.
Mrs. Emma Sewald, 59, yellow fever, German.
Melsier Deltz, 47, yellow fever,--.
Hawkins L. Waller, 3030 [sic], yellow fever, Ky.
Jacob Twig, 27, yellow fever, Wis.
Wm. T. Moore, 37, yellow fever, Ky.
Wilhelmina Witte, 26, yellow fever, German.
Clara T. Gifford, 8 y. 9m., yellow fever, City.
Margaret Lindsey, 29, yellow fever, Pa.
P.A. Gost, 34, yellow fever, U.S.

Jas. McCabe, 30, yellow fever, Ireland.
Mr. Pert [?], 28, yellow fever, --.
Thomas Carroll, 32, yellow fever, Ireland.
Pablo Polisco, 32, yellow fever, Poland.
James Conly, 42, yellow fever, Ireland.
Margaret Besthiers, 34, yellow fever, France.
Mrs. J.T. Kirkman, 24, yellow fever, Ill.
Augusta Hankel, 6m., teething, Texas.
Mary Kruse,--, unknown, --.
G.T. Urnstein, 24, congestion bowels, Gr.
    Of the above, 8 females, 12 males, no colored, 5 City Hospital, 1 Israelite; 17 yellow fever, one not known, 2 other diseases, 8 natives, 8 foreign, 4 unknown nativity, 5 were patients of the Howard Association.

Issue August 24, 1867
Died of yellow fever, August 6, 1867, in the town of Tuxpan, Mexico, John M. Lockett, formerly of this state.

The *New Orleans Times* says: W.N. Ledyard, who died the other day in Galveston, was, until his removal to Texas, for many years identified with the interest of Mobile. The *Mobile Tribune* says:
    Mr. Ledyard was a great favorite with his numerous friends -- those who knew him as a school-fellow and as a comrade in the army of Northern Virginia.

The epidemic -- We regret to learn of the demise of two captains of vessels in port, Captain F.J. Runnels, master of the schooner *Letitia* from New York, and Capt. J.A. Nickerson of the schooner *E.C. Howard*, also from New York. Capt. Runnels was buried yesterday evening, and Capt. Nickerson is to be buried this morning at 7 o'clock from Kuhn's wharf.

Mortuary Report. -- The following is a list of the names of the persons buried yesterday, August 23d, 1867, furnished by the City Sexton:
Boy, Jesus, 9, yellow fever, Mexico; Mrs. R/B. K. Smith, 49, yellow fever, Delaware; Andrew Gilchrist, 25, yellow fever, Scotland; James Schendon, 22, yellow fever, Liverpool; Morris Almar, 25, yellow fever, France; F/E. Voight, 39, yellow fever, --; Capt. F.V. Runnels, 35, yellow fever, N.H.; E. [?] W. Rodefeld, 26, yellow fever, German; E. [?] White, 36, yellow fever, German; James Kirkpatrick, yellow fever, Ireland; J.P. Rogers, 43, yellow fever, S.C.; John H. Keys, 26, yellow fever, Me.; Samuel Vogel, 23, yellow fever, German; M.J. Cordray, 21, yellow fever, Ala.; Unknown man, yellow fever, --;

Daniel McGinnis, 46, Intermittent, City; Arthur Collier, 3m., spasm, City; Rosina Vogt, 13m., teething, City.

Three females, 16 males, 1 negro, Howard Association 3, City Hospital 4, Israelite Association 1. Fifteen yellow fever, four others.

Issue August 25, 1867

Died in this city on the 22nd inst. of yellow fever, Clara Fay Gifford, aged 8 years and 9 months, youngest daughter of G. C. and Mary C. Gifford. New England papers please copy.

Died: Daniel G. Price, of Philadelphia, of congestion. The friends and acquaintances of the deceased are respectfully invited to attend his funeral on this (Sunday) morning at 10 o'clock from J.P. Davie's hardware store.

Died at Galveston, Texas, on Monday morning, August 19th, of congestion of the brain, Calvin G. Lownds, a native of Norfolk, Virginia; aged [?]9 years and 15 days. N.O., Natchez and Baltimore papers please copy. Dr. Lownds engaged in the 1st National Bank of Texas...

Died at Chappell Hill on the 16th day of August 1867, infant daughter of D.C. and Audora Smith, aged 1 year, 3 months, 5 days.

Killed. -- The leader of a squad of U.S. soldiers killed a man named W.R.A. Vivion, an Englishman, on the 11th at the house of Mr. Alderman, in the edge of Collin county. The leader of the band of soldiers shot him in the back, the bullet passing through the body. Before he fell, one of the men struck him with the butt of a gun. He died in about two minutes. The soldiers then went off towards Dallas, of which county Vivion was a resident. The *Dallas Herald* learns that the immediate --- of the order for Vivion's arrest was a charge of having killed a freedman some weeks previous.

On the 10th, at Jefferson, Judge D.B. Bonfoey, collector of U.S. Internal Rev., killed Col. W.H. Fowler, Deputy U.S. Internal Rev. Collector. Judge B. entered the office of Colonel F. placed a pistol to his head and fired, killing him instantly. Col. Fowler was an Alabamian, and removed to this state last winter.

Rumor says that a negro woman was the only witness of the murder, and that after Fowler fell, Bonfoey placed a cocked pistol in his hand and left the room announcing that he had killed Fowler in self defence. We trust that this rumor has done Bonfoey injustice.

Echoes from Houston. Eds. News. -- Since my report of yesterday, the following deaths have occurred in the city: James B. Flemming, yellow fever; Charles Whitcomb---; Mrs Joseph H. Shepherd, congestive fever; Fred VanAlstyne, yellow fever.

Mr. Flemming was a member of the Davis Guards, and participated in the gallant defense of Sabine Pass on the 8th of September, 1863, under the command of the heroic Dick Dowling. He was lately an efficient member of the city police force. There seems to be some difference of opinion as to his disease. If yellow fever, it makes the first death among our citizens from that malady.

Mrs. Shepherd died after an illness of some two weeks duration. She was an amiable and accomplished lady, whose death will be deeply lamented by a large circle of friends.

Charles Whitcomb was an inmate of Dr. Howard's infirmary, but I have been unable to learn his disease.

Fred VanAlstyne was a nephew of the late W.A. Van Alstyne, and has always been esteemed as a citizen.

There are quiet a number of cases of yellow fever in Harrisburg at this time. Tom Vapid.

MORTUARY REPORT: The following is a list of the names of the persons buried yesterday, August 24th, 1867, furnished by the City Sexton:
Edward Jones, 22, yellow fever, Penn.
Eharly Polus, 38, yellow fever, France.
Margaret Safferin, yellow fever, Tenn.
John Craik, 45, yellow fever, Ireland.
Capt. J.A. Nickerson, 25, yellow fever, Mass.
Michael Daly, 40, yellow fever, Ireland.
Thomas Harris, 25, yellow fever, Ireland.
Patrick Downey, 28, yellow fever, Ireland.
Wilhelm Beisswenger, 42, yellow fever, Germany.
J.B. Berthlers, 43, yellow fever, France.
Christie Ivers, 34, disease of heart, Ireland.
John Murphy, 34, yellow fever, Ireland.
Wm. McCulloch, 45, yellow fever, Tenn.
Rosine Diermmermann, 24, yellow fever, Germany.
Fritz Norther, 34, yellow fever, Germany.
_____ Hohetable, 35, yellow fever, England.
Chas. Solomon, 25, yellow fever, Germany.
Annetta Polus, 28, yellow fever, France.
Kunigundi Schmidt, 13, yellow fever, Germany.
Frederick Gelger, 35, yellow fever, Germany.
Joseph Schmidt, 64, yellow fever, Germany.
Patrick Mullin, 36, yellow fever, Ireland.

Mrs. T.V. Hide, 43, yellow fever, Georgia.
H. Winkin, 28, yellow fever, Germany.
Michael Patten, 40, yellow fever, Ireland.
Carter Tinker, 65, chronic dysentery, U.S.

Issue August 27, 1867

Died in this city of yellow fever on August 11th, James Newell, in the 13th year of his age. Also in this city, on August [?], 1867, of yellow fever, Miss Georgia Alexander, in the 26th year of her age. Montgomery, Alabama papers please copy.

Mortuary report. The following is the list of burials Sunday, August 25th, 1867:
Maurice Kiely, 50, Ireland, yellow fever.
Anna Sieport, 21, Germany, yellow fever.
John Gould, 17, England, yellow fever.
A. Isaac, 32, Poland, yellow fever.
Mrs. Porter, 28, Germany, yellow fever.
Gustave Volat, 37, Germany, yellow fever.
Wm. Joentzen, 27, Germany, yellow fever.
J.E.[?] Harmon, 31, New York, yellow fever.
Charles Davis, 26, Virginia, yellow fever.
P.A. Straboch, 36, Germany, yellow fever.
John Cassady, 22, Ireland, yellow fever.
C.A. [?] Roache, 45, Ireland, yellow fever.
Josepha [?] Brakoff, 17, Germany, yellow fever.
Wm. Jacobs, not known, yellow fever.
Jacob/John Watson, 28, not known, yellow fever.
[?] White, 25, Kentucky, yellow fever.
Joseph Davidson, 21, Alabama, yellow fever.
John Welch, 50, Ireland, yellow fever.
James Payne, 21, New York, yellow fever.
William Gore, 36, Ireland, yellow fever.
Jimmy Saffern, 3, Texas, yellow fever.
Thomas Hubbell, 28, Ireland, yellow fever.
Miss M. Marian, 25, France, yellow fever.
Henry McGee, 43, Ireland, yellow fever.
Mary Augustine, 15 days, Texas, yellow fever.
L[?]enz Austerburg, 33, Ireland, yellow fever.
Thomas Cassedy, not known, yellow fever.
Delaware [?] Home, 21, Virginia, yellow fever.
Thomas Hest, 32, Denmark, inflammation of the bowels.
Daniel G. Price, 31, Pennsylvania, congestion.

Monday, August 26, 1867

John Coleman, 75, Va., yellow fever.
D.H. Smith, 35, Mass., yellow fever.
Henry Saffern, 43, Ireland, yellow fever.
[?] Hicheblum, 33, Germany, yellow fever.
Wm. Colson, 28, England, yellow fever.
Chas. Sands, 32, Ireland, yellow fever.
Robt. Smith, 28, do, yellow fever.
Wm. Sweeney, 21, Mass., yellow fever.
Louis G. Leer, 25, Germany, yellow fever.
Jas Payne, 21, N.Y., yellow fever.
Dr. R.H. Barnett, 37, Ky., yellow fever.
J.S. Gillespie, 51, Pa., abscess in neck.
H. H. Westerlage, 27, Germ'y, cong. brain.
[?] Schmidt, 13 mos. Galv'on, not known.
----- John, not known, yellow fever.
Wm. Grassoper, 37, n.k., yellow fever.
Rich'd Maddison, 30, Scotland, yellow fever.
Geo [?] Lyon, 27, not known, yellow fever.
Wm Carter, --, Germany, yellow fever.
Br. Lt. Col. Wm. S. Abert, 35, Washington, D.C., yellow fever.
Fredrika Drawe, 40, Germany, Typ's fever.
Oscar Ortz, 22, Germany, cong'n brain.

Died on Sunday, August 23rd, of yellow fever at the residence of Judge Dean in Galveston, Mr. Jacob P. Watson, aged about thirty years, and a member of Batts, Dean & Watson... Mr. Watson was a native of Prince Edward Co., Virginia and late of Washington county, Texas... Richmond and Petersburg, Virginia papers please copy.

Brevet Colonel Wm. S. Abert was interred yesterday by the military. He was, we believe, awaiting orders at this point when the fever came upon us. His wife preceded him to the grave only a few days. They leave two children in our midst in sad orphanage. Of our citizens buried yesterday, we report several well-known and worthy members of society. Among them were Louis G. Leer and H.H. Westerlage, who were attended to their last resting places by the members of their Fire Companies and Society of Odd Fellows. Also, J.S. Gillespie, who was interred by the Masonic Fraternity.

Died of congestion of the brain on the morning of the 24th inst. a few miles down the Island, Thomas G. Stone, youngest son of D.C. & Mary Stone, aged about five years...

Funeral Notice: [note: paper folded] [??] Neil, are respectfully invited to attend the funeral of his wife, Mrs. Agnes N. Neil, today at 9 o'clock from his residence, corner Broadway & 15th.

Echoes from Houston. List of interments for August 25th 1867: Gustave Hamer, 21, yellow fever; Fanny Rottenstein, 8, yellow fever; H.P. Allen, 45, gastritis; Wilhelmeiene Elbert, 13, disease unknown; Mr. O'Neil, delirium tremens.
List of interments for August 26th:
Chas. Baumberger, 38, yellow fever; R. O'Riley, yellow fever; Peter Rhein, 8, yellow fever; Helen Schuster, 5, congestive fever; Mary Altebrun, 2, congestive fever.

Yellow fever in Corpus Christi: Among the dead are the Mayor, two clergymen, three doctors, two druggists, and five undertakers. Mr. Maltby, of the *Advertiser*, was severely afflicted in the loss of his wife and sister.
The following is a list of deaths that have occurred. It is possible that a few have been overlooked:
July 3rd: Mr. Snyder, came from Indianola, sick.
July 25th: Mr. Drinkard, not fever.
July 26th: Rev. Wm. H. McPhail, Mrs. John Pollan.
July 27th: J.N. Morgan.
July 28th: Mr. Perry; a Pole, name unknown; Mr. Sterne.
July 30th: H.H. Eastwood.
August 1st: Rev. Wm Mitchell, Clymer, Clayton, [note: page folded] child of Mr. Larkin.
August 6th: Marcella Swift, Mrs. McClannahan.
August 7th: Mr. Smith, Patrick Dunn, Daniel Cahill, a Pole name unknown, Jane L. Marsh, Mrs. Christopher Dunn.
August 8th: John W. Scott, widow Clark, James Rankin, Christopher Dunn, F.J. Cromer, Frank Stillman, H. Fisher, Rebecca Hughes, (child), T.M. Lawrence.
August 9th: Jas. Gibbs, Benj. Gibbs, Mrs. Hughes, F. Riddir, Owen Clymer, G. Headen, McFarlane, Miss A. Dann.
August 10th: H. Sinclair, Carrie Sims, two Poles (unknown), Mrs. John Kelly, ____ Kelly (child), Charles Fields, Dr. G.F. Johnson, Mrs. Mary Grace Maltby, George Meuley, Jas. Almond, Mr. Chas. Weidenmueller, John Pollan, Jr., Dr. George Robertson, Agnes Rankin.
August 11th: Mr. Stone (a Mexican), Lizzie Riggs, Louisa Dryer, Mrs. Vetter, Mrs. Geo. A. Ludewig.
August 12th: Dr. E. Merriman, A. DeRyee, Mrs. Schultz, J.M. Sims.
August 13th: Mrs. Matthew Headen, Mrs. Gibbs, Mrs. John Dunn, Mrs. F. Riddir, Jos. Dunn, J.M. Myers, George Adolphe Ludewig, infant of Dr. G.F. Johnston, Michael Whelan, Mrs. Michael Whelan.

August 14th: John Gallahan, Rinaldo Allen.

P.S. Seven more deaths as we go to press at 5 P.M. Total to date 88.

Yellow fever at Lavaca: The *Commercial* of the 16th announces the death of Rev. W.T. Harris, pastor of the Methodist church in that place, on the 14th...

Issue August 28, 1867

Mortuary Report -- The following is a list of burials Tuesday, August 27th, officially reported by the City Sexton:

Loius Meyer, 25, France, yellow fever.

P. Battell, 38, Ireland, yellow fever.

Edward Pousoyer, 24, France, yellow fever.

Unknown man, yellow fever.

Chas. McWilliams, 35, Ireland, yellow fever.

Cora Wilson, 3, Texas, yellow fever.

Mrs. Agnes W. Neill, 34, Ky, yellow fever.

Mary Woit, 51, Germany, yellow fever.

Charley Scott, 25, Virginia, yellow fever.

Arthur Maratsky 21, Germany, yellow fever.

Lucinda McCauley, 34, Virginia, yellow fever.

P...ix [?] Price, 26, not known, yellow fever.

Francis Mobin, 22, Germany, yellow fever.

Mrs. Alice Smith, 35, Norway, yellow fever.

Jennie V. Neitsch, 9, Texas, brain fever.

Laura Ada Garner, 4, Texas, yellow fever.

Karl Hgen, 6, Germany, yellow fever.

Wm. Gastman, 26, Germany, yellow fever.

James Sullivan, 33, Ireland, yellow fever.

Mrs. J.G. Whann, 52, Scotland.

Otto Krausse, 17, Germany, yellow fever.

James Telter, 25, Scotland, yellow fever.

Elvira Brawn, 27, Germany, yellow fever.

Total interments 23.

A terrible accident happened at Mr. Pollard's in this county [Fayette?] on Friday last. His two sons, in company with a hired person, were in an outhouse loading a gun, which was prematurely discharged, the load entering some kegs of powder. The effects of the explosion were instantaneous. All persons were wounded, and one of the young Pollards being struck by a beam on the neck was so severely injured that he has since died.

We learn from the stage driver that Phocian Tate killed a man in Columbus, yesterday.

Yesterday morning about 10 o'clock, Capt. Leddy, in command of the Barge *Dwyer*, was knocked overboard by the tiller and drowned. Some negroes on board and a sailor endeavored to rescue him in a small boat which they launched, but were too late. Capt. Leddy had been a long time captain of the ship *Fannin*, which was in New York and Galveston trade prior to the war...

Judge Alvan Reid died yesterday evening. He has been a citizen a great many years, and was well known in the community.

The Fowler murder: We have already announced the killing of W.H. Fowler, Deputy U.S. Revenue Collector, by his principal, Judge Davis B. Bonfoey, at Jefferson, in this state, on the 10th... He was buried with Masonic honors... He leaves a wife and three daughters. He was an Alabamian and removed to Texas last winter... [note: condensed].

Echoes from Houston... Since my report of yesterday the following interments have taken place:
Aug. 26--A. Wilson, 35, yellow fever; Betty Floyd, colored, 104, old age.
Aug. 27--Jesse, colored, 28, typhoid fever.
Mr. Johnson, reporter of the *Journal*, is one of the new cases. Owing to the indisposition of Mr. Stanley, I am unable to supply the usual thermometric and hygrometric report. Tom Vapid.

Issue August 29, 1867

Died in this city at 10 o'clock A.M. on the 28th inst. of yellow fever, Loren Kent, Collector of Customs, port of Galveston, aged 28 years. Funeral from his late residence on Broadway at 10 o'clock A.M., 29th inst. Illinois papers please copy.
The office of the Internal Revenue was closed yesterday out of respect to Gen. Kent.
The Epidemic -- Gen. Kent, our much esteemed Collector of this port, is reported among yesterday's deaths... Gen. Kent, by his obliging disposition and gentlemanly deportment, was held in the highest estimation by all our citizens.

Among those who have fallen victims to this fatal epidemic, after having lived through similar visitations in former years, we must now number Judge Alvan Reed, formerly sheriff of this county, but more recently one of our magistrates. [note: see Reid].

Died in this city yesterday morning of the prevailing disease, Mr. Geo. M. Straub. Mr. Straub was confidential clerk of Messrs: Arnold, Bros. & Co., of this city, and had charge of their business in their absence. Pennsylvania and New Jersey papers will much oblige by copying the above.

Died on the 9th inst. at the residence of Col. Robert <u>Williams</u> in Matagorda from congestive fever, Miss Nettie Webb, in the 19th year of her age... Corpus Christi papers please copy.

Echoes from Houston... J.B. Beckman, proprietor of the Exchange Hotel at Millican, shot and killed Jack Coleman, at that place, on Sunday evening. The verdict of the coroner's jury was "justifiable homicide."
The following is a list of the deaths in this city up to the hour of closing my letter:
August 28--Infant son of Ed. <u>Williams</u>, 2 yrs, teething; Marcus Devons, 26, yellow fever; Jno. Dulemon, 43, yellow fever.

Mortuary Report. The following is a list of the names of the persons buried yesterday, August 28th, 1867, furnished by the City Sexton:
Thomas Grady, 24, Ireland, yellow fever.
G. Pultiz, 29, Ireland, yellow fever.
Charles <u>Williams</u>, 12, Louisiana, yellow fever.
Elizabeth Reese, 21, England, yellow fever.
William Laughley, 22, U.S., yellow fever.
John Bale, 20, U.S. yellow fever.
William Delaney, 24, Ireland, yellow fever.
William Otther, 23, Germany, yellow fever.
Thomas Green, 25, Ireland, yellow fever.
P.E. Noughton, 36, Ireland, yellow fever.
Peter E. Ward, 29, New York, yellow fever.
Harrison Bates, 24, Alabama, yellow fever.
John Fisher, 28, U.S., yellow fever.
W.H. Clune, 35, New York, yellow fever.
Infant of J. Briggs, 2 days, Gal., yellow fever.
C.C. Corbett, 26, Virginia, yellow fever.
Ellen McDonald, 13, Tennessee, yellow fever.
Harry Pike, 28, Ireland, yellow fever.
Bertha Dawrwmik, 87, U.S., yellow fever.
Henrietta Dawrwmik, 5m., U.S., teething.
Michael Harrison, 30, Illinois, yellow fever.
Mrs. Ellen Crockett, 42, Ky., yellow fever.
Peter Carson, 8, Galveston, yellow fever.
George Straub, 24, Pennsylvania, yellow fever.
[?]Macoob, 23, Germany, yellow fever.
Isaac Waiss, 10, Galveston, yellow fever.
Charles Wells, 27, Germany, yellow fever.
Charles Blum, 24, Germany, yellow fever.
Mary Stephens, 20, Texas, yellow fever.
Alvan Reid, 44, N.Y., congestion brain.

John Brook, 53, Germany, congestion brain.
Marion Sterling, 55, Alabama, debility.
Jessie Ritzler, 4, Gal., congestion brain.
Edward Lawrence, 28, Eng., consumption.

Issue August 30, 1867

Died on Thursday, 29th inst., at 2 o'clock A.M., F.O. Snow, of yellow fever. Boston, New Orleans & San Antonio papers please copy.

Capt. F.O. Snow, a gentleman who has made many warm friends during the short time he has been in business here, died yesterday morning at 2 o'clock.

The *Waco Register* of the 24th says Rev. W. McK Lambdin was lying dangerously ill.

Gen. Loren Kent was buried by his brethren of the Masonic fraternity, yesterday morning.

Mortuary Report. The following is a list of the names of the persons buried yesterday, August 29th, 1867, furnished by the City Sexton.
Antone Riser, 44, Germany, yellow fever.
Henrietta Klatt, 33, Germany, yellow fever.
Millian Atluke, 33, Germany, yellow fever.
Capt. F.O. Snow, 40, U.S., yellow fever.
Infant of Mr. Sangston, Galveston, stillborn.
John Gillis, 45, Canada, yellow fever.
Thos. McKernin, 27, Ireland, yellow fever.
Mrs. W.B. Crawford, 52, Tenn., yellow fever.
John Spelter, 32, New York, yellow fever.
Miss F. Frank, 29, Germany, yellow fever.
Daniel Beichatal, 28, Penn., yellow fever.
Gertrude C. Rhea, 8, La., yellow fever.
George Hogg, 45, Scotland, yellow fever.
Peter Lew, 50, Germany, yellow fever.
Dennis Healy, 49, Ireland, yellow fever.
August Muller, 17, Germany, yellow fever.
W.H. Cratch, 26, Ireland, yellow fever.
Thos. Gartland, 27, yellow fever.
Mrs. Ann Lewis, 65, Wales, yellow fever.
Grace Stevenson, 4?, Texas, yellow fever.
Fred. Berry, unknown, unknown, yellow fever.
Dolly Alexander, 18m, city, yellow fever.
Mrs. N. Muller, 27, Germany, yellow fever.
Wm. Clifford, 4 1/2, Galveston, yellow fever.

G. Picon, 25, Louisiana, yellow fever.
Catherine Wall, 28, Ireland, disease heart.
E.L. Higyueir/Higyneir, 21, N.Y., yellow fever.
A. Bateman, 18, Germany, yellow fever.
Mary Ann Dean, 5 1/2, Galveston, yellow fever.
Gen. Loren Kent, 28, Illinois, yellow fever.
Mary Boudineau, 20, France, typh. fever.
Mr. Hodges, 23, Louisiana, yellow fever.
Mrs. C.J. Hamilton, 33, Mich., yellow fever.
Sampson Neil, 25, yellow fever.
Frank Warren, 36, Maryland, yellow fever.
Infant of Mrs. Buck, 2 hours, city, unk'n.
P. Wilson, 48, Illinois, yellow fever.

Issue August 31, 1867
Judge James Armstrong died in Williamsport, Penn., Friday, aged 74.

The Cholera has made its appearance in Carroll county, Miss., and one of those who died was Col. J.M. Hamilton.

Died in Galveston, August 30th, at the residence of Maj. Bolling, William Bulger, of yellow fever, aged 35. Rochester, New York & Montgomery, Alabama papers please copy.

Died on Friday, August 3rd, Ben. H. Price, of yellow fever, aged 27 years, a native of Harper's Ferry, Virginia. Richmond, Va. & Baltimore, Md. papers please copy.

Died at Peach Point, Brazoria county, on Tuesday morning, August 20th, Rosa Estelle Pebry/Perry of congestion of the brain, aged 5 years, 4 months.

Mortuary Report. The following is a list of the names of the persons buried yesterday, August 30th, 1867, furnished by the City Sexton]:
Anna T. Delesman, 27, Germ'y, yellow fever.
Cornelius Cahill, 27, Louisiana, yellow fever.
Frank Orega, 23, Mexico, yellow fever.
Charley Kremer, 32, Germany, yellow fever.
Kate King, 28, Ireland, yellow fever.
G.W.D. Honey, 12, U.S., yellow fever.
Fintine Oleran, 8, U.S., yellow fever.
A.C. Blash, 23, Canada, yellow fever.
H. VanLanton, 32, Germany, yellow fever.
Ida VanLanton, 28, Germany, yellow fever.
Charley Scham, 23, France, yellow fever.

Morris Kleinson, 26, Poland, yellow fever.
B.H. Price, 27, Virginia, yellow fever.
Agnes Jackson, 27, Scotland, yellow fever.
Mrs. M. Courbat, 47, France, yellow fever.
J.F. Wainwright, 2 1/2, La., inflam. bowels.
Anna Deitzel, 25, Germany, yellow fever.
Frederike Oppa, 29, Germany, yellow fever.
Wm. Bulger, 35, New York, yellow fever.
B. Goldstein, 32, Poland, yellow fever.
Nelly Joseph, 18 mos., Texas, yellow fever.
Charley Miller, 23, Ohio, yellow fever.
Alfred Meredith, 24, R.I., yellow fever.
Alfred Mungen, 35, yellow fever.
William Schaffeir, 26, N.Y., yellow fever.
Miss Grundler, 17, Germany, yellow fever.
H.I. Watrus, 5, Galveston, yellow fever.
S.A. Auterside, 2, do., congestion brain.
James Hall, 32, Massachusetts, yellow fever.
Mary Gerlaff, 46, Germany, yellow fever.
Charles Smith, 19, yellow fever.
Frank Williams, 40, S.C., billious fever.
Wilhelm Piehorst, 17, Grmy, yellow fever.
John Maloney, 41, Ireland, yellow fever.
John Randolph, 30, Switzerland, yellow fever.
Henry Harrison, 32, Germany, yellow fever.
Total 36.

Issue September 1, 1867

Died at the residence of her parents in this city on Wednesday evening the 28th of August at 8 o'clock of yellow fever, Gertrude Clifford Rhea, born in the city of New Orleans on the 17th of November 1858, and daughter of John S. & Mrs. Susan Rhea.

Died on Saturday morning, August 31st, of yellow fever, Mr. James F. Milhouse, formerly of San Antonio, late of the firm of Burns, Gee, & co. of this city. San Antonio papers please copy.

Echoes from Houston -- The following is the Sexton's report for yesterday and this morning:

August 30--Mrs. A. Seigle, 31, Germany, yellow fever; Charles Wilson, 21, Sweden, yellow fever; John McConnell, 9, Texas, yellow fever; Thomas R. Roots, 32, Va. herniceous fever; Hendrick Rayless, 43, Ala. irritative fever; Washington Grant, 9 mos., Texas, croup; Infant of Mrs. Cooper, premature birth, caused by yellow fever in the person of the mother.

August 31--Betsey McKinney, f.w.c., 21, N.C. yellow fever; Mr. Campbell, 35, yellow fever; John K. Knox, 30, Penn., yellow fever; Mary McConnell,13, Texas, yellow fever; Lucy Seal, f.w.c., 23, Texas, febris typhoides.

A man named Theodore Bennett was brought up from Harrisburg yesterday, charged with the killing of one John L. Horton at that place on Wednesday last. The preliminary examination of the accused will take place at 1 o'clock to-day before Judge Fuller. Tom Vapid.

John Hamilton, son of Gov. A.J. Hamilton, of Texas, is reported to have died of yellow fever in New Orleans on the 28th inst.

The epidemic -- during this epidemic there have been thirteen connected with our office, including their families, taken sick. One, Col. Milliken, who was assistant foreman, died early yesterday morning. Two of Rev. Mr. Carnes' children are sick, which accounts for the limited extent of our editorial.

Ex-Mayor Haviland. -- Capt. Haviland's death at Sour Lake has been reported in this city for the last two or three days, but the best information we can get on the painful intelligence is that he was not expected to live when the dispatch left Sour Lake, and there is therefore very little ground to hope that he is now living.

Death on the *Harris*. The carpenter of the steamship *Harris*, John Reily, died on board yesterday morning about 1 o'clock. He ate a hearty supper and was a corpse before morning. His disease was reported yellow fever, but some of the passengers reported it to be cholera. [note: see issue September 3, 1867 for an article that appears to be concerning this same death, but does not give the victim's name.].

Mortuary Report -- The following is a list of the names of the persons buried yesterday, August 31st 1867, furnished by the City Sexton:
John Schonbacker, 23, Ger., yellow fever.
Daniel Clearay, 29, Ireland, yellow fever.
James Broose, 25, U.S., yellow fever.
James McGibbon, 31, yellow fever.
Mrs. Fannie M. Foltz, 32, Tenn., yellow fever.
Col. Chas. A. Milliken, 34, N.Y., yellow fever.
Infant of I. Holstein, 1 day, Galveston, yellow fever.
Wm. Murphy, 24, Ireland, yellow fever.
John Reiley, 33, England, yellow fever.
Rudolph Schultz, 12, Galveston, yellow fever.
James F. Millhouse, 20, Ky., yellow fever.
Alford Patterson, 24, Georgia, yellow fever.
Wm. M. Alexander, 23, Pa., yellow fever.

Frederich Goos, 45, Germany, yellow fever.
Geo. McLane, 25, Ga., yellow fever.
Fred. Klink, 31, Germany, yellow fever.
Luis Hartu/Bartu, 8, Tenn., yellow fever.
M.R. Demerest, Tenn., yellow fever.
J.C. Adams, U.S., yellow fever.
Fred. Wally, 31, Switzerland, yellow fever.
O[???] Veinnig, 45, England, yellow fever.
L[?]uis Frier, 23, Germany, yellow fever.
Stewart Richardson, 21, Ireland, yellow fever.
Adolph ____, 48, Germany, yellow fever.
Joseph ____ , yellow fever.
Eugene Kemmerlin, 18, France, yellow fever.
Charley Curtis, 25, N.Y., yellow fever.

Issue September 3, 1867

Died in Galveston, September 1st at 9 o'clock of yellow fever, William Magruder, aged 4 years, 9 months, only son of Mrs. [?] Pilkington. *New Orleans Times* please copy.

In memoriam for Mr. T. Mather.

The following are interments for Sunday, Sept. 1st, as reported by the City Sexton:
Thomas Moran, 23, Ireland, yellow fever.
John Orange, 34, Prussia, yellow fever.
Wm. G. Parish, 25, Indiand [sic], yellow fever.
John Gibbon, 35, Ireland, yellow fever.
Fred. Jordan, 23, England, yellow fever.
John Broadley, 48, Eng., cong. brain.
C.W. Bernhard, 50, Germany, cong. brn.
Negro man, Africa, unknown.
Jacob Kenkele, 28, Germany, yellow fever.
Mrs. Lawrence, 22, England, yellow fever.
Adolph Sherer, 21, Bederie, yellow fever.
M. Douglas, colored, unknown.
Sophia Artz, 27, Germany, yellow fever.
Rosa Perry, colored, yellow fever.
--- Kennedy, unknown, yellow fever.
Joseph Thompson, 28, Nova Scotia, yellow fever.
John Campbell, 26, Mississippi, yellow fever.
Mrs. Epperson, colored, yellow fever.
George Hale, 27, New Jersey, yellow fever.
R. Wilson, 24, England, typhoid fever.

Eliza Davis, colored, unknown.
Mary Ann White, colored, Tex., yellow fever.
Mrs. Jalonick, 30, Bohemia, yellow fever.
Wm. Pfleger, 37, Germany, yellow fever.
Thomas Sargeant, 28, Ky., yellow fever.
Miss Julia R. Bradford, 16, La., yellow fever.
Amelia Deltz, 16, Germany, yellow fever.
Miss M. Montgomery, 12, Texas, yellow fever.
Frederick Gatta, 19, Germany, yellow fever.
Five U.S. soldiers.
    Of the above twenty seven of yellow fever, and three other diseases.
Total deaths, exclusive of soldiers, thirty.
    Monday Sept. 2d.
Ladwig Klatt, 33, Germany, yellow fever.
Mr. Bertrand, 39, Germany, yellow fever.
Mrs. Mollie E. Ruse, 22, not kn'n, yellow fever.
Susan Caruvay, 105, N.C., yellow fever.
Anna Seidelman, 24, Germany, yellow fever.
Mr. Wood, 24, U.S., yellow fever.
Meta Schmidt, 18 mos. Texas, yellow fever.
I. Johnson, not known, U.S., yellow fever.
Geo. Harley, 4 1/4, Houston, conges. brain.
John Ford, 15 mos., city, water on brain.
G.W. Rey, 28, U.S., yellow fever.
Mr. Hefferman, 28, not kn'n, yellow fever.
Wm. M. Pilkington, 4 3/4, Houston, yellow fever.
Peter Smith, 24, Germany, yellow fever.
Bernard Rogers, 25, Ireland, yellow fever.
John Falkehagen, 1 1/2, city, yellow fever.
John Rettsher,__, not kn'n, yellow fever.
Katy A. Leonard, 9, Ireland, yellow fever.
Thomas S. Jones, 45, N.Y. dumb ague.
Mr. Ditterman, Germany, 38, yellow fever.
T. Mather, 52, New York, yellow fever.
Artemiser Jane Honey, 23, Ala, yellow fever.
Davy Wren, 4, Texas, yellow fever.
D.S.J. Harm, 1 1/2 La., yellow fever.
Henry Sheettze, 23, Germany, yellow fever.
Two U.S. soldiers.
    Of the above, 5 females, 20 males. The Howard Association buried five.
There were 4 from the Charity Hospital, and 4 from the city Hospital, and 2
colored.
    There were 21 deaths from yellow fever and 4 from other diseases.

We deeply sympathize with Col. Diamond, one of the editors of the *Houston Journal*, in the loss of another child, a small boy, ten years and one month old. It is indeed, a severe affliction to be bereft of two lovely children in so short a time.

We now learn definitely from Capt. Fowler that Capt. Haviland was dying at Sour Lake when he left there on last Wednesday morning and he doubtless died during that day. He was afflicted with dropsy of the chest and there was not the least hope of his recovery. Capt. Fowler ordered a metallic case to be sent from Houston, but in consequence of the heavy and continuous rains, dispatches inform us that the train was delayed at Liberty till Sunday morning, caused by the washing away of the culverts on the road beyond Liberty. Hence the case could not have reached Sour Lake till Sunday night, and the presumption is that the remains of Capt Haviland had to be buried before the case arrived. Mrs. H. and two of her children were with Capt H. at his death.

Capt. Haviland was one of the oldest and most respected citizens of Galveston...

The epidemic -- Among the many deaths which our surviving citizens have lately been called upon to mourn, none has been more universally lamented than that of our highly esteemed fellow citizen, T. Mather, one of the comparatively few of our old citizens who have fallen victims to this terrible scourge. We believe he never remained in our city during any previous epidemic, and his many friends have greatly to regret that Mr. Mather was prevented from leaving during the present epidemic.

That cholera case -- The man who died on board the S.S. *Harris* on her last trip from New Orleans, and who was reported by some of the passengers to have had cholera, we are informed by the officers of the boat, had genuine black vomit, his case undoubtly yellow fever. [note: see issue September 1, 1867 for an article that appears to be concerning this same death, but gives the victim's name as John Reily.].

Issue September 4, 1867

Gen. Griffin did not leave yesterday for New Orleans, as reported, in consequence of his son suddenly taken sick. It is reported that he has asked for the removal of headquarters from New Orleans to this city.

Obituary: At a meeting of the board of trustees of Chappell Hill Female College, August 26th, the following resolutions were unanimously adopted: Whereas it has pleased God, in his wise Providence, to remove from this life on the 12th inst. our late beloved and highly esteemed President, the Rev. John Carmer...

Died in this city of congestion of the brain, Geo. W., son of Charles W. and Susan Hurley, aged 4 years and 3 months, a native of Houston.

Victim of the epidemic at Corpus Christi, Rev. J.P. Perham, President of the Howard Association.

Echoes from Houston—The following list is furnished by Mr. Pannel, the City Sexton:

Sept. 1st, Frank Vaugh, 22, Indiana, yellow fever; Oliver Wendhance, 10, yellow fever; Locana Luca, 30, Mexico, yellow fever.

Sept. 2d, M.E. Weiss, 46, yellow fever; Thomas Wilcox, 28, yellow fever; Louisa Cloe, colored, febris maligna; man unknown, colored, yellow fever; child unknown, 7, typhus febris.

The epidemic — We regret to hear of the death of M.F. Thompson. He had been considered almost out of danger at one time -- but yesterday evening about 3 o'clock he breathed his last. He was one of our most enterprising and valuable citizens.

We regret exceedingly to hear of the death of our young friend John S. Spann. He was a sterling young man and gave promise of a life of much usefulness.

The *LaGrange Democrat* says Dr. J.[?] P. Brown was severely and, it is feared, mortally stabbed, in that place on the previous Monday by L. Lindsay, an attorney.

Mortuary Report--The following is a list of names of the persons buried yesterday, Sept. 3d, 1867, furnished by the City Sexton:
Wm. R. Garrett, 42, U.S., yellow fever.
P.H. Bloxon, 21, U.S.Q.M.D., yellow fever.
Henry Schultz, 23, Germany, yellow fever.
Col. Brendt, 25, Virginia, yellow fever.
L. Baker, 28, Germany, yellow fever.
W. Boyd, unknown, N.Y., yellow fever.
Capt. A.B. Rich, 28, Mass., yellow fever.
Chinton Villets, 18, Penn., yellow fever.
Henry E. King, 23, Germany, yellow fever.
L.M. Fowler, 3 months, city, congestion.
Wm. Migel, 27, Galveston.
Antone Bergham, 47, Germany, typhoid.
J.M. Reidner, 47, Germany, yellow fever.
John Stranlak, 26, Moravia, yellow fever.
Kitty Elizabeth Golledge, 10 mos., Galveston, teething.

Carolina Delabarre, 10, Galveston, y. fever.
Will Carter, 19, Texas, yellow fever.
J. Duke, 31, Germany, yellow fever.
Man unknown from the Island below.
     do.   found in the cemetery.
Louisa Collins, 18, Galveston, yellow fever.
Louisa Wilson, 15, Georgia, congestion.
John Miller, 28, Germany, yellow fever.
Conrad Struve, 27, Switzerland, yellow fever.
Antone Honeycut, 25, Germany, yellow fever.
Louis Decody, 34, Belgium, yellow fever.
John S. Spann, 22, S.C., yellow fever.
James Drammed, 21, New York, yellow fever.
Charles Edgard, 22, Galveston, spasms.
F. Lewis, 24, unknown, yellow fever.
Edward Hunt, 34, England, yellow fever.
P. Mattison, 22, Sweden, yellow fever.
Elizabeth H. Sterrett, 27, Phil., yellow fever.
Joseph M. Leroy, 39, France, yellow fever.
C. Nosholson, unk., unk., yellow fever.

Issue September 5, 1867

Died in this city on the morning of the 4th inst. of yellow fever, Miss Emma Victory. Boston papers please copy.

Died in this city on the morning of the 3rd inst. of yellow fever, Elizabeth H. Sterret, of Philadelphia, wife of Col. W. B. Sterrett. Philadelphia papers please copy.

Died in this city of the prevailing epidemic, Dr. R/H. H. Hanna, aged 24 years... His funeral on this Thursday morning at 10 o'clock from the Catholic Church.

A letter from Lavaca dated yesterday says: "The fever continues about the same. George Finlay's family are much afflicted. His brother is dying of consumption -- his sister will probably die today, and his two children are both very ill -- the last three have fever." *Ind. Bulletin.*

The *Savannah News & Herald* regrets to hear of the death last Friday at his sea island residence of Pierce Butler, well known in Georgia and Florida. His disease was congestive chills and his death was very sudden and unexpected. He was about fifty years, leaves but one child, a daughter...

We find the following in the *Lavaca Commerical*: The town is nearly deserted. Since our last report we have heard of the death of Mrs. William Mennefee, Charles W. Hoyle, and Robert, eldest son of the late Dr. Woolfolk.

Died in this city on the 2nd inst., Mr. Thadeus Mather. The deceased was born in Huntington, Long Island, on the 23rd day of July, 1815, and was, consequently, 52 years old when he died. He moved to Galveston with his family some years before the war, and engaged in mercantile business...

Deaths by yellow fever in Houston: Interments for September 3rd: Maj. Thomas Johns, Mrs. Martha Neal, Mrs. Esther Kehl, 42, W.A. Newton, 44, Geo. Pelham, F.M.C., 28.

Coroner Hanney held an inquest yesterday upon the body of Mr. J.M. Slapp, a printer in the *Bulletin* office, found dead and partially mutilated in the bay flats near the city hospital. Mr. Slapp had been sick with the yellow fever in the hospital, and twice escaped from it.

Two of the children of M.F. Thompson, whose death is so generally deplored, are down with the fever.

We have heard of the death of Dr. Hanna. He was an ornament to his profession, and a most estimable gentleman. Cut off in the prime of manhood, and in the midst of usefulness, his death is a sad and painful event.

At a late hour last night, we received the sad intelligence of the death of Dr. Rowe, Assistant Surgeon U.S.A. and Surgeon in charge of the Military Hospital. His funeral will take place this morning at 10 o'clock.

Mortuary Report--The following is a list of the names of the persons buried yesterday, Sept. 4, 1867, by the City Sexton:
Emma Victoria, 23, Mass., yellow fever.
Oscar Freshchimer, 23, Prussia, yellow fever.
Alfred Spanberg, 40, Sweden, yellow fever.
Dr. G. Ulrich, 61, Germany, yellow fever.
Frederick Pfleger, 67, do., yellow fever.
Matilda Wessendor, 6 1/2[?] city, yellow fever.
George Campbell, 3, Texas, yellow fever.
Daniel E. Adams, 28, Maryland, yellow fever.
M.F. Thompson, 36, Georgia, yellow fever.
J.M. Slapp, 43, Maryland, yellow fever.
Timothy Duryer, 25, Ireland, yellow fever.
James Moore, 19 [?], Missouri, yellow fever.

Rebecca J. Babrman/Bahrman, 10, city, yellow fever.
Ernest Kupenix, Germany, yellow fever.
Rosa King, unknown, U.S., yellow fever.
Matilda Prendler, 2, Germany, yellow fever.

In addition to the above. Mr. R. Augustus Tompkins, whose body arrived from Harrisburg on the steamer *Era*, yesterday, was also buried by the City Sexton. He was a brother to Capt. Tompkins of the firm of Tompkins & McMurphy.

Issue September 6, 1867

Died of yellow fever on Sunday at 10 1/2 A.M., Thos. Sargent, of Kentucky, 27 years old. The deceased, though a native of Kentucky, has been, since the war, a resident of this state. Though no loving father and mother, gentle sister or brother were with him in his last hour, the spirit of a sister Mary hovered over him, enticing him to the happy world in which she lives. Louisville, Kentucky papers please copy.

We learn that Dr. Towsey is now down with the fever. Dr. Gantt has been sick for several days and is very low. His family are all down, and we regret to learn two of his children are in a very critical condition. We are happy to learn that the Dr. is improving.

We regret exceedingly to have to announce the death of Capt. Dan. Richardson, at Harrisburg, who is reported to have died there, day before yesterday, of the prevailing sickness.

We refer our readers to the "Special Notice" regarding the business of T. Mather & Co. Mr. Mather, in his will, provided for the continuance of the business, which will be conducted by the surviving partner, W. Warren, for the purposes and in the manner set forth in the notice mentioned.

A convict by the name of Wheeler was shot dead on the 12th, while attempting to escape from the Penitentiary.

We have to announce among the deaths yesterday, the only child of Gen. Griffin, a boy some 5 or 6 years old, whose sickness we mentioned as preventing his father from going to New Orleans on the last trip of the *Harris*.

Mr. Codling, who has kept a wall paper store on Market street near the old theater, also died yesterday afternoon. He was a worthy member of the fraternity of Odd Fellows. He will be buried this morning at 8 o'clock. His brother-in-law, Mr. Leer, died in the same house a week or ten days since.

Mortuary Report--The following is a list of the names of the persons buried yesterday, Sept 5, 1867, furnished by the City Sexton.

Harry King, 45, Germany, yellow fever.
John Crawford, 48, Ireland, yellow fever.
Fred. Guffus, 34, Germany, yellow fever.
Loiusa Mickegan, 19, Ga., yellow fever.
Mary Celesto Stevens, 6 1/2, N.Y., yellow fever.
Dr. Chas. H. Rowe, 26, Conn., yellow fever.
Dr. R.H. Hanna, 24, Miss., yellow fever.
Michael Cullen, 23, Ireland, yellow fever.
Emily Hanks, 3, U.S., yellow fever.
John McDonnell, 20, Ireland, yellow fever.
--- Mays, 24, Germany, yellow fever.
Wm. Guigus, 38, Germany, dysentery.
Lawiya Roberts, 19, Eng., yellow fever.
John Geban, 13, Maryland, yellow fever.
Samuel Jackson, yellow fever.
Mrs. Patten, 38, Ireland, yellow fever.
Thomas Patten, 12, Ireland, yellow fever.
Kate Daley, 29, Maryland, yellow fever.
George Bell, 25, U.S., yellow fever.
Henry Green, 30, Ireland, yellow fever.
Mary Phelan, 25, Ireland, yellow fever.

Echoes from Houston -- The following, I believe, includes all the interments of yesterday:

Sept. 4 Julius Hohl, 57, typhus abdominalis; Geo. Schmidt, 5, febris billiosa; Mich'l Barrett, yel. fev., no certificate; Mrs. M.J. Neil, 29, yellow fever; John, f.m.c., 40, yellow fever; Fritz Koz, 28, yellow fever; Jno. Umberfield-- no certificate; John Callahan, 35, Jaundice; Child of Mr. Stewart, 4, convulsions; Tustus Hall, 51, typhus fever; Mr. Schnaver-- yellow fever. Tom Vapid.

Issue September 7, 1867

List of Houston interments: F. Ael, 29, febris typhoides; F. King, 32, apoplexy; L.A. Klein, 9, billious remittent fever; Henry Clayton, 23, yellow fever; J.C. Dawson, 22, yellow fever; Kate G. Celif, 5, yellow fever; M. Riordan, 50, yellow fever.

We learn that Dr. Gantt is very low and will hardly survive another day.

Died at her home in Galveston on the 28th of August, Mrs. N.B. Crawford, in the 52nd year of her age, of yellow fever; born in Knox county, Tennessee in the year 1815; the wife of Dr. J.W. Crawford, who died in Washington county, Texas, in the year 1856; the daughter of Maj. Jesse Bartlett and Francis Calloway, who emigrated to Texas in an early day. Maj. Jesse Bartlett was one among the first Texians to resist Mexican oppression and served as an officer in the army under Sam Houston... Mrs. Crawford was one of the oldest Texians in the state and resided the largest portion of her life in Washington, Texas. Some years previous to the war, she removed to Hempstead, where she remained until the close of the war, and removed to Galveston, where up to her death, she kept the hotel known as the Crawford House. She leaves a daughter and many relatives...

Died in this city, September 6th at 8 o'clock A.M., aged 2 years, 10 months and 6 days, Janet Willie, only daughter of James and Mary J. Owen.

Col. Ira R. Lewis departed this life on the 24th ult., in his 67th year, at the residence of his son-in-law, Maj. Austin Bryan, Independence, Washington county. He was a native of Ohio; born on the 25th of September, 1800. Studied law in the offices of the celebrated Mr. Longworth of Cincinnati. He married in that city, emigrated to Mississippi and Louisiana, and thence to Texas. He landed at Matagorda Bay, shipwrecked (losing everything) with his wife and two youngest daughters in March 1831... One of the founders of Matagorda... He leaves a wife and three daughters to mourn him: Mrs. Axson of New Orleans; Mrs. Hancock of Austin City; and Mrs. Bryan of Independence. His youngest died during the war... [note: condensed].

The epidemic — Yesterday very many new cases were reported, which, with the bad weather, may, we fear, increase the mortality.
    J.C. Wilson, marine clerk in the Customhouse, died yesterday. He was a young man of fine promise and a great favorite with his comrades. He was a native of Maryland, and came out from Baltimore to this city.

Mortuary Report—The following is a list of the names of the persons buried yesterday, Sept. 6, 1867, furnished by the City Sexton:
Edward Lacon, --, --, yellow fever.
Mr. Maitag, --, Germany, yellow fever.
Mrs. Bridget Smith, 35, England, yellow fever.
August Coon, 27, Germany, yellow fever.
A. Howel, 36, France, yellow fever.
James Codling, 28, St. Louis, yellow fever.
Miss A. Burton, 18, Tennessee, cong. brain.
Andrew Voigt, 28, Germany, yellow fever.
Negro boy, Texas, yellow fever.

James E. Wilson, 21, Maryland, yellow fever.
Henry O'Keefe, 23, Ireland, yellow fever.
Sally Green, 28, Mississippi, yellow fever.
Negro boy, Texas, yellow fever.
H.B. Thomasson, 26, Penn., yellow fever.
Regina Cook, 23, St. Louis, yellow fever.
Wm. Jackson, 25, England, yellow fever.
Emma Thompson, 12, New York, yellow fever.
Negro woman, Virginia, yellow fever.
Amina Doe, 24, Maine, yellow fever.
A.L. Ford, 27, New York, yellow fever.
George Pelium, 25, Scotland, yellow fever.
Thomas Murry, 34, Ireland, yellow fever.
C.C. Griffin, 5, Wash'gton, D.C., yellow fever.
Adam Acom, 9, Missouri, yellow fever.
Miss Lundh, 40, Sweden, yellow fever.
Jennette Owens, 3, Galveston, yellow fever.
Two U.S. soldiers.
One man in quartermaster's employ.

Issue September 8, 1867

Houston Interments: Emil Zacho, 27, Denmark, yellow fever, treated at the city hospital. Mrs. Mitchell, 40, yellow fever, treated by Dr. B. Powell. Mrs. Hedgebeth, 38, yellow fever, treated by Dr. Robinson. M. Olson, 46, Norway, hemorrhage of lungs, treated by Dr. J. Cowling.

Horrible Tragedy at Marshall -- The *Jefferson (Texas) Jimplecute* of the 27th says that it is deeply pained to learn that an attempt was made to murder Mrs. Bonfoey in bed at Marshall that morning. The injuries she received were believed to be fatal... A man was arrested on the same day. Mrs. B. was the wife of the man who has recently been committed for the murder of Col. Fowler at Jefferson.

T.W. Folts, of Ayers & Childress, is among the many convalescents. We hear Col. Lawther has relapsed. Drs. Towsey and Welch were both in bed yesterday with fever, their services can not well be spared at this juncture. We hope they may speedily recover. The death of Dr. Gantt yesterday morning is a sad loss to his family and the community. He had been a professor in the Galveston Medical College since its establishment.

Mortuary Report--The following is a list of the names of the persons buried yesterday, Sept. 7, 1867, furnished by the City Sexton:
Mary Gambalu, 22, Germany, yellow fever. [note: see note at end of report].
Sarah Shline, 33, England, yellow fever. [note: see note at end of report].

Chas. Smith, 21, New York, yellow fever. [note: see note at end of report].
A. Thalinger, 31, Germany, yellow fever. [note: see note at end of report].
Thos. Vaughan, 17, Georgia, yellow fever.
R.W. Tompkins, 4, Texas, spasms.
Dr. W.H. Gantt, 43, Mo., yellow fever.
Howard Burton, 21, Tenn., yellow fever.
Capt. M.E. Price, 39, Virginia, yellow fever.
Mrry [sic] H. Blakeman, 51, Conn., yellow fever.
Jas. McGregor, 53, Maine, yellow fever.
Fred Boss, 21, Germany, yellow fever.
John Lakeman, 25, New York, yellow fever.
Edward Flanagan, 32, Ireland, yellow fever.
Francis Gaines, 25, Western Iles, yellow fever.

The 4 first named were buried the night before, after the sexton's report was made out, and appear in the report as interred on the 6th. [note: this note applies to the four names beginning at the top of the report on the previous page.].

Issue September 10, 1867

The *Tyler Reporter* records a fight there recently between Mr. I.H. Murry, of Smith county, and Corporal Crawley, Co F, 20th Reg. U.S.A., in which the latter, it is feared, was mortally wounded, being cut with a pocket knife in several places about the neck and face...

To the Officers and Members of the Galveston Typographical Union No. 28. Tribute of respect for John R. Pointer, Charles A. Milliken, Wm. G. Casseady, Charles Zadow, J.M. Reidner, and J.M. Slapp... [note: condensed].

Galveston Mortuary Report: The following are the interments for Sunday, September 8th, as reported by the City Sexton:
Frederike Miller, 28, German, yellow fever.
Ellen Ryan, 42, Ireland, yellow fever.
Mathew Healey, 45, Ireland, yellow fever.
Patrick Warly, 30, Ireland, yellow fever.
Robert Loriwen, 26, Ireland, yellow fever.
L.[?] McDowell, 45, U.S., yellow fever.
H.H. Sture, 26, Ohio, yellow fever.
Stedman Clarke, 39, U.S., yellow fever.
Edwin Carroll, 21, Mass., yellow fever.
Jas. Moran, 28, Ireland, yellow fever.
R. Slick, 28, Germany, yellow fever.
Fred Michal, 25, Germany, yellow fever.
Joseph Griflin, 30, N.C., yellow fever.
Bethany Hide, 22, Georgia, yellow fever.

A.D. Wood, 22, Penn., yellow fever.
Wm. Philips, 30, Ky., yellow fever.
Wm. Davis, colored, not known, country.
Kate Baldwin, 3, Texas, yellow fever.
Anna Roderfelt, 2, Germany, yellow fever.
Joseph M. Baker, 30, Scotland, yellow fever.
Robert Shilling, 17, Texas, yellow fever.
Blonde Curry, 20 ms, U.S., yellow fever.
Thos Harold, 26, England, yellow fever.
Jas. Butler, 21, N.J., yellow fever.
Wm. Wolff, 27, Germany, yellow fever.
Jas. Andrews, 25, N.O., yellow fever.
Seven U.S. soldiers buried.
    Mortuary Report for Monday, September 9th:
Joseph Barton, 26, U.S., yellow fever.
Mr. Eruries, 40, Portugal, yellow fever.
Kate Micklejohn, 16, Georgia, yellow fever.
Mr. Micklejohn, 43, Georgia, yellow fever.
August Laugerhouse, 34, Grmny, yellow fever.
Mariah Simmons, 17, N.O., yellow fever.
Anne Pasco, 30, St. Helena, yellow fever.
Rebecca Homes, 24, Ohio, yellow fever.
William Cunnier, 21, Ireland, yellow fever.
C.A. Macmurphy, 35, Georgia, yellow fever.
P.A. Strohback, 53, Germany, yellow fever.
Mrs. Anna Ready, 19, N.Y., yellow fever.
August Rumpa, 29, Germany, yellow fever.
Belsey Auseley, 21, Kentucky, yellow fever.
Charley Sanders, 8, Texas, yellow fever.
Mary Westerlage, 11 mos., Ohio, yellow fever.
Mary A. Wicktorick, 27, Moravia, yellow fever.
William Elwood, 26, Ireland, yellow fever.
Archibald Green, 37, Canada, yellow fever.
Edward Maloney, 31, New York, yellow fever.
..... Gantt, 11, Texas, yellow fever.
Henry Jones, 26, England, yellow fever.
John Fehrinz, 26, Germany, yellow fever.
John W. Savage, 32, Virginia, yellow fever.
Henry Irordop, 28, Sardinia, yellow fever.
John Crane, 25, Ireland, yellow fever.
Theodore Schultz, 24, Germany, yellow fever.
W.F. Ready, 32, Ireland, yellow fever.
W. Bretschneicher, 25, Gmy, yellow fever.
Three U.S. soldiers.

The Epidemic: The number of new cases Sunday and yesterday is very great, but the streets are lively with convalescents who are coming out by scores. The heavy mortality indicated by the Mortuary Report of Sunday was unexpected. It was increased by the unusual number of soldiers, constituting over a fifth of the interments... Dr. Welch has been very low, but it is pleasing to his friends to know that he is considerably better. Dr. Towsey is improving.

Dr. Alexander, who was attacked Sunday morning, had a bad night, but was better yesterday.

Dr. Adams, assistant surgeon U.S.A., died of yellow fever in the afternoon yesterday. This makes three army physicians that have died during the present sickness, namely, Dr. Taylor, Dr. Rowe, and Dr. Adams...

A son of Dr. Gantt, aged 11 years, was buried yesterday, the father having been buried only two days before.

Mr. C.A. Macmurphy, a brother of G.L. Macmurphy, of the firm of Tompkins & Macmurphy, died and was buried yesterday. He was a most estimable gentleman, whose loss will be mourned by every one who knew him. No one possessed a nobler heart, a more irreproachable name than he.

Mr. Shropshire of the firm of Shropshire & Co. took the prevailing fever on Saturday, but is reported to be doing well.

Capt. Swisher of the firm of Hewitt, Swisher & Co. also took the fever on Saturday, but we are glad to hear that indications are favorable.

Col. Lawther is recovering slowly from a relapse.

Issue September 11, 1867

San Saba, August 18, 1867: Our "red neighbors of the forest" visited us a few days since, getting a few horses off Ruff & Simpson's creeks, also some from the vicinity of town. A few days before they killed Ben Smith (son of Taylor Smith) and scalped him. This was done near Camp San Saba... Smith's body was found in the water. *Georgetown Watchman.*

Died on the night of the 9th inst., Mr. J.L. Hadley, of Ohio. Mr. Hadley was a partner of Mr. Hiram Close in the foundry business and had been living in this city about two years. He died of the prevailing epidemic.

[Died] On June 27th, 1867, in Toodlesaike, Tennessee, Col. Jas. Campbell, of Brazoria county. His death was occasioned by a railroad accident, his death occurring in a few hours after. He was 57 years old. He was a native of North Carolina, and moved from Louisiana to Texas in 1835. He was a planter of Brazoria and universally respected.

We sympathize with our friend, Col. C.C. Gillespie, of Houston, on the loss of his father, J.P. Gillespie, whose funeral, we see, took place there at 10 o'clock A.M. on the 9th.

Mortuary Report for Tuesday, September 10th:
Dennis Donovan, 24, Ireland, yellow fever.
Peter Morgan, 37, Ireland, yellow fever.
Denis Twohey, 35, Ireland, yellow fever.
A.G. Gonzaros, 40, West Islands, yellow fever.
Mrs. Nelion, 19, Ireland, yellow fever.
P. Schaefer, 35, Germany, yellow fever.
Mrs. M. Gosch, 29, Germany, prematurely confined.
Henry Jones, 40, Canada, yellow fever.
Brvt. Maj. S. Adams, 28, Maine, yellow fever.
Henry McKintosh, 15, England, yellow fever.
J.E. Peters, 8 mons., New Orleans, teething.
Mary F. Stow, 23, Illinois, yellow fever.
Wm. R. Storm, 25, Norway, yellow fever.
Jas. W. Watkins, 5, Louisiana, yellow fever.
Thos. Hennessy, 26, Ireland, yellow fever.
C.W. Crewel, 45, Maine, yellow fever.
Mrs. R.F. Cordua, 30, Ireland, yellow fever.
Henry Brown, 30, Germany, yellow fever.
Mary Ricke, 22, Alabama, yellow fever.
Wm. Langerhausen, 10 mos., Texas, consumption.
Two U.S. soldiers, and one yard man.

Houston Correspondence We regret to learn from the following letter that our correspondent [Tom Vapid] is down with the prevailing fever, but we are much gratified to be informed that he is doing well and has all necessary attention.

Houston, Texas. Tom Vapid is down with the yellow fever, is doing very well, and is in good hands. L'Inconnier.

Necrologue on Mrs. Annie Pascoe/Rascoe, born at St. Helena, 1837, died at Galveston Sept. 1867. [note: poem follows].

The epidemic -- At the Custom House we were pleased to see yesterday, J.M. Kishpaugh, Deputy Collector, up and in the discharge of his duties, having fully recovered; also the chief clerk, Mr. McGuire. Mr. Crooks, Weigher and Gauger and Mr. Stone, clerk, are convalescent. There have been four deaths viz: Gen. Loren Kent, D. Smith, Mr. Wilson, and Strawback.

In a previous mortuary report, Miss Mary McIntosh, 15 years of age, native of England, was incorrectly reported.

Issue September 12, 1867

Died of yellow fever in the city of Corpus Christi, Texas, August 6, 1867, after a severe illness of four days, Mrs. Mary Doretha, consort of G.W. McClanahan. The deceased was born in Charlotte, North Carolina, October 16, 1833, was a daughter of Dr. Harris of that place and received much of her literary education as well as moral and religious training from the late Rev. Dr. Johnston of Charlotte... Removed to Texas in the fall of 1853 and at Victoria, shortly after her arrival, from yellow fever, lost her first husband, C.C. Shive; to whom she had been married but a few months. After this she was, for several years, successfully employed in teaching the higher branches in the Victoria Female Academy. On the 17th of October 1858, she was married to G.W. McClanahan, with whom she lived happily as a wife and a mother up to her death. In 1860 she attached herself to the M.E. Church South. Five motherless children.

We notice among the deaths in Houston the name of Mrs. Reese, the wife of the Methodist minister of that city. She died on Saturday last. We regret to learn that Mr. Reese is also sick and considered in a critical situation.

Mr. M.F. Thompson, well known as the genial host of the Washington Hotel, was among the victims of yellow fever in Galveston this week. He was a prince among landlords and the absence of his cheerful, good-natured countenance from the hospitable board of the Washington will be sadly felt by his numerous friends and patrons throughout the State.

LETTER FROM HOUSTON, dated September 10, 1867: "Tom Vapid" your former correspondent has delegated "Yours truly, Bolivar <u>Ward</u>" to run a quill for him while he (said Thomas) is lying between blankets in company with "Yellow Jack" thinking of the joys when you and I were boys and while he exclaims, "Oh why was I tempted to roam." Tom will not suffer for want of attention.

The following is the official list of interments, Tuesday, September 10th: J.P. Gillespie, 65, yellow fever; C. Buckley, yellow fever; Knolte, 28, yellow fever; H. Fisher, 28, yellow fever; A. Loritz, 5, yellow fever; J.H. Murbot, Jr., 5, yellow fever; Bettie Clark, 37, yellow fever; John Aitken, 34, yellow fever; T.C. Dixon, 66, dysentery; James Morris, colored, con. of bowels; Chas. Wann, 53, general debility; Peter Smith, colored, 1 1/2 teething.

We are pleased to see on the streets again, Dr. E.F. Stewart, A.W. Wood, C.G. Hutton and Capt. McCheerg. Among those down we may mention Rev. Mr. Rees, Rev. Mrs. Cross, Major R.W. Dowling, Capt. Wallace, Maj. S.C. Timpson, Dr. J.R. Hand, Dr. Connell, R. Stuart (Stuart & Mair), Mr. Harper, our postmaster and his assistant, Mr. Barrels. Bolivar <u>Ward</u>.

Mortuary Report for Galveston, a list of the names of persons buried September 11th:
William Douglas, 26, Alabama, yellow fever.
M.A. Kembel, 56, New York, yellow fever.
William Petre, 26, Germany, yellow fever.
Joseph Lindsey, 25, U.S., yellow fever.
John Lyons, 24, Ireland, yellow fever.
Frederick Summers, 65, Germany, old age.
Thos. Burton, 50, Ireland, yellow fever.
Hattie S. Porter, 33, Conn., yellow fever.
Chas. Templeton, 36, U.S., yellow fever.
Felix Saunders, 5, Texas, yellow fever.
Henry Evans, 37, South Carolina, yellow fever.
Jackson Crowder, 39, Alabama, yellow fever.
J.B. Roberts, 28, Kentucky, yellow fever.
Catherine Allen, 30, Ireland, yellow fever.
William Short, 36, England, yellow fever.
Adolph Nordhousen, 25, Germany, yellow fever.
Eliza Jane Young, 36, Maryland, yellow fever.
Three U.S. soldiers, 2 white, 1 black. Total 20; males 17, females 3, yellow fever 19, other diseases 1; 5 negroes.

Death of Capt. Haviland: The exact time of Capt. Haviland's decease we have, heretofore, been unable to state, in consequence of the want of communication with Sour Lake. We now, however, learn that he did not die on the day Capt. Fowler left there (the 27th) as was supposed but on the next day, the 28th of August at 2 P.M. Mortification had taken place even before his death. He was buried at Sour Lake on the 29th.

I, Wm. Andrews, do hereby certify that I, in company with Thomas Duke, did, on or about 25th May, examine a certain lot of blankets, offered for sale at Messrs. Murdock & Milby's auction room, Indianola. Said blankets were left by persons who came from Vera Cruz on or about the 20th of May on schooner *Margarita*. Three days subsequent, I left Indianola for my home on Hynes Bay and on the evening of the same day I was attacked with yellow fever. My companion, Mr. Duke, was attacked on the 4th day with the same disease and died a few days after. Wm. Andrews.

Issue September 13, 1867
Died on the 9th inst. at the residence of her father, W. Joel Bryan, of Brazoria county, Mrs. Mary A. Trueheart, wife of Dr. Chas. W. Trueheart, Galveston.
The announcement of the death of Mrs. M.A. Trueheart, wife of Dr. Chas. W. Trueheart of this city, is of very sad import. We, with his numerous friends, sincerely sympathize with him in this, his great affliction and bereavement.

Miscellaneous Texas Newspaper Abstracts - Deaths — Vol 2

Alleyton -- The *Columbus Times* says the yellow fever prevails at Alleyton. There were five or six cases, one of whom, Mr. Drew, brother to the proprietor of the Alleyton Hotel, died on the 4th. A great many of the citizens were leaving for the interior.

Sickness at Brenham: The *Enquirer* of the 7th says Mr. Ephraim died there at the residence of Mr. Sam Levinson on the previous Wednesday. On the 6th, Mr. Shyhagan, died of the same disease (yellow fever). Some two weeks since Mr. Marks and Capt. Devine, recently from Galveston, died of yellow fever at Brenham...

LETTER FROM HOUSTON, SEPTEMBER 11, 1867: "Tom Vapid" sends his regards to you and your readers. We understand Dr. J.R. Hand, buried here today had his life insured for $3,500, by Henry L. Allen. Dr. Hand has been with us but a little while, engaged in the drug business.

I herewith send you the names of 17 persons buried on Tuesday, September 10, 1867:
J.P. Gillespie, 65, yellow fever.
Knotte, 28, yellow fever.
H. Fisher, 28, yellow fever.
J.H. Murbot, Jr., 5, yellow fever.
Bettie Clark, col'd, 37, yellow fever.
T.C. Dixon, 66, dysentery.
A. Lantz Deforhu, 5, yellow fever.
J.C. Buckley, 35, yellow fever.
John Aiken, 34, yellow fever.
Mrs. Sar'h Windham, 34, yellow fever.
John Dobler, 38, yellow fever.
M. Rohen, 28, yellow fever.
M. Marchinska, 30, yellow fever.
Chas. Wann, 53, general debility.
James Morris, colored, 60, con. of bowels.
Peter Smith, colored, 1 1/2, teething.
Thos. Ness, 24, billious and remit. fever.

List of interments for Wednesday, September 11th 1867:
Margaret Ripp, 36, typhus fever.
Michael Matthews, 35, black vomit.
M. Coniff, 35, febris billiosa.
B.J. Denaro, 35, yellow fever.
Wm. Warchester, 34, yellow fever.
C.J. Drescher, 26, yellow fever.
Huey Carey, 35, yellow fever.
Dr. J.R. Hand, 35, yellow fever.

H.S. Craddock, 30, yellow fever.

H. Swann, 27, congestive fever.

We regret to announce the death of Mr. Allen Gardner Spenser, aged 62, an estimable gentleman, who came among us a short time since. This will cause many regrets from his friends here, in Brooklyn and New York. We deeply sympathize with his son, A.W. Spenser, conductor on the Texas Central Railroad.

Dr. E.N. Covey, Dr. Connell, Mr. N. Carpenter (of R. Marsh, Denman & Co.), Maj. Burk of Galveston, and J. Waldo are all doing very well... Bolivar Ward.

List of names of the people buried September 12, 1867 for Galveston:

Mr. Crane, 35, New York, yellow fever.

Bradford Curry, 27, England, yellow fever.

Thos. J. Kurty, 20, Pa., yellow fever.

Dennis Russell, 31, Ireland, yellow fever.

Mike Condon, 30, Ireland, yellow fever.

Reuben Green, 26, Virginia, yellow fever.

Emanuel J. Dalton, 4, Georgia, yellow fever.

Lucy Withers, 19, Virginia, yellow fever.

Leon Burnell, 25, France, yellow fever.

George W. Jones, 33, U.S., yellow fever.

John Healey, 30, Ireland, yellow fever.

Cornelius Codnen, 45, Ireland, yellow fever.

Mrs. Decro, 32, France, bilious fever.

James B. Wright, 26, Vt., yellow fever.

Texana Perry, 18, Texas, yellow fever.

Wm. Wyllie, 26, Scotland, yellow fever.

E. Lawrence, 30, England, yellow fever.

Unknown man, 22, Germany, yellow fever.

The Fever On The *Delaware* — We are indebted to Lieut. Thos. H. Redgate, of the Revenue Cutter *Delaware*, for the following intelligence:

Chief Engineer George W. Jones of the cutter died at 10 p.m. Wednesday of yellow fever, and was buried yesterday morning in the "Soldiers Rest." There have been three officers attacked. The remaining two, Lieut Dickinson and Engineer Detmar, are both improving. Lieut. E.L. Dean is in command. The vessel is anchored in Bolivar Channel.

Sickness at Brenham -- The *Enquirer* of the 7th says Mr. Ephraim died there at the home residence of Mr. Sam Levinson on the previous Wednesday. His physician pronounced the case yellow fever. On the 6th, Mr. Shyhagan died of the same disease. Some two weeks [note: paper folded] and Capt Devine, recently from Galveston, died of yellow fever at Brenham. These facts have created some uneasiness and some stampeding. But Brenham is a very healthy locality and we cannot think the fever will become epidemic there.

Among the burials yesterday will be noticed the name of Miss Texana Perry, the eldest daughter of Mr. Pat Perry, whose death took place some two weeks ago. Miss Perry was universally beloved. But this is but one instance of distress which pervades nearly all families in our city.

Issue September 14, 1867
We learn from New Iberia that there has been since the commencement of the epidemic at that place, ninety-eight deaths in all, among them Mr. Harvey Hopkins.

Death of Dr. S. Adams. He came among us a stranger and until the epidemic was hardly known beyond his own happy little home and his immediate circle of brother officers... He obeyed the calls at all hours of the night of the poor who came for his professional services... What sympathy can we offer to that heart-broken young wife, who but a few days since was so bright and happy in the cheering society of that fond and doting husband?...

Gen. Chas. Griffin was attacked by yellow fever night before last and had a very high fever all night and yesterday, but in the evening Dr. Randall thought the danger about over. Later we hear the General is still improving.

Information has been received from Harrisburg by Gen. Sherman that Major John A. Williams, Superintendent of the B.B.H.&C.R., was attacked with the same fever night before last. Mr. Graves, Secretary of the Road, is also down, as well as the agent at Alleyton. Dr. Thompson is also sick with the fever at Harrisburg. There were five new cases and three deaths on Thursday.

Officer P.A. Stout of the City Police died last night about 8 o'clock. He was apparently well in the morning.

Dr. E.S. Alexander was very low at last accounts.

Major T. E/F.[?] White of the firm of White & Ledyard has entirely recovered from a violent and long continued illness, having been in the clutches of yellow jack some two or three weeks. He will probably be able to visit his business office some time today. He will sadly miss his estimable partner, Col. W.N. Ledyard, whose demise we have chronicled some weeks since.

LETTER FROM HOUSTON, SEPTEMBER 12, 1867:

Richard is himself again. We have reference to our friend Richard W. Dowling, who is out again from his siege with Yellow Jack.

We learn that Dr. Hand, whose death was announced yesterday, also had $10,000 insured in the St. Louis Mutual Life Insurance Company.

Mr. O.C. Drew, Teller of the National Bank; Col. O'Connell, Commandant of the Post, and Mr. J.W. Gillian, are down with the fever.

Burials for September 12th:
A. Jones, 66, general debility.
Catherine Lister, 26, billious remittance.
A.G. Spencer, 62, yellow fever.
Son of M. Hyman, col, still-born.
Geo. W. Parker, 9, yellow fever.
Mrs. A. Lanotte, 35, yellow fever.
James Cannon, 37, enteritis.
Among the dead at Navasota are Allen Post; Drs. Beesby, Jones, James Williams and J.E. Tubbs. As ever, Bolivar Ward.

Mortuary Report for Galveston for Friday, September 13th, as reported by the City Sexton:
Jas. Sheridan, 28, Ireland, yellow fever.
J. Hall, 21, ..., yellow fever.
Arthur Beyer, 4, Texas, cong. brain.
William C. Astell, 13, Indiana, yellow fever.
Edwd. M. Sanderson, 4, Texas, congestion.
Dew Noyce, 3, Texas, yellow fever.
Wm. Lawrence, 28, New Jersey, yellow fever.
Louis Nerney, 30, France, yellow fever.
Henry Savage, 25, Ireland, yellow fever.
Clara D. Massie, 65, Virginia, yellow fever.
Sarah Dockrel, 26, Ireland, yellow fever.
Mena Heyan, 40, Germany, gen. debility.
Three U.S. soldiers.

Issue September 15, 1867

Letter from Houston, September 13, 1867:
...Mr. Fred Moore (Hutchins House) and Mr. Lanatte are doing finely... Col. O'Connell, Commandant of the Post, and his wife are very ill with the fever. Everything that can be done for them is being done.

The following burials have taken place here today, Friday, September 13th:
Infant of Mrs. Botts, 4 days, convulsions.
Major Harlan, unknown.

Patsey Church, colored, 72, frac. thigh bone.
Mr. Redsall, 48, yellow fever.
Infant of Mr. Redsall, 8 months, yellow fever.
Mrs. M.A. Morbert, 30, yellow fever.
Ada Collins, 8, yellow fever.
Lewis Smith, 21/24, yellow fever.
Wm. Kraft, 17, yellow fever.
One man from City Hospital.

Capt. J.F. Wallace, appointed by Gen. Griffin as Assessor and Collector for this county, will be buried tomorrow morning. Geo. W. King, of the *Telegraph*, is down sick with the fever. Mr. M. Bawsel, the efficient Deputy Postmaster of this city, we regret to learn, died tonight. He has been with us but [a] year... [He] is from Washington, D.C., and leaves a wife and three little children. Mr. B. will be buried by Holland Lodge #1 F & A.M., he being a member in good standing. Bolivar Ward.

Mr. Swisher and Col. Shropshire are yet in a critical state, but at noon yesterday in both cases, the indications were exceedingly favorable and we are informed that, in all probability, they will commence to improve from this time.

Gen. Griffin, at noon yesterday, still had fever, but his case was not considered at all dangerous, the symptoms being favorable. The remedies applied seemed to promise timely efficacy.

Mrs. Bonfoey, who was so cruelly attacked and wounded while in her bed, some days since, at Marshall, died on the 1st.

Mortuary report for Galveston; interments for Saturday, September 14th:
Mr. Spocet, unknown, Tennessee, yellow fever.
Mrs. Thompson, 35, U.S., yellow fever.
Charles Bryant, 20, Texas, yellow fever.
Mrs. M.F. Rosell, 60, New York, dropsy.
John Orthman, 42, Germany, inf. bowels.
Patrick Shield, 42, England, yellow fever.
Harry Adams, 24, New York, yellow fever.
Walter Spann, 10, Georgia, yellow fever.
Lawrence Elston/Biston, Sweden, yellow fever.
Calvin John Barr, 9, Texas, yellow fever.
J.S. Knight, 22, Philadelphia, yellow fever.
Alexander G. Barr, 5, Texas, yellow fever.
William Hgen, 50, Germany, yellow fever.
Dr. E. S. Alexander, 45, Vt., yellow fever.
Lucy Davis, 2 1/4[?], New Orleans, yellow fever.

Mike Hussey, 7 days, Galveston, Lock Jaw.
Alex. Ramsey, 3, U.S., yellow fever.
Mrs. M.E. Koenig, 51, Germany, debility.
Two U.S. soldiers and one yard man.

Dr. E.S. Alexander was buried yesterday evening. His death was lamented as a public calamity. He had been unremitting in his attendance by the bedside of the sick up to the hour the fever seized him, and many are now alive and breathing the invigorating air in health and strength through his skill.

Capt. Howard Finley was also buried yesterday. He had many friends and comrades who will mourn his untimely demise. He had in the famous Hood Brigade encountered the deadly perils of a hundred battles, sieges and skirmishes and now falls a victim, in the prime of his manhood, to the scourge that spares neither the brave or the timorous.

Issue September 17, 1867

Died, September 16, 1867, Dominick Holland, of Dublin, Ireland; aged 24 years. Philadelphia papers please copy.

Brevet Maj. Charles Griffin died of yellow fever in this city on Sunday last about 11 o'clock A.M. He was a native of Ohio and was at the time of his death, *pro tem* commander of the Military District of Louisiana and Texas in place of Sheridan, removed and awaiting the arrival of Gen. Hancock, who has recently been appointed the position by the President... Our people do not permit political differences to affect their human sympathies. Therefore, there was just as much regret when Gen. Griffin was stricken with the fever, just as much pleasure felt and expressed at the favorable reports of his condition, from time to time, and just as much sorrow at his death, as though his had been a representative instead of an imposed and unwelcome authority... it [yellow fever] tore from him a lovely and promising child... beloved wife.

Mortuary Report for Galveston; a list of names of the persons buried Sunday, September 15th, 1867:
Infant of Mr. Enne, Galveston, still born.
August Wigers, 23, Germany, yellow fever.
George Willis, 30, Virginia, yellow fever.
Carolina Hunt, 23, S.C., yellow fever.
William Stewart, 24, Maryland, yellow fever.
William Carover, 38, Germany, yellow fever.
Stephen Boyce, 30, Tennessee, yellow fever.
Lieut. Dickerson, 32, U.S., yellow fever.
Mrs. Noyes, 23, Alabama, yellow fever.

Henry Rucker, 19, Virginia, yellow fever.
Cornelius Meyers, 32, Ireland, yellow fever.
Mr. Gillas, 35, Prince Edwd Isle, yellow fever.
Bvt. Maj. Gen. Chas. Griffin, Ohio, yellow fever.
Two U.S. soldiers.
   Lieut. Dickerson was an officer of the navy on board the U.S. revenue steamer *Delaware*.

The following are the interments for Monday, September 16, 1867, Galveston, as reported by the City Sexton:
Mrs. Mary Mills, 38, England, yellow fever. [note: see end of this report.].
Reinholdt Fultz, 18, Germany, yellow fever.
Frank ....., Mexico, yellow fever.
Augustine Pavel, 48, Ger., yellow fever.
Wm. McCondelt, 19, Eng., yellow fever.
Emily Sephus, 42, Georgia, yellow fever.
Mrs. Jane A. Bacal/Baral, 24, Canada, yellow fever.
Geo. Burke, 56, Ala., yellow fever.
Ellen Reynolds, 23, Ireland, yellow fever.
A. Miller, 35, U.S., yellow fever.
Thos. Holland, 22, U.S., yellow fever.
Anna Augusta Wolf, 39, Galveston, cramps.
Geo. Wheill, 35, Va., yellow fever.
Four U.S. soldiers.
First name on the list belongs to Mortuary Report of the previous day.

Capt. Howard Finley -- The report which was current on the streets, exciting universal regret, through the city on Saturday, that this gentleman had succumbed to an attack of fever and had been buried, proves untrue. We had it stated to us as positive fact by as many as four persons, and not only gave it the credence to again repeat it ourselves, but made mention of it in this column in Sunday's issue. We are glad to be able to say that Capt. Finley is improving.

Mrs. Carolina M. Kennison, wife of Alphona Kennison, died ---- [note: not clear] will be buried this morning at half past seven o'clock. Mr. Kennison himself is ill with the fever.

We have the following intelligence from Harrisburg, received late yesterday evening. Major John --[?] Williams died last night (Sunday night) and was buried this afternoon. Mr. Graves, Secretary of the B.B.B. & C.R.R. [--?] black vomit and it can't [--?] Dr. Tompkins is improving.

The wife of Capt. <u>Peacock</u>, one of our long resident citizens, we regret to learn, died yesterday evening, of the fever.

Issue September 18, 1867

Died in this city on the 16th of yellow fever, Mrs. Bettie, wife of Capt. Thomas <u>Peacock</u>, aged 31 years. Liberty & Shreveport papers please copy.

Died in Galveston, Texas, on the 14th of August, 1867, of yellow fever, Jas. Pratt, a native of Nova Scotia, aged 25 years. Serg. Pratt enlisted as a Private in the Lone Star Rifles in August 1861... [note: condensed].

Letter from Houston, September 16, 1867: ... Dr. Haynes and Dr. Massie, wife and child, William Dobbins and Capt. Greene, Secretary of the Houston Direct Navigation Company, are all down with the fever.

In the death of Col. John A. Williams, which occurred at Harrisburg last night, Texas has lost a good man and a splendid soldier. At the time of his death he was Superintendent and Engineer of the B.B.B. & C.R.R. and VicePresident of the Columbus & San Antonio Railroad. It appears as but yester eve when we heard him promise to "love and honor" her whom he now leaves a widow. Twice in one short week has death visited Gen. Sherman's family, leaving him two widowed daughters. May God bless them now in this hour of affliction.

Among those who have died in Louisiana the past week that have acquaintances in Galveston who will feel sad to hear of their death, we mention Hiram Tomlin, late of the 5th Co., Battalion Washington Artillery; Thomas Wilbur Compton, and Joseph A. Steele...

List of burials, [Houston], September 15th:

Jos. Jamison, 8, yellow fever.
Matilda D. Mahan, 12, yellow fever.
L. Verfleu, 21, yellow fever.
Wm. Daly, 22, yellow fever.
John Pister, 22, yellow fever.
Wm. McCarthy, 23, yellow fever.
R.J. French, 27, yellow fever.
Mr. Regan, 29, yellow fever.
J.H. McMillan, 31, yellow fever.
Dr. E.N. Covey, 35, yellow fever.
Jerry Collins, 37, yellow fever.
Mrs. K. Kirch, 52, yellow fever.
Rev. Wm. Rees, .., yellow fever.
Isaac Ashes, .., yellow fever.
Daniel O'Mal, .., yellow fever.
E. Jennings, 25, hemorage.
John Flynn, 47, congestion of brain.

John Lewis, f.m.c., 26, typhoid fever.
Two men unknown.

Interments, September 16th:
Fred Moore, 22, yellow fever.
Geo. Lang, 23, yellow fever.
F. Schamer, 23, yellow fever.
L.F. Burbank, 28, yellow fever.
G.W. Davis, 30, yellow fever.
J. Kanivoski, 45, yellow fever.
G.W. Douglass, 46, yellow fever.
A. Lovengadt, ..., yellow fever.
Child of C. Aerson, 3, unknown.
M. Fox, 14, unknown.
Child of S. Priester, 10 months, unknown.
Mrs. Moss, 34, congestion of bowels.
J.W. Tibbs, 26, unknown.
Child of Clara Wright, still born.
Col. O'Connell, died this evening at the Hutchins House.
Yours, Bolivar Ward.

Two Notorious Outlaws Killed. Owensville, Robertson co., Texas. For the past three months one Bob Scivils and Capt. Hunt, alias Bob Leach, have been committing outrages upon the whites and blacks of this county, of every name and nature known to the dark catalogue of human crime. Armed to the teeth... Sheriff Logan of this county did everything a man could do to effect their apprehension, but without success. Capt. Randall most signally failed...

At last Capt Randall gave a peremptory order to one Ben Brown, a noted horse thief catcher... taking them dead or alive, and not to return without the murderers or their scalps, with the ears on, unless they had fled the State... Leach was surprised while asleep and captured without resistance, about the 12th ult. at Bryan City. Scivils was shot dead the day following, a few miles from that place, while in the act of drawing his revolver... The bodies of the outlaws were respectably buried with their "har" on. Among the posse was one Deeson who had been shot three times by Hunt and crippled for life...

Mortuary Report for Galveston, interments for Tuesday, September 17th:
Caroline Kennison, 24, S.C., congestion.
George D. Baker, 1 month, Galveston, yellow fever.
Mrs. Betty Peacock, 31, La., yellow fever.
Walter Burkhardt, 11 mos., Galveston, yellow fever.
Mrs. McDonald, 36, Ireland, yellow fever.
John Rogers, 36, Ireland, yellow fever.
Mrs. Cameron, ..., U.S., yellow fever.

E. Baum, 35, Germany, yellow fever. [note: see end of this report.].
Jacob Vanpell, 25, U.S., yellow fever.
Robert Barr, 45, Scotland, yellow fever.
John Williams, 15, Galveston, brain fever.
John Johnson, 27, Norway, yellow fever.
Dr. Wm. Hunter, 44, Minnesota, yellow fever.
Gusta Volst, 6 mos., Texas, cholic.
Mrs. Magdaiane Oligschlaeger, 94, Germany, old age.
One U.S. soldier.
E. Baum (the 9th named) died at Millican and was brought here for interment.

A dispatch in our paper of yesterday from Columbus stated that there was no train from Harrisburg. We learn from Gen. Sherman that the train did arrive at Alleyton on Monday, though after night, owing to the engine getting out of order. Thus far, the trains have made regular trips every day, and if all the machinists are not taken sick, will continue to do so. This road has indeed been unfortunate in the loss of Col. Williams, the superintendent and Capt. Archie Graves, the secretary of the company. The chief machinist is also sick and most of the employees. It is now with the utmost difficulty that hands enough can be got to keep the trains running. The conductor, Mr. Briscoe, is sick. Mr. Ross, the assistant engineer, is now Gen. Sherman's principal dependence.

Issue September 19, 1867
Letter from Huntsville, September 14, 1867:
...Among those dead of general acquaintance, we number Dr. Moore, B. Cunningham, Mr. Wright, Col. Rouls, Mrs. Neil, and could name others... Robert Campbell.

Letter from Houston, September 17, 1867:
Mr. Bawsell, Assistant Postmaster of this city, whose death was announced a few days ago, had his life insured in the St. Louis Mutual for $2500.

We are sorry to note that Major Dowling and S.K. Mclihanny are down with a relapse.

Mr. Dobbins, that was buried today, had gotten over the yellow fever, but in the goodness of his heart, undertook to nurse his friends [?]– his strength proved inadequate to the task, a relapse ensued, and today he has gone to return no more.

Mr. Link, of the *Baptist Herald*, and M.P. Gillespie, of the *Telegraph*, are in bed with the yellow fever.

Mr. Warner and Mr. Taylor of the *Bureau* are among the new cases under treatment for the Yellow Jack.

Bvt. Lieut. Col. J.D. O'Connell, 17th U.S. Inf., was buried today with military honors. We hear his youngest child was buried in the same coffin with him...

P.J. Mahan and wife have been ill several days. They lost a bright and promising daughter a few days ago...

List of burials for September 17, 1867 [Houston]
Joseph Qweib, 29, yellow fever.
W. Dobbins, 28, yellow fever.
W.H. Kessler, 27, yellow fever.
Joseph Shield, 26, unknown.
B.C.[?] Linden, 24, yellow fever.
E. Keil, 24, yellow fever.
Henry Mack, colored, 20, remittent fever.
Chas. Butler, 4, yellow fever.
Lieut. Col. J.D. O'Connell, yellow fever.
W. Beller, 21, yellow fever.
Capt. Warren, who is now in command of this post is down with the fever.
As ever, Bolivar Ward.

Delayed letter from Houston, interments for September 11, 1867:
Mary L. Windham, 12, yellow fever.
John Fox, 16, yellow fever.
John Downey, 20, yellow fever.
Joe Trewald, 25, yellow fever.
Thos O'Conner, 25, yellow fever.
Louis Guinnand, 25, yellow fever.
Ed. Malley, 27, yellow fever.
Sam. Malone, 27, yellow fever.
M. Bawsell, 35, yellow fever.
J.F.[?] Wallace, 35, yellow fever.
Henry Terchs, 37, yellow fever.

The epidemic in Houston: From the *Telegraph* of Tuesday: ...Among the deaths on Sunday was that of Rev. Wm. Reese, pastor of the Methodist Church in this city, and for some time past one of the professors of the Houston Academy... His wife died Saturday, September 7th, and he followed her to the grave a week after, a willing victim...

Mortuary Report for Galveston, names of the persons buried Wednesday, September 18th:
John Foley, 30, Ireland, congestion.
John Grassman,..., Bohemia, yellow fever.
John Leach, 35, U.S., yellow fever.
Mrs. Joana McKenna, 60, Ireland, yellow fever.
Wm. Pasahatag, 25, Ger., yellow fever.
John Griffith, 35, Ireland, yellow fever.

Infant of Wm. Love, city, still born.
One U.S. soldier, one laborer.

Yellow fever in LaGrange, letter dated the 12th inst. "We have had about one hundred deaths from yellow fever in LaGrange, and the citizens have scattered it all over the county. The deaths are from seven to fifteen per day in LaGrange. Many of the oldest citizens have died of it. Mr. Thompson, editor of the *Democrat*, has it, and Mr. Matthews of the *New Era* has died of this fatal disease."

We regret to learn from the *Register* that Rev. William McK Lambdin, an able and much beloved minister of the Methodist church, died at Waco on the 11th...

Issue September 20, 1867

The following have died at Hempstead recently: Mr. Voorhies, John Scherly, John Kalsh [?], John Erving, Mrs. J.B. Stephenson. J.E. Muller, John Conner, A. Londermilk, Col. J.J. Hollowell, Mary Green, — Kelser, Mary Coleman, Nanny Wright, J.E. Green, Thomas McGehre.

Yellow fever at Hempstead: The *Countryman* of the 14th says the yellow fever was increasing at Hempstead. Mr. G.C. Morrison, of Baltimore, died of it that morning. On the previous Sunday the death, by fever, of one of the Registrars, F.M. Miller, produced a general move of the well citizens towards the country.

Letter from Houston, September 18, 1867:
Mrs. O'Connell, buried today, was the wife of the commandant of the post, who was buried yesterday. The bodies have been placed in metallic cases, laid in vaults, and will be forwarded to their friends North. They have an interesting little son of three years, who is recovering from the fever.
W.C. Tomlinson and T.A. Fowler, of the *Telegraph*, Dr. J.S. Roberts and Mr. Beman, with Gray, Smallwood & Co., are ill.
"Tom Vapid" got out to his gate today, but soon returned. Don't get a relapse, Thomas.
Mr. Kessler, who died yesterday, was the Engineer of Liberty, #2 Steam Fire Engine Co.
The survivors of Hood's Old Brigade will feel sad to learn that the Rev. O.M. Menifee died recently in the interior of the state.

Interments (Houston) September 19, 1867:
Jasper Schmidt, 31, yellow fever.
C.S. Duncan, 28, yellow fever.
Emily Peters, 10, yellow fever.

.... Dobbins, ..., yellow fever.
Mrs. J.V. O'Connell, 22, yellow fever.
Mr. Messner, ..., unknown.
Mr. Kerhe, yellow fever.
Mrs. Fox, ..., yellow fever.
Capt. <u>Warren</u>, 25, yellow fever.
An Israelite, ..., yellow fever.
Dick Eans, ..., yellow fever.
Mrs. Ephraim, (Hempstead).

Capt. <u>Warren</u> was in command of the post at the time of his death.

Mr. Tracy, the energetic proprietor of the *Telegraph*, has placed us under obligations for the following list of deaths in Hempstead: Out of 70 cases 37 so far have died. Only five so far are out of danger. Mr. Voorhies, yellow fever; Jay <u>Dixon</u>, congestion; Kate <u>Dixon</u>, do; George Brookman, 18 mos., yellow fever; John Schelley, John Irby, do; John Kane, congestion; Mrs. T.B. Stevens, do; E.F. Miller, board of registration, yellow fever; John Connor, J.L. Hollowell, C. Loudermilk, Mary <u>Green</u>, Mary Coleman, Thomas McGehee, Jr., Mr. Kaiser, Nannie Wright, Maj. J.E. <u>Green</u>, Board of Registration, Mrs. D.H. <u>Coleman</u>, James A. Lester, G.C. Morrison, Mrs. J.E. <u>Green</u>, J.E. Herbert, W.P. McConnell, Dr. John Lark, Nelly <u>Coleman</u>, William Brink, child of Col. Hallowell, Mrs. J. Ephraim, Mary Young, Susan Frost, Miss <u>Coleman</u>, Daniel Winter, eight freedmen. As ever, Boliver Ward.

Obituary: Died in Lavaca on Sunday morning, the 8th of September, Rev. Alexis Renoux, a native of Digne, in France, at the early age of 26. [note: condensed].

Killing -- The *Gonzales Inquirer* of the 14th says Charles W. Mason, assessor and collector, was shot and killed on the previous Sunday by Wm. Baltzell, a citizen of that place. They were both intoxicated.

We learn that several cases of fever have occurred across the Bay, at and near Frank White's settlement, on Nueces Bay. We regret to announce the death of Mrs. Ed White and child.

Zeb. French and Theo. Carter, county and district clerks at LaGrange, have died with yellow fever. Twelve died on Wednesday and fourteen on Thursday.

Galveston Mortuary Report. The following is a list of the names of the persons buried Thursday, September 19, 1867:
Robert Allen, 2, Galveston, congestion.
C.R. Deboer, 12 days, Galveston, jaundice.
Wm. L. Foster, 3 1/2, Galveston, yellow fever.
Chas. Bradley, 24, Tennessee.

Mary Loomis, 3 weeks, Galveston, yellow fever
One U.S. soldier.

In Corpus Christi, out of a population of less than a thousand, from 100 to 129 have died. At Victoria there have been a few cases, but the *Commerical* says the disease has not spread and probably will not become epidemic there. Rev. C. Moore, pastor of the Presbyterian Church at Victoria, died with the fever on the 2d. Miss Mattie Hubbell of Indianola, and two or three strangers, have also died of the fever at Victoria.

Issue September 21, 1867
Died in Harrisburg on the 18th inst. at 9 1/2 o'clock P.M. of yellow fever, Archie R/K. Graves, aged 35 years. Richmond, Virginia, and Mobile, Alabama, papers please copy.

The *Crockett Sentinel* of the 10th inst. says a man named Brinberry killed Mrs. Isaac Earle on the San Pedro in Houston county. The killing is said to be an act of deliberate murder.

Letter from Houston, September 19, 1867, ... Miss Mariana Cross, a promising young daughter of the pastor of the Episcopal church in this city, died this A.M. We buried her at sun down beneath the shades of a wide spreading oak, there to remain until that great day.
    Houston Mortuary Report of interments for September 19th:
Mrs. Harbin, 32, yellow fever.
Emanuel Jones, 45, yellow fever.
Miss Mariana Cross, 11, yellow fever.
F.N. Marbut, 37, yellow fever.
S. Oleary, ..., yellow fever.
Kasper Schmidt, 31, yellow fever.
James Sargent, 20, yellow fever.
John S. Lattimer, 20, yellow fever.
Son of Mrs. Buckmeyer, 5, yellow fever.
F. Evans (colored) 38, yellow fever.
Jewish girl, 14, yellow fever.
Valentine Lanter [note: page folded], 48, typhoid abd.
E. Reis, 29, hem. bowels.
Fred. Randolph, 44, gastritis.
E.W. Torbert, 23, typhoid fever.
Henrietta Cohn, 2, infl'n bowels.
Child of Mrs. Lunceford, 1, chron. diarr'a.
Child of Mrs. Gearson, 1 1/2, teething.
Ludwig Rachye, 40, —.
Mary J.C. Read, 25, —.

Child of Mr. Blake, 2 1/2, ----.
　　Dr. Haynes, a promising young physician, and Capt. Hewett, with Abbott, Chandler & Co., we learn have died. Bolivar Ward.

Mortuary Report for Galveston, Friday, September 20th:
Anthony Wiener, 30, Germany, yellow fever.
Samuel Kossoner, 44, Germany, yellow fever.
Julius Dice, 20, yellow fever, Germany.
Patrick J. Cusick, 5, S.C., cong. brain.
Capt. W.A. Bowen, 40, Fla., imfl. bowels.

Issue September 22, 1867
Died in this city on the 21st inst. of yellow fever in his 23d year of his age, Mr. Alonza Allen, of Virginia. He was a brave soldier in the Confederate Army. He leaves a sister in Virginia and many friends to mourn his loss. Charlottesville and Richmond papers please copy.

From Houston: Ed. Terrell, the conductor on the Texas Central Railroad, is down with the fever at Millican. The mortality of that city has been estimated as high as 70%. S. Beman, ex-jumpiest, (Sam Patch, Jr.); Capt. J.E. Foster, I. Colman, and Charley Marston, are all, we learn, down with the prevailing disease...

Mortuary Report--interments for Saturday, Sept 21, 1867:
William Lewis, 27, Wales, not known.
Christine Marhzen [?] 26, Germany, yellow fever.
Phil Sheridan, 30, Ireland, yellow fever.
Kana [?] H. Weihrmann, 32, Germany, yellow fever.
Mr. D. Beckman, --, --, unknown.
Henry Reed, 1y., Texas, yellow fever. ·
Emma I. Prosch [?] 23m, Texas, diarrhea.
Milly Day, 25, Virginia, yellow fever.
Ida Aschoff, Texas, yellow fever.

The following is the list of interments for Houston, September 20, 1867:
Jas. Chapgake, 1, yellow fever.
Mary Fox, 12, yellow fever.
Louis Kirch, 14, yellow fever.
F.M. Mills, 23, yellow fever.
Dr. R.H. Haynes, 23, yellow fever.
Mrs. Dreyfus, 27, yellow fever.
Frank Webber, 32, yellow fever.
J.H. Crantford, 33, yellow fever.
M. Archer, 30, yellow fever.

Pat ......, 31, yellow fever.
Mrs. Mary Turner, 37, yellow fever.
Frank Macer, 43, yellow fever.
Child of M. Cohen, 1, teething.
.... Hewitt, 40, meningitis.
Colored woman, unknown.
Ann McGraw, ..., unknown.
.... Jennings, ..., unknown.
Son of Mr. Fox, ..., unknown.
J.H. Crantford was a member of the Typographical Union.
L.J. Warner, chief clerk in the Freedman's bureau, died here this morning.

Issue September 24, 1867

Died in New Orleans, September 21, 1867, A.C. Holt, Jr., aged 11 years, son of Dr. A.C. Holt and Mary Williams.

Died August 21, 1867, on Lake Bruin, Tensas Parish, Louisiana, Thomas Wilbur Compton, aged 31 years, second son of the late Thomas A. Compton.

Mortuary Report for Galveston for Monday, September 23d:
Robert Guy, 24, U.S., yellow fever.
Patrick Ryan, 24, Ireland, yellow fever.
Charley Ferguson, 29, Ala., consumption.
Infant of A. Woods, 3 hours, unknown.
One U.S. soldier.

Mortuary Report for Galveston buried Sunday, September 22d:
Patrick Murphy, 27, Ireland, yellow fever.
John Harrington, 28, Mass., yellow fever.
Jacob H. Lawson, 41, Sweden, yellow fever.
Samuel Grey, 17, England, yellow fever.
James Bergen, 24, Conn., yellow fever.
Robert Gibson, 24, New York, yellow fever.
One U.S. soldier.
Sally Simms, 85, Virginia, old age.

Letter from Houston: A. Tapana and R.F. George, druggist, are among the new cases of fever. Sam Beman -the jumpiest- is not down with the fever as we have reported. We were misinformed.
Interments September 21, 1867:
Child of Mr. Lanotte, 6, yellow fever.
Peter Cole, 9, yellow fever.
Daughter of Mrs. Jordan, 11, yellow fever.
L.J. Warner, 23, yellow fever.

Henry Brown, col., 25, yellow fever.
Geo. Friends, 30, yellow fever.
Mrs. Aug. Haske [?], 37, yellow fever.
Mrs. Roe, 50, yellow fever.
Mrs. Lunceford, –, yellow fever .
Mrs. Brashear, –, yellow fever.
H.G. Mare, –, yellow fever.
Henry Grimm, 60, consumption.
Man from hospital, –, yellow fever.

We hear of many new cases today. We mention Drs. Moody and Powell, Major Denny, J.H. Murchie, Wm. Webb, (with W.A. Ellis) Capt. Gault, cashier in the Texas Express Company and Captain Foster, formerly of Harrisburg.

Issue September 25, 1867

A private telegram was received in this city yesterday, dated Houston, Texas, September 15th, communicating the sad intelligence that Dr. E.N. Covey died of yellow fever on the morning of that day. Dr. Covey was a native of Maryland, and formerly of the U.S. Army...

Mortuary Report for Galveston, for Tuesday, September 24th:
August Kline, 36, Germany, yellow fever.
Margaret A. Coglin, 8, Texas, yellow fever.
John Silier, 28, Italy, yellow fever.
Geo. Driscol, 24, England, yellow fever.
Jacob Johnson, 28, Germany, yellow fever.
John G. Pfluger, 24, Texas, yellow fever.
Eli Dufour, 29, Canada, yellow fever.
Mrs. Buckley, .., Ireland, not given.
One U.S. soldier, yellow fever.

Letter from Houston, September 23rd: The following is the list of interments September 22nd:
Miss C.B. Adams, 11, yellow fever.
Jas. Cavanaugh, 18, yellow fever.
Miss Sarah Talley, 52, yellow fever.
Wm. Reynolds, 25, yellow fever.
C.C. Webster, yellow fever.
Fannie Powell, 5, yellow fever.
John Flood, 9, yellow fever.
Wm. Woodal, colored, 89, yellow fever.
Henry Nash, 32, yellow fever.
Mr. Blake, 29, yellow fever.
Jas. F. Eppinger, 43, yellow fever.
John Williams, 2, diarrhea.

Nelson, colored, 3, cholera morbus.
John Bullock, 35, cong. of lungs.
    David Link, brother of the Rev. Mr. Link, publisher of the *Baptist Herald* in this city, was buried today. He was a good soldier in the Rockbridge Artillery in Va...
    Joseph Pauska, Esq., of this city, died today. His funeral takes place tomorrow.
    Interments for September 23rd:
Peter Larkin, 33, yellow fever.
Mrs. Winne Faysoux, 38, yellow fever.
David Link, 30, yellow fever.
A. Waters, colored, 30, yellow fever.
Chas. Munroe, 26, yellow fever.
Chas. Havers, 26, yellow fever.
R. Page Boyce, 25 [?], yellow fever.
Mary Redsall, 7, yellow fever.
John Thompson, 25, yellow fever.
Jos. Taylor, 23, yellow fever.
Colored man, ..., yellow fever.
Henry Hoffman, 2 days, spasms.
    Maj. Richard W. Dowling is dead. E.Y. Ammerson, a compositor in the *Telegraph*, is dead. Particulars by next mail. Bolivar Ward.

A few days since James Finn shot and killed James McCauly at the camp of government employees, to which both belonged, near San Antonio. Both were New Orleans roughs. Finn was arrested by the military and turned over to the civil authorities.

Mr. Thule, a German, was killed by Indians five miles west of Castroville, on the 13th. The cavalry gave pursuit, but being badly mounted, the Indians escaped.

Sickness in LaGrange: letter from Mr. [J.A.] Haynie: As to the Taylor Simons, all are dead but one, and he is nearly so. Several deaths today (14th), yesterday 12, day before 18. You ask who is dead. It would be easier to tell you who is not. Bob Bennell, Tom Patton, Hill's wife, N.C. Harrison from Houston, son of Dr. Milinberg [?], Amos Huff, a german girl. Among the dead of yesterday are Frank Cox, Mrs. W.B. Price, Miss Annie Moore, Mr. Rosenfield, Mr. Merram, Mr. Schroeder, Mrs. [?] Melcher, Mrs. Hermes and child, Mr. Ternanakle, Mr. Trombusky, young Matchee, Giles Ryan. Thus far 87 in all. V. Korn is among the dead and has left a helpless family. Only two negroes have died up to this time, but the disease is spreading among them. Old Mr. Denny Moore and his wife died in the Christian hope; also Mrs. Hord...

Mr. Haynie's next letter is dated the 15th. He says: "I have just seen W.G. Webb and family. They are convalescent, and I think will get well. A load of provisions came in yesterday, and, for a time, made us all happy... We had 11 deaths yesterday, and up to this hour (12 o'clock) today only 5, namely, Henry Homuth, Mrs. Koening, Dr. Milenberg's son, a German girl and Dr. Warren...

The sickness still increases as fast as subjects present themselves. This morning there are fifteen or twenty new cases among the freedmen. August Frede's wife was buried this morning and Amos J. Bursteed by moonlight last night. I am literally in the city of the dead. The stench is almost intolerable. Ninety-four have died in twenty days or less. I am now the only well man in town to visit the sick and see the dead buried. I have been up for 10/15 successive nights, nearly all night. I sleep from 3 to 7 a.m. J.A. Haynie.

The reward of $1,000 by the Sheriff of Harrison for the murderer of Mrs. Bonfoey is still offered in the Marshall papers.

Issue September 26, 1867

Letter from Houston, September 24, 1867... Maj. R.W. Dowling, latterly known as "the Hero of Sabine Pass", was followed to his grave, at a late hour this evening, by a large concourse of mourning friends. He was a highly respected citizen, a friend to the poor, a christian gentleman, a devoted husband and father, generous to a fault. Cut down in the prime of life, only 29 years of age; his loss will, indeed, be felt by the entire community and his friends abroad. He was buried from the Catholic church, of which he was a member...

Mrs. Minor Bawsell, buried today, was the widow of our Deputy Postmaster, whose death was announced ten days since. She leaves three little orphan children in this cold, bleak world...

Interments for September 24th:

Richard Rowe, 50 years, yellow fever.
Jno. Maloy, 42, yellow fever.
Dr. Repp, 35, yellow fever.
Joseph Pauska, 32, yellow fever.
E.H. Inglehardt, 30, yellow fever.
R.W. Dowling, 29, yellow fever.
E.Y. Ammerson, 25, yellow fever.
Mrs. Bawsell, 23, yellow fever.
Albert Milhe, 22, yellow fever.
Julias Lanatie, 10, yellow fever.
A.A. De Baligathy, 15 months, yellow fever.
Child of Mrs. Jenny, 1m., yellow fever.
One female and one male, unknown on account of certificate. Bolivar Ward.

Mortuary Report for Galveston. A list of names of the persons buried Wednesday, September 25th, 1867:

H. Tennekohl, 35, Germany, yellow fever.

Charlotte Shaw, 16, U.S., black vomit.

Alex. L. Roy, 25, Canada, yellow fever.

J.M. Greenhow, 48, England, consumption.

Silas Cooke, 34, Md., yellow fever.

Bernard Dunn, 31, England, yellow fever.

Jas. Creighton, 23, New York, yellow fever.

Jas. McDonald, 5 1/2, Texas, cong. brain.

Mary How, 8 days, city, unknown.

A. Blessing, 28, Germany, yellow fever.

Bill and Steve Coxe, two notorious desperadoes, were recently arrested by the military in Lamar county. Dick Copeland, one of the same gang, has been executed by the citizens there.

Clarksville Standard of the 14th: A negro attached to the Donoho House, in Clarksville, informed James Donoho that a person, who had threatened his life, was prowling outside. Mr. D. deemed suspicious circumstances and fired and killed him. There was a mistake. He killed Hamilton Sivley, living five miles east of town, who was drinking and wandering...

I am called upon to record the mournful intelligence of the death of Miss Emma Holliday, of Millican, Texas, who for a long time was a most faithful and affectionate student of Port Sullivan college. She died at her mother's, Mrs. A.A. Holliday's. Widowed mother and large family of brothers and sisters.

Issue September 27, 1867

Letter from Houston, September 24, 1867:... two hundred and fifteen deaths in this city since August 13, 1867, from yellow fever, have occurred to date. Mr. Foley and Mr. Middleton are down with the fever... the following is the list of interments, September 25, 1867:

George Grant, 35, yellow fever.

... Nourse, (Nourse & Yeaton) 35, yellow fever.

Henry Taylor, 29, yellow fever.

Robert McKay, 28, yellow fever.

James Kelly, 27, yellow fever.

Geo. Frederick, 23, yellow fever.

Son of Mr. Sonza, 12, yellow fever.

Betsy Bryant, colored, 12, yellow fever.

Texana Dechaumes, 9, yellow fever.

W. Kranzeman, 6, yellow fever.

Anna Veight, 5, yellow fever.

Robert, colored, 2, yellow fever.
Child of Mrs. Bowers, 6, yellow fever.
R. Mitchell, colored, yellow fever.
Man unknown, no certificate.
Total, 15, yellow fever 14.
R.C. Brashear, 22, and Mr. Scott, 30, were the two names "unknown" yesterday. So Mr. Tracy, of the *Telegraph*, informs us. Rev. L. Steiner, Rabbi of the Hebrew congregation in this city, died this evening. As ever, Bolivar Ward.

Mortuary Report for Galveston, for Thursday, September 26, 1867:
Mrs. Anna Petick, 60, England, yellow fever.
Thomas Cannon, 26, Ireland.

Issue September 28, 1867

The *Telegraph* mentions among the deaths in Houston the name of Mr. Joseph E. Gregory, Secretary of the Central Railroad... He was father to Mr. E.C. Gregory, one of the oldest and most respected citizens of Houston.

Mortuary Report for Galveston, burials for Friday, September 27, 1867:
Oliva Thompson, 8, New Mexico, yellow fever.
George Cross, 21, Scotland, yellow fever.
Frank Rodfld[?], 30, Germany, yellow fever.
Edward Hood, 30, Ireland, yellow fever.
John Spooner, 25, U.S., yellow fever.
N. Johnson, 8 ms., teething, Galveston.
John Smith, 32, Eng., inflammation bowels.

Letter from Houston, September 26, 1867:
Joseph E. Gregory, Secretary and Treasurer of the T.C. Railroad, departed this life today. He will be buried tomorrow at 10 o'clock A.M. from the "Old Capitol Hotel." Mr. Gregory has been a resident of this city for the past ten years... He was taken ill with the yellow fever on Monday, A.M.; was thought to be out of danger until last evening, when he began to sink; death intervened, leaving a wife, kindred and many friends to mourn his loss.

Mrs. R.B. Harvey (Dr. Powell's mother-in-law) died today at the "Old Capitol Hotel" of yellow fever. The doctor and his estimable lady are, indeed, afflicted. Sunday they buried a bright and interesting little daughter of six summers, Fannie, today their mother, and while we write, Mrs. Powell and two children are very ill.

The following is the list of interments for Houston, September 26th:
John Hackett, 50, yellow fever.
... Stanter, 25, yellow fever.
E.S. Femeick, 23, yellow fever.

Pat McKune, 25, yellow fever.
Mrs. Nourse, 30, yellow fever.
Henry Hobem, 32, yellow fever.
Miss Carrie Asher, 12, yellow fever.
Mike Hart, 26, yellow fever.
Chas. Wood, 23, yellow fever.
A. Harris, 32, yellow fever.
Ada Rawley, 5, yellow fever.
W.G. Beagple, 35, yellow fever.
H. Hickey, 24, yellow fever.
Rev. L. Steiner, 31, yellow fever.
M. Flort, 30, yellow fever.
Child of Mr. From, 10, yellow fever.
Child of J. Peschk, 2, yellow fever.
Child, colored, yellow fever.
Martha Taylor, colored, 7, yellow fever.
John Hughes, 37, yellow fever.
Man from hospital, yellow fever.
R. Getchell, 61, consumption.
Sallie P. Dolen, 6, Dropsy.
L. Latney, colored, cong. chill.

The following tribute from "Tom Vapid", to the memory of the gallant Dowling, is this day published: Died at his residence, in Houston, Texas, on the 23rd of September, 1867, Richard W. Dowling, aged 29 years. The 8th of September, 1863, will long be gratefully remembered by the people of Texas, as the day when a fleet of twenty-seven vessels of the United States, with a naval and military force of some 15,000 men, under a noted General, were driven away from Sabine Pass by forty-two Irish-Artillerists.

On that memorable day a carefully planned and elaborately appointed expedition, intended to carry ruin and desolation into the heart of rebellious Texas, was frustrated by the unparalleled boldness and intrepidity of a young lieutenant of artillery and his forty two stalwart followers. For four years we have silently celebrated the anniversary of this glorious day in our memories; but the 8th of September, 1867, alas! is swiftly followed by a wail of sorrow!

The far-off echoes of the guns of Fort Griffin have served as funeral salvos for the warm-hearted hero Dick Dowling. Houston, September 26, 1867. Tom Vapid.

Issue September 29, 1867

The following is the list of interments (Houston) for September 27th:
Mrs. R.B. Harvey, 50, yellow fever.
Fannie Herron, 25, yellow fever.
Mary E. Conway, 6, yellow fever.
Mrs. M. Conway, 26, yellow fever.

Anna Dipperman, 12, yellow fever.
George Herron, 25, yellow fever.
John Frome, 43, yellow fever.
William E. Mullen, 28, yellow fever.
.... Pitrousky, 27, yellow fever.
J.E. Gregory, 37, yellow fever.
M.D. Grant, 30, yellow fever.
J. Steele, 21, yellow fever.
S. Graham, 28, yellow fever.
Child of R. Robinson, ..., yellow fever.
Child of Mr. Myers, 3, yellow fever.
Italian, unknown, yellow fever.
T. Jackson, 20, col., yellow fever.
G.W. Mossgrove, 25, congestion.

Mortuary Report for Galveston, for persons buried the 28th of September 1867:
George Stewart, 44, Alabama, yellow fever.
James McGuinil, 29, Ireland, yellow fever.
F.M. Cat, not known, U.S.
Two U.S. soldiers, disease not given.

Issue October 1, 1867
Letter from Houston, September 28, 1867: C.C. Beavans, the attentive manager of the Mason's News Depot, in this city, was taken with the fever this evening. The patrons of this depot will find Mr. Ernest Wagner (Grimes) ready to wait on them.

Today in the *News*, you announce Mr. J.E. Gregory, deceased, as father of Mr. E.C. Gregory. This is a mistake, as he is a younger brother of Mr. C.E. Gregory, who, at the present time, is on North with his family.

Capt. W.W. Purdom died here today. He is a brother of Maj. R.H. Purdom. Capt. Purdom is from Nashville, Tennessee; and at one time, was connected with the *Journal*, published in this city. By some mistake, Dr. Moody had his funeral notices printed and coffin ordered today. He was supposed to be dead, but revived. He is exceedingly low, and his life is despaired of. Dr. Moody was in charge of the city hospitals, and was a faithful physician in the discharge of his duties.

Dr. A.M. Barbisch, who was buried today, went down below Harrisburg to nurse his family, who were sick. While there he was taken ill, his body being brought here for interment.

The following are the interments for September 28th:
Jno. A. Allen, 24, typhoid fever.
Dr. A.M. Barbisch, 38, yellow fever.
Mrs. M.M. Anderson, 81, yellow fever.

... Darmon, ..., yellow fever.
Maximillian Loefler, 3, yellow fever.
Aug. Metze, 12, hem. kidneys.
Chas. Richter, 68, typhoid fever.
Jno. Kregar, 48, yellow fever.
Wm. Goldsmith, 18, yellow fever.
Henry Gerds, 4, cramp colic.
Cath McCarthy, 29, yellow fever.
B. Jacobs, 26, yellow fever.

Mortuary Report for Galveston, interments Sunday, September 29, 1867:
Mr. A.C. Ross, 33, Ohio, disease of the heart.
W.O. Hallauran, 26, Ireland, yellow fever.
John Welch, 30, U.S., yellow fever.
Mr. Sweeney, 32, Ireland, yellow fever.
John Stewart, 47, not known.
Joseph F. Baudenon, Galveston, not known.
James Cassidy, 25, American, yellow fever.
Charley Pierce, 24, Kentucky, yellow fever.
Infant of T.O. Moore, 1 hr., unknown, city.
Two U.S. soldiers, not given.

Interments for September 30th:
Mrs. Mary P. Johns, 22, Georgia, yellow fever.
Phil Stockton, colored, 2, U.S., yellow fever.
Henry Schneider, 30, Germany, yellow fever.
William Rodefeldt, 35, Germany, yellow fever.
John Wilkes, 28, Scotland, yellow fever.
Chas. E. Jones, 18, Texas, yellow fever.
Wm. Ruby, 45, England, yellow fever.
Wm. Horl, 20, Germany, yellow fever.
Geo. Johnson, 17, Hanover, yellow fever.
Gertrude Pierce, colored, 16 ms., city, teething.
One U.S. soldier.

We have to announce another severe loss to the B.B.B. & C.R.R., Mr. A.C. Ross, for many years Assistant Engineer under Col. Williams, died suddenly at 12 o'clock on Saturday night...

Issue October 2, 1867
Mortuary Report for Galveston, interments for Monday, October 1st:
A.W. Hughes, 27, Canada, inflammation of bowels.
J. Connally, 25, Ireland, yellow fever.
One U.S. soldier.

Died at Brenham, Texas, on the 26th of September of yellow fever, Thomas Henry Eldridge, aged 21 years. Norfolk, Virginia papers please copy.

Died at his residence in LaGrange, Texas, on Sunday, September 22nd, Benjamin Shropshire, aged 41 years, a native of Bourbon county, Kentucky, but a resident of Texas for sixteen years. Lexington and Paris, Kentucky papers copy.

Benjamin Shropshire, a native of Bourbon county, Kentucky, was left an orphan at the age of seven years, with limited means. At the age of about 18 years he entered Cumberland College, at Princeton, Kentucky, and by spending all of his patrimony completed his collegiate education, and prepared himself for the practice of law, and came to Texas in 1851, locating at LaGrange, where he practiced his profession successfully until the unfortunate political troubles commenced in our country, when he warmly espoused the Southern cause, and served most of the four years of the war in the Southern Army. He leaves a wife and four children... [note: condensed].

A letter from Bryan City, dated the 23rd inst., says: The fever is very bad at Millican and very fatal. There have been some thirty deaths in that place in the last ten days, and among the number I regret to say are Mr. Shepard and Mr. Thompson, of the firm of Marchbank & Co., Mr. W.W. Simmons, of Simmons & Smith, Dr. Hardy, Maj. Reynolds, hotel keeper, George Clements, of the livery stable, and Dr. Yates. The senior Mr. Haswell, of the firm of Haswell & Son, also his family and clerk are down, but late accounts say they are doing well. There are now not enough left to bury the dead. I am glad to say that Mr. Ed. Terrell, the efficient conductor of the T.C.R.R. has entirely recovered...

Sickness at Chappell Hill: We have been furnished with the following list of the names of persons who have died at Chappell Hill of the yellow fever to wit: E.A. Hammond, Mrs. E.A. Hammond, Mr. ... Hall, Sr. and wife, Mr. ... Hall, Jr. and wife, John Smith, Mr. Vail, Rev. Mr. Myers, Miss Julia Davy, Willie Davy, Mrs. Gale Aleck, J.M. Donald, Mrs. Wright, Mrs. Crawford, Miss Crawford, Mr. Hester, Jas. Degges, P.G. Smith, Mr. Smith, Henry Smith, Miss Melissa Smith, Miss Helen Smith, Mrs. Mary Drake, Miss Maggie Drake, Miss Gertrude Drake, John Drake, Jas. Drake, Mrs. Thos. Chappell, Mrs. Chadwick, Wesley Gardner, Henry Umblan, Mrs. Mary Glass, Miss Mollie Glass, Mrs. Thomas, Wm. Thomas, Dudley D. Haller, Gamlow Stanchfield, F.M. Williamson, Miss Emma Atkinson, John Crockett and wife, Henry N. Stone. Wm. Forshee and four other colored men. The entire number of cases of yellow fever in Chappell Hill up to September 29th was 125. Total number of deaths 49, or 2 deaths out of every 5 cases, which is indeed a most terrible fatality...

Issue October 3, 1867

Mortuary Report for Galveston for persons buried Wednesday, October 2nd:
Geo. Crawford, 24, Ireland, yellow fever.
Theo. Baker, 22, New Orleans, yellow fever.
Pat Callahan, 28, Ireland, not known.
Infant of W.D. Stone, 1 m., city, inflammation bowels.

Death at Millican: The *Bryan News Letter* of the 28th ult. gives the following list of deaths by yellow fever at Millican since its last issue:
Dr. Young; Mr. Domidy, clerk with Crenshaw; Mr. Fanner, clerk with Tabor & Luce; S. Bar, merchant; Jas. M. Shepherd, of Marchbanks & Co.; F.A. Thompson, of Marchbanks & Co.; Henry Fisher; Maj. Reynolds; Dr. O.P. Yates; Mr. Williamson, clerk of Loggins.

Sickness at Huntsville: The following is the list of deaths since the 19th, the date of the previous report: September 21st: Mrs. Penland, Mrs. J.P. Keneymore, and child of Mr. Nusbaum, all of yellow fever.
September 22nd: Negro woman, yellow fever.
September 23rd: Theodore Heflin and Mrs. Fullenwider, yellow fever.
September 24th: Capt. Keneymore and a child of Dr. Dixon, yellow fever.
September 25th: W.H. McWaters, Miss E. Price, Dr. W.P. Kittrell, one Federal soldier and a negro girl, all yellow fever.
September 26th: Miss Lizzie Stranahan, R. Burns, ... Jemison, Thos. Laprelle, all of yellow fever.
September 27th: James Logan, William Daniels and a negro man, all of yellow fever.
Dates unknown: Geo. Elmore and a negro named Harry, all of yellow fever. Among the young men who have lately died in the community, the loss of none will be more deeply felt than that of Theodore Heflin...
The death of Dr. W.P. Kittrell has cast a gloom over our community...
We regret to learn that Dr. G.M. Baker is seriously ill, six miles from town, at the place of Mr. Charles Abercrombie...

Issue October 4, 1867

We have the following from the *Norfolk Journal*: John Hobday, Sr., one of our very oldest citizens, and a soldier of the war of 1812-14, was "gathered to his fathers" yesterday morning at four o'clock, at his residence on North Court street. Mr. Hobday had arrived at the extreme age of eighty-seven years, and his decease was the result of natural decay. The departure of this venerable sire leaves but one other representative of the era of 1812 in our midst -- Mr. Charles A. Grice. The funeral of Mr. Hobday takes place from his residence [note: page folded].

Issue October 5, 1867

Died of yellow fever on Wednesday morning October 2d at 3 o'clock, Theodore Baker, aged 22 years, a native of New Orleans. *New Orleans Times* please copy.

Sherman Courier: Mrs. Beatty, a widow lady, aged between 40-50, residing in the neighborhood of Squire Noel's, in the North-west portion of this county, unfortunately killed herself on last Wednesday, in a most remarkable manner. It seems that she was in the act of getting on a horse when a common sewing needle, which was stuck in her dress, caught in the saddle and was driven in her body near the breast, slightly piercing her heart. She lived only about half an hour.

Sexton's report for Galveston, for Thursday and Friday, 3rd and 4th:
August McDonald, 1, Texas, cong. brain.
Mary Rodefeldt, 17, Germany, yellow fever.
Mary McErlain, 26, Ireland, yellow fever.
Geo. Barnett, 25, Ireland, yellow fever.
John Jones, 33, Germany, yellow fever.
Alice Honney, 2, Louisiana, pneumonia.
Onney Riley, 22, Texas, typhoid fever.
Unknown man found drowned.

Issue October 6, 1867

Brenham Mortuary Report from the commencement of the epidemic, furnished by Dr. J.S. Watkins: Strangler at Crumpler House, stage driver, do., Capt. Devine, U.S.A., S. Hagan, J.H. Beck, Mrs. J.H. Beck, in the country --- Ephraim, Thomas Eldridge, Miss Wilcox, Miner's child, D.C. McIntyre, Margaret McIntyre, Amanda McIntyre, Sallie McIntyre, Daniel McIntyre, Mrs. H.E. Lockett, --- Higgins, --- Putnam, --- Kolmy, Kolmy's child, Miss Mary Compton, in the country, --- Dwyer, Dwyer's son, negro in jail, Mrs. Powers, Mrs. D.W. Jones, Mrs. Souter, Mr. Souter, W.H. Farrell, Mrs. Breedlove, F. McNeese, a woman at Koch and Gehrman's, --- Ettinger, --- Boyle, Mrs. Boyle, --- Brenning, Mrs. Brenning, --- Williamson, W.H. Chadwick, Tobe Wallace, Mrs. R.P. Blount, Dr. Gilden's son, Mrs. J.P. Key, Frank Smith, Jno. Sherrill, Judge Stamps near Independence, --- Spears, J.H. Wheeler, Peter Crow, Judge Horton, Henry Stone, at Union Hill, Miss Rial, N. Rial, Dutch tailor, man at hospital, --- Brooker, --- Green, of Wood & Green, Richard Ford, --- Thompson, two children of Mr. Thompson's, --- Esterberg, Brenning's child, Miss Sansum, Miss Cook, --- Gehaman, Aycock, Aycock's son, in the country, --- Hammitt, Mrs. T. Ton, two men at Zeip's bakery, a painter at do., Dr. Violet, at Keke's, a German girl at Breedlove's, Lt. Lambert, --- Kline, George Racy, a negro at Dwyers, Capt. Walker, congestion of lungs, Mrs. Reddick, cong. bowels, Mrs. Watson, cong. brain, D. McCord, cong. brain,

Keke's daughter, diphtheria, Mrs. Thacker, unknown, Watson's child, unknown, Witteburg's child.

Sexton's report for Galveston, Saturday, September 5th:
John J. Kelley, 11 months, New York, dropsy of brain.
George E. Brandis, 15 months, Texas, cholera infantus.
C. Washington, 2 days, unknown.
Fritz Veschir, 30, Germany, yellow fever.

Issue October 8, 1867
Mortuary Report for Galveston, persons buried Monday 7th:
Chas. Ward, 1 week, yellow fever.
Chas. Schafer, 21, Germany, yellow fever.
J. Harkman, 23, Germany, yellow fever.
F. Jacobson, 24, Denmark, yellow fever.
R. O'Connor, 23, Ireland, yellow fever.
Dice Hall, 25, Texas, cancer.
R.D. Gownston, Texas, unknown.
Thos. Regan, 21, Ireland, chron. splenitis.

Sickness in the interior and Houston: A letter from Mr. H.L. Allan to Mr. Whitmarsh, President of the Houston Firemens Charitable Association, dated the 3d inst., says the mortality had increased in consequence of the Norther, and the new cases numbered thirty. At the Crumpler Hotel, there were a dozen sick. The following interments are given:
Dwyer's child, 10 years; — Elliot; Mrs. D. Ford, 28 years; Wm. Ridge, 27 years; Kollmey's child, 10 years; Mrs. Joseph Smith, 20 years; Strickland's child, 8 years; George Arrington, colored; .... Souters, colored; negro man, unknown. In addition, a lady, a stranger, and a negro were buried...

The *Telegraph* reports as follows: The following is the list of interments for Friday, October 4th:
Mrs. H. Hobaen, 34, yellow fever.
Simon Ehrenworth, 19, yellow fever.
Son of Col. Carter, 6, yellow fever.
Mary Williams, colored, 22, yellow fever.
Child of Mrs. Redsall, 12, yellow fever.
Mrs. Redsall, 45, yellow fever.
Child of Mr. Gibson, 4, yellow fever.
Child of Mrs. Kanivoski, 2 1/2, yellow fever.
Julia Mitchell, colored, 18, yellow fever.
Mrs. Gibson, 45, yellow fever.
...Col. Carter's whole family have been down, but all are reported convalescent but one child, Frank, who was buried on the 4th.

The *Telegraph* gives the following burial on the 3rd:
Mrs. Jas. Burrell, 25, yellow fever.
Henry Rosenfield, 27, yellow fever.
Frank Diamond, 2, yellow fever.
Jno. A. Diamond, 12, yellow fever.
R.S. Cuthbertson, 11, yellow fever.
Patrick O'Neal, 60, yellow fever.
Mrt. Eliza Praeger, 22, yellow fever.
Jacob Hirsch, 27, yellow fever.
Wm. H. Whalen, 9, yellow fever.
Mr. Dow, 28, yellow fever.
D. Jefferson, 9, yellow fever.
D.W.C.W. Castle, 23, yellow fever.
Child N. Jenkins, colored, 2, yellow fever.

There is a report here, founded upon a few words written on the back of a letter, that our fellow-citizen, Mr. A.B. Thompson, died at Chappell Hill a few days ago. We have waited two or three days with the hope that this report might prove to be untrue. But we are now without any such hope.

Two children of James H. Hughes, of Harrisburg, have died of yellow fever, namely Sue Eugenia and Jonathan Lowry, the former on the 26th September, aged 14 years and 11 months, the latter on the 28th of September, aged 12 years, 8 months.

Issue October 9, 1867
Mortuary Report for Galveston, for persons buried Tuesday, October 8, 1867:
Henry A. Swartout, 31, yellow fever.
Anna Voight, 42, heart disease.
Edward A. Brown, 22, from Houston.
Mary Hamburg, 15, yellow fever.
Safer Bohle, 63, yellow fever.

The following is a list of deaths from yellow fever at Chappell Hill from the 2nd to the 6th of October:
A.B. Thompson, Thos. Crawford, Chas. Carmer, R. Elgin, Mrs. R. Elgin, Carrol White, John D. Rogers, James D. Haynie, Phil Howerton, Miss Mary Junker, Miss --- Hall, Miss ... at Dr. Davis', Dr. McCartney.

From Houston: The list of interments for yesterday are as follows:
Mrs. M. Simpson, 25, yellow fever.
John D. Meneilley, 22, yellow fever.
John Dennis, 35, yellow fever.
Daughter Dechaumes, 10, yellow fever.

Child of Mr. Voight, 10, yellow fever.
Mrs. B. Jordan, 32, yellow fever.
Mrs. N. Brenson, 43, yellow fever.
Robert Killough, 27, yellow fever.
Charles Finkleman, 23, yellow fever.
Child A. Hadley, colored, 10, yellow fever.
J.L. Dunooski, 66, congestive fever.
   The following are the interments this morning:
Petters Vonters, 38, yellow fever.
Mr. Bexter, 35, yellow fever.
Hannah Patrouke, 23, yellow fever.
Mrs. Caroline Geiselman, 41, yellow fever.
O. Day, 45, yellow fever.
Lizzie Diamond, 7, debility.
   Two young men, well known in the city, Edward Brown, of the firm of
Harrell & Brown, and A.P. Pruitt, an attache of the H.&T.C.R.R., met near the
corner of Congress and Fannin streets yesterday afternoon, and it is said,
after a brief altercation of words, were drawn into a personal encounter, which
resulted in the death of the former and the dangerous wounding of the latter...

Issue October 10, 1867
Mortuary Report for Galveston buried Wednesday 9th:
Negro man, Michael, U.S., yellow fever.
Fred. Himb, 21, German, yellow fever.
Henry Hard, 33, England, yellow fever.
Man, unknown, German, yellow fever.
G.A. Pratt, 37, Vermont, yellow fever.
Aug. Hasselmier, 9, Galveston, yellow fever.
P.P. Wixon, 23, New York, yellow fever.
Mary Carville, 7, con. brain, Galveston.
Otto Harber, 1 day, not known, yellow fever.

Letter from Houston; the following is a list of interments for October 7th:
J. Baxbra, 25, yellow fever.
Peter Dougherty, 21, congestion brain.
Elizabeth Diamond, 3, gen. debility.
Sallie Frome, 16, yellow fever.
Robert Rogers, 35, yellow fever.
William Evans, 25, yellow fever.
Wife of Nat Wilson, ..., yellow fever.
Mary Buckholtz, 52, yellow fever.
James Clark, 27, yellow fever.
Jennett Jomes/Jones, 40, yellow fever.
Owen Rickmiles, 28, yellow fever.

Betsey Wallace, 35, yellow fever.
Two paupers, City Hospital, yellow fever.
Francis Repp, 10 mos., teething.
Mr. McQuinney, 35, chron. dys.
Mary Miller, 7, convulsions.
Child of Mrs. Mays, 1 week, convulsions.
Child of H. Wells, 6 weeks, convulsions.
There are several new cases reported today. Captain Hugh T. Scott has just died.

Mortality at Huntsville:
September 27th: Jas. Logan, Wm. Daniels, a negro man, child of Col. Neil, negro child, Amos, f.m.c., J.C. Outlaw, ... Slack, convict at penitentiary, ... Welch, ... Lockier; yellow fever. Thos. Bird, convict at penitentiary, killed.
September 28th: Henry Mosely, mortally stabbed; Mrs. Nusbaum, infant of Mr. Davidson, man at Murphy's Hotel; yellow fever.
September 29th: Child, name unknown, David Randolph, H. Gillespie; yellow fever.
September 30th: C.P. McRoy, Mrs. Kenedy, Dr. G.M. Baker, Wm. Birdwell, child of J. Rhodes, Henry Lee Hume, S.P. Butler, Miss Matilda Wynne; yellow fever.
October 1st: Mrs. Yoakum, Miss Kate Fullen, Caroline Wynne, (f.w.c.); Clinton Smith, child of Mrs. Burns, Tom Patterson, James Mitchell, Geo. Patterson, Wm. Mitchell; yellow fever.
October 3rd: Col. A.M. Branch, Martin Gibbs, Benton Oliphant, Rose, f.w.c., William Ferguson, Col. James Gillespie; yellow fever.
October 4th: Judge James Smither, Mrs. F.B. Bailey; yellow fever.
October 10th: Scotch child, negro woman, Rev. Mr. Fullenwider; yellow fever.
Dates unknown: George Elmore, and Harry, f.m.c.; yellow fever. Total number of deaths, yellow fever, 100; other diseases, 16.

Issue October 11, 1867
Letter from Concrete: John Bell killed Walt Edwards and Charley Thee. [note: condensed].

Died at Millican, September 29th, of yellow fever, Lizzie L., daughter of Geo. D. and Eliza Haswell.

    Died at Bryan, September 28th, of chronic diarrhea, George D., only son of Geo. T. and Susan Haswell.

Mortuary Report for Galveston for persons buried Thursday, October 10th:
Christian Schach, 21, typhoid fever.
Fritz Tiesan, 31, typhoid fever.

Bryan, October 6, 1867: The fever is still bad at Millican. The following are some of the deaths of last week: Dr. Bailey and Dr. J.J. Roberts, Mr. and Mrs. Campbell, Mrs. Bridge and her two children, Mrs. & Miss Bettie Simmons, James Swaine, the T.C.R.R. conductor. Miss Ella Yates, and two Miss Sawyers died here. They contracted the fever at Millican.

Houston, October 9, 1867: There were four additional interments after my letter was posted. There names are reported by the City Sexton as follows:
Robert Sayles, 35, yellow fever.
J. Haynes, colored, 42, yellow fever.
Pat Courtney, 31, yellow fever.
E. Greer, colored, 3, yellow fever.
  The interments up to the hour of mailing today (3 P.M.), are reported to be:
Hugh T. Scott, 35, yellow fever.
Emeline Faulnier, 22 mos., yellow fever.
Cora Dean, 21, yellow fever.
Mr. Greer, yellow fever.
Robert Miller, 7, yellow fever.
Mr. Goldsmith, 16, yellow fever.
William Casala, 20, yellow fever.
Jordan, colored, 50, yellow fever.
Infant of Mrs. Burbank, 2 m., yellow fever.
Robert Robinson, 35, yellow fever.
Patience Prindle, 18, dropsy.
  Capt. Hugh Scott, whose death was briefly noticed by me yesterday, was well known in Houston, where, during and subsequent to the war, he made a large number of acquaintances. He was, I believe, a native of Tennessee, and came here during the war as an officer, and was assigned to duty in Houston by Gen. Magruder. Before the war closed, he was married to Miss Milby, a daughter of Wm. Milby...

Issue October 12, 1867
Mortuary Report for Galveston, for October 11th:
Lochlin Campbell, 29, Scotland, yellow fever.
Francis Ward, 24, New York, yellow fever.
George Lane, 21, U.S., yellow fever.
Samuel Porter, 45, U.S., yellow fever.
Negro child, unknown.
Alice Lee, 3, Texas, dysentery.

The following is the list of interments at Houston for October 10th for the day previous:
Calvin Holt, 29, yellow fever.

Willie Davis, colored, 11, yellow fever.
James Clark, 27, yellow fever.
H.T. Scott, 35, yellow fever.
Arad Goldsmith, 16, yellow fever.
Wm. Casala, 20, yellow fever.
Miss Cora Dean, 21, yellow fever.
Emeline Sauliner, 22 mos., yellow fever.
Michael Greer, 28, yellow fever.
Robert Miller, 7, yellow fever.
Jourdan, colored, 50, yellow fever.
Robert Robertson, 35, chronic dysentery.
Lawrence Dowling, 50, phthisis.
Patience Prindle, 18, dropsy.
Child of Mrs. Burbanks, 2 mos., diar.

We are informed that young Prewitt, who was so severely wounded in his recontre with Ed. Brown, is not expected to recover. At the present writing, 7 P.M., the 9th, his life is despaired of. He is said to be suffering under brain fever, caused by a severe contusion of the head... Since the above was put in type, we learn by a passenger on the steamer from Houston that Mr. Prewitt died yesterday about 11 A.M.

Issue October 13, 1867
The death of Col. J.J. Diamond, after the loss of so many of his family, presents one of those instances of total family desolation which have so often attended the ravages of the present epidemic... Col. Diamond had lost three of his children before his own death, and a fourth child was buried the same day with himself...

Bastrop: ...James M. Turner and lady died there last month from what was regarded as yellow fever. They had come from the infected districts. Mr. Foushee and Mr. Hink, who died above Bastrop, were also from the infected districts. Dr. Sayres, reports that Mr. & Mrs. Organ, Mrs. Thompson and Willie and Mattie Aldridge and Mr. Evans, who had the fever, were from below...

From the *Houston Telegraph* of October 11th: Mortuary Report; the following is the list of interments for Thursday, October 10, 1867:
Miss E. Diamond, 19, yellow fever.
M. McDougahl, 38, yellow fever.
John Bergin, 19, yellow fever.
Catherine Williams, 32, yellow fever.
Anstinia Hirsch, 8, yellow fever.
Col. J.J. Diamond, ..., yellow fever.
A.P. Pruitt, ..., gunshot wound.

Child at A. Coleman, 5, convulsions.
Child of Mr. Ewings, ..., no certificate.
Man unknown, ..., no certificate.
Man unknown, ..., no certificate.

Victoria: The *Lavaca Commercial* of the 14th says the yellow fever was epidemic in Victoria. It publishes the following list of deaths, which includes but few of the Germans who have died, and none of the colored people: Mr. Ripley, Rosa Hardy, Mrs. Ross, Willie Boreland, Willie Mitchell, Mr. Silvestine, Sarah Kane, Mrs. Coffee (not fever).

Issue October 15, 1867

Letter from Concrete on yellow fever in Victoria: Dr. Ragland is dead; Samuel Gaylord is dead; Mrs. Addison Hall is dead; Col. Stapp is sick, his son dead; Mr. Womack is recovering; his daughter is dead; Rev. Mr. Thurmond is dead; Mr. Glass is very ill; Mr. Mitchell's son Willie is dead. Many others are dead, whose names my informant did not recollect, a great many children have died.

Died at Galveston, September 13, 1867, of yellow fever, Emanuel Joseph Dalton, aged 4 years, oldest child of E.R. and Caroline Dalton. Savannah, Georgia and Richmond, Virginia papers please copy.

The *Waco Register* learns that a young man named Anderson, shot and killed a man named Varnell, at Palton's Mill, in McLennan county, a few days since. They met as strangers, got into a conversation, quarreled, and fought, with the result just stated. Anderson is still at large.

The *Waxahachie Argus* says John Smith was murdered a few days since, at his house, by a traveling stranger, calling himself Robert Smith. No cause for the murder is known, unless the murderer wished to obtain a very fine horse belonging to the deceased. The murderer has not yet been arrested.

Mortuary Report for Galveston for Monday, October 14th:
Peter Charlotte, 34, France, yellow fever.
Edward Ochbrih, 5 1/2, Texas, typhoid fever.

The following list of interments, after three o'clock to-day, is furnished by the City Sexton [Houston]:
Mrs. Willers, 63, yellow fever.
John Griffin, 24, yellow fever.
Alfred Bessenger, 51, yellow fever.
Alice Smith, 12, yellow fever.
Mr. Warren, 40, yellow fever.

P. H. Glaze, M.D., 60, consumption.
Mr. Welsch, no certificate.
Mexican, no certificate.

There were only four interments yesterday; all yellow fever. The *Telegraph* of Saturday morning gives the following as the burials on Friday:
John Prain, 45, yellow fever.
James Moran, 30, yellow fever.
Son of Mr. Jourdan, 11, yellow fever.
Child of Moses, col., 18m, yellow fever.

Issue October 16, 1867
Mortuary Report for Galveston:
John King, 21, U.S., yellow fever.
Mr. Meally, 20, Ireland, from amputation.
W.H. Kinkard, 22, Illinois, yellow fever.
Mary A. Landwith, 8 months, Texas.

Very many old friends and acquaintances will be pained to hear of the death of Mr. Joseph H. Cherry, who for many years, has been engineer of the Morgan line of boats.

Issue October 17, 1867
Letter From Huntsville: I was led into an error in my last, in stating that Mrs. D.G. Campbell, a daughter of Mrs. Yoakum, was among the dead. The lady is alive and getting well. The blunder was caused by negroes reporting her buried in the night, to prevent the children knowing anything about their mother's death. I made no authentic inquiries, but took the statement for a fact. I make the correction with unfeigned pleasure.

The epidemic seems to have run its course here. One death here this morning, Jo. F. Rhodes; one yesterday, the wife of Dr. Heflin of Andrew Female College; and one the day before, Mrs. Evans, an old lady.

You were mistaken in saying the new Financial Agent of the penitentiary had taken the fever; it was Dr. D.C. Dickson; the new one, Major Garretson, not having yet taken hold, owing to Dr. D's sickness. Col. Gillespie, the Superintendent, also Gov. T's appointee, died of the disease some days since...

Died on Thursday, September 26th, of yellow fever, near Brenham, Henry Napier Stones, aged 23 years, oldest son of Ben and Mary J. Stones of Brenham, Texas. Nashville, Tennessee papers please copy.

Died in this city at 2 o'clock P.M., yesterday, the Rev. John Owen, acting rector of Trinity Church.

The Rev. John Owen, the minister who had in charge the congregation of the Rev. B. Eaton, in this city, during the past two or three months, died yesterday evening, and is to be buried this morning, from the Trinity Church. In the short space of time Mr. Owen has been here, he has endeared himself to his congregation by his zealous and faithful ministrations to the distressed, the sick and dying, who have sought his counsel and assistance.

Mortuary Report for Galveston for October 16th:
Charity Miles, 35, yellow fever, Georgia.
Unknown man, 45, yellow fever, U.S.
Edward Bohme, 42, typhoid, German.
Paulinest Pecklape, 55, inflammation of bowels, German.

Our Galveston readers will be deeply pained to learn that their old fellow citizen, Mr. Michael Seeligson, is dead. He died on the 9th inst. at Goliad, where he has resided for the last 14 years. He had been sick with the yellow fever about one week. There was no physician in Goliad experienced in the treatment of the disease. Mr. Seeligson was one of the earliest citizens of Galveston, having made his residence here as early as 1839. He was elected Mayor of the city in 1853, but resigned before the expiration of his term, and removed to Goliad... He was in his 70th year at the time of his death. He left a wife and seven children to mourn their heavy loss.

THE FEVER AT VICTORIA, Clinton, October 12, 1867:
Eds. News: I herewith send you a list of interments at Victoria, from the advent of yellow fever until yesterday morning—83 deaths. There may be cases not reported, and the list may be incomplete and defective, but it is the best I can get. I have no report from the U.S. troops encamped at Freedom's Lake, six miles below Victoria, on the west side of the Guadalupe. You will observe Maj. Lathrop has fallen a victim; he was respected and esteemed as a judicious and humane officer. Dr. John H. Ragland was one of the most self sacrificing and charitable citizens.

Mrs. Viola Case and Mrs. Lowe have recovered and are waiting on the sick; Mr. Glass is recovering, Mr. Womack quite ill; Loring Wheeler convalescent. Mrs. A.P. Cunningham very sick; Mr. Perry, formerly of Mobile, and Mr. Gervis, Austrian, recovering; Mrs. Beaty and family all recovering; Mr. Mitchell and wife both sick. Two hundred or more cases under treatment. Yours in haste, L.

There were 88 interments at Victoria, up to Friday morning, 11th inst., as follows: Miss Mattie Hubble, Rev. George C. Moore, J.A. Rupley, Benj. Scott, Mrs. Victor M. Rose, Miss Rosa Hardy, Willie Borland, H.S. Gaylord,

Louis Silverstein, L. Kahn, Miss Sarah Kahn, E. Fitz, Mrs. E. Fitz, W. Mitchell, Mrs. A. Hall, A.P. Cunningham, Mrs. Harrison, W. Womack, Mrs. L. Coffee, Miss L. Coffee, Rev. O.B. Adams, J. Vanderburg, Rev. J.H. Thurmond, Dr. John B. Ragland, infant of Mr. Mitchell, Maj. Lathrop, U.S.A., post commandant; A.S. Crocker, superintendent of railroad; A.B. Hersaldt, Mr. Rosenthal, H. Horwitz, Mrs. Miller, J. Beohn, H. Fischer, E. Luter, M. Luter, August Luter, — Luter, Fannie Luter, Miss Luter, A.J. Stamm, Mrs. Shier, Mr. Wallace, registrar, Mrs. Rouff, Mrs. Shroder, C. Schmidt, Mr. Kaiser, Rev. Mr. Schall, two children of Mr. Schall, child of John Gild, Mrs. F. Mack, Miss Mary Walker, U.S. soldier, Mrs. G. Peifer, negro Jeff, E. Voight, — Smith, Mrs. Kahn, child of Mr. Ditiechs, Keneck's child, Mr. Oblitz, Grooej's boy, F. Palm, one from hospital, Mr. Pinneman, German boy, Mrs. Schroll, Mrs. Schiner, C. John, Mary Klumdenst, one Mexican, one Mexican child, five negroes, Mrs. Spicy, colored, Mrs. Fidler, Geo. Washington, colored, C. Knodge, Mrs. Petticolas and child, Mr. G. Floyd.

Issue October 18, 1867
Mortuary Report for Galveston for October 17th:
Rev. J. Owen, 65, England, jaundice.
George T. Parker, 45, swamp fever.
Mrs. Caroline Hergesele, 32, Germany, yellow fever.
Unknown man, found dead on the beach.

Maj. S.H. Lathrop, U.S.A., 35th Inf., commanding post at Victoria, died at that place on the 7th of yellow fever. He was a native of Maine.

Tribute of Respect for Rev. John Owen.

Issue October 19, 1867
Mortuary Report for Galveston for October 18th:
Fred Niederman, 18, yellow fever, Germany.
Emiline Bowers, 18, Lock Jaw, Galveston.

We have been informed by Mr. Thomas L. Gillespie, a friend of the deceased, that Patrick McCaffrey, a native of Ireland and citizen of New Orleans, a seaman, who last boarded at the corner of Celeste & Tchoupitoulas St's., while a passenger on board the steamer *J.H. Whitelaw*, jumped overboard and was drowned near Galveston, Texas, on the evening of October 16, 1867.

Issue October 20, 1867
Mortuary Report for Galveston for October 18th:
Mary Jones, colored, 40, U.S., consumption.
Peter Campe, 19 months, Ky., teething.

Judge E.F. Buckner, formerly of Louisville, but for many years a resident of Mississippi, committed suicide at Brandenburg, KY, a day or two since, near the residence of Mr. Nathan Shrewsbury, where he was boarding, by blowing his brains out with a double-barrel shot gun, which he fired attaching the trigger to a twig, having placed the muzzle against his head. The deceased was about sixty-five years of age, and had a daughter living in Houston, Texas.

Issue October 22, 1867

Suicide of Judge Buckner. Particulars of the event.

From the Louisville *Courier*. A special dispatch in the *Courier* a few days since, from Brandenburg, mentions the suicide of an aged and estimable gentleman, Judge E.F. Buckner. Letters in yesterday's mail give us some particulars of the melancholy occurrence.

The deceased was a brother of Col. Robert Buckner, formerly jailer of J[?]son county. He resided one time in Mississippi, but more recently in Texas...

Judge Buckner came to Kentucky some three months since to see some relatives in Meade county, and took boarding in the house of Nathan Shrewsbury, near Brandenburg. His health seemed to get worse. His body and mind became morbidly sensitive.

On Tuesday morning last, he took a shot gun to his head. He died almost instantly.

In the trunk of the deceased was a letter... I have no country, no family, no home, no money, no hope, no health...

Obituary. Died, at Sterling, Robertson county, Texas, September 23, 1867, B. Frank Steele, after an illness of a few days. Mr. Steele was born in West Liberty, Ohio co., Virginia, April 23, 1843...

We learn that Mr. C.M. Seymour, who was buried yesterday in our cemetery, was a native of New York and 40 years of age. He has left a wife and two children to mourn their sudden bereavement.

Issue October 23, 1867

Mr. L.L. Bailey was killed on the 24th ult. near Clarksville by Hugh Jones.

Died of diphtheria near Hempstead on Monday the 14th inst., Harry, youngest son of Col. Jos. McCarty, aged 3 years and 6 months.

Mortuary Report for Galveston for October 22nd:
John Shoult, 29, Germany, yellow fever.
Mary Jane Weeks, 6 days, city, hives.
Unknown man, 41, unknown, cong. fever.

O.L. Daly, 29, Ireland, yellow fever.
Louis Chas. Frederick, 6 w., city, jaundice.

Robbery and murder. A letter in the *Clarksville Standard* says Col. Hugh Rogers was met by three robbers in Davis county, not long since, taken from his horse, blindfolded, carried into the woods, tied to a tree and robbed of his money, watch, horse, and two mules... They also brought a negro man and tied him up, shot him dead and took his mule.

Killed — On Sunday evening, Sergeant Reagan, of the U.S.A., stationed at this place, shot and killed Ed. Russell, a soldier. Insubordination is reported to have been the cause. We know nothing of the particulars.

Issue October 24, 1867

Jefferson Texas Clarion of the 9th: On Saturday morning last, Lt. Allanson, commander at this post, despatched a wagon load of supplies for the use of the forces at Boston, in Bowie county. The wagon and team were guarded by Corp's Hardenbrook, Gavin, and the teamster Mooney. The team and escort reached Douglassville in safety, but after proceeding about a mile or such a matter beyond Douglassville, in Davis county, they were attacked by a squad of men... the teamster, Mooney, killed dead, one of the corporals fatally wounded and left for dead...

Death of D.B. Bonfoey — We have heretofore stated that this man, the murderer of Capt. Fowler, of Jefferson, had been admitted to bail by Judge Winston Banks, at Clarksville, in the sum of $12,000. We now learn from the *Marshall Republican* that he gave the bond, returned to his home in Marshall, and died on Thursday night, Oct. 10th. The *Republican* says his death was caused by mental depression. It will be remembered that his wife was cruelly murdered in bed, at Marshall, soon after the murder by Bonfoey...

Our dispatches bring the sad and startling intelligence of the death of George Wilkins Kendall, recently, at his residence near Boerne, Kendall county in this State. In him the *New Orleans Picayune* loses one of its founders and its chief...

Mortuary Report for Galveston for October 23rd:
John Quin, 35, Ireland, yellow fever.
William Drury, 57, Ireland, chronic dysentery.
Antoine Arnold, 43, yellow fever.

Issue October 29, 1867

Mortuary Report for Galveston for October 28th:
Thomas, colored, Alabama, yellow fever.

Mr. Jackson, U.S.
Isaac January, colored, not known.
Bernard F. Rickter, 2 years 3 months, Galveston, teething

Issue October 30, 1867
LETTER FROM HUNTSVILLE, October 24, 1867:
   Although yellow fever, as an epidemic, has run its race in our village, there are occasional new cases occurring every day or two. The wife of Gen. Besser died with it on the 21st inst., and Mrs. John Buckley on the 23rd. I was surprised to hear yesterday that Mr. Alt. Richardson, of Houston, who was "civilized" in the Bayou city years ago, and has been here some days on a visit to his brother was down with the disease, but doing well at present... Business continues at a stand still. No schools, and with the decease of President Heflin and Madame Otey, both of Andrew Female College, it will be a task to set that institution at work again soon...

Died at Brashear City, Louisiana, October 25th, with the prevailing epidemic, William H. Eastesbrooks. The deceased was a nephew of Capt. J.Y. Lawless and son of Mrs. Mary Eastesbrooks of Bristol, R.I....

Died on the 14th inst. of congestive chill at the residence of his uncle, Col. Terry M. Bryan, across the bay, in this county, Stephen F.A. Bryan, aged 27. He was the oldest son of Austin Bryan.

The Indians killed an old man named Leeper and the wife of Mr. Hamilton near Weatherford about two weeks since. They took off two of the Hamilton children and left a third severely wounded. They also wounded Mr. James Hefflinger so severely that it is thought he will die.

Bastrop. The *Advertiser* says... Mr. Turner died there of yellow fever, as was supposed, on the 15th ult., since which time there has been but one death of a citizen from any cause...

Suicide: A man named John Handley was found drowned in about 4 feet of water near the New Wharf, yesterday morning, his hands and feet tied...

Issue November 1, 1867
Out West. Concrete, October 25, 1867. Eds. News-- On the 12th inst., at Mission Valley store, Neall Brown was killed by Wiley Pridgeon... Neall Brown was a fine looking youth of 19 years. He fell dead, shot through the heart, at his mother's feet, in his own yard.

Issue November 2, 1867

The fever at Victoria:

Oct. 13-Mr. Frederich, D. Crampton, J. Hahn, Mrs. C. <u>Steiner</u>, child of H. <u>Mitchell</u>.

13th-child of B. Owen.

14th-J. Pilgram, Miss R. Linch, Mrs. Hannecke, Miss A. Schrader, Mrs. J.G. Krapf.

15th-Mrs. Jantsch, Miss M. Jantsch, C. Grehmeier, Mrs. Badnoche.

16th-L. Earnst, U.S. soldier, C. <u>Steiner</u>, J. Golla.

17th Miss A. Thomas, Mrs. D. <u>Stapp</u>, Miss O Finger.

18th-child of F. Waschko, H. Becker, Miss M. Becker, Miss F. Spawa, F. Wacker, L. Gethleman.

19th-Mrs. Newman, Mrs. Reiman, Miss R. <u>Stapp</u>.

20th-Miss A. Porch, child of M. Schafer, W.T. <u>Mitchell</u>, Theo Lesage, Fiedler, U.S. soldier.

21st-Mrs. J. Szowr; P. Scheiner.

22d-Child of J. Fritz, Mrs. Lt. Cloudius, M. Wilmar, Miss Bilstein.

23d-R. White.

24th-P. Sitterb, L. Lythe, G. Schellentrager, L. Cockes, J. Lapez, and 14 negroes.

Issue November 3, 1867

Died in Robertson county, October 5th, 1867, Mary Ellen, aged 3 years, daughter of Mrs. Sallie A. & Dr. W.H. Farmer.

Fever in Eureka -- The *Houston Telegraph* of the 18th says: We are informed by Dr. Riddle, who was a part of the time practicing physician at Eureka, that the following persons have died there since the epidemic:

B. F. Smith, 23.

Peter McElvaine, 25.

Martha Trim, 12.

Mr. T. Trim, 48.

John Simon, 60.

Wm. Davis, alias G. Thomas, 24.

Neal McKeithan, 14.

Geo. Palmer, 16.

Dennis Duggan, 34.

colored child, 18 months.

John Shively, of Nelson, Winconsin [sic], went into his field last week, and opening a stock of wheat, found it wet. He said he would look at the other and if that was wet too, he would hang himself. It was wet, and he shot the top of his head off.

Issue November 6, 1867

Waco Register: A sprightly little son of Dr. J.M. Moore, of Owensville, was killed in a very distressing manner on the 30th ult. The little boy was with his father at a saw mill near town, and just as the engine started the boy was in the act of getting over one of the large bands. He was caught up and carried over the wheel with such force as to completely sever the head from the body. He was about six years old.

Navasota Mortuary List. The following list contains the names of those who have died in the city during the prevailing epidemic up to the present date.
July: Girl child of Sam Moore's, freedman, died July 27th, 1867; girl child of Dick Slaven, date unknown.
August: Mr. Walker's daughter, August 5th; Stevens, a youth at Mrs. Cade's, August 9th; Capt. B. Donnelly, August 15th; Thomas Thorp/Thorn, August 16th; Bennerman, stranger, August 19th; Dr. J.W. Russell, August 24th; James [note: page folded] Cook, August 24th; Kate, child of Fred Miller, August 24th; Cornelia Buffington, August 26th; Peggy, freedwoman, August 26th; John Smith, freedman, August 27th; John Giesler, August 28th; John W. Cook; Miss Jessie Williams, August 30th; Mrs. Woodward, August 31st.
September: P. Thompson, Sept. 2nd; Stanhope Smith, Sept. 3rd; Mrs. J.R. Goodwin, Sept. 3rd; Jack Cole, Sept. 3rd; Wm. R. Jones, Sept. 3rd; Jesse Goodwin, Sept. 3rd; W.J. Jones, Sept. 4th; Jesse Tubb, Jr., Sept. 5th; Dr. J. Hamilton Jones, Sept. 6th; Mr. Davis, writing master, Sept. 7th; Mary, German girl, Sept. 7th; Wm. Cook, Sept. 7th; Charles Fox, Sept. 7th; Charles Baptist, German, Sept. 5th; Sam Cook, Sept. 7th; Mr. Miller, German, Sept. 7th; Ferdinand Miller, German, Sept. 7th; Henry Swift, Sept. 7th; Miss Smith, Sept. 7th; Miss Carrie Smith, Sept. 7th; D.D. Greer, Sept. 8th; Dr. Beasly, Sept. 8th; J. Goodman, Sept. 8th; Miss E. Williams; Miss Ann Cook, Sept. 8th; Col. Morse, Sept. 8th; Franklin Viegel, Sept. 8th; Herman Viegel, German, Sept. 8th; J.E. Williams, Sept. 9th; C.C. Bass, Sept. 9th; Allen Post, Sept. 9th; Dick Morris, Sept. 9th; Robt. Dixon, Sept. 9th; freedman (name unknown), Sept. 9th; Mr. Roberts (telegraph office) Sept. 9th; George (Mexican), Sept. 9th; Mr. Wadlington, Sept. 9th; Annie N. Ireson, Sept. 1st; Charles Priest, Sept. 5th; Mrs. J. Miskell, Sept. 2nd; Gustave Schrader, Sept. 10th; Wm. Pye, Sept. 10th; Dr. A. Campbell, Sept. 10th; German, unknown, Sept. 10th; Wm. Bass, Sept. 10th; Mrs. Dr. P.H. Smith, Sept. 11th; Mrs. Wadlington, Sept. 11th; Frank Smith, Sept. 11th; two freedmen, Sept. 9th; Frenchman, name unknown, Sept. 9th; Mercer Cordios, Mexican, Sept. 10th; John Hart, Sept. 10th; H. Ballinger, Sept. 12th; Tommie Blackburn, Sept. 12th; Mr. Taylor, Sept. 12th; Rufus Moore, Sept. 13th; Ella Fisher, Sept. 13th; Mrs. Tubb, Sept. 13th; Mrs. L.F. Hamilton, October 1st; E.B. Alston, Sept. 14th; Wm. H. Shelton, Sept. 14th; J.R. Goodwin, Sept. 14th; Belle Harris, Sept. 14th; Mr. Musgrove, Sept. 14th; Mrs. Beasly, Sept. 15th; D.E. Harris, Sept. 15th; Lucy Harris, Sept. 15th; Mrs. Lewellyn, Sept. 15th; Mrs. Musgrove, Sept. 15th;

George Dunaway, Sept. 15th; Eugene Freeman, Sept. 15th; Mrs. Clarke, Sept. 15th; colored child, Sept. 16th; Jim George, freedman, Sept. 16th; freedman, name unknown, Sept. 16th; Kate Davis, Sept. 17th; John Ade, Sept. 17th; Griffe, colored child, Sept. 17th; E. Ackerman, Sept. 17th; Col. E.P. Blackburn, Sept. 18th; James Williams, Jr., Sept. 18th; Mrs. Gillen, Sept. 18th; Miss Jennie Moore, Sept. 20th; Miss Ann Greer, Sept. 20th; Miss M. McCarty, Sept. 21st; Mittie Goodwin, Sept. 31st; David Cook, Sr., Sept. 21st; Mr. Wharton, Sept. 21st; Eugen Wohl, Sept. 21st; Sol Brown, Sept. 22nd; Jack, freedman, Sept. [??]; Jacob, freedman, Sept. 24th; Mrs. E.D. Johnson, Sept. 24th; Mrs. Brown, Sept. 25th; freedman at Bennet's, Sarah A. Brown, Sept. 26th, John Harris, Sept. 26th; China Harris, Sept. 27th; T.W. Brown, Sept. 27th; Mrs. T.S. Nettles, Sept. 27th; Tom Nettles, Sept. 28th; Mr. Goodman's child, Sept. 27th; Mollie Stevens, Sept. 28th; Mrs. Goodman, Sept. 28th; Mrs. Susan Harris, Sept. 29th; Miss Mary Godsey, Sept. 29th; L. Rainey, freedman, Sept. 29th; Noah Tabb, freedman, Sept. 29th; Mrs. Ashforth, Sept. 20th; ___ Stewart, Sept. 30th; child of Mr. Kintz, Sept. 30th; Thomas Cook, Sept. 30th; Kidd, freedboy, Sept. 30th; Hannah Botts, freedwoman, Sept. 11th.

October: Dr. Paul Smith, Oct. 1st; Mrs. M.A. Glass, Oct. 2nd; Mrs. Jane Ross, Oct. 3rd; Dr. Pryor H. Smith, Oct. 5th; ___ Clark, Oct. 8th; Calvin Huckaby, Oct. 9th; ___ Farley, Oct. 10th; Child, colored, Oct. 7th; ___ Dennis, Oct. 7th; Mrs. Godse[?], Oct. 12th; Mrs. McEachern, Mr. Walthal, Martha, colored, Oct. 13th; J.A. Winders and child of W.M. Stacy, Oct. 17th; Mrs. Tom Clarke, Oct. 16th; A. Ireson, Oct. 19th; Gen. T.E. Blackshear, Mary McCann, Oct. 21st; Thomas Lyle, Oct. 22nd; Neal McCann, Oct. 16th; J. McCann, Oct. 24th; child of Mrs. Huckaby, L.L. Singletary, freed boy at Newbrans, Oct. 25th.

It will be understood that our city has had no sexton during the epidemic; that being the case, there are a great many we have not made note of. We trust if it is not correct, that someone will give us a correct statement, for our next issue, of those we have omitted.

The following names were handed in after the above list was in type: Mr. McEachern, Welcome, colored, Oct. 14th; Eppy McEachern, Oct. 17th; E.R. Brigancy, Oct. 14th; Jas Cane, date unknown; Mrs. Lucy Atchinson, Oct. 22nd; Miss Delia Lowry, Oct. 23rd; L.F. Hamilton, Oct. 28th.

BRENHAM MORTUARY REPORT, from 11th August to 18th October, 1867:
August 11th: J. Marks, died at Crumpler House.
September: Sept. 4th, Ephraim, an Israelite, died at Sam Levinson's; Sept. 6th, Shyhagin, a saloon keeper, died at the McIntyre Hotel; Sept. 8th, G. Razy, a carpenter, at Mrs. Sherroll's; Sept. 12th, Shwizer, a stage driver, at Crumpler House; Sept. 13th, Mrs. D.W. Jones, Brenning's child, and a German woman at Koch's; Sept. 15th, Frank McNeese; Sept. 16th, Capt. Walker, at Crumpler House, Wilder, a carpenter, at Keeke's, Mrs. Reddick; Sept. 17th, Kline, a carpenter, Mrs. Thompson's child; Sept. 18th, Mr. Boyle,

Mrs. Brenning; Sept. 19th, John Brenning, a gunsmith; Sept. 20th, Mullens, express agent, Maj. Jas. H. Beck, Mrs. Thetis Power; Sept. 21st, Aemil Kreith, at Giess', Mrs. Breedlove, Mr. Winkle, little girl at Boyle; Sept. 22nd, Mr. Dwyer; Sept. 23rd, G. Souter; Sept. 24th, D.C. McIntyre, W.H. Chadwick, Wm Pritman, Ida Ryol, Mr. Williamson, E.T. Terrell, H. Higgins, Frank Bein, Mr. Loftis, blacksmith at Souter's, Mr. Ettinger; Sept. 25th, Mrs. Blount, Dr. Eddins; Sept. 46th [sic], Peter Crow, Mr. Taylor, Noah Ryol, Margaret McIntyre, Thos. Eldridge, Mrs. H.E. Lockett, Tobe Wallace, Henry Stones, Mrs. Boyle, Witteberg's boy; Sept. 27th, Amanda McIntyre, Kolny's son, Miss Sanderson, Wheeler, a carpenter, son of D.C. McIntyre; Sept. 28th, Mrs. Tonn, Mr. Sherroll; Sept. 29th, Mrs. J. Smith, J.M. Spears, G.W. Horton, John Dwyer, Robert Ford, John Green, Mr. Moodyman, Laura Sanderson; Sept. 30th, Hammett, a carpenter, Thompson's child, Mr. Booker, man at Trumbull's warehouse.

Oct. 1, Mrs. S.G. Souther, Mr. Gehrman, Mr. Dwyer, Mrs. Ledgerman. Oct. 3rd, Mr. Elliott, at Brophy's, Mrs. Ford, Wm Ridge, Kolmy's child, S.M. Strickland, Sr., S.M. Strickland, Jr., Thomas Campbell, Wm Banding. Oct 5th, Mrs. R. Ford and her child, a German girl, at hospital. Oct. 6th, Harriet McIntyre, Captain N.B. Roff, Wm Sedgwick, brakeman on W.C.R.R. Oct. 7th, Joshia Barnett. Oct 8th, Hammet, Weekmaster, Mr. & Mrs. McFarland and child, Mrs. Bookr, Dr. Kay, Mr. Cole. Oct 10th, Mr. McFatter, Mrs. Vanness. Oct. 11th, Mr. Mayfield, a saddler, Mrs. Wm Ridge, Miss Witteberg, ___ Barnes. Oct. 13th, Geo Barnett. Oct. 15th, Preston Gilder. Oct. 16th, N.H. Porter, James Blount, Rogers' child. Oct. 17th, Dr. Rhodes, Mr. Hammond, and Mr. McIntyre, at hospital. Oct. 18th, Mr. Fisher.

To the above let us add the following, the precise date of whose deaths we have not obtained: Mr. Thompson, Mr. Aycock, Mr. Booker, Frank Smith, sister-in-law and step-son of J.L. Miner, a German woman at Breedloves's, Tom, the Wild Irishman, Lieut. Lambert and Mr. Green, partner of Dr. Warren...

The fever at Rio Grande City. Mr. VanMerick sends us the following list of those who have died up to the 16th inst. Anselmo Reyes, Mrs. Anselmo Reyes, son and daughter, Dr. Reiley, W.S. Garner, Albert, a Maximilian soldier, Wasson, do, Mr. Forbes, a Q.M. clerk, Dorvotes Elisondo, Refugio Guiturres, Jose Ma. Garza, Antonio Topia, Rafel Cortes and two children, Quintara ___, Jr., Dna. Tiburcio Cenel, Dna. Cecelia Marulanda, son of [?], Augustin Villarial, Mrs. Salinas. [note: the list contains more names that are illegible]. *Corpus Christi Advertiser.*

FROM BROWNSVILLE: The *Rio Grande Courier* of the 17th, contains further particulars of the storm of the 7th... The following is a list of killed and wounded at Brownsville: Killed: M. Diamond, Filmono Raladez, Juan Gonzales de Gongosa, Pablo Major, Alveda Morton, Margt. O'Hara, a Mexican woman and baby, names unknown, three others, names unknown, and a man named Tucoman who died of his wounds. Wounded: Somers Kinney, leg broken, Antonio Espinosa, Vicente Garcia, San Juana Flores, Helena Portillo, Petra Hernandez, Francisco Peres, Dolores Pefia, Francisco Fernandez, Zepeenia Mondosa, Francisco Galavez, Juana Porea, Bernardo Conde, Frank Brown, Luz Pefia, Francisco Mola. Five others, names unknown, badly wounded, and over 40 others more or less injured...

Below we give a list of persons supposed to have been lost at Brazos: Harris Blakesly and wife, Mrs. Cornelia White, Henry Vanhusen, Byrsold, Jack Anderson, George ..., late member of Battery I 1st U.S. Artillery, Mrs. Fischer, Mrs. Meade and child, James Sales, mate of schooner *Volumnia*, Harry, sailor, and four soldiers of Co. B 41st U.S. Inf... On the above the *Corpus Advertiser* makes the following comment: Mr. Sayles, (not Sales) mate of the *Volumnia*, arrived in Corpus Christi via Padre Island, as published by us last week.

Private letters from Brownsville state that the fever is disappearing almost as suddenly as it came. Mr. Sturges died there on the 6th.

The Diamond family: The following is a correct list of the deaths in the families of the late Col. J.J. Diamond, of his brother William, and of his niece, Mrs. Burton. The three families comprised some twenty-five persons. The first deaths occurred at the place of Maj. Scott, a mile and a half east of the Houston Courthouse, whither they had gone for the summer. We copy the deaths from a communication in the *Houston Telegraph* as follows:

Arthur L., son of Col. J.J. Diamond, aged 10 years; John A., son of Col. J.J. Diamond, aged 12 years; Frank, son of Col. J.J. Diamond, aged 2 years. Infant of Col. W.W. Diamond; Emma, niece of Col. Diamond, aged 15; Col. J.J. Diamond.

The family moved to town. Arthur, son of Mrs. Burton; Mrs. Burton, niece of Col. Diamond; Sally Diamond, aged 17; Col. W.W. Diamond; Lillie, niece of Col. Diamond, aged 5 years.

Death of Dr. Heflin — Huntsville has been deeply afflicted in the recent loss of some of her best citizens. None has left a larger vacancy than Rev. R.T. Heflin, D.D. the able and energetic President of Andrew Female College, who has fallen a victim to yellow fever. His son, a promising young man, died there, of the same disease, a few weeks ago. Dr. Heflin came to Texas from North Carolina, where he edited the *Raleigh Christian Advocate* and was widely known and highly esteemed.

Issue November 8, 1867

Died at Sour Lake Hotel, Harden county, Texas, on the 31st of August, Erastus Adgate Patterson, of Hudson, Columbia county, New York, in the 30th year of his age. N.Y. and Milwaukee papers please copy.

TEXAS ITEMS: The *Columbus Times* of the 2d says: We regret to learn that a young man named Cleveland Coffee, son of Mr. L.M. Coffee, formerly Sheriff of Colorado county, was accidentally thrown from his horse on Monday, 21st, and received injuries of which he died, Monday, 28th.

A little negro boy living on the plantation of Mr. Isam Tooke, took a fit on Thursday last, fell into the fire, and was so badly burned that death ensued.

FEVER AT MILLICAN: The *Bryan News Letter* of the 2nd says: The following additional names of those who have died of the fever at Millican, and not heretofore published, has been handed us. The mortality in proportion to the inhabitants has been as great at that place as anywhere the fever has visited this season. The total number of whites who have died up to the 25th of October, was 61, and of blacks 20: Mrs. Carevon and son, Alex. McKeig, Miss Jackson, Claiborne Hays, Michael Monaghan.

Issue November 9, 1867
Died in the city of Galveston on the 9th day of August, 1867, of yellow fever, Major Robt. W. Keyworth, in the 36th year of his age... True to his country, family, friends, his comrades on the battle field and the "lost cause." He idolized his wife and the little ones of his own and others who called him father...

Stephen Schaefer: The *Dallas Herald* pays a warm hearted tribute to the memory of Stephen Schaefer, who died in this city, not long since, of yellow fever. He used to live in Dallas, and when the war broke out, joined Capt. Good's battery, the first company raised in that place, "and remained with it until the surrender, in 1865, never having been absent from his command during the entire war."...

Yellow Fever on a Galveston Steamship. The steamer *Ariadne*, Capt. Parrish, which arrived this morning from Galveston, reports that on the 1st inst., Albert Farrell, steward; Samuel Lee, fireman; Robert F. Cambell, a passenger, and the ship's porter were taken sick. On the 11th, at 5 P.M., Albert Farrell died, and on the 12th, Robert F. Campbell, Corporal in Co. E, 17th U.S. Inf. died. The steamer left in the hospital at Galveston, Edmund Brooks a fireman... *New York Evening Post*, 17th.

Issue November 10, 1867
Departed this life at his residence in this county on the 30th of August last, Geo. W. Thatcher, in the 59th year of his age. He was born in Frederick county, Virginia, on the banks of the beautiful and fast rolling Shenandoah, on the 8th of January, 1808, but removed with his father in early youth to Ohio; resided for a time in Mississippi, where he married a daughter of the late James S. Montgomery; emigrated to Texas with his family about the

beginning of the Revolution, and has resided on his plantation, near Eagle Lake, till the date of his death... Mr. Thatcher lingered in illness for two years from an attack of paralysis, which caused his death...

Just two months from the date of his father's death, the fatal shaft was hurled at George M. Thatcher. He was just entering upon manhood, when he was suddenly carried off by a congestive chill... He was residing with his widowed mother... He was born on the 22nd of October, 1849 and died on the 30th of October 1867.

Issue November 13, 1867

Deaths in Lavaca during the epidemic: Rev. H.S. Thrall sends the following report to the President of the Howard Association of this city: Mary Daly, D. Bellfield, Laura J. Bramen, Mrs. Desha, B.A. Whitney, C.F. Gordon, W. Boyd, J.J. Bramen's child, negro girl, Rhoda Patrick, Mina Hangaella, W.H. Prouty, J. Richard's infant, Rev. W.T. Harris, Octav Finlay, Virginia Finlay, S. Burke, R. Banks, Mrs. V. Heyck, Dr. J. Beauchamp, Fannie Harris, Orlando Jackson, C. Gilbert, G. Patton, Olivia Forbes, J. Maxwell, Sarah, Rev. Renoux, Catholic Priest, Lizzie Norris, Stephen Smith, J.G. Guessnard, E. Hawes.

We sincerely sympathize with our friend Hon. R.V. Cook, of Colorado county, in the loss which he has sustained by the death of an only child - a son, aged six years, who died at Columbus 23d October of congestion of the brain... [note: the father writes] "This is the first great sorrow of my life, and a more afflicting one could not have been laid upon me..."

Issue November 14, 1867

From Huntsville. We have published from time to time, as they were received, the lists of death at Huntsville, from the 9th of August to the 1st of November... There were but two deaths at Huntsville, from November 1st to Nov. 5, namely, Miss Jardine, aged 12, of jaundice, and Seth Matthews, aged 20, of yellow fever.

The following are given from memory: J.C. Rawls, 63; B.F. Wright, 60; wife and child of Arch. Branch; wife of Rev. Mr. Kimball; wife of W.E. Watkins; wife of Howell Garrett; Mr. Byrd, 55; Chas. Wyser, 38, consumption; Mr. Quarles, 45; R.P. Stone, 55; Mollie Fearhake, 4.

A gentleman named Mynatt, came up from below about the 4th of August, with well-marked symptoms of the disease, and on the 9th died at one of the taverns... Soon after, Mr. Wanekey, who was of the number, but had not been further than Houston—where the disease was not then epidemic—took the disease, and in about four days died. His was a clear case of the black vomit. Then Mr. Fancher, a young lawyer, died on the following day... He had been exposed to the sun and had overheated himself by a ride of some ten miles. That night he went to bed sick. After death, his skin turned as yellow as a pumpkin.

The next marked case was the wife of Mr. Adickes, whose residence adjoins the tavern where Mynatt died, and who went to her rest some few days after Mr. Fancher.

There was a rumor that Fancher visited Mynatt during the sickness of the latter, but this the writer cannot verify.

Col. J.C. Rawls and Capt B.F. Wright, who both came to town early, in the epidemic, but saw no cases, went to their homes, and died in a few days of the disease, as I have understood. Anyhow, Fancher died the day after Wanekey, with black vomit.

Issue November 15, 1867

We learn from Mr. G. Colberg, of Anderson, that the venerable Mr. Fanthrop of that place, and his wife both died of yellow fever last week, but with a few hours interval between their deaths. Mr. Fanthrop was 77 years of age and was one of the oldest, and perhaps the oldest Texan at the time of his death, having lived here for near fifty years. He had accumulated a large fortune, which, of course falls to an only child, the present wife of Major Stone of the same place.

Died of yellow fever on October 3, 1867, at his residence in Huntsville, Walker county, Texas, Hon. Anthony M. Branch, in the 45th year of his age. The lamented subject of this notice was the son of Samuel Branch, Esq., of Buckingham county, Virginia, and a native of said county and state. He graduated at Hampden Sydney College at a period of life which gave earnest of his future prominence and usefulness and came to Texas, settling in Huntsville, in 1847 [note: last number of date not clear]... He was elected to represent the people of his county, and senatorial district, in both branches of the Legislature. In 1863 he was called from the field, where he had made a gallant soldier, and sent by his constituency to the Lower House of the Confederate Congress. [note: condensed].

Issue November 19, 1867

Many citizens of Galveston are deeply pained to hear of the death of Mrs. Sydnor, wife of Col. John S. Sydnor, who are numbered among the early settlers in this city...

Died in the town of Brenham, Texas, of yellow fever, October, 17, 1867, Dr. M.A. Rhodes. Dr. Rhodes was educated at West Point, Georgia; was a dentist by profession; served in the confederate army during the whole of the war; came to Texas soon after the surrender and established himself in business at Brenham. On the 12th of September, 1867, he was married to Miss Julia Gilder, eldest daughter of Dr. A.J. Gilder, of Brenham... Dr. Rhodes was attacked first with the fever about the 18th of September, but a few days after his marriage, and suffered under two relapses before he died. He leaves a young and devoted wife... Georgia papers please copy.

Issue November 20, 1867
Died on the [?]th of November 1867, at the residence of his father, in Grimes county, Texas, Shelby Mays Hammond, aged 4 1/2 years, son of Capt. F.M. Hammond and May E. Mays.

The *Waxahachie Argus* says a negro was killed on the night of the 6th on the plantation of Henry Panwell in the eastern part of Ellis county. He was stabbed... the bloody deed was done by a brother freedman, named Jeff. The one who was killed bore the name of George.

A letter from Gab. Felder brings the sad intelligence that Rev. J.W. Shipman died at the house of the former, 6 miles from Chappell Hill, on the 14th inst. at 10 minutes before 9 o'clock. He was buried there the next day... He leaves a wife, to whom he was recently married, and three children...

Issue November 21, 1867
Gonzales: The *Inquirer* says Mr. W.J. Jarvis, an industrious mechanic and respectable citizen, was killed a few days since at Hodge's steam saw mill, near Gonzales. He was at work on machinery and was caught in it and crushed to death.

James White killed James Kindred at Hopkinsville, Gonzales county, on the 9th.

Yellow fever at Goliad: The following appears in the *Goliad Guard*: "We give a list of all who died since the fever broke out, and their names as far as we know, viz: C. Inman, J.B. Thrift, Wm. B. Bawer, Mrs. Hitchins, Mrs. Barnidina and child, Mrs. Jno. Decker, Miss Whitby, A.R. Lane, M. Seeligson, Jno. Kraft and daughter, Miss Weilder, Capt. A.N. Smith, son of Mrs. Welch, a German and his wife at the Robbins House, Mrs. Arnold and Dr. E.M. Fant; Spence Goffe, f.m.c."

We learn by a note on the back of a letter that Mr. Leckenby, the Postmaster of Richmond, died on the 16th inst.

Issue November 22, 1867
The Bureau Agent at Cotton Gin, Freestone county, Texas, a Lieutenant Culvert, with his clerk or Sergeant, were killed two miles north of the town of Springfield, in Limestone county, a few days since by a man named Stewart and his son. Stewart had some misunderstanding with his hands, some freedmen, a short time previously, and the difficulty had been referred to

parties selected by Stewart and the freedmen to be settled by arbitration... Stewart would not permit the parties to take away his property, and the agent then came, and the fatal affray was commenced by the agent himself, who first shot Stewart, wounding him severely, whilst Stewart was inside his house. The Sergeant and agent both fired at the inmates of the house, also wounding Stewart's wife. Stewart, in self defence, then fired upon and killed the agent; and Stewart's son, a lad of about fourteen, shot and killed the Sergeant.

Issue November 23, 1867
McKinney Enquirer... very recently Mr. Fenton, living on Denton Creek, in Wise county, lost two little boys, carried off by the Indians. About the same time Mr. Leeper and Mrs. Hamilton were killed in Parker and several children of the latter carried off...

Issue November 26, 1867
Charles Eastwood, aged 47, died suddenly Monday morning at the residence of Mr. Chas. Thompson, in this city, of paralysis. Mr. E. was a resident of the city of New York, and came out 1st mate of the Brig. *Ocean Wave*, which was wrecked on our beach in the hurricane of the 3rd of October. He was struck with paralysis on the voyage out, and was speechless and almost helpless when brought ashore; but it will be some consolation to his friends to learn that he met with an old schoolmate, in the person of Mr. Thompson, who took him to his house and tendered him every kindness in his power.

His brother, Capt. Francis Eastwood, learning his condition, came out on the *Tybee* to carry him back to his friends. He found him improved in health, so much so that their passage was engaged, and they would have sailed on the *Tybee* this evening. He retired Sunday night feeling very comfortable, but on going to his room Monday morning he was found dead. He was buried by the Masonic Fraternity, of which he was a member... Galveston, Nov. 25th, 1867.

Issue November 27, 1867
Mrs. M.V. Friedeman, who lived somewhere in the western end of the city, died yesterday about 2 o'clock, very suddenly.

Maj. Thompson of the 4th cavalry has been killed at Fort Mason where he was commanding... a party of couriers from Ft. Mason while drunk at a store near the Post got into a dispute with a party of citizens, who knocked two of them over the head with their six shooters -- the soldiers not being armed. Major Thompson with his wife, in an ambulance, drove up on the scene and ordered the arrest of the citizens, whereupon a sargeant, who attempted to execute the order, and the major, were both shot by some of the citizens, who immediately fled...

Issue November 28, 1867

Departed this life at his late residence in Bryan City, Brazos county, Texas, on Monday the 18th inst., B.P. Hollingsworth, attorney-at-law and of the late firm of S.P. and B.P. Hollingsworth, in the 41st year of his age. Was born in Franklin county, Tennessee and moved to Texas in 1845; lived in Rusk county for several years and finally settled in Austin in 1856. He leaves a wife and two little daughters to mourn his loss.

Mortuary Report for Galveston for November 27, 1867:
George Street, 45, New York, apoplexy.
R. Edler, unknown, Germany, intermittent fever.
Louis V. Nicholas, 30, Virginia, yellow fever.
Mrs. K.F. Friedeman, 36, Virginia, yellow fever.
Unknown man, Texas, not known.
Albert E. Illias, 29 1/2, Texas, intermit. fever.
Mike Furlong, 29, Ireland, yellow fever.
Unknown man, 50, not known.
Mrs. W. Walstein, 30, Germany, yellow fever.

Issue November 30, 1867

Riot in Brenham. Fatal encounter between citizens and soldiers, Brenham, November 27, 1867: A difficulty occurred here since supper between the soldiers and three citizens, John Watson, John Farquhar, and Thomas Autrey from Washington, who came to town this p.m. The soldiers suspected John G. Gee to be with the party from Washington and went to the hotel to arrest him when Farquhar and Autrey started out the door. Feliz Farquhar was killed dead and Thomas Autrey was seriously wounded. Watson was not fired at, but is still here and not under arrest.
  Since the transmission of the above, Autrey has died.

Issue December 1, 1867

Died in Galveston November 30, 1867, Patrick Ducey, a native of County Tiperary, Ireland, aged 38 years. The funeral will take place today at 1 1/2 o'clock P.M. New York & Flushing papers please copy.

Issue December 3, 1867

Died, Monday morning, December 2nd, of hemorrhage of the bowels, Henry VanHuesenn. His body will be sent to Houston for interment.

Died in this city on the 2nd day of December 1867 of chronic inflammation of the liver, Thos. Curphey, a native of Douglass, Isle of Man, aged 33 years and 7 months.

The intelligence of the death of Sarah C., the wife of Col. John S. Sydnor, has brought sadness and sorrow to the hearts of all those who knew her well. She was a native of Virginia, and as her health had not been good for some time, she left our city in early summer, her friends indulging the hope that travel and her native air would restore it. She died at Richmond on the 13th day of November 1867...

Issue December 5, 1867

The *Trinity Advocate* says W.A. Ratliff was killed by W.N. Fitzgerald in Palestine on the 23rd ult.

Maj. Ira W. Chaflin, 6th U.S. Cavalry, died at Mt. Pleasant on the 18th ult.

Issue December 6, 1867

Died of yellow fever, October 24th, 1867, Richard Rodgers, youngest child of Dr. & Mrs. R.R. Peebles, at their residence near Hempstead, Austin county, in the 8th year of his age...

Died of yellow fever at Chappell Hill, October 18, 1867, Robert W. Carnes, youngest child of R.W. and P.E. Carnes. Robert was born in Galveston, March 4, 1859, aged 8 years and 8 months.

Died at Chappell Hill, Washington county, Texas, of yellow fever, November 1, 1867, Mr. J.H. Carlisle, after an illness of a few days. He was born at Louisburg, North Carolina, January 21st, 1814 [1844?] and was a noble young man, remarkable for generosity of heart, strength of mind and devotion to duty. During the epidemic he devoted himself to the suffering and dying. He was well attended during his own short sickness and the community was deeply affected by his death. The spot where he sleeps will be remembered by the friends he made in his far off new home. Louisburg, North Carolina papers please notice.

Died at Lake Hill, Fort Bend county, Texas, on Wednesday the 24th day of July, Mrs. Jennie N. Fulshear, wife of Churchill Fulshear, Jr, and daughter of Maj. John & Mrs. N.E. Wimberly of Alabama.

Issue December 7, 1867

Died at the residence of his brother-in-law, N. Mayblum, in Richmond, Fort Bend county, Texas, Lewis M. Franklin, a native of Cincinnati, Ohio, after a short illness, of congestion of the brain.

Another bright eye is closed; another noble heart is cold! To the already extensive list of victims from the fearful epidemic that has spread woe throughout our land, another name is to be added. Lewis V. Nicholas breathed his last, at the residence of his cousin, Mr. J. Harris, in this city on Wednesday, November 27th. He was born in Albemarle county, Virginia, and was 34 years of age...

Issue December 11, 1867

The *Lavaca Commercial* records the death of Maj. Ben. White at Texana. He was one of the 300 of Austin's colonists; was 86 years old at the time of his death, November 22nd.

From the *States Rights Democrat* of LaGrange: We feel sad, indeed, when we look down the long column of familiar names and see numbered with the death such men as Quinn Menifee, preacher in charge of LaGrange M.E. Church; Ben Shropshire, judge of this Judicial Dist.; Parker Hood, Sheriff of the County; Theo. Carter, & Zeb. French, the former District and the latter County Clerk. There appears the name of Charley Smith, Leslie Savage, old Uncle Henry Moore, John Carragee, Jas. Nicholson, and others...

Issue December 12, 1867

The *Trinity Advocate* announces the death at Palestine on the 1st of Hon. James M. Perry, an old influential and respected citizen. He was a native of Tennessee and came to Texas and settled in Palestine about 20 years ago... He leaves a widow and five children.

Brother Kills Brother. Brazoria, December 6, 1867: Our county has just been the scene of a most unfortunate and terrible affair between two brothers, John C. and George Jackson, sons of the late Maj. Abner Jackson. It seems that George and his half brother, Lewis M. Strobel, were living together at the Lake Jackson place, the late residence of Maj. Jackson, which had been set apart by the county court as the family homestead. John was residing on one of the plantations belonging to his father's estate, near Sandy Point. John became displeased with his brother George about some business matters, some several months ago, and was in the habit of showing his displeasure towards him whenever they met...

George fired upon him (John) with both barrels of the gun, and also with his six-shooter. Several of the shots were fatal, and John fell from the horse lifeless... [note: condensed from a long article].

Issue December 14, 1867

George Parr, county clerk of Live Oak, was murdered on the 22nd ult. by a man named J.M. Watkins.

Brenham Banner of the 5th says Thos. Autrey died this morning at 8 o'clock of wounds received at the hands of the soldiers.

Issue December 18, 1867

We welcome the reappearance of the LaGrange *New Era*. It is now published by N.C. Rives and edited by B. Timmons. Jas W. Matthews, the former editor, died of yellow fever at LaGrange, September 4.

Issue December 21, 1867

The *State Gazette* reports an unfortunate difficulty at Webberville on the 14th between young Sam Harris and a negro named Charley Stewart. The negro had threatened the life of Harris on account of his refusal to employ him on the farm of his father. On meeting, the parties commenced shooting, and Harris was finally wounded dangerously in the breast. The negro was unhurt...

Died at her residence, near Hempstead, Austin county, Texas, on Thursday, 1st of August, Mrs. Lizzie McCarty, wife of Col. J. McCarty, and daughter of Dr. Charles Baldwin, of Virginia, aged 33 years...

Issue January 3, 1868

Died in this city on December 23, 1867, David L. McNeill, born in North Carolina, aged 42 years, 8 months.

Issue January 5, 1868

Died on the 3rd inst., Mary Falvel, youngest daughter of Capt. and Mrs. L.A. Falvel, aged 16 years.

Issue January 11, 1868

Died in this city on the night of the 9th inst., David H. Grove, in the 50th year of his age. The deceased was a native of North Carolina, but moved to Galveston in 1847, where he has mostly resided with his family...

The *Henderson Times* of the 4th contains an obituary of Judge W.B. Ochiltree, who it says, died at Jefferson on the 25th ult. He was a native of North Carolina, about 30 years ago he came to Texas...

Issue January 15, 1868

The *Semi Weekly Examiner* of the 10th says that news had reached Waco that Mr. Charles Gill, a resident of Bosqueville, was murdered by a negro on the 9th and that the murderer escaped.

The *Jefferson Intelligencer* says Judge Ochiltree had for sometime been in feeble health, but that his death was unexpected. He died at his residence in Jefferson, December 27th. The same paper says he was born in Cumberland county, North Carolina, October 18, 1811.

Judge Key, of Gonzales, died there on the 7th. He was an old and prominent citizen. During the war he commanded the Fourth Texas Regiment in Virginia.

A gentleman named Heating, from Georgia, died at Mt. Pleasant recently. He was cared by and buried by the Masons.

Issue January 18, 1868

Died in this city on the 17th inst., Bettie Blackiston, daughter of J.D. & W.S. Roberdean, aged 15 months. Baltimore (Md.) & Alexandria (Va.) papers please copy.

Died: Owensville, Texas, January 12, 1868. After a severe illness protracted through many months, Mrs. Elizabeth Olive Lawdermilk, died in this place on the morning of the 7th inst. Mrs. Lawdermilk's maiden name was Echols. Her father's family originally settled in South Carolina and her mother's in Virginia. This ancestry is most suggestive of the character of the lamented deceased, whose father's name, especially, was the very synonym of integrity, truth, and virtue, among the people of Monroe county, Mississippi, where he spent the best years of a long and useful life. Mrs. Lawdermilk leaves a bereaved husband and five children...

Issue January 24, 1868

INDIAN RAID: A letter from Gainesville, Texas, dated January 12, 1868, reports a murderous and destructive Indian raid into Cook county. On Sunday the 5th about one hundred Indians appeared in that county and, dividing into squads, commenced their usual work of murder and robbery. During Sunday and Monday they killed a Mr. Long, a young man named Leatherwood, Mr. Menesco and it is supposed, Mrs. Carrolton, who is missing, Mr. Thomas Fitzpatrick and wife, and Arthur Parkhill. Three of Fitzpatrick's children, Miss Carrolton, and Mrs. Edward Shegog were captured. Mrs. Shegog and Miss Carrolton escaped, however, before the Indians left the county, but they killed the infant child of the former. They even encamped near the town of Gainesville, and sent a party through it in the night. Mrs. Shegog says they were continually driving in horses to the encampment near town. They cut off this lady's hair and stripped her of clothing.

Issue January 26, 1868

Another of Galveston oldest citizens of Texas has gone to his final re-ting [resting] place. On the 14th inst., Joseph Stowe died at his late residence in this city, in the seventy-third year of his age. The deceased was born in the state of Massachusetts, and moved to the state of New York, while young, and was reared in that state; he afterwards moved to and resided for a time in the state of Alabama from whence he emigrated to Texas in the year 1837 and he continued to reside in this state up to the time of his death. He fought under Gen. Jackson at the memorable battle of New Orleans...

Issue January 31, 1868

Homicide -- Philip Werdehausen, an old Galveston citizen, residing at corner of H. and 36th street, was arrested yesterday. On Tuesday, Werdehausen came home slightly intoxicated and was met at the door by his son-in-law, Stephen Lauser, and wife. The old man was struck by his son-in-law and fell. He seized a stick of wood and struck the young man over the head; he died yesterday evening.

Issue February 1, 1868

Died in this city, January 31st at 6 P.M., C.L. McCarty, aged 53 years, a native of Ireland. His funeral will take place from the residence of his son, W.C. McCarty, #171 West Church st. at 3 P.M. today. Hagerstown (Md.) papers please copy.

C.L. McCarty, an old and popular citizen died last night after a severe illness of several months.

Issue February 2, 1868

Valentine Cook, of DeWitt county, one of Terry's Rangers and the only son of the late Rev. Thomas F. Cook, was murdered and robbed in Lavaca county near a place called Hope on the 16th.

Maj. J.W. Scott, an old Texan and citizen of Houston, died in that city on the 30th. He served as Lieutenant and Paymaster in the days of the Republic.

Issue February 7, 1868

On the 25th ult., E.D. Dennis and Dan. Dennis were killed near Hickory, Mississippi, by negroes. One of these gentlemen, had discovered that a freedman named Dyers, had killed his hogs, and obtained a warrant for his arrest. An officer went to execute the warrant, taking several white men to assist him. After hunting the freedman for some time, the party gave up the search and were returning when they were attacked by some six or eight negroes in ambush. The two gentlemen above named were killed on the spot, and Mr. B. Griffin received a shot in the leg, breaking the bone... The murderers, after shooting Ed. and Dan. Dennis, then beat them with the butt of their guns. On arriving there they were fired upon by the murderers, wounding Mr. Lyle mortally...

Issue February 8, 1868
MURDER OF TEXAS EMIGRANTS: Brownsville papers give the particulars of the cowardly murder of two of the recent emigrants from Waco to Tuxpan. When near the city of Victoria, the two unfortunate gentlemen, named Pillow and Cook, fell in with a couple of Mexicans... the Mexicans shot their American companions in the back.

Issue February 11, 1868
We learn that the body of young David Grove, who drowned some two weeks since, while landing at night from the *Whitelaw*, at Morgans Point, has been recovered.

Issue February 15, 1868
City Intelligence: Last night about half past seven o'clock, Mrs. Giddings, wife of Col. G.H. Giddings was accidently killed. Col. G. with his family had arrived in a hack at the front of the theater and Col. G. and two little daughters had reached the ground, when the horses took fright and started off. Another little daughter and Mrs. Giddings were in the hack when it started and the little girl jumped out without being hurt. When she reached Tremont street the lady jumped out or was thrown out and in the fall received injuries which caused her death within twenty minutes. [note: see issue February 16, 1868].

Issue February 16, 1868
Further particulars of the accident -- a young mother in the agonies of death surrounded by her children uttering cries of despair... The funeral yesterday from the Episcopal Church was attended by a large number of friends. [note: see issue February 15, 1868].

Issue February 18, 1868
A party of Mexicans made an attempt, a few days ago, to rob the premises of Mrs. Snider, at White's ranch. They first fired several shots into the lady's room, and tried to cut a way into the house with an axe, but without success... Mrs. Snider's husband died last fall of yellow fever.

Gen. McCook has issued an appropriate communication on the death of Mrs. Margaret Hayes, who was accidently killed, a few days since, on the Mexican side of the Rio Grande, opposite to Brownsville by the discharge... [note: page creased] this side, of a musket in the hands of a member of the United States garrison guard... Amongst those who attended the funeral of Mrs. Hayes, at Brownsville, on the 14th, were Gen. McCook, all the officers at the post, and a detachment of the 26th Infantry.

Issue February 19, 1868

Mrs. Anna R. Beaumont died after a long and painful illness. She was among the earliest settlers of this county. Surviving consort.

Funeral notice: The funeral of Mrs. Anna R. Beaumont, wife of Mr. J.K. Beaumont, will take place at 3 o'clock P.M. on Wednesday, February 19th. Friends and acquaintances are respectfully invited to attend the funeral of the deceased, to take place from her late residence, on Postoffice street, near the machine shop of the Galveston, Houston, & Henderson railroad.

The *Texas Ranger* says D. McKinney, lately from Austin, shot Clay Searcy, of Anderson, in Navasota on the 13th. McKinney, is reported to be a desperado, and the Ranger says he behaved in an outrageous manner towards Searcy before shooting at him. During the preceding part of the same day he had drawn his pistol on several bar keepers for refusing to furnish him liquor without pay. Searcy was not killed, but we presume he cannot recover. McKinney was sent to jail at Anderson. The Ranger tells the sequel: Mayor Jones sent a party to Anderson to bring down McKinney for trial. On the way back with the prisoner, in a strip of woods, the guard was halted by a crowd of sixty armed men. They were ordered to lay down their arms and give up the prisoner. When the guard protested and remonstrated, they were ordered peremptorily to hush up. The men were all disguised and blackened, and all spoke in broken English and Dutch. McKinney was hung to a limb, and the rope or limb broke and he fell down. He was then tied securely and hung over ten feet high, and left hanging.

A woman named Wagner was killed by them [Indians] near Kerrville last week.

Robert Harper, of Covington, for many years a leading member of the Louisiana Legislature and the law partner of L.Q.C. Lomar/Lamar, of this state, committed suicide at his house a few days ago.

Liberty Gazette. We regret to record the death of another old Texian. Reason Green, died in this county, 11th inst., in the 68 year of his age. He lived in this county since 1825.

Issue February 21, 1868

The *Indianola Bulletin* of the 20th says the steamer *W.G. Hewes*, in running down the bay on the 15th, carried a small boat under her wheel. There were two persons in the boat, James Miller and his son, Alexander. The younger was killed immediately and the elder badly injured, was picked up by the steamer's boat and taken on shore.

Tribute of respect from the Masonic Hall, Chappell Hill, Texas, to the memory of our deceased brethren: Rev. Thomas Wooldridge, Hon. James W. McDade, J.A. Haynie, J.R. Moore, E.W. Rodgers, W.D. Crockett, J.E. Crockett, and T.J. Jackson.

Died on the 9th of February of paralysis at the plantation of B.G. Marshall, Duncan Marshall, aged 63 years, former servant of B.G. Marshall... He leaves a wife and four children and a number of grandchildren...

Issue February 23, 1868
Extract from a letter dated Burnett, Burnett county, February 15, 1868: Three men, I omitted to mention, Barton, Miller, and Vaughan, of McLennan county, were killed by Indians a few days ago.

The same party shot and scalped an old lady, Mrs. Friends.

From Houston. We are sorry to learn of the death of Rev. George Rottenstein, a noble masonic brother.

Issue February 26, 1868
TERRIBLE INDIAN ATROCITIES: Letter dated Belton, Bell county, Texas, February 15th, 1868:

I just heard through Mr. W.O. Phillips, of Llano county, the particulars of the most heart rending atrocities lately committed in that county by Indians. They went to a house on Legion Creek, and took prisoner Mr. Boy's and William Johnson's wives, four children and a Miss Walker. A Mrs. Friend, who was at the house, fought them, was shot and scalped, and left for dead but recovered and went one mile the same night, and is now thought to be in a fair way to get well of her injuries.

The savages traveled one night with their prisoners, and then put them to death by knocking the brains out of the married women with their muskets, and dashing the children's heads against the rocks, and scalped them all. Miss Walker was taken to their second camping place and there killed, as the others had been, and when found, her body was partly consumed by hogs, as was the case of the others. Doubtless they suffered the pangs of death before it came to their relief.

The fiends killed, while on their exit, an old man by the name of Smith, who was found on the road alone...

Issue February 27, 1868
The *Waco Register* reports the murder of Mr. Isaac T. Eichelberger, while out with his wagon in a cedar brake some fourteen miles from Waco on the 19th. No clue to the murder [has] yet been obtained.

Issue February 28, 1868

An inquest was held yesterday on the body of P.A. Lawson, who was found dead, about three miles west of the city, with a folded handkerchief tied around his head over his eyes. The deceased was a native of Lower Canada; had been in Galveston about two years; about 36 years old.

Issue March 3, 1868

Departed this life on the 16th day of December, 1867, Eugenia Gracia Gaines, after a painful illness of sixteen days, the beloved wife of Col. W.P.B. Gaines, residing near Columbia, Brazoria county, in this state. Willow Glen, February 24, 1868. [note: mentions husband and children].

Issue March 4, 1868

The *Journal* of the 3rd says J.A. [sic] Patrick killed J.J. Harrison in Joe Grant's saloon at Houston on the 2nd. Both men are natives of Georgia.

Issue March 5, 1868

We regret that Mr. Honey, clerk of our Supreme Court, received a telegram yesterday that his father had been killed by a fall from his horse at his home in Wisconsin.

Major Holmes, formerly an officer in the Confederate Army, died at the Rosseu House in Toronto on the 26th ult.

Issue March 6, 1868

An innocent man killed... It is well known that, for several months past, we have had a squad of soldiers encamped on the public square... These soldiers began to frequent constantly, grogshops and lager beer saloons... They entered the hotel and commenced beating in the doors and firing into the rooms. In one of the second story rooms asleep was a physician by the name of Cunningham, living near Belmont. The noise roused him and he opened the door and asked them what they meant. They pushed open his bedroom door and dragged him out and after beating him severely the Sergeant ordered him to repeat the Lord's prayer and give three cheers for the Union, which the poor fellow did. They then brought him out into the street and finally shot him dead. His brains and parts of his skull were scattered in front of the Keyser pavement...

Issue March 7, 1868

Hon. George W. Glasscock, of Austin, died at Webberville, on the 28th inst. in consequence of injuries received by being thrown from a mule. Buried at Austin on the 1st with Masonic honors.

Issue March 12, 1868

Mr. Henry T. Driskill was murdered in Crockett lately by Ed. Wingate. The victim is represented as an estimable man, the murderer as an abandoned and reckless character.

Issue March 13, 1868

Georgian killed in Texas: A private dispatch to a gentleman in this city, from Houston, Texas, reads as follows: Rough Harrison was murdered by J.H. [sic] Patrick at one o'clock today. Communicate the intelligence to his family. We are informed that the Harrison referred to was raised in the vicinity of Athens, and is very respectably connected there. The other party, J.H. Patrick, we learn, was raised about Carnesville, in Franklin county... *Atlanta Intelligener.*

Letter from Houston. Monday night a policeman named Adams was shot in the market place by a man named Murchie. I learn the wounded man has since died.

Issue March 14, 1868

Died, Friday morning at 5 o'clock, March 13th, of teething, Emma, youngest daughter of Fredinand and Emma Flake.

We learn that Mr. Honey, of Fond du Lac, Wisconsin, father of G.W. Honey, Clerk of the Supreme Court, was not killed as was first supposed, by a horse, but that some one had attacked him while in his stable, and killed him, in a most brutal manner. His pocket book, which contained some sixteen or eighteen dollars, was taken. Mr. Honey was an old man of sixty and bore an excellent character.

Issue March 17, 1868

The *Era* announces the death of Dr. S.D. Wilkinson, a highly esteemed citizen of Fayette county.

Henry Deringer, the author, in 1820, of that most efficient instrument, the Deringer pistol, died in Philadelphia, February 26th, aged eighty-two years and five months.

Chapter of accidents -- A young man named John Neugent, a citizen of Galveston of some twenty years standing, was engaging in loosening a rope at the head of the mast of the sloop *Comet*, lying at Kuhn's wharf yesterday evening, when the mast fell with him and he was fatally injured by the concussion. Several of his teeth were knocked out of his jaws and fell from his mouth when he was being transferred to the wharf. He recovered consciousness when on the wharf, but we understand that the surgeon, who was immediately called, pronounced the case fatal.

Issue March 18, 1868

The *Waco Register* has a notice of the death of J. DeCordova at Kimball, Bosque county, on the 26th January 1868. He was born at Kingston, Jamaica, June 6, 1808.

Issue March 20, 1868

A negro man waylaid and killed, by shooting him with a pistol, young Reid Leverett, of Jasper county, Georgia, on the night of the 29th ult.

The *Times* has an affecting account of the death of Mr. Oliver Loring/Loving, who left Parker county, last summer, for New Mexico, with a drove of beeves. After proceeding about six hundred miles, he was attacked by Indians near the Pecos river on the 6th of August and mortally wounded. He was not found until the 12th and was then taken to Ft. Sumner, where he died on the 25th of September. His remains were brought back and reinterred at Weatherford, on the 8th, by the Masonic fraternity, attended by the largest procession ever witnessed in the place. He was an old and much esteemed citizen.

Issue March 22, 1868

The *San Antonio Herald* learns that Capt. Peter Tumlinson, an old citizen of Atascosa county, was waylaid and killed recently. The *Herald* also reports the death of George Kluppenbach, delegate elect to the Convention from Comal and Hays.

The brother-in-law of Dr. Cunningham, M.H. Beaty, makes a statement concerning the murder of the former by a squad of United States soldiers at Gonzales on the 25th [?] ult., which entirely confirms the account copied by us from the *Inquirer*. It seems to have been one of the most brutal murders ever recorded. Mr. Beaty has always been a Union man.

Died at her father's residence in Polk county, March 11, 1868, Lilly Josephine, second daughter of Capt. W.D. and Mrs. Fanny Mitchell, aged eleven years, two months. She fell a victim to one of the severest maladies known to the human body, rheumatism of the heart.

Issue March 25, 1868

The *Sherman Courier* of the 14th says a squad of soldiers went from that place, the previous week, to Pilot Grove, in the same county of Grayson, for the purpose of arresting several persons, two of whom, Clark and Dixon, resisted and were killed.

Issue March 26, 1868

It was stated that the soldier who murdered Dr. Cunningham at Gonzales, recently, had been committed to jail; but that was a mistake.

Issue March 28, 1868

Major Justinian Alman of the U.S. Army was drowned in the river near Jefferson on the 17th. He and several other officers were going down the river in a skiff, when they met a steamer, under the wheel of which they were carried by the suction. A last accounts the body of Major Alman had not been recovered. He leaves a wife, and is said to have been a useful and popular officer.

The *San Antonio Herald* learns that the report of the killing of Peter Tomlinson, is untrue.

Issue March 29, 1868

Died at his residence in Montgomery on Friday, 20th inst., Reubin J. Palmee, aged 37 years and 6 months. The deceased was a native of Appomattox county, Virginia, whence he emigrated to Texas in 1856, and settled in this place, devoting himself to the pursuit of his profession; lawyer; Methodist. His disease (consumption) had for many months confined him to his room, so that he was prevented the enjoyment of the public worship of the sanctuary... Three orphan children mourn his loss... Father and mother sweetly sleep together in our village graveyard. A Friend, Montgomery, Texas, March 23, 1868. *Houston Telegraph* please copy, and present bill to Messrs P.J. Willis & Bro.

Died at his residence in Travis county, Texas, Mr. W.H. Gilbert, aged 53 years. Mr. Gilbert has been in feeble health for some time. On the 4th of March he was taken violently ill with congestive convulsions, or chills, having three during fifteen hours, and died on the 9th of March.

The *Hempstead Countryman* says that John Catron, an Irishman, was killed on the Central road on the 19th. He was intoxicated and fell off a hand car, which was being run by a party of Irishmen, all of whom were drunk, and was run over and so injured that he died the next day.

The *Henderson Times* announces the death of Gen. Andrew Miller on the 14th, in the 84th year of his age. The *Times* says he was doubtless the oldest of the public men of the State, with the exception perhaps of ex-President Burnet, of this city.

The *Telegraph* says Mrs. Kate Fitzgerald of Houston committed suicide by drowning on the 25th. She was seen to jump into the Bayou at the Galveston railroad bridge, but was not gotten out until life was extinct. She was the wife of Mike Fitzgerald of the Houston police.

Issue April 1, 1868

Napoleon Bonaparte, an old freedman, known by the name of Bony, was killed up at Judge Varnell's on the Areonoso last Friday night 20th inst. The Judge had in his employ a negro man named Gus Randall...

Dr. Garnett, who lived fifteen miles below Goliad, was drowned last week in attempt to cross the river... Dr. G. lost his wife last summer and leaves several small children.

Issue April 2, 1868

The *Dallas Herald* learns that several parties of Indians were in Wise county during the last moon... They killed a Miss Bowman within eight miles of Decatur and stole a large number of horses.

Issue April 7, 1868

The *Telegraph* of the 4th contains an account of the hanging of Sam Johnson, freedman, on the 3rd for the murder of Dick Taylor...

Issue April 10, 1868

Serious shooting affair: On Friday morning last at Reed's Prairie, some twelve miles hence, a difficulty arose between Wm. Sapp, Jr., and _____ Saunders, relative to a matter of which we known nothing, in which Mr. Saunders was killed. On Saturday evening, _____ Stewart, brother-in-law of Mr. Sapp and half brother of Mr. Saunders, procured a writ for the arrest of Mr. Sapp, and with a party composed of six men, surrounded a house in which Mr. Sapp was known to be. The arresting party, we understand, reached the house after night-fall, and remained in close proximity to the house during the night, and at early dawn firing commenced, but by which party it was inaugurated, or what conversation took place, if any, we are not informed. Neither are we informed as to the duration of the difficulty. Mr. Wm. Loggins and Mr. _____ Stewart belonging to the arresting party were killed, and one white man and one negro wounded.

On the other side, Mr. _____ Bell was killed, and Messrs. Wm. Sapp, Sr. and Wm. Sapp, Jr. were seriously wounded, the former in the left breast and the latter in the right leg... (from the *Hempstead Countryman* of the 8th).

Negro Killing: One day last week an altercation took place on the premises of Mr. Ed. Thompson, in this county, resulting in the death of one negro at the hands of another. Gus. Thompson, F.M.C., it seems, in protecting his wife from the assault of her brother, used a rail too heavily, and disjointed his brother-in-laws neck, causing his immediate demise. The last seen of Gus. he was passing Leona, in route for a city of refuge. His wife, it is said, took passage on one of the Trinity boats for some other place. (*Centerville Conservative*).

The *Guard* says Dr. A. Seitz, a German physician of Goliad county, met his death by his own hands, as is supposed, a few days since.

The *Independent* announces the death of Rev. Wesley Sorelle, one of the oldest and most respected citizens of Hunt county.

Issue April 12, 1868
The *LaGrange New Era* learns that Mr. Ellis Shropshire was killed on the 4th inst., 3 miles below Lyon, on the Navidad, by James Hazle.

Issue April 14, 1868
Died last night at 9 o'clock, Frank Wheeler, son of Maj. Frank M. and Flora M. Spencer, aged 14 months... funeral from the residence of the family at 4 o'clock this afternoon.

Issue April 15, 1868
We clip the following account of the murder and robbery of W.R.D. Ward, of Marshall, and the attempted murder of Mr. Ely, from the *Marshall Daily Flag*, of the 4th.
   Tyler, April 4, 1868. To the operator at Marshall: W.R.D. Ward and Mr. Ely attacked, and Mr. Ward killed on the road ten miles below Henderson, on the Nacogdoches road. Mr. Ely badly shot and robbed. We are in pursuit. The murderers are Willis Hoe and Harris Robinson. Inform their friends. We have not heard from them since we left Jamestown. It occurred on the evening of the 2nd instant. Henry Miller, C. Boggs.
   Col. Ward and Mr. Ely left this place a few days since and had a considerable quantity of money with them, for which one of them has been murdered and the other badly wounded. Col. Ward is an old resident of this place, and one of the earliest settlers in Texas. Mr. Ely is a citizen of Shreveport, and the father-in-law of Mr. W.T. Brooks, proprietor of the Brooks House... *Shreveport Southwestern,* April 8th.

Died in this city April 13, 1868, Willie Harris, infant son of Wm. H. and Sarah Baker. *New Orleans Times* and *Houma Civic Guard* please copy.

Sudden death: We regret to learn that Col. Minor, collector of Customs for this port, died suddenly at his residence on Broadway, yesterday evening... He leaves a wife to mourn his loss... He came here from Hamilton, Ohio.

Little Frank Spencer was yesterday taken to the grave after having just entered upon the second year of his brief existence.

The *Bastrop Advertizer* says the young German, Louge, who was accidently shot in that place on the 24th ult., died of his wounds on the 7th inst.

Issue April 18, 1868
Frank Staffel, a fruit dealer of Brenham, was found, says the *Banner*, dead in his room on the morning of the 11th.

Issue April 23, 1868
We learn that it was "Uncle Charley" one of the oldest and, in slavery times, one of the best negroes on the plantation of the late Judge Felder of Washington county, who was killed recently by a fellow freedman.

Tribute of respect: To the memory of brother Henry R. Cartmell, who departed this life at his residence, in the town of Washington and state of Texas, on the 3rd day of March 1868, A.L. 5868. The deceased was one of the oldest members of the Masonic Fraternity in the state... He was born in the town of Winchester, Virginia, September 22, in the year 1800. At an early day he emigrated to the state of Tennessee and made the city of Nashville his home... He continued a true and faithful member of Cumberland Lodge until the 19th March 1836, when he moved to the state of Texas...

Issue April 24, 1868
The *Messenger* says Shelton Howard, charged with the murder of George F. Eber on the 6th inst., was lodged in jail at McKinney on the 11th.

Issue April 25, 1868
The *Register* (Waco) announces the death on the 19th of W.D. Williams, an esteemed citizen of Waco.

Issue April 28, 1868
From Nashville: News has just reached here that Littleton Lincoln, of Marshall county, while visiting his brother-in-law near Columbia, Maury county, was taken from the house on Sunday night by a party of six men and shot dead, and his body thrown into a cove.

On the 11th inst., says the *Mt. Pleasant (Texas) Press*, the prisoners confined in the jail at that place broke out, and all but one escaped. This one, named Landtroop, was shot by the guard and died next day.

Issue April 29, 1868
At a place called Terripin Neck, 40 miles above Vicksburg, a man named Keenan was murdered by two negroes.

From Houston: Mr. J.P. Franck, an enterprising citizen near Goose Creek, died there a short time since.

Issue May 1, 1868

A few days ago, near Des Arc, Arkansas, as Miss Sallie Kennedy was assisting in burning logs, her clothes caught fire, and she was so badly burned that the skin on her hands fell down over her fingers and her fingernails came off. She died the next day. Her sister was also badly burned in attempting to extinguish the flames.

Issue May 2, 1868

The *Rusk Observer* says Dr. T.J. Warren, charged with the murder of James W. Bates of Tyler, has been held to bail in the sum of $50,000.

The *Countryman* reports that on Wednesday afternoon last, B.B. Lee was shot and killed by Joseph Farr in the saloon kept by G.H. Wheeler at Hempstead. Farr left and has not been arrested.

Georgetown Watchman. We are reliably informed by a gentleman just down from Bell county that on Tuesday night last an attempt was made to arrest some supposed horse thieves, when a difficulty took place which resulted in the killing of one Shackleford and one of the attacking party by the name of Jackson. No further particulars.

Gen. W.H. Stevens – The body of Gen. Walter H. Stevens – who is remembered with respect and affection by many in Galveston, where he was living at the breaking out of the war – was recently interred at Hollywood Cemetery, Richmond, with Masonic honors. Gen. Stevens was a native of New York, a graduate of West Point, and when the war commenced in 1861, an officer in the United States Navy. Resigning this position, he joined the Confederate Army... He died of yellow fever at Vera Cruz, November 12, 1867.

Death of Hon. W.C. Rives – A telegram from Charlottesville, Virginia, announces the death at that place on the 29th ult., W.C. Rives, formerly Minister to France and Senator from Virginia, aged 75.

Issue May 3, 1868

The *Mt. Pleasant Press* has an account of a brutal murder on the road between Mt. Pleasant and Sulphur Springs, in Hopkins county, on the 18th ult. Two men overtook a young gentleman and his sister, riding in a buggy, and offered the young lady indignities of the most shocking character. The brother, being unarmed protested, referring to his defenseless condition, when one of the men shot him, causing instant death. A party was soon out in pursuit of the murderers, and the *Press* learns that they had been overtaken and hung. Their names were Fry and Green. The young lady escaped further indignities by flight.

The stage driver informs us that on the 2nd inst., Bruno Durst, son of W.E. Durst, formerly of this place, was killed at Navasota... From the *Centerville Conservative*.

We understand that Sergeant Dwyer, charged with the killing of Dr. Cunningham, at Gonzales a few weeks since, has been sent to that place for trial, the District Court now being in session there.

Church services -- The funeral sermon of the late Mrs. Outerside will be preached at 11 a.m. The community are respectfully invited to attend.

Issue May 5, 1868

The *Courier* reports several murders: The killing of Peacock and Sanders by Lee and Dixon at Pilot Grove, and also of Dr. Thompson of Grayson. Suspicion in the latter case attaches to Wm. Young and Neely Heron, both of whom have left. Pursuit has been made.

The *Liberty Gazette* of the 1st says: Jack Branch, freedman, who had just served 2 years in the penitentiary for thief and Paul, another freedman, were shot and killed in the neighborhood of Martin Jones, last Saturday, for killing and carrying away beef that did not belong to them.

On last Wednesday morning on Gen. Harrison's place, about ten miles from Waco, on the east bank of the Brazos, a negro by the name of Peter Riddle shot and instantly killed another negro by the name of Hamp. Harris.

The *Jefferson (Texas) Times* gives a somewhat different version of an affair which we have recently noticed. A young man named Gilead and his sister, traveling in a two-horse wagon, had camped for the night on Saturday, in the upper edge of Titus county. They were soon after joined by two drunken men, who conducted themselves so badly as to force the young man and his sister to remove their camp half a mile further on where they were again intruded upon. Then, to be entirely rid of their annoyance, they abandoned their wagon, and started to a house not far off; but they had only advanced a few yards when they were ordered to halt, but not obeying the command, the young man was shot in the back of the neck and instantly killed. The lady was then attacked, but obtaining protection by her cries for help, her assailants fled in the direction of Sulphur Springs, at which place they dined the next day, and then proceeded to Black Jack Grove; but in a ravine near that place they were confronted by some men who had gone in search of them, and on their showing resistance, fired and killed the murderer, and severely wounded his accomplice. The dead man (whose name we have not yet learned), was left lying in the road, and the other, Green, was taken to

Sulphur Springs, where he has a brother in the grocery business. [note: see issue May 3, 1868].

Issue May 6, 1868
Gonzales Inquirer of the 2nd has the following: Mr. James Minter, who formerly resided a few miles above this place, was shot and killed by a desperado in Live Oak county a few days since...

Issue May 7, 1868
Waco Register records the drowning of a man named Hardin in the Tehuacana Creek; the suicide of William Lynch, of Limestone county, by shooting himself with a pistol...

Two young men, named Cooper, sons of a Mrs. Wirt by a former husband, killed a young man named Wirt, son of Mrs. Wirt's husband by a former wife, in Denton county, recently.

Issue May 8, 1868
Neil McLennan, Sr., who died in McLennan county on the 27th of February last at the advanced age of 81 years, was an "old Texian" having come to the country in company with several brothers in 1835. He was a native of Scotland and came to the United States in 1801. Those families did good service in the struggle for the independence of Texas. One of his brothers was murdered by Indians, and several children carried into captivity. Mr. McLennan located on the Bosque in 1846, where he lived till the day of his death. He was a man of strong clear intellect and untarnished honor, unaffectedly charitable, courageous and hospitable.

Waco Register: We learn that there were seven persons in all killed in the Perryville affair last week. Only two Shoonovers were killed, the father and son, George. The other son, Peter, escaped. A man named Jackson, not mentioned in our last, was killed, the Jackson reported killed in our last was Ed. Jackson of the attacking party...

The *Austin Gazette* announces the death of Mrs. Eliza Crosby, wife of Capt. Stephen F. Crosby, of that city, on the 2nd inst...

Issue May 9, 1868
Judge W.S. Oldham died in Houston day before yesterday.

Died in this city on the 8th inst. at one o'clock A.M. at the house of Philip Dubie, her brother-in-law, Mrs. Margaret Doyle, in the 32nd year of her age; a native of Ireland. Her remains were taken to New Orleans for interment at 9 o'clock A.M. on Monday the 11th inst. *New Orleans Times & Mobile Tribune* copy.

Serious Affray: Early this morning, two vegetable dealers in the second Ward Market had a difficulty, resulting in the shooting of Joe Antonio by Louis Faute with a dragoon size repeater, Colt's patent. The ball entered his back near the backbone, and the wound, it is thought will prove fatal. Faute was arrested and his examination will take place in the morning before Recorder Johnson. The parties are both Dagoes.

Issue May 10, 1868

Serious accident: Mr. Joe Lewis, a painter, in attempting to get off of a street car at the west end of the road yesterday about noon, was caught, thrown upon the track and run over by the car, whereby his left leg below the knee was badly crushed and three fingers of his right hand cut off by the car wheels. He was sent to the City Hospital...

Issue May 12, 1868

Homicide: An Italian named Guilelmo Mangealo was killed last night between 9 and 10 o'clock at the corner of Market and 22nd st. He was killed by Frank Saccaro, a vegetable and fruit dealer, also an Italian...

The *Trinity Advocate* learns that Col. J.J. Cook, of Cook's Ferry, on the Trinity, was killed a few days since by Mr. J.D. McCauley.

Bastrop Advertiser announces the death in Bastrop on the 4th of Dr. W.H. Stamps...

Issue May 13, 1868

The *(Henderson) Times* reports the murder in that county on the 1st of Mr. James Brewster, a dwarf, not more than 36 inches in height, by one Joe Cocke.

The *Telegraph (Houston)* announces the death of Mr. George Onderdonk, a useful citizen, on Saturday night last. About six o'clock he was injured by a refractory horse, and died about 9 o'clock the same evening.

Issue May 14, 1868

We are informed by a correspondent that a man named Osburn residing at Anderson committed suicide by cutting his throat with a razor in a barber shop at Navasota yesterday morning. The deed was done on account of a woman...

In the death of Mr. T.M. Bagby, day before yesterday, Houston lost one of her foremost citizens.

The *Belton Journal* reports the killing of Mr. W.B. McKaughan, by Mr. Spencer, his brother-in-law, in the neighborhood of Belton on the 15th. The difficulty was about family affairs.

We learn from the *Telegraph* that Mr. T.M. Bagby, of Houston, whose death we notice elsewhere, died at 7 o'clock P.M. the 12th, and that he had been a citizen of that place for about thirty years.

Issue May 15, 1868

The *San Antonio Herald* has an account of the killing of the notorious Billy Thompson, recently, by Mr. Walton in Atascosa. Mr. Thompson is the man who killed Mr. James Minter in Live Oak a short time ago.

Issue May 16, 1868

Mr. James Martin was brutally murdered by negroes near Allendale, S.C., last Wednesday...

Issue May 17, 1868

The *Brownsville Ranchero* of the 10th announces the finding of the bodies of James Moore and Henry Walden, carpenters, who had been employed on the garrison buildings at Brownsville...

Issue May 19, 1868

Fatal stabbing affray: A row concurred in the Lager Beer Saloon corner of Centre and Mechanic streets, yesterday afternoon, resulting in the probable killing of one of the parties. Ed. Williams, a sailor, lately engaged as a hand on board a lighter, was stabbed in the right side just below the ribs with a broad knife by James Brennan, a pugilist. The wounded man was carried to the drug store of Dr. Goodall on Market street, where his wound was examined and dressed by Drs. Goodall and McGill...

The *Trinity Advocate* reports the body of a young man named J.K.P. Able was found near Magnolia in Anderson county a few days since.

The *San Antonio Herald* says Mr. Walker, of Atascosa county, was killed recently by a man named Montgomery, near Lockhart.

Suicide: A man named D.D. Osborne, a saddle and harness maker, from North Carolina, came from Anderson to this place, and on Friday morning went to the barbers shop and got shaved. He then took a razor from the shelf and cut his throat from ear to ear, ran out of the side door, and fell to the ground, where he died. *Navasota Ranger* of the 7th.

Issue May 20, 1868
At Greenville, Mississippi, on the 13th, a difficulty occurred in the yard of the Campbell House between Major E.P. Byrne and Dr. T.G. Polk, when Col. Hinds attempted to stop the quarrel. In this, however, he was prevented by Dr. O.M. Blanton, who stealthily approached him from the rear, and with a six inch knife inflicted three stabs. Col. Hinds dropped dead at once...

Issue May 21, 1868
We deeply sympathize with our friend Dr. J.E. Scott, of Dallas county, who, the *Herald* says, lost a promising little son by drowning on the 9th...

Issue May 23, 1868
We learn that Mr. H. Clay Searcy, who was shot at Navasota about 3 months ago by a man named Dan McKinney, died of his injuries on Sunday last at the residence of his father-in-law, Gen. J.W. Barnes, near Anderson.

Issue May 24, 1868
The *Trinity Advocate* contains an account of the murder of Mr. R.J. Masters, a highly respected citizen of Anderson county, on the 14th in Houston county, sixteen miles from Crockett. He was killed on the road by three traveling strangers.

We learn from the *Trinity Advocate* that J.D. McCauley, charged with the murder of J.J. Cook of Anderson county, recently, has been examined and discharged.

It seems that Mr. D.D. Osborne, who committed suicide in Navasota, recently, was from North Carolina. He left a letter stating that he had relatives in Dodson, Charlotte and Huntsville, North Carolina...

Issue May 27, 1868
We learn from a passenger by the Central train that Mr. L. Springfield shot and killed Mr. Clinton Fort, a lawyer of Bellville, at Hempstead, yesterday morning.

We understand that Mr. Gray, a well known citizen of Robertson county, was killed on Friday last by a negro employed on his farm... The negro fled and was followed by a number of citizens to Bryan of where he was captured on Saturday morning and executed.

Issue May 28, 1868

The *Clarksville Standard* has an interesting obituary notice of Maj. Edward West, an old Texian, who died there on the 10th, in the 67th year of his age. He was born in Campbell county, Virginia, in 1802, and came to Texas in 1835.

Issue May 29, 1868

The *Crockett Sentinel* says the name of the murderers of Mr. Master's are Geo. Miller, C. Bowels, and James F. Lee. They were caught within eighteen miles of Carthage, Panola county. Bowels says he has a mother and two sisters living in Austin. All of them were summarily executed... Lee was from Bradley county, Tennessee...

Issue May 31, 1868

From the *Bryan News Letter* of the 30th: On Sunday night last, a young man named Graham, living about eight miles from this place, was foully murdered by three brothers, Andrew, Thomas and Amos Walker.

Issue June 4, 1868

Died at Galveston at 11 1/2 o'clock A.M., May 31st, Miss Ellen McDonnell, second daughter of B. and Winifred McDonnel. *New Orleans Times* and Chicago papers please copy.

Died on Sunday morning, May 25th, of congestion of the brain, Benjamin Sidney, son of Robt. M. and Sallie F. Franklin, aged 21 months.

Issue June 5, 1868

Houston Telegraph: We are informed that J.O. Cassidy shot and instantly killed Mr. Ghans, a dry goods merchant at Brenham, on Tuesday morning last.

Issue June 7, 1868

The *Crockett Sentinel* reports that a negro man named West Wooten was killed by Col. P.V. Green at Pennington in Trinity county on the 29th ult.

Issue June 9, 1868

The *Waxahachie Argus* reports the assassination of Capt. Robert Blackwell, on his way home from Weatherford on the 29th ult.

Notice of the untimely death of Mr. Robert Hardie, Jr.

Issue June 10, 1868
Col. John Ashe, an old citizen, died in Charleston on the 30th ult. He was born in 1776...

Issue June 11, 1868
The death of Mrs. Maclin will be felt by all our citizens...

Issue June 12, 1868
The *Waco Examiner* reports the death of two of the most estimable ladies of that city, Mrs. L.G. Davenport, wife of Rev. Mr. Davenport, and Mrs. Trice.

Issue June 17, 1868
The *Inquirer* reports the death of A.J. McKean, a worthy citizen, on the 10th at Prairie Lea.

Issue June 19, 1868
The *Corpus Christi Advertiser* has notices of the killing of William Ashton by Richard Miller on the 8th at San Diego, Duval county, and of the murder of Mat Dunn, a young and respectable citizen of Nueces county, on the 12th. He is supposed to have been murdered by Mexicans.

The *Victoria Advocate* announces the death on the 10th of Rev. Joel T. Case, formerly pastor of the Presbyterian church, in that place...

Issue June 21, 1868
The *Brazos Signal*... Capt. T.C. Robinson committed suicide on the 17th by taking morphine. He left a note requesting that affairs be closed up for the benefit of his wife, who is now in Mississippi.

Issue June 23, 1868
From the *Weatherford (Parker county) Times* of the 17th... A traveler afoot on the Buchanan road was fired on and killed instantly by some party unknown... from papers on the deceased, it is thought his name was Thomas Bird, formerly of Dakotah, and that he was direct from Austin. Suspicion fell on a negro named Joe Williams...

Issue June 24, 1868
Mr. William N. Sparks, who has been confined to his bed with rheumatism for nearly fourteen years, died at his residence in this city, yesterday evening... His funeral will take place this morning from his late residence at 9 o'clock, conducted by the Masonic fraternity of which he was a member.

Miscellaneous Texas Newspaper Abstracts - Deaths --- Vol 2

Issue June 26, 1868

We learn from the *Gazette* that Maj. W. Oldham, of Burleson, who had just arrived in Austin a few days since, fell into a gully at the end of Congress Ave., and was so injured that he died in a few hours after being found.

Issue June 27, 1868

Died at the residence of Dr. W.P. Craddock, Lowndes county, Mississippi, on the 26th inst., Annie Somerville, infant daughter of Albert and Annie Somerville of this city.

Issue June 30, 1868

The *Lavaca Commercial* of the 24th... In September last a traveler was murdered 12 miles west of New Braunfels. Recently it has been ascertained that the murdered man was the Rev. James K. Tanzy of the M.E. Church South. His horse, branded 85 with a half circle over it, has not been found...

Dr. Charles F. Thornton, a young well known and prominent citizen of Cincinnati, committed suicide by stabbing himself with a penknife on the 22nd. He was a grandson of the late Gen. Harrison, President of the United States.

Sunday morning between 2 & 3 o'clock, Bill Harris, a freedman, was found on Winnie Street near the Episcopal church by a watchman, shot through the body. He was carried to a house and died about 10 o'clock the same morning...

Issue July 1, 1868

Henderson Times of the 26th says a house occupied by Mr. T.J. Cornelius, 200 yards from the family residence, and 2 1/2 miles east of town, was burned down the night previous. Mr. Cornelius was burned to death. He had been a lunatic for many years. He leaves a widow and several children.

Issue July 2, 1868

The *Journal* says 2 negroes recently tried at Belton for the murder of a freedman named Antley Myers were acquitted by the civil authorities.

Issue July 4, 1868

Died on June 26th, far away from her home and her father, little Annie, only child of Albert and Annie Somerville, aged 9 months, 18 days. Houston papers please copy.

A letter from our correspondent at Richmond, Texas, informs us that Mr. W.L. Hathaway, an old citizen of that place, committed suicide on Tuesday afternoon last... The deceased was a brother-in-law of Mr. J.J. Dunn, foreman of the *Houston Telegraph* office...

372

Issue July 5, 1868

Died in this city on the 8th inst., Mrs. Ann Lane, late of Houston, Texas. *New York World*, Houston, Galveston and New Orleans papers please copy.

Issue July 7, 1868

Mr. B. Crone, one of our oldest citizens, as well as most quiet and worthy, was buried from the Cathedral Sunday. His age at his death was 76 years.

Died at 4 o'clock P.M., July 6th, 1868, Virginia, youngest child of J.H. and Minnie Hutchins, aged 1 year, 8 months and 10 days. The funeral will take place from their house in this city at 4 o'clock this afternoon, and their friends and acquaintances are respectfully invited to attend.

Died in Giles county, Tennessee, June 20th, of inflammation resulting from wounds received at Brenham in April 1867, Mr. Ben Stones, of Brenham, Texas, aged 53 years... Since his removal to Texas from Tennessee, in 1836, he has been favorably known as a capable merchant and a good citizen... Notice: The business of Ben. Stones, at Brenham, will be continued as formerly until further notice. Mary J. Stones.

Issue July 8, 1868

John Dodd, a notorious desperado, was killed a few days ago near Gonzales...

The *San Antonio Herald* of the 2nd says a well but not very favorably known frenchman of that place named Lecomte de Waretime was shot and killed on the night of the 1st.

Issue July 9, 1868

The *McKinney Enquirer* of the 14th records the murder of two brothers, Tom and Dol. Waters, on the 26th ult. in the Eastern part of Collin county.

The *Enquirer* mentions a painful rumor that Major Dougherty of Collin was killed by Indians recently, while on his way to Kansas with cattle.

Issue July 15, 1868

The *Austin Republican* learns that Wm. I. Shepherd, wife, and child, were murdered by Indians on the 2nd, seven miles southeast of Blanco city, near the road leading to San Antonio...

Issue July 16, 1868

From the *Jefferson Times* of the 4th inst: On Tuesday evening, Mr. Harry McDonald committed suicide in this city by taking strychnine. The deceased was a blacksmith by trade and is said to have a family and relatives in the city of New York.

Issue July 17, 1868

The *Waco Examiner* reports the shooting of Mr. W.A. Gleason by Mr. C.L. Merriman on the 11th while the former was sitting on the porch of his residence at Waco. He died on the following Sunday.

Issue July 18, 1868

Indians -- The *San Antonio Herald* says the bodies of a man named Sheppard and his wife and child were found on the 8th, scalped, on the road between San Marcos and Middletown. A brother of the deceased Sheppard is missing. About 125 horses were stolen on this raid.

Issue July 19, 1868

Died on the 18th inst. at San Antonio, Charles E. McCarthy of hemorrhage of the lung, native of Ireland, late of this city, in the 26th year of his age. New Orleans papers please copy.

Issue July 21, 1868

Died on Sunday morning the 19th inst. at half past 3 o'clock, Rebecca, wife of Capt. Aaron Burns, in the 74th year of her age. New Orleans, Philadelphia, & Wilmington, Del. papers please copy.

We learn by private letter of the murder of N.G. Seales at Sempronius, Austin county, Texas, on Saturday evening by S. Austin Middleton.

Issue July 25, 1868

Died on the 23th July, 1868, Mary Elizabeth, daughter of Andrew and Elizabeth Gover, aged 1 year, 5 months and 11 days.

Issue July 26, 1868

The *Telegraph*, yesterday morning, announced the killing of Col. H.M. Ashby at Knoxville, Tennessee.

Dr. J.H. Herndon, who lately removed from Austin to San Antonio, committed suicide at the latter place on the night of the 18th by stabbing himself to the heart with a small scalpel or knife. The *Herald* says he had been deranged for some two weeks. He was buried by the Odd Fellows.

Mr. J.R. Goode was killed at Columbus, Texas, a few days ago by Mr. J.M. Bowen...

Issue July 28, 1868

A duel took place a short distance below the barracks in the parish of St. Bernard, Louisiana, on the 25th, between Messrs. Paul E. Laresche, Jr. and Sandford Boussiere, both of New Orleans. Laresche was wounded and died in a few minutes.

Issue July 29, 1868

Death of Dr. E.M. Walker: We regret to learn as we do from the *Gonzales Inquirer* that this eminent and useful citizen died suddenly at his residence near San Marcos a few days since.

Natchitoches Times: On Sunday evening an old negro man named Tom Sloan died on the street near the town ferry, not, like Brick Pomeroy's man and brother, of too much freedom and too little grub, but of an excess of grubyea, of the delicacies of the season: to wit, two big watermelons and a pot of honey, which being devoured for his midday meal, made him a "cold corpus" and sent him to Abraham's bosom before sun-down.

Killing: The *Bastrop Advertiser* says two twin brothers, Neill and Richard Northcross, were killed on the 22nd, twelve miles north of Bastrop. One of the brothers was a son-in-law of a Mr. Gentry, who was about to remove to Kentucky, and the difficulty arose about the separation. His wife at first determined to go with her father, but had finally concluded to remain.

Mr. Gentry, father-in-law of Northcross, received a flesh wound from a pistol shot in the back of the left shoulder from the hand of his son-in-law. The parties engaged in the killing of the Northcross brothers are G.W. Gentry, his son, T.M. Gentry, and nephew, George Gentry, son of Elias Gentry, and Robert Arnold, who, we are informed, proffered his services in case of a difficulty if Gentry would defray his expenses to Tennessee. Richard and Neill Northcross were originally from Franklin county, Alabama, but lately from Tippa [sic] county, Mississippi, have been residents of this county for about 18 months; about 24 years of age.

Another murdered radical: We copy as follows the last issue of the *Brenham Banner*: The Austin Convention's Report on Lawlessness has charged to political causes the death of Reading W. Black of Ulvade. This is about as bold and brazen a falsehood as the muddy headed fools could well have put on paper. The facts of that case we know, and we know that politics had no more to do with it than with the thousand and one cases occurring every day in the world, where men provoke personal difficulties and pay the forfeit with their lives. Wall is a man beyond the middle age of life, and has a family of children nearly grown. He wanted to marry Meldy McKinney, a girl of 16 or 17, and sister to Black's wife. Black opposed the wedding; abused Wall violently, brought on a personal collision, and got himself killed.

Issue July 31, 1868

We are glad to learn from the *McKinney Enquirer* that the report of the murder of Maj. F.M. Dougherty, of Gainsville, by the Indians, is untrue. He arrived safely in Kansas with his cattle.

Issue August 1, 1868

Mr. A. Gillette, known among his friends and comrades by the name of Dick Gillette, was murdered Thursday on the banks of Cedar Bayou by some person or persons unknown...

Under the head of cases of persons killed for their loyalty, the last crime report mentions W.H. Upton, a man who had been largely engaged in beef stealing, and who, the Texas Ranger declares, sold stolen beeves in Navasota a day or two before he was hung...

The second crime report. Committee room, Austin, Texas: In our report of the 30th ultimo, it was stated that Milton Biggs, a loyal man, was murdered in Blanco county last year. Subsequent investigation shows that Claiborne Biggs, the son, was murdered as described, that circumstances point to certain rebel outlaws as the murderers, and that the father and the other members of the family understand that their lives are in danger, and have left the county for safety...

We would also state that Mr. Wade was murdered in Red River county instead of Lamar, as previously reported...

The Hon. A.O. Cooley, a worthy citizen of Gillespie county, and a prominent republican, was shot and wounded on the 10th inst. at home by an assassin from a distant county. We also learn that W.H. Upton, a Union man, was hung by a mob on the 3d inst. in Brazos county.

Issue August 2, 1868

Drowned on Monday morning last, a man by the name of Thomas Slocum...

From the *Grenada (Mississippi) Sentinel*... Mr. Robert McSwine, a most estimable gentleman who lives near Grenada, had discharged from his service a worthless negro named Tom McLean. This negro was stimulated by the Loyal Leaguers to assassinate Mr. McSwine, which he did on the night of the 20th ult. by shooting him in the back with a double-barrel shotgun...

The late crime report says: "The Hon. A.O. Cooley, a worthy citizen of Gillespie county, and a prominent republican, was shot and wounded at home on the 10th inst. by an assassin from a distant county... The person who wounded Cooley was a mere boy named T.B. Nixon."

Issue August 4, 1868
Died suddenly on the 2nd inst. of congestion of the bowels at 11 o'clock A.M., Capt. Thomas M. Deane, general agent of the Louisiana Equitable Life Insurance Co. New Orleans papers please copy.

Sam Houston Webb, son of a citizen of Williamson county, died from getting a bean down his windpipe, a few days since...

Issue August 7, 1868
Capt. Henry Parker, an old and esteemed citizen, died night before last and was buried yesterday at 4 P.M.

By private letter from Kansas City we learn that Charles McCally, of Chambers county, Texas, was killed on the night of the 4th July last. He was a soldier in the 5th Tx. Regt. Hood's Brigade...

Issue August 9, 1868
The *Huntsville Republican* gives an account of the murder there on the 4th inst. of Sheriff A.J. Edwards by a young man named Wooten. The body of the sheriff was pierced with 5 pistol balls. One shot from the young man's pistol passed through the body of his uncle, Shelby Wooten.

Issue August 11, 1868
We regret to learn of the death of Capt. J.H. Hamilton of Houston on the 9th inst.

Issue August 18, 1868
Departed this life on Sunday the 16th of August at 4 o'clock P.M., Mrs. M.C. Dial, consort of Dr. Wm. H. Dial, of this city. Mrs. Dial was a daughter of Judge Wm. J. Adair of Alabama and has a large connection in West Tennessee. Memphis & Alabama papers please copy.

Died in this city, August 16th at 11 o'clock P.M. of rheumatic neuralgia, Mrs. Mary Stevens, aged 57 years. Deceased was born in Baltimore. New Orleans & Baltimore papers please copy.

Issue August 20, 1868
Death of Josiah Taylor... by telegraph we learn that his demise took place last evening at half past 8 o'clock at the town of LaGrange, in Fayette county...

Letter from Matagorda: Mr. Thomas Jamison died at his residence on Caney in April last. He was one of the "Old Three Hundred" who emigrated to Texas in 1824...

Dr. L.H.W. Johnson came to this state from New Orleans in 1835, and at one time was at the head of his profession in this place. About 1842 he left here and spent most of his time in Houston and Millican until 1865 when he returned. He died at Live Oak, in this county, in June.

Mrs. Elizabeth E. Campbell died in this city on the 25th of July, in her 85th year. She came to this state from Arkansas in 1829...

I regret to announce "another man killed". On Tuesday last a man named Rhodes was killed by Mr. Trammel on Col. Hawkins plantation...

Issue August 21, 1868

A young man named Clark, who was employed as a laborer near Long Point, Washington county, met with an accident a few days since, which caused his almost instant death. He drove a yoke of oxen into the woods for the purpose of getting timber to make cotton baskets, and coming near the oxen one of them kicked him in the region of the heart, which caused internal hemorrhage. He is reported to have been an industrious man, and had relatives living in some northern state.

Issue August 22, 1868

Wm. E. Thompson, a former resident and merchant of New Orleans, died on the 18th at his plantation below this city.

Issue August 23, 1868

The *Brenham Inquirer* says: We learn that a shooting affair took place in the prairie, some five miles south of this place, on Thursday last, in which an old man named Gid. Kesee shot a German named Frank Phol dead upon the spot...

Issue August 26, 1868

Died at Hot Springs, Arkansas, on the 13th of August 1868, Charles Henry Hughes, aged 35 years, after a short illness of only 3 days...

Issue August 28, 1868

Died with consumption at Lake Hill, Fort Bend county, Texas, Capt. Wm. G Wimberly, of Russell county, Alabama, on the 3rd of August 1868. *Jefferson Jimplecute* and *Columbus Ga. Inquirer* please copy.

Issue September 1, 1868

Chappell Hill, August 26, 1868: In the Monday's issue of the *Tri-Weekly News* there is a paragraph copied from the *Brenham Enquirer* reporting the killing of a German near Brenham on the 13th day of this month by Mr. Gideon Keesee, Sr...

Issue September 2, 1868

Indians -- We learn from the *Dallas Herald* that the Indians visited Wise county a few days ago, killing four persons, taking prisoner one young lady, wounding a boy mortally, and stealing some 75 or 100 head of horses, making their exit without molestation. Mrs. Russell and two sons and a man named Foyster, of Denton county, were the killed. A son of Mr. McDaniels was lanced three or four times, and was expected to die. Mr. Chisholm, of Denton, was wounded by them. The young lady taken captive was a daughter of Mrs. Russell. There were marks of desperate fighting in her house.

This is a terrible affair, and unfortunately, such are far too common on our frontier. What a pity that the surplus military energy and talent of the country cannot be given to its defence.

Issue September 3, 1868

The *Texas Observer* says W.E. Hartless was found dead on the 22nd ult. near his home, 13 miles from Rusk on the Henderson road. Strong suspicion rest upon his wife and her son, Henry Mitchell, and they have been arrested.

Issue September 6, 1868

Huntsville Times, 5th... A friend informs us that on 16th ult. Mr. Alex Taylor, of Montgomery county, mortally wounded himself with his shot gun, dying soon after... He was a son of Capt. Wm. S. Taylor, one of the surviving heroes of San Jacinto...

Died at the residence of Col. E.S. Jemison, of Tennessee Colony, Anderson county, Texas, on the night of the 25th of August, John Allen Adams, formerly a citizen of New Orleans, Louisiana, but for two years previous to his death a resident of said Anderson county. The deceased was attacked with pneumonia on the 19th day of August...

Issue September 9, 1868

The *San Antonian* of the 2nd reports the murder of Mr. Spangenberg, Mr. Pickel, Miss Pickel, and a child of three years old, by a party of Mexicans near Boerne on the night of the 29th ult...

Issue September 10, 1868

Died on the 8th inst. at her residence in this city after a protracted illness, Mrs. R.A. McCracken, of Evansville, Indiana. Evansville papers please copy.

Issue September 18, 1868

We sympathize with Mr. Wm. G. Barrett, of the *Harrison Flag*, in the loss of his wife.

Murder on the Trinity: A letter from our travelling correspondent informs us that early on Sunday night, 13th inst., at Calhoun's Ferry, 12 miles from Huntsville, Mr. Hall, Mrs. Hall, a girl, 12 years old, sister of Mrs. Hall, and a traveler named something like Wicknow, were all murdered. The bodies of Mr. Hall and wife were thrown into the river, and the bodies of the girl and the traveler were thrown into the well...

Issue September 20, 1868

The Hall Murders: We have already mentioned the recent murder of Mr. Chas. Hall, and wife, her sister, and a stranger, supposed to be a man named Murray from the San Jacinto river, somewhere at Calhoun's Ferry, on the Trinity. We now hear that a negro has been arrested...

Issue September 23, 1868

Henry Miller, a horse thief, was hung recently in McNairy county, Tennessee, by some unknown persons...

Issue September 25, 1868

The *State Gazette* says a deep gloom has been cast over society in Austin by the death of Mrs. Eliza H. Major, wife of Gen. James P. Major, late of the Confederate Army, second daughter of Dr. John G. Chalmers, deceased...

Obituary: Mr. John Cross Jones was born on the 14th of November 1824 in Cape Girardeau, Missouri, was married in 1855, became a citizen of our state in 1859, and died at his residence in Grimes county, Texas, the 9th September 1868...

Issue September 26, 1868

The *Anderson Gladiator* says Mr. M.D. Ball, its publisher, who was killed on the 19th by Mr. Briggs Goodrich, had threatened to kill the latter some half hour before the shooting occurred...

Issue September 27, 1868

The *Henderson Times* of the 23rd has an account of the killing of four men near Mt. Enterprise, Rusk county, recently. First, Mat Shaddon was killed by John Elliott in a quarrel about an estate. They were brothers-in-law. This was on the 13th. Some days afterwards, four brothers of Shaddon set out to hunt his murderer and killed Haydon Phillips because he would not tell where Elliott was, Phillips protesting that he did not know. Immediately after Ben Phillips, a son of Haydon Phillips, was shot and killed. Asa Irwin, a son-in-law of Haydon Phillips, was also killed at the same time and place.

Siedie Joseph, infant, colored, died of lockjaw.

John Clark, native of Ireland, died of pneumonia, at the city hospital.

Issue September 29, 1868

The *Houston Evening Times* of the 28th announces the death of Col. Scott Anderson at his home near Eagle Lake of congestive chill on Friday evening last.

Issue September 30, 1868

The *Examiner* chronicles the death of Mr. P. Paulson, a prominent member of the Norwegian settlement in Bosque county...

In the death of Gen. Thomas C. Hindman, Arkansas, loses a very valuable citizen...

Mrs. Rebecca Hildreth, aged 97 years, died in Louisville on the 21st inst. She dressed the wounds of the old continental who were hurt at King's Mountain, North Carolina, in 1780...

On the 18th inst., while returning from a Democratic barbecue given at Whittaker Springs, Louisiana, Messrs. David Toadvine and George Shules were waylaid and assassinated by some radicals. Both these young gentleman were residents of Jackson, Louisiana...

Issue October 1, 1868

Died in this city on Wednesday evening, September 30th, 1868, F. Markey, aged about 41 years. The funeral will take place at 3 o'clock this evening from his late residence, corner of Market and Centre streets.

Issue October 3, 1868

Mr. John B. Ramsey, 106 years old, has just died in Florida.

Col. D.C. Glenn died in Mississippi on the 19th inst...

Issue October 4, 1868

It was reported recently that a party from Montague county had overtaken some horse thieves in Grayson. Still more recently the dead bodies of two white men and one negro were found near where the thieves were said to have been overtaken. The *Sherman Courier* says the bodies correspond with the description of the thieves. The names of the whites killed, or found dead, were William Estes and John Bridges. The negro's name was Morgan...

The *Clarksville Standard* reports the killing at that place on the 24th of John P. Duty, who was lately arrested for sundry offenses by W.C. Harris...

Issue October 6, 1868

Died at his residence in Lavaca county, Texas, Dr. M.M. Wilkins, of consumption, aged 49 years, 11 months and 10 days; a native of Mobile, Alabama. Mobile papers please copy.

Issue October 8, 1868

We regret to learn that Mr. Edward Ware, who on Saturday morning shot himself in the mouth at his residence corner Canal and Franklin streets, has since died at Hotel Dieu. *(New Orleans Times* of the 6th)

Issue October 11, 1868

The *Hempstead Countryman* reports a horrible outrage committed recently by a negro man upon Mrs. Wentz, a German lady, living near Waller's store. The negro was tried by the citizens, found guilty and hung.

Issue October 13, 1868

James Clarke, a barkeeper at the Exchange Hotel, fell dead yesterday without any apparent cause... Mr. Clarke was about 38 years of age... was formerly employed in the grocery house of Smith & Zeigler, New Orleans. We believe he had no family.

William P. Fitzgerald, a boss carpenter well known to many of our citizens, whose residence is on Market street near the railroad depot, was stabbed in the Imperial barroom about 5 o'clock yesterday evening by Maj. Tom Ochiltree. He has a wife and two children.

Issue October 14, 1868

Mr. A.M. Tubbs of Kaufman was shot and killed recently in his own yard.

Issue October 16, 1868

Died on Thursday, October 15th, Miss Margaret Moore, aged 18 years and 10 months, daughter of A. & Thos. S. Moore. New Orleans & St. Louis papers please copy.

Issue October 18, 1868

Mortuary Report:

October 11th: Mr. Adams, 72 years of age, consumption. Alice West, 10 months old, disease not stated. Infant of William Yunker, 1 day old, lockjaw.

October 12th: Jas. Clark, 35 years, disease of heart.

October 14th: Amelia Fink, 23 years, intermittent fever.

October 15th: Mrs. Elihu R. Arnetchey, 70 years, old age. Infant of C.H. Lenard, still born.

October 16th: Miss Margaret Moore, 19 years, convulsions. Jos. Wright, 50 years, inanition. Peter Yunker, 5 days, lockjaw. Infant of W. Farmar, 3 weeks old, negro, disease not stated.

Issue October 20, 1868

The *Texas Ranger* of the 17th gives a horrible account of the murder of the youngest son of the editor, Capt. J. Lancaster, on the 13th of last month.

Died in New Orleans on the 13th inst. at 10 o'clock, 10 minutes, O.J. Noyles, aged 68 years.

A Little Rock, Arkansas, special says Marcus Houston was assassinated on the steamer *Hesper*, while lying at the wharf there on the night of the 8th inst.

Mr. George W. Mensman, a native of New Orleans and highly respected man, died last Friday.

Issue October 22, 1868

Maj. E.D. Smith died at Brownsville on the 16th. He had lived on the frontier more than 1/3 of a century... He leaves a wife and two daughters, one of them the wife of Col. J.S. Ford, and the other the wife of Capt. Michaelowski, late of the U.S. 1st Artillery.

Died in this city on the 21st of October 1868, Capt. Joseph I. Sargent, aged 48 years. The funeral takes place at 10 o'clock A.M., today. Cincinnati papers please copy.

The *Brandon (Mississippi) Republican* chronicles the death of two venerable ministers of the gospel, Rev. Jacob Carr and Rev. Hardy Mullins.

Lieut. Churchill of the 14th Inf. died at Jackson, Mississippi, on the 14th.

Issue October 25, 1868

Killing and burning: The *Jefferson Jimplecute* of the 16th has the following: We regret to have to chronicle another bloody affair which occurred on Wednesday night. A body of armed men, thought to have numbered at least fifty, attacked the plantation of the late Willis Whitaker, about 12 miles from this city, in Davis county, and killed some six or seven freedmen and burned the gin and mill on the premises...

The *Columbus Times* of the 16th says: On last Saturday, the Hon. I.B. McFarland, Judge of the District Court for this District, pronounced the sentence of death upon John Thomas, f.m.c., who had, a few days previous, been tried and found guilty of rape upon a German lady in this county.

Accidentally killed: Says the *Hempstead Countryman* of the 23rd: We are pained to hear of a shocking accident befalling one of the members of the family of Mr. J.H. Kuttner, his brother being shot and instantly killed, accidentally, by a friend in San Antonio. Mr. Kuttner left for that place yesterday to settle his brother's estate.

Mortuary Report:
October 18th: Joice Lindsay, 27 years old, dysentery; infant of Mr. Ringh, stillborn. Bridget Tarphey, 40 years, inflammation of the bowels.
October 20th: Harmon Stern, 27 years old, chronic diarrhea.
October 22nd: Capt. Jos. I. Sargent, 44 years, dropsy. Mrs. Renetta, colored woman, 23 years, consumption.

Issue October 28, 1868

Aaron Butler, one of the early settlers of Liberty county, Mississippi, died recently at the advanced age of 91 years.

Issue October 30, 1868

Killing and arson: About sunrise on Thursday of last week, a body of armed men numbering about fifty made their appearance on the plantation of Willis Whitaker, twelve miles above Jefferson in Davis county, and killed seven negroes, wounded three others, burned the gin house with 40 bales of cotton, and the corn cribs, containing near 2,000 bushels of corn. One of the negroes was found hanging...

Jefferson Times... the same paper says a Mr. Linton, son of a widow lady, also living in Arkansas, was killed not long since by the same negroes...

Issue October 31, 1868

The *San Antonio Express*, a radical paper, plainly intimates that the loss of G.W. Smith, killed at Jefferson, is not much to be lamented.

Mr. J.M. Dillon, a clerk in the revenue department, was stabbed and killed instantly, at Indianola on the night of the 26th by Duncan Barr, a Scotchman, who lately resided in Tres Palacios, Matagorda county. Barr escaped and has not been arrested...

Our *Commercial* editor, Mr. John E. Thornton, has just returned to the city from the sad task of consigning to the tomb the remains of his beautiful and accomplished wife, formerly Miss Laura O. West, daughter of Maj. West, an old Texan, and step-daughter of Rev. H.E. Thrall. She died at Victoria...

Issue November 1, 1868

Mortuary Report:
October 25th: L. Sunaseites, 35 years, Hepatitis chronic; Fred Wachemouth, 59 years, consumption.
October 26th: Henry Butler, 25 years, fits, negro; Willie Franklin, 16 years, lockjaw, negro.
October 28th: J.B. Shorter, 38 years, inflammation of bowels; infant of Julius McAvoy, still born.
October 29th: J. Ducros, 30 years, inanition; Rebuen Kennedy, 105 years, old age, negro.
October 31th: George Anderson, not known; infant of Mrs. Hinkell, 6 days, lockjaw.

Issue November 3, 1868

The *Bastrop Advertiser* reports the explosion of a boiler in the steam mill of Wesley McGuire ten miles south of Bastrop, killing one employee named Patrick Doyle, and wounding several others.

Issue November 4, 1868

Died in this city at 10 o'clock A.M. yesterday, Mr. John Shackelford, aged 56 years... his funeral today at 3 o'clock P.M. from his residence on Broadway.

From the *Marshall Flag*:... Capt. W.H. Mullins, of Tyler, committed suicide by shooting himself on the 24th ult...

Frank Craig, son of a widow lady of Marshall, was accidently shot in Shreveport, says the *Marshall Republican*, on the 25th, and killed by Sam. Burton.

The *Inquirer* says Frank Frisby, a somewhat notorious character, was shot and killed by some parties unknown, in the lower end of Gonzales county, on the night of the 25th.

The *Rusk Observer* says the suicide of Col. Mullins has cast a gloom over that community, where since 1859, until the last few months, he resided. He was 34 years of age, a native of Sumner county, Tennessee...

Issue November 5, 1868

Miss Kate Hayden, danseuse, was burned to death at the Louisville varieties last week.

Issue November 6, 1868

Obituary: of the death of Mr. John Shackleford... he died Tuesday, in his 56 year... He was a native of Virginia, but had lived in Texas nearly a third of a century.

Dr. J. Whittlesy, city physician of Columbus, Georgia, died on the 25th.

W.C. Turner and Dudley Hopkins, well known citizens of Enterprise, Mississippi, died last week.

John R. Norton, a well known and much respected citizen of Savannah, died in New York on the 26th.

W.M. Plant, of the house of Plant brothers of St. Louis and well known in that city, died on the 27th inst.

An old man named Mapes was murdered in Cooper county, Missouri, last week, whereupon a mob arrested his wife and hung her brother.

Died... little Mary, only child of Col. O.P. and Margaret Bowels, who died in Bryan on the 27th ult., aged 3 years, 6 months, 8 days.

Issue November 7, 1868

The *Belton Journal* gives the particulars of the killing of T. Eberhardt, a Private of Co. A 17th U.S. Infantry, at that place on the 26th ult.

Died in Brazoria, Texas, October 31st, Mrs. Lucy M.J. Weir. She was a firm Christian.

Issue November 8, 1868

From the *Bonham News*: John White killed W.P. Seitz, about 4 miles from Bonham, on the 28th ult. White is expected to die of wounds given him by Seitz.

Mortuary Report: Interments: Henry Dodge, died November 1st, aged 56 years, chronic diarrhea. Infant of Theodore Neitsch, died November 2nd, stillborn. John Shackleford, died November 4th, aged 56 years, congestive chill. Clundia Hyde died November 5th, aged 27th, disease unknown. John Lewis died November 6th, aged 39 years, chronic diarrhea; Christina Idleman died November 6th, aged 1 year, cramps; Nina Rost, died November 7th, aged 6 weeks, cramps.

Issue November 11, 1868
Col. Samuel Abbott of Cuachita county, Sebron Jameson of Columbia county, and Col. H.M. Lernay of Lafayette county, Arkansas, have recently died. They were old citizens.

Issue November 12, 1868
The *LaGrange New Era* announces the death on the 4th of Col. S.C. Ferrill, an old citizen of that county...

Death of John T. Stanley... from the *Bastrop Advertiser*... He died a few days since at Chappell Hill, Texas... He was a native of Maine.

Mr. Fortinberry, Mrs. Vicks, and a young man whose name is not known, were murdered recently in Decatur and Wise counties by the Indians...

"Old Aunt Sookey" (colored) aged 110, died in Augusta, Georgia, on the 4th inst.

Dr. J.W. Vance and Maj. W.D. Hilton, both of Bossier Parish, Louisiana, died last week.

Mrs. Sallie Sutherland, a venerable lady of Augusta, Georgia, died on the 3rd inst. near there, aged 104.

Judge Thurlow of the Probate Court of Limestone county, Alabama, who was mortally wounded by a negro mob in Huntsville, died on the 27th.

Issue November 15, 1868
Died, early in the morning of Thursday, 5th November, at the residence of his brother-in-law, Mr. W.N. Sheridan, in Houston county, in his 31st year, Zac. C. Wilson, son of Rev. D.R. Wilson, and son-in-law of Mr. Thomas P. Collins, merchant, of Crockett, leaving his wife (the second time a widow) just at the completion of her 26th year...

Mortuary Report as reported by M. Cahill, City Sexton:
7th: Phresilla Howes, aged 35 years, cholera morbus.
8th: S. Estabrooks, aged 35 years, malenaria.
10th: P. Carney, aged 49 years, ascites; Hastilla Quales, aged 2 months, whooping cough; Juliana Williams, negro, aged 26 years, disease not known.
11th: Mary Ann Pingh, aged 26 years, dysentery; Anna Maria Flowers, aged 17 months, inflammation bowels.

Issue November 17, 1868
Mr. James T. Shelton, formerly mayor of Mobile, died in that city on the 2nd inst.

The *Bastrop Advertiser* announces the death at his residence in that place on the 14th of Dr. J.N. Williams. He was a member of the Masonic & Odd Fellows fraternities...

Issue November 19, 1868
Mr. S.W. Smith, living 3 miles from Rusk, was shot from ambush and killed, a few days since. The observer says his dying declaration fixed suspicion on his son-in-law, W.H. Norris, who has been arrested.

Issue November 22, 1868
Mortuary, city of Galveston:
November 11th: Anna Keast, 64 years, dysentery.
November 16th: Jas. Ardale, 39 years, disease of heart; Mary Miller, 9 months, consumption; infant of R.M. Tevis, stillborn.
November 17th: Infant of A. Gilbert, 2 days, croup; David P. Miller, 7 days, not known; Robert Sennott, 35 years, consumption; P.M. Mitchell, 45 years, meningitis.
November 18th: Wm. Henry Divine, 18 months, inflammation of bowels.
November 19th: Mrs. Louis Gonzales, 26 years, hemorrhage of lungs.
November 20th: C. Kearson, 30 years, dysentery.
November 21st: Dr. E. Brake, unknown age, unknown disease.

Issue November 26, 1868
H.W. Rozar, a radical member of the late (so called) Georgia Convention, was run over by a train of cars at Chattanooga and instantly killed, Saturday last.

A young man named Branch, while out hunting in Washington Parish, Louisiana, a few days ago, was accidentally shot for a deer by his companion, and the wound proved mortal.

Issue November 28, 1868

The local of the *Civilian* learns from Capt. J. Hawthorne, of the steamboat *Crescent*, that a child of Mr. W.H. Cockey died at sea on the *Crescent* during her last trip from this city to Indianola. The body was interred in the cemetery at the latter place.

Henry T. Brooke, for the last 26 years connected with the press of New Orleans, died there last Wednesday.

Rev. A.P. Williams, an eloquent minister of the Baptist church, was killed last week near Glasgow, Missouri, by his horse falling over an embankment.

Issue November 29, 1868

Mortuary Report: The following is the weekly report of Mr. Cahill, City Sexton of Galveston:

November 22nd: A. Lochuby, aged 50 years, died of consumption.

November 25th: Francis J. Flagg, aged 21 months, croup; Fred Peterson, aged 24, diarrhea.

November 26th: Laura Branch, negro child, aged 8 days, croup.

November 27th: Mrs. Christian Woern, aged 26, diarrhea.

November 28th: Dennis Toohay, aged 52 years, phlebitis.

The 1st, 3rd and last of the above died at the city hospital.

Issue December 2, 1868

James G. Campbell, a prominent member of the bar and formerly associate justice of the Supreme Court of Louisiana, died at his residence in Natchitoches, a few days ago.

A notorious horse thief named Reynolds shot and killed a man named Benjamin Avent, near Holly Springs, Mississippi, Sunday week, and was captured and hung up to a tree by the citizens.

On the 14th instant, a man named Casteel, living near Des Arc, Arkansas, was taken from his home and hung. He was charged with being unable to distinguish his own hogs from his neighbor's.

Issue December 3, 1868

Capt. Edward B. McFarland died in Savannah, Georgia, on the 25th of lockjaw.

A young man by the name of Martinez fell into a boiling kettle at his grandfather's sugar house a few miles above Thibodaux (Louisiana) last week, and perished before he could be extricated.

Issue December 4, 1868

Judge W.P. Palfrey, well known throughout Louisiana, died a few days since.

Issue December 5, 1868

Mr. Harry Williams, an old and much esteemed citizen of New Orleans, died there last Tuesday.

Issue December 6, 1868

Mortuary Report for Galveston from 29th November to 4th December:
November 29th: Joseph Mekyger, aged 22 years, native of Germany, died of typhoid fever.
December 1st: Joseph Rebina, aged 28 years, native of Scotland, died of consumption.
December 3rd: Geo. Burke, aged 20 months, died of convulsions.
December 4th: H. Myers, aged 63 years, native of Holland, disease not stated. John H. Westcott, aged 28 years, native of Ohio, died of lung disease.

Issue December 11, 1868

Died at 3 o'clock P.M., December 10, 1868, Nicholas Murphy, infant son of Wm. and Mary Murphy... funeral this evening from residence, Ave. K, between 26th & 27th sts., at 3 o'clock.

Issue December 13, 1868

Mr. Shirley Sledge, age 91, and for 37 years a citizen of Troup county, Georgia, died last week.

Weekly Mortuary Report: The following is a list of interments in the various cemeteries of this city made by Mr. Cahill, the City Sexton, [Galveston] from the 5th to the 11th, December 1868:
December 5th: T. Marsh, 34 years, Germany, dysentery.
December 6th: Infant of Mr. Gover, 10 days, spasms; Josie Trask, 1 year, teething; Wilby Trask, 1 month, inflammation bowels.
December 8th: D.W. Coelor, Germany, 34 years, brain fever; Kate D. Baker, 2 years, consumption.
December 9th: Dan Corderay, negro, age and disease unknown.
December 10th: R. Einbeck, Germany, 18 years, diarrhea; Margaret Silva, 23 years, dropsy.
December 11th: Michael S. Murphy, 10 months, spasms; D.B. Arnold, 65 years, pneumonia; Amelia Bowers, negro, child, 8 days, lockjaw.

Issue December 15, 1868

We regret to have to report the loss of Capt. John Davidson, one of our pilots, and Mr. Joe White, boat keeper of one of the pilot boats...

Issue December 17, 1868

The editor of *Vedette* reports having just returned from Gainsville, Cooke county, where there was much excitement on account of the killing of Mr. Cloud by Mr. Mosby.

Jack Cox, an old negro, died near Baltimore, recently, aged 110 years.

Yesterday afternoon, the body of Mr. White, one of the men drowned Sunday evening, was found on the bay shore.

Issue December 18, 1868

Mr. Matthew Pierce of New Kent county, Virginia, died at Quitman, Mississippi, a few days since.

Mr. Thomas R. Price, an old merchant of Richmond, Virginia, died on the 13th inst.

A meeting of the bar at Houston on Wednesday, passed a tribute to the memory of Col. Eli H. Baxter, whose death we recorded a few days since.
    The remains of Eli Baxter arrived in the city yesterday and were finally interred in the Episcopal Cemetery. *Houston Telegraph*.

Houston letter. Dr. A.J. Hay, our oldest physician, except Dr. McCraven, died day before yesterday.
    The remains of A.J. Hay were followed to their last resting place by friends and relatives. *Houston Telegraph*.

The wife of A.C. Miller died this morning, it is charged, from injuries she received from her husband.

Issue December 19, 1868

We learn that D.C. Isreal, formerly on the police in this city, was murdered in Brownsville on the 3d inst.

Coroners inquest on the body of Mrs. Miller, who died yesterday morning, the jury decided that she came to her death partly by the abuse and maltreatment, by her husband A.C. Miller...

Dr. Arthur E. Peticolas, late of Richmond, and superintendent of the Eastern Lunatic Asylum, of Virginia, committed suicide.

Issue December 20, 1868

Died on Saturday, December 19th, Maria Elperdeim, daughter of Mr. &. Mrs. Prat, aged 15 years & 2 months. Funeral service will take place this day (Sunday) at 3 1/2 P.M. at St. Mary's Cathedral.

The *Ranchero* gives an account of the attack at Clarksville... W.H. Phelps and Hammond were buried the next day.

Mortuary Report for the 12th to the 19th:
December 12th: Fred. Vogclar, aged 25 years, pneumonia, Germany.
December 13th: Nicholas Gingler, aged 79 years, old age, Germany. James A. Jones, aged 21 years, cholera morbus, Arkansas.
December 15th: E. Raftis, aged 19 years, Typhoid fever, Ireland; Rudolph Barkman, aged 2 years, not known, Germany.
December 16th: Infant of James Monroe, aged 24 hours, disease not known; Robt. White, aged 35 years, drowned, Persia.
December 17th: Mrs. A.C. Miller, aged 30 years, disease not known, Georgia; Samuel Brains, aged 45 years, bad cold, Africa.
December 19th: Louis Burdin (col.) aged 25 years, pneumonia; Mary Pilaut (col.) aged 40 years, abscess.

Issue December 22, 1868

Another murder: A man named Israel, who came out here from Galveston as a juror to the District Court of the U.S., left a few days ago for the interior of Texas... Last Thursday his dead body was discovered near the Laguna of Tio Cano. *Ranchero.*

We have to announce the death of another of the early citizens of Galveston, Mrs. Farish, consort of Mr. Oscar Farish, died at 3 P.M. on the 20th inst. Sister of Hamilton Stuart, editor of the *Civilian*.

John Pemberton, a worthy citizen of New Orleans, died last Friday.

Col. John S. Hogan, of the *Memphis Appeal*, is dead.

Capt. Ed. Farrell, the Kentucky guerrilla, died in the Louisville city hospital on the 13th from old wounds.

The *Savannah Morning News* announces the death, by heart disease, of Judge Thomas S. Gholson, of Virginia, in that city.

Mr. George Mixer of South Carolina, son of Daniel Mixer, who built the Charleston Hotel, died in New York on the 7th.

Obituary in *Oshkosh (Wis) Times* of the 8th inst. Died in this city on Wednesday, December 2d, of dropsy of the heart, Wm. R. Wilson, Sen. of Galveston, Texas, aged 58 years.

Issue December 23, 1868
From the *Memphis Avalanche* of the 12th inst: Account of the suicide of Frederick Kornick, an Israelite from St. Louis. [note: includes letter to father].

Issue December 24, 1868
Judge Culver, a native of Kentucky, died in St. Joseph, Missouri, a few days ago.

Mrs. Mattie Filmondson/Edmondson, died at her residence, Washington County, Virginia, on the 3rd October last, aged ninety years. She was the daughter of Mr. Wm. Moore, deceased, who lost a leg at the battle of King's Mountain. She had one hundred and three lineal descendants, all within three hours ride of her residence.

Contains an account of the murder and robbery at Clarksville, Texas, at the mouth of the Rio Grande... killed were George T. Hammond and Wm. H. Phelps and severely wounded Robert R. Ryan...

James Callahan, aged 105, has just died in Bourbon county, Ky.

Issue December 25, 1868
Drowned: On last Monday, a German named August Earnest was drowned while attempting to cross Cummins' Creek...
On last Thursday, Oscar Delany, colored drayman, was drowned while watering his horse at Brooks' Ferry... *Gonzales Inquirer.*

Another Old Texian Gone. Capt. E. Luter, an old Texan, and for over 20 years a worthy citizen of this place, died at St Marys, Sunday the 6th inst. He left a wife and several small children... (*Goliad Guard*)

Died near Independence, Washington county, Texas, on the morning of the 25th July, 1868, Capt. Tasetas T. Clay, aged 44/41 years. Capt. Clay was born in Daviess county, Kentucky; when he had arrived at the age of six years, his father moved from that county to the then province of Texas, and settled with his family in Cole's Settlement Austin's Colony. The high order of mind possessed by Nestor Clay, his father, together with his devotion to the interests of the settlers of the colony, soon placed him among the leaders in those interesting events that culminated, a few years later, in making Texas a nation. It was during these years that the subject of this notice received his earliest impressions of men and things. His father and mother having died, he with his two sisters, were sent to his grandfather, Capt. Johnson, in Daviess county, Kentucky, in the fall of 1835, where he remained until he received his education. In 1845 he returned to Washington county, Texas, settling near Independence, where he resided up to the time of his death... Capt. Clay married the daughter of Mr. Samuel Seward, one of the earliest settlers of Austin's colony, and settled near Independence, where his honorable bearing and strict integrity gained him the confidence and esteem of all who knew him. In 1859 he embarked in the mercantile business, and up to the breaking out of the war was doing a remunerative business... in the latter part of the summer of 1861 he left his home as 1st Lieut. of Co. I, 5th Reg. Texas Volunteers, for Virginia... leaves wife and four children. [note: this obituary contains a lengthy account of Capt. Clay's military service].

We are pained to have to record the death of Mrs. S.E. Murrah, widow of the late Ex Gov. Murrah, at the residence of Judge Samuel Earle.

We learn from a gentleman by the name of Hunter, from Gonzales, and also C.A. Russell, of Helena, that Capt. J. Littleton and a man by the name of Stanard were waylaid and shot near Leesburg, from which they both died on Friday the 3rd inst. *Goliad Guard.*

Suicide. The *Henderson Times* of the 16th says Hep Graham, a clever gentleman, committed suicide at his residence in Nacogdoches county, a few days since. He was about 25 and had been married about a month.

Issue December 27, 1868
Report from Brenham on the death of Dr. E.W. Cade by Mr. Rome Campbell in a shooting affair which occurred in that place on the 21st inst... Dr. Cade was in the habit of taking a spree periodically...

We learn that on the evening of the 14th inst. a party of white men went to the plantation of Gen. J.E. Harrison, near the line of McLennan and Falls counties, and robbed Flanders Beata, a freedman, of about seventy-five dollars. They also shot at him as he made a leap to get out of the house, but being in a stooping posture he escaped unharmed. They also fired at his son Spencer, slightly wounding him in the neck.

After robbing and shooting the above named parties, they passes by the cabin of Israel Butler, another freedman, and shot at him, cutting off his middle finger. They then passed on to where Robert Harrison lived... placing his pistol against Bob's head, killed him dead. *Waco Examiner.*

In Oakville, Ala., last Friday week, Dr. James was shot dead by three men in mask.

Further particulars of the murder of two customs inspectors, George T. Hammonds and William H. Phelps, and the serious wounding of Robert R. Ryan...

Mortuary Report for the week ending Dec. 26:
Dec. 19—Maria Elperdiern, 15, typhoid fever.
Dec. 20—Mrs. Angelina Farish, 46 years and 6 months, general debility; Mrs. Octavia Hughs, 29 years, typhoid pneumonia; Jury, c.m., 15 years, consumption.
Dec. 22—J. Haley, 50 years, diarrhea; Victoria A. Jay, 1 year, inflammation of bowels.
Dec. 24—Robert Douglas, 72 years, old age; Aurelia A. Fraqua, 1 month, lockjaw.
Dec. 26—John Kile, c.m., 28 years, neuralgia; colored man, name unknown, 25 years.

Issue December 29, 1868
Our usually quiet town was this evening the scene of a fatal affray. An old man by the name of Porter and his son, got into a difficulty with a man named Dave Hicks, in which Porter was fatally shot in the head, and his son-in-law, a brother of Hicks, received two flesh wounds... *Texas Press*.

On Friday last, about 11 o'clock a.m., Mr. S.U. Smith, living three miles from town, was foully murdered near his own house, while walking in the road, on his way to visit a neighbor. He was shot from ambush, the whole load of nine slugs, each weighing over an ounce, entering his stomach, caused a frightful wound, from the effects of which he died the next day.
     From the dying declarations of Mr. Smith, suspicion attached to his son-in-law, W.H. Norris, who was promptly arrested by Deputy Sheriff J.B. Long.
     Messrs. Priest and Wilson appeared for the State and Messrs. Guinn [note: Robert Henry Guinn] and Gregg for the defendant. *Rusk Observer*.

Issue December 31, 1868
George W. Reynolds, associate editor of *Brenham Banner*, shot and killed a soldier, N. Davis.

NEU BRAUNFELSER ZEITUNG
Published at New Braunfels, Texas.

[German to English translation by Eva Lia Graubard
of Temple and Houston, Texas.]

Issue November 19, 1852
Mrs. Priscille Underwood, of Jefferson county in Indiana, is 93 years old, mother of seventeen children, forty grandchildren, great grandmother of 132, and a great, great grandmother of four.

Comal county. Letters of Administration of the estate of G. Heusinger, dec., have been granted to W. Heusinger.

Louis Hipp, from Seguin, died a little while ago, 15 miles below Victoria.

Son of Johann Heifrich Petri from Comal, near New Braunfels, hasn't been seen since March 1848. Please, his parents are looking for him.

Issue November 26, 1852
Blake H. Thompson, who murdered Finnan in Austin, was seen in Lewisburg, Conway county. The governor and friends posted $2000 for bringing Thompson to Justice.

Issue December 3, 1852
On 26 December 1852 at the courthouse there will be a probate hearing of Jacob Heim. New Braunfels. 30 November 1852. John Arnold adminstrator.

Administrators notice. Comal county. Estate of George Wenzel, dec. Ignaz Wenzel, admin.

Issue December 10, 1852
Administrators notice. Comal county. Estate of Mrs. Helene Klemm, dec. Charles Bonnet, admin.

Administrator notice. Guadalupe county. Estate of Christian Henze, dec. Caroline Henze, admin.

Issue December 17, 1852
Notice of death. Died after six months of sickness. My wife died 4 December, 47 years and 21 days. Louis Kraz. Independence, 6 October 1852.

Estate Sale J.J. Coll. New Braunfels. U. Raundorf, admin.

Rent of farm. Estate of J.J. Coll.

Issue December 24, 1852

Administrators notice. Comal county. Estate of Wilhelm Klinger, dec.
Dorothea Klinger, admin.

Issue January 7, 1853

Administrators notice. Comal county. Estate of Arnold Henckel, dec.
Mathilda Blumberg, admin. M.A. Dooley, her attorney. New Braunfels.

Settlement of Estate. Heinrich Metzing, dec. Dorothea Metzing, admin.

Settlement of Estate. Adolph Benner, admin. of the Estate of Samuel Amend,
Christian Schmidt, Frederick Schmidt, Carl Volk, Frederick Behrens, Wilhelm
Heischbach and Leopold Neckmann, dec. Comal county. C. Seabaugh,
Clerk.

Born January 2, 1853 to Dr. Th. Koester, a son, New Braunfels.

Issue January 14, 1853

Born January 6, a son to Th. Schwab in New Braunfels.

Died on 7th January, a son of Dr. Th. Koester, New Braunfels, six days old.

Issue January 21, 1853

Where is Albert Hegmann from Wiesbaden? He arrived by ship 21 December
1849 with a wife and 3 children and one sister in Galveston. He did not say
where he was going. Franz. Moureau, New Braunfels, Comal county.

Issue January 28, 1853

Born January 24, a son to G.F. Holekamp.

Issue February 4, 1853

Monthly Church notice. German Prot. New Braunfels. (January 1853)

Baptized

2 January, Hulda Mina Marie Emile Staats, born 29 October 1852.
2 January, Charlotte Auguste Orth, 8 April 1852, by Santa Clara.
9 January, Ernestine Karoline Sophie Friedrike Boges, born 4 October 1852.
9 January, Heinrich Karl Bages, born 18 March 1852, by Santa Clara.
23 January, Johanne Antoniette Gruene, born 21 December 1852, in
Comaltown.

Married
9 January, Georg Scholl with widow Katharina Knetsch.
9 January, Leopold Beisele with Babette Vogel, new arrival from Bruchfal in Baben.
9 January, Johann Krams with Auguste Lonise Florentine Ultwein, both live in Friedensthal.

Died
7 January, the unbaptized son of Dr. Th. Koester, 6 days old.

Married
New Wied, on 18 January 1853, Hans Sqecht and Lizette Schmidt.
In New Braunfels, 25 January 1853, Carl Ruehn and the widow Henriette Peters.

Born
To Julius Dresel in Sisterdale, 9 October 1851, a son named Carl, and on 21 January 1853, a daughter named Hedwig.

Round Top. Fayette county. On 16th January, Stephen Townsend was murdered by Baughbe. Baughbe was arrested and handed over to the sheriff of Fayette county. Baughbe is living now 18 miles from Little Rock, Arkansas, and nearby brothers and sisters live.

Issue February 11, 1853
Born on January 15 to J.J. Gross by Wacoe Spring, Comal county, a son.

Born 28 January to L. Bromme, New Braunfels, a daughter.

Died on 25 January, Th. Schwab, by New Braunfels, a son, 19 days old.

Issue February 18, 1853
Settlement of estate of Justus Kellner, dec. Comal county. Mrs. Wilhelmina Kellner and Charles Rossy, adm.

Admin. Notice. Estate of Wilhelm Besserer, dec. Comal county. Mrs. Helene Besserer, admin.

Issue February 25, 1853
Admin. Notice Constantine Fritsch. Comal county. J.F. Arnold, admin.

Issue March 4, 1853
Monthly church notice German Prot. New Braunfels, Comal county, Texas. (February 1853).

Baptized

6 February, Heinrich August Karl Kohler, born 18 December 1852 in Comaltown.

13 February, Ernst Friedrich Otto Herrmann, born 27 January 1853.

20 Ferbruary, Wilhelmine Albertine Koroline Neb, born December 20, 1822 [sic] in Comaltown.

20 February, Johann Karl Bogt, born 18 September 1852.

27 February, Philipp Franklin Setac, born 18 December 1852.

27 February, Otto Heinrich Simon, born 9 December 1852.

Issue March 25, 1853

Born to businessman Franz Moureau in New Braunfels, a daughter 23 March 1853. Her name is Hulka Amalie.

Issue April 1, 1853

Monthly News. German Prot. Church, New Braunfels, Comal county. (March 1853).

Baptized

17 March, Marie Louise Katharine Meda Alma Runge, born 28 (April) [sic] 1852 in Guadalupe county.

27 March, Heinrich Ferd. Albert Nolte, born 10 February 1853.

27 March, Gustav Louis Johann Sutor, born 14 August 1852.

27 March, Friedrick Wilhelm Karl Zuehl, born 24 August 1852 on the third Santa Clara.

28 March, Elise Thiele, born 26 December 1852.

28 March, August Frederike Jonas, born 28 January 1853.

Married

12 March, John Lauritz Buaas from Austin with widow Helene Besserer of this town.

20 March, Wilhelm Christian Bunnas and Dorothea Kretzmeyer, both from Hortontown, Guadalupe county.

Married by Justice of Peace H. Seele

20 February, Heinrich Schulz and Ernestine Hoffmann.

13 March, David Trapp with Mrs. Marie Anna Braum.

19 March, Wilhelm Julius Reuter and Mrs. Wilhelmine Caroline Heusinger.

Issue May 6, 1853

Monthly report. German Prot. church, New Braunfels, Comal, Texas.

Baptized
3 April, Adolf Ferdinaud Behrendt, born 15 February 1853 in Schumansville.
10 April, Catharine Jakobine Wetz, born 7 April 1853.
17 April, Heinrich Julius Chistoph Dedebe, born 23 March 1853 in Comaltown.
20 April, Charlotte Emilie Von Stein, born 20 April 1851.

Married
17 April, George Lang and widow Rosine Blessing.

Admin. Notice. N. Heinrich <u>Jonas</u> and Louise Heinrich, dec. Comal county. Carl <u>Richter</u>, admin.

Issue May 13, 1853
Administrators notice. Estate of Louis Brentano, dec. New Braunfels. Wm. Brentano, admin.

Admin. Notice. Estate of Heinrich <u>Jonas</u> and Louise Jonas, dec. Carl <u>Richter</u>, admin. Comal county.

Issue May 20, 1853
Administrators notice. Comal county. Estate of August Tweele. Margaretha Bernhard, admin.

Issue June 3, 1853
Hermann Seele, admin. of the estate of Henry Bevenroth, dec., filed fiscal account. Comal county.

Monthly report. German Prot. Church, New Braunfels, Comal county, Texas. (May 1853)

Baptized
14 May, Friedrich Christoph Twiesel/Zwiefel, born 15 March 1853 at Comaltown.
15 May, Franz Albert Boelker, born 9 November Guadalupe county.
16 May, Karoline Jung, born 7 March 1853.
16 May, Elise Hermine Theodore Auguste Adolphine Seekap.
22 May, Henriette Nolte, born 30 April 1853.
29 May, Ernst Kupserschmidt, born 11 April 1853 Comaltown.
30 May, Marie Wilhelmine Schmuck, born 8 October 1852.

Married

13 May, Johann J. H. Koebler and Henriette.Emille Bretzke in Comaltown.

15 May, Johann Zacharias Hartung and Louise Karoline Sahm, by Four Miles Creek.

27 May, Johann F. Krause and Margarethe Heiss.

17 May, Karl Steubing and Maria Weil.

22 May, Heinrich Burgfeld and widow Frederike Jonas.

23 May, Johann George Froehich and Marie Sander.

22 May, Friedrick Eberling and Sophie Leichner on the first Santa Clara.

Died

10 May, Barbara Hafner from Wuertemberg, 21 years, brain fever.

Married by Justice of the Peace Seele

5 May, Carl L. Legn with Miss Ellen Hill.

8 May, Dr. Christian Baer with Josephine Brentano.

29 May, Johannes Ulfens with Miss Sophie Hoffman.

Issue June 10, 1853

Born 6 June, Postmaster N. Benner at New Braunfels, a son.

Issue June 17, 1853

Administrators notice. Comal county. Estate of Wersdoerfer, dec. Anna Maria Hofacker.

Issue July 1, 1853

German Prot. Church, New Braunfel, Comal county, Texas

Baptized

2 June, August Ebel, born 11 January 1853 on the upper Guadalupe.

5 June, Mina Preusser, born 19 September 1853 at Eight Miles River.

7 June, Rudolf Georg, born 30 December 1853 [sic].

26 June, Rosine Therese Schlather, born 21 November 1852 at Horne's Farm.

Married

5 June, Heinrich Breistadt with widow Elisabeth Mueller.

Died

23 June, Johannette Christiane Henriette, daughter of Adam Kunzge, 1 year, 1 month.

Issue July 29, 1853

Married by Justice of Peace Herman Seele:

5 June, Christian Damman and Rosa Ferlen.

2 July, 1853 Dr. Hermann Starke and Auguste Klose.

6 July, 1853 Johann Lobe and Marie Klose.

11 July, 1853 Julius Hermann Griesenbeck and Emilie Becker/Beder.

Issue August 19, 1853

Born, a son to C. Meyer in New Brausfels, 9 August. Name Otto.

Issue September 2, 1853

Monthly Bulletin of the Prot German Church in New Braunfels, Comal county, Texas. (July 1853)

Baptized

4 July, Johann Heinrich, child of Christian and Elizabeth Bosnig, born 16 June 1853.

4 July, Konrad August, child of Johann Jacob & Katharine Gross, born 15 January 1853.

4 July, Heinrich Wilhelm, child of Jacob and Katherine Blieder, born 27 February 1853.

5 July, Anna Frederike Konradine child of Hans Heinrich Dietrich and Bernhardine Elisabeth Knibbe, born 25 January 1853.

10 July, Dorothe Sophie, child of Georg Andreas & Elisabeth Katharine Pape, born 8 May 1853.

17 July, Heinrich, child of Joseph & Margarethe Batz, born 25 December 1852.

Issue September 16, 1853

Married by Justice of Peace, September 11, 1853. Micheal Heimor with Justine Leisch.

Administrators notice. Comal county. Estate of August Rudloff. William Wiedenfeld.

Issue September 23, 1853

Died 14 September, my son Heinrich, born 24 January of this year. G.F. Holekamp.

Issue September 29, 1853

Married by Justice of Peace Moegen, Karl Klemm and Johanna Micheln on 13 September 1853.

Issue October 21, 1853

Gillespie county, Texas. Estate of Christoph Feuge, dec. Fredrickburg. Johann Metzger, admin.

Estate of Henry Roeser, dec. Comal county. Wm. Seckatz, admin.

Issue November 4, 1853

Protestant Church at New Braunfels, Comal county, Texas.

Baptized:

11 September, Koroline Wilhelmine, born 1 August 1853. Parents Wilhelm Schulz and Wilhelmine, maiden name Vogt.

11 September, Ferdinand, born 14 July 1853. Parents August Weinert and Heinrietta, maiden name Briestadt.

25 September, Auguste and Wilhelmine, born 10 June 1853. Parents Friedrich Neumann and Christine, maiden name Lenz.

25 September, Heinrich Ernst August, born 4 May 1853, on the third Santa Clara. Patents: Heinrich Grobe and Karoline, maiden Hennings.

25 September, Anna Agnes, born 2 September on the third Santa Clara. Parents: Ernst Binneu and Wilhelmine, born Hegebaum.

2 October, Christian Friedrich, born 6 September 1853 in Comaltown. Parents Heinrich Puls & Augustine, maiden Stathemann.

18 October, Pauline Katharine Mathilde, born 4 June 1853 in the hills near Friedrichsburg. Parents: Konrad Kapmeier & Wilhelmine, maiden Meyer.

23 October, Wilhelmine Auguste, born 25 June 1853. Parents: Johann Heinrich Boges and Lisette Ernestine, maiden Schmidt.

Married

30 October, Johann Andreas Lindenau from Schchmanneville, and Wilhelmine Knetsch from here.

In this month no deaths were recorded.

Issue November 11, 1853

Born 24 February 1852, a daughter to Mr. Gustav Adolph Leabelin in Schmannsville, named Clara Elvira.

GLOSSARY

Apoplexy - Stroke.

Bilious fever - Malaria.
Brenham, Texas - Settled by German immigrants. Became county seat of Washington county in 1844.

Cholera - Acute infection which chiefly involves the small intestine. A germ gains entrance into the body through polluted water. The main symptoms are severe, constantly flowing diarrhea, vomiting, collapse, cramps in the muscles, and suppression of the flow of urine.
Comal county, Texas - Established in 1846. Earliest settlers were Germans.
Comal Town, Texas - In Comal county. Separated from New Braunfels by the Comal River. Settlement began in 1846.
Congestion of the Brain - Concept that too much blood in the brain caused a stroke. Used before the use of the sphygmomanometer to determine blood pressure.
Congestive Fever - Most severe and dangerous form of malarial fever. Can destroy life in a few hours. Frequently characterized by stupor, delirium, a marble-like coldness of the skin, vomiting, jaundice, or hemorrhage from the nose or bowels.
Consumption - Tuberculosis. Also called "TB" and hemorrhage of the lung. Disease may be chronic; quick or galloping. Fever, loss of weight, night sweats, and severe cough are characteristic.

Debility - weakness, feebleness, exhaustion
Delirium tremens - a mental and nervous disorder accompanied by violent trembling and terrifying hallucinations, usually caused by prolonged and excessive drinking of alcoholic liquor.
Dropsy - bloating or puffiness of the skin. Not itself a disease, but only the symptom of a morbid condition of the blood, kidney, liver or heart.
Dumb ague - a malaria without the characteristic chills.

Flux - Diarrhea.

Galveston, Texas - Galveston, located on Galveston Island, was made a port of entry in 1837, and became the county seat of Galveston county in 1839. During the Republic, Galveston was the metropolis of Texas.

Harrisburg, Texas - In Harris county. Established 1825. Santa Anna burned the town in 1836. Harrisburg was the first railroad terminal in Texas. Harrisburg was annexed into Houston in 1926.

Hemorrhage of the Lung - See consumption.

Howard Association - Organization of men who had had yellow fever and thought to be immune to another attack. The men nursed, provided food and clothing to those who had yellow fever. They were very active in providing assistance during the yellow fever epidemic of 1866-1867.

Inflammation of the Bowels - Dysentery. Frequent, scanty and bloody stools.

Monomania - Insanity on one subject.

New Braunfels, Texas - Site on west bank of Guadalupe River and Comal River, at their junction.

Pleurisy - Inflammation of the pleura, which is the membrane that lines the lungs. It may occur as either an acute or a chronic process. In acute pleurisy the pleura becomes reddened, then covered with an exudate; the disease may progress to the second stage, in which a copious exudation of serum occurs. The symptoms are a stitch in the side, a chill, followed by fever and a dry cough.

Putrid sore throat - Diphtheria, mononucleosis or strep.

Remittent fever - Malaria.

Republic of Texas - As a result of the defeat of the Mexican army on April 21, 1836 in the Battle of San Jacinto, the Texas Revolution ended in victory and the Republic of Texas was formed. Although never recognized by Mexico, the Republic of Texas functioned as a nation for nine years. Sam Houston was the first President of the Republic. On December 29, 1845 Texas entered the Union as the 28th state and the Republic ceased to exist.

Santa Clara Creek - Creek that starts in Guadalupe county, and travels about twelve miles to Cibolo Creek.

Yellow Fever - A viral illness believed to have been brought to the United States during the time of the slave trade. Symptoms include headache, abdominal pain, and vomiting, followed by liver and kidney failure. Jaundice, the result of liver damage, is another common sign of this disease. Early Texas newspapers had almost daily accounts of deaths due to this disease, commonly referred to as "the epidemic" and "yellow jack", during the warmer months of the year. These accounts tell of the widespread devastation brought on by this disease that took thousands of lives in Texas. Many of these reports included the deaths of entire families and towns. It appears from these reports that more lives were taken by yellow fever than from Indian attacks and natural disasters combined. The occurrence of yellow fever was

405

attributed to a lack of proper drainage systems and hot weather. Many cities, including New York, Philadelphia, and New Orleans, were successful in ridding their communities of yellow fever as a result of implementing sewerage systems. Newspapers covering cities such as Houston, Galveston, Indianola, and Rio Grande City reported hundreds of deaths each week during the month of August. Remedies, such as carbolic acid, and yeast and charcoal, were plentiful but ineffective. It was also thought that adjustments in personal behavior would aid in avoiding the disease or hastening death once it was contracted. In 1881 Carlos Finlay, a Cuban physician, promoted that yellow fever is transmitted by mosquito bites. His theory was verified in 1901 by an investigative group that included American bacteriologist Walter Reed, who also proved the agent to be a virus. A yellow fever vaccine was developed in 1939. However, there remains no known treatment once the disease has been contracted. Today, there are many South American and African countries where yellow fever is considered endemic.

NAME INDEX

Ashby 374
Ashe 371
Asher 319
Ashes 305
Ashforth 340
Ashley 88, 171
Ashton 371
Askew 72
Astell 301
Atchinson 340
Atkins 230
Atkinson 10, 39, 43, 322
Atluke 278
Aubrey 48
August 227
Auguste 227, 263
Augustine 137, 272
Auld 14, 184
Auseley 293
Austerburg 272
Austin 146, 350, 393, 394
Auterside 280
Autrey 348, 351
Avent 389
Axson 290
Aycock 324, 341
Ayers 291
Ayrick 61
Babrman 288
Bacal 304
Bache 51
Bachelder 41
Bacon 95
Badnoche 338
Baehr 260
Baer 401
Bagby 368
Bages 397
Bahn 211
Bahrman 288
Bailey 62, 101, 102, 180, 328, 329, 335
Baily 35, 135
Bake 110

Baker 61, 87, 107, 215, 237, 265, 285, 293, 306, 323, 324, 328, 362, 390
Baldis 89
Baldridge 156
Baldwin 58, 105, 253, 293, 351
Bale 277
Balford 89
Baligathy 316
Ball 4, 5, 85, 185, 380
Ballinger 339
Ballou 235
Baltzell 310
Banding 341
Banett 85
Banks 262, 336, 344
Banner 152
Bannerman 239
Baptist 339
Baptiste 88
Bar 323
Baral 304
Barbee 167
Barben 27
Barber 91
Barbisch 320
Barclay 159
Barker 12, 136, 153
Barkley 70, 163
Barkman 392
Barnes 66, 82, 84, 91, 341, 369
Barnett 138, 273, 324, 341
Barnidina 346
Barns 157
Barr 1, 302, 307, 385
Barrels 296
Barret 22
Barrett 83, 85, 189, 289, 380
Barrington 15
Barrm 51
Barron 42
Barry 83, 202
Bartlett 115, 290
Bartley 67

Barton   60, 80, 122, 163, 293, 356
Bartu 282
Bascom 103
Bass 210, 339
Bassett 54
Batch 68
Bateman 37, 99, 279
Bates 158, 215, 256, 277, 364
Battell 275
Battle 96
Batts 273
Batz 402
Baudenon 321
Baudin 201, 202
Baudman 263
Baughbe 398
Baughn 171
Bauhoff 257
Baum 307
Baumberger 274
Baumgarten 225
Bawer 346
Bawsel 302
Bawsell 307, 308, 316
Baxbra 327
Baxter   37, 87, 159, 165, 391
Bayles 200
Baylor 33, 150, 204, 222
Beagple 319
Beard 26, 187
Beasely 143, 167
Beasly 339
Beatty 107, 324
Beaty 28, 333, 359
Beauchamp 344
Beaumont 355
Beavans 320
Bechsoppf 201
Beck 324, 341
Becker 338, 402
Beckman 277, 312
Beckum 58
Becllmann 53

Beder 402
Bedford 88
Beesby 301
Beeson 215
Behrendt 400
Behrens 397
Beichatal 278
Bein 341
Beisele 398
Beisswenger 271
Belden 29, 241
Bell 4, 13, 25, 45, 80, 103, 113, 132, 134, 145, 164, 202, 224, 289, 328, 361
Beller 308
Bellfield 344
Bellows   138
Beman 309, 312, 313
Bennell 315
Benner 397, 401
Bennerman 339
Bennet 55, 340
Bennett   23, 31, 98, 115, 178, 189, 219, 281
Benton 76, 255
Beohn 334
Bergen 313
Bergham 285
Bergin 55, 330
Berimendi 96
Berkowitz 126
Bernhard 282, 400
Berry   139, 249, 263, 264, 278
Berthlers 271
Bertrand 283
Besberd 264
Beshard 256
Bessenger 331
Besser   337
Besserer 398, 399
Besthiers 269
Bevenroth 400
Beverly 66
Bexter 327

Beyer 301
Bheringer 50
Bickerstaff 90
Bickley 68
Biggs 376
Bilstein 338
Bingham 151
Binneu 403
Bird 135, 328, 371
Birdwell 328
Bishop 31, 106
Bishor 200
Biston 302
Biven 103
Black 8, 11, 69, 82, 84, 149, 157, 158, 171, 228, 375, 376
Blackburn 124, 339, 340
Blackiston 352
Blackmore 88, 90
Blackshear 340
Blackwell 170, 177, 370
Blagge 247
Blain 188
Blair 21, 64, 65, 68, 69, 188, 246
Blake 312, 314
Blakeman 292
Blakemore 178
Blakesly 342
Blakey 87, 156
Blanding 228
Blanton 187, 369
Blash 279
Bledsoe 93, 102
Blessing 317, 400
Blessman 34
Blessmann 31
Blieder 402
Blobel 55
Block 54, 235
Blossman 121
Blount 324, 341
Bloxon 285
Blum 257, 277
Blumberg 397

Blunt 26
Bobb 27
Bobo 63
Bodden 219
Bodine 184
Bodman 216
Boelker 400
Boges 397, 403
Boggiss 163
Boggs 9, 362
Bogt 399
Bohannon 33
Bohle 326
Bohme 333
Bolling 279
Bond 49
Bonds 216
Bone 55, 67, 163
Bonet 265
Bonfoey 270, 276, 291, 302, 316, 336
Bonnet 396
Bonney 80, 130
Booker 17, 185, 341
Bookr 341
Boon 154
Boone 34, 67
Boons 256
Borden 196
Bording 259
Boreland 331
Boring 219, 224
Borland 333
Bosnig 402
Boss 292
Boston 265
Botts 301
Boudineau 279
Bouldin 207
Boussiere 375
Boutsch 268
Bowden 72
Bowels 370, 386
Bowen 59, 66, 177, 312, 375

Bower 154
Bowers 178, 318, 334
Bowles 59
Bowlin 256
Bowls 156
Bowman 53, 361
Boy 356
Boyce 303, 315
Boyd 61, 94, 188, 285, 344
Boykin 88
Boyle 205, 324, 340, 341
Bracewell 80
Bracken 54, 108
Bradberry 174
Bradbury 236
Bradford 88, 283
Bradley 95, 310
Bradshaw 90, 177-179
Bragg 127
Brains 392
Brake 388
Brakoff 272
Bramen 344
Branch 328, 344, 345, 388
Brandis 325
Brash 177
Brashear 109, 160, 213, 249, 314, 318
Brassel 127
Brassell 127
Braum 399
Braush 263
Brawn 275
Bray 13
Brazle 150
Breedlove 40, 324, 341
Breedloves 341
Breese 202
Breistadt 401
Brendt 285
Brenham 17, 22
Brennan 122, 266, 368
Brennin 34
Brenning 324, 340, 341

Brenson 327
Brentano 400, 401
Bretschneicher 293
Bretzke 401
Brewer 2
Brewster 77, 367
Brickman 267
Bridge 73, 329
Bridges 382
Briestadt 403
Brigancy 340
Briggs 191, 277
Brigham 97
Brinberry 311
Brink 310
Briscoe 56, 259, 307
Brissett 52
Britchsnider 260
Britt 84
Brittle 21
Britton 13
Broach 192
Broadley 282
Broadwell 88
Brobst 68
Brock 260
Brockington 91
Broker 50
Bromme 398
Brook 278
Brooke 59, 105, 389
Brooker 324
Brooking 144
Brookman 310
Brooks 97, 343, 362, 393
Broose 281
Brophy 341
Brotherton 139
Brown 20, 29, 34, 53, 62, 88, 98, 115, 122, 135, 136, 151, 160, 161, 164, 178, 201, 203, 255, 256, 263, 285, 295, 306, 326, 327, 330, 337, 340, 342
Browning 81, 89, 184

Brownlee 86
Bruce 132, 256
Brudow 116
Bruin 169
Brumley 237
Brunow 116
Bruton 140
Bryan 32, 54, 187, 209, 251, 290, 297, 337
Bryant 24, 135, 137, 190, 242, 302
Bryson 190
Buaas 399
Buchanan 88, 182
Buck 31, 152, 203, 279
Buckholtz 327
Buckley 296, 298, 314, 337
Buckmeyer 311
Buckner 10, 171, 335
Buell 90
Buffington 339
Bulger 279, 280
Bulkley 231
Bullard 24, 190
Bullerty 266
Bullock 65, 97, 141, 315
Bumbuhl 265
Bunch 157
Bundick 35
Bunnas 399
Burbank 306, 329
Burbanks 330
Burch 263
Burdet 26
Burdit 26
Burger 193
Burgfeld 401
Burguess 261
Burk 299
Burke 14, 41, 55, 129, 201, 304, 344, 390
Burkhardt 306
Burleson 149, 157
Burnell 299

Burnes 135
Burnet 206, 263, 360
Burnett 77, 160
Burney 67
Burnham 143
Burns 169, 181, 280, 323, 328, 374
Burr 160, 262
Burran 64
Burras 23
Burrell 326
Burrus 92
Bursteed 316
Burtis 143
Burton 92, 174, 178, 290, 292, 297, 342, 385
Burwell 142
Busby 21
Bush 200, 233, 263
Butler 48, 51, 52, 56, 62, 72, 129, 140, 197, 230, 286, 293, 308, 328, 384
Buttler 38
Byrd 63, 171, 344
Byrne 173, 369
Byrsold 342
Cabanis 53
Cabannis 53
Cabban 233
Cabell 6
Cabler 99
Cade 339, 394
Cahill 122, 274, 279, 388, 389, 390
Cain 56
Cairnes 8
Calaveros 171
Calder 16
Caldwell 6, 11, 14, 20, 37, 38, 56, 77, 184, 187
Calhoun 33, 380
Callahan 289, 323, 393
Calloway 290
Calvillo 7

Cambell 343
Cameron 130, 142, 306
Camp 100
Campbell 6, 15, 31, 36, 90, 94,
100, 185, 256, 281, 282, 287, 294,
307, 329, 332, 339, 341, 343, 369,
378, 389, 394
Campe 334
Cana 266
Canall 257
Canby 115, 222
Cane 209, 231, 340
Canfield 28, 36, 192, 193
Cannada 14
Cannedy 74
Cannon 256, 301, 318
Canter 69
Capers 199
Caperton 135
Cardel 51
Cardenas 127
Careleman 257
Carevon 343
Carey 2, 298
Carleton 38
Carlisle 349
Carlos 108
Carlson 226
Carlton 188, 259
Carmer 284, 326
Carmichael 47
Carnes 281, 349
Carney 388
Carover 303
Carpenter 125, 299
Carr 93, 106, 216, 383
Carragee 178, 179, 350
Carrall 51
Carraway 167
Carrer 243
Carroll 14, 269, 292
Carrolton 352
Carson 6, 45, 158, 183, 277

Carter 138, 139, 162, 178, 179,
265, 273, 286, 310, 325, 350
Cartmell 363
Cartwright 92, 94, 97
Carty 200
Caruvay 283
Carver 85
Carville 327
Casala 329, 330
Case 333, 371
Casey 6, 110
Cash 190, 212
Cason 257
Cassady 272
Casseady 252, 253, 292
Cassedy 272
Cassidy 29, 181, 321, 370
Castanie 34
Casteel 389
Castle 326
Castleberry 28, 168
Castledine 186
Castro 10
Cat 320
Cate 266
Cathings 68
Catron 360
Cattinger 202
Cavanaugh 265, 314
Celesto 289
Celif 289
Cenel 341
Chacon 244
Chadwick 322, 324, 341
Chaflin 349
Chalmers 240, 380
Chamber 162
Chambers 37, 67, 170, 205
Chance 57
Chanch 23
Chandler 56, 157, 312
Chapgake 312
Chapman 56, 152
Chappell 212, 322

Charlotte 331
Chassaigne 51
Chaste 256
Chavis 27, 44
Cheek 55, 156, 157
Cheers 249
Cheesborough 266
Chenault 31
Cherry 86, 122, 332
Chester 105
Chevalic 199
Chevallie 110
Childress 257, 291
Childs 43
Chiles 42
Chisholm 70, 379
Chism 64
Christian 88
Christiana 201
Christopher 3
Churchill 383
Ciaaro 108
Cimmarger 262
Cinckle 201
Clapp 222
Clar 55
Clark 1, 14, 35, 54, 78, 110, 122, 140, 166, 171, 184, 210, 215, 248, 257, 274, 296, 298, 327, 330, 340, 359, 378, 381, 383
Clarke 109, 292, 340, 382
Clay 200, 393, 394
Clayton 274, 289
Clearay 281
Clement 23, 193
Clements 16, 52, 122, 322
Clesser 259
Cleveland 55, 133, 156, 239, 252
Clifford 278, 280
Cline 152
Clinton 202, 204
Close 225, 294
Cloud 43, 170, 188, 245, 248, 391

Cloudius 338
Clune 277
Clymer 274
Co--- 122
Cobb 136
Cobern 233
Coburn 151
Cochran 20, 21
Cocke 77, 152, 153, 367
Cockes 338
Cockey 389
Codling 288, 290
Codnen 299
Coelor 390
Coffee 27, 211, 331, 334, 343
Coffin 19, 121, 122
Coglin 314
Cohen 313
Cohn 311
Coit 48
Colberg 345
Colbert 5
Coldwell 176, 247, 248
Cole 122, 215, 313, 339, 341, 393
Coleman 13, 40, 160, 273, 277, 309, 310, 331
Coll 396, 397
Collier 270
Collin 122, 209
Collins 58, 88, 102, 122, 179, 232, 286, 302, 305, 387
Colmac 47
Colman 47, 102, 312
Colquitt 165
Colson 273
Colt 367
Coltant 185
Coltart 14
Colton 66, 105, 180
Colvin 48
Compton 169, 262, 263, 266, 305, 313, 324
Conard 178

Conde 342
Condon 299
Condor 264
Conger 20
Coniff 298
Conklim 267
Conly 269
Connally 321
Connell 296, 299
Connelly 60
Conner 176, 309
Connolly 255
Connor 245, 310
Conoly 216
Conring 238
Conway 319
Cook 2, 15, 20, 21, 86, 180, 185, 189, 251, 291, 324, 339, 340, 344, 353, 354, 367, 369
Cooke 38, 55, 57, 317
Cooley 376, 377
Coombs 184
Coon 290
Cooper 5, 114, 136, 161, 258, 263, 280, 366
Cope 65, 66
Copeland 317
Corbett 277
Cordios 339
Cordova 12
Cordray 269
Cordua 295
Corley 245
Cornelius 372
Cornett 210
Corry 170
Cors 201
Cortes 341
Cosgrave 94
Cossa 226
Cotton 138, 178, 230
Coulson 114
Council 174, 235
Courbat 280

Courteney 28
Courtney 28, 329
Coutret 121, 122
Covey 299, 305, 314
Cowling 291
Cowser 70, 163
Cox 75, 178, 315
Coxe 317
Coyle 83
Coyne 264
Craddock 299, 372
Cradler 167
Craft 79
Craig 215, 385
Craik 271
Crain 87, 245
Cramar 54
Cramor 54
Crampton 338
Crane 88, 201, 293, 299
Cranston 247
Crantford 312, 313
Cratch 278
Crawford 30, 34, 135, 140, 251, 256, 257, 278, 289, 290, 322, 323, 326
Crawley 292
Creary 261
Creighton 317
Crenshaw 34, 142, 323
Crewel 295
Crittendon 16
Crocheron 138
Crocker 334
Crockett 277, 322, 356
Cromer 274
Crone 373
Cronin 257
Cronkrite 116
Crooks 295
Croom 178
Crosa 171
Crosby 366
Cross 296, 311, 318, 380

Crossland 121
Crossman 14, 185, 191
Crow 235, 324, 341
Crowder 297
Crowly 134
Cruger 2, 61
Crumpler 217, 324, 325, 340
Crutchfield 115, 116
Culbreath 126
Cullen 16, 289
Cullin 90
Culp 93
Culver 393
Culvert 346
Cummin 11
Cummins 393
Cunnier 293
Cunningham 28, 142, 181, 307, 333, 334, 357, 359, 365
Cuppler 257
Curphey 348
Curry 266, 293, 299
Curtail 49
Curtis 141, 282
Cusick 312
Cuthbertson 326
Cutliff 38
Dabbs 1
Dabney 191
Dacy 230
Dagget 21
Daggett 94, 188, 189
Dale 231
Daley 289
Dalian 252
Dallam 49
Dallas 196
Dally 59
Dalton 75, 76, 190, 299, 331
Daly 49, 271, 305, 336, 344
Damman 402
Damon 93
Daniel 97, 242, 245
Daniels 323, 328

Dann 274
Danzay 50
Darby 266
Darling 226
Darmon 321
Darnall 76, 243
Darnell 49
Daross 63
Davenport 371
Davidson 126, 272, 328, 390
Davie 201, 220, 262, 270
Davis 3, 20, 32, 54, 55, 87, 92, 97, 110, 131, 154, 158, 242, 253, 261, 262, 272, 302, 306, 326, 338, 339, 340, 395
Davy 322
Dawrwmik 277
Dawson 11, 33, 194, 215, 243, 289
Day 180, 266, 312, 327
De Gongosa 341
De la Garza 131, 169
De St. Romes 94
De Waretime 373
Dealy 209
Dean 94, 179, 188, 245, 273, 279, 299, 329, 330
Deane 257, 377
Dearer 141
Deboer 310
DeBrow 261
Dechanne 53
Dechaumes 317, 326
DeChene 13
Decker 346
Decody 286
Decoe 262
DeCordova 29, 359
Decro 299
Decrow 122
Dedebe 400
Deeson 306
Deforhu 298
Degener 126

Degeurs 24
Degges 322
DeGraffenried 255
Degurs 190
Deitzel 280
Delabarre 286
Delaney 277
Delany 175
Delesman 279
Deltz 268, 283
Demerest 282
DeMorse 127
Denaro 298
Denman 299
Denney 169
Dennis 83, 326, 340, 353
Denny 314
Depew 33, 34
Depperman 160
DePruy 227
Deputy 140
Deringer 358
Derwin 268
DeRyee 274
Desha 344
DeSilver 205
Detmar 299
Devine 298, 299, 324
Devons 277
DeWarren 178
DeWitt 229
Dewney 255
Dial 85, 98, 377
Diamond 284, 326, 327, 330, 341, 342
Diamond Bessie 67
Dibble 250
Dice 312
Dick 91
Dickerson 130, 151, 303, 304
Dickey 204
Dickhart 200
Dickinson 179, 299
Dickson 139, 332

Diderich 18
Diermmermann 271
Dieterich 98
Dietrich 402
Dilks 262
Dillon 385
Dinsmore 197
Dinter 122
Dipperman 320
Dismuke 48
Ditiechs 334
Ditmar 125
Ditterman 283
Divine 388
Dixon 296, 298, 310, 323, 339, 359, 365
Dobbins 305, 307, 308, 310
Dobler 298
Dobson 235
Docket 257
Dockrel 301
Dodd 373
Dodge 387
Doe 291
Dolan 47, 89
Dolen 319
Dolson 11
Domidy 323
Donald 322
Donelson 42
Donley 252
Donnell 64
Donnelly 339
Donoho 317
Donovan 11, 295
Dooley 14, 397
Dora 266
Dorcher 45
Dormey 233
Dormy 233
Dorr 52
Dossatt 141
Doswell 183
Dougan 53

Dougherty 327, 373, 376
Doughty 126, 236
Douglas 297, 395
Douglass 254, 306
Dow 238, 326
Dowd 204
Dowdy 236
Dowell 258
Dowling 271, 296, 301, 307, 315, 316, 319, 330
Downey 271, 308
Downing 184
Downs 47
Dowsey 260
Doxey 178
Doyle 174, 234-236, 247, 367, 385
Dozell 71
Dozier 138, 200
Drake 322
Drammed 286
Drawe 273
Drescher 298
Dresel 398
Dressel 252
Drew 298, 301
Dreyfus 312
Drinkard 274
Driscol 246, 314
Driskill 358
Drury 336
Dryer 274
Du Fallois 1
Dubie 367
Dubner 267
Ducey 348
Ducros 385
Duffy 161
Dufour 29, 192, 314
Duggan 108, 199, 338
Duke 286, 297
Dulemon 277
Dummerry 262
Dummitt 156

Dunaway 340
Duncan 67, 76, 140, 158, 172, 196, 197, 204, 309
Dungan 131
Dunham 153
Dunn 60, 132, 206, 274, 317, 371, 372
Dunnington 6
Dunooski 327
Dupuy 227, 228
Durant 247
Durham 133, 156
Durr 255
Durst 365
Duryer 287
Dutton 31
Duty 150, 382
Dwier 234
Dwyer 234, 324, 325, 341, 365
Dwyers 324
Dyer 247
Dykemann 50
Eagely 201
Eager 189
Eans 310
Earl 29
Earle 63, 311, 394
Earley 97
Earnest 393
Earnst 338
Easley 161
Eastesbrooks 337
Eastland 194
Eastwood 261, 274, 347
Eaton 10, 239, 267, 333
Ebel 401
Eber 363
Eberhardt 386
Eberling 401
Eccles 172
Echols 48, 352
Eddar 206
Eddins 341
Eddy 197

Farrell 3, 236, 324, 343, 392
Faulnier 329
Faute 367
Fay 104
Faysoux 315
Fearhake 344
Fehrinz 293
Felder 142, 346, 363
Femeick 318
Fenner 126
Fenton 347
Ferguson 18, 313, 328
Ferlen 402
Fernandez 342
Ferrill 387
Feuge 403
Fidler 334
Fiedler 338
Field 226
Fields 274
Fiers 210
Files 67
Filmondson 393
Finch 135
Findley 145
Finegan 264
Finger 338
Fink 122, 200, 383
Finke 1
Finkleman 327
Finlay 125, 160, 236, 286, 344, 406
Finley 256, 268, 303, 304
Finn 315
Finnan 396
Finnegan 262
Finnin 137, 148, 157
Fischer 334, 342
Fisher 16, 17, 55, 64, 147, 232, 274, 277, 296, 298, 323, 339, 341
Fisk 100
Fitch 8, 256
Fitz 70, 334

Fitzgerald 17, 104, 257, 349, 360, 382
Fitzgerld 147
Fitzpatrick 352
Flagg 389
Flake 358
Flanagan 292
Flatau 96
Fleming 265
Flemming 266, 271
Flesher 143
Flett 260
Flewellen 158
Flint 213
Flock 221
Flonrnoy 8
Flood 36, 259, 314
Flores 131, 342
Flort 319
Flourney 74
Flournoy 8, 74
Flowers 388
Floyd 334
Fly 138
Flynn 305
Foley 221, 308, 317
Folger 19
Follet 160
Folts 176, 291
Foltz 281
Fonda 263
Fondi 262
Fonleron 264
Foote 122
Footh 178
Forbes 341, 344
Forbus 109
Ford 96, 283, 291, 324, 325, 341, 383
Forester 155
Forlson 136
Forrest 83, 157, 199
Forrester 133, 134
Fort 369

Fortinberry 387
Foscue 91
Fossett 65
Foster 64, 124, 166, 310, 312, 314
Fountain 141
Foushee 330
Fowler 184, 270, 276, 284, 285, 291, 297, 309, 336
Fox 8, 89, 306, 308, 310, 312, 313, 339
Foy 75
Foyey 79
Foyster 379
Francis 4
Franck 363
Frank 244, 253, 278
Frankland 21, 188, 189
Franklin 33, 88, 94, 177, 178, 253, 349, 370
Franks 109, 186
Fraqua 395
Frauget 201
Frazier 82, 233
Frede 178, 316
Frederich 338
Frederick 209, 317, 336
Fredo 178
Freeman 340
Freil 29, 116
French 130, 175, 178, 241, 305, 310, 350
Frescher 53
Freshchimer 287
Friedberger 177
Friedeman 347, 348
Friend 248, 356
Friends 314, 356
Frier 282
Frillman 158
Frisby 385
Fritsch 398
Fritz 338
Froehich 401

From 319
Frome 320, 327
Frosh 238
Frost 107, 310
Fry 19, 27, 191, 364
Frye 237
Fullen 328
Fullenwider 323, 328
Fuller 7, 15, 16, 281
Fulshear 349
Fultz 304
Fundi 262
Furlong 348
Fushe 49
Gaffin 246
Gage 102, 133
Gaines 115, 292, 357
Galavez 342
Gallahan 275
Gallighan 88
Gambalu 291
Gamble 142
Ganehill 171
Ganes 88
Gangawa 54
Gantt 288, 289, 291, 292, 293, 294
Garcia 82, 342
Gardenier 39
Gardner 178, 299, 322
Garland 258, 261, 263
Garner 12, 16, 19, 27, 50, 57, 64, 92, 95, 124, 190, 222, 225, 275, 341
Garnett 361
Garretson 332
Garrett 94, 109, 285, 344
Gartland 278
Garvin 251
Garvland 251
Garza 17, 131, 169, 341
Gaskill 200
Gastman 275
Gaston 256

Gate 153
Gates 136
Gatewood 69
Gathings 68
Gatta 283
Gauger 295
Gaugler 126
Gault 314
Gavin 336
Gay 141
Gaylord 331, 333
Gazlay 23
Gearson 311
Geban 289
Gebhard 209
Gee 280, 348
Geers 77
Gehaman 324
Gehrman 324, 341
Geiselman 327
Gelger 271
Genois 45
Gentry 12, 50, 375
George 161, 313, 339, 401
Gerdes 240
Gerds 321
Gerlaff 280
Gervis 333
Getchell 319
Gethleman 338
Ghans 181, 370
Gholson 392
Gibbon 282
Gibbs 179, 257, 274, 328
Gibson 113, 217, 264, 313, 325
Giddings 354
Giesler 339
Giess 341
Giffeths 180
Giffney 252
Gifford 136, 201, 268, 270
Gilbert 102, 344, 360, 388
Gilchrist 269
Gild 334

Gilden 324
Gilder 341, 345
Gilead 365
Gill 35, 88, 351
Gillas 304
Gilleland 13
Gillen 340
Gillespie 10, 251, 273, 294, 296, 298, 307, 328, 332, 334
Gillet 27
Gillett 60
Gillette 151, 376
Gillhe 264
Gillian 301
Gillilan 161
Gillis 278
Gilly 225
Gingler 392
Ginseng 210
Gladwin 3
Glascoe 261
Glass 125, 322, 331, 333, 340
Glasscock 357
Glaze 332
Gleason 28, 193, 374
Gleen 36
Glenn 125, 381
Goacher 129
Gobel 178
Godfrey 2
Godse 340
Godsey 340
Goebel 178, 179
Goeffert 122
Goggan 259, 260
Goldman 125
Goldsmith 321, 329, 330
Goldstein 280
Golla 338
Golledge 285
Gomet 201
Gongosa 341
Gonzales 95, 191, 267, 388
Gonzaros 295

Gooch 246
Good 343
Goodall 368
Goodbread 92
Goode 375
Goodlow 201
Goodman 339, 340
Goodrich 85, 210, 380
Goodridge 183
Goodwin 24, 339, 340
Goodwyn 24
Goos 282
Gordon 184, 223, 249, 344
Gore 272
Goree 159
Gorman 106, 160, 188, 254
Gormond 35
Gosch 295
Goss 213
Gost 268
Gould 158, 159, 268, 272
Gover 374, 390
Gownston 325
Grady 277
Graham 77, 158, 259, 320, 370, 394
Granadez 241
Grant 2, 38, 41, 50, 235, 264, 280, 317, 320, 357
Grape 263
Graphy 69
Grassman 308
Grassoper 273
Graves 133, 141, 155, 232, 267, 300, 304, 307, 311
Gravis 37
Gray 60, 64, 65, 68, 69, 80, 82, 91, 155, 209, 239, 309, 370
Grayson 193
Green 16, 35, 52, 82, 90, 167, 188, 194, 200, 217, 243, 268, 277, 289, 291, 293, 299, 309, 310, 324, 341, 355, 364, 365, 370
Greene 36, 305

Greenhow 317
Greenlaw 228
Greenwell 66
Greer 268, 329, 330, 339, 340
Gregg 164, 256, 395
Gregory 171, 172, 175, 207, 239, 318, 320
Grehmeier 338
Gresham 143
Grey 26, 95, 313
Grice 323
Grider 87
Griesenbeck 402
Griffin 62, 166, 176, 202, 284, 288, 291, 300, 302, 303, 304, 331, 353
Griffith 308
Griflin 292
Grimes 6, 84
Grimm 314
Grinder 211
Grisham 161
Grobe 403
Grobecker 216, 218
Groce 27, 45, 101
Grodbread 201
Groebaker 222
Groebecker 222
Groesbeck 57
Groesbecker 218
Grooej 334
Groot 263
Grosjean 23
Gross 398, 402
Grove 351, 354
Grover 106
Gruene 397
Grumbles 132
Grundler 280
Gubner 49
Guerin 85
Guessnard 344
Guffus 289
Guigus 289

Guinn 234, 235, 395
Guinnand 308
Guiturres 341
Gutor 399
Guy 313
Gwin 234
Gwinn 132, 234
Habermehl 205
Hackett 318
Hackney 244
Hadgel 55
Hadley 40, 294
Haenel 212
Hafner 401
Hagan 18, 192, 324
Haggard 67
Haggerty 93
Hagler 89, 213
Hahn 338
Hahu 257
Hale 184, 282
Haley 95, 395
Half 141
Halkrauth 257
Hall 62, 84, 96, 98, 99, 108, 115,
122, 139, 173, 174, 193, 242, 256,
280, 289, 301, 322, 325, 326, 331,
334, 380
Hallauran 321
Haller 122, 150, 262, 322
Hallins 254
Hallowell 310
Halton 209
Ham 66, 67
Hamberlin 51
Hamblin 55, 57
Hamburg 326
Hamer 274
Hameun 232
Hamilton 58, 72, 148, 171, 175,
226, 247, 248, 256, 279, 281, 337,
339, 340, 347, 377
Hammet 341
Hammett 341

Hammitt 324
Hammond 322, 341, 346, 392,
393
Hammonds 395
Hampshar 34
Hampshire 34
Hampton 115, 130, 165
Hancock 16, 110, 290, 303
Hand 160, 188, 296, 298, 301
Handley 337
Hangaella 344
Hankel 269
Hanks 136, 289
Hanna 122, 286, 287, 289
Hannar 115
Hannay 165, 236, 237, 240
Hannecke 338
Hanney 287
Hansborough 62
Hansford 24, 25, 190
Hapson 257
Haraldson 144
Harber 327
Harberg 266
Harbin 311
Hard 94, 187, 188, 196, 327
Hardeman 131
Hardenbrook 336
Hardie 371
Hardin 52, 154, 200, 366
Hardwick 72
Hardy 112, 322, 331, 333
Harigel 178, 179
Harkman 325
Harlan 301
Harley 283
Harm 283
Harman 220
Harmon 254, 272
Harold 293
Harper 140, 153, 296, 355
Harrell 172, 327
Harrington 147, 182, 313

Harris 24, 66, 67, 76, 150, 152, 156, 164, 171, 208, 212, 213, 217, 248, 256, 271, 275, 296, 319, 339, 340, 344, 350, 351, 362, 382
Harrison 100, 104, 122, 158, 160, 168, 178, 218, 219, 266, 277, 280, 315, 334, 357, 358, 365, 372, 394
Hart 54, 88, 139, 319, 339
Hartless 379
Hartshorn 188
Hartu 282
Hartung 401
Harvey 198, 267, 318, 319
Hasdorff 172
Haske 314
Haskell 172
Haskins 10
Hasselmier 327
Haswell 322, 328
Hatfield 161
Hathaway 372
Hauser 76
Havers 315
Haviland 281, 284, 297
Hawes 122, 344
Hawkins 39, 262, 378
Hawley 66, 225, 255
Hawthorne 389
Hay 99, 391
Hayden 57, 66, 386
Hayes 112, 354
Hayne 1, 46
Haynes 305, 312
Haynie 113, 175, 315, 316, 326, 356
Hays 81, 110, 112, 343
Hazelrigg 161
Hazen 103
Hazle 362
Headen 274
Healey 292, 299
Healy 278
Heard 93
Heating 352

Hebbins 24
Hedgebeth 291
Hefferman 283
Hefflinger 337
Heflin 323, 332, 337, 342
Hefner 78
Hegebaum 403
Hegler 213
Hegmann 397
Heim 396
Heimor 402
Heinrich 400
Heisenbach 397
Heiss 401
Helen 232
Helfenstein 220
Heller 214
Hellman 178
Helm 231
Helterich 229
Hemingway 171
Hemphill 114, 142, 160
Henckel 104, 397
Henderson 12, 16, 85, 243
Hendrick 133, 155
Hendy 56
Heniker 22
Heninger 22, 189
Hennessy 295
Henniker 189, 190
Henninger 21
Hennings 403
Hennise 93
Henry 98, 180
Henson 78, 115
Henze 396
Heran 156
Herbert 249, 250, 310
Herd 122
Hergesele 334
Herman 178, 207
Hermann 256
Hermes 178, 315
Hernandez 342

Herndon 374
Heron 365
Herring 19, 21, 134
Herrmann 399
Herron 105, 319, 320
Hersaldt 334
Hertz 257
Herzfield 201
Hest 272
Hester 322
Heusinger 396, 399
Heuston 187
Hewett 312
Hewitt 294, 313
Hewson 240, 241, 245
Heyan 301
Heyck 344
Heyman 260
Hgen 275, 302
Hicheblum 273
Hick 257
Hickey 10, 319
Hicks 88, 91, 122, 144, 395
Hide 151, 257, 272, 292
Higginbotham 6, 60
Higgins 324, 341
Higginson 17
Hightour 241
Hightower 68
Higyneir 279
Higyueir 279
Hildebrands 261
Hildeger 53, 54
Hildreth 381
Hill 33, 70, 80, 88, 122, 135, 150,
182, 187, 194, 211, 244, 267, 268,
315, 401
Hillard 251
Hilton 387
Himb 327
Hindman 85, 381
Hinds 239, 369
Hine 172-174
Hines 95

Hink 330
Hinkell 385
Hinkle 89
Hinton 47
Hipp 111, 132, 396
Hirsch 326, 330
Hitchins 346
Hittle 178
Hoa 25
Hoback 200
Hobaen 325
Hobday 323
Hobem 319
Hobson 59
Hockley 60
Hodge 60, 65, 346
Hodges 190, 279
Hoe 362
Hofacker 401
Hoffman 53, 54, 71, 267, 315,
401
Hoffmann 399
Hoffmaster 22, 189
Hoffmeister 23
Hoffmester 22
Hogan 41, 54, 156, 221, 392
Hogg 56, 278
Hohetable 271
Hohl 289
Hoke 246
Holbein 196
Holbrook 111
Holden 261
Holderman 187
Holekamp 397, 402
Holiday 136
Holland 65, 257, 303, 304
Holliday 137, 317
Hollingsworth 348
Hollowell 23, 309, 310
Holman 92, 94, 95, 97, 138, 183,
210, 256, 260
Holmes 357
Holstein 281

Holt 80, 157, 164, 241, 313, 329
Homberg 122
Home 272
Homes 256, 293
Homuth 316
Honey 256, 279, 283, 357, 358
Honeycut 286
Honney 324
Honora 126
Hood 6, 174, 178, 180, 239, 309, 318, 350, 377
Hooker 68
Hope 139
Hopkins 300, 386
Hopson 55, 169
Horan 255
Hord 315
Hordes 228
Horl 321
Horn 82, 139
Horne 401
Hornsby 39, 40, 43, 100
Horton 104, 122, 144, 281, 324, 341
Horwitz 334
Hoskins 108
Hoston 26
Hough 178, 179
Houghton 46
Housa 260
House 182
Houston 40, 97, 158, 159, 290, 383, 405
How 317
Howard 6, 31, 36, 176, 193, 195, 196, 199, 202, 271, 363
Howards 89
Howe 113, 114, 152, 267
Howel 157, 290
Howell 31, 63
Howerton 326
Howes 388
Hoyle 287
Hubbell 272, 311

Hubbie 123
Hubble 123, 333
Hubert 24, 52, 196
Hubins 24
Huchcock 47
Huckaby 340
Huckins 202
Hudgens 15
Hudgins 17, 86
Hudson 145, 255
Hueston 20
Huff 89, 315
Huffman 55, 93, 248
Huffmans 175
Huffmaster 18
Huggins 38
Hughes 88, 214, 233, 274, 319, 321, 326, 378
Hughs 395
Hulin 256
Hulsman 161
Hume 328
Humphrey 122
Humphreys 2, 122, 182
Hunt 8, 58, 78, 107, 142, 180, 263, 286, 303, 306
Hunter 53, 93, 103, 173, 226, 307, 394
Hurlbert 159
Hurlburt 157
Hurley 285
Husbands 159
Hussey 260, 303
Huston 26, 192
Hutchins 301, 306, 373
Hutton 13, 296
Hyde 70, 140, 163, 261, 268, 387
Hyen 263
Hynes 26
Idelman 257
Idleman 387
Illias 348
Inconnier 295
Inglehardt 316

Ingram 46, 140, 141
Inman 346
Irby 310
Ireson 339, 340
Irordop 293
Irvin 111, 145
Irwin 381
Isaac 272
Isbel 94
Isheutreger 54
Island 23
Israel 392
Isreal 391
Ivers 271
Ives 111
Jack 30-35, 68, 191, 194, 195
Jackson 3, 15, 17, 40, 42, 43, 64,
71, 88, 92, 204, 207, 208, 213,
232, 247, 248, 280, 289, 291, 337,
343, 344, 350, 353, 356, 364, 366
Jacobs 88, 158, 159, 272, 321
Jacobson 325
Jaeger 20
Jalonick 283
James 53, 184, 187, 206, 394
Jameson 4, 214, 387
Jamieson 131, 154
Jamison 26, 237, 244, 305, 378
Janes 10, 23, 215
Jantsch 338
Jardine 344
Jarvis 346
Jasper 95
Jay 232, 395
Jeaneau 19
Jeannotat 200
Jeffers 184
Jefferson 38, 75, 326
Jeffry 79
Jeffrys 79
Jelks 217
Jemison 323, 379
Jenkins 99, 100, 126, 143, 144,
200

Jennings 305, 313
Jenny 225, 316
Jett 37, 99
Joentzen 272
Johaima 261
Johen 201
John 186, 261, 273, 334
Johns 287, 321
Johnson 5, 14, 31, 76, 82, 88,
95, 111, 113, 129, 130, 135, 141,
149, 163, 164, 165, 167, 175, 186,
199, 211, 240, 259, 274, 276, 283,
307, 314, 318, 321, 340, 356, 367,
378, 394
Johnston 148, 203, 240, 274, 296
Jolly 256
Jomes 327
Jonas 399-401
Jones 5, 19, 56, 68, 80, 85, 86,
89, 102, 107, 108, 109, 122, 143,
145, 163, 165, 170, 181, 184, 198,
200, 217, 222, 242, 244, 259, 266,
271, 283, 293, 295, 299, 301, 311,
321, 324, 327, 335, 339, 340, 355,
365, 380, 392
Jope 122
Jordan 92, 160, 188, 212, 220,
282, 313, 327
Jordon 62
Joseph 268, 280, 282
Jourdan 52, 332
Joy 16
Jung 400
Junker 326
Kahn 334
Kaiser 310, 334
Kale 122
Kalsh 309
Kaminski 6
Kane 310, 331
Kanivoski 306, 325
Kapmeit 403
Karnes 5, 203
Kath 256

Kauder 217
Kauffman 133, 145, 187
Kaufman 18, 207
Kavanaugh 150
Kay 248, 341
Kearson 388
Keast 388
Keays 197
Keazer 230
Keef 142
Keeke 340
Keenan 363
Keesee 379
Kehl 287
Keigher 265
Keil 308
Keith 45, 102, 177, 249
Keke 324
Keley 253
Kell 135
Kelley 122, 325
Kellner 398
Kellogg 88
Kelly 6, 31, 72, 144, 242, 255, 259, 266, 274, 317
Kelser 309
Kelsey 56
Kelso 261
Kelton 256
Kembel 297
Kemmerlin 282
Kemp 122
Kemper 29, 36, 54
Kenard 31
Kendall 48, 102, 336
Keneck 334
Kenedy 328
Keneymore 323
Kenkele 282
Kennark 246
Kennedy 14, 238, 282, 364
Kenner 69
Kennison 304, 306
Kenny 87

Kenser 243
Kent 276, 278, 279, 295
Keohn 50
Keoys 197
Ker 141
Kerhe 310
Kerr 226
Kesee 378
Kessler 308, 309
Ketchum 46, 213
Key 64, 324, 352
Keys 269
Keyworth 343
Khun 264
Kibbe 125
Kiefer 178
Kiely 272
Killough 327
Killum 138
Kimball 344
Kindred 346
King 26, 53, 128, 153, 169, 189, 260, 262, 279, 285, 288, 289, 302, 332
Kink 200
Kinkard 332
Kinney 28, 43, 60, 89, 101, 193, 342
Kinsey 91
Kintz 340
Kirby 87, 198, 214, 222
Kirch 305, 312
Kirk 179
Kirkland 31, 33, 192, 195
Kirklane 192
Kirkman 265, 269
Kirkpatrick 269
Kiruin 141
Kishpaugh 295
Kittrell 323
Klapt 257
Klatt 278, 283
Klein 24, 190, 289
Kleinker 259

Landwith 332
Lane 138, 268, 329, 346, 373
Lang 228, 246, 253, 306, 400
Langerhausen 295
Lanotte 301, 313
Lansing 186
Lanter 311
Lapez 338
Laprelle 323
Lard 131
Laresche 375
Lark 310
Larkin 25, 54, 274, 315
Larsson 41
Lathrop 333, 334
Lattimer 311
Laudrum 9
Laugerhouse 293
Laughley 277
Laughlin 7, 165
Lausen 267
Lauser 353
Lavine 227, 261
Lawdermilk 352
Lawler 223
Lawless 80, 337
Lawrence 183, 274, 278, 282, 299, 301
Lawson 313, 357
Lawther 252, 291, 294
Lay 257
Layton 97, 140
Le?maird 96
Leabelin 403
Leach 306, 308
Leake 122
Leatherwood 352
Leckenby 346
Lecuyer 236
Ledbetter 170
Leddy 276
Ledgerman 341
Ledyard 260, 262, 269, 300

Lee 122, 181, 198, 225, 247, 252, 329, 343, 364, 365, 370
Leeper 337, 347
Leer 273, 288
Leesemann 179
Legn 401
Leiberman 262
Leichner 401
Leight 226
Leimiller 203
Leisch 402
Leman 212
Lenard 383
Lennox 83
Lenox 183
Lenz 403
Leonard 177, 256, 283
LePert 206
Lernay 387
Leroy 286
Lesage 338
Lester 310
Letson 30
Lettemer 257
Lettson 30
Leu 207
Levei 253
Levenhagen 30, 32
Leverett 359
Levi 124, 125, 254
Levine 178
Levinson 298, 299, 340
Levy 260
Lew 278
Lewellyn 175, 339
Lewis 1, 3, 19-22, 49, 59, 67, 88, 90, 92, 142, 164, 187, 189, 211, 213, 261, 278, 286, 290, 312, 367, 387
Lewson 30
Libby 243
Lichtenstein 261
Lidstone 265
Lightfoot 65

Lilly 102
Lincecum 238
Linch 338
Lincoln 200, 363
Linden 308
Lindenau 403
Lindley 172
Lindsay 177, 285, 384
Lindsey 268, 297
Lineham 230
Link 307, 315
Linn 107, 124, 125, 127
Linton 384
Lipscomb 143
Lister 301
Little 62, 178, 228
Littleton 394
Livingston 216
Lobe 402
Lochuby 389
Lockett 152, 243, 269, 324, 341
Lockhard 54
Lockhart 98, 99, 161
Lockier 328
Locklin 188
Lockman 264
Loeb 254
Loefler 321
Loessin 179
Loftin 58, 213
Loftis 102, 341
Logan 3, 51, 203, 306, 323, 328
Loggins 323, 361
Lomar 355
Londermilk 309
Long 163, 212, 259, 264, 352, 395
Longacor 64
Longworth 290
Loomis 311
Loring 359
Loritz 296
Loriwen 292
Lothrop 31, 33, 195

Lott 106, 137, 141
Loudermilk 310
Louge 362
Loughridge 178
Louis 110
Lounds 266
Love 93, 145, 163, 196, 309
Lovelace 200, 248
Lovengadt 306
Lovin 71
Loving 81, 359
Lovins 71
Lowe 202, 333
Lowell 213
Lownds 266, 270
Lowrey 31, 32
Lowry 27, 326, 340
Lowther 138
Luca 285
Luce 323
Lucky 150
Ludewig 274
Luguire 100
Lunceford 311, 314
Lundh 291
Luter 334, 393
Luxton 83
Lyle 169, 340, 354
Lynch 9, 171, 256, 257, 366
Lyon 88, 273
Lyons 17, 199, 246, 263, 297
Lythe 338
Lytle 131
M'Clellan 70
M'Connell 184
M'Coullough 183
M'Gee 242
M'Laughlin 184
Macdonald 9, 57
Macelmurray 206
Macer 313
Mack 334
Macklin 224
Maclin 371

Macmurphy 293, 294
Macnamara 139
Macoob 277
Madden 122
Maddison 273
Magrouz 257
Magruder 282, 329
Mahan 212, 305, 308
Mahon 125
Mair 296
Maitag 290
Maix 202
Major 341, 380
Malincrodft 201
Malitz 125, 148
Malley 308
Malloy 165
Malone 250, 308
Maloney 141, 280, 293
Maloy 316
Maltby 274
Man 87
Mangealo 367
Mann 183, 209, 260
Manning 246, 247
Manson 31
Mapes 386
Mapson 261
Maratsky 275
Marbut 311
Marchbank 322
Marchbanks 323
Marchinska 298
Marckmann 177, 178
Marcus 257
Mare 314
Maren 259
Marhzen 312
Marian 272
Marid 253
Marion 79
Markey 381
Markham 8
Marks 35, 266, 298, 340

Markun 55
Marr 248
Marsh 141, 274, 299, 390
Marshall 42, 43, 104, 105, 169, 231, 356
Marston 184, 312
Martin 1, 61, 70, 94, 187, 188, 199, 257, 368
Martinez 389
Marulanda 341
Marx 201
Mason 84, 229, 310, 320
Massey 260
Massie 301, 305
Master 370
Masters 369
Masterson 268
Matchee 315
Mathee 201
Mather 214, 282-284, 287, 288
Mathews 41, 145, 178, 179, 188
Matlock 247
Matschke 178
Matthews 298, 309, 344, 351
Mattison 286
Maulding 25
Maury 264, 268
Max 256
Maxey 69, 200
Maxwell 344
Mayberry 91
Mayblum 349
Mayfield 146, 341
Maynard 112
Mayne 122, 124
Mays 159, 199, 289, 328, 346
McAllister 131
McAshan 168
McAulay 27
McAuley 240
McAvoy 385
McCabe 269
McCaffrey 334
McCally 377

McCampbell 73
McCann 228, 340
McCarten 229
McCarthy 305, 321, 374
McCartney 326
McCarty 335, 340, 351, 353
McCauley 39, 275, 367, 369
McCauly 315
McChane 264
McCheerg 296
McChellan 187
McClanahan 249, 252, 296
McClannahan 274
McClarty 216
McClellan 179
McClelland 218
McCloud 83
McClung 163
McClure 106
McClutchin 71
McCollum 67
McCondelt 304
McConnell 14, 280, 281, 310
McCook 354
McCord 324
McCormick 225, 247
McCoun 77
McCracken 91, 380
McCraven 391
McCreary 122
McCulloch 106, 114, 271
McCullough 16, 70
McCutchan 147
McDade 137, 253, 356
McDaniel 27, 29, 44
McDaniels 379
McDonald 11, 84, 211, 260, 277, 306, 317, 324, 374
McDonnel 370
McDonnell 268, 289, 370
McDonough 94
McDougahl 330
McDowell 292
McEachern 340

McEbine 214
McElvaine 338
McErlain 324
McFadden 93
McFadin 110
McFail 79
McFarland 53, 134, 136, 341, 384, 389
McFarlane 274
McFatter 341
McGary 226
McGee 272
McGehee 177, 310
McGehre 309
McGehu 80
McGibbon 281
McGill 260, 368
McGillick 268
McGinnis 270
McGoven 141
McGown 178
McGrath 122
McGraw 313
McGregor 149, 292
McGrew 126
McGuinil 320
McGuire 62, 72, 295, 385
McHanks 97
Mclihanny 307
McIntosh 206, 295
McIntyre 324, 340, 341
McIver 92, 94, 154
McKaughan 368
McKay 317
McKean 371
McKee 200
McKeig 343
McKeithan 338
McKelvey 80
McKenna 308
McKenney 115
McKenzie 26
McKernin 278
McKinney 74, 355, 369, 376

McKinnie 175
McKintosh 295
McKnight 197
McKune 319
McLain 254
McLane 282
McLean 92, 253
McLees 133, 155
McLennan 366
McLeod 114, 267
McMahan 20, 21, 23, 171, 231, 237
McMahon 122
McMillan 144, 305
McMiller 143
McMullin 225
McMurphy 288
McMurty 202
McNair 205
McNamara 125
McNeel 73, 81
McNeese 219, 324, 340
McNeil 73, 81, 223
McNeill 141, 351
McPhail 274
McPherson 258
McQuinn 257
McQuinney 328
McRoy 328
McSween 70
McSwine 376
McWaters 323
McWilliams 275
Meade 342
Meador 153
Meadows 34, 92
Meally 332
Means 99
Mehin 94
Meier 210
Meinert 179
Mekyger 390
Melcher 178, 315
Melchoir 125

Melton 139
Melvin 200
Menard 186, 202, 263
Mendenhall 256
Meneilley 326
Menesco 352
Menifee 175, 309, 350
Menifer 180
Mennefee 287
Mensman 383
Mercer 12, 28, 105
Meredith 224, 280
Merram 315
Merrem 178
Merriman 274, 374
Merryman 161
Messer 259, 260
Messner 310
Metze 321
Metzger 403
Metzing 397
Meuley 274
Meyenberg 178
Meyer 126, 178, 179, 259, 275, 402, 403
Meyers 304
Michael 207
Michaelowski 383
Michal 292
Micheln 402
Michie 194
Mickegan 289
Micklejohn 293
Middleton 10, 187, 252, 317, 374
Migel 285
Milam 14, 185, 264
Milby 297, 329
Milenberg 316
Miles 333
Milhe 316
Milhouse 280
Milican 75
Milinberg 315
Millar 160

Miller 2, 23, 49, 54, 55, 58, 72, 78, 79, 82, 98, 122, 124, 135, 153, 163, 164, 167, 197, 201, 208, 217, 254, 264, 266, 280, 286, 292, 304, 309, 310, 328, 329, 330, 334, 339, 355, 356, 360, 362, 370, 371, 380, 388, 391, 392
Millhouse 281
Milligan 34
Milliken 281, 292
Mills 50, 76, 108, 200, 216, 218, 222, 304, 312
Milner 242
Milsted 177
Milton 207
Miner 324, 341
Minor 135, 362
Minter 366, 368
Miskell 339
Miskill 232
Mitchel 187
Mitchell 149, 213, 244, 274, 291, 328, 331, 333, 334, 338, 359, 379, 388
Mix 264
Mixer 392
Mixon 111
Mize 157
Mobin 275
Mockett 34
Moegen 402
Moench 268
Mola 342
Moller 202
Monaghan 343
Mondosa 342
Monges 6
Monroe 392
Monseratte 121
Monsey 26, 28
Montgomery 115, 134, 218, 283, 343, 369
Moody 125, 127, 314, 320
Moodyman 341

Mooman 95
Moon 175
Mooney 257, 336
Moore 2, 5, 11, 19, 23, 29, 34, 41, 52, 58, 59, 80, 94, 95, 96, 99, 122, 150, 170, 178, 181, 196, 216, 234, 241, 255, 256, 268, 287, 301, 306, 307, 311, 315, 321, 333, 339, 340, 350, 356, 368, 382, 383, 393
Morales 41
Moran 267, 282, 292, 332
Morbert 302
Moreland 9
Morgan 6, 123, 153, 154, 161, 200, 208, 250, 274, 295, 332
Morian 206
Moriarty 52
Moro 200
Morrill 255
Morris 22, 32, 35, 54, 187, 195, 215, 230, 254, 265, 339
Morrisett 60
Morrison 75, 77, 122, 176, 245, 246, 309, 310
Morriss 137
Morrow 174
Morse 68, 93, 204, 224, 225, 339
Morton 176, 178, 265, 341
Mosby 391
Moseley 150, 156
Mosely 24, 25, 190, 258, 328
Moses 166, 264
Moss 257, 306
Mossgrove 320
Mott 20, 21
Moureau 397, 399
Mueller 401
Muir 51
Muldrew 147
Mull 208
Mullen 320
Mullens 341
Muller 254, 278, 309
Mulligan 88

Mullin 271
Mullins 86, 383, 385, 386
Munden 168
Mungen 280
Munger 136, 137
Munroe 315
Munson 150
Munyan 231
Murbot 296, 298
Murch 192
Murchie 314, 358
Murdock 297
Mure 94, 141
Murphree 229
Murphy 36, 67, 88, 108, 191,
193, 194, 228, 261, 262, 266, 271,
281, 313, 328, 390
Murrah 394
Murray 380
Murrell 36, 59, 157
Murry 257, 291, 292
Musgrove 179, 339
Myer 53, 173
Myers 93, 198, 274, 320, 322,
390
Mynatt 257, 344, 345
Mynett 63
Naff 79
Nagle 263
Nancy 54
Napp 138
Nash 158, 210, 258, 314
Navarro 108
Neal 287
Neb 399
Neckmann 397
Negries 263
Negroes:
    Amos 328
    Anderson 123, 232
    Antoine 123
    Arnold 31
    Arrington 325
    Ashworth 140

Negroes (continued):
    Aunt Bettie 68
    Aunt Sookey 387
    Aunt Winnie 241
    Autville 123
    Bateman 123
    Battese 88
    Beata 394
    Bell 87
    Betsey 30
    Betts 176
    Blackly 237
    Bob 70
    Bonaparte 361
    Bony 361
    Botts 340
    Bowers 390
    Branch 365, 389
    Brown 314
    Bryant 317
    Burdin 392
    Burney 232
    Butler 385, 394
    Carter 178
    Cash 251
    Castro 193
    Charley 363
    Church 302
    Cloe 285
    Coburn 234
    Corderay 390
    Cox 391
    Daniels 123
    Dave 81
    Davis 283, 293, 330
    Delany 393
    Desforges 85
    Dick 176, 245, 246
    Dolley 267
    Douglas 282
    Dr. Jim 139
    Dunn 49
    Dyers 353
    Ebley 123

Negroes (continued):
Pilaut 392
Rainey 340
Ralph 81
Randall 361
Renetta 384
Riddle 365
Robert 318
Rose 328
Rutledge 123
Seal 281
Shelton 232
Simon 233
Sloan 375
Smith 296, 298, 339
Sookey 387
Souters 325
Spence 251
Spencer 394
Spicy 334
Stamps 267
Stephens 173
Stewart 351
Stockton 321
Strickman 257
Tabb 340
Taylor 319
Thomas 336, 384
Thompson 361
Todd 262
Turner 123
Uncle Charley 363
Wallace 233
Walter 123
Warren 29
Washington 334
Waters 315
Welcome 340
White 283
Wiggins 176
Wilder 213
William 232
Williams 123, 325, 371, 388

Negroes (continued):
Wilson 80
Winnie 241
Woodal 314
Wooten 370
Wynne 328
Young 123
Neibor 206
Neibou 262
Neibour 257, 266
Neighbors 133
Neil 274, 279, 289, 307, 328
Neill 275
Neitsch 275, 387
Nelion 295
Nelson 69, 87, 89, 102, 213, 226
Nerney 301
Ness 298
Neterson 232
Netherly 158
Nettles 340
Neugent 358
Neumann 403
New 88
Newbrans 340
Newcome 237
Newell 210, 257, 272
Newlands 2
Newman 141, 174, 237, 338
Newton 25, 287
Ney 261
Neyland 81
Nibbs 36, 58
Nicholas 348, 350
Nichols 70, 122, 150, 170, 250, 263, 266
Nicholson 94, 100, 178, 350
Nickerson 269, 271
Nicolls 65
Nieburh 266
Niederman 334
Niles 15, 46
Nitsche 257
Nix 63, 100

Nixon 65, 377
Noah 183
Noble 59, 66, 238
Nobles 55
Noel 324
Nolan 19, 55
Noles 112
Nolte 399, 400
Nordhousen 297
Norr 110
Norris 344, 388, 395
Northcross 375
Northcut 95
Norther 271
Northway 128
Norton 71, 178, 386
Norwood 99
Norwoode 152
Nosholson 286
Noughton 277
Nourse 317, 319
Nowlan 230
Nowlin 230
Noyce 301
Noyes 303
Noyles 383
Nunn 167, 169
Nusbaum 323, 328
Nushon 263
Nuttenhaver 134
O'Brian 190
O'Brien 18, 112, 264
O'Clair 258
O'Connell 301, 306-309, 310
O'Conner 308
O'Connor 325
O'Daniel 206
O'Hara 341
O'Keefe 291
O'Leary 198
O'Mal 305
O'Neal 152, 165, 326
O'Neil 257, 274
O'Riley 274

Oberle 261
Oblitz 334
Ochbrih 331
Ochiltree 85, 351, 352, 382
Odom 64, 65
Odum 156
Oelsner 244
Ogden 86
Ohrmnair 257
Oldendroff 201
Oldham 366, 372
Oleary 311
Oleran 279
Oligschlaeger 307
Oliphant 328
Oliver 12
Olson 291
Onderdonk 367
Oppa 280
Opperman 200
Orange 282
Orega 279
Organ 330
Orth 397
Orthman 302
Ortz 273
Osborne 69, 369
Osburn 368
Osgood 215
Osker 205
Osterman 219
Oswald 16
Otey 337
Otther 277
Outerside 365
Outlaw 328
Overman 45
Owen 13, 182, 184, 191, 192,
290, 333, 334, 338
Owens 112, 125, 187, 291
Pace 184
Page 63, 214
Painter 201
Palauis 267

Palfrey 390

Palm 334

Palmee 360

Palmer 338

Palton 331

Pannel 285

Pannell 39

Panwell 346

Pape 402

Pardue 103

Parish 15, 88, 282

Park 142

Parker   79, 99, 185, 243, 255, 301, 334, 377

Parkhill 352

Parr 350

Parrish 343

Parsons 114

Pasahatag 308

Pascal 21

Pasco 293

Pascoe 295

Patch 312

Pate 132

Patill 89

Patrick 229, 242, 259, 344, 357, 358

Patrouke 327

Patten 272, 289

Patter 213

Patterson 96, 281, 328, 342

Patton 9, 10, 39, 178, 315, 344

Pauli 178

Paulson 381

Pauska 315, 316

Pavel 304

Payne   14, 165, 185, 189, 272, 273

Peabody 159

Peacock 305, 306, 365

Peak 252

Pearsall 207

Pearson 83

Peas 80

Pebry 279

Pecklape 333

Peebles 72, 349

Pefia 342

Peifer 334

Pelasho 135, 136

Pelium 291

Pelter 266

Pelzer 178

Pemberton 392

Pendergast 245

Pendleton 241

Penland 323

Penn 60, 168, 177

Pennington 93

Penny 203

Pentecost 72

Perdue 159

Peres 342

Perham 285

Perkins 102, 135, 138

Perry   87, 101, 112, 122, 132, 140, 187, 249, 265, 268, 274, 279, 299, 300, 333, 350

Perryman 83

Pert 269

Peschk 319

Peters   64, 122, 255, 295, 309, 398

Peterson 389

Petick 318

Peticolas 391

Petoi 200

Petre 297

Petri 396

Petticolas 334

Pettus 41

Petway 130

Peyton 19, 21, 22, 189

Pfeffereorn 178

Pfleger 283, 287

Pfluger 314

Phehwe 74

Phelan 289

Phelps   16, 392, 393, 395
Philabeaucourt 11
Philips 293
Phillips   85, 88, 145, 178, 356, 381
Phol 378
Pickard 63
Pickel 379
Pickens 91
Pickett 248
Picon 279
Piehorst 280
Piejat 124
Pierce 7, 157, 321, 391
Pike 277
Pilant 22, 186, 187, 189, 191
Pilgram 338
Pilkin 239
Pilkington 4, 5, 282, 283
Pillman 221
Pillow 354
Pinchback 38
Pinchboak 175
Pinckney 48, 51, 115
Pingh 388
Pinkard 188
Pinkney 56
Pinneman 334
Pipkin 54
Pister 305
Pither 55
Pitrousky 320
Pitts 74, 137
Planed 257
Plant 386
Pledger 190
Plehwe 74
Plenwe 74
Ploem 257
Plumly 265
Plummer 255
Plympton 233
Poe 84, 90
Poinsett 52

Pointer 254, 292
Polan 261
Polisco 269
Polk 369
Pollan 274
Pollard 170, 275
Polus 271
Polvgt 266
Pomeroy 375
Pool 80
Pope 170, 237, 238
Porch 338
Porea 342
Porter 126, 196, 272, 297, 329, 341, 395
Portillo 342
Posey 133
Post 79, 301, 339
Potter 21, 94, 178, 188
Potts 68
Pound 264, 266
Pousoyer 275
Pouvais 13
Powel 182
Powell 155, 200, 218, 247, 291, 314, 318
Power 341
Powers 6, 7, 77, 91, 111, 221, 224, 264, 324
Praeger 326
Prain 332
Prat 392
Pratt 73, 262, 305, 327
Praytor 140
Preacher 261
Prendler 288
Prescott 184
Preston 68, 72
Preusser 401
Prewitt 330
Prey 256
Price   39, 178, 215, 270, 272, 275, 279, 280, 292, 315, 323, 391
Pridgen 81

Pridgeon 337
Prier 11
Priest 339, 395
Priester 306
Prigmore 176, 247, 248
Prindle 329, 330
Pritman 341
Proctor 39
Proffitt 259
Prosch 312
Prouty 344
Province 93
Pruett 96
Pruitt 248, 327, 330
Puls 403
Pultiz 277
Pumpelly 16
Purdom 236, 320
Putnam 324
Pye 339
Qinn 58
Quales 388
Quarffle 233
Quarles 344
Quin 188, 336
Quinby 218
Quinn 182
Quino 131
Quintara 341
Quitte 197
Qweib 308
Raadel 23
Raby 214
Rachye 311
Rack 178
Racy 324
Raftis 392
Ragland 72, 134, 148, 331, 333, 334
Ragsdale 45, 61, 90, 232
Rain 86
Rains 184
Rainwater 145
Raladez 341

Ramerschautz 54
Ramey 200
Ramorez 193
Ramsey 255, 303, 381
Randall 248, 300, 306
Randle 127, 220, 244
Randolph 187, 230, 280, 311, 328
Randon 239
Rankin 80, 113, 274
Ransom 15, 185
Rascoe 295
Ratcliffe 53
Rather 31
Ratliff 349
Raundorf 396
Raunscheutz 53
Rawley 319
Rawls 344, 345
Ray 101
Rayfield 86
Rayless 280
Raymond 145, 184, 234
Rayner 53, 103
Razy 340
Read 51, 134, 311
Ready 293
Reagan 178, 179, 336
Rebina 390
Reddick 324, 340
Redgate 299
Redsall 302, 315, 325
Reed 109, 156, 250, 276, 312, 361, 406
Rees 296, 305
Reese 16, 84, 277, 296, 308
Reeves 53, 213
Regan 305, 325
Reichel 178
Reid 7, 27, 276, 277
Reidner 285, 292
Reiley 281, 341
Reily 16, 88, 281
Reily.] 284
Reiman 338

Reinermann 34
Reis 311
Reissner 253
Remer 88
Remington 130
Renfro 95
Rennall 251
Renoux 310, 344
Repp 316, 328
Rettsher 283
Reuter 399
Rey 283
Reyes 341
Reynold 87
Reynolds 20, 25, 41, 61, 136, 178, 191, 203, 304, 314, 322, 323, 389, 395
Rhea 11, 278, 280
Rhein 274
Rhinehart 17
Rhodefield 263
Rhodes 51, 143, 328, 332, 341, 345, 378
Rhoton 4
Rial 324
Rice 6, 17, 213
Rich 213, 285
Richard 344
Richards 65, 101, 257
Richardson 65, 105, 195, 251, 282, 288, 337
Richers 177, 178
Richmond 105
Richter 321, 400
Rick 39
Ricke 295
Rickets 190
Ricketts 24
Rickey 181
Rickmiles 327
Rickter 337
Riddir 274
Riddle 338
Ridge 20, 325, 341

Ridgely 25
Ridgeway 32, 38, 41
Riggs 207, 274
Rigin 246
Riley 188, 251, 324
Ringh 384
Riordan 289
Ripke 252
Ripley 331
Ripp 298
Riser 278
Ritchie 158
Ritters 143
Ritzler 278
Rivers 158
Rives 351, 364
Roach 88
Roache 272
Robbins 85, 346
Roberdean 352
Roberson 150
Roberts 50, 139, 177, 232, 289, 297, 309, 329, 339
Robertson 68, 130, 139, 140, 153, 171, 192, 257, 274, 330
Robinson 6, 8, 20, 22, 54, 55, 57, 79, 84, 90, 147, 154, 171, 204, 207, 211, 224, 241, 254, 258, 263, 268, 291, 320, 329, 362, 371
Roby 65
Rodefeld 269
Rodefeldt 321, 324
Roderfelt 293
Rodfld 318
Rodgers 182, 349, 356
Roe 314
Roeser 403
Roff 173, 341
Roger 164
Rogers 19, 51, 110, 134, 160, 269, 283, 306, 326, 327, 336, 341
Rogillio 218
Rohen 298
Rolata 201

Rooney 257
Roots 65, 280
Roring 224
Rose 86, 91, 172, 200, 247, 333
Rosell 302
Rosenfield 315, 326
Rosenthal 334
Ross 4, 20, 46, 183, 241, 307, 321, 331, 340
Rossy 398
Rost 387
Rothschild 67
Rottenstein 214, 274, 356
Rouff 334
Rouls 307
Rowe 200, 287, 289, 294, 316
Roy 317
Rozar 388
Rozell 168
Rubel 78
Rubrio 17
Ruby 321
Rucker 304
Rudloff 402
Ruehn 398
Ruff 294
Rumpa 293
Runge 399
Runnells 96
Runnels 32, 53, 54, 62, 195, 269
Rupley 333
Ruschau 124
Ruse 283
Rush 265
Rusk 16, 92, 139, 146
Russel 38, 266
Russell 48, 49, 203, 299, 336, 339, 379, 394
Rust 231
Ruter 147, 150, 151
Rutherford 2, 170
Ruthven 212
Rutor 147

Ryan 73, 88, 127, 182, 191, 254, 292, 313, 315, 393, 395
Ryol 341
Saber 255
Sabner 253
Saccaro 367
Saddler 235
Safferin 271
Saffern 272, 273
Sahm 401
Sale 147
Sales 342
Salinas 341
Salmon 87, 153, 261, 262
Salsbury 193
Sample 137
Sampson 116
Sanchez 7
Sander 401
Sanders 144, 293, 365
Sanderson 153, 301, 341
Sandord 214
Sands 273
Sandusky 197
Sanford 86, 91, 205
Sangston 278
Sansum 324
Sapp 361
Sargeant 283
Sargent 288, 311, 383, 384
Sartwell 161
Satterfield 166
Sauliner 330
Saunders 24, 98, 214, 297, 361
Sauters 258
Savage 178, 197, 200, 293, 301, 350
Savery 103
Sawyers 329
Sayers 177, 178
Sayles 329, 342
Sayres 330
Sayrt 257
Scarborough 32

Schach 328
Schaefer 295, 343
Schafer 325, 338
Schaffeir 280
Schall 334
Scham 279
Schamer 306
Scheiner 338
Schellentrager 338
Schelley 310
Schendon 269
Scherly 309
Scheuer 225
Schimpf 34
Schiner 334
Schinl 201
Schivarke 179
Schlather 401
Schleight 203
Schmidt 31, 122, 271, 273, 283,
289, 309, 311, 334, 397, 398, 403
Schmuck 400
Schnaver 289
Schneider 321
Scholl 398
Scholtz 179
Schonbacker 281
Schonholts 257
Schrader 338, 339
Schramber 254
Schrimp 130
Schriver 261
Schroder 253
Schroeder 178, 179, 315
Schroll 334
Schuelder 267
Schugart 125
Schultz 274, 281, 285, 293
Schulz 399, 403
Schuster 274
Schwaah 261
Schwab 397, 398
Schwartz 178
Schweiger 209

Scivils 306
Scoby 168
Scott 9, 38, 55, 61, 128, 141,
174, 190, 192, 202, 251, 274, 275,
318, 328, 329, 330, 333, 342, 353,
369
Scull 172
Scurry 16
Seabaugh 397
Seales 374
Searcy 355, 369
Seawell 163
Sebring 194
Seckatz 403
Secres 96
Sedgwick 341
Seeberger 178, 179
Seekap 400
Seele 399-402
Seeligson 119, 250, 333, 346
Seely 212
Seguin 11
Seibrat 57
Seidelman 283
Seigle 280
Seitz 362, 386
Sellers 247
Selman 180
Seneschall 49
Sennott 388
Sephus 304
Setac 399
Settle 188
Sewald 268
Seward 394
Sexon 256
Seymour 252, 335
Shackelford 385
Shackleford 364, 386, 387
Shaddon 85, 381
Shanks 92, 104
Shannon 170
Sharp 112
Sharpe 20

Shattuck 201
Shaver 202
Shaw 47, 149, 168, 194, 317
Shawnee Bill 158
Shea 52, 53
Shean 47, 257
Sheettze 283
Sheffield 30
Shegog 352
Shelton 186, 339, 388
Shely 50
Shepard 322
Shephard 16
Shepherd 211, 271, 323, 373
Sheppard 374
Sherer 282
Sheridan 301, 303, 312, 387
Sherman 205, 300, 305, 307
Sherrel 145
Sherrill 324
Sherroll 340, 341
Sherwood 190
Shield 302, 308
Shields 235
Shier 334
Shiley 55
Shilling 293
Ship 160
Shipman 44, 187, 346
Shire 222
Shive 112, 296
Shively 338
Shline 291
Sholiboh 203
Shoonovers 366
Short 141, 178, 200, 201, 257, 297
Shorter 385
Shotwell 62, 268
Shoult 335
Shrewsbury 335
Shroder 334
Shropshire 178, 294, 302, 322, 350, 362

Shules 381
Shultz 37, 38, 100
Shumaker 261
Shwizer 340
Shyhagan 298, 299
Shyhagin 340
Sibley 115, 125
Sidney 370
Sieport 272
Silier 314
Silva 390
Silversand 266
Silverstein 334
Silvestine 331
Simington 163
Simmler 32
Simmons 17, 33, 173, 175, 257, 293, 322, 329
Simms 248, 313
Simon 122, 178, 338, 399
Simons 20, 23, 315
Simonton 236
Simpson 17, 36, 37, 40, 255, 294, 326
Sims 102, 274
Sinclair 274
Singletary 340
Sitterb 338
Sivley 317
Skailes 146
Skinner 250, 251
Slack 328
Slapp 287, 292
Slaughter 95, 96, 152, 207
Slaven 339
Sledge 48, 262, 390
Slick 292
Sligar 109
Sloan 15, 93
Sloat 16, 43, 45
Slocum 109, 376
Smallwood 309

Smith   26, 37, 40, 41, 59, 61, 68, 88, 89, 93, 97, 99, 100, 101, 103, 106, 109, 110, 122, 123, 129, 131, 132, 137, 140, 141, 150, 161, 171, 176, 178, 180, 183, 185, 187, 210, 226, 239, 245, 253, 260, 264, 265, 269, 270, 273, 274, 275, 280, 283, 290, 292, 294, 295, 302, 318, 322, 324, 325, 328, 331, 334, 338, 339, 340, 341, 344, 346, 350, 356, 382, 383, 384, 388, 395

Smither 328

Smithers   11

Smyth 95, 96

Smythson 77

Snediker 88

Sneed   19, 81

Snell 148, 149, 164, 176

Snider 354

Snow 278

Snyder 216, 218, 274

Solomon 57, 271

Somerville 372

Sommers 7

Sonza 317

Sorelle 362

Souter 324, 341

Souther 341

Southern 129

Southmayd 41

Soyre 266

Spaight 204

Spanberg 287

Spangenberg 379

Spanish Pete 122

Spann   139, 285, 286, 302

Sparks 371

Spawa 338

Spear 250

Spears 324, 341

Speers 249

Spelse 79

Spelter 278

Spence 261

Spencer 63, 106, 170, 301, 362, 368

Spenser 299

Sperry 41

Spocet 302

Spooner 214, 318

Spotts 153

Springfield 369

Sqecht 398

St Clair 109

St. Blondine 265

St. John 253, 254

St. Romes 94

Staats 20-22, 397

Stacy 340

Staffel 363

Stafford 54, 134, 143, 167

Stamann 202

Stamm 334

Stample 201

Stamps   324, 367

Stanard   394

Stanchfield 322

Stanfield 96

Stanley 183, 276, 387

Stansbury 19

Stansel 74

Stanter 318

Stanton 245

Stanwood 229

Stapp 80, 106, 125, 331, 338

Starke 402

Starr 74

Starratt 65

Starrs 46

Statenboro 73, 81

Stathemann 403

Stauffle 200

Steadman 173

Steele 214, 222, 257, 305, 320, 335

Steger 41

Stegger 41

Stein 400

Vanward 208
VanZandt 36, 49, 50, 84
Vapid 271, 276, 281, 289, 295, 296, 298, 309, 319
Varnell 331, 361
Varner 95, 191
Vasques 12
Vasquez 13
Vaugh 285
Vaughan 81, 292, 356
Vaughn 200
Vedder 3
Vedre 141
Veight 317
Veinnig 282
Veitgen 266
Verfleu 305
Verner 87
Veschir 325
Vetter 274
Vicks 387
Victoria 287
Victory 286
Viegel 339
Villarial 341
Villets 285
Violet 324
Vivion 270
Vlake 200
Vogclar 392
Vogel 269, 398
Vogt 270, 403
Voight 64, 269, 326, 327, 334
Voigt 255, 290
Volat 272
Volk 397
Volst 266, 267, 307
Vonters 327
Voo 203
Voorhies 309, 310
Vorrith 191
Vose 44, 101
Voss 101
Vott 254

Wace 184
Wachemouth 385
Wacker 338
Waddill 264
Waddle 268
Wade 65, 79, 376
Wadlington 339
Wadsworth 45
Wages 128
Waggoner 253
Wagley 66
Wagner 253, 264, 320, 355
Wagnor 253
Wail 261
Wainwright 255, 280
Wair 256
Waiss 277
Wakeley 50
Waldeman 61
Walden 368
Waldo 299
Walker 50, 64, 68, 122, 134, 142, 143, 165, 167, 202, 207, 221, 248, 324, 334, 339, 340, 356, 369, 370, 375
Wall 84, 140, 154, 279, 375, 376
Wallace 55, 77, 89, 129, 296, 302, 308, 324, 328, 334, 341
Waller 268, 382
Wallis 16, 204, 207, 226, 258, 263
Wally 282
Walsh 172
Walstein 348
Walter 172, 178
Walters 227, 229, 230
Walthal 340
Walton 49, 100, 238, 368
Wampler 73
Wanberg 256
Wanekey 344, 345
Wann 296, 298
Wannie 53
Warchester 298

Ward 84, 90, 161, 200, 217, 268, 277, 296, 299, 301, 302, 306, 308, 310, 312, 315, 318, 325, 329, 362
Warden 128
Wardick 144
Wardon 242
Ware 103, 195, 382
Waretime 373
Warly 292
Warner 307, 313
Warren 279, 288, 308, 310, 316, 331, 341, 364
Waschko 338
Washington 5, 30, 88, 139, 160, 325
Wassoms 264
Wasson 341
Waters 30, 220, 232, 373
Watie 46
Watkins 295, 324, 344, 350
Watrous 11
Watrus 280
Watson 97, 186, 198, 272, 273, 324, 325, 348
Wayland 35, 61
Wayne 113
Weathered 69
Weaver 51, 138, 157
Webb 83, 178, 277, 314, 316, 377
Webber 14, 184, 312
Webster 246, 314
Wedemeyer 219
Weekmaster 341
Weeks 171, 335
Weems 260
Weidenmueller 274
Weigand 20
Weigert 200
Weigher 295
Weihrmann 312
Weil 261
Weilder 346
Weinert 169, 178, 403

Weir 386
Weiser 48
Weisiger 220
Weiss 263, 285
Welch 93, 272, 291, 294, 321, 328, 346
Welkes 234
Well 147, 175, 241
Wells 95, 161, 162, 186, 191, 192, 223, 260, 277, 328
Welr 88
Welsch 41, 332
Welschmeyer 6
Welsh 250
Wendhance 285
Wentz 382
Wenzel 396
Werdehausen 353
Wersdoerfer 401
Wertheimer 125
Wessendor 287
West 50, 370, 383, 385
Westcott 74, 390
Westerlage 268, 273, 293
Westoff 126
Weston 138, 159
Westphall 262
Wetz 400
Weyers 21
Whalen 326
Whann 275
Wharton 191, 204, 205, 222, 223, 340
Whartons 32
Wheeler 16, 32, 104, 112, 152, 288, 324, 333, 341, 362, 364
Wheelock 164
Wheelwright 255
Wheill 304
Whelan 274
Whetstone 22
Whistler 16
Whitaker 384
Whitby 346

Whitcomb 271
White 12, 23, 41, 56, 74, 111, 115, 154, 178, 215, 221, 248, 260, 269, 272, 300, 310, 326, 338, 342, 346, 350, 354, 386, 390, 391, 392
Whitehead 246
Whiteside 44
Whitett 83
Whithy 113
Whiting 5, 63, 78, 266
Whitmarsh 325
Whitney 6, 344
Whitson 197
Whittlesey 97, 181
Whittlesy 386
Wicknow 380
Wicktorick 293
Wiedenfeld 402
Wiener 312
Wigers 303
Wigginton 186
Wilbanks 69
Wilbar 154
Wilbergard 266
Wilcox 285, 324
Wild Bill 79
Wild Irishman 341
Wilder 340
Wilhelm 55
Wilke 265
Wilkerson 122
Wilkes 321
Wilkie 178
Wilkins 3, 59, 336, 382
Wilkinson 198, 358
Willburn 168
Willerford 178
Willers 331
Willett 214
Williams 6, 48, 57, 58, 69, 88, 98, 108, 161, 171, 181, 198, 210, 256, 257, 266, 277, 280, 300, 301, 304, 305, 307, 313, 314, 321, 330, 339, 340, 363, 368, 388, 389, 390

Williamson 99, 216, 322, 323, 324, 341
Willingham 69
Willis 200, 213, 216, 303, 360
Wilmar 338
Wilson 4, 23, 24, 29, 33, 38, 42, 45, 55, 74, 78, 130, 132, 135, 164, 174, 199, 200, 208, 213, 234, 235, 252, 254, 259, 265, 275, 276, 279, 280, 282, 286, 290, 291, 295, 327, 387, 393, 395
Wilson, 54
Wimberly 216, 349, 378
Winder 94
Winders 340
Windham 225, 267, 298, 308
Wingate 58, 158, 358
Winkelman 124
Winkin 272
Winkle 341
Winkleman 122
Winter 242, 310
Winters 76
Wintzel 254
Wirt 366
Wiseman 158
Withers 299
Witschke 179
Witte 268
Witteberg 341
Witteburg 325
Wittenberg 220
Wixon 327
Woern 389
Wohl 340
Woit 275
Wolf 183, 304
Wolfe 92
Wolff 260, 293
Wollasten 8
Wolstenholme 179
Wolston 244
Womack 331, 333, 334
Womble 208

Wood   82, 157, 163, 164, 253, 256, 283, 293, 296, 319, 324
Wooddy   22
Woodfolk   74
Woodley   57
Woodruff   40, 41, 228
Woods   23, 65, 83, 313
Woodward   128, 163, 250, 339
Wooldridge   356
Woolf   98
Woolfolk   287
Wooten   377
Wren   283
Wright   24, 65, 140, 233, 299, 306, 307, 309, 310, 322, 344, 345, 383
Wyatt   23
Wyllie   299
Wynne   140, 267, 328
Wyser   344
Yager   201
Yancy   65
Yarington   164
Yates   193, 322, 323, 329
Yeates   200
Yeaton   317
Yell   148, 173
Yerger   149, 237
Yoakum   328, 332
York   95
Young   31, 50, 69, 70, 78, 129, 135, 163, 232, 233, 257, 297, 310, 323, 365
Yunker   383
Zaadoc   262
Zacho   291
Zadow   264, 292
Zamora   126
Zanders   178
Zansford   80
Zeigler   382
Zeip   324
Zellers   178
Zimmerman   264

Zuehl   399
Zumlin   239
Zwiefel   400